CREATING STYLIZED
CHARACTERS

3dtotal Publishing

CREATING STYLIZED
CHARACTERS

3dtotal Publishing

3dtotalPublishing

Correspondence: publishing@3dtotal.com
Website: www.3dtotal.com

Creating Stylized Characters © 2018, 3dtotal Publishing. All rights reserved. No part of this book can be reproduced in any form or by any means, without the prior written consent of the publisher. All artwork, unless stated otherwise, is copyright © 2018 3dtotal Publishing or the featured artists. All artwork that is not copyright of 3dtotal Publishing or the featured artists is marked accordingly.

Every effort has been made to ensure the credits and contact information listed are present and correct. In the case of any errors that have occurred, the publisher respectfully directs readers to the www.3dtotalpublishing.com website for any updated information and/or corrections.

First published in the United Kingdom, 2018, by 3dtotal Publishing.

Address: 3dtotal.com Ltd, 29 Foregate Street, Worcester, WR1 1DS, United Kingdom.

Reprinted in 2022 by 3dtotal Publishing.

Soft cover ISBN: 978-1-909414-74-7
Printing and binding: Gutenberg Press Ltd (Malta) www.gutenberg.com.mt

Visit www.3dtotalpublishing.com for a complete list of available book titles.

Editor: Marisa Lewis
Template design: Joseph Cartwright
Cover design: Matthew Lewis

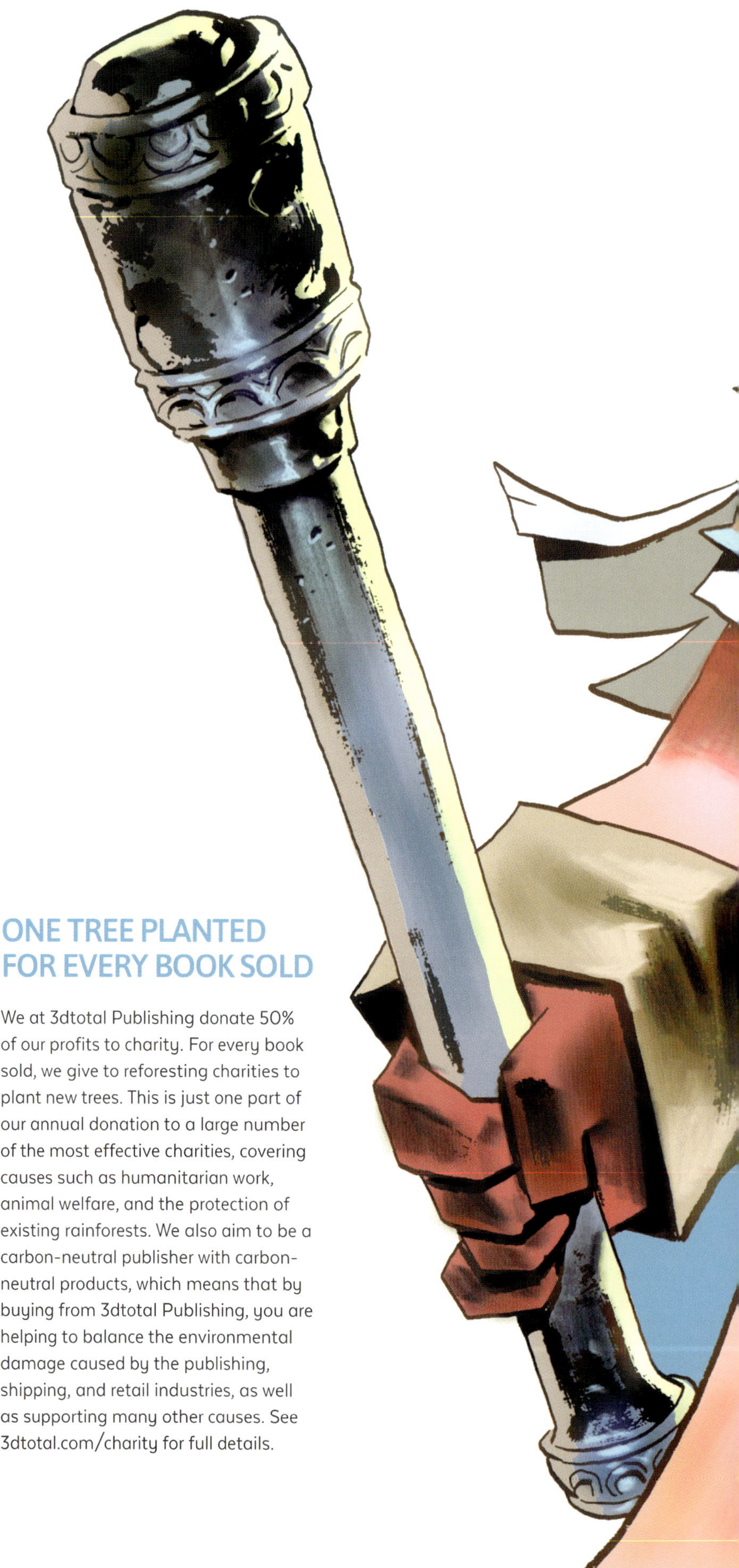

ONE TREE PLANTED FOR EVERY BOOK SOLD

We at 3dtotal Publishing donate 50% of our profits to charity. For every book sold, we give to reforesting charities to plant new trees. This is just one part of our annual donation to a large number of the most effective charities, covering causes such as humanitarian work, animal welfare, and the protection of existing rainforests. We also aim to be a carbon-neutral publisher with carbon-neutral products, which means that by buying from 3dtotal Publishing, you are helping to balance the environmental damage caused by the publishing, shipping, and retail industries, as well as supporting many other causes. See 3dtotal.com/charity for full details.

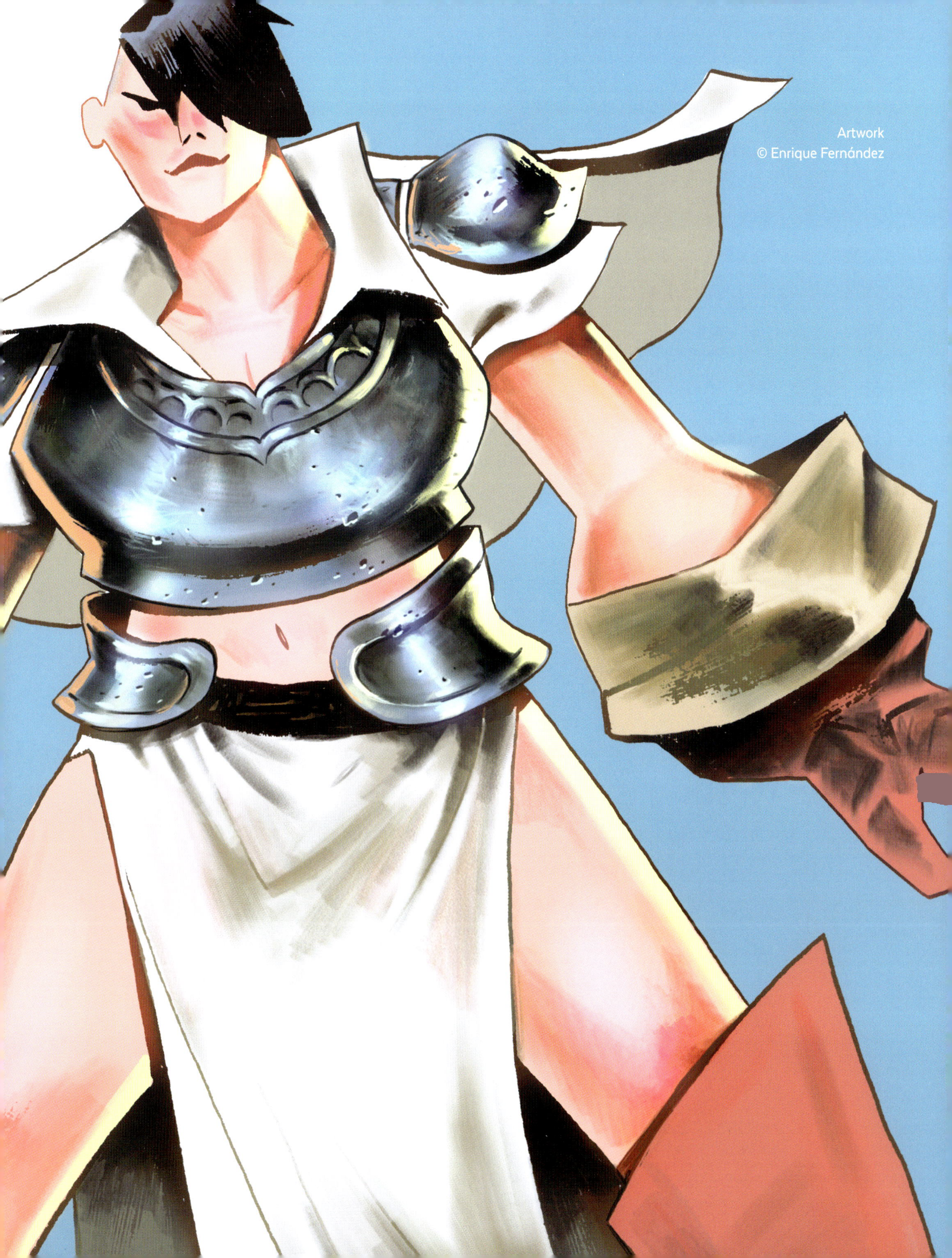
Artwork
© Enrique Fernández

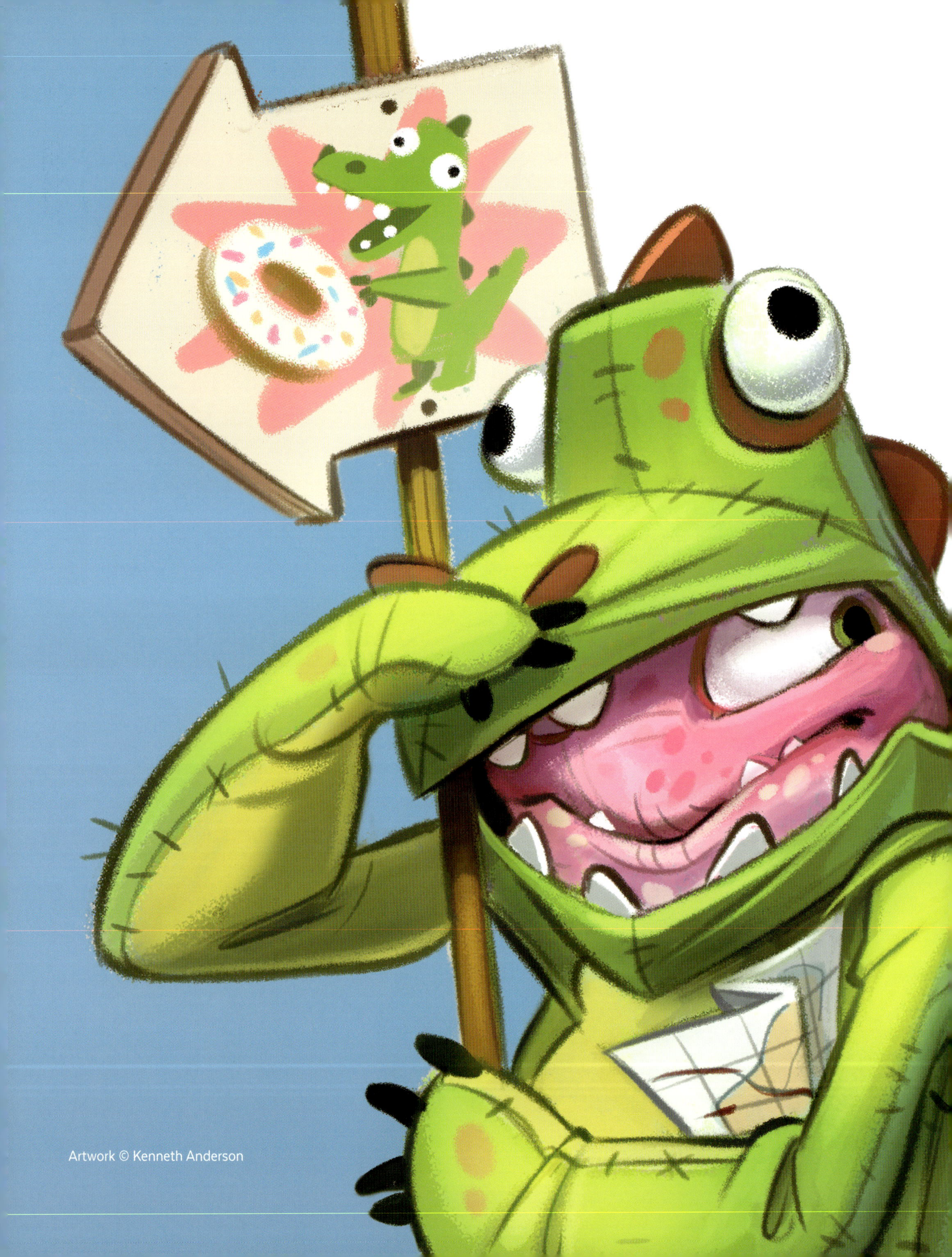

CONTENTS

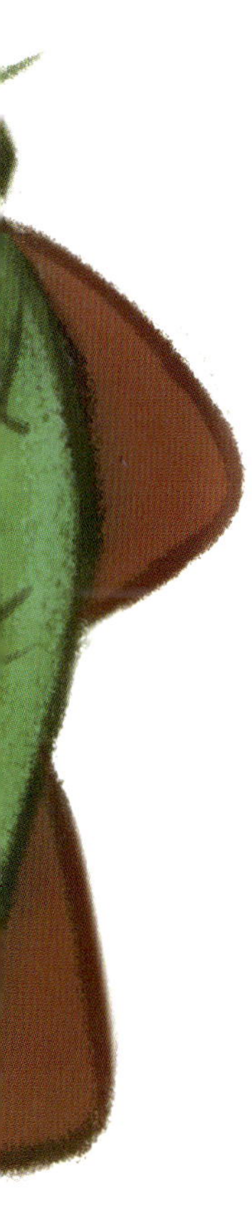

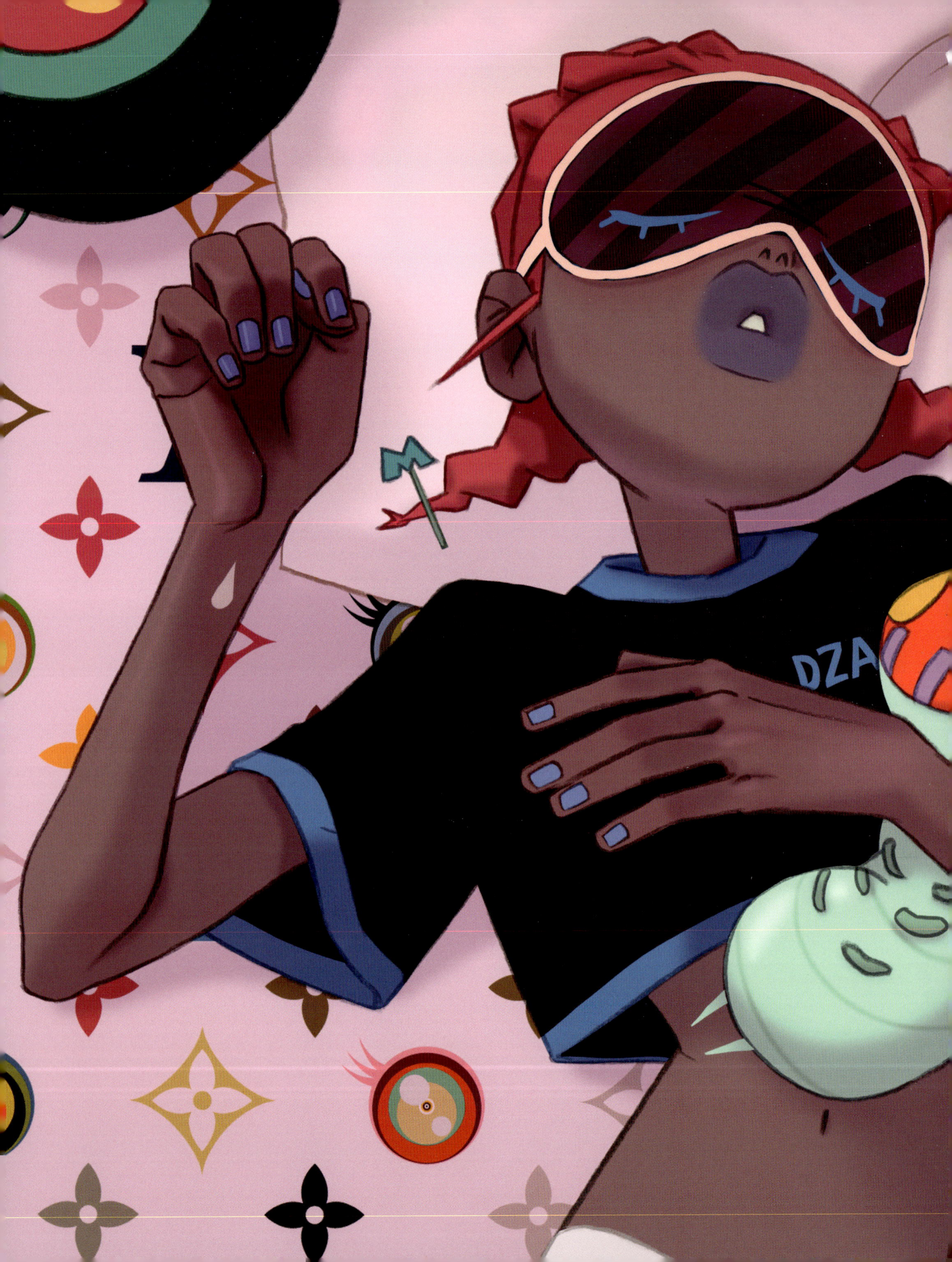
DZA

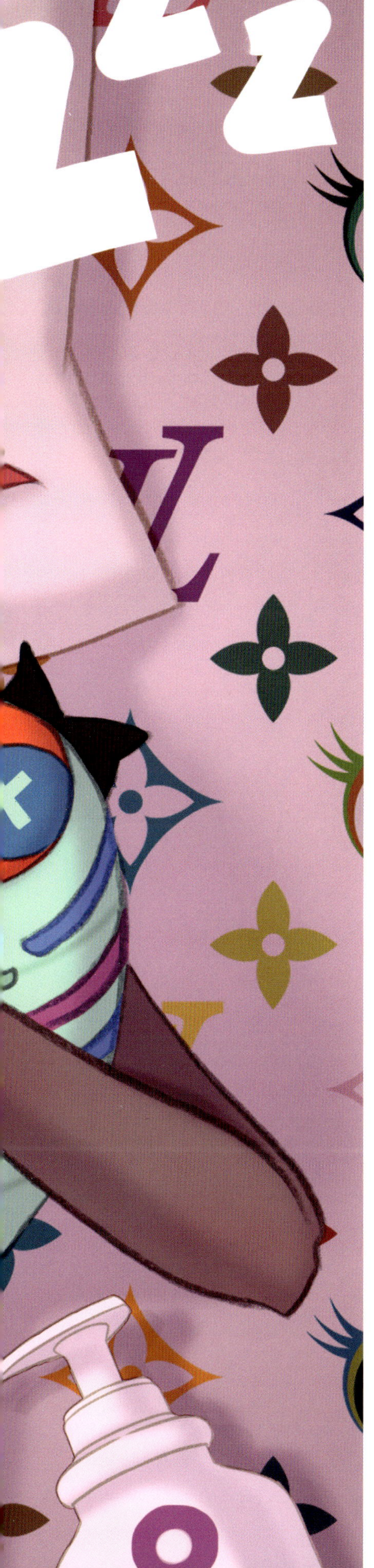

FOREWORD

I was always into character design. I used to copy my favorite cartoon characters as a child, then come up with ideas for creating my own characters for existing universes. I must have designed a dozen *Sailor Moon* warriors! I have now been freelancing and creating characters for many years, and there are a few common questions that people ask me. They are usually "How do I find my own style?" and "How do I stay motivated?"

"HOW DO I FIND MY OWN STYLE?"

I strongly believe that style is not just a set of features. It's not like you decide that from now on you are going to draw noses like *this* and use colors like *this*. Style is something that naturally arises from the artist's vision, so your vision should come before everything. To develop your vision, you must research, experiment, and absorb a lot of material, digest it, and apply it to your project. At first you'll just pick up the most "snazzy" things, the things that are obviously cool and easy to understand. But if you keep using those elements in your work for some time, you'll quickly get tired of them. This is why, when you're ready for them, you'll start to look for more and more sophisticated ideas and inspirations.

"HOW DO I STAY MOTIVATED?"

So how can you find motivation for practice? It's crucial to have artists to look up to when you are studying, but you can't just rely on outside help. Generally you have to love what you are doing. Find a small spark of love and blow it up. If you can't enjoy things, no amount of advice will help you, and you will only end up hurting yourself and quitting. Enjoy your workplace, enjoy your tools, enjoy even a small doodle that turned out well.

I feel like we all have sort of "sockets" inside us that are waiting to be filled by certain puzzle pieces. These pieces are taken from things that inspire us; some of them might be known to us from beginning, but most of them will have to be carved out and discovered through hard work. If you make it to the end, you'll see something really amazing: your ultimate favorite art style. And it will be yours.

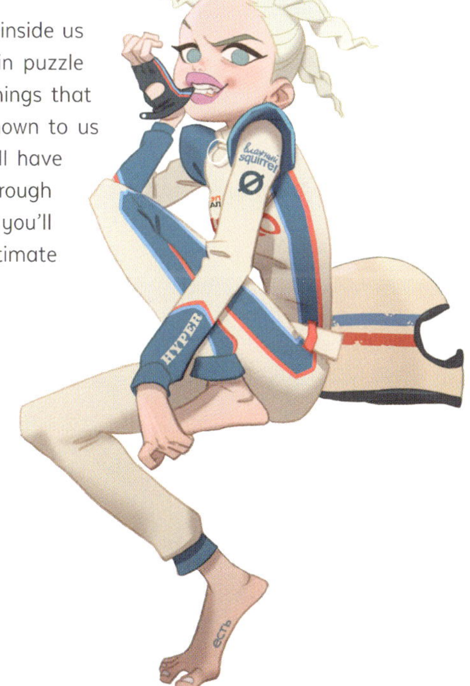

Good luck on your journey!

ANNA CATTISH
Artist, Character designer

annacattish.com
instagram.com/anna_cattish

Artwork © Anna Cattish

INTRODUCTION

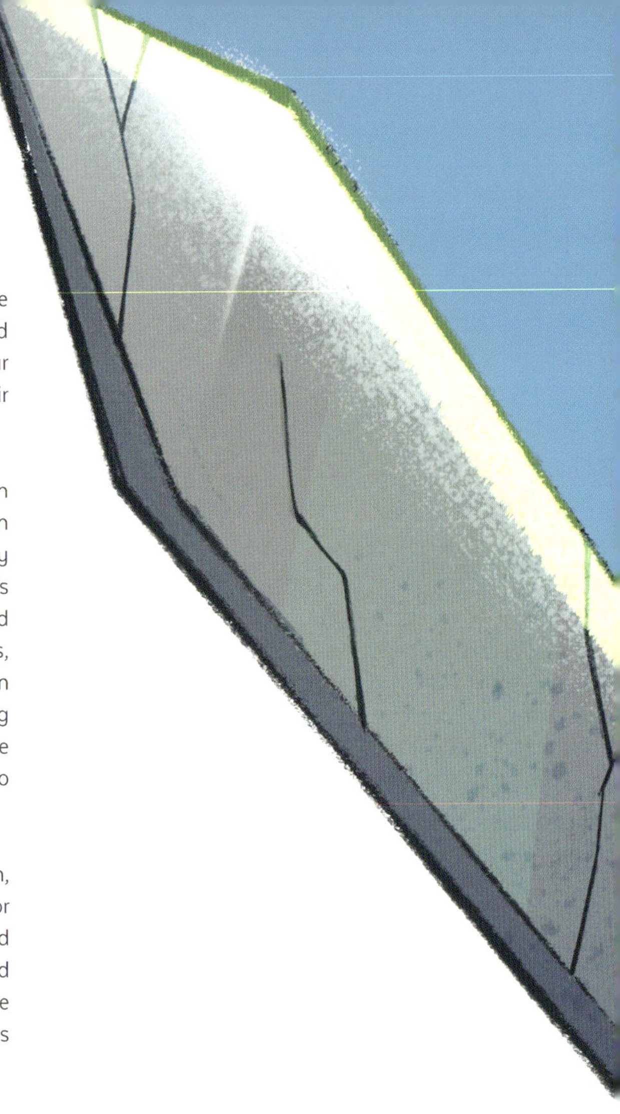

Character design forms the backbone of so many things that we enjoy: our favorite childhood animations, popular comics, memorable book illustrations, and beloved gaming franchises. Whether they are heroes, anti-heroes, villains, or sidekicks, our favorite characters are often those who don't just tell a great story through their plot and actions, but through their appearances.

An artist's personal style is something unique that makes their work stand out from the crowd, but in the field of character design specifically, an artist's stylization choices are a way to make a unique character with an appearance and personality that a reader or viewer will vividly remember. There is a reason why so many people's early love of drawing began with copying their favorite characters: memorable and effective stylization, that is, the successful simplification and exaggeration of forms, proportions, and details. Perhaps a character had distinctive features that stuck in your mind, or a shape that was really fun to draw, or a costume with intriguing details that fondly reminded you of their setting or story. All those aspects were decided by character designers and visual development artists whose goal was to bring that character to life in the most original and exciting way possible.

In this book, talented character designers from across the industries of animation, illustration, comics, and games will share their knowledge and approaches for building a character from scratch. The book's first section will get you acquainted with fundamentals related to body shapes, gestures, expressions, color theory, and common character design methods. We recommend that you start here before moving on to the step-by-step projects, so you have an overview of the process before you begin.

Each of the six main projects in the book is by one artist, interpreting the brief for one core character, which will be developed from research and thumbnails up to a final posed and colored design. Then, as an additional exercise, the artist will create three spin-off variations of their main character: for example, the character in a different genre, at a younger or older age, or in the form of an animal. These will give you some ideas for how the distinctive features and personality of a character can be translated into different scenarios, and how you can flesh out a sense of story across different variations of the same character theme. You do not need to use specific software or a particular drawing tool to follow this book, as it is focused on ideas rather than techniques, so you can adapt what you learn to whatever medium you prefer.

Character design is engaging and appealing by its very nature, because its aim is to connect with *you*, the viewer, and tell you a story. A strong design is one that not only intrigues and pleases the eye, but is true to the character's spirit and helps the viewer to engage with the character's world. We hope you find this book inspiring, fun, and educational, and that it helps you in making your own unique and memorable creations.

MARISA LEWIS
Editor, 3dtotal Publishing

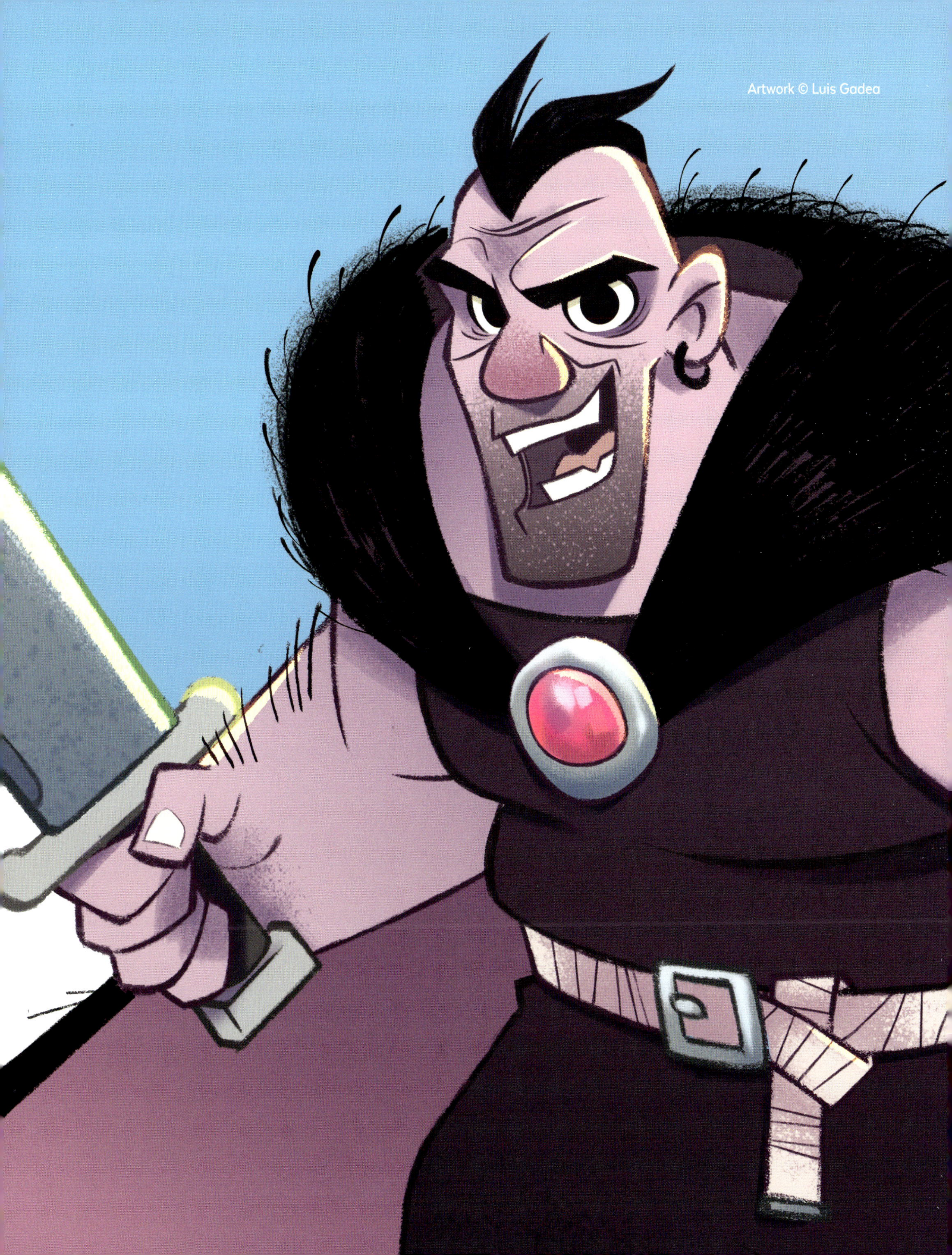
Artwork © Luis Gadea

GETTING STARTED

Before jumping into any major character design projects, let's begin with the fundamentals. In the following chapters, skilled professional artists will introduce you to the essentials of shape language, gestures, facial expressions, and color theory. You will learn how to apply these ideas in a universally useful workflow for designing stylized characters, which will then be applied throughout the rest of this book.

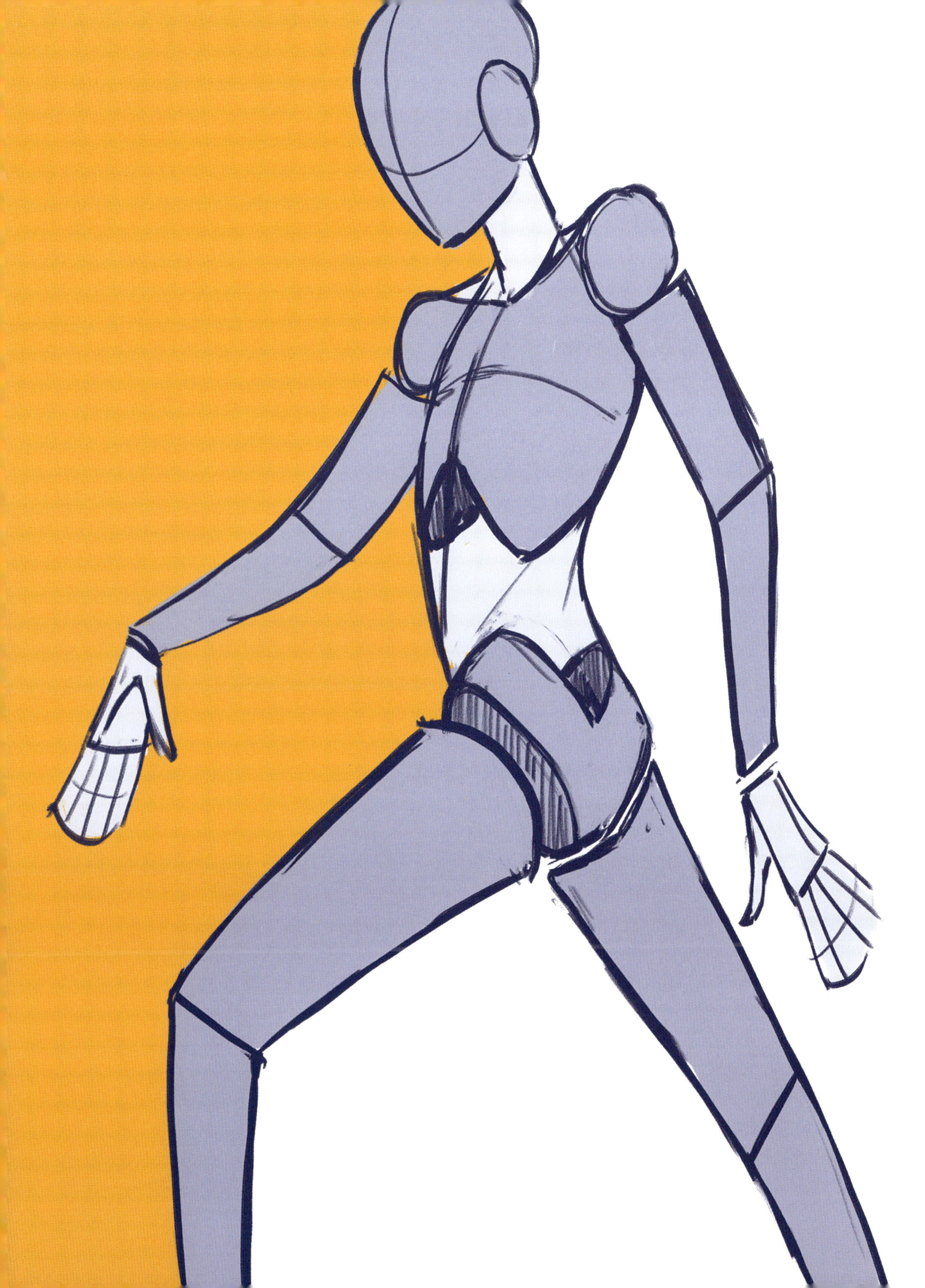

STYLIZED FIGURES

BY IDA HEM

FOUNDATION IS KEY

Humans are one of the most difficult subjects to draw. We see them on a daily basis, so if there is something slightly "wrong" about your representation, it is very apparent. Understanding how the body is built and moves is a must as a character designer, because our main goal is to make the audience believe that the character is real. How can they believe, if a character doesn't look right? A strong foundation is key, and a lack of knowledge will show in your work. You can't hide behind a style,

which is something many artists are or have been guilty of, as it will affect your versatility.

This doesn't mean that every character you design needs to have defined **anatomy**. For example: in a classic comic-book style, anatomy is more realistic and defined, but in the field of animation, characters are heavily simplified due to the high production costs, resulting in greater **stylization**. This is also because of the appeal of stylized

characters to a wide audience, particularly children. However, even if your character has noodles for arms, the viewer must still be able to visualize their underlying skeleton, which leads us back to the importance of understanding how the body is built and moves.

This chapter will give you a brief overview of how the body is constructed, and then show you how to stylize the figure in order to create appealing character designs.

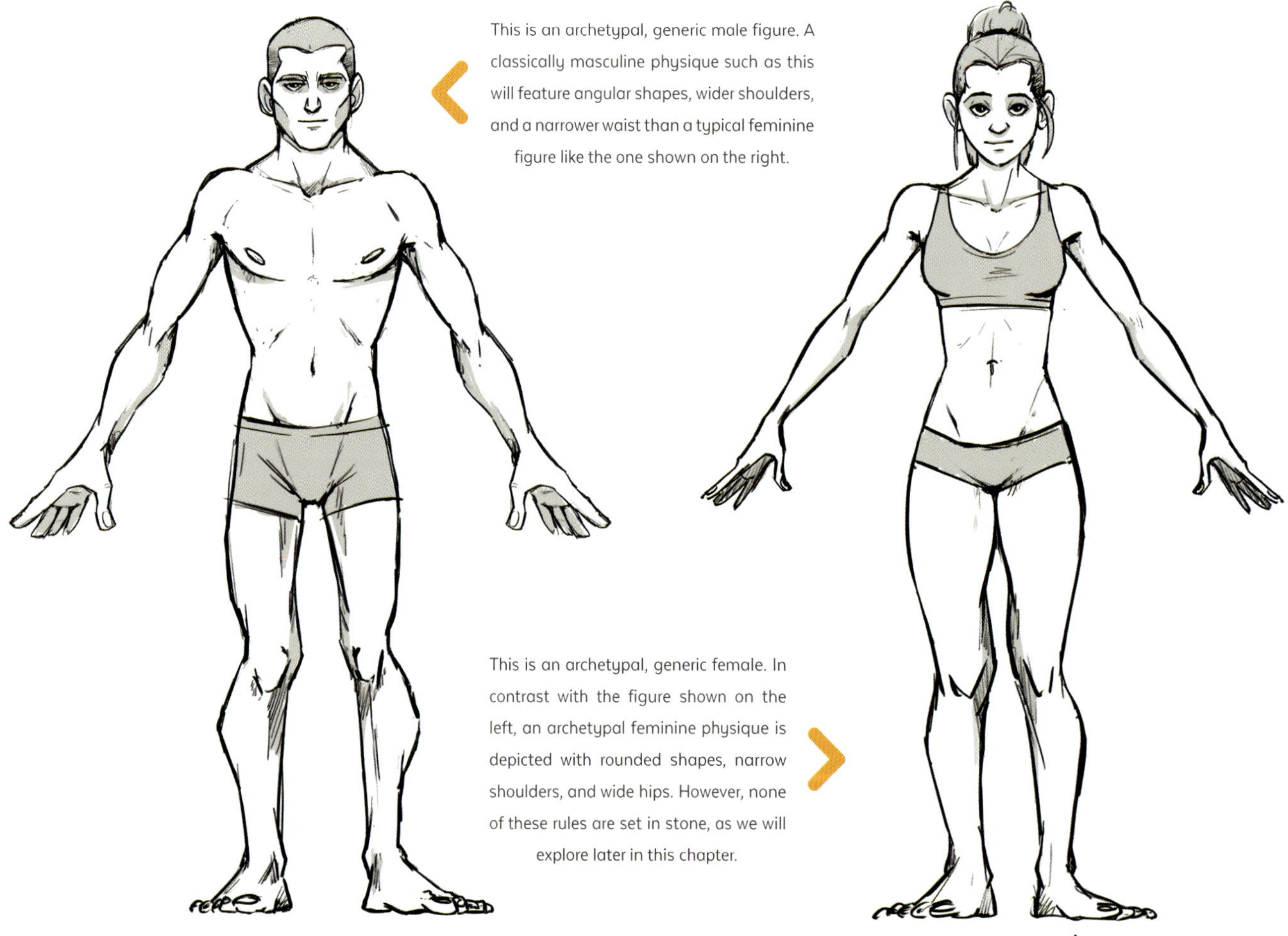

This is an archetypal, generic male figure. A classically masculine physique such as this will feature angular shapes, wider shoulders, and a narrower waist than a typical feminine figure like the one shown on the right.

This is an archetypal, generic female. In contrast with the figure shown on the left, an archetypal feminine physique is depicted with rounded shapes, narrow shoulders, and wide hips. However, none of these rules are set in stone, as we will explore later in this chapter.

SIMPLIFYING SHAPES

Every artist works differently, so there is no universal method for drawing a body "correctly." However, there are notable body masses and landmarks that will be the same no matter what approach you may choose.

It can be counter-productive to start your character off with a high level of detail; establishing where a character's eyes are before even knowing how to pose their body may leave you with a weak end result. Instead, working from big to small shapes, or from **macro to micro**, builds up a strong initial foundation for your design. Constructing a body can seem daunting because of what looks like an endless amount of muscles and joints, but it can be broken down very simply.

You can separate the body into **six basic parts**, as highlighted in the figures below: the chest, pelvis, shoulders, legs, arms, and head. By dividing the body into shapes, you can see the "bigger picture" more easily. Once you have an understanding of how to separate the body into different shapes, it will be easier to draw your character in more appealing and tangible poses, as well as taking those shapes and exaggerating them to make a more interesting, stylized design.

Bony landmarks, or parts of the skeleton which help to visibly define the surface of the body, are useful for working out where to split the body into sections (for example, at the hips or collarbones). Making these landmarks more or less pronounced also helps to convey a character's physique.

You can estimate the realistic base **proportions** of a figure by counting out how many lengths of the character's head fit into their overall height. An average male figure may measure between seven and eight "heads" tall, unless heavily exaggerated; similarly, an average, unexaggerated female figure may measure between six and seven-and-a-half heads. This common rule of thumb can help you to quickly map out a whole figure or change a character's proportions. For example, a superhero character may be up to nine heads tall to make them appear more impressive.

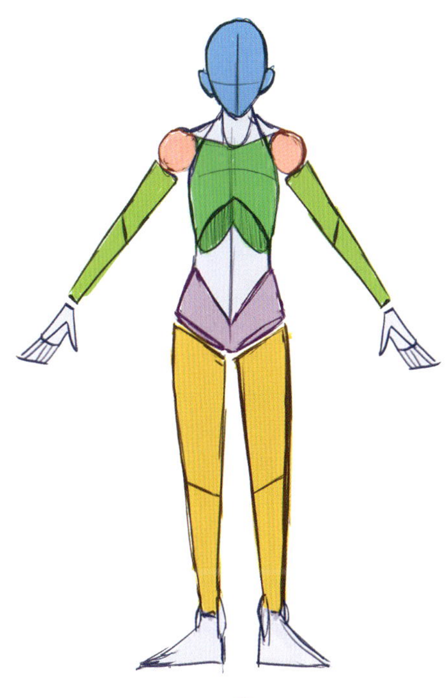

By visualizing the different parts of the body as shapes, it is easier to see how the body is built. For example, in this sketch the complex pelvis is simplified into a solid piece of underwear. The body is now easier to stylize and pose, as we can see in the figures to the right.

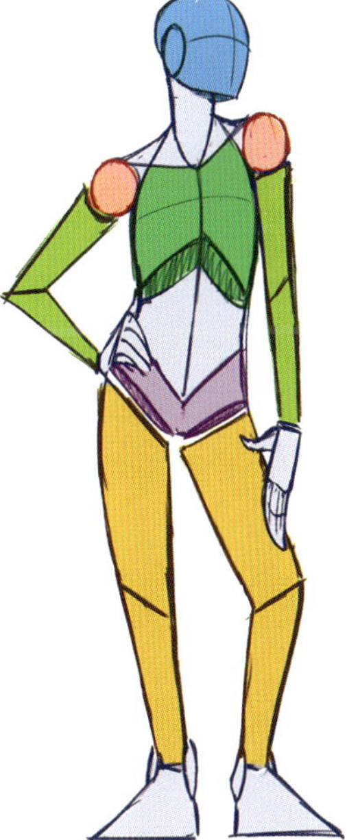

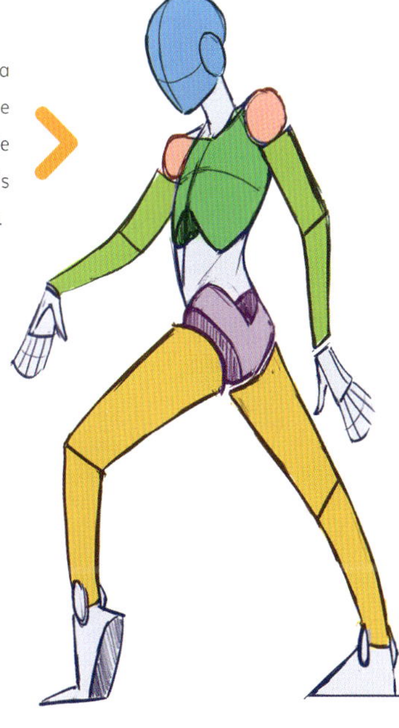

An effective way of creating a dynamic figure is by twisting the shoulders and hips in the opposite direction of each other. Contrast is key to creating more visual appeal.

Contrapposto is an Italian term used for when the weight of the character is shifted onto one leg, and the angle of the hips and shoulders move opposite each other. Posing a figure in this way makes it feel more natural.

A house cat may have a different type of anatomy than a human, but can just as easily be broken down into the same basic shapes. Focus on taking the most recognizable aspects of the body, such as the chest, front legs, back legs, and head, and simplify them until they are just a geometric mass.

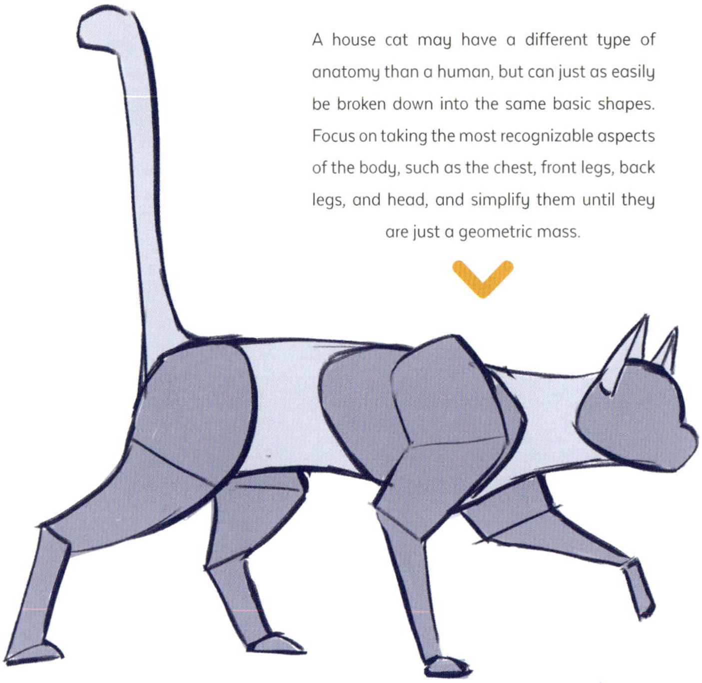

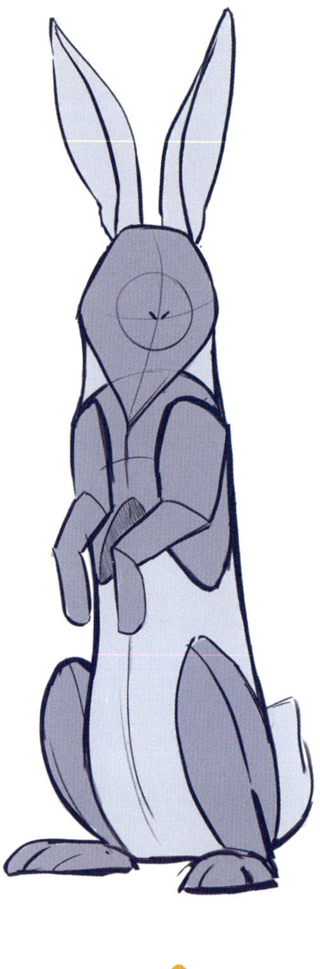

A rabbit is a more challenging animal than a cat to break down, because small furry animals' postures often obscure their anatomy. However, despite being a different animal, the shapes are almost the same. This is because the basic skeletal structure is very similar between many different species. The only difference may be that the spine is longer, or the back paws are bigger.

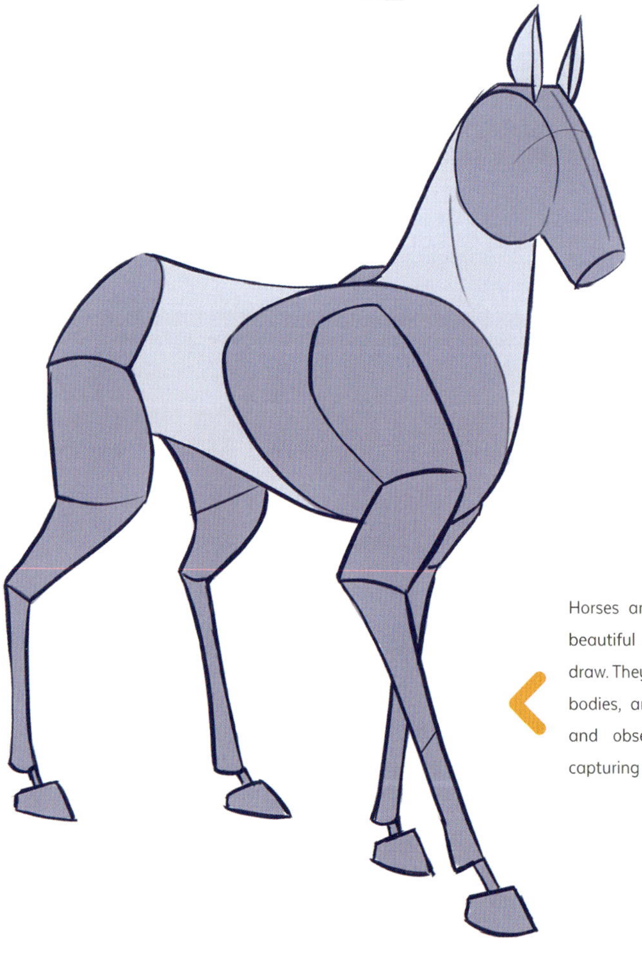

Horses are known for being elegant and beautiful animals that are challenging to draw. They have long legs, almost cylindrical bodies, and thick, strong necks. Research and observation is always helpful for capturing the anatomy of a more complex animal such as this.

DIFFERENT BODIES

The best thing about humans is that we are all unique, and we are all built **differently**. Though there are useful guidelines, such as the proportions I mentioned earlier, there is no universal template on how to draw a body. Using the "heads" system of measurement is a great starting point when beginning the learning process, but keep in mind that it may end up becoming a limiting template to follow, potentially resulting in similar, repetitive characters.

On these pages you will see a range of potential shapes and sizes for human characters of different genders and ages – and even some non-humans – but of course there are countless other possibilities which you will discover as you work and research. There are as many different body types as there are **personalities**. Expanding your knowledge on how to emphasize proportions and shapes will go a long way, and being able to draw a wide range of characters with different forms and body types is a highly desired skill to have as a character designer.

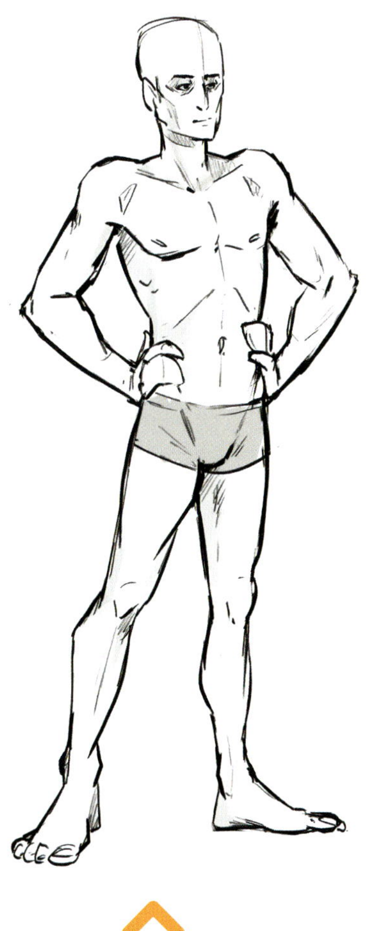

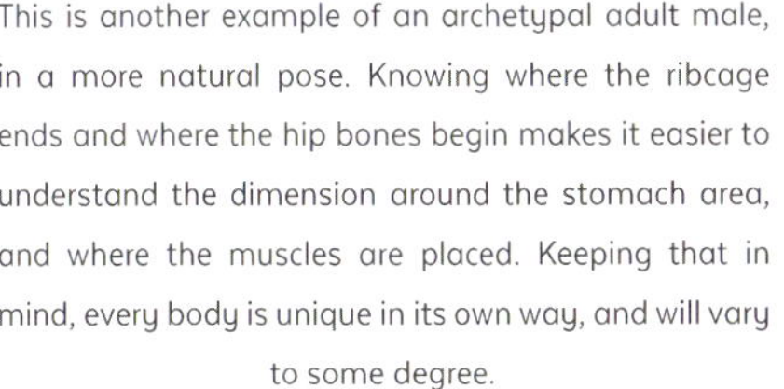

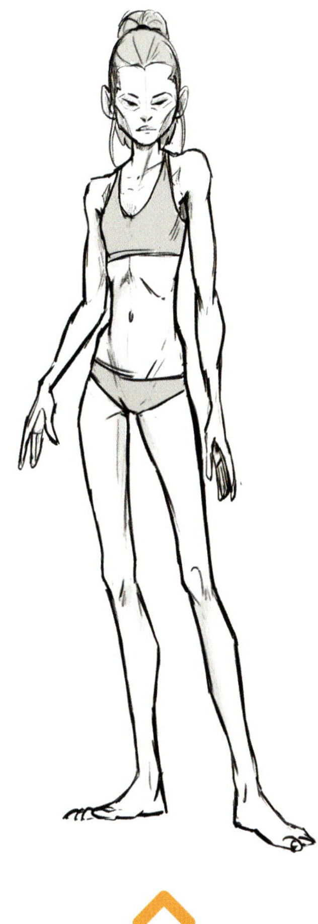

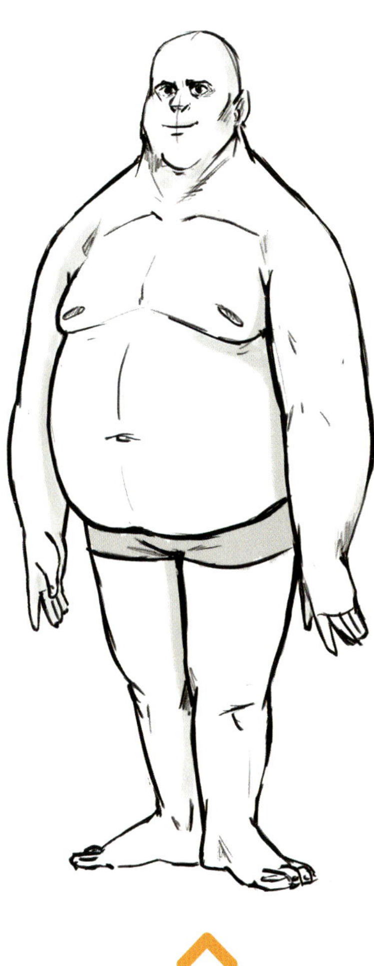

This is another example of an archetypal adult male, in a more natural pose. Knowing where the ribcage ends and where the hip bones begin makes it easier to understand the dimension around the stomach area, and where the muscles are placed. Keeping that in mind, every body is unique in its own way, and will vary to some degree.

Here is an example of an underweight adult female. Notice how bony landmarks like the hip bones, shoulders, ribcage, and knees are more highlighted and defined. This makes the body more angular, in contrast to the softer, rounded forms of the female figure shown on page 14.

This is an example of an overweight body type for an adult male. The bony landmarks that are usually found on the body may not be that visible anymore, so you are working with simplified, round shapes. Instead of using the bones as anchor points for the anatomy, consider gravity and how the excess body masses move in relation to the skeleton.

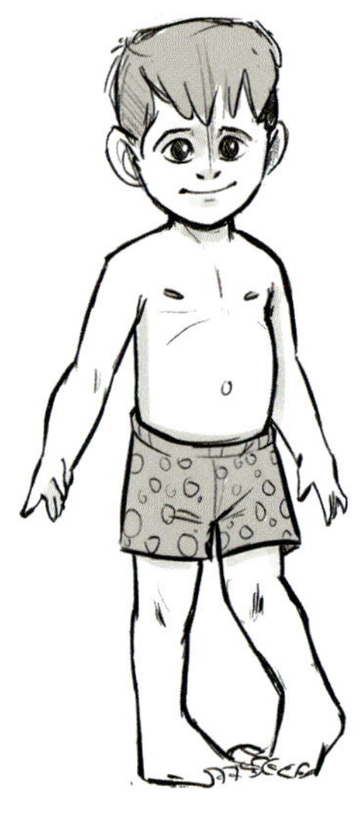

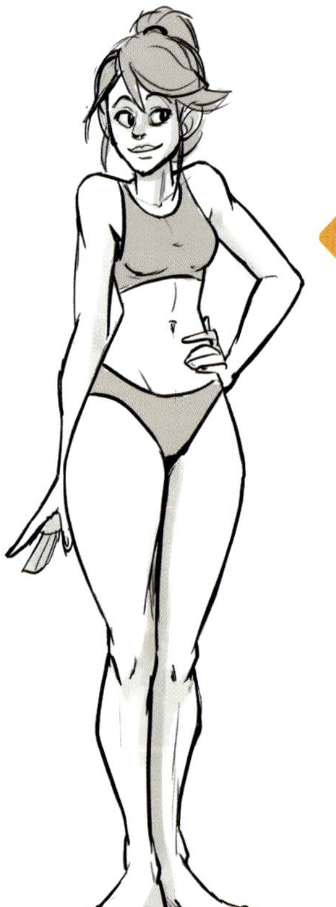

This is a young female adult with a fuller figure. In contrast to a more overweight character, gravity comes less into play. You can slightly see the underlying bone structure, but this body type will be more rounded out around the hips, shoulders, knees, and ankles, giving the character a less defined and softer look.

This is an example of a boy around three to four years old. In contrast to adults, a child may only be four heads tall, so the head is rather large in comparison to the body. A key visual element of a child is their soft features, so utilizing round shapes is an effective choice.

This is an example of how an older male's body shape could look. Obviously an elderly character can range anywhere from underweight to overweight, but a distinguishing feature of elderly characters is often the extra skin, such as around this man's neck and belly, as skin becomes looser with age.

This is an example of a female adult with a slim, pear-shaped body. Like many female characters, this design utilizes soft, round shapes to emphasize a classically feminine look. Her hips are slightly on the wider side, creating the pear-shaped figure, but other female characters may have a bigger chest and smaller hips, or equally wide hips and shoulders.

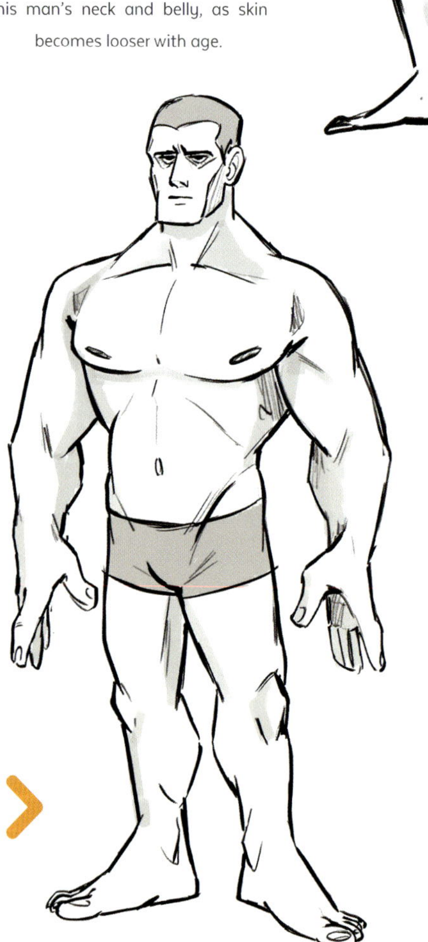

This is an adult male with defined muscles and a strong, solid body shape, further enhanced by widening his shoulders and narrowing his hips. These top-heavy proportions are typically used for male action heroes and superhero characters.

EXAGGERATING SHAPES

Now that we have seen how complex figures can be simplified into a more manageable structure, let's look at how to take that a step further and create stylized designs using basic geometric shapes to create **shape language**. Using basic shapes as a starting point for a design is a more flexible approach than limiting a character to realistic proportions, and results in more imaginative outcomes. This is where you can put your creativity on display. Deriving a design from a shape is an extremely common technique that will be used throughout this book, and also goes back to the idea of working **macro to micro**, focusing on the big picture before refining the details.

The most commonly used shapes are circles, triangles, and squares, or some variation of these. Each shape has different traits that can speak to what kind of personality your character has. For example, a **circle** doesn't have any edges, so a round character will look softer and kinder. A **triangle** has sharp edges, and will come across as dynamic or even dangerous. A **square** comes across as solid and compact, so is often used for characters that are physically strong. Using these three shapes, you can make a design with shape language that highlights your character's personality, making for a stronger design.

The concept of shape language isn't only used to showcase a character's personality, but also to create a distinct and unique design that will make the audience remember your character. Mickey Mouse is a good example of this idea, utilizing circles to successfully create an iconic silhouette.

Two key aspects of designing using shape language are **exaggeration** and **contrast**, ideas which you will encounter throughout the projects in this book. You can simply exaggerate and contrast the six basic body parts identified previously, or you can group some together to form larger contrasting forms, but these two elements are crucial for making your designs more stylized and visually interesting. For example, you could create exaggeration and contrast by giving your character a tiny head and a huge body, or a short torso with long legs. Don't restrict yourself to a realistic body frame, because it will result in a less interesting outcome.

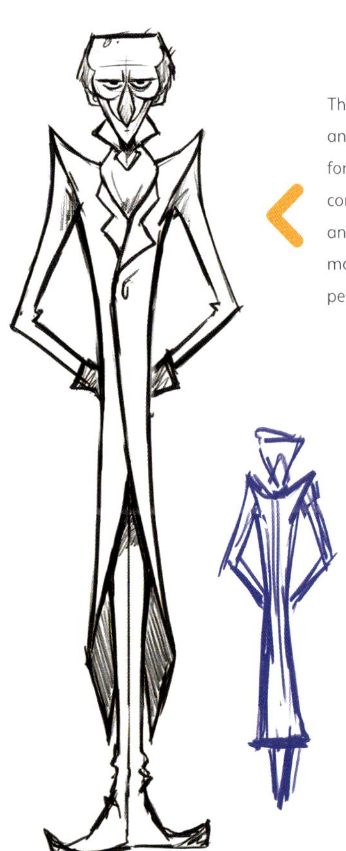

This design is an unfriendly character. Angles and sharp edges are effective tools to use for this type of design because they often come across as dangerous. Making him tall and slim achieves an almost snake-like feel, making us feel like we can't trust him. Deriving personalities and features from animals is a common character design technique.

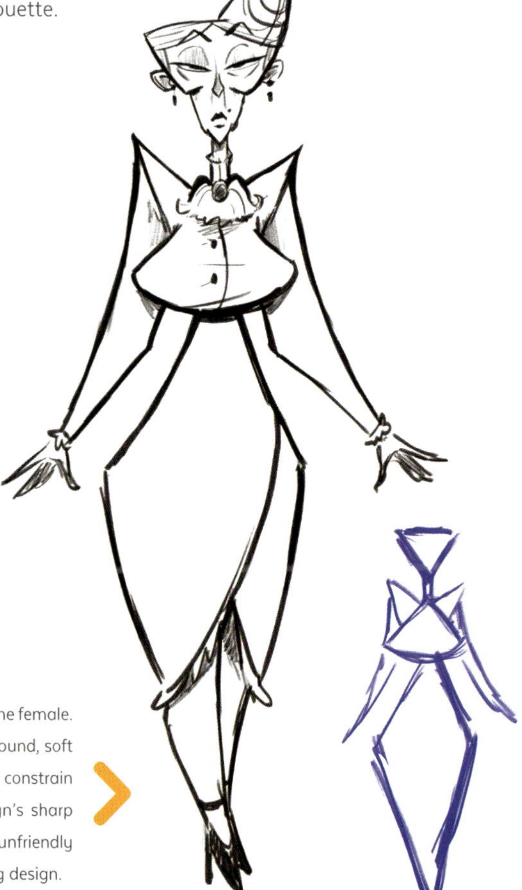

This is another villainous character, this time female. People will more often than not connect round, soft shapes to female characters, but don't constrain yourself to those perceptions. This design's sharp angles help to emphasize the character's unfriendly demeanor, making for a more interesting design.

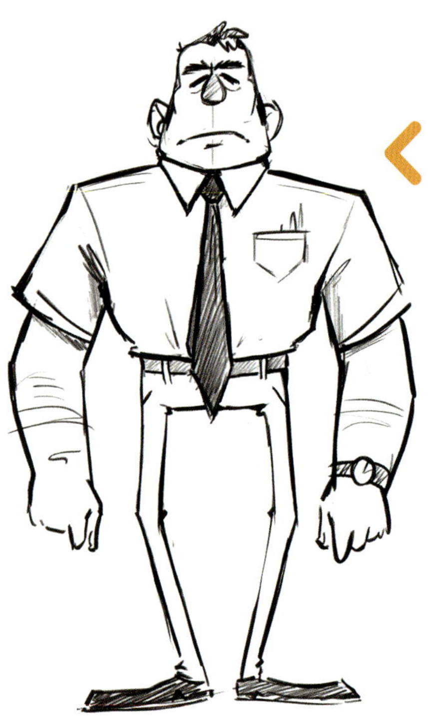

You can make a design unique by experimenting with contrasting shapes. In this case, I make the character's legs long and skinny in contrast with his short, blocky torso. The character still comes across as a stubborn and stern man, due to the squared shapes in his design, but the contrast is what makes him interesting and unique.

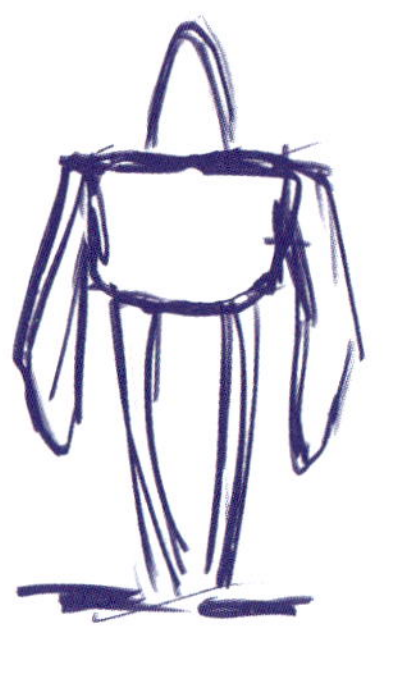

This design feels friendly and solid as it combines a circle and a square. A nun is a good choice of character to demonstrate this down-to-earth and friendly shape language. This design also shows that you can exaggerate shapes to the point where you no longer need to define where landmarks such as the elbows are. Instead, they are rounded off to make the entire arm a half-circle, emphasizing the character's friendly feel.

This design utilizes both circles and sharp edges to describe a unique body shape. You should use the shapes to explain a character's personality; in this case, a strong female warrior who may come across as mean and angry, but perhaps has a softer side, suggested by the unexpected rounder edges.

This design is based on a square, but has a slightly top-heavy chest to emphasize the muscular aspect of the character. A technique you can use to make your design more unified is repeating your main shape elsewhere in the design. In this case, I turn the shape upside down and repeat it as the nose.

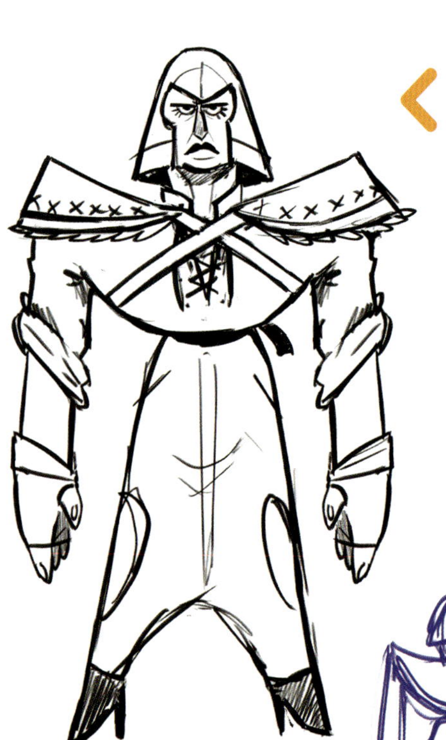

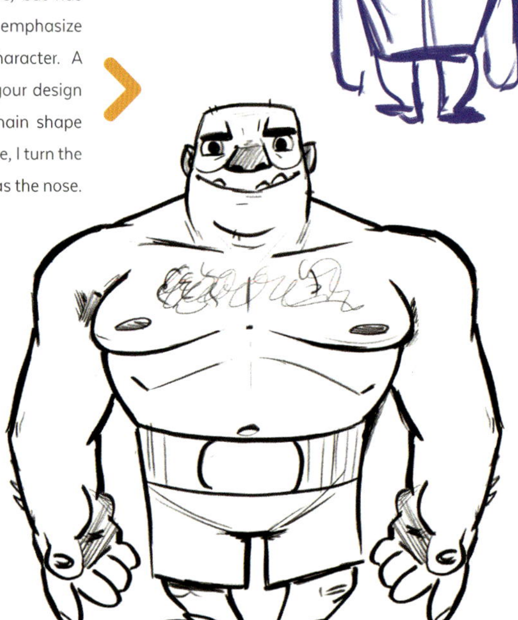

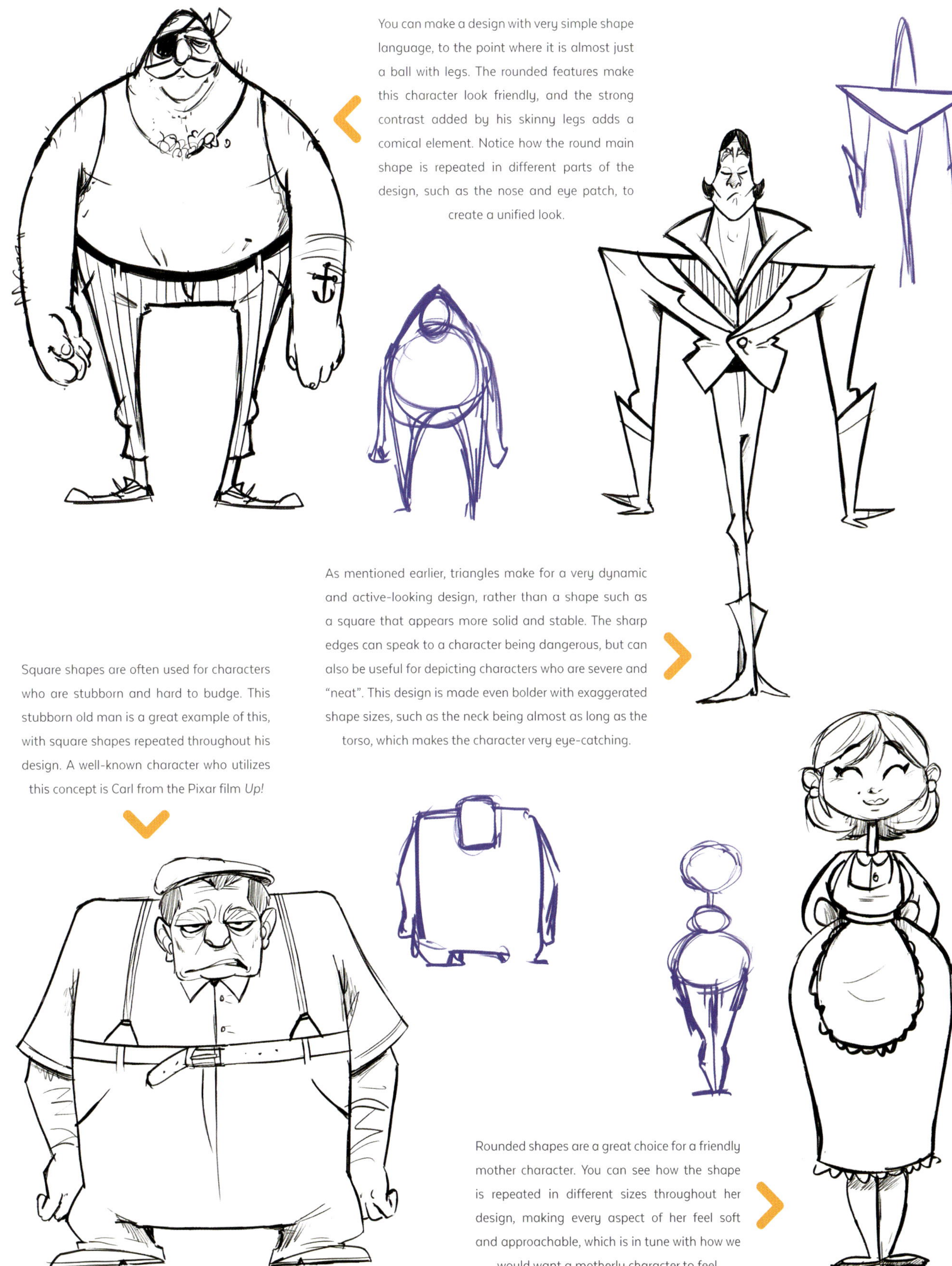

You can make a design with very simple shape language, to the point where it is almost just a ball with legs. The rounded features make this character look friendly, and the strong contrast added by his skinny legs adds a comical element. Notice how the round main shape is repeated in different parts of the design, such as the nose and eye patch, to create a unified look.

As mentioned earlier, triangles make for a very dynamic and active-looking design, rather than a shape such as a square that appears more solid and stable. The sharp edges can speak to a character being dangerous, but can also be useful for depicting characters who are severe and "neat". This design is made even bolder with exaggerated shape sizes, such as the neck being almost as long as the torso, which makes the character very eye-catching.

Square shapes are often used for characters who are stubborn and hard to budge. This stubborn old man is a great example of this, with square shapes repeated throughout his design. A well-known character who utilizes this concept is Carl from the Pixar film *Up!*

Rounded shapes are a great choice for a friendly mother character. You can see how the shape is repeated in different sizes throughout her design, making every aspect of her feel soft and approachable, which is in tune with how we would want a motherly character to feel.

GESTURE & POSE

BY IDA HEM

WHAT IS GESTURE?

Now that we have a better understanding of anatomy, shape language, and how to stylize the figure, it is time to discuss **gesture**. What is it and why is it useful? The general idea of a gesture is conveying an emotion, action, or some kind of non-verbal communication. For example, visually explaining someone's feeling of happiness through their **body language**. Gesture is not only used for emotions, but also for creating poses, conveying your character's personality, or showing a specific action.

Gesture drawings are quick and loose sketches. This ensures that they are full of life and energy, and will let you explore many different options without wasting time on details. In many ways, gesture drawing can be considered the non-technical part as far as character design goes, because it

is all about **emotion** and **personality**. This part of the creative process is especially useful and important because showcasing your character's personality using only one drawing will help you to sell the idea behind them. If your audience can't tell what kind of person your character is, they have no reason to become invested.

When I studied this particular art form for the first time in college, the one big mistake I made was not looking at the bigger picture of the figure. When gaining an understanding of anatomy, it is useful to separate the different body parts into different sections, but when producing a gesture you have to make sure all those parts work together in unison. Instead of drawing the head, and then the torso, and then the legs, and so forth, utilizing the

concept of the **line of action** will ensure a much more dynamic pose and visually pleasing flow.

The line of action is a curved line that runs down your character's spine, giving you a visual guide that helps to pose your character with a sense of force. The line of action will always be curved in a **direction**, depending on what you are trying to portray; this is often an S- or C-shaped curve derived from the natural flow of the spine, and can vary from strong to subtle in the extremity of its curves. A mistake a lot of beginners make is leaving the line of action vertically straight, resulting in a rigid torso and a stiff pose. It is easy to forget how flexible the spine is, which is why you should always draw the line of action first and use that as a guide for the rest of your pose.

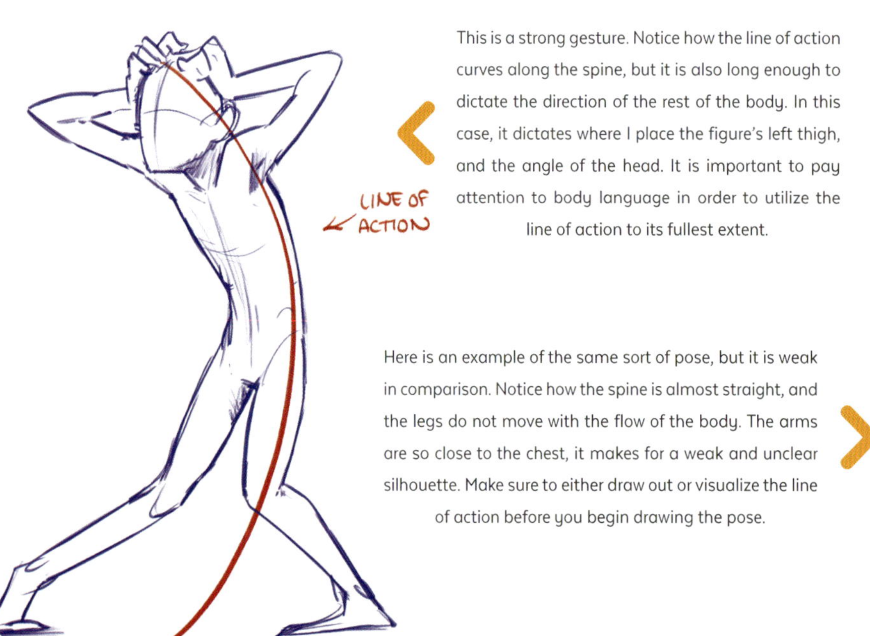

This is a strong gesture. Notice how the line of action curves along the spine, but it is also long enough to dictate the direction of the rest of the body. In this case, it dictates where I place the figure's left thigh, and the angle of the head. It is important to pay attention to body language in order to utilize the line of action to its fullest extent.

Here is an example of the same sort of pose, but it is weak in comparison. Notice how the spine is almost straight, and the legs do not move with the flow of the body. The arms are so close to the chest, it makes for a weak and unclear silhouette. Make sure to either draw out or visualize the line of action before you begin drawing the pose.

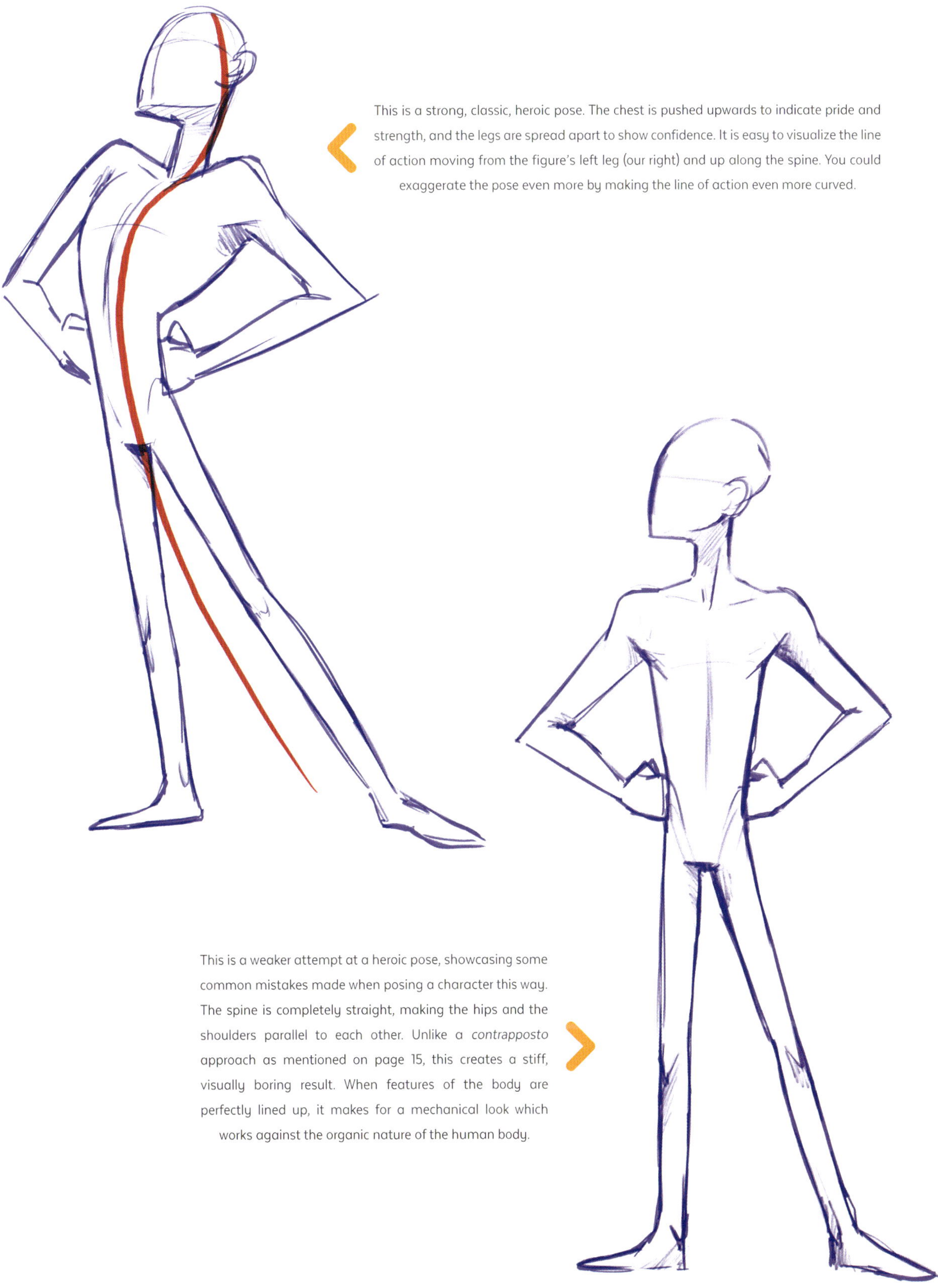

This is a strong, classic, heroic pose. The chest is pushed upwards to indicate pride and strength, and the legs are spread apart to show confidence. It is easy to visualize the line of action moving from the figure's left leg (our right) and up along the spine. You could exaggerate the pose even more by making the line of action even more curved.

This is a weaker attempt at a heroic pose, showcasing some common mistakes made when posing a character this way. The spine is completely straight, making the hips and the shoulders parallel to each other. Unlike a *contrapposto* approach as mentioned on page 15, this creates a stiff, visually boring result. When features of the body are perfectly lined up, it makes for a mechanical look which works against the organic nature of the human body.

SQUASH AND STRETCH

Squash and stretch is a principle commonly used in animation and cartoons. It helps to describe the organic nature of the character, and expresses a sense of motion that will make your characters feel alive. For example, a rock would not need any "squash and stretch," because it is completely solid and rigid. In contrast, the volumes of a subject like the human body usually have the capacity to squash and stretch. When you stretch a subject, notice how it becomes thinner, instead of just longer, creating a heightened sense of action and drama. When you squash a subject, it becomes shorter and thicker, much like a rubber ball, creating tension as if it is about to spring back into shape. Consider how you can use squash and stretch techniques to "push" - or exaggerate - a pose or expression to make it more clear and effective.

As you look through the poses and expressions in this book, pay attention to how the character is being stretched out or compressed down to create a more vivid impression of life and weight, and try to incorporate the same ideas into your own characters.

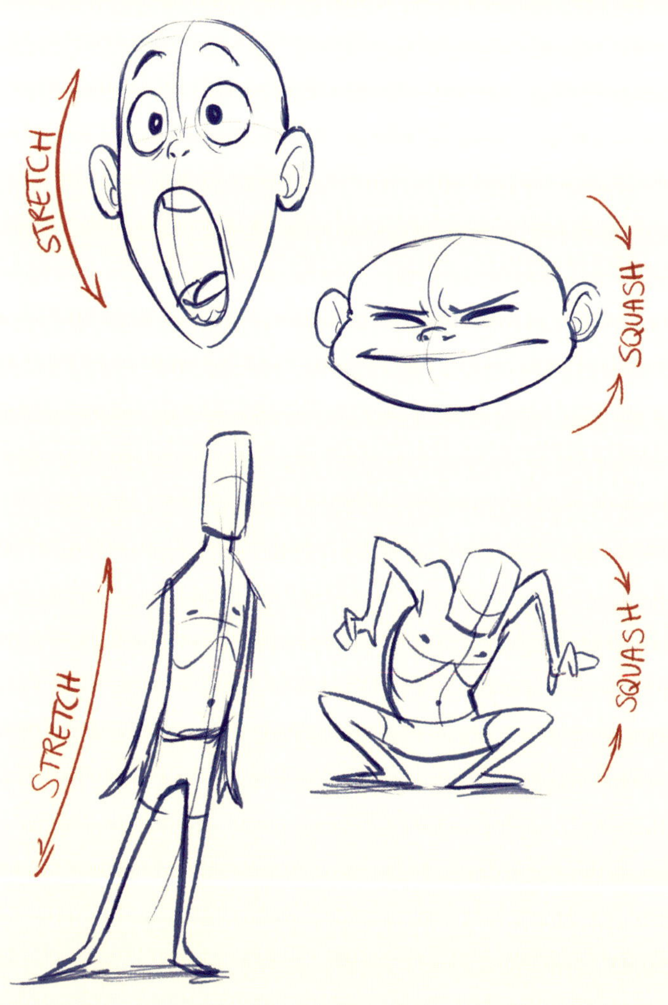

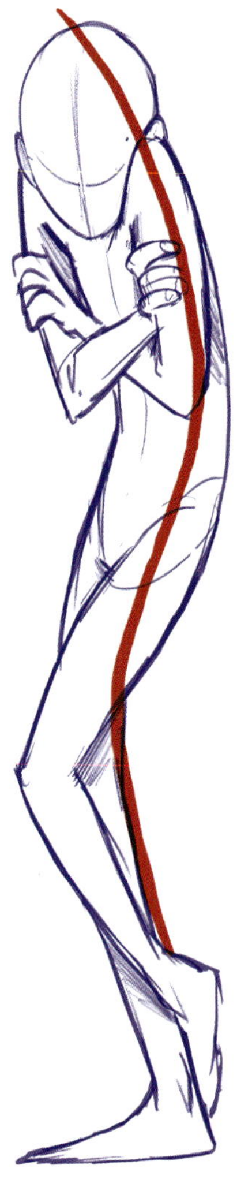

A figure doesn't necessarily need an active, action-packed silhouette with lots of movement to have a strong pose. Poses with an inactive silhouette can suggest a lack of confidence which may work in your favor, depending on what you are trying to portray. In this case, the pose is a very shy character, with the shoulders pulled up to hide the neck, and their limbs crossed to appear as small as possible.

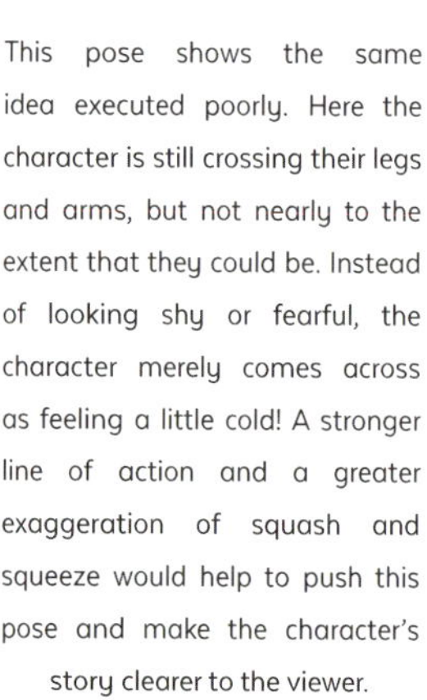

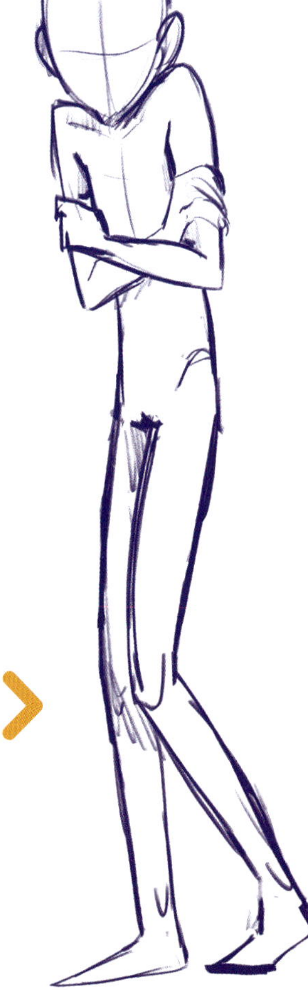

This pose shows the same idea executed poorly. Here the character is still crossing their legs and arms, but not nearly to the extent that they could be. Instead of looking shy or fearful, the character merely comes across as feeling a little cold! A stronger line of action and a greater exaggeration of squash and squeeze would help to push this pose and make the character's story clearer to the viewer.

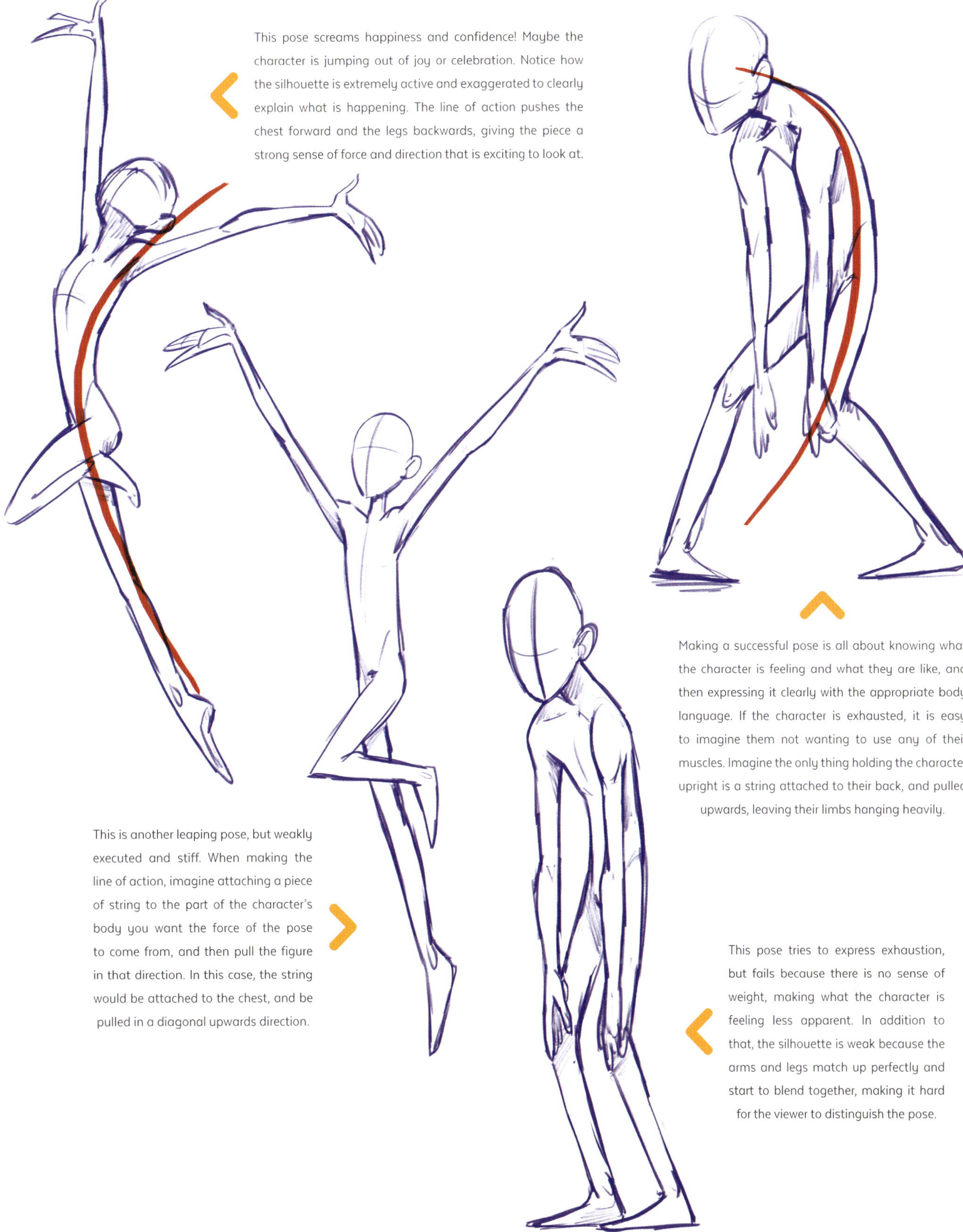

This pose screams happiness and confidence! Maybe the character is jumping out of joy or celebration. Notice how the silhouette is extremely active and exaggerated to clearly explain what is happening. The line of action pushes the chest forward and the legs backwards, giving the piece a strong sense of force and direction that is exciting to look at.

This is another leaping pose, but weakly executed and stiff. When making the line of action, imagine attaching a piece of string to the part of the character's body you want the force of the pose to come from, and then pull the figure in that direction. In this case, the string would be attached to the chest, and be pulled in a diagonal upwards direction.

Making a successful pose is all about knowing what the character is feeling and what they are like, and then expressing it clearly with the appropriate body language. If the character is exhausted, it is easy to imagine them not wanting to use any of their muscles. Imagine the only thing holding the character upright is a string attached to their back, and pulled upwards, leaving their limbs hanging heavily.

This pose tries to express exhaustion, but fails because there is no sense of weight, making what the character is feeling less apparent. In addition to that, the silhouette is weak because the arms and legs match up perfectly and start to blend together, making it hard for the viewer to distinguish the pose.

BUILDING UP FROM A GESTURE

So far this book has covered basic construction, different body shapes, how to take those shapes and exaggerate them for a stylized outcome, as well as what a gesture is and how to capture it. Once you have an understanding of all these concepts, you can use them to create characters with a **bold, clear pose** and silhouette by combining the techniques together in a step-by-step approach. The first step is establishing the **line of action** to which you can then add contrasting and exaggerated shapes, to help you generate the gesture. This is so you have a clear understanding of the character and their attitude from the beginning. The second step is to identify the six key body parts on top of the gesture, often starting with the core forms of the torso, pelvis, and head, to make sure the anatomy will be fleshed out appropriately for the pose. This is where you can start to push and further **exaggerate** the character's underlying shapes to create a stylized shape language. The third step is to finalize your character on top of the gesture and building blocks, refining their costume and surface details.

Always draw the line of action first. It will dictate where the body goes. Add building blocks over your gesture, keeping anatomical structure and shape language in mind, and then flesh out your design according to the pose.

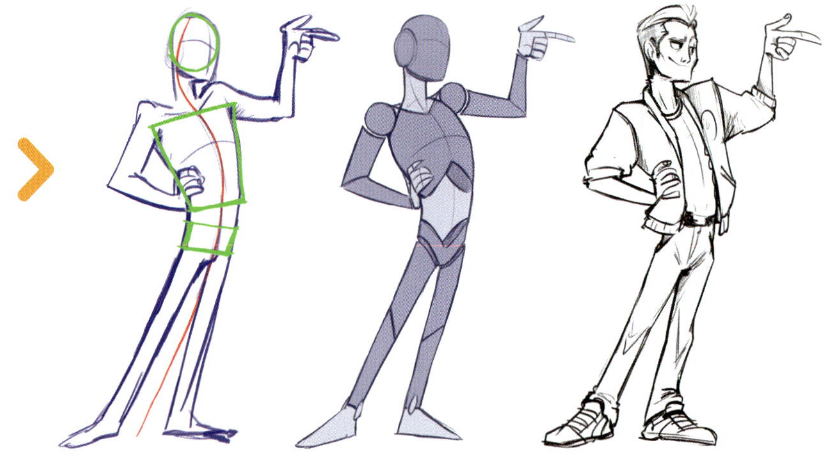

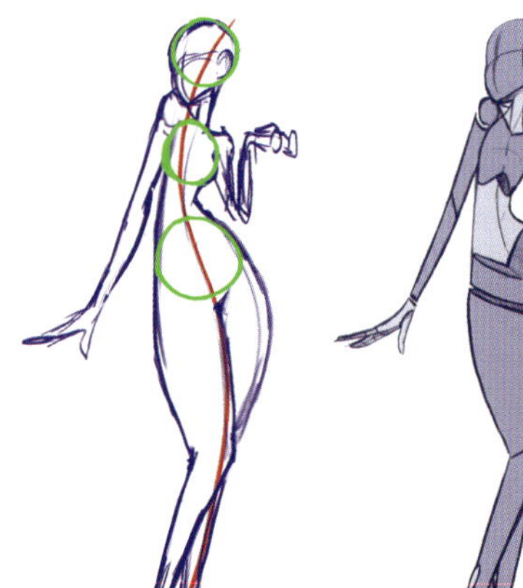

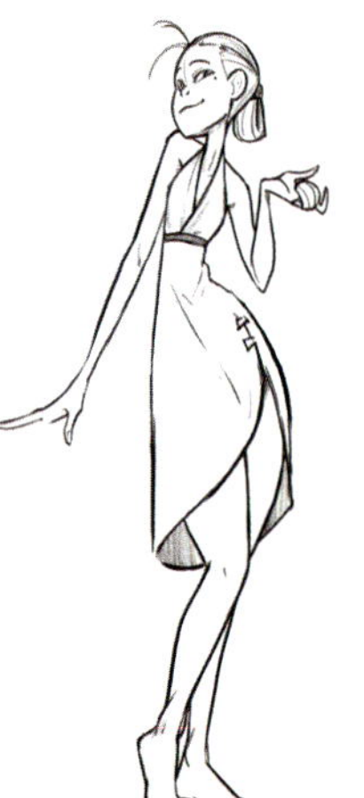

Curving the line of action in an S-shape is a great way to achieve an elegant, flowing pose such as this one. Establishing that strong S-shape in the first step is important because it follows all the way through to the final design.

NOTE

The stylization process used in the character projects of this book deals with basic shapes and gestures slightly differently than shown here. This is because the characters created on pages 68–247 are built up from standard T-poses in order to make the basic shape construction simple for you to follow. Lines of action and gestures are then tackled later in the process when poses are explored. After building up your character in a generic T-pose, you can then use the step-by-step process described above to test out various poses and gestures. As you will learn later, many artists explore gestures at thumbnail stage, so being able to quickly build basic shapes up from a line of action is very important.

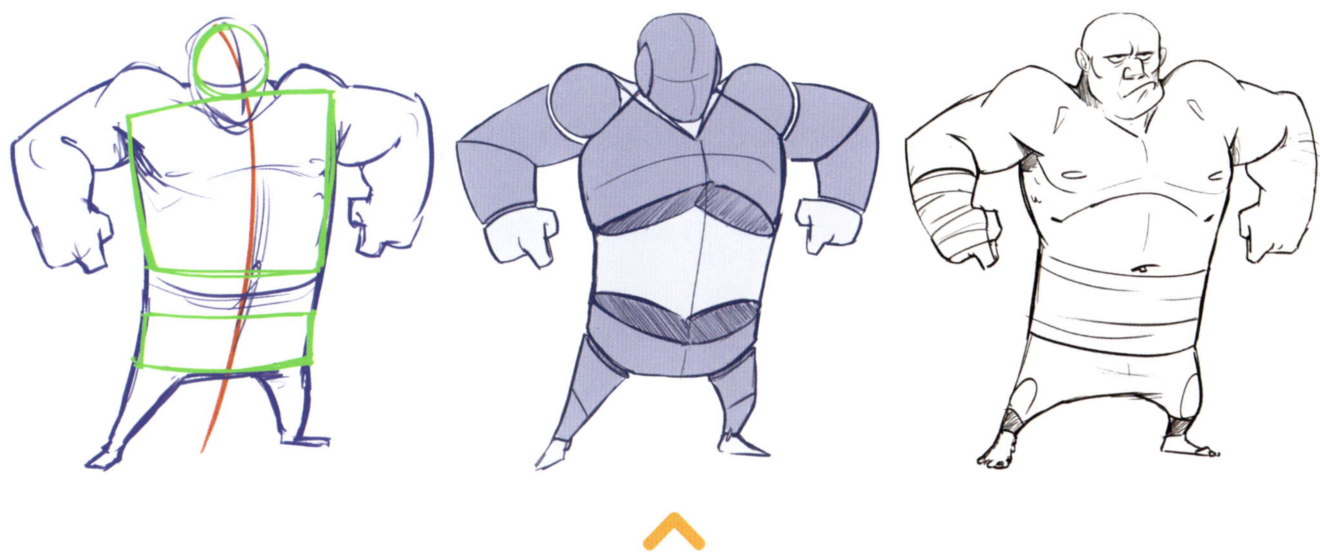

Even if the character is heavily exaggerated, the core shapes of the
human body are still the same, as you can see in the heavily stylized
but still defined anatomy of this square character. The line of action
also doesn't have to be extremely curved in order to be effective.

The same rules apply for animals and non-human characters as for humans.
Establish the flow of the spine with a line of action, then build up the masses
of the body according to your research and studies into that creature. This fox
has a strong triangular shape language, which makes it look cunning, but the
flowing line of action also helps to make it look graceful and stealthy.

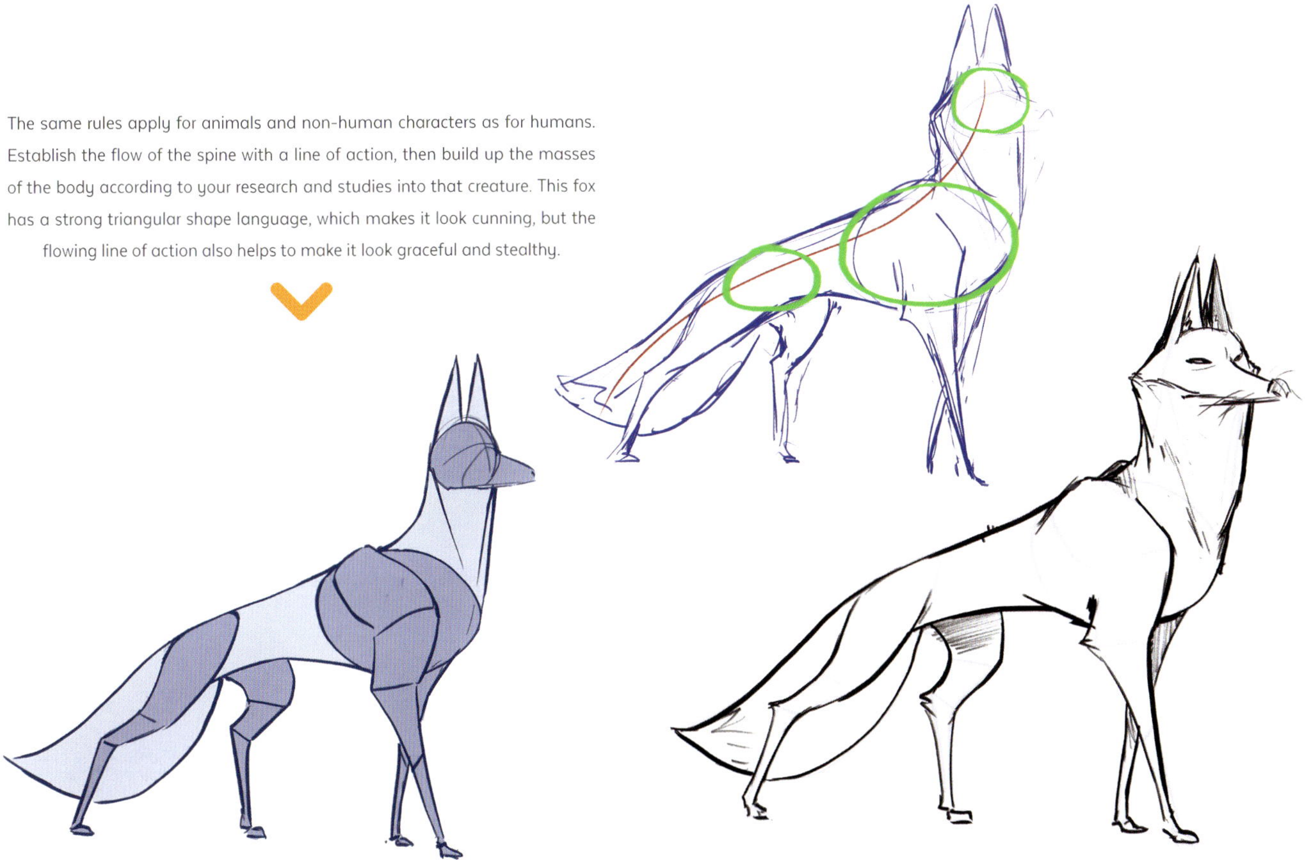

CAPTURING GESTURES

Now that you know what a gesture is and how to use one to create a character design, how do you use references and your imagination to create a character? Creating art is an extremely personal process, and every artist has their own unique way of approaching it. This process will differ from many other artists, so while you read this section, know that it is good to develop your own way of capturing gestures to suit your artistic needs. It is preferable to draw gestures using **reference**, because drawing from life will always create a better result and there is much to learn from it.

While drawing from reference, there are two important aspects to keep in mind – **observation** and **interpretation**. What is the pose telling us, and how do we expand upon

that idea? In many ways, gesture drawing is about emotions and storytelling. The aim is to express the character's mood and energy in a quick conceptual way, so you don't have to draw exactly what you see. Interpret the pose and "push" it (emphasize and exaggerate the defining aspects of it), to further highlight the important parts. When observing, try to figure out where the subject is leaning their weight. Where is the line of action? How are the shoulders placed in relation to the hips? The important part is to not just draw what you see, but to capture the entire subject as one single entity.

Drawing from your **imagination** is completely different. It may be more fun and may be better fuel for your creativity, but it is extremely important to always

bounce back to reference to make sure you are improving without leaving behind the **fundamentals**. If you do not have a strong understanding of how the body is built and how it moves, it will be extremely apparent using this technique. Keeping that in mind, drawing from imagination comes with a whole different set of challenges. Instead of **observing** and **interpreting**, you are **creating**. The same concepts still apply to gestures drawn from imagination. A good gesture should have a clear story or action, accurate weight balance, and a line of action to follow. Use these concepts as guidance to make your gesture stronger.

In this section I will show some examples of stylized gestures captured from everyday, less stylized poses.

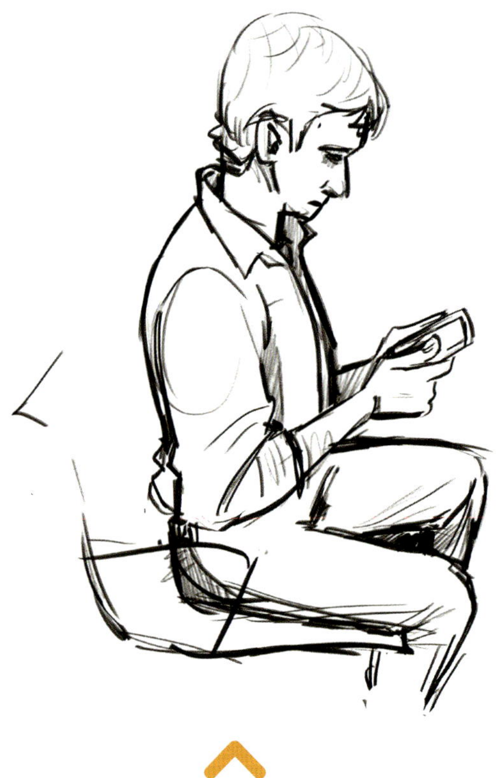

This is a quick sketch based on a reference. I observed the person and noticed he was sitting with an extremely straight posture while looking down at his phone.

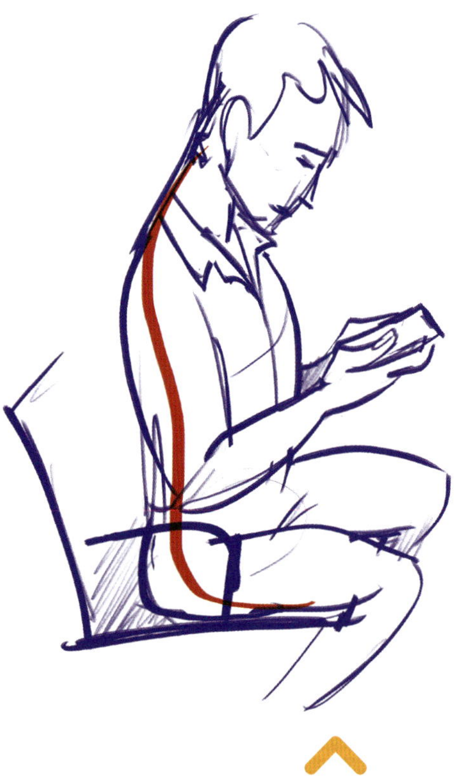

In the simplified gesture, I emphasize the straightness of the man's back and contrast it with the curved shapes of his arms and legs. I even simplify the outline of the seat to flow visually with the more stylized gesture.

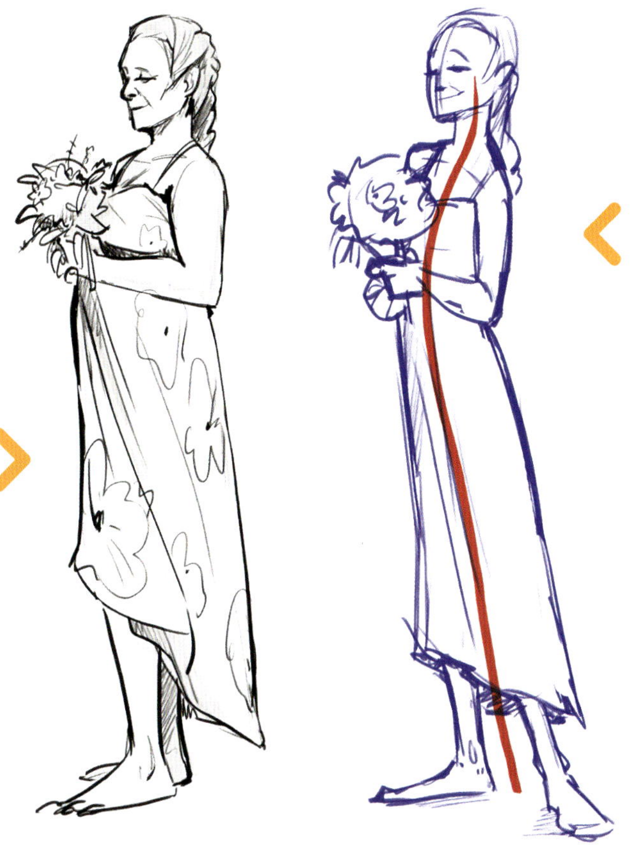

When I capture the gesture I keep the strong sense of flow to her back and dress, making the pose stronger by pushing the interesting parts of it, while adjusting some features like the stance of her feet for a more exaggerated result.

This is a straightforward observational sketch of a woman holding a bouquet. She has a robust, straight posture, standing upright and alert like she is watching something.

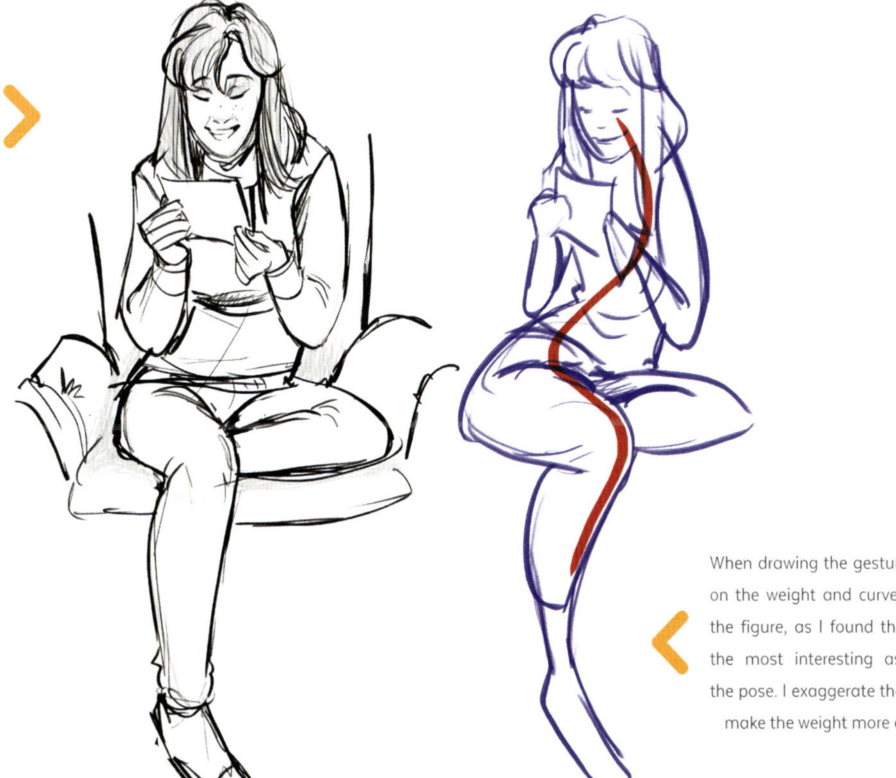

In this observational sketch, I noticed the woman was leaning her weight on her left side, while her spine was curving in the opposite direction for balance.

When drawing the gesture, I focus on the weight and curved flow of the figure, as I found them to be the most interesting aspects of the pose. I exaggerate the curve to make the weight more evident.

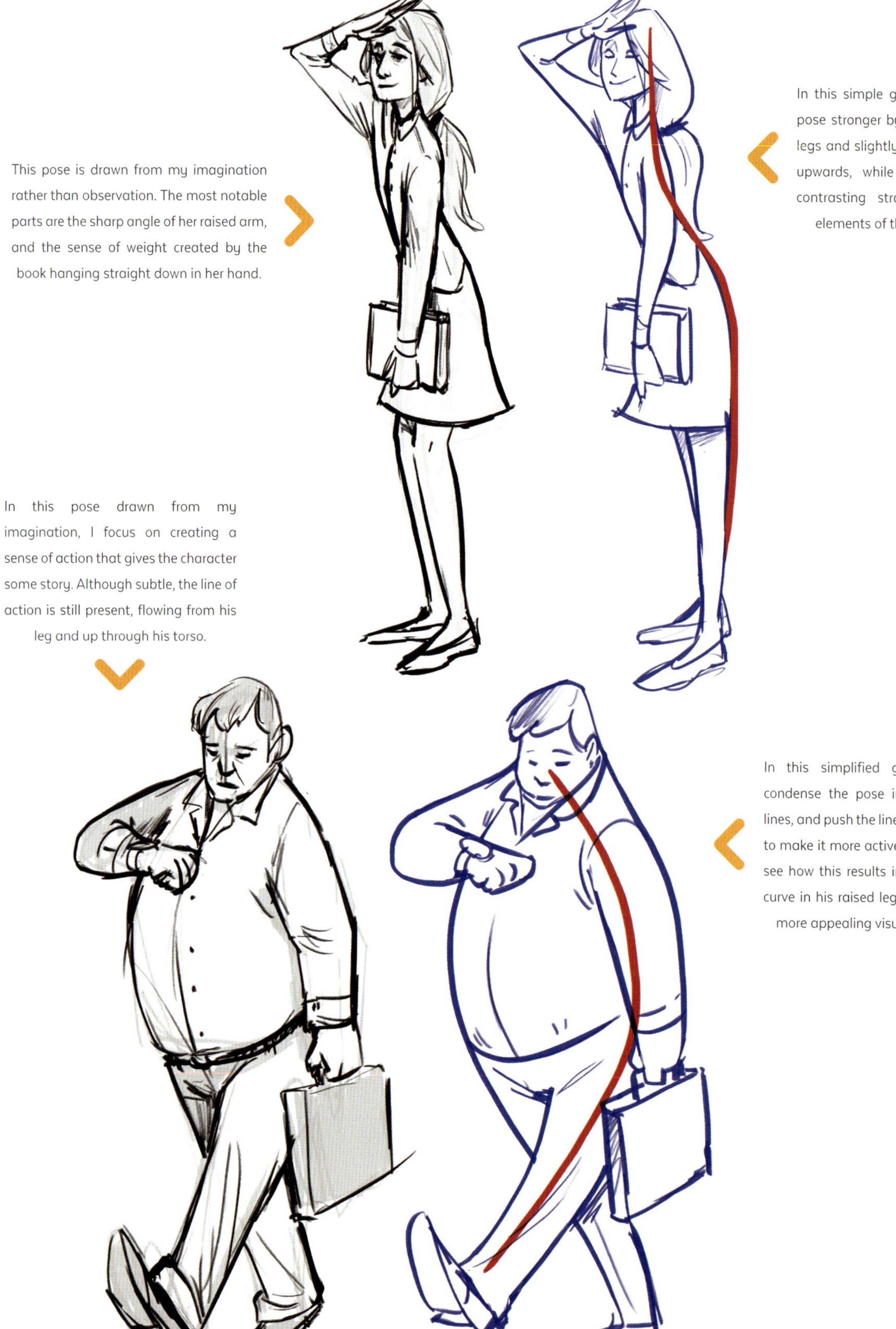

This pose is drawn from my imagination rather than observation. The most notable parts are the sharp angle of her raised arm, and the sense of weight created by the book hanging straight down in her hand.

In this simple gesture, I make the pose stronger by straightening the legs and slightly pushing the spine upwards, while emphasizing the contrasting straight and curved elements of the original pose.

In this pose drawn from my imagination, I focus on creating a sense of action that gives the character some story. Although subtle, the line of action is still present, flowing from his leg and up through his torso.

In this simplified gesture, I condense the pose into fewer lines, and push the line of action to make it more active. You can see how this results in a slight curve in his raised leg, creating more appealing visual flow.

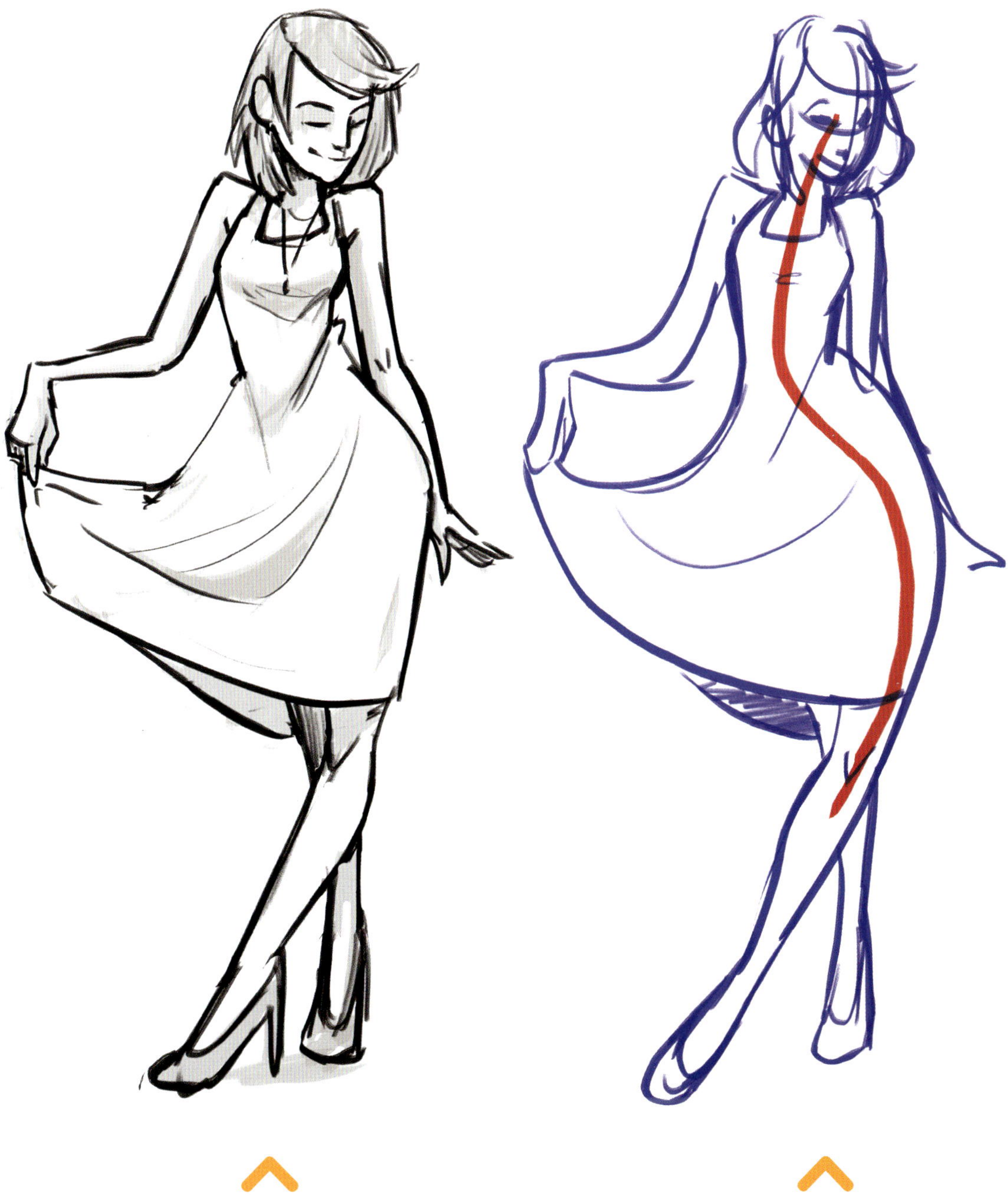

I drew this graceful, feminine pose from my imagination, with an emphasis on *contrapposto*. The line of action here could be imagined as a strong S-shaped curve; this works especially well for posing elegant female characters.

Simplifying the outline of the character is important when making a quick gesture. A lot of detail is not always needed, or indeed effective. You can see how I have streamlined and simplified the shapes of her leg and dress to achieve a clearer gesture.

EXPLORING PERSONALITY & GESTURE

One of the biggest advantages of gesture drawings is that they do not require a lot of detail, so you can sketch them out quickly. This allows for an easier brainstorming session, enabling you to explore much more widely when developing your character; you will notice that many of the artists in this book explore gesture as early as the thumbnailing stage.

Posing your character and drawing their expressions is one of the most important parts of getting to know their **personality**. While sketching them for the first time, the character should be the one to reveal themselves, with their personality and temperament emerging from their **backstory** and manifesting organically in their poses. What feels right? Maybe there

are some aspects to the character that you didn't even consider before stumbling over it while sketching out the poses. The key word here is **exploring**. It is hard to explain what kind of person your character is with only one pose, so it helps to make a wide range of different gesture sketches. There is a trial and error arc to this process, so don't expect every pose to be perfect.

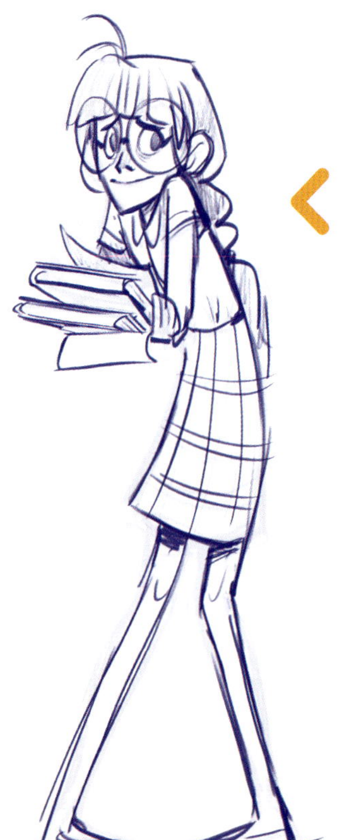

When looking at this gesture, you can immediately tell what kind of person this character is. She is smart and insecure, but kind-hearted. Curving her back as if she is making herself as small as possible is a great indicator of the insecure aspect. The pose speaks to her character, which makes it a strong pose.

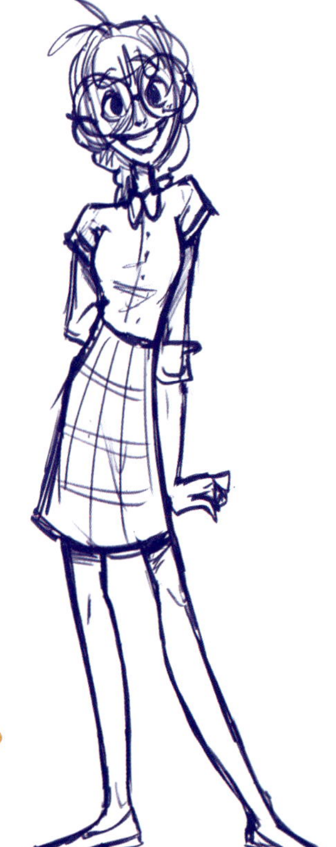

When you are making poses for a specific character, you have to keep their personality in mind. The pose may be technically strong, but if it doesn't correspond with their personality, it will render the pose weak no matter how well it is drawn. This pose is weak because it is generic and does not communicate much about this character, whom I imagine to be very bookish, awkward, and shy.

Here is another example of a pose that looks good but is a wrong choice for the character's personality. As mentioned earlier, puffing up the chest and spreading the legs is an indicator of outgoing confidence, which directly conflicts with her established personality.

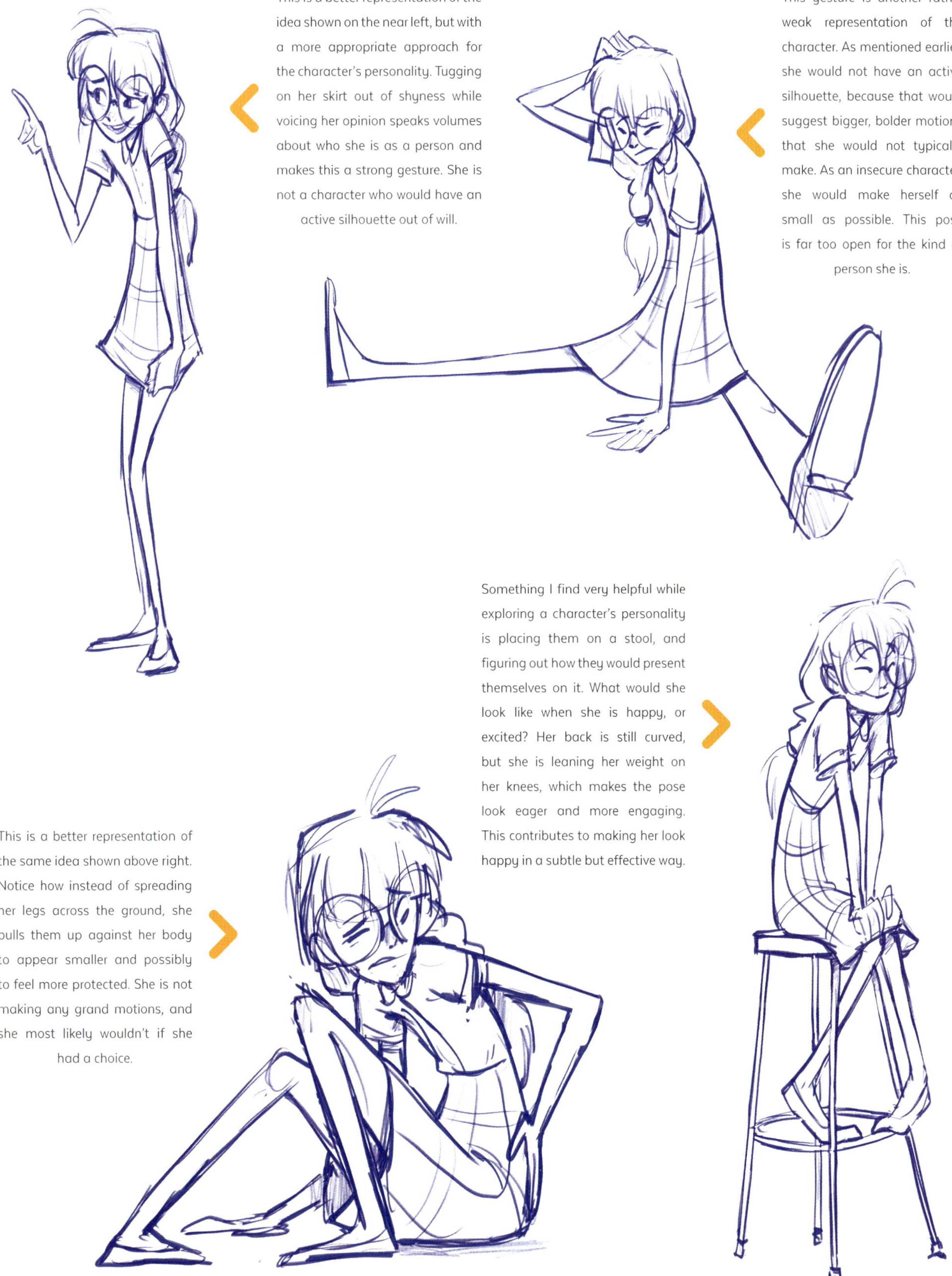

This is a better representation of the idea shown on the near left, but with a more appropriate approach for the character's personality. Tugging on her skirt out of shyness while voicing her opinion speaks volumes about who she is as a person and makes this a strong gesture. She is not a character who would have an active silhouette out of will.

This gesture is another rather weak representation of the character. As mentioned earlier, she would not have an active silhouette, because that would suggest bigger, bolder motions that she would not typically make. As an insecure character, she would make herself as small as possible. This pose is far too open for the kind of person she is.

This is a better representation of the same idea shown above right. Notice how instead of spreading her legs across the ground, she pulls them up against her body to appear smaller and possibly to feel more protected. She is not making any grand motions, and she most likely wouldn't if she had a choice.

Something I find very helpful while exploring a character's personality is placing them on a stool, and figuring out how they would present themselves on it. What would she look like when she is happy, or excited? Her back is still curved, but she is leaning her weight on her knees, which makes the pose look eager and more engaging. This contributes to making her look happy in a subtle but effective way.

FACES & EXPRESSIONS

BY VARUN NAIR

BASIC CONSTRUCTION

The foundation of drawing heads, caricatures, and character designs is to be able to simplify the shape of the head before you start thinking about the individual features of the face. One of the challenges of this is in giving the impression of three-dimensional features on a two-dimensional canvas. Much like when we looked at simplifying the shape of the human body, almost every human head can be broken down into a basic square, rectangle, circle, triangle, or a combination of two shapes.

It is always useful to start drawing the head with a sphere, because it immediately puts you in a three-dimensional space and allows you to imagine and draw the rest of the facial features around it. This would be followed by a line that goes across the center of the sphere, usually indicating the brow. Then it is possible to define the front and side planes of the face, which creates a basic three-dimensional head, before "sculpting out" the forms of the facial features. We will look at the basic construction here.

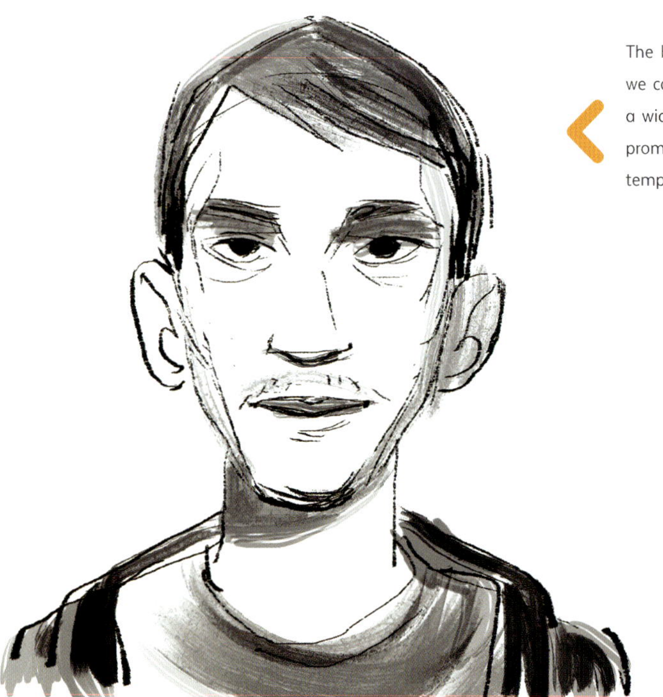

The basic shape of this face is a rectangle. On a male face we can emphasize the overall skeletal landmarks by drawing a wide chin and cheekbones, and making the jaw area more prominent. This character also has deep eye sockets, and the temple bone around the eye is emphasized. Even for the smaller features, a masculine face has a blocky overall feel.

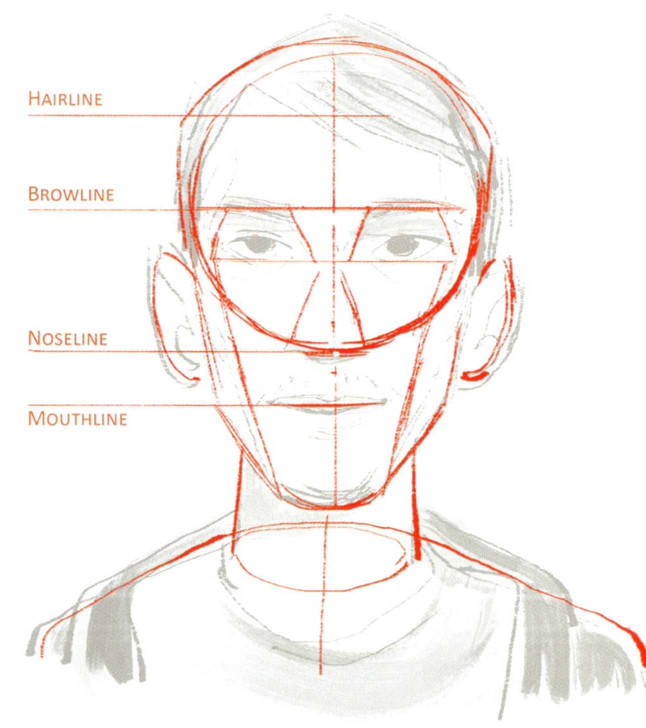

Here we see the basic construction of the head, starting from a sphere and building the overall rectangular shape. Mark out the key areas such as the browline (center of the sphere), nose, mouth, and hairline, then draw the eye sockets and basic indications of the nose and lips. Attach basic shapes for the ears and a simple cylinder for the neck, and you will have a solid foundation for a head drawing.

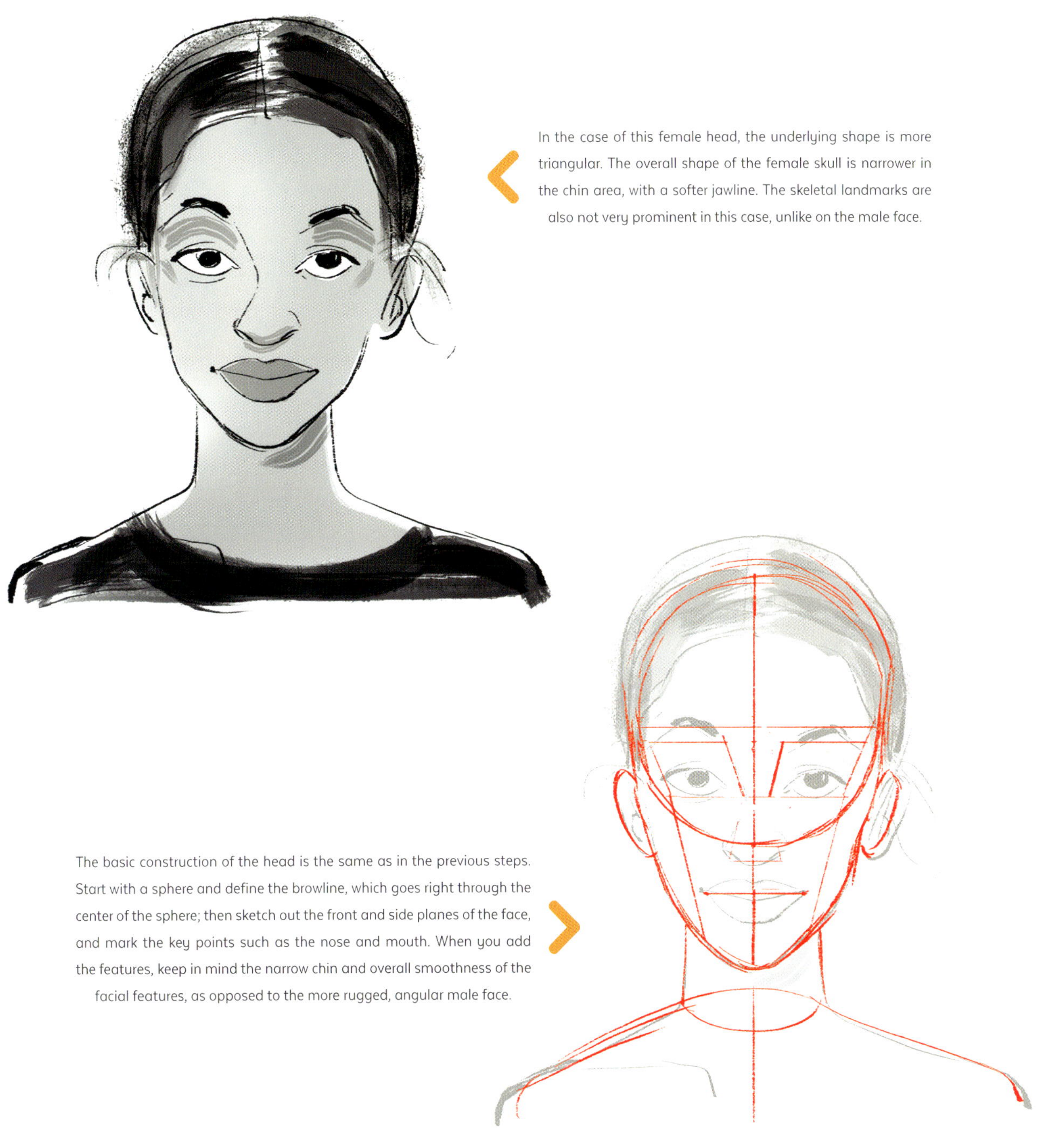

In the case of this female head, the underlying shape is more triangular. The overall shape of the female skull is narrower in the chin area, with a softer jawline. The skeletal landmarks are also not very prominent in this case, unlike on the male face.

The basic construction of the head is the same as in the previous steps. Start with a sphere and define the browline, which goes right through the center of the sphere; then sketch out the front and side planes of the face, and mark the key points such as the nose and mouth. When you add the features, keep in mind the narrow chin and overall smoothness of the facial features, as opposed to the more rugged, angular male face.

Drawing and studying heads helps you to build a library of simple shapes and proportions in your head – knowledge which comes in handy when you are designing your own character. As a character designer you are the equivalent of a **casting director** in a movie. When you are handed a character description, you decide which actor would be suitable for this role. In this case, you draw the character that would best fit the description and the story. In many cases, you might not get a solid description of the character's physical attributes. At this point you would be required to provide a variety of options of faces with different shapes and features. We will look at some more faces at different angles over the next two pages.

The central division of the starting sphere helps you to visualize the overall shape of the head, even at an angle. When sketching a three-quarter view, the main challenge is to keep the proportions of the face correct. The strong angular features of this face emphasize the character's masculine characteristics, giving him a tough overall look. The firm jaw, bulky chin, and swooping hairstyle also add personality to this sketch.

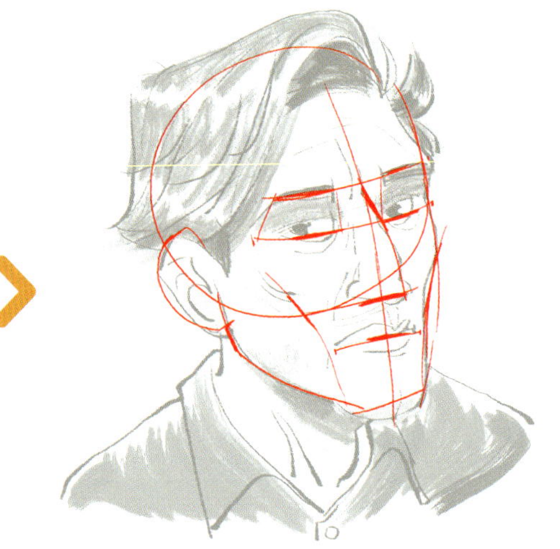

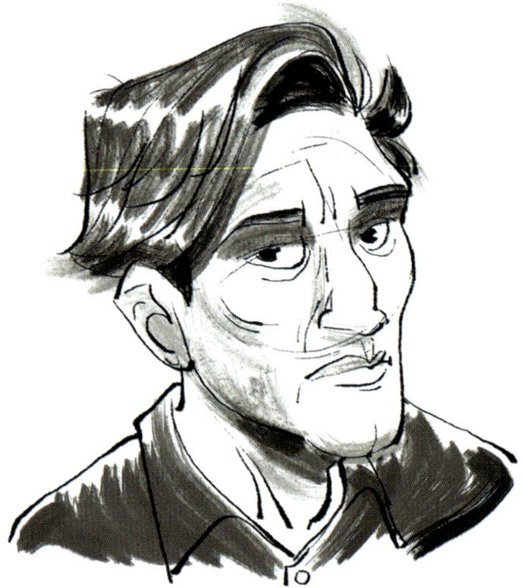

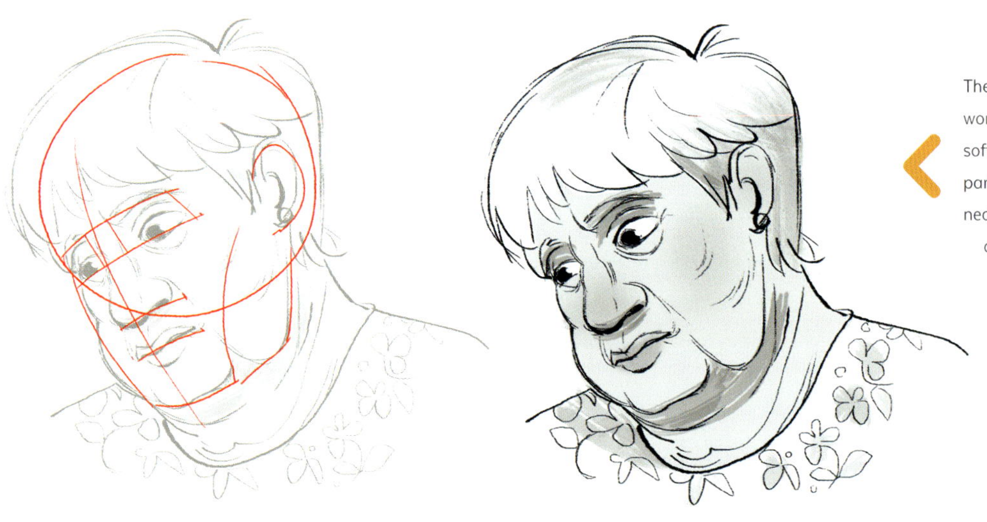

The overall shape of this elderly woman's head is rounded, with really soft features. The flesh on the lower part of the face and the folds on the neck help to emphasize the age on an older character such as this one.

The same principles can be applied to characters with different ages and features. The overall basic shape of this male character is a square. The emphasis on the cheekbones and the subtle tilt of the eyelids indicate his Asian origins, while the eye bags, receding hairline, and folds on the face and neck give the impression of him being middle-aged.

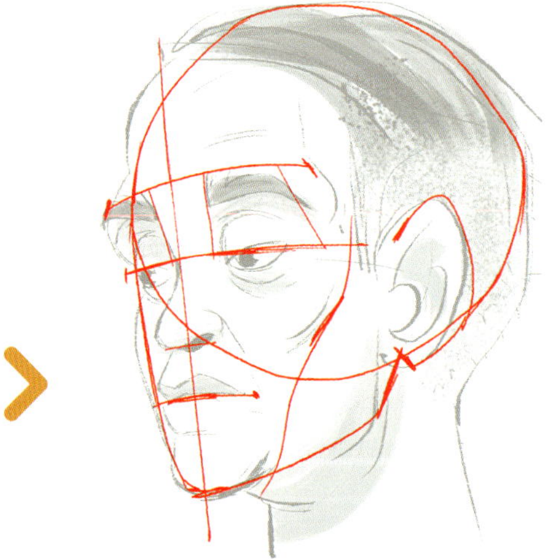

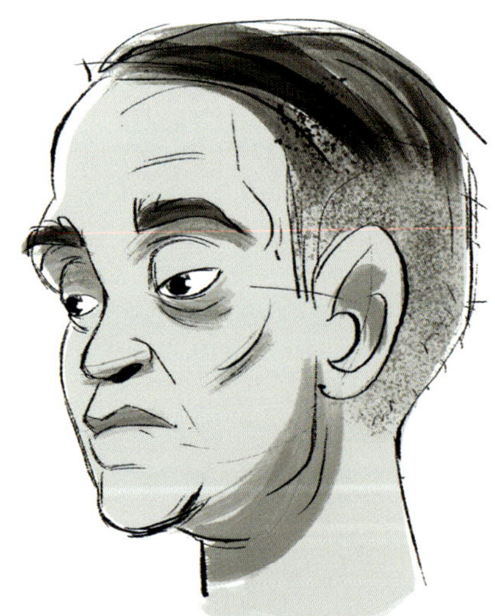

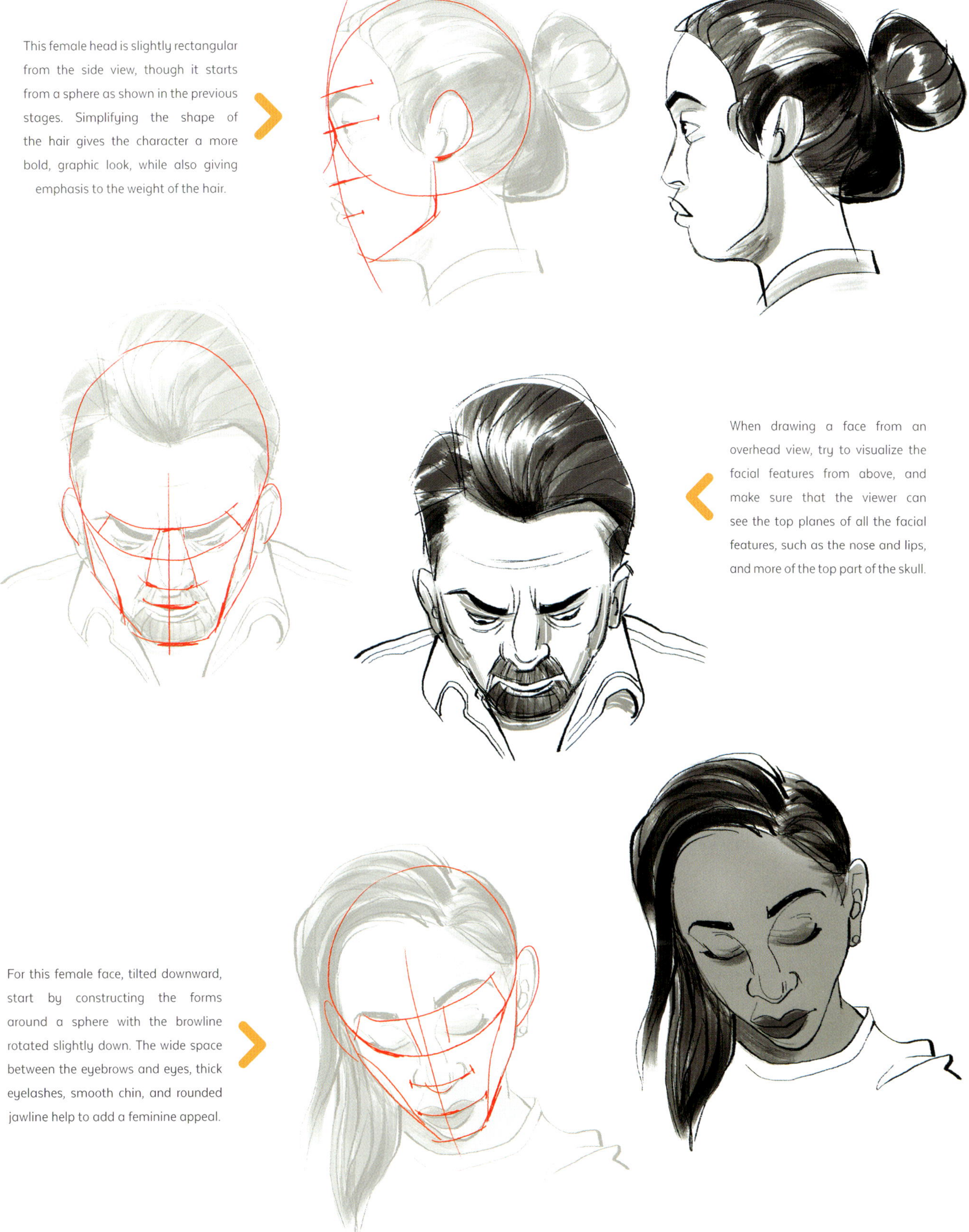

This female head is slightly rectangular from the side view, though it starts from a sphere as shown in the previous stages. Simplifying the shape of the hair gives the character a more bold, graphic look, while also giving emphasis to the weight of the hair.

When drawing a face from an overhead view, try to visualize the facial features from above, and make sure that the viewer can see the top planes of all the facial features, such as the nose and lips, and more of the top part of the skull.

For this female face, tilted downward, start by constructing the forms around a sphere with the browline rotated slightly down. The wide space between the eyebrows and eyes, thick eyelashes, smooth chin, and rounded jawline help to add a feminine appeal.

EXAGGERATING SHAPES

The human brain perceives various shapes differently, and certain shapes evoke certain feelings and emotions. As a designer, this "shape language" is a tool that we can use to manipulate the emotions of the audience and convey a point about the story or character. For example, we naturally perceive round, soft shapes to be friendly and approachable, while sharp and pointy shapes are dangerous and threatening. Thus round shapes could be used to design a friendly character, while sharp shapes could be used to design a villain. But once we understand how to use shapes, it is possible to break these rules to enhance the story and create suspense; for example, by having a villain who has a soft and cuddly look to deceive the people around them.

The small gray thumbnail shapes in this section show the underlying geometric shape of each face, with red lines indicating how the eyes, nose, and mouth are proportioned within it.

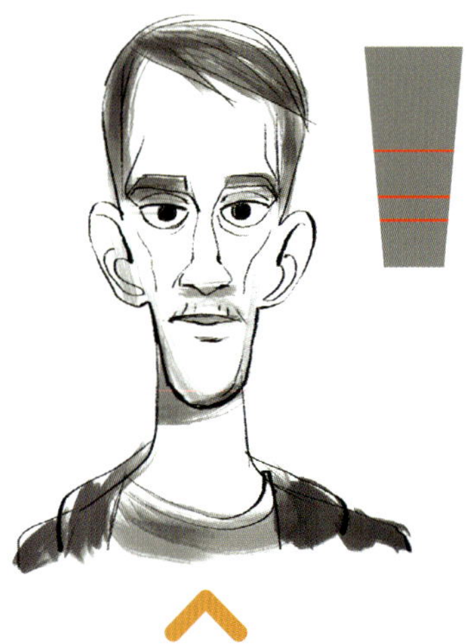

To make a more exaggerated version of the male character from page 34, start by pushing the basic rectangular shape of the head a bit more. Mark out the key areas of the head around a sphere, constructing it exactly the same way as shown previously, but create a caricature by more strongly emphasizing the wideness of the chin and cheekbones, and the overall blocky feel of the face.

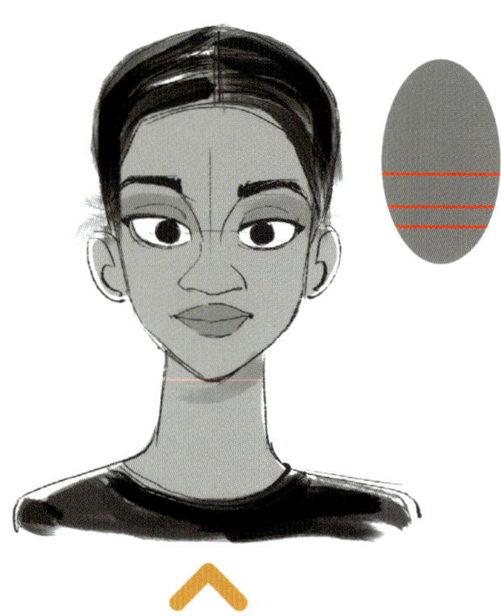

For this caricatured version of the female face from page 35, start from a sphere and sketch out the triangular shape, defining the key facial landmarks as before. This time, exaggerate elements such as the scale of the eyes and nose, and the distance between the eyes and brows, to make her features more striking while retaining a smooth look.

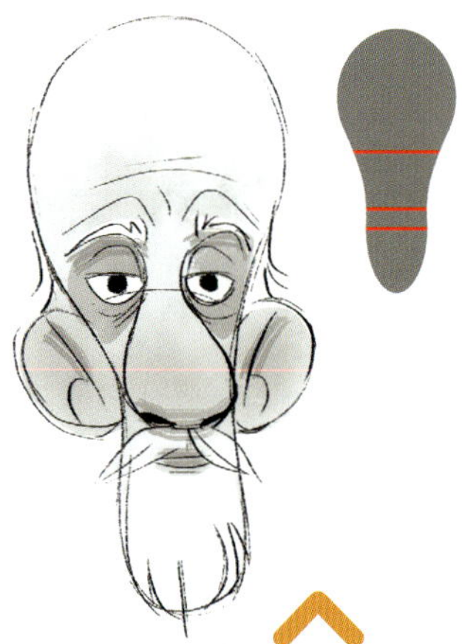

This elderly man has a pear-shaped head. The scale of the nose and ears is exaggerated to give his character a slight goofiness, yet his facial hair, the size of his head, and overall aged appearance give him a sense of wisdom and knowledge.

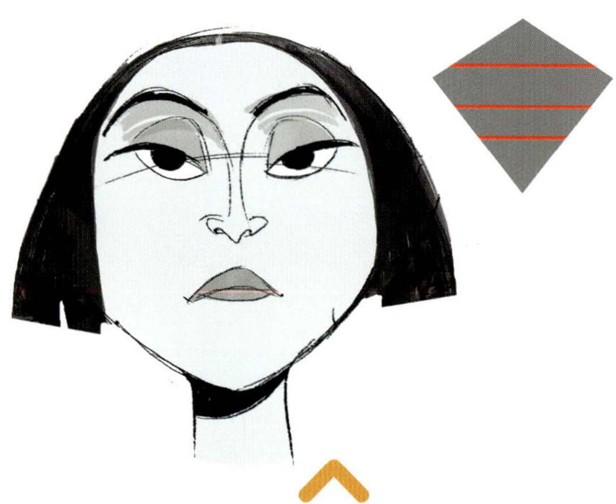

Here we have a kite-shaped head – a dynamic overall shape. The neat, flat hair with pointed sides, and her pointy nose and chin, give her a very stern and serious look. She could be an FBI agent.

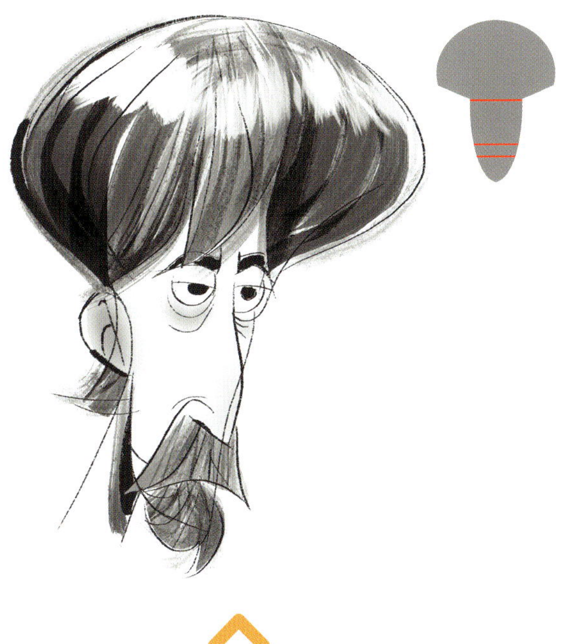

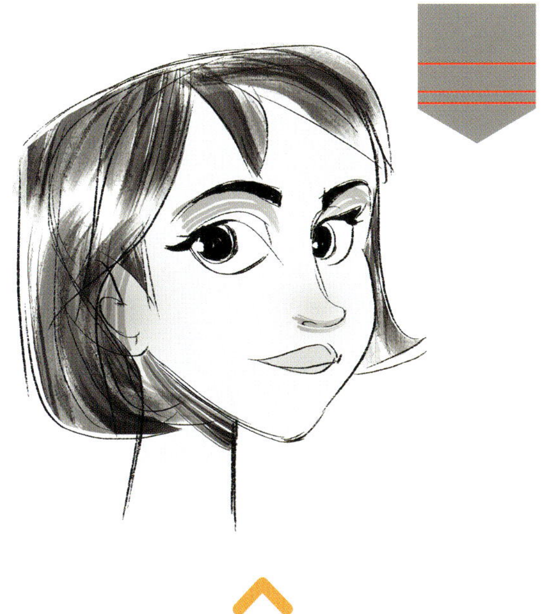

This man's mushroom-shaped head gives him a shabby, comical look, which is enhanced by his hair shape and facial hair. Other features, such as the eyes and ears, are toned down to make sure that the hair shape stands out and gives him an interesting, scrawny silhouette.

This character has an overall triangular shape for her face, though her hair makes her head appear more square. The edges of these shapes have been softened to give her a friendly look. The large scale of her eyes, the softness of her facial features, and the curves of her hair make her look young, friendly, and approachable.

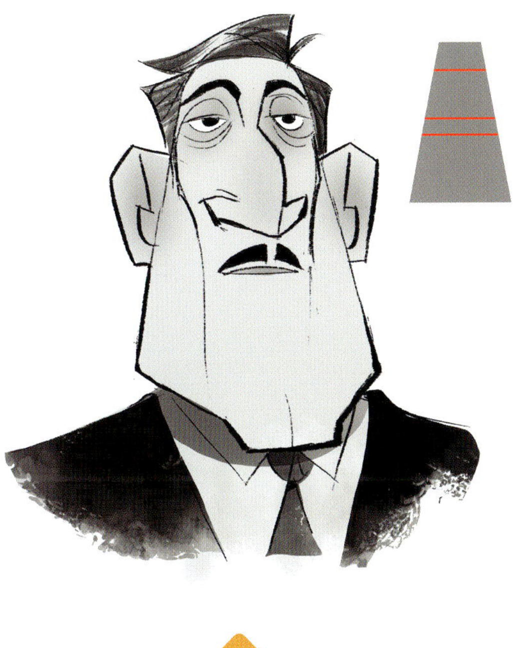

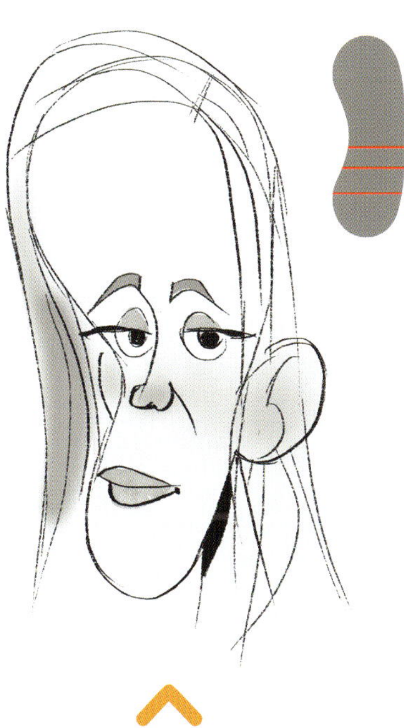

This macho man has rough, choppy facial features. The overall shape of the head has a lot of weight at the bottom to emphasize the bulkiness of this character. The shapes of the hair, nose, ears, jaw, and chin are sharp, almost knife-like, to further push the idea of a tough, severe character.

This girl has a bean-shaped head, giving her a funny, foolish appearance. Her forehead and ears have been exaggerated in this case, to enhance that look, while her other facial features are toned down and kept close to normal scale to further emphasize her head shape.

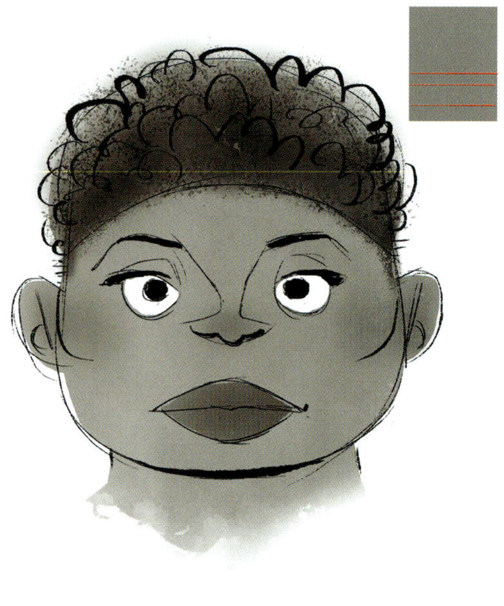

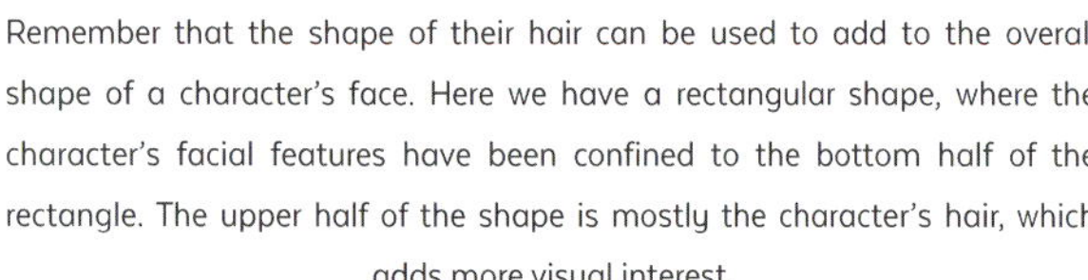

Remember that the shape of their hair can be used to add to the overall shape of a character's face. Here we have a rectangular shape, where the character's facial features have been confined to the bottom half of the rectangle. The upper half of the shape is mostly the character's hair, which adds more visual interest.

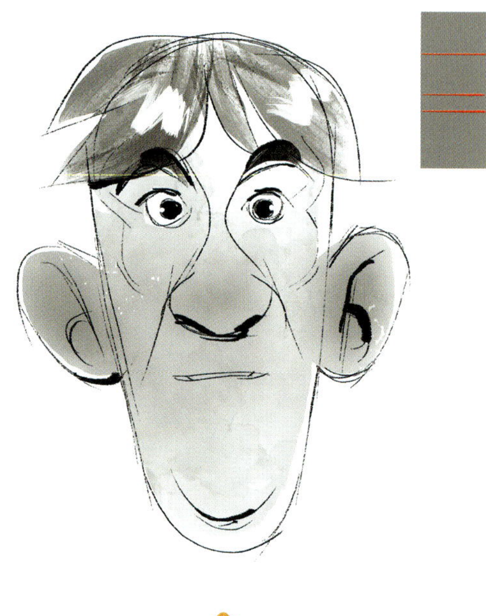

The basic shape of this head is a rectangle. On the diagram in the top right you can see that I have arranged the facial features with uneven spacing, because characters with facial features that are equally spaced tend to look boring and less appealing. In this case, the eye line of the character is very high up, giving him a naive look. The scale of the nose and ears are increased to enhance his light-hearted personality.

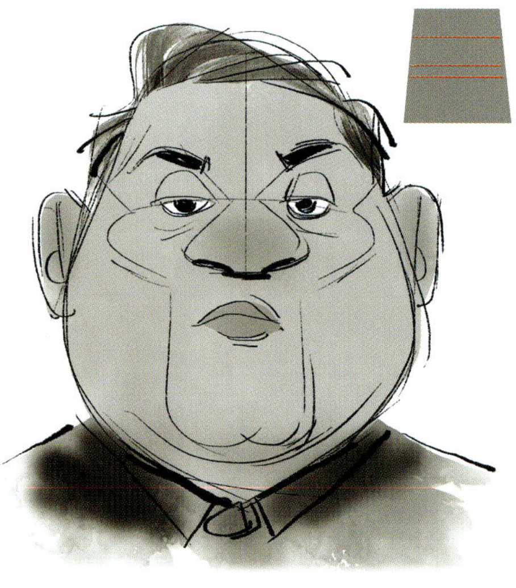

The basic shape here is a trapezoid with a thicker bottom. This is a self-contained, reserved character, and so his facial features are confined in close proximity to each other. This leaves a lot of room around his face, giving him a more bulky look, and a sense of thickness and weight.

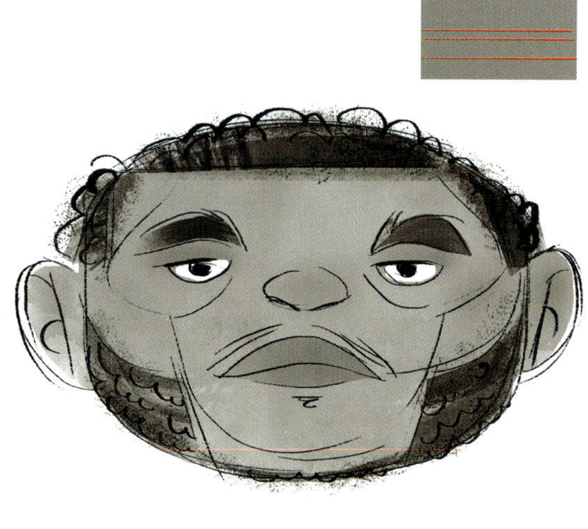

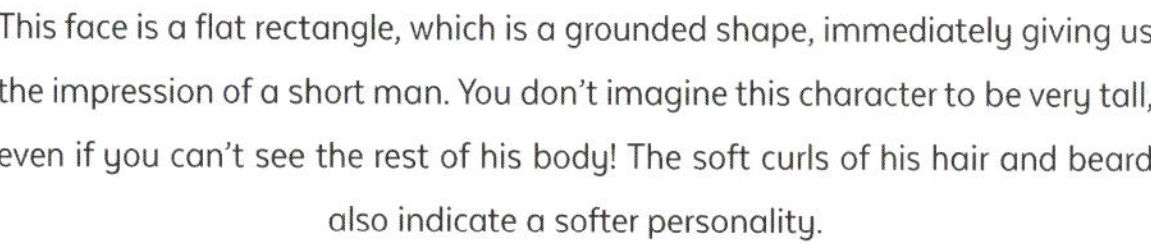

This face is a flat rectangle, which is a grounded shape, immediately giving us the impression of a short man. You don't imagine this character to be very tall, even if you can't see the rest of his body! The soft curls of his hair and beard also indicate a softer personality.

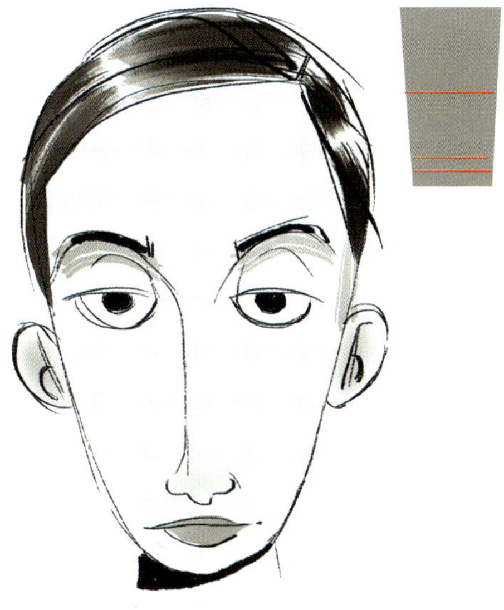

Here the character is a trapezoid with a thicker top. Most of the facial features are confined to the lower end of the shape, while the top half of the head consists of just her forehead and eyes, giving the impression of a brainy character – perhaps a manipulative villain.

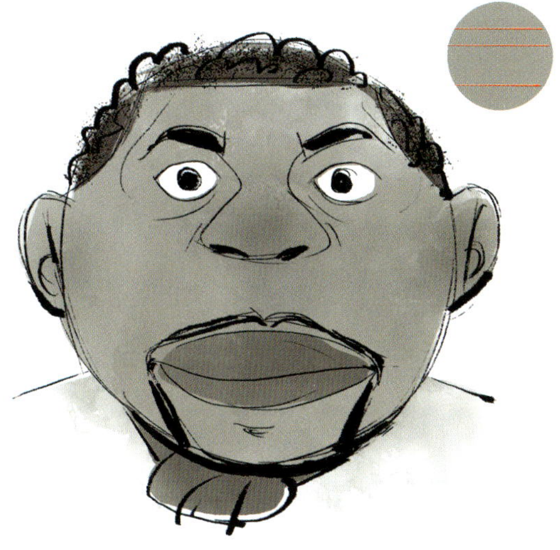

The basic shape here is a circle. The eyes and nose are close together and the mouth is way down at the bottom, making it stand out. The scale of the mouth also makes him look like a "big-mouthed," chatty guy.

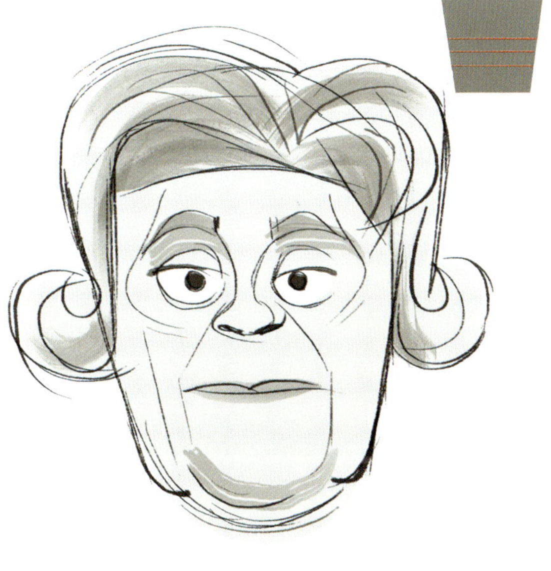

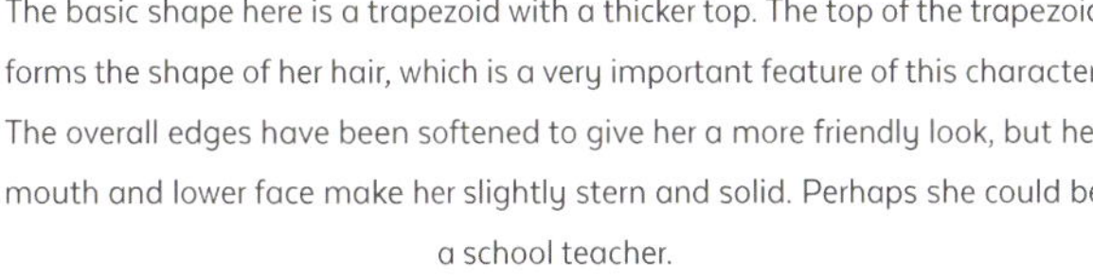

The basic shape here is a trapezoid with a thicker top. The top of the trapezoid forms the shape of her hair, which is a very important feature of this character. The overall edges have been softened to give her a more friendly look, but her mouth and lower face make her slightly stern and solid. Perhaps she could be a school teacher.

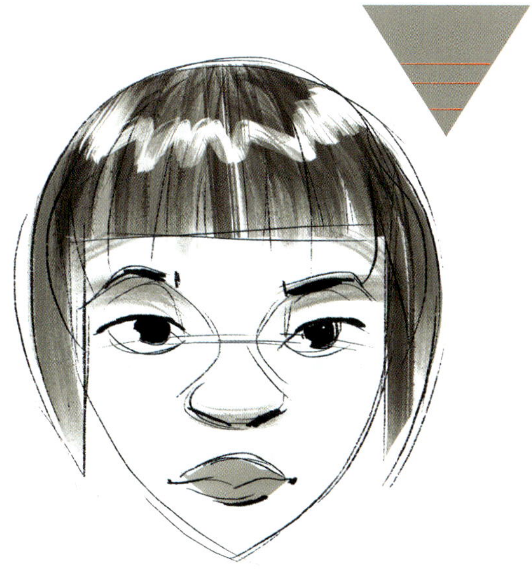

This child character has a large rounded head and big eyes to indicate her youth, but her basic face shape is a triangle. Retaining that sharpness in her facial features makes her look more dynamic. The sharp edges of her hair and chin make her look like an agile character, and give her a serious look despite her age.

EXPRESSIONS

One of the most important qualities to have as a character designer is the ability to show how a character feels – to communicate to the viewer what the character is thinking. The overall shape of the head and facial features help to show a character's personality, and their facial expressions show the viewer how they feel. The **primary** features used to create an expression could be broken down into two parts: the **eye area** and the **mouth area**. The eye area includes the eyes, eyebrows, and the areas around them; the latter includes the mouth and lips. Other features such as the **cheeks**, **nose**, and **forehead** could be considered **secondary**, as they react to the way the primary features move on the face.

Creating believable expressions takes a lot of experimentation and practice. It is helpful to research facial muscles to improve your understanding of how the features move. When you are drawing an expression, it is always handy to keep a mirror nearby, and to make the expression yourself as you draw. You will always get better results

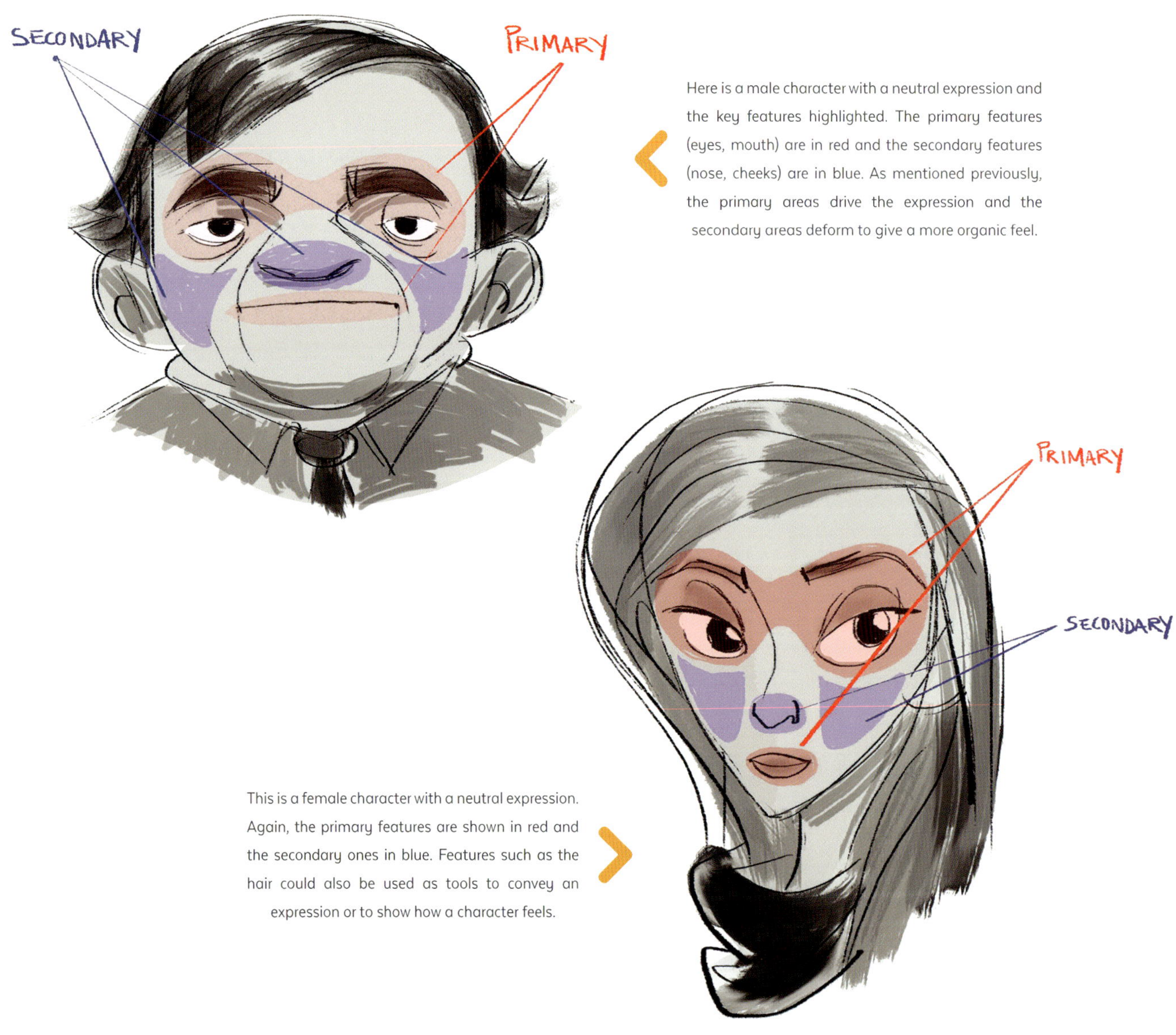

Here is a male character with a neutral expression and the key features highlighted. The primary features (eyes, mouth) are in red and the secondary features (nose, cheeks) are in blue. As mentioned previously, the primary areas drive the expression and the secondary areas deform to give a more organic feel.

This is a female character with a neutral expression. Again, the primary features are shown in red and the secondary ones in blue. Features such as the hair could also be used as tools to convey an expression or to show how a character feels.

when you can "feel" the expression that you are trying to draw – even though it might make you look stupid at times! When creating expressions, try to find the simplest statement using the primary features, then consider how the secondary features will react to them; this will make the expression look believable and add more life to the character.

Below you can see some examples of basic expressions and an explanation of how they have been achieved. Refer to the table below for a quick summary (which is by no means exhaustive when you consider the full range of human emotion) of ways in which primary and secondary features can be moved to create certain expressions.

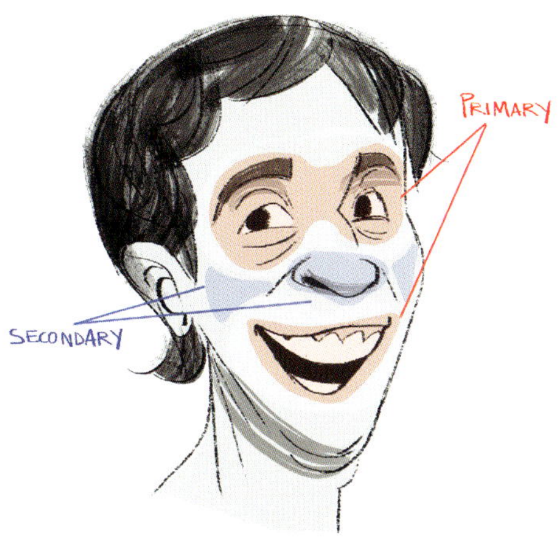

This character has a happy, silly expression. His raised eyebrows and big smile are the primary features; the nostrils, revealed teeth, and folds around his nose and eyes react to the movement of the primary features.

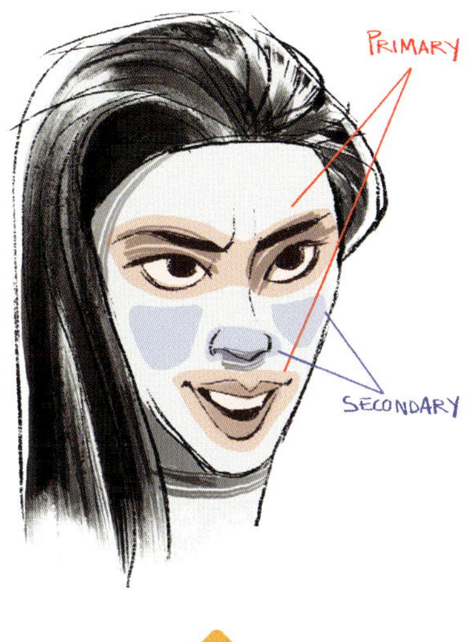

This female character has a sinister expression. Her lowered eyebrows suggest anger, while her smile shows she has an evil plan in mind. Tilting her forehead forwards so she is looking up through her browline slightly also adds a sinister feel.

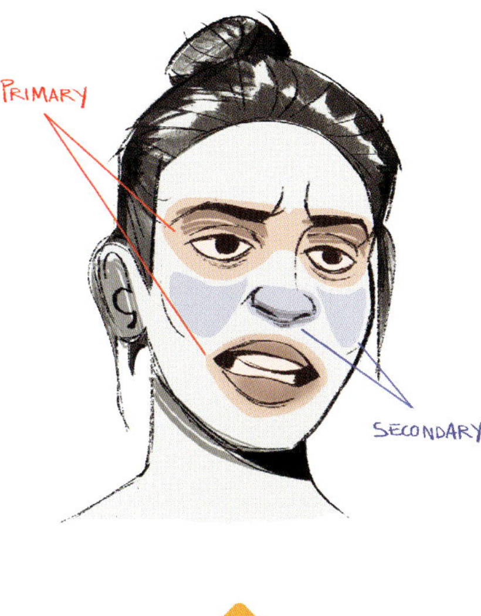

This character is quite embarrassed and worried, indicated by her eyebrows pulling together and by her clenched teeth.

HAPPY	SAD	DISGUSTED	SURPRISED	ANGRY	AFRAID
Corners of mouth go up	Corners of mouth go down	Upper lip goes up	Mouth opens	Mouth narrows	Mouth opens
Cheeks go up	Inner corners of eyebrows go up	Nose wrinkles	Eyebrows go up	Lips can press together; or in pure rage a character could be yelling	Corners of mouth go down slightly and stretch outwards
Eyes narrow	Brow can wrinkle	Brow goes down	Eyes widen		Eyebrows go up and pull together
Wrinkles can form around the eye	Tears can form	Eyes narrow		Eyebrows go down and pull together	Upper eyelids go up
Tears can form	Head can point downwards	Head can lean away		Eyes narrow	Forehead can wrinkle

EXAGGERATING EXPRESSIONS

Like you saw with gestures and poses in the previous chapter, a strong expression helps the audience read the character quicker and adds **dynamism** and **interest**. To make more dramatic expressions, exaggerate the primary features by pushing their shapes, and hold back on some of the other features to find a stylistic balance between them. In order to make exaggerated expressions, it helps to study them in a more realistic form, then simplify them to find the **boldest statement** for a more stylized look. In the examples discussed here you can see the features involved in the expression and how they can be **manipulated** to create something more exaggerated and stylized.

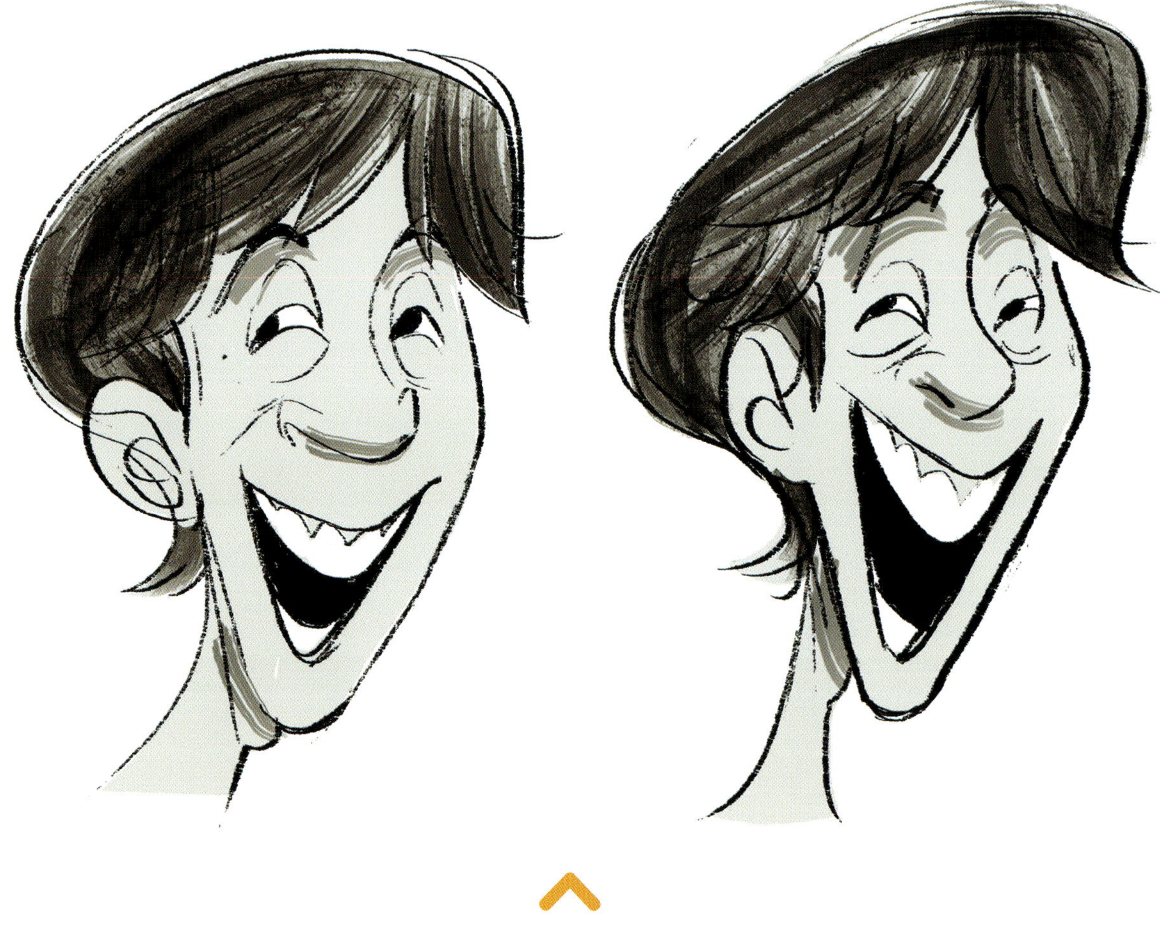

The face on the left here is a more stylized version of the happy male you saw on the previous page. You can see how the primary features – raised eyebrows and a large smile – have been exaggerated to emphasize this emotion. The eyes are more narrow to show the extreme movement of the cheeks moving up. In the expression on the right, the primary features are pushed almost (but not quite) to the point of breaking the character's face. The triangular shape of the mouth is more pronounced, the eyes are even narrower, and the eyebrows are raised almost beyond visibility. The overall shape of the hair and the head is also exaggerated to enhance the fun, happy expression of this character.

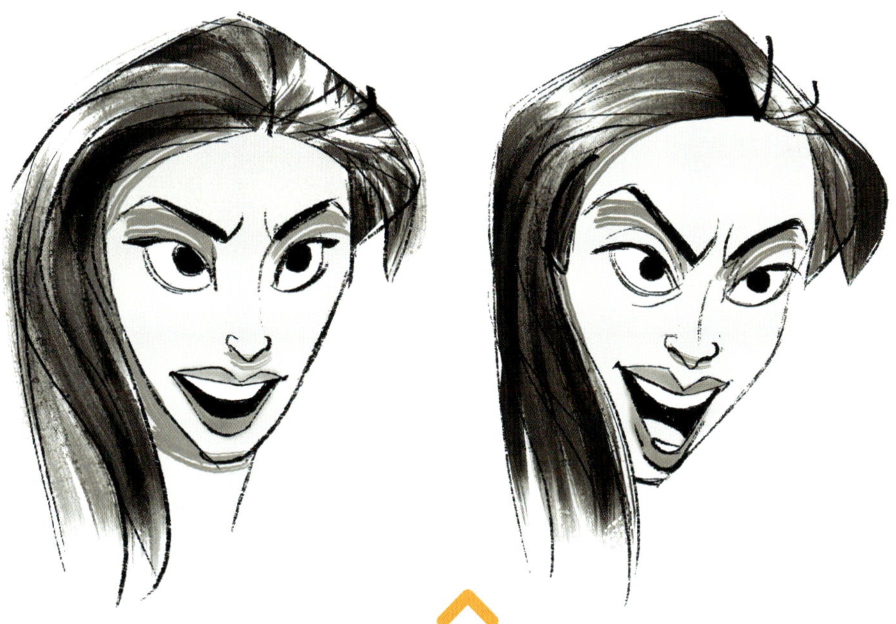

The face on the left is again a stylized version of one of the characters on page 43. You can see how the angle of her eyebrows has been made more severe, and the triangular shape of her face enhanced to reflect her unfriendly nature. The sleek shape of the hair makes her look graceful yet villainous. In the more stylized version on the right, every single one of these aspects is pushed to make the expression more dramatic: her eyebrows are even sharper; her smile is more pronounced; and her angular face is highlighted by the placement of her hair.

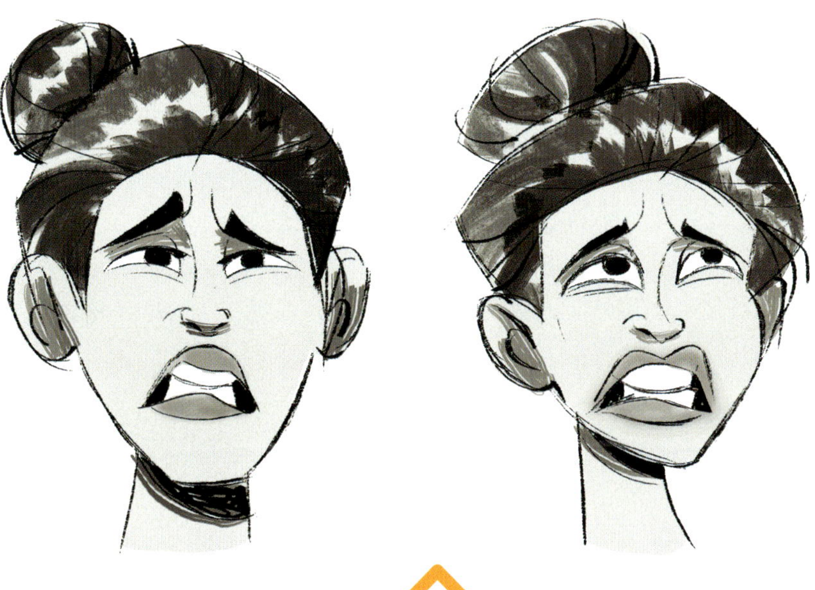

In the more exaggerated versions of the worried character from page 43, the eyebrows and teeth are pushed more, while secondary features such as her furrowed brow and areas around her eyes and nose help to add a more authentic feel to the expression. Notice how in the right-hand version her eyes are now pointing upwards and to her left, which usually shows that someone is in thinking about a specific memory, perhaps the cause of her embarrassment.

On the next few pages are some examples of exaggerated expressions so that you can observe how a range of emotions can be captured on the faces of stylized characters.

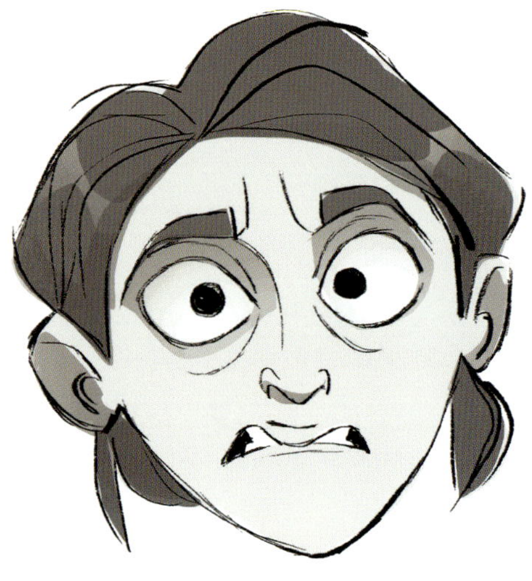

This character has just seen something scary! His wide-open eyes and mouth capture his shock and horror, and the angle of his eyebrows shows his dismay at what he is seeing.

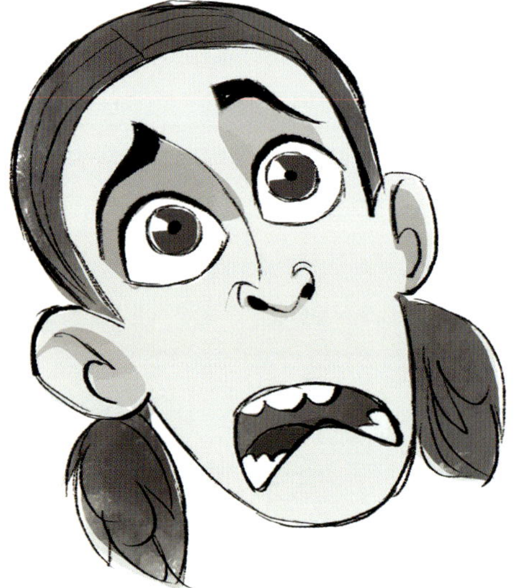

This female character is frightened of something. Her worried eyebrows and mouth, and wide eyes with small, shocked pupils, help to convey this fear.

This girl is terrified of what she is seeing. Her eyes and mouth are wide open and her eyebrows are worried. She looks as if she is inhaling, about to scream.

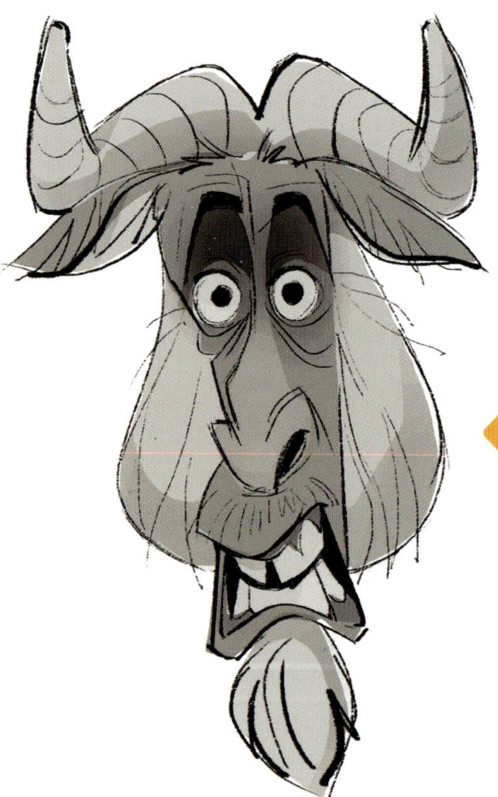

This nervous wildebeest has gotten himself in trouble. The raised eyebrows and startled eyes give a sense of shock and disbelief. His grimacing mouth and clenched teeth show how scared he is.

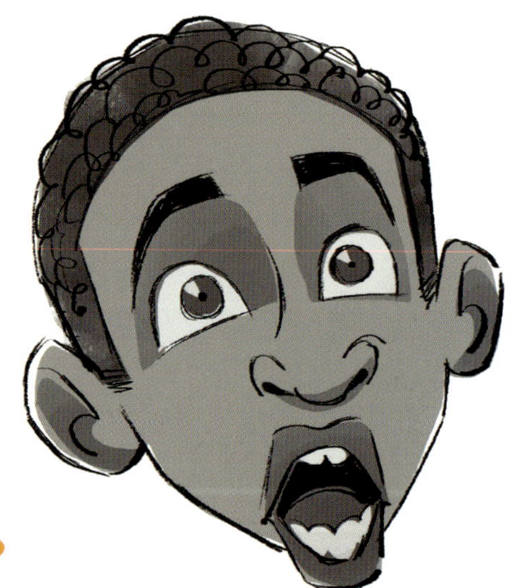

This boy just heard the ice cream truck. His surprise and awe are captured by his raised and arched eyebrows, and his open eyes and mouth.

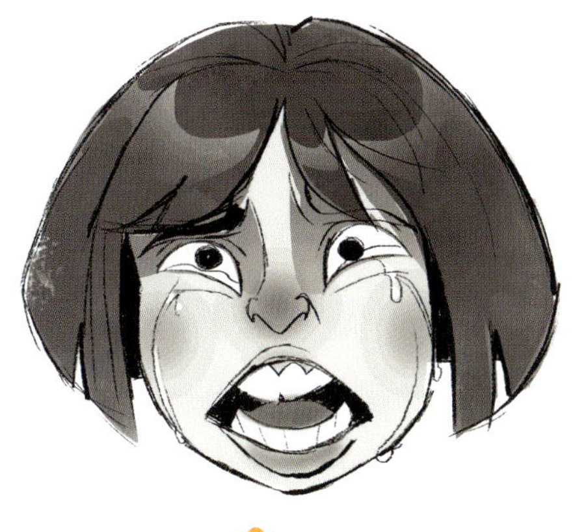

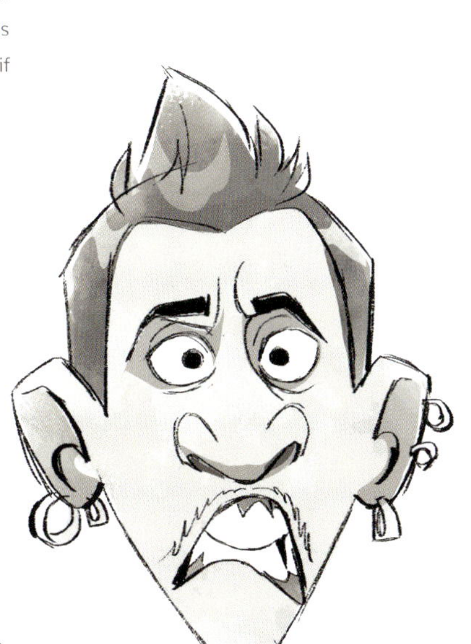

This character is sad, with his head lowered and his hair falling on his face. His eyebrows are compressed together, and the open mouth captures him in the moment he is about to cry. The swelling of the nostrils and folds around his eyes help to convey this idea further.

This character is caught at a sensitive, tearful moment: her eyebrows are worried, her hair falls messily over her face, and her mouth is open as if she is about to say something to defend herself.

This punk character is disgusted by something or someone. The frowning eyebrows give him a sense of worry, while his teeth are biting together hard, showing how uncomfortable he is. His flared nostrils add a lot to his look of disgust; in this case, this secondary feature is as important as the primary ones.

This little boy is not happy to hear something. His brows are lowered but his eyes are wide and staring, creating an angry, sulky frown.

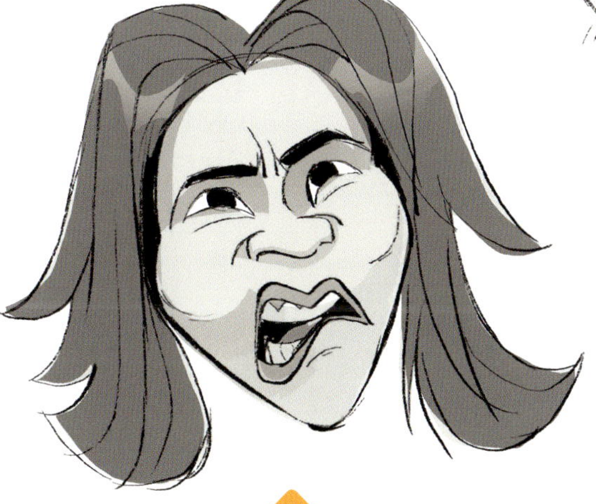

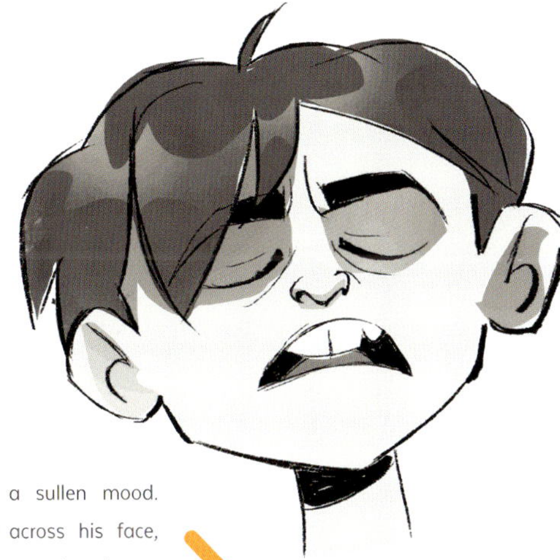

This woman is quite disgusted, as shown by her lowered eyebrows, flared nostrils, and the grimacing shape of her mouth with the subtle action of biting her lip.

This boy is in a sullen mood. The hair falling across his face, compressed eyebrows, closed eyes, and frowning expression show that he is unenthusiastic and gloomy.

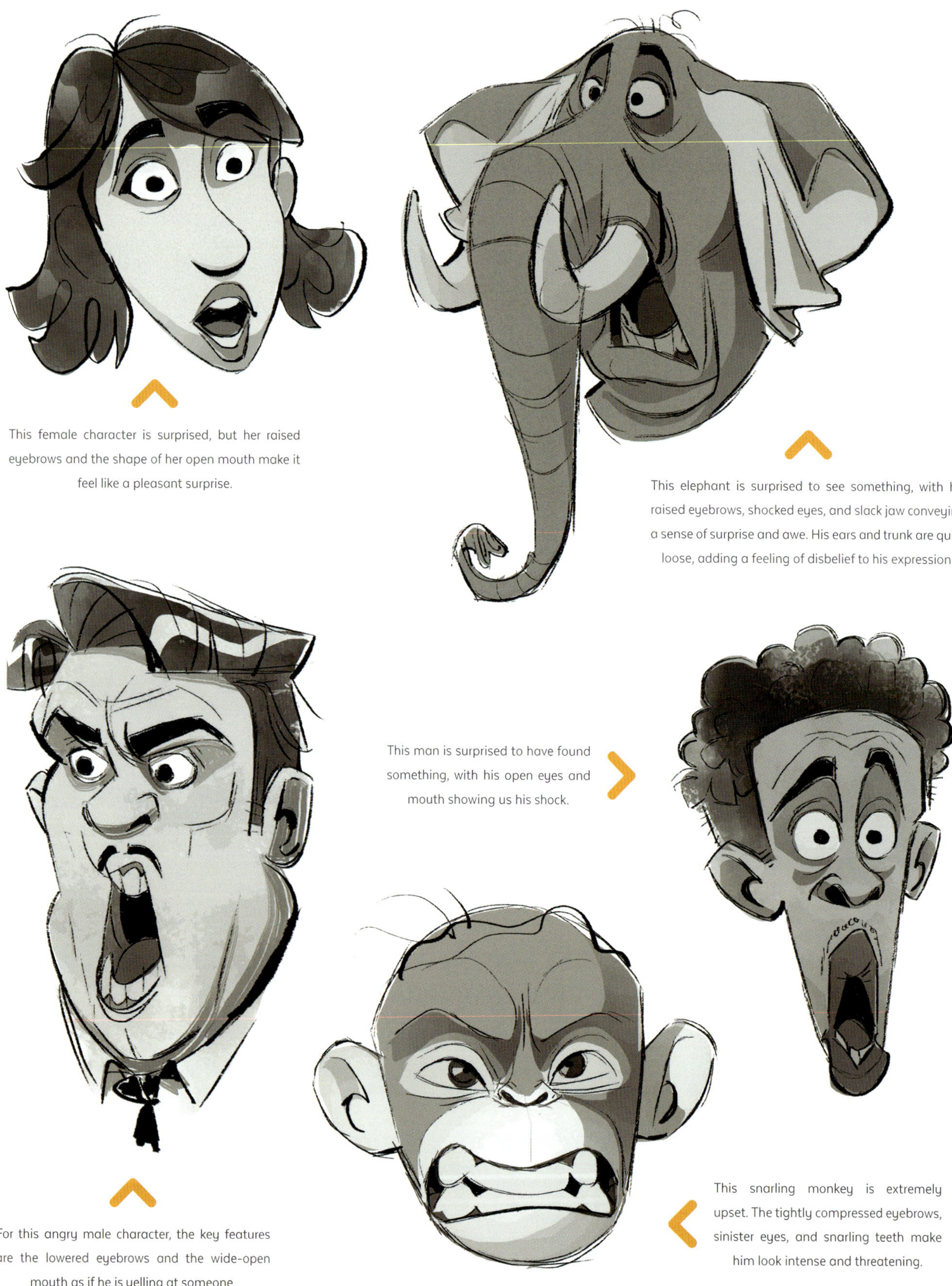

This female character is surprised, but her raised eyebrows and the shape of her open mouth make it feel like a pleasant surprise.

This elephant is surprised to see something, with his raised eyebrows, shocked eyes, and slack jaw conveying a sense of surprise and awe. His ears and trunk are quite loose, adding a feeling of disbelief to his expression.

This man is surprised to have found something, with his open eyes and mouth showing us his shock.

For this angry male character, the key features are the lowered eyebrows and the wide-open mouth as if he is yelling at someone.

This snarling monkey is extremely upset. The tightly compressed eyebrows, sinister eyes, and snarling teeth make him look intense and threatening.

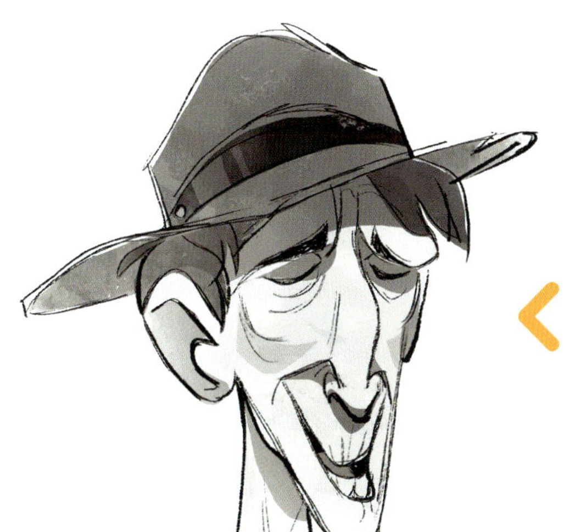

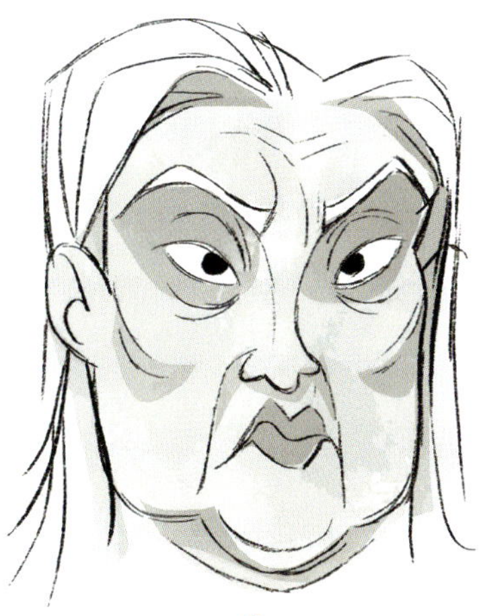

This humble old man's closed eyes with squeezed eyebrows give a sense of contentment. It is always interesting to exaggerate the facial muscles and folds on an elderly character, such as those around his smile.

This elderly woman is not happy with something, as conveyed by her lowered eyebrows and angry, down-turned mouth. The square shape of her head and hair reinforces her stern expression.

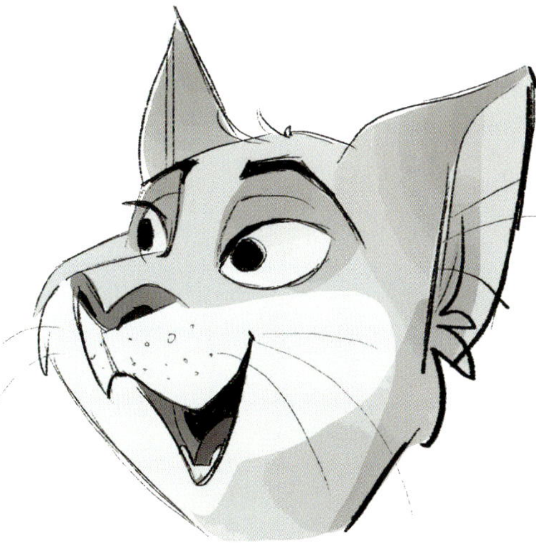

This kid has been faced with the dreaded broccoli! His closed eyes, tightly squeezed eyebrows, and the action of biting his tongue show his disgust. His nostrils are flared and his head is subtly tilting away, which helps to sell the idea further.

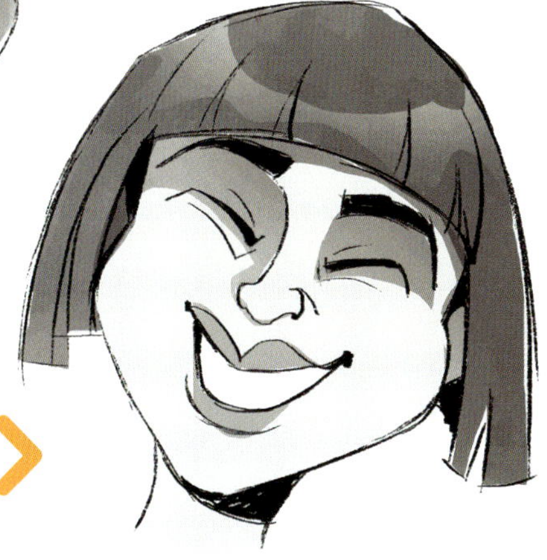

For this happy little girl, the raised eyebrows, big smile, and closed eyes show how elated and excited she is.

This happy cat follows the same principles as the human characters. Her eyebrows are raised but relaxed, her smile is wide open, and her ears are perked up.

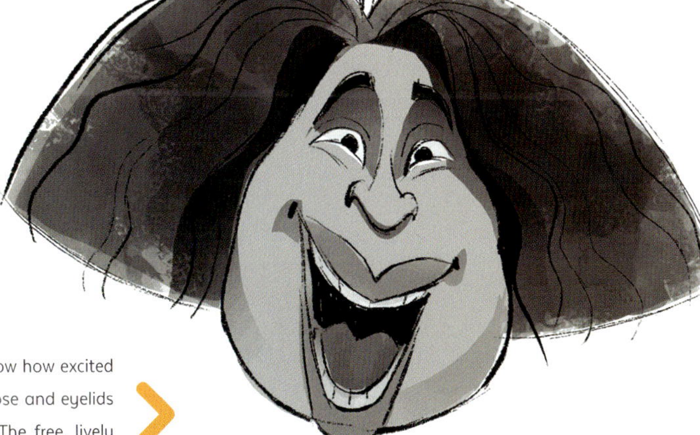

This lady's raised eyebrows and wide open laugh show how excited and happy she is. Secondary features such as the nose and eyelids move up to make this expression more believable. The free, lively shape of her hair also helps to convey this emotion.

COLOR THEORY

BY IRIS MUDDY

There are many different ways of putting color theory into practice, depending on schools of thought and artists' individual preference. As you study color theory, you will come to think of an image's color palette as a specific world and **atmosphere** that you can create and influence with your decisions, and the same applies to character design. Thinking of colors and their relationships to each other gives you the power to manipulate **mood**, **feeling**, and many other ethereal aspects that really elevate your creations from just being good to having a lasting **emotional impression** on the viewer.

Because there are so many ways to ineffectively use color and lose focus when working with it, you must try to constantly be aware of how you can make better use of elements like value and chroma (see the definitions box below), how you group values and colors, and how you create variation and harmony. A definite path to using color more meaningfully is being observant of light and color in life around us: in photography, film, paintings, fabric, objects, and nature. In this introduction to color theory we will first look at **color wheels** and then how a range of color palettes can be applied to characters to create visually pleasing designs that enhance the audience's understanding of that character, their personality, and their story.

USEFUL COLOR TERMS

There are three qualities that define a color, and it is useful to know these terms if you intend to delve deeper into color theory.

Hue is what we typically think of when we hear the word "color." For example, whether a color is basically red, yellow, blue, and so on.

Value is a color's lightness or darkness. For example, bright green or dark green.

Chroma is a color's "colorfulness" or purity, relative to its brightness. For example, pastel pink has lower chroma, while deep magenta has higher chroma.

THE COLOR WHEEL

The color wheel is a great tool for visualizing colors and deciding on different arrangements of colors. When we discuss **color harmony**, we are referring to different fixed ratios between areas of the color wheel, which are common tools for artists. The color wheels on the next page illustrate some of the most commonly used approaches to color harmony, showing different ways in which you can create strong color combinations.

If, like myself, you find yourself working and thinking more intuitively when it comes to color, then it may not work for you to carefully study the distances between your choices on the color wheel before diving into your art. However, understanding these concepts will still help you to make solid, informed choices.

You can also use the color wheel for **gamut masking**, a method which helps to create harmonious color palettes by selecting limited portions of the color wheel. Lines, triangles (see example on opposite page, far right), squares, and rectangles are drawn within the wheel to section off areas of color. From this reduced assortment of colors, you can choose which one will be the best dominant tone, and let the others play more of a supportive role. This can be a challenging and informative way to work with color and discover new color schemes.

The color wheel can also help you simplify the process of moving towards warmer or cooler hues relative to your starting point, if you decide that you would like to adjust the hues or color temperature of your palette.

Finally, it is worth noting that most color wheels you see are subjective, and are not accurate representations of the distribution of the color spectrum. You may find that some color wheels are more useful or appropriate than others. Study each of the color wheels on the following page carefully and consider how you might be able to incorporate the theories into your color selection when designing characters.

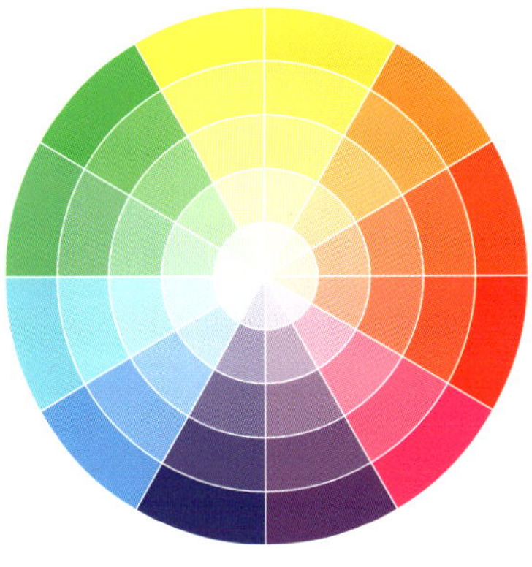

This is quite a **standard color wheel**, but remember that all color wheels are subjective and may look slightly different.

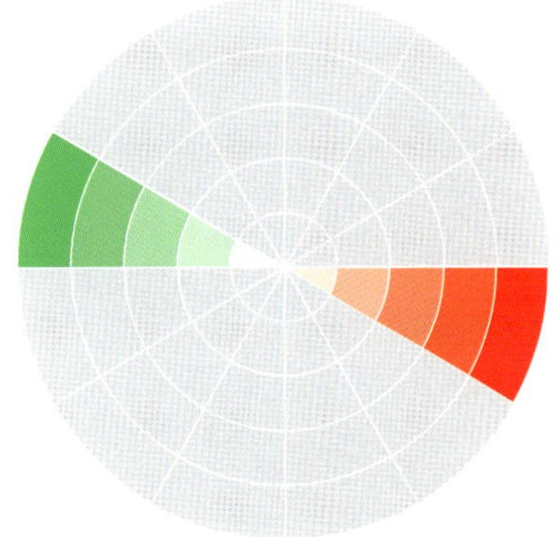

Complementary colors are opposite each other on the color wheel. Green and red are a popular example of a complementary color combination. These two colors could be used roughly equally, or one color could be a smaller contrasting accent.

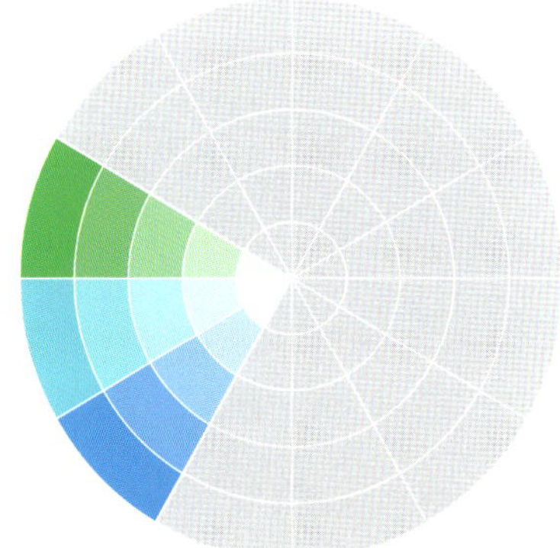

Analogous colors are three colors that sit beside each other on the color wheel. For example, blue, blue-green, and green. This is a useful way to create a subtle, almost monochromatic palette with no extreme changes in hue.

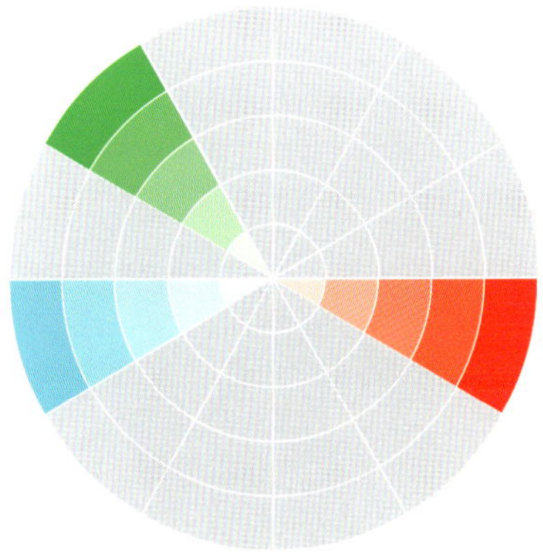

Split-complementary color schemes combine aspects of the above approaches. Instead of using the opposite color as a direct complement, it uses the two colors either side of it. This red, blue-green, and yellow-green palette would create a similar, but more nuanced, effect as the common red and green complementary palette.

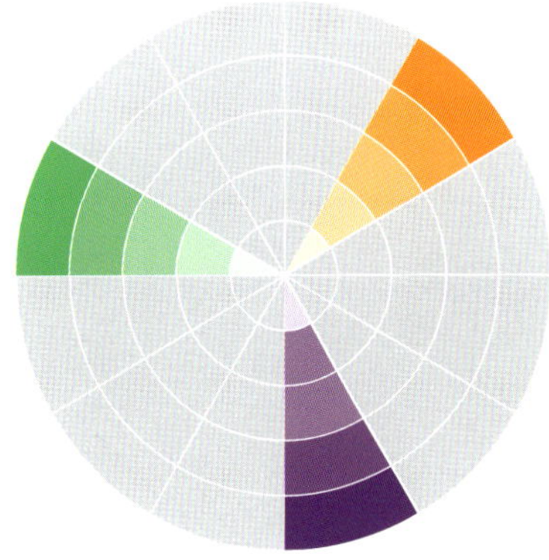

Triadic color schemes use colors that are situated in a triangle across the color wheel. For example, orange, purple, and green form a triadic color scheme. This is a useful way to create a very varied palette for a character without the colors becoming too disorganized.

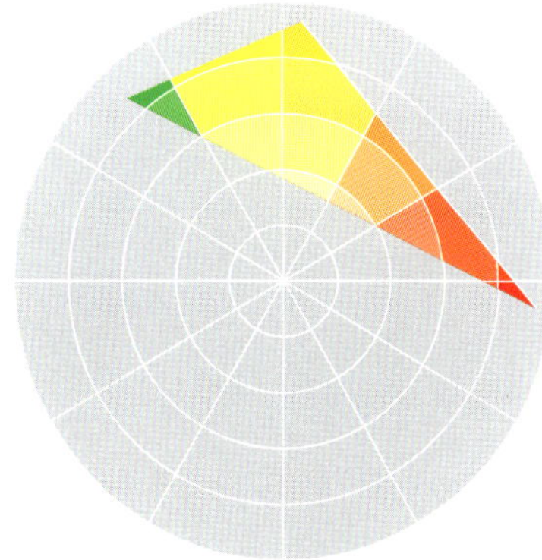

An example of **gamut masking**, in which your chosen palette is limited to a section of the color wheel. Here the masked-off area covers a range of yellows and oranges, with accents of red and green, creating a harmonious yet limited color palette to work with.

REMEMBER THAT YOU DON'T HAVE TO GO BRIGHT

When designing a character, it is often a good approach to emphasize the colors quite heavily on the areas that you want to be the focal points (such as using an eye-catching color on an important element), while reining in the others. This can make the whole palette stronger by creating visually interesting color variation, but should not be used to the extent that it becomes distracting.

When starting out with art, it is hard to judge how to create harmonious and appealing color combinations. An easy trap to fall into is using every color as a bold, bright, loud statement, which doesn't pay off in the end. Grays and earth tones provide a world of opportunity to let other colors shine. This is often an idea that takes a while to set in. Most of us don't start out appreciating how much of a role these colors play.

SAMPLE PALETTES

Depending on the complexity of your character design, you will very likely be using more than just two or three colors; you will have to bring in more tones and extra **accents** to flesh out your character and make them more unique and original. This is where developing a palette can become very challenging. Peppering seemingly random color choices throughout the image can cause a lack of **unity** and make your design feel disjointed. It is important to think about grouping elements together, and how to use these groups purposefully. Let's look at the range of color palettes below to see examples of strong or weak color harmonies.

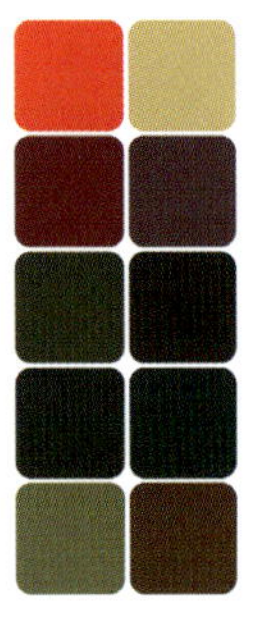 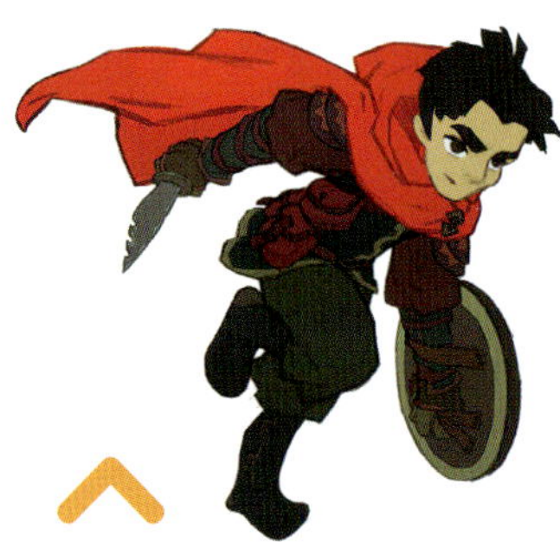

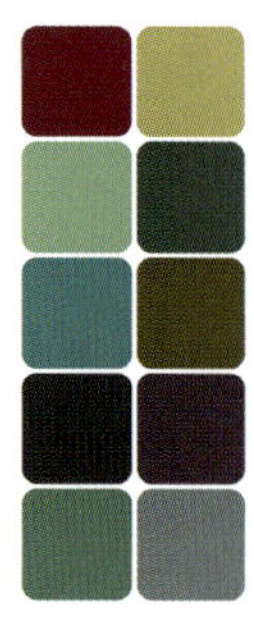 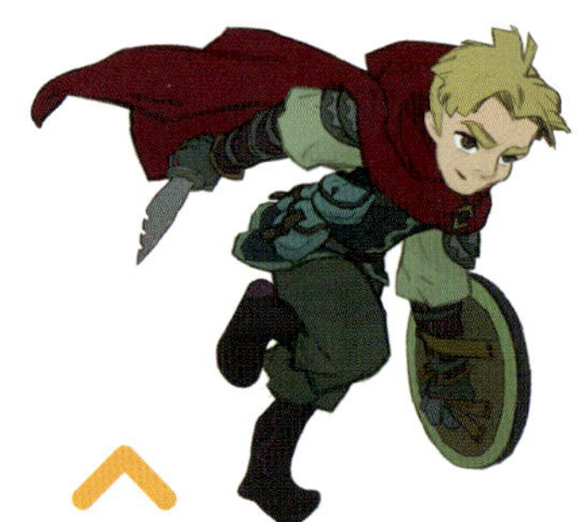

In this case, the bright red of the cape is intentionally the strongest element. Other elements are given a reddish hue to add unity with the cape. Subdued and dark greens, with a couple of lighter neutral tones, add interesting contrast without becoming distracting.

One of my favorite main color combinations is a cooled-down version of the well-known red and green complementary pair. A few neutral colors and dark mauves add small variations to a combination that is already proven to work.

 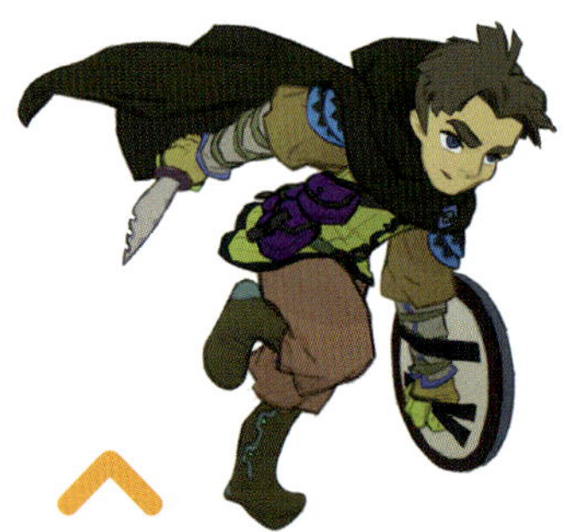

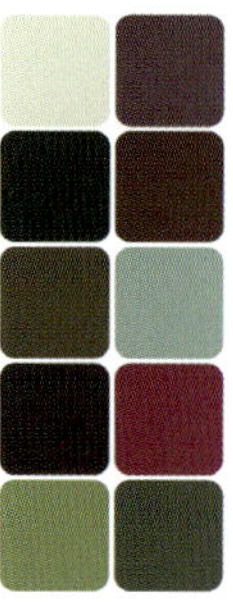 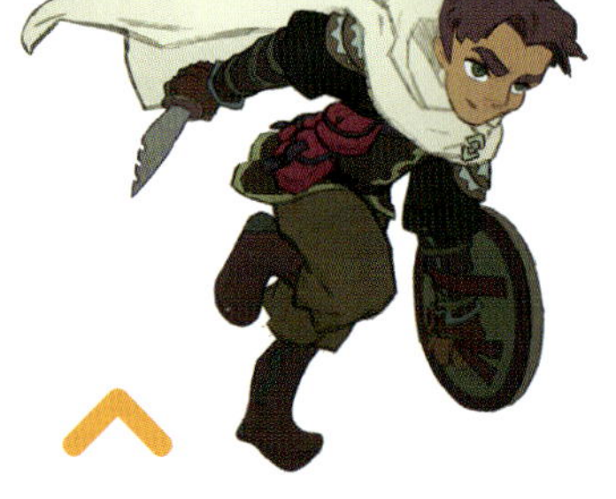

This palette is an example of clashing color choices. The purple bags are random and garish, and the contrast in the shield area is too high, considering it is not a focal point of the design. Compared to the previous color schemes, this is not a successful design.

I particularly enjoy playing with different neutral tones, and having their subdued nature bring out other more vibrant elements, such as the pink pouches. Even in a neutral palette, consideration should still be given to the interplay of warm and cool hues within it.

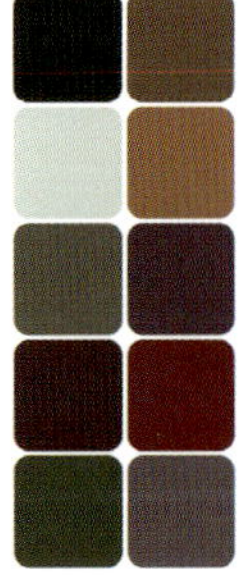 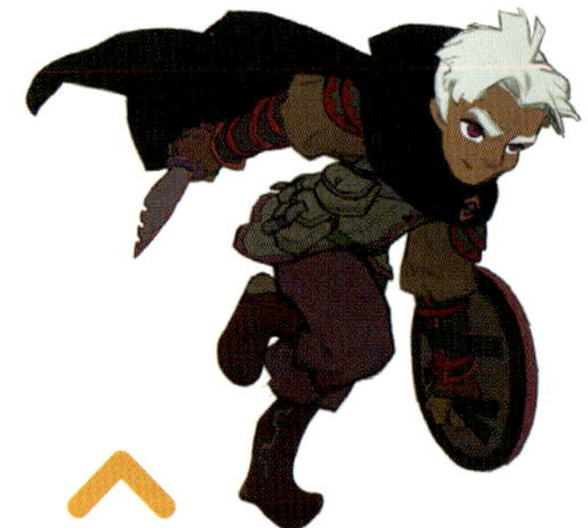

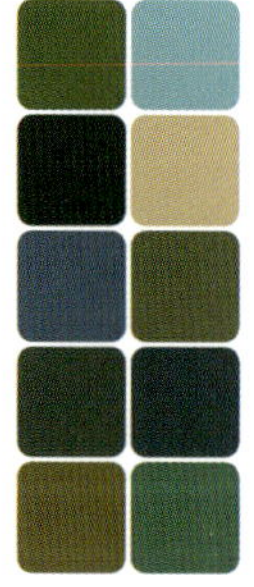 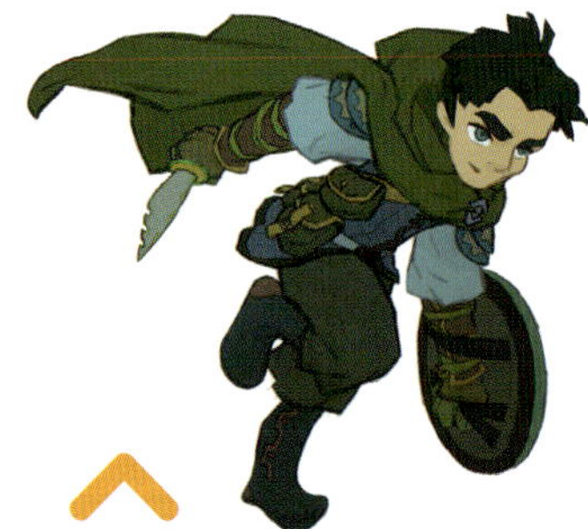

This variation, although similar to the very first one in some ways, has much less appeal. Unity is good, but too much of it can be boring, which makes the areas with contrasting colors and tones (the character's head and arms) seem too jarring.

This palette is more harmonious, but includes many steps of the transition between yellow-green and teal (on his shirt, sleeves, and bags) and looks a bit sloppy as a result. More restraint and consideration for contrast and temperature would help.

CREATING MEANING WITH COLOR

Color has the potential to communicate so much about a character. Depending on what the situation calls for, there are many possibilities to consider drawing from, ranging from **emotional symbolism** to representing something physically present in the character's surroundings. From one culture to another, certain colors' meanings and positive or negative attachments can vary greatly. Certain hues can suggest elements of the **environment** a character comes from or is adapted to, such as water, soil, vegetation, sky, animals, structures, or anything else that is significant in that context. A palette can strongly **evoke** a certain season or climate. Darker, richer colors carry a more intense mood than bright or light ones.

Ask yourself questions about what you are trying to **express**, because that train of thought will intuitively direct you towards potential colors. It is especially useful to seek reference images that "feel" a particular way, and then think about what causes that effect. It is also always best to explore beyond your first ideas for a character's palette, because that's usually when the more interesting, **unexpected choices** will come about. For example, I instinctively chose a classic, passionate hero's red cape for the rogue boy on the previous page, but it is still possible to approach the same design from a different angle and achieve interesting results, as the other palettes show.

As we have seen already, different tones, temperatures, and juxtapositions can hugely change how colors come across and make the viewer feel. The selection below is by no means exhaustive, but it can be useful to understand some of the moods and meanings associated with a color before you begin. You can use some of these ideas as starting points for your own research.

This bright, sea-green turquoise color is often associated with calm, soothing feelings. It is said to provide energy and balance. It is a peaceful color, with a vibrant, positive tendency.

Orange, like red and yellow, is very energetic and intense. It is warm, welcoming, and upbeat. It is associated with motivation and encouragement, and evokes images of fire and sunsets.

Brown is associated with warmth, nature, wood, stability, earth, and dependability. It evokes feelings of home and comfort. It can be very versatile when used in different tones.

Yellow is so vibrant that it can't help but be associated with joy, positive energy, opportunity, and spontaneity. Its warmth and connection to our symbolic idea of a sunny day makes it inherently linked to feelings of summer and heat.

Purple or violet can be associated with spirituality, imagination, and mystery. It feels magical, creative, and innovative. It can even feel related to psychic experiences. It is an unusual, inspiring, cryptic color.

Red is possibly one of the first colors we attach meaning to, and one with the most meanings attached to it. It can mean love, emotion, intensity, passion, and drawing attention. It can also represent fire, lust, rage, power, anger, or danger.

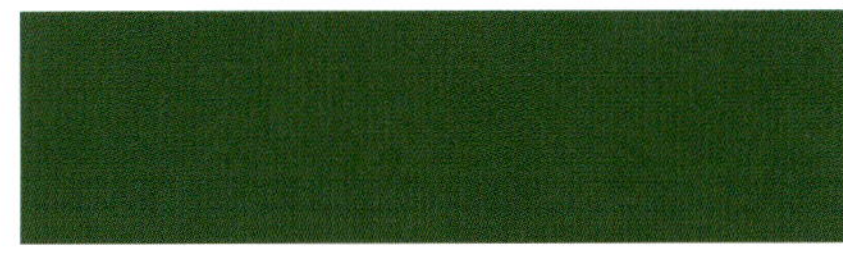

Greens in general can be seen as representing growth and strong vitality. They are associated with renewal, health, verdant nature, foliage, luck, and regeneration. Green is also associated with envy.

This icy, neutral gray could be seen as a formal and conservative color. It has a cold aspect to it, harboring little emotion. It can be associated with solitary, lonely feelings.

Blue is a color that carries associations with wisdom, knowledge, trust, serenity, harmony, and integrity. It can also be cool, aloof, depressed, gloomy, and tranquil.

SAMPLE PALETTES

We will now look at examples of color schemes and meaning in the context of different characters. It will often take experimentation and adjustment to find the ideal colors for your character designs.

Sometimes very different palettes may make for equally strong designs, but carry different meanings which may or may not suit the character and their backstory. Sometimes these different meanings may

even open up new ideas for the character which had not occurred to you before. On these pages you can observe how different color schemes can change a character and their personality.

FRUIT SELLER

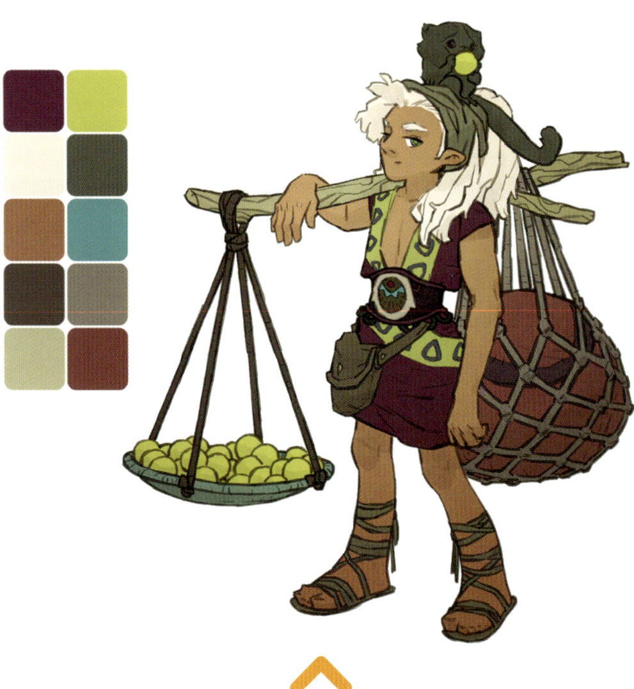

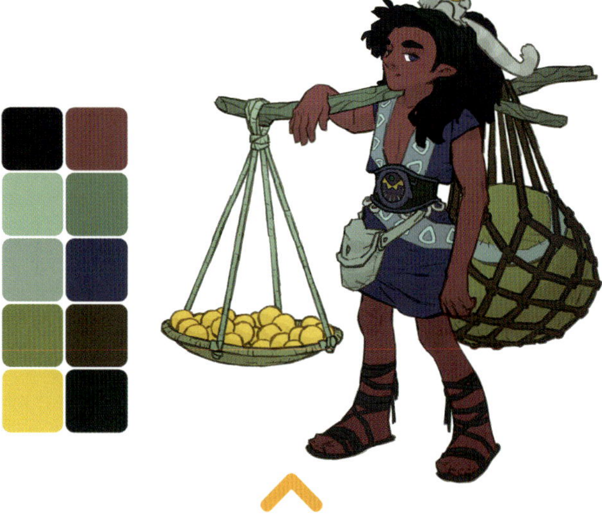

This more blue-green version embodies comfort more than the other two palettes. The temperatures and colors are more laid back, and deep blues can feel magical or restful. In this palette, the yellow is especially zesty, while one or two areas of warmer green keep the yellow from feeling too far off from the main blue.

This character's palette needs to embody a feeling of lightness and agility as well as strength. He seems unusual, alluring, and tricky. This palette uses contrasting brighter and deeper tones, with a slightly askew version of the purple and yellow complementary pair, mixed with various neutrals, to represent that identity.

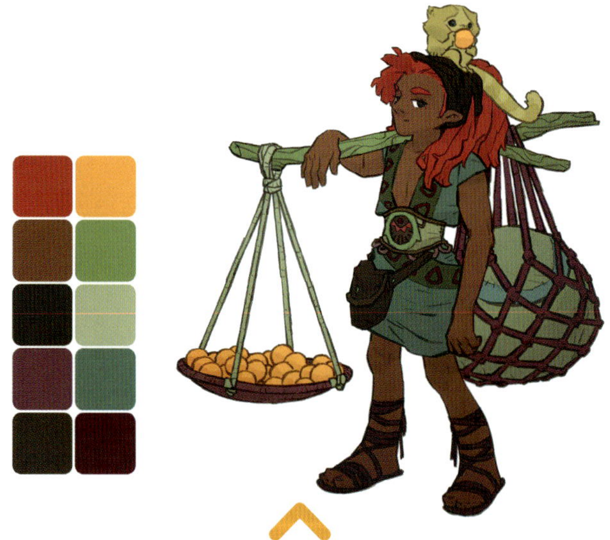

LEARN MORE

There are many useful resources, tools, and methods available to help artists learn about color. I recommend reading James Gurney's books and website, learning about gamut masking (see page 50), and visiting www.huevaluechroma.com. Curating and analyzing an "inspiration folder" can play a huge part in helping you to understand what you want to achieve with color, and which traits you consider to be powerful in the images that you look at, whether they are photographs or paintings.

Whenever I use red and green together, I really try not to make it feel like Christmas! This can be achieved by reaching out to nearby colors, like the dusty mauve and yellowish orange, to add some complementary visual treats. This creates more appeal and breaks the stereotypical associations of that color combination.

ELF WARRIOR

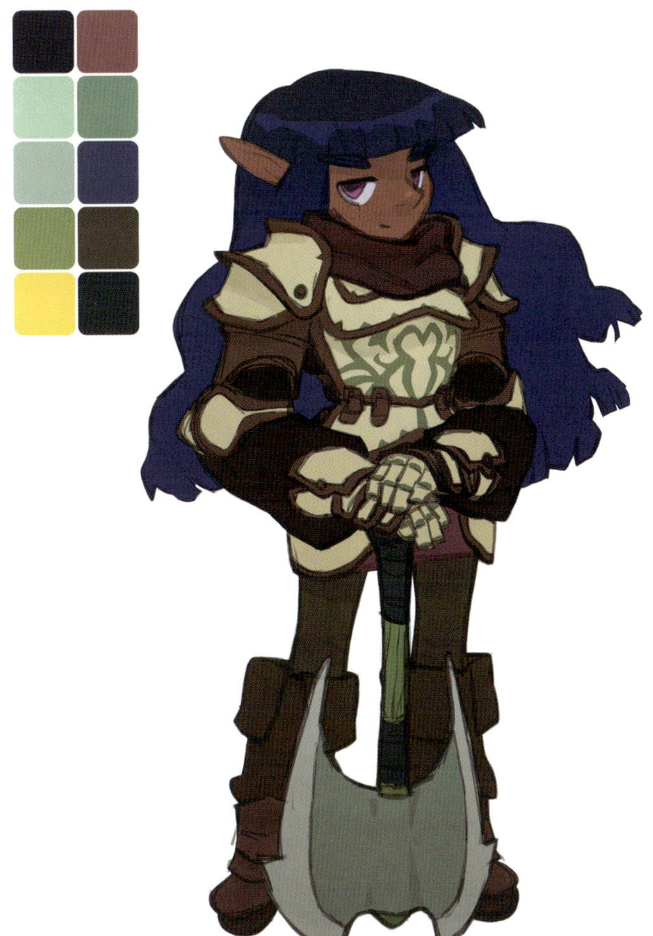

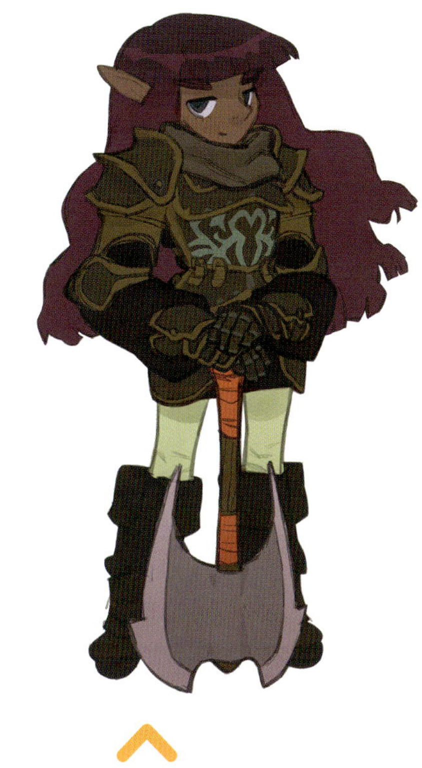

While this variation feels less royal and high-ranking than the one on the left, these colors embody more of an earthly power. The warm tones give her a feeling that brings her closer to town and forest settings. It is as if the feeling her proud expression carries is changed by the colors she wears, compared to the other two palettes shown here.

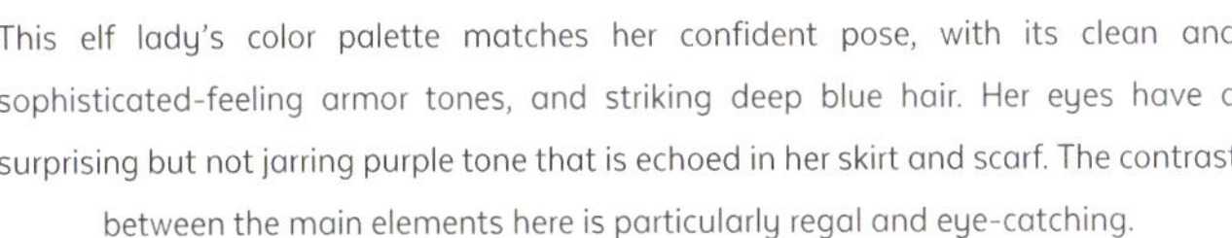

This elf lady's color palette matches her confident pose, with its clean and sophisticated-feeling armor tones, and striking deep blue hair. Her eyes have a surprising but not jarring purple tone that is echoed in her skirt and scarf. The contrast between the main elements here is particularly regal and eye-catching.

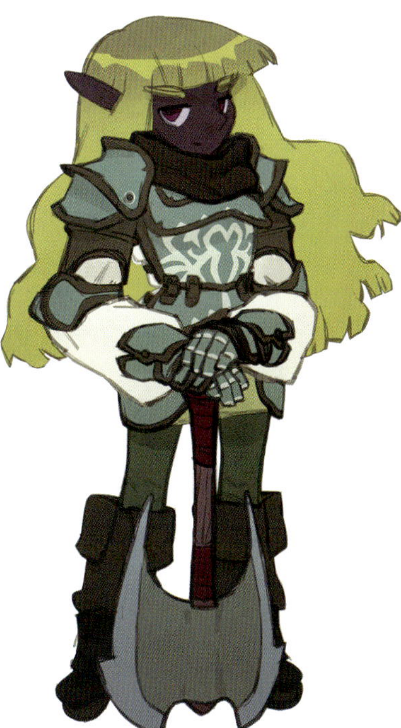

This mostly cool, neutral palette has a couple of warmer colors that create a feeling of unease (such as the purple eyes and yellow-green hair). She feels like she knows something we don't, and carries less warmth than the other two. Her clean, bright sleeves and more decorative armor almost indicate some higher level of cleverness.

WISE DWARF

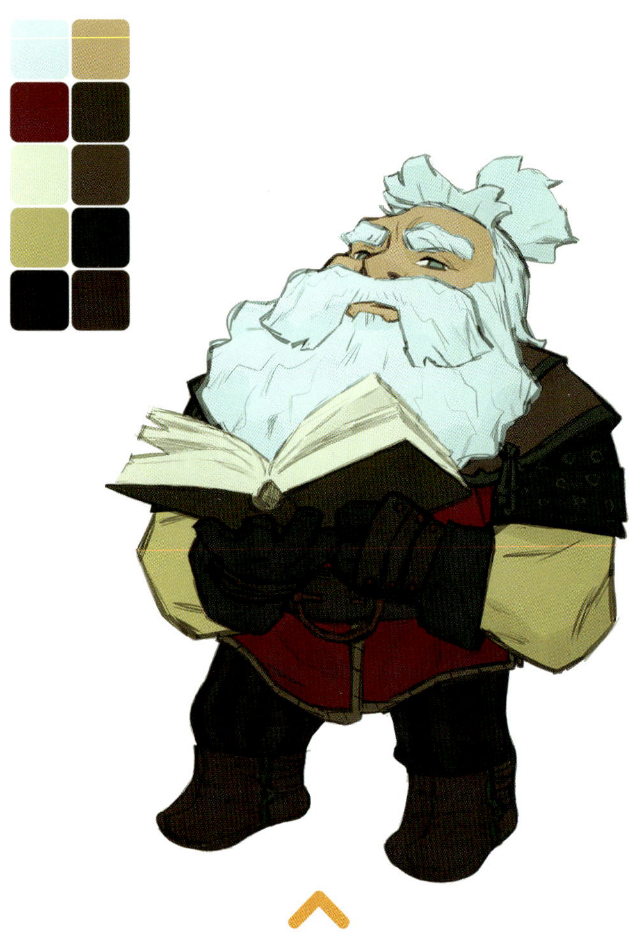

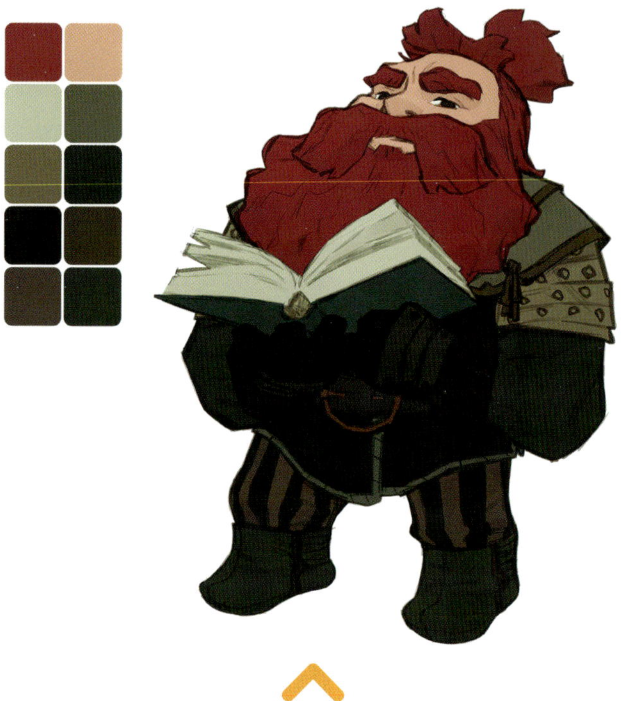

This mostly cool green palette, with a couple of neutrals and a strong red, feels more rough and lively than the other two palettes – even sneaky, too. He looks like he might know a thing or two about the town's surroundings, and possibly the taverns and pubs.

This fellow needs to look wise but approachable and authentic. The earth-toned clothes he wears, paired with the wine-colored tunic, give him a seasoned but refined air. He looks like he might teach adventurers about weapons he has mastered through battle and training.

KEEP NARRATIVE IN MIND

As you can see on these pages, changing a character's color palette can vividly alter the sense of their personality, environment, and role. While choosing a harmonious and balanced color scheme is important, don't forget to consider the narrative element of your character. Are they supposed to be subtle and camouflaged? Are they wealthy and ostentatious? Make sure that your color choices are practical for your character and the story you want them to tell.

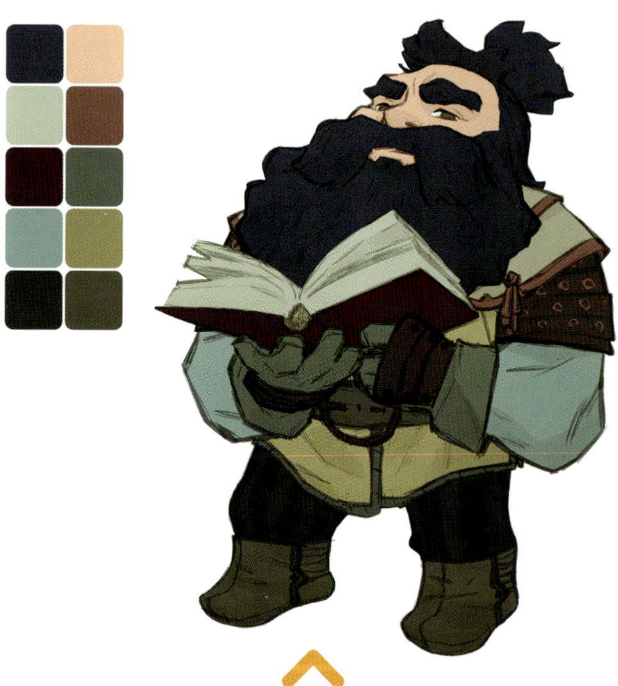

The bluer variation of this character instantly seems like someone who is more likely to be reading about spells, mana, and enchantments, simply because of the cooler, lighter tones in his clothing, paired with the deep blue hair and beard.

FALCONER

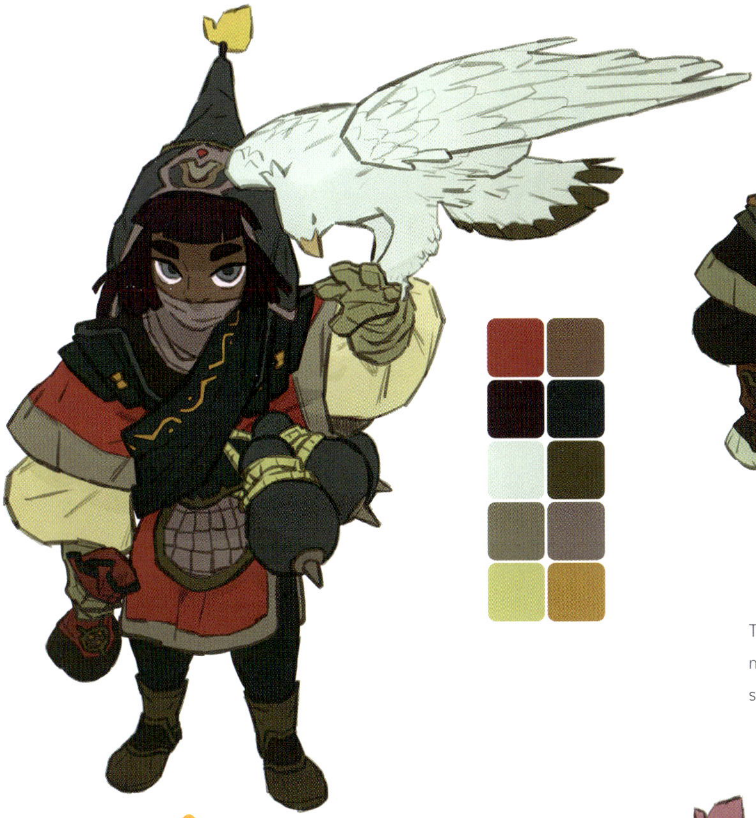

The contrast and deep vibrant colors make this character stand out and feel like she is in charge of her surroundings. The darkness of the palette gives her an air of strength, and the very light and clean bird seems to evoke pride in her role.

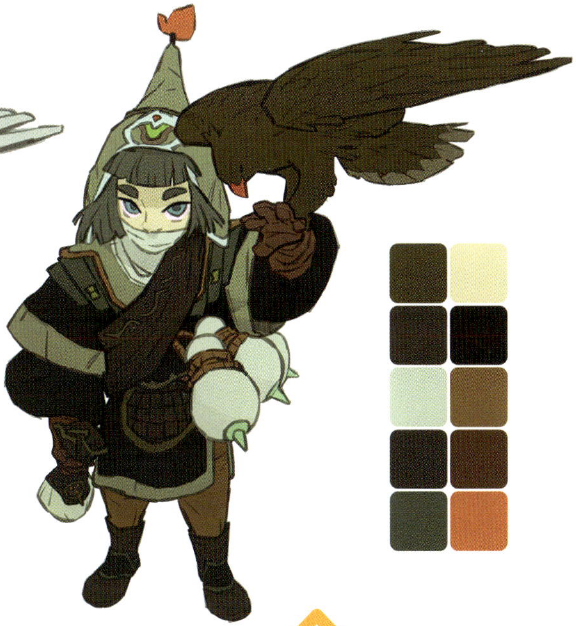

This palette seems more inspired by a swampy area: a place with moss, trees, and many plants. The character could blend in there, stealthily hunting. This alternative version is well characterized by this palette, even if she doesn't have the heroic feeling of the first.

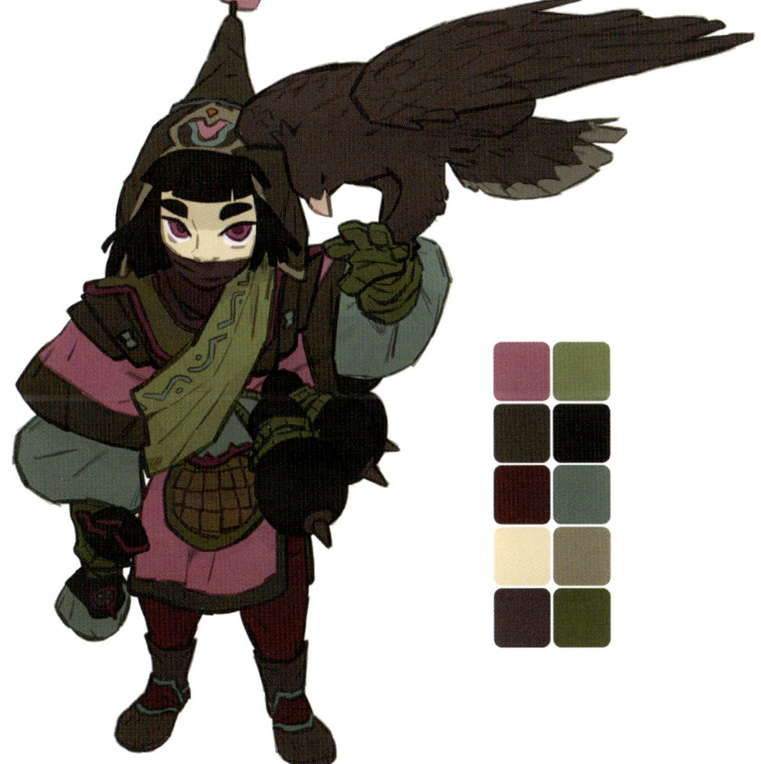

This palette is dark, deceitful-looking, and even somewhat poisonous with its mix of greens and pinks. The character now seems more like a ninja or assassin. Her bird also seems very stealthy. There is an air of mystery about her that is less present in the other two.

THE STYLIZATION PROCESS

BY AMANDA JOLLY WITH CONTRIBUTIONS FROM KÉVIN ROUALLAND & HICHAM HABCHI

The process of designing and stylizing a character is never completely linear or identical from one artist to another, but there are some essential stages that many character designers will have in common. Paying attention to these key milestones of the design process will help you to create characters that are more appealing, unique, and thoughtfully fleshed out. In this chapter, discover the key components of the stylization process. The core steps shown here will be applied in depth throughout this book, so make sure to acquaint yourself with these ideas now, and try testing them out on some character designs of your own.

01 THE IDEA

The first step in creating any character is to know who that character is. We can determine this through asking ourselves a series of questions. Who is the character to the story? What is the character's motivation? What kind of person or archetype is this character? Every aspect of a design begins with knowing the *purpose* of the design; it makes each step from that point forward more clear and focused. If you are working as a character artist, some of this information will usually come to you in the form of a brief outlining the character's personality, role, and appearance. However, there will be gaps for you to fill with your own research, interpretation, and ideas. Different artists have different methods for generating and developing ideas. The tool used in this book will be a mind map, which allows you to write down your thoughts and expand upon them based on the foundations you already have. While you may just want to start drawing, it is important to incorporate this explorative stage into your process, whether it be through a mind map, bullet points, or key words.

When you stylize a character, what you are really doing is determining which elements of that character to **exaggerate**. That exaggeration immediately tells the viewer what to think about that character, and why. In stylizing a character, you are also trying to make one that is memorable, one that stands out, one that is iconic. So much of what will strike a viewer is what you have chosen to exaggerate. Exploring the key traits of a character early on will help you to ensure that you maximize the areas of exaggeration within the confines of the brief.

EXAMPLE

Let's look at the design process for a character who is the sidekick to a hero. This sidekick is a jolly fellow who enjoys a good joke and meal, but is also skilled in a fight. The story is set in sixteenth-century France. Using these key facts, you can explore the concept further to provide the character with more background and distinct traits.

Kévin Roualland says: For this character, I focus on the main characteristics and try to find some context. What defines him as an actor, and what can I add to give him more credibility and volume?

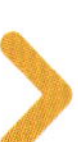

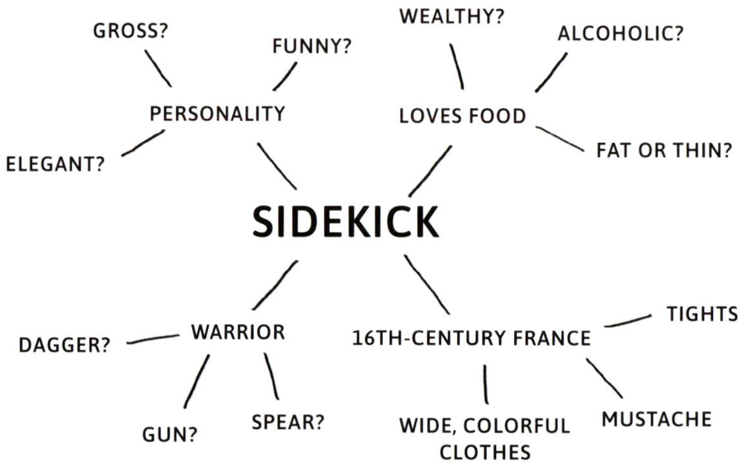

02 RESEARCH

Once you know what you want out of your character, research begins. Research is the most essential step of the design process, and one sadly overlooked by many artists due to a misguided notion that researching equates to a lack of creativity. The opposite is true. Not only does research make a design ultimately seem grounded in reality, it also provides the artist with innumerable design avenues which they would not have known or remembered on their own. Usually what we recall of an animal, article of period clothing, or a person's ethnicity is not as interesting or accurate as what we would find if we simply dug into it with research.

Gathering a visual library from research is key, because this is where stylization is born. Like with the idea stage discussed above, you have a much better chance of exaggerating or placing emphasis on the right elements if you have carried out your research. Research will also help to ground your designs in reality, making them more believable, even if the concept is based in a fantasy or sci-fi world.

Use books, websites, social media, magazines, documentaries, and real-life observations in your research. It is useful not only to look at the images you find, but to really study and sketch them. This will help you to become familiar with the shape language, construction, and texture of the different elements before you incorporate them into your character.

EXAMPLE

You can now begin looking up reference material that suits the needs of this sixteenth-century sidekick character. Look into costumes from that period, as well as architecture, art, and patterns from that location. Research actors or types of people who come to mind when you picture that description, and see how those real people are formed. You have now built yourself a visual library using research.

Kévin Roualland says: Looking at references helps me to find a look and personality for the character, adding more accuracy to my portrayal. If a character lives in an existing period and in an existing place, you can't fool around without cultural background.

USE MOOD BOARDS

Hicham Habchi says: I usually spend an hour or two looking through websites such as Pinterest or Flickr, collecting inspiration for subjects, moods, colors, and styles, which I put together in a patchwork of images called a "mood board" that I can refer to as I work.

03 THUMBNAILS

The sad truth is, your first idea will almost never be your best or most exciting one. That is disappointing if you were hoping to save time, but it also makes perfect sense. Your first idea – or first several ideas – will likely be whatever concepts had seemed most obvious to you. If we are trying to make a character that is uniquely memorable, these obvious choices likely won't pass the test. A useful approach to this obstacle is to avoid wasting time on detailed drawings. Instead, work small and fast, creating tiny thumbnails that focus on the exaggerated shapes founded in the research from the previous step. Your goal in this stage should be to get down as many ideas that are dissimilar, while still feeling true to the character. The purpose of this is to give yourself **options**.

Different artists have different methods for producing thumbnails. Some find that silhouettes are the best way to work out shapes, while others use sketchy outlines. Find a technique that works best for you, as long as it is effective for making small, quick images. Once you have created your thumbnails, you should step back and judge the advantages and disadvantages of each one in the context of the brief. Which aspects of the character did you want to highlight when you planned the idea and carried out your research? Which thumbnails achieve this? This will not always be a linear process: sometimes you will draw a dozen thumbnails and one will stand out as being ideal; other times you will draw six thumbnails and take the best bits from three of them; sometimes you might make two or more rounds of thumbnails before hitting upon a concept you are satisfied with. This will result in a strong design that is worth the effort.

EXAMPLE

For the sidekick character, you might focus on keeping most of his shape language curved or rounded, as he is supposed to be sweet and heroic. However, he is also meant to be formidable in combat, so maybe he is tall and broad, or maybe he is short and stocky; maybe he is loose and wiry, making him nimble, but with a slightly fuller belly due to his love of food. This is how you give yourself options, as if you are a casting director auditioning vastly different actors until you see someone you like.

KEEP YOUR CAST IN MIND

It is important to keep the idea of a cast in mind. When you create a character, it is unlikely that they will be the only character in the project. This character will be sharing visual space with others, and because of that, it is important to create a cast that has as much variety as the options you give yourself in the character thumbnails. You don't want anyone confusing your sidekick with the villain (unless that is a specific plot point), so always keep in mind how these characters can most clearly represent themselves, either alone or amongst others.

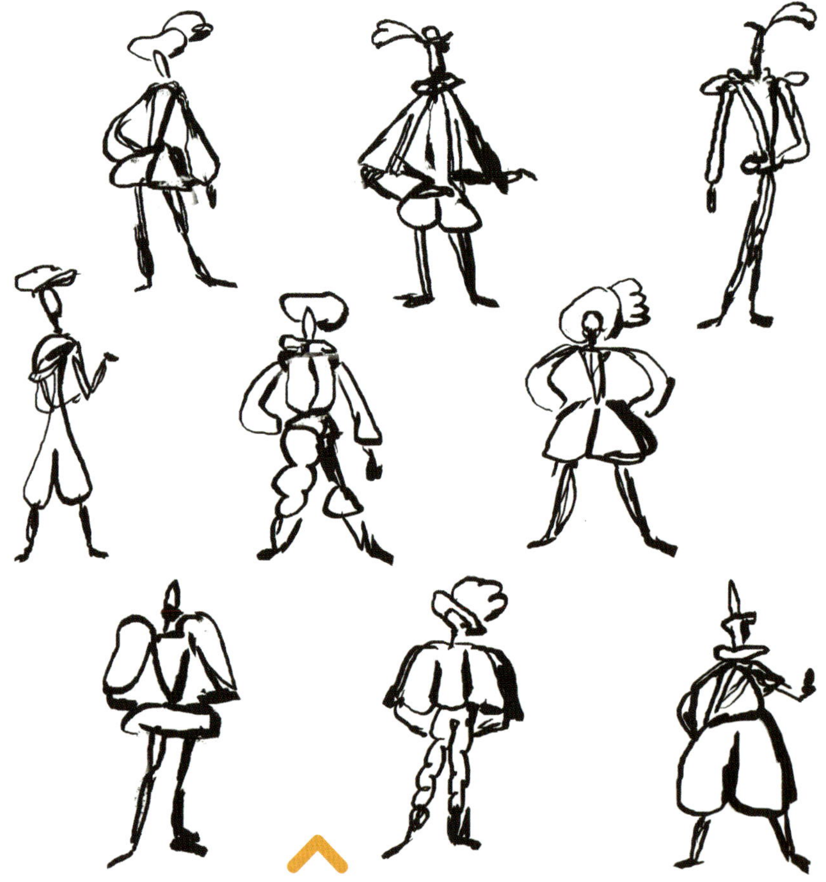

Kévin Roualland says: At this stage I use my references to guide my thumbnails, but also start to add my own thoughts about the character. I try to move away from clichés about the character's shape and size, and find interesting ratios and proportions.

04 BASIC SHAPES

Once you have selected the thumbnail you like the most (or combined more than one thumbnail), you can begin refining the shapes and elements of the character. Often your initial design may be little more than a mess of shapes piled together in interesting proportions, so there can be a lot of work to do at this stage! This is the moment when you can really ensure that you are getting the best out of the good "seed" idea that you had in your thumbnail. Usually this will involve honing the character's shape language - a concept we learned about in the Stylized Figures chapter - to help you communicate their personality.

Now that the basic forms and shape language of your thumbnail have been blown up to a larger scale, you must ensure that the clarity of the design has not been lost, or it will only be lost further once you move on to adding secondary details like props and accessories. These checks could be carried out by overlaying the design with basic geometry, to see how the parts of the character relate to each other in their simplest forms, and by creating a black silhouette of the design to ensure that its shapes are clear and bold. Often artists will test gestures out at this stage to test their design. For the purpose of simplifying the process for this book, and to focus on how basic shapes can be used to build up a character, we have saved gestures and poses until later in the workflow. As you develop your own way of working you will probably find that you merge some of these steps and go back and forth more.

EXAMPLE

Here you can see how the design is taking shape. When scaling the character up and starting to refine his forms, it is important not to lose the clarity and appeal of the thumbnail that captured his jolly personality in the first place. Viewing the character in silhouette is a useful way to check this.

Kévin Roualland says: I picture the character as thin, geometric, and mustached, with a bit of a belly since he likes hanging out in taverns and eating at banquets.

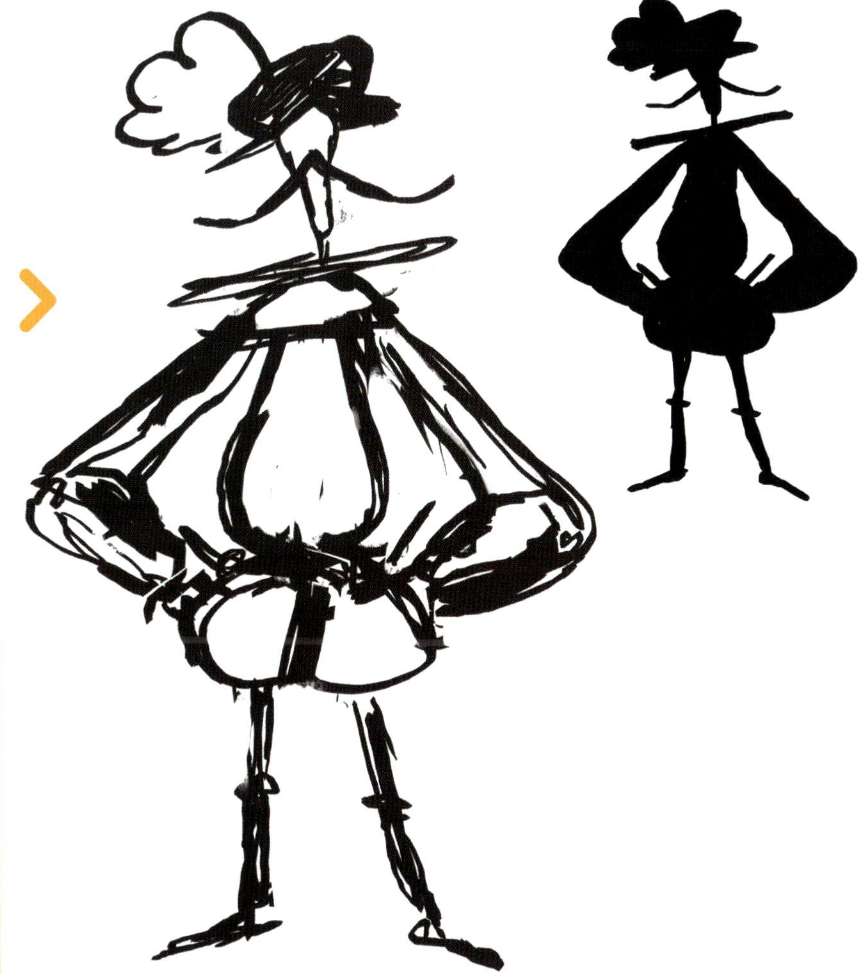

VARIETY IS KEY

Visuals of any kind, and particularly stylized ones, are most interesting when they contain a variety of proportions. It is much more compelling to design and look at characters who have some small, some medium, and some large sections to them, than characters with no visual variety who seem like they could just be folded in half!

05 ADDING DETAILS

This stage brings out the best of the design, lets you really work out the details of a costume so that the eye focuses where you desire, and solidifies aspects like facial features and physical details. You may find it useful to draw directly on top of scaled-up copies of your loose thumbnail, as this allows you to retain the appeal of the rough thumbnail that you loved, while fleshing it out and making the design truly "finalized."

This is where some of your early research into costuming, accessories, and patterns may come back into play, helping you to add finishing touches to the character that really give a sense of the story and setting they inhabit. It is always best to establish a strong underlying structure for the character first, as discussed in the previous steps, before trying to tackle a rendition that is more refined – even though cutting corners and jumping ahead can be very tempting!

EXAMPLE

The character's physical features, costume, and accessories are now fully realized and as good as finished. In this neutral pose, you can clearly see the various elements and proportions of the design: a paunchy stomach contrasted with long, agile arms and legs, and a costume with period-appropriate weapons and accessories. Details such as the ruff and mustache help to break up his skinny silhouette and make the whole design more interesting to look at.

Kévin Roualland says: Here the character starts to take shape, without a final facial expression and pose, but with most of his visual complexity decided. The wildly contrasting shape language helps to convey his comical personality, and can be further exaggerated in his final pose.

KEEP IT FLUID

It may happen that some details don't work out when you proceed to the next stage of posing the character, but you can always move back a step or two in the process to iron out any problems or try different approaches.

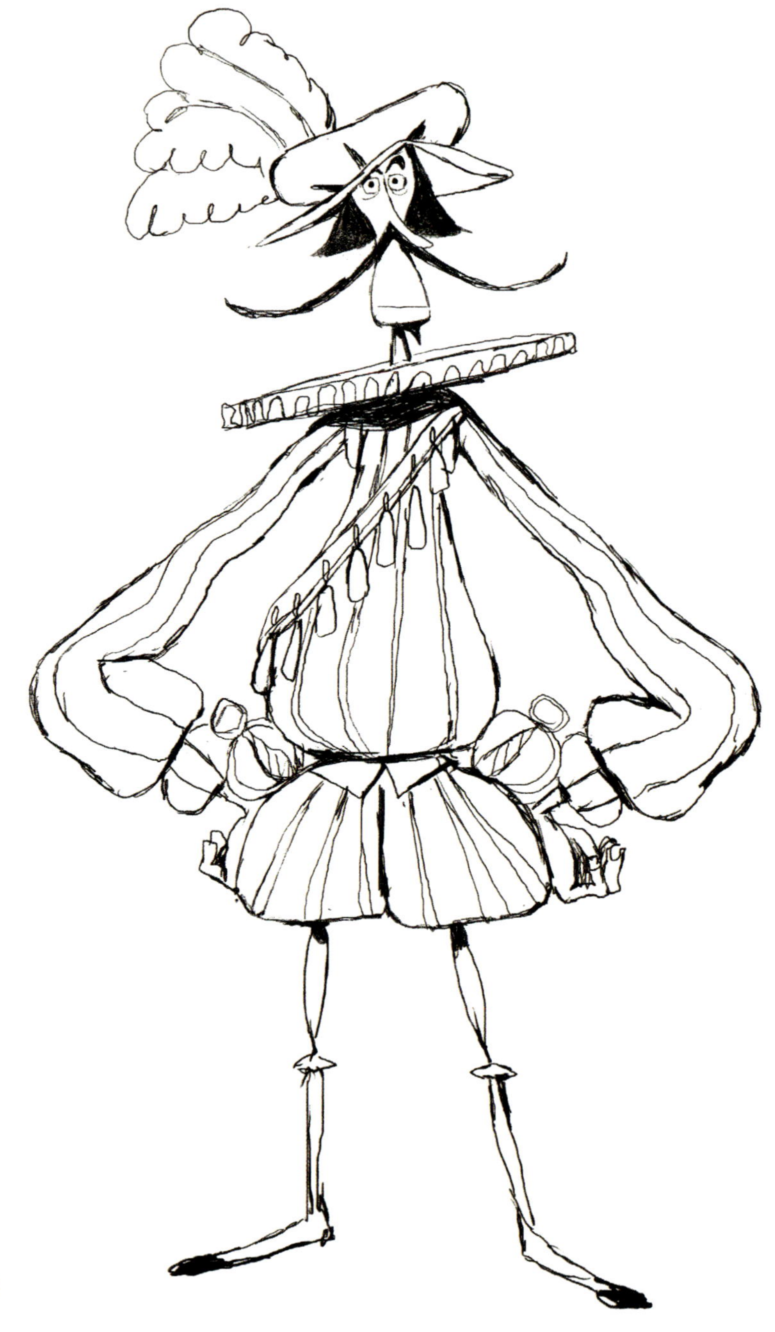

06 EXPRESSIONS & POSING

Upon creating a design that is working for you, the most critical stage is conveying your character's attitude through posing and "acting." In character design, the "character" aspect is often given little consideration compared to the "design" element.

However, if you think again that creating characters is akin to a casting call, you have created this character presumably because they will act. This character must have a personality, and that personality should be as distinct as their trousers, mustache, sword, or other details you added in the previous step.

Refer back to the Gesture & Pose and Faces & Expressions chapters to ensure you understand some useful approaches for creating poses and facial expressions. Practice and study are essential here. Think about acting you have witnessed that gets those traits across, or stand up yourself and feel such movements in your own limbs. It will help give that last bit of credibility to a character who otherwise doesn't look like he could exist in our reality. It also puts your character through posing paces that can work out any persisting kinks in the design. This relatable human touch makes a stylized character a believable one that viewers come to love.

EXAMPLE

If we return to the idea of our jolly sidekick, he most likely doesn't stand stiffly or scowl at people. He probably stands relaxed, smiles, and perhaps has a small amount of swagger in his movements. His posture and movements will also depend on his body shape and physique, which we developed earlier – for example, if he was tall, stout, or paunchy, his movements might be limited.

Kévin Roualland says: I try to achieve the most fitting expression and pose for the character: one that suits his entire being as an actor, but also one that suits his shapes so we can fully appreciate his design. The central pose gives the best sense of his comedy sidekick role, warrior's weapons, and love of food.

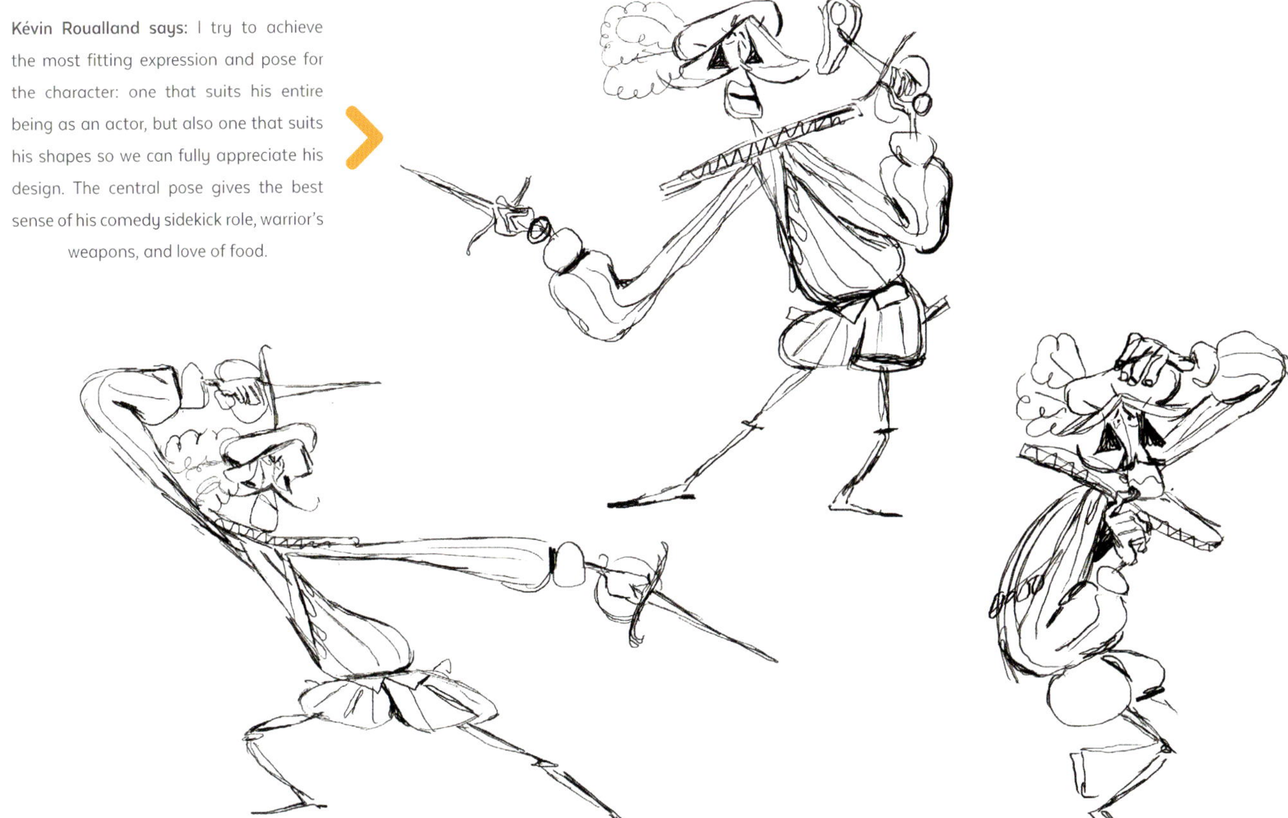

07 VALUES & COLOR

As you learned in the Color Theory chapter, working with color and value is a good way to lead the eye to the most important parts of a character, as well as visually linking them to other characters in the project. The viewer's eye will immediately be drawn to anywhere with strongly contrasting values in a design. The same goes for highly textured areas, which can pull focus, and low-textured areas, which can allow the eye to rest. If we have a cast in which certain characters have been deemed as "good" or "evil," giving the characters who fall within each category a similar color scheme can immediately let the audience know where that character's loyalties lie or what to expect from their personality.

START WITH THE BASICS

Hicham Habchi says: If you are finding it hard to come up with a color palette, try starting with one color to establish the mood of the character, then diversify to add more contrast and attract attention to focal areas. Filling out your character in grayscale first helps to create contrast between elements for good readability and balance.

EXAMPLE

Similar to the thumbnailing process, this stage is about quickly and efficiently exploring a wide range of options from which you can derive the best solution for the character. Rather than drawing the character over and over again, save yourself time by creating multiple copies of the design that you can overlay with different color combinations. If you created a mood board during your research phase, now is the time to return to it for some color inspiration. Planning your design in grayscale first is a valuable method for judging the best balance of light and dark tones for your character.

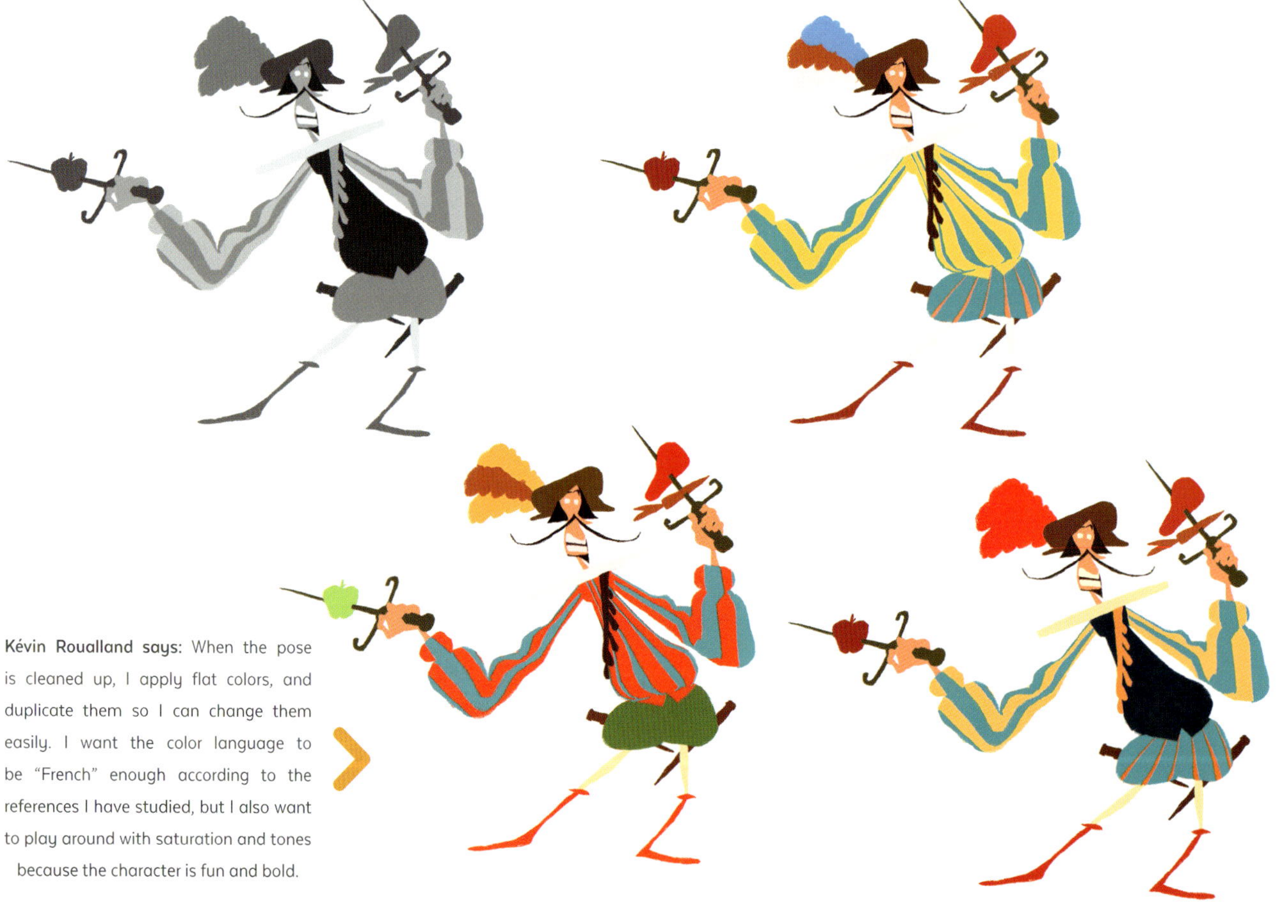

Kévin Roualland says: When the pose is cleaned up, I apply flat colors, and duplicate them so I can change them easily. I want the color language to be "French" enough according to the references I have studied, but I also want to play around with saturation and tones because the character is fun and bold.

08 FINAL DESIGN

Your final design should synthesize all the work and research you have put in previously, resulting in the most memorable and appropriate shape language, color palette, and pose for the character's personality and backstory.

EXAMPLE

The final design clearly captures the brief of a jolly, food-loving, sixteenth-century sidekick while also offering an interpretation that is unique and perhaps not what would be immediately obvious.

Kévin Roualland says: When I finalize the image, I make sure to keep the best possible overall harmony of shapes. The food on his daggers keeps the character close to the original description, and each of his accessories helps to further push the character's pose and fun personality.

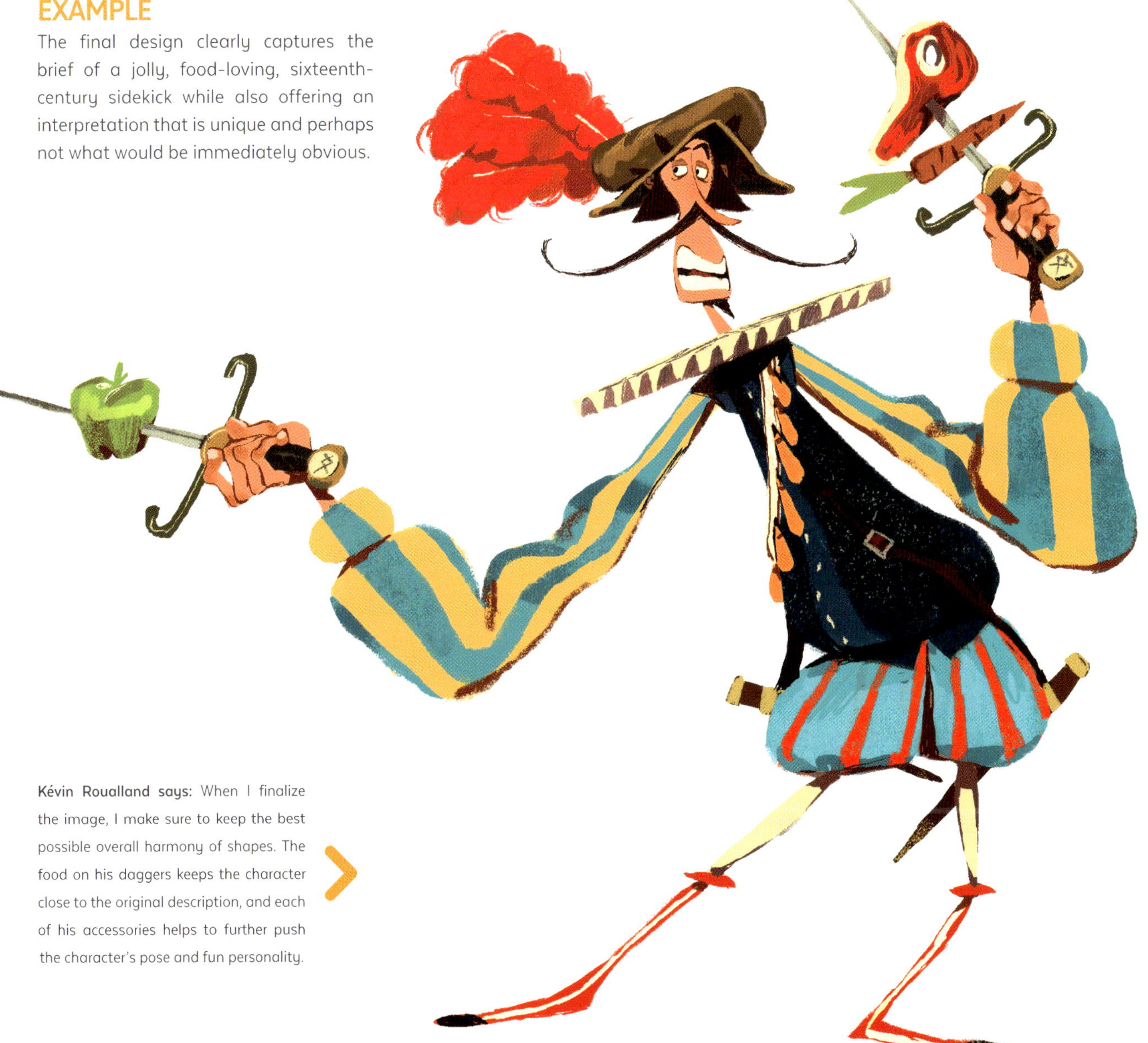

CHARACTER PROJECTS

Now that you have covered the basics needed to start creating entire characters, let's move on to in-depth character development projects. In the following chapters, six talented artists will show you how to create a range of fun, exciting character designs. Each stage of the process is broken into bite-sized chunks so you can clearly follow along with every new development, from research and early sketches to choosing a color palette and pose. Though each project will follow the same overall arc that you covered in the Stylization Process chapter, each artist brings their own unique expertise and visual style to the process, offering insight that will help you to discover your own style and ways to create characters.

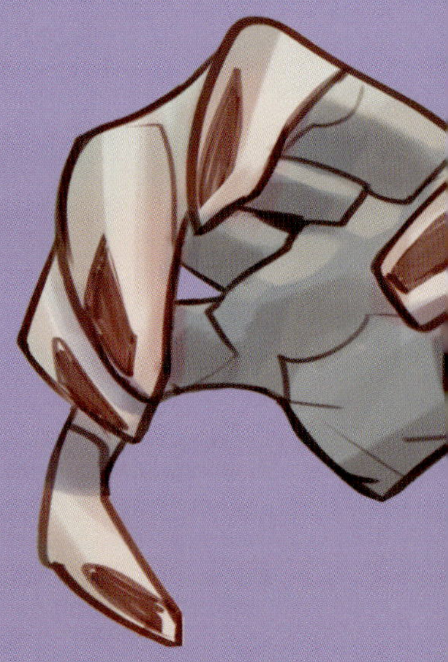

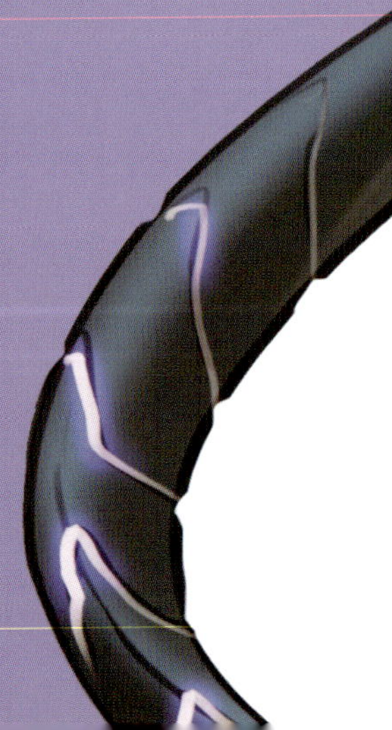

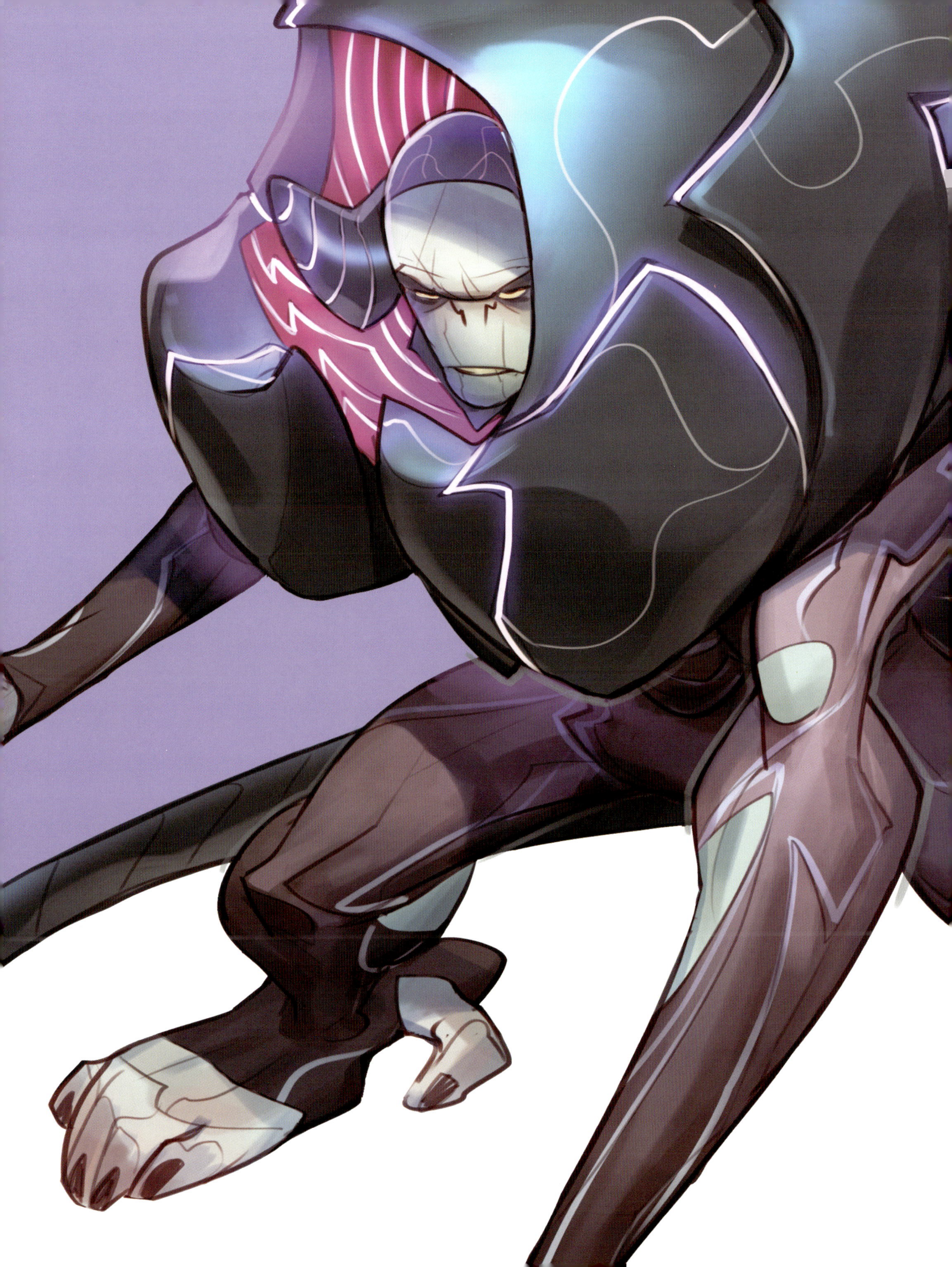

ALIEN EXPLORER

BY KENNETH ANDERSON

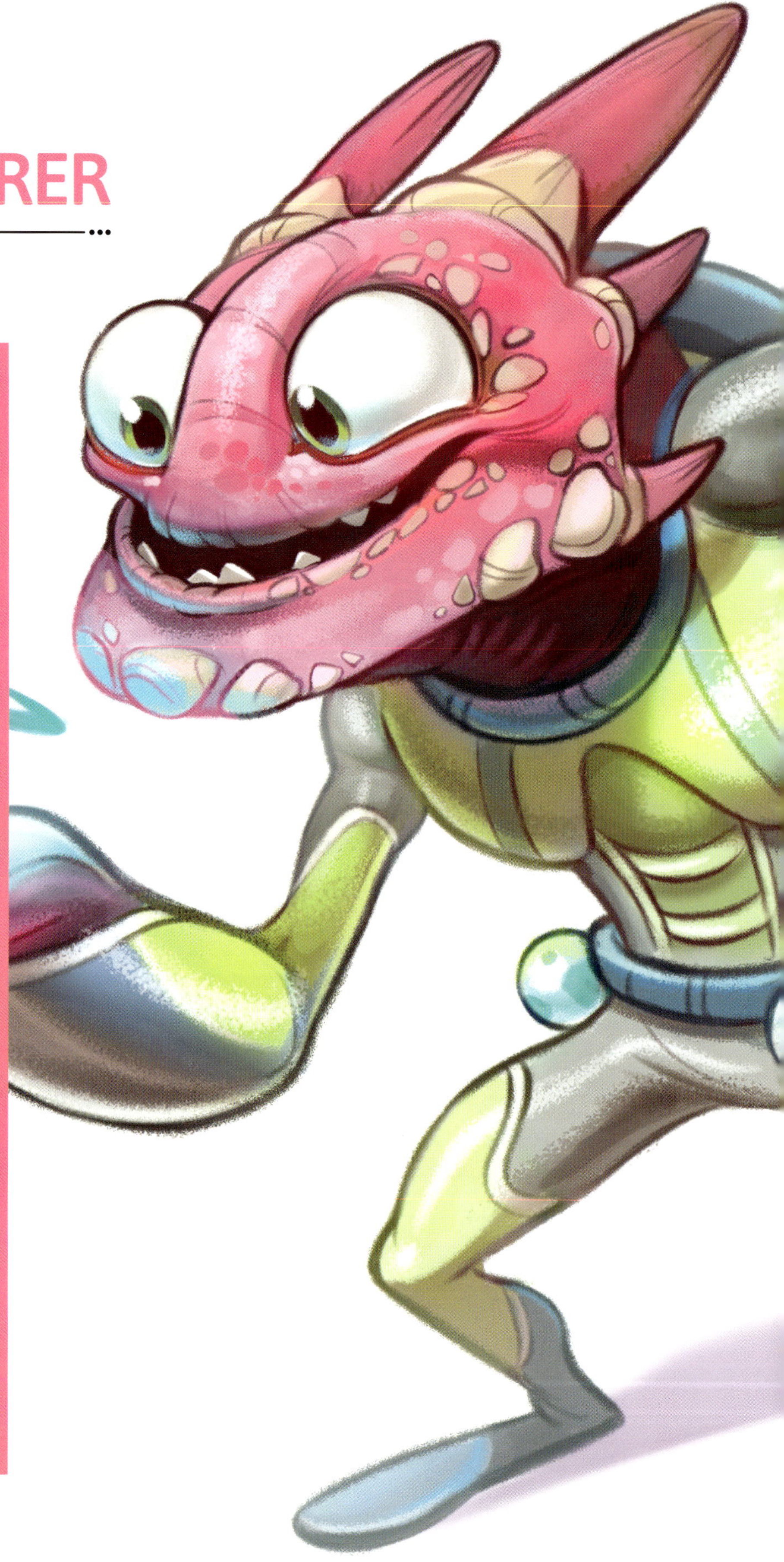

In this chapter, illustrator Kenneth Anderson creates a friendly alien explorer with a futuristic suit and gadgets.

VARIATIONS

- YOUNG ALIEN
- DISGUISED VISITOR
- QUADRUPED ALIEN

FOCUS

Kenneth's style uses bold shapes and expressive facial features to create fun, relatable characters. This approach would work well for creating characters for comics, animation, and video games.

Make sure you pay attention to using clear shapes and bold gestures, and do plenty of research into real-world references to create designs that are memorable and full of personality.

THE IDEA

My character theme for this project is an alien explorer. I want to avoid a cliché alien design and bring something visually unique to this idea, which is where the reference I use will help. The character is going to be bipedal, with some sci-fi flair, and maybe draw some inspiration from reptiles or amphibians to distance the design from looking too human.

With this in mind, I think through possible research ideas. I want to look at frogs, lizards, and even unusual fish for inspiration. I also need to decide on the tone of the design: humorous or serious? The character is friendly, so I am leaning towards the design being humorous and fun.

Concept: A friendly alien explorer or adventurer

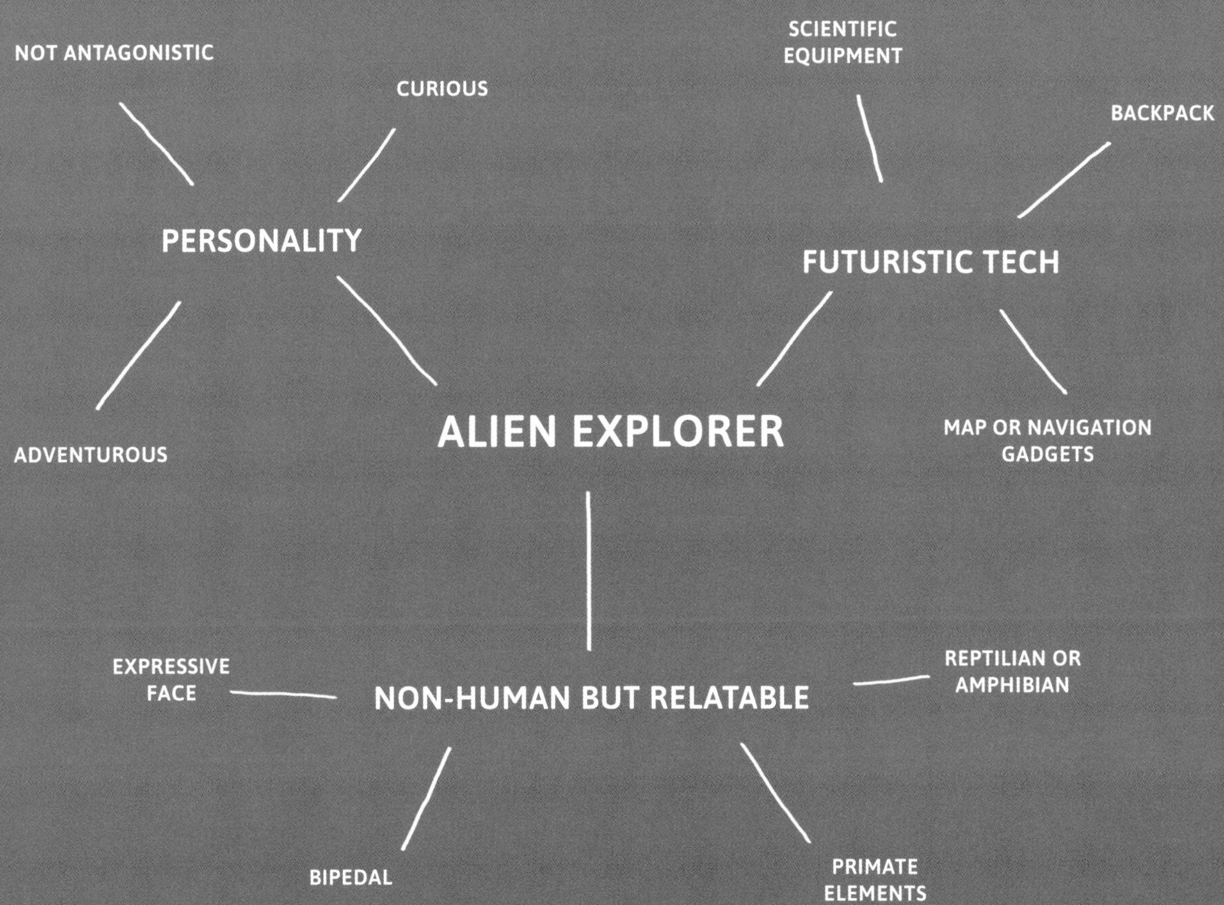

RESEARCH

I initially search the internet for images relating to keywords such as amphibian, reptile, and fish. I keep my pool of reference quite broad at the start to see what new ideas might come into my head. As I start looking into other subjects – insects, crustaceans, deep-sea creatures, and even gibbons – I think about how I might synthesize all these inspirations into a working design.

Then I start to narrow in on particular references and specific species. I know the character will need to emote and be capable of facial expressions, making them appealing to an audience, and not so "alien" that the design isn't relatable. My choices reflect this, while also giving me some range and unusual features I can draw upon.

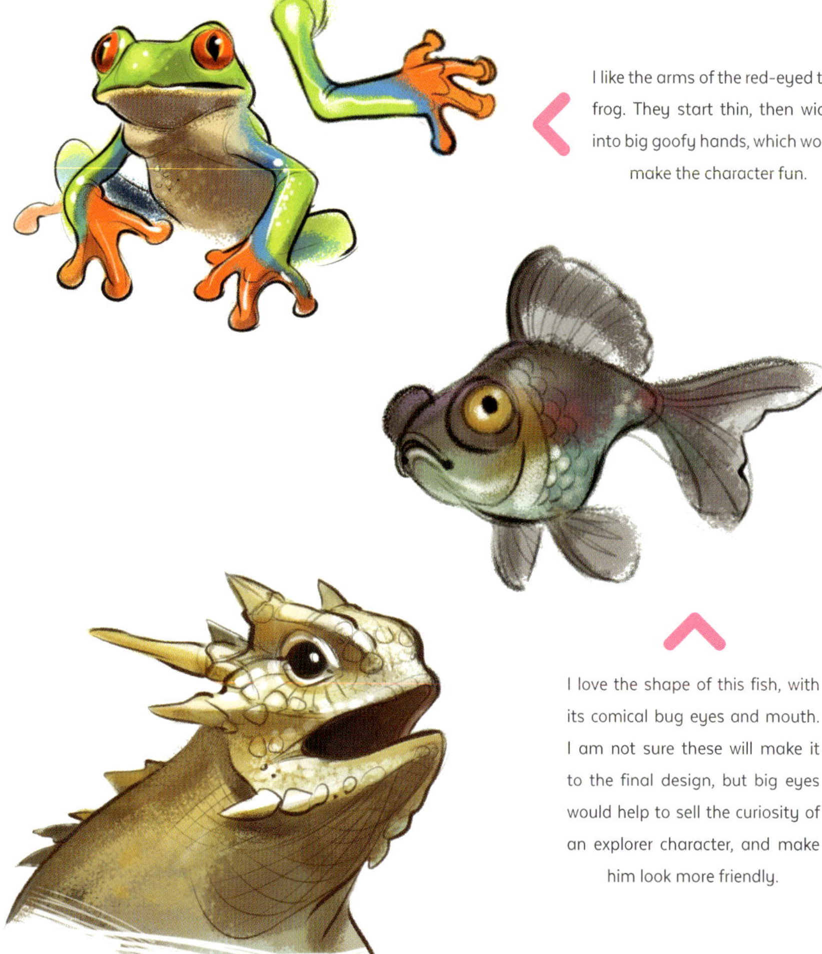

I like the arms of the red-eyed tree frog. They start thin, then widen into big goofy hands, which would make the character fun.

I love the shape of this fish, with its comical bug eyes and mouth. I am not sure these will make it to the final design, but big eyes would help to sell the curiosity of an explorer character, and make him look more friendly.

Horned lizards have really interesting features, with a combination of spikiness and rounded forms. I like how nonthreatening they look, despite their horns, due to their large eyes and smiley mouths.

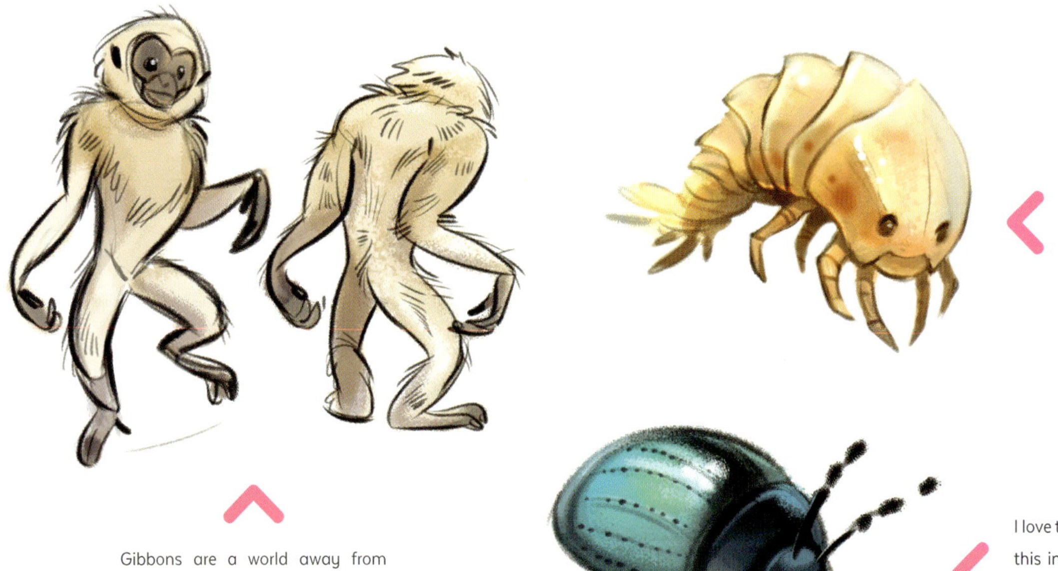

Gibbons are a world away from lizards, but their gangliness might be a good foundation for the character's overall body shape and the way it moves.

Crustaceans might provide an interesting and unusual springboard for costume ideas. I want my costume and accessories to be "alien," and not like things we might immediately recognize as clothing or equipment.

I love the color and transitions in this insect. I might try to bring some of this into the character's costume or skin.

THUMBNAILS

I keep my thumbnails loose and varied at this point, creating as many options as I can. I explore different body shapes and focus on creating an interesting design, drawing from my earlier reference sketches. I think about the head and the overall silhouette, and also the costume – what does my character wear? Do they need a suit that keeps them alive on other planets? Do they need a weapon or other equipment?

Some thumbnails have a bulbous, humanoid head shape, but I lean away from them in favor of the more endearing reptilian shapes. I decide to keep the tone playful, with a bit of an edge of toughness; the small lizard-like spikes will help to add that sharper element. The character is an explorer, so I see them as hardy but not a threat. I want them to be curious, perhaps a scientist or anthropologist studying new worlds – and possibly us! The far middle-left thumbnail, holding a ray gun, strikes a good balance between all these aspects.

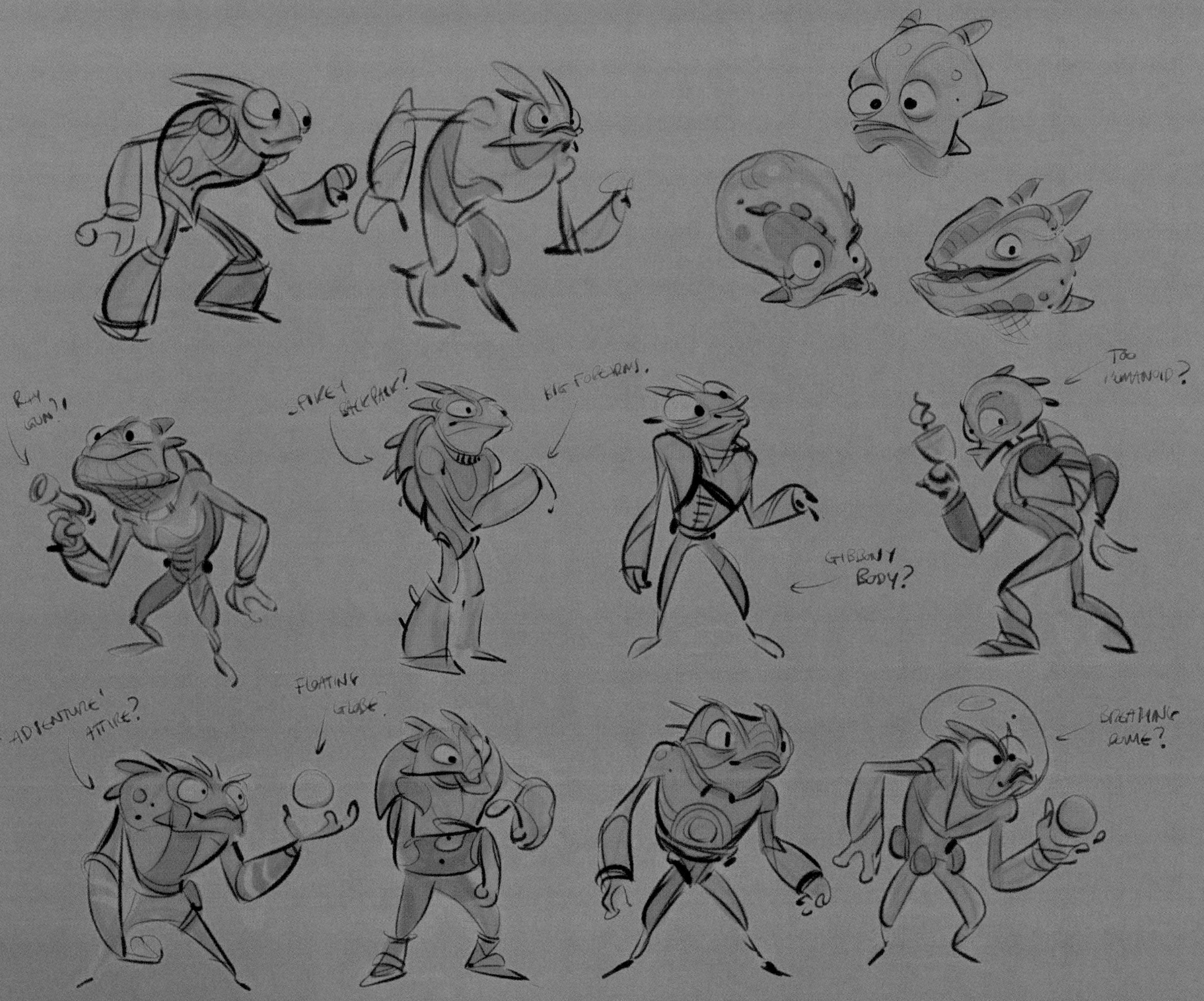

BASIC SHAPES

To reflect the playful but edgy tone I am going for, I lean towards rounded and amphibian shapes, with some contrasting sharpness in the points, just to add a bit of ambiguity as to how dangerous (or not) this character might be.

I develop round-versus-straight shape language with flowing forms. I want one shape to dominate and the other to be its contrast. Too much of one or the other will be boring to look at; too much variety and the design will lose unity. How all the shapes tie together is key – the silhouette helps me to keep that on track.

I experiment and combine elements from a few thumbnails to find a design with a strong silhouette and interesting features. Giving him three rounded digits on each hand is a frog-like touch that adds to his benign non-human appeal. At this stage I also explore how pronounced I want to make the spines on his head.

I work out the straight-versus-curved shape language, to flesh the character out from the basic shapes. I also think about the rhythm of the design, and how the shapes flow together.

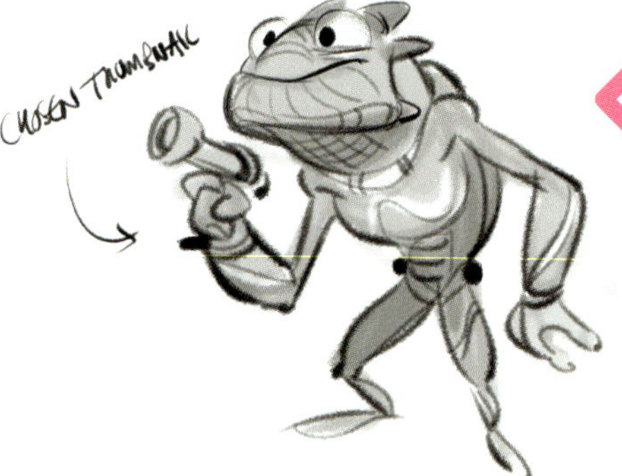

My chosen thumbnail has a clear dominant triangle shape language, with rectangles as secondary shapes. I think this makes the character look quite dynamic.

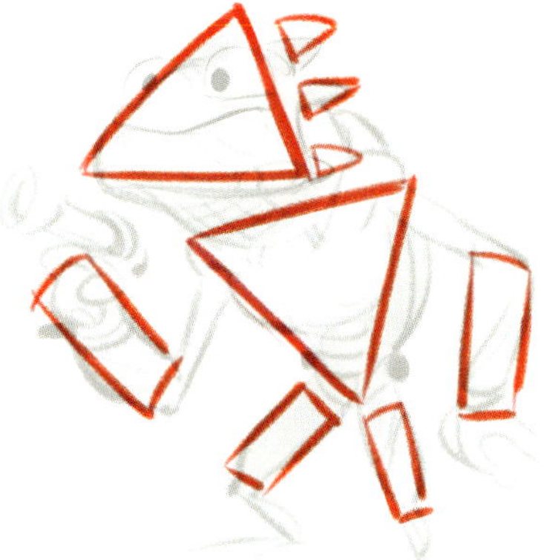

By rounding out the forms and smoothing out hard points, I keep the design "friendly" while the underlying triangle gives a sense of dynamism and possible danger that fits an alien species.

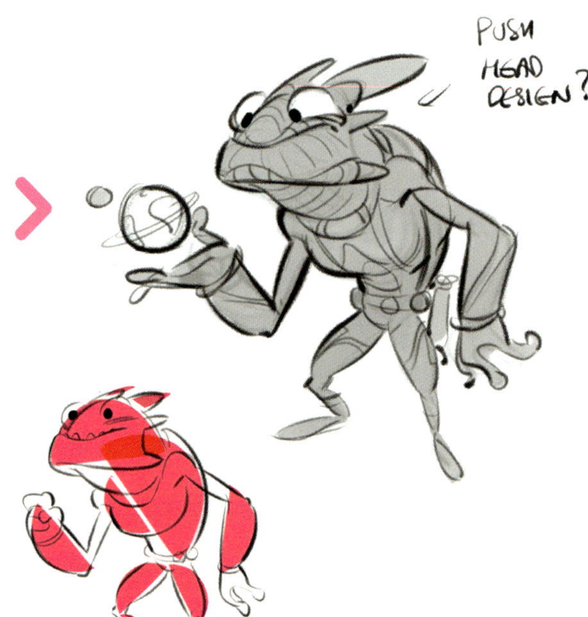

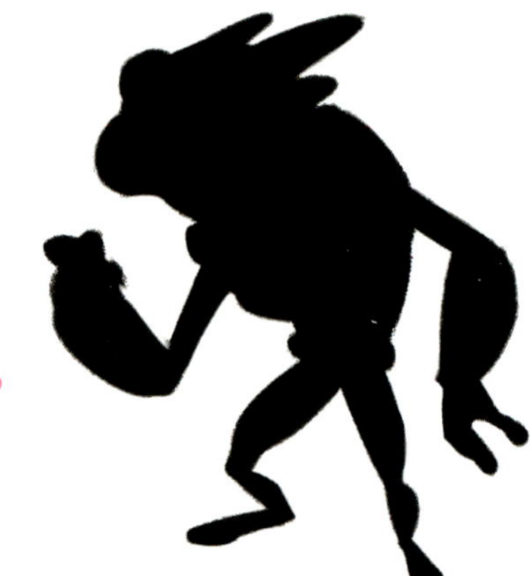

I think my silhouette is working well. It's obviously not human, and suggests a suited creature of some kind, with some ambiguity in the shapes, which I like.

DETAILS

Now I draw inspiration from my research to influence the character's costume and anatomy. I want frog-like hands and a spiked lizard-like head, combined with an almost crustacean shell. I see this shell as a kind of backpack or breathing apparatus.

In my thumbnails, I played around with the idea of a helmet so the character can breathe on other worlds – but I remembered that frogs can breathe partly through their skin! I decide this is how the character breathes: the backpack filters out hostile air, while he absorbs the good gases though his skin. All these features will help to convey an intrepid character who is well suited to life in an alien habitat, and is able to thrive in places that a human could not.

I play with scale texturing to sell his alien nature and add visual interest to his design. Do I keep it just on his skin, or add it on his costume too?

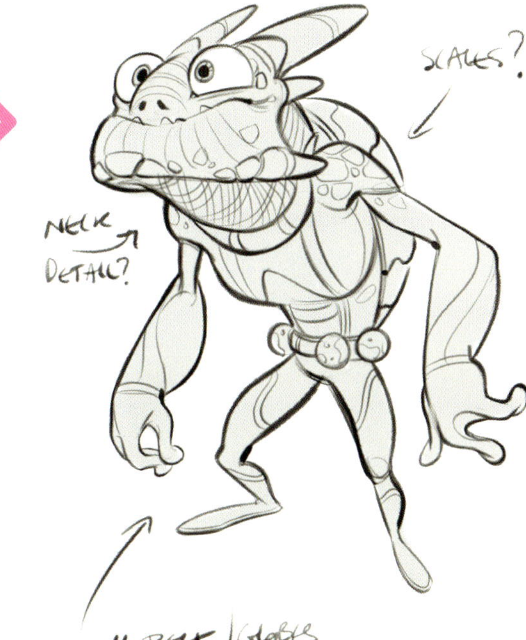

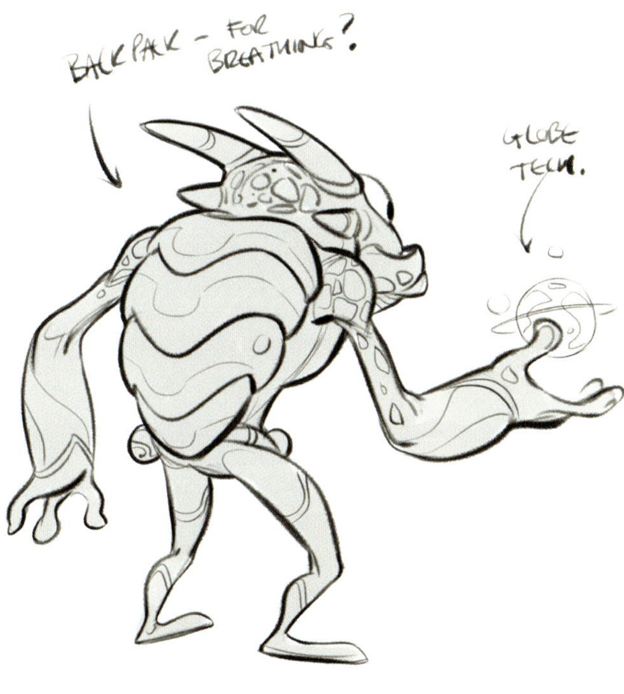

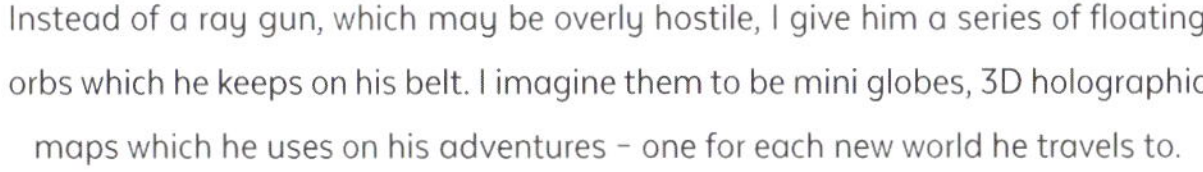

Instead of a ray gun, which may be overly hostile, I give him a series of floating orbs which he keeps on his belt. I imagine them to be mini globes, 3D holographic maps which he uses on his adventures – one for each new world he travels to.

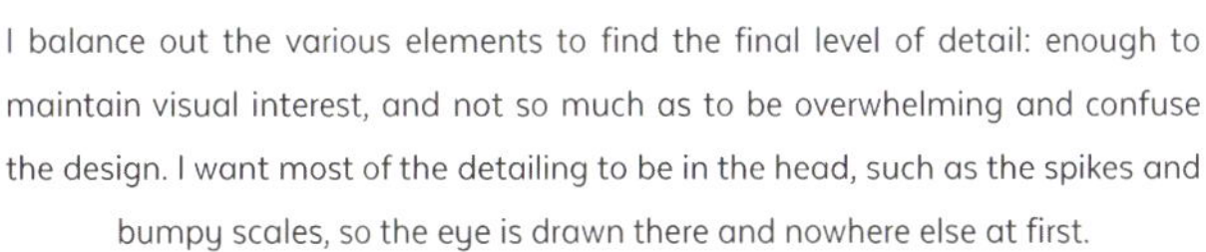

I balance out the various elements to find the final level of detail: enough to maintain visual interest, and not so much as to be overwhelming and confuse the design. I want most of the detailing to be in the head, such as the spikes and bumpy scales, so the eye is drawn there and nowhere else at first.

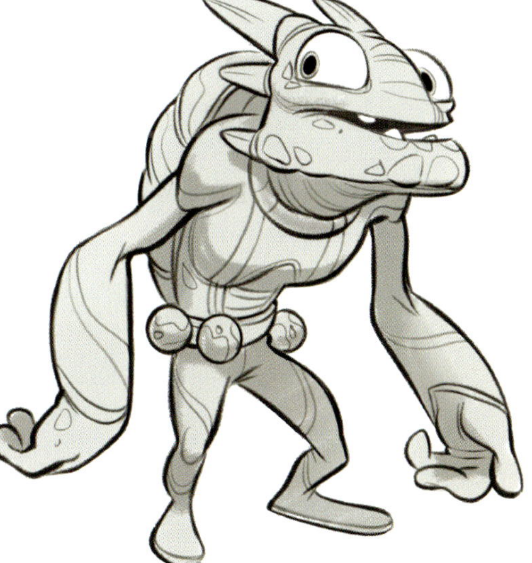

FACIAL EXPRESSIONS

Any facial expressions need to convey the character's personality – intelligent, curious, essentially friendly – and be emotive enough to appeal to an audience. Even though I want the character to be an amicable creature, I explore angry expressions too to test the range in the design. It is important to find out a design's limitations.

One of the most important expressions, especially if I want the character to be relatable, is a smile. If he couldn't pull off a believable smile, I would have needed to start over! The wide open grin and keen, focused eyes in this expression really help to capture his eager, optimistic personality.

I use squash and stretch principles to bend the character's jaw in ways that are cartoony, yet believable, to see how far I can exaggerate his mouth shape. Here he's scared or startled by something, but I will more likely use a cheerful expression for the final image.

Even a happy character gets angry sometimes. The character has big lidless eyes, so I need to find a solution for showing this emotion. I "cheat" a bit by giving him lowered brows to achieve a frown, which works, though I would rather show him smiling in the final design.

POSING

I want my character to show the energy and enthusiasm of an explorer. It's a role that can't be passive, but always engaged in action and curiosity. I sketch out a range of options, all showing the character's inquisitiveness. It is not just the action that is important – *how* a particular character executes an action is what gives them personality.

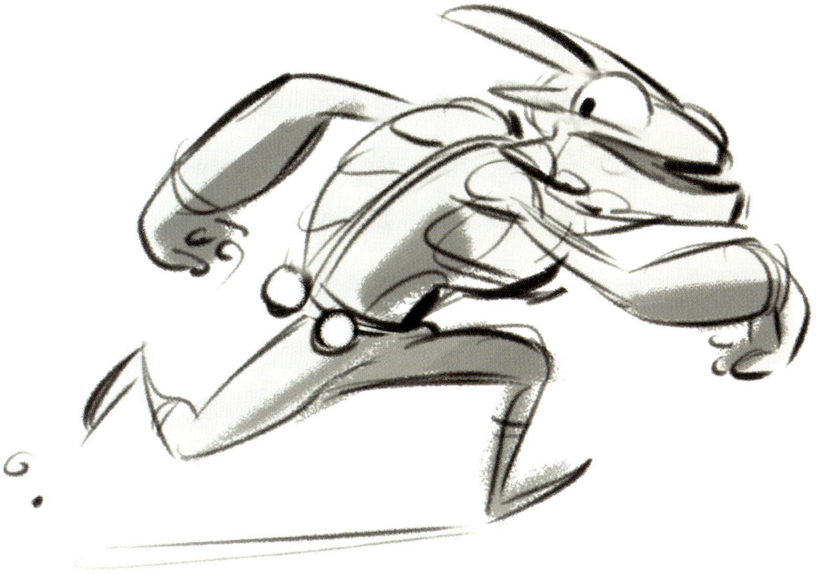

What is my character running from? Did his curiosity get the better of him? I want his arms to partially mimic those of a gibbon, adding a comical agility to this pose.

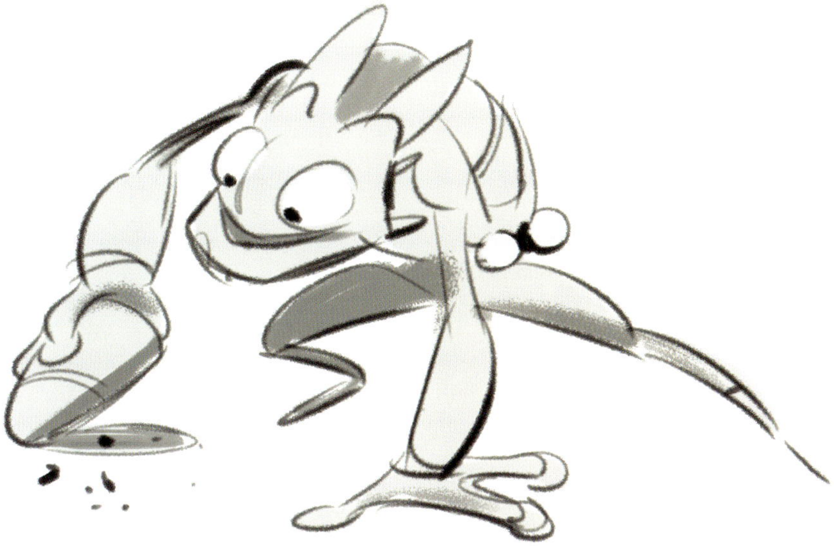

As a child I remember being fascinated by lifting up rocks and seeing what was under them. I imagine my character doing the same as he explores other worlds. This pose is a strong one for showing his inquisitive nature, as well as showing off the agile, frog-like nature of his limbs.

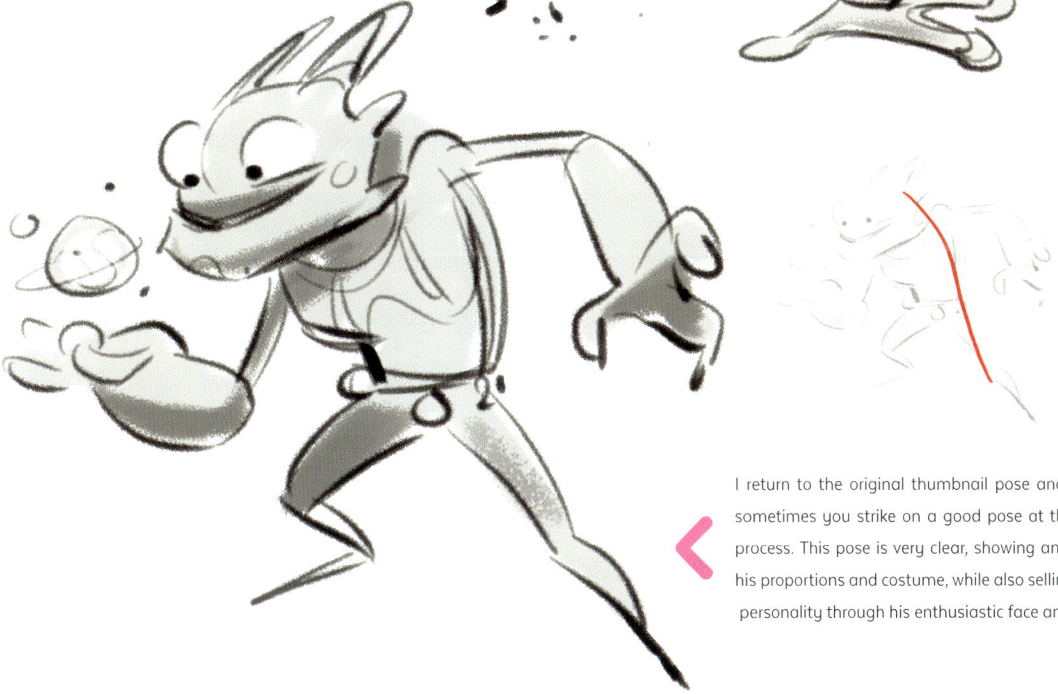

I return to the original thumbnail pose and create a variation – sometimes you strike on a good pose at the early stages in the process. This pose is very clear, showing an unobstructed view of his proportions and costume, while also selling his cheerful, curious personality through his enthusiastic face and eagerly raised arm.

VALUES & COLOR

I want a strong value structure in the design to lead the viewer towards the focal point; in a character design, this is usually the face. I also want the colors and tonal patterns to suggest "alien" or at the very least "non-human." The amphibian references will be useful here.

With values roughly decided, I explore some color options, some safe, some a bit different. I want to explore a range of options and not just settle for the first color that comes into my head!

When adding the values, I realize that the two stripes on his chest almost read as "backpack straps," which I think is a fun nod to human explorers. I decide to keep this detail as it enhances the character.

I want the head to contrast with the character's body, as the viewer's eye needs to be drawn there. I choose my tonal range and distribution with that in mind: most of the contrast is around the head, with points of tone (the scales) breaking up the forms and giving the eye clear points to wander over.

I start with a split-complementary color palette of pink, aqua, and orange. This harmonizes visually while also containing subtle variety, but the blue color could be too safe for the character - too expected for an amphibian- and reptile-inspired alien.

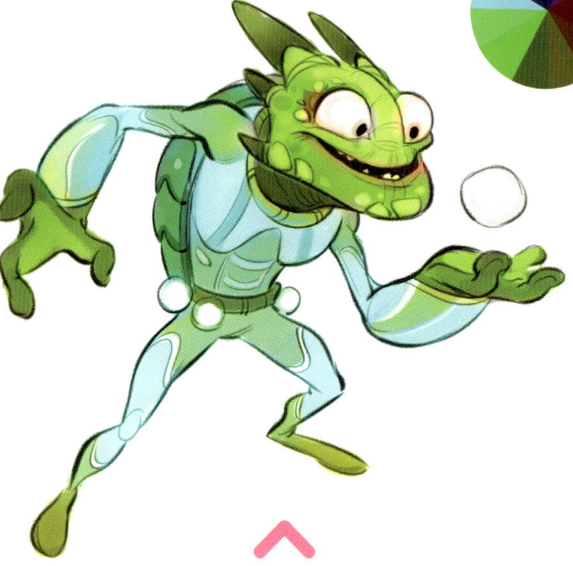

A harmonious color scheme is difficult to get wrong but it can look bland. I do want the character to be harmonious and non-threatening, but this blue and green palette does not emphasize his alien nature or suggest his adventurous streak.

I eventually choose a triadic color scheme, using pink, green, and blue hues. This adds variety and visual tension by using colors that harmonize but are dissimilar enough to be really striking, making the design dynamic. I just need to be wary of balancing these colors and their saturation, so their brightness doesn't offend the eye!

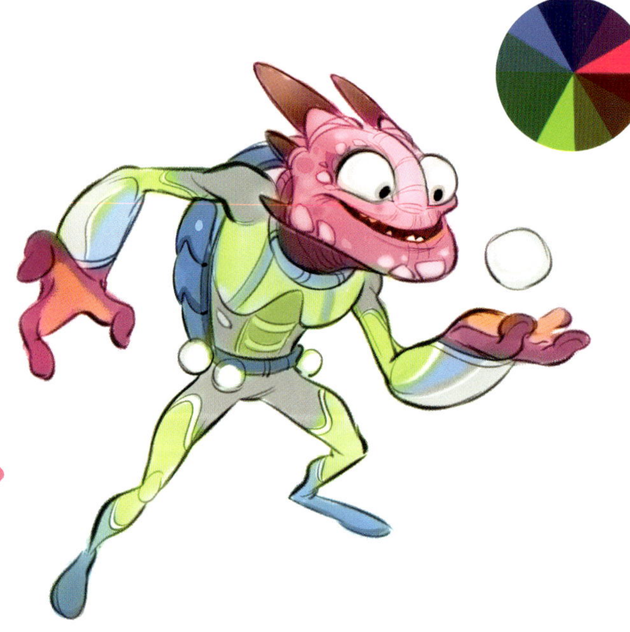

FINAL DESIGN

This final design fulfills my aim of creating an alien explorer. The character definitely comes across as alien, as his outlandish colors and combination of physical features do not resemble any existing Earth creature. Different elements of the design communicate his role as an explorer. By starting with a varied pool of reference, but keeping an overall theme in mind, coming up with something I might not have drawn straight from my imagination was much easier. The different combined elements of amphibians, crustaceans, and lizards were not so different that they couldn't synthesize well. The slight sheen on his skin is reminiscent of amphibian creatures while the two-tone color transitions hark back to the beetle I looked at in the research stage. The light-hearted visual style, punchy colors, and excitable pose all capture this character's curious and enthusiastic personality, while the details of his protective suit and holographic gadgets help to convey his adventurous role in a fun, colorful sci-fi setting.

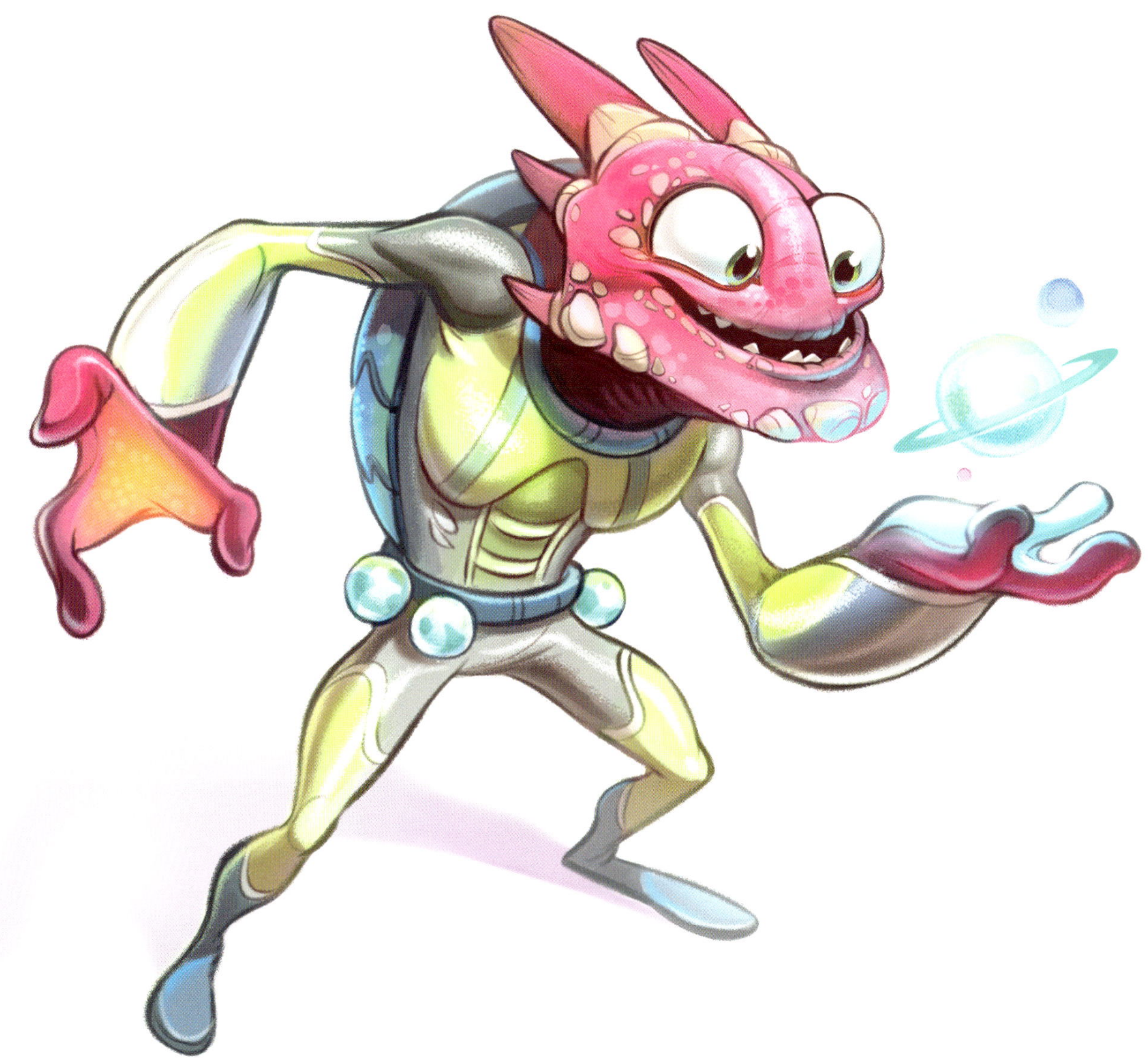

Final artwork © Kenneth Anderson

VARIATION 1:
YOUNG ALIEN

IDEAS & RESEARCH

For this version, I will be re-designing the character as a young alien. To "age down" the character, I return to some familiar reference points: frogs, lizards, and fish. This time I look for key elements that I could bring to the character to make him appear younger. I want to make him more vulnerable-looking, so I play with the idea of transparency in his skin; maybe his organs show through his body slightly. My idea is that as he ages, he hardens and develops tough scales and spikes. I don't want to completely lose sight of this endpoint, so I need to hint at it in this stage of the character's development.

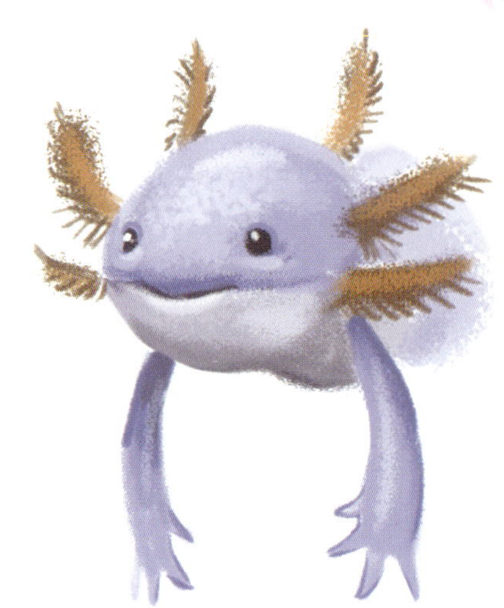

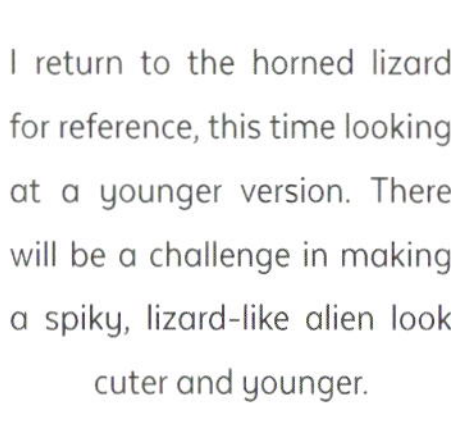

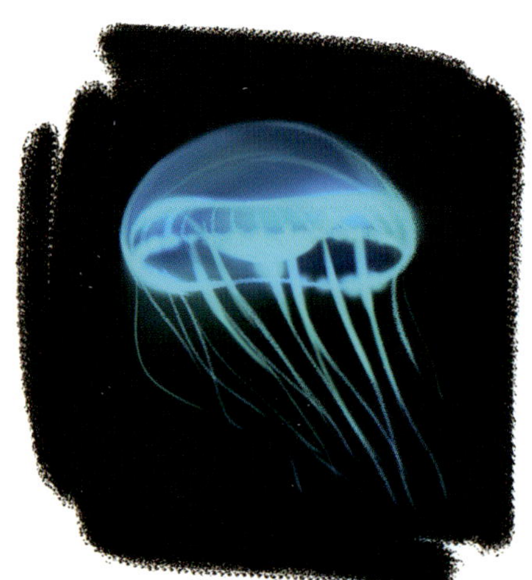

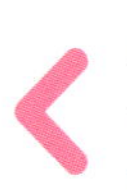

The axolotl has a strong mix of unusual traits: the external "gills" on its head could be primitive spikes in development, its skin is slightly translucent, and overall it is a cute and appealing animal.

Glass frogs are the perfect reference for transparent bodies. I want the character's arms to have a similar radiance and refraction of light, and I'd like to play around with what can be seen inside.

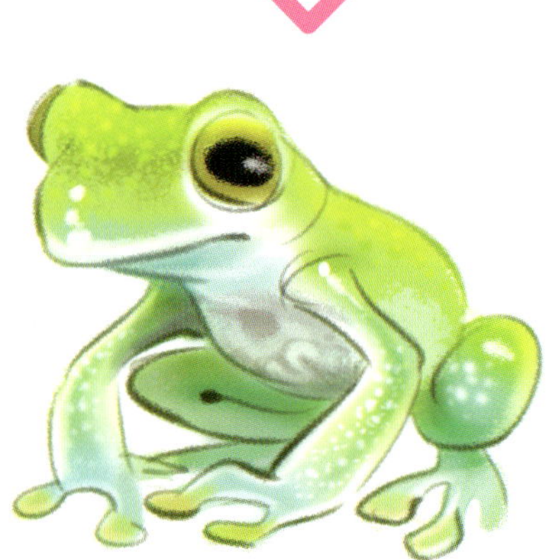

The pink colors of the axolotl are already almost perfect for my character, but I am unsure at this point whether I want to match my original design's colors, or do something different such as this more blue example.

Glowing jellyfish are fascinating; I am keen to see if I can make this idea work with the squashy, radiant appearance of this younger character, but I'm not yet certain how to incorporate these features.

Glass frogs also look shiny and permanently wet. This might be an interesting contrast with the skin of the adult version, emphasizing the vulnerability of the younger design.

I return to the horned lizard for reference, this time looking at a younger version. There will be a challenge in making a spiky, lizard-like alien look cuter and younger.

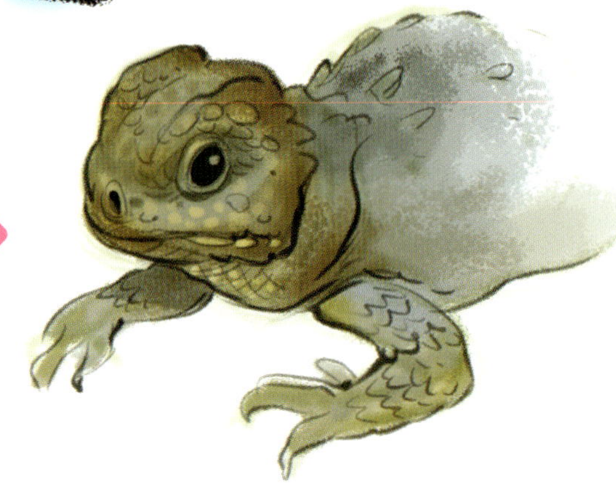

CHANGES

I decide to keep the overall shapes of the new character very similar to the original, while playing with proportions to emphasize a change in age and development. A bigger head, bigger eyes, and softer skin will all help to sell this. I also want to push the original gibbon influence, as it would fit the idea of the young version of the character being a bit more awkward.

Children and baby animals generally have larger head-to-body ratios than adults. I will adjust these proportions to convey the younger age of this version of the character.

I intend to experiment with translucency when rendering the final design, suggesting that the character's body is vulnerable and less developed.

The spikes on the character's head should be less sharp, in keeping with the much rounder shapes of this version in general. The design should not feel spiky and threatening at all.

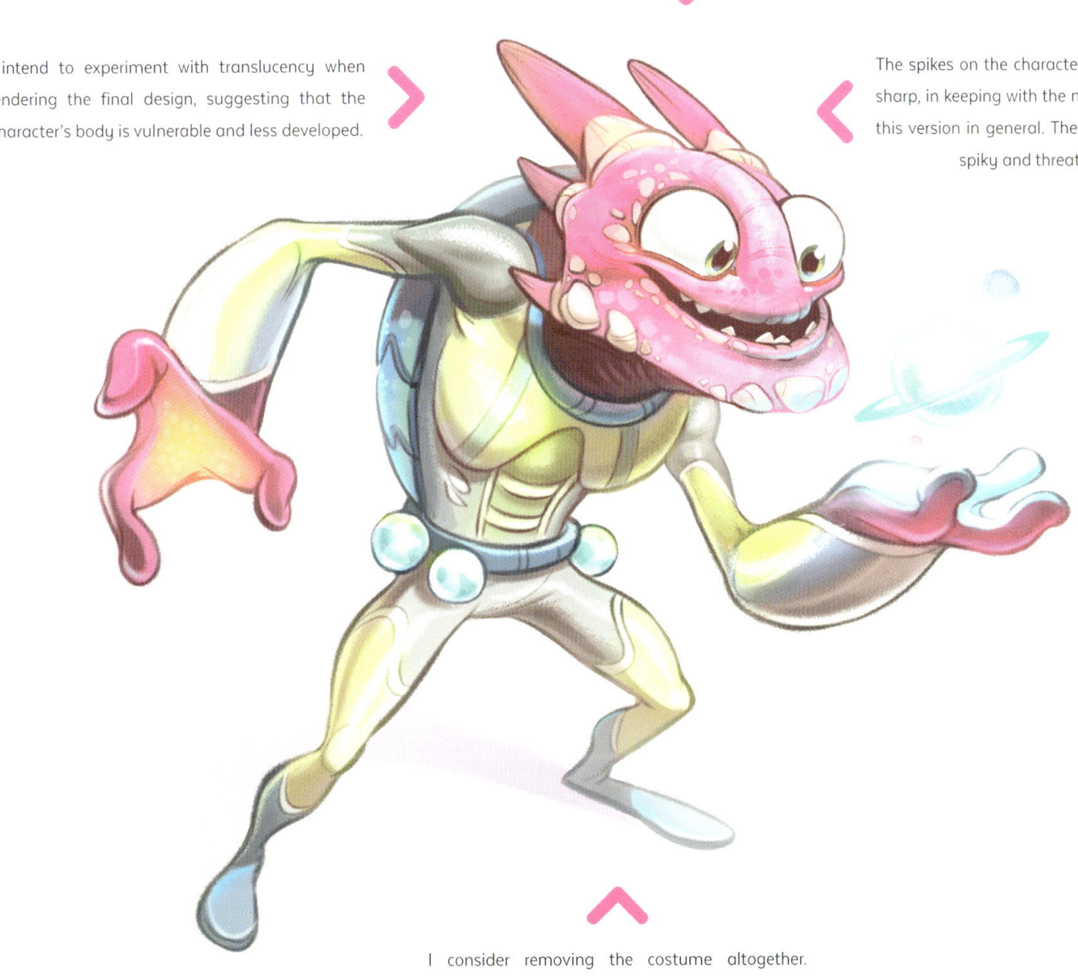

I consider removing the costume altogether. Perhaps the suit that the main character wears is only worn when visiting other worlds, and is unnecessary at this stage in its growth?

THUMBNAILS

Drawing influence from the new reference material, I sketch a range of thumbnails that are somewhat stunted, more rounded, and more childlike versions of the main character. Some of the thumbnails stray a bit too much from the defined body shape; I need to find a balance between looking different and at the same time being recognizably the same character. The top-left and bottom-middle thumbnails are definitely on the right track.

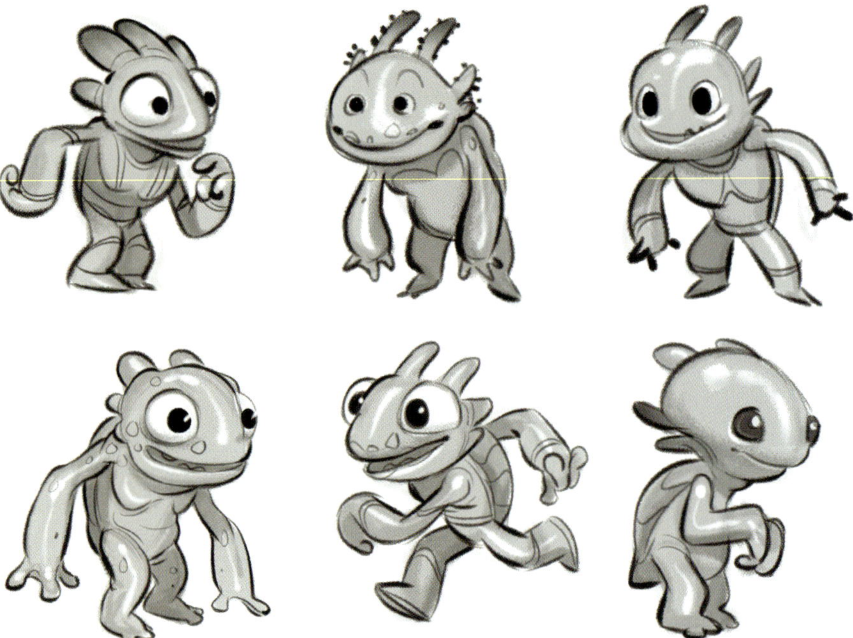

BASIC SHAPES

I combine elements of the top-left and bottom-middle thumbnails in order to create a character that looks less physically developed while still having some distinct features of the original design, such as the horns, somewhat reptilian head shape, and large eyes. The overall forms lean more towards the amphibian inspirations than the tougher, scaly creatures that I researched for the adult version. These will help to give the baby alien a soft, endearing look.

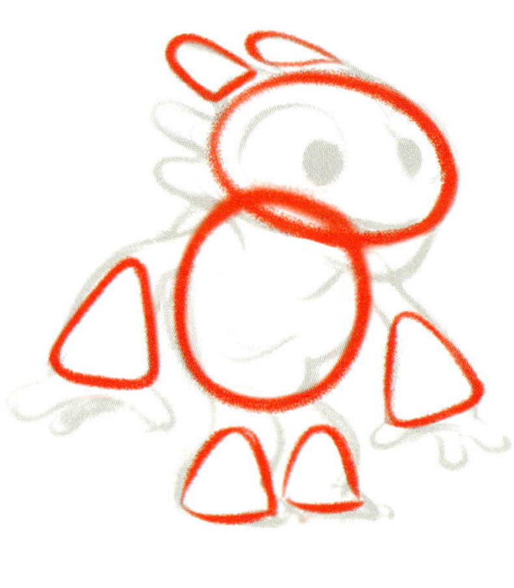

The new character has very similar basic shapes to the original one, but they are now more rounded, stunted, and less harsh. Rounded shapes like ovals are definitely the new dominant theme, helping to sell the idea of a younger, softer character.

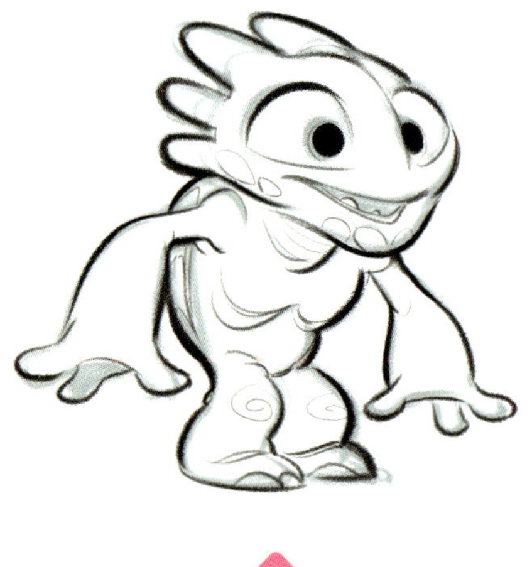

I develop the forms further, making sure that the shapes work well together and read as childlike. The head is large in relation to the body, conveying the character's young age.

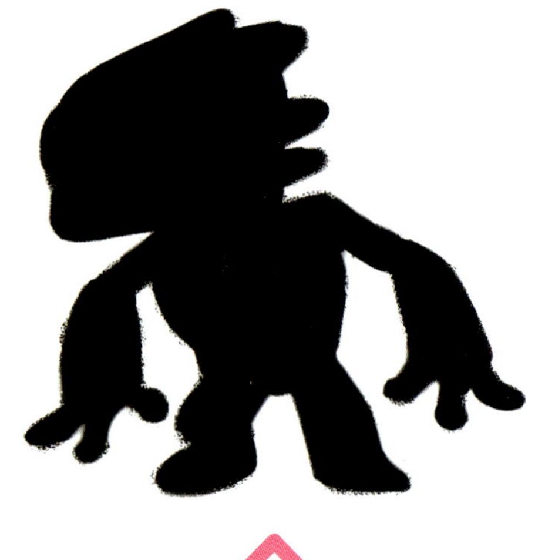

In silhouette, the character clearly reads as round and soft, with only the back of his head hinting at his future spiky nature. Features such as his frog-like limbs and three-fingered hands are distinctly legible and relate back to the original design.

DETAILS

With fewer spikes and no costume, I need to think of other details to bring life to this character. Vulnerability is the idea I keep coming back to; I need the details to reflect that, while also hinting at how his skin might evolve with time by adding some faint bumps and scale patterns to his face, shoulders, and arms.

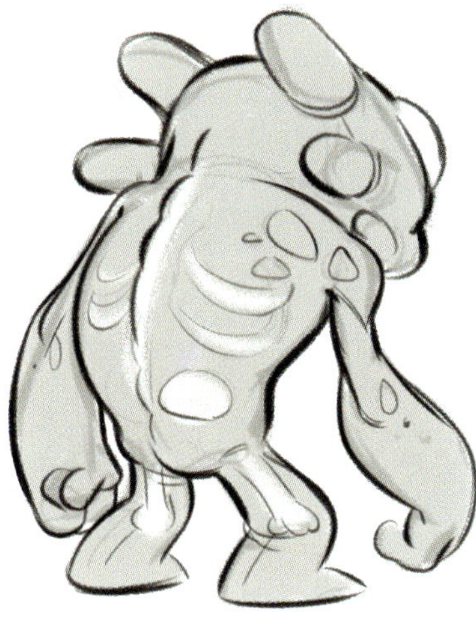

Here I play with seeing the bones in the legs, and the organs in his belly, much like the glass frogs from my earlier research.

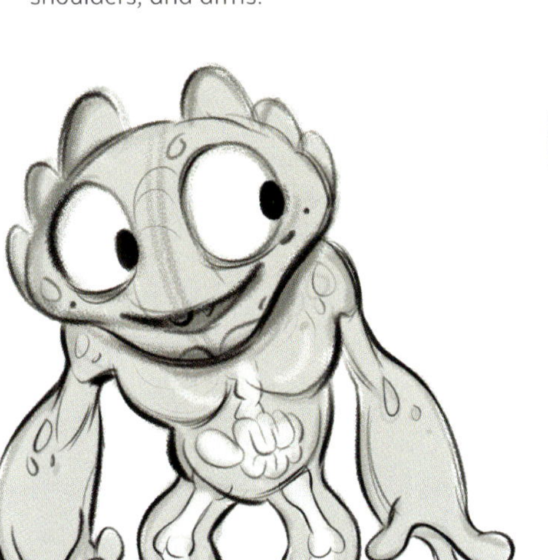

I need to be careful that I don't go overboard with the transparency – I want it to be clear, but subtle enough that it's not the main feature of the design.

EXPRESSIONS & POSING

I play around with poses that are childlike while also having similar traits to the adult character. I want him to still be curious, hinting at his adventurous nature, and maybe to show the viewer where his love for exploration began.

I return to the rock-lifting idea, as I want to compare how he does it as a child with how he does it as an adult. Coupled with a similarly captivated facial expression, it is still a very strong and charming pose for showing his curious nature.

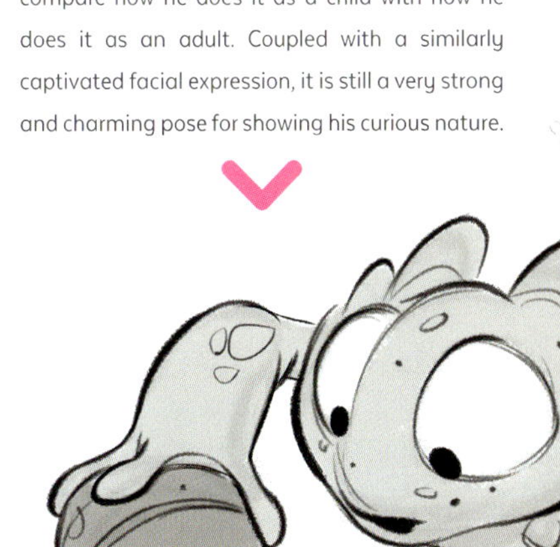

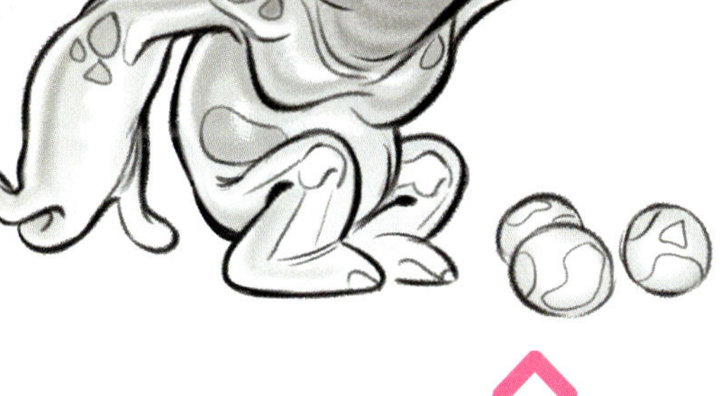

Here the character is discovering the glowing orb maps for the first time, and his interest in exploration is born. The joyful smile and clear interaction of this pose are great for conveying a sense of inquisitive, childlike wonder, so I will use it for the final image.

VALUE & COLOR

As with the adult version, I use values to lead the viewer's eye to the character's face, as I want that area to have the highest point of contrast and the most visual and tonal interest. However, as the character is no longer in costume, the overall tone and color choices must be different to reflect his youthful and translucent skin. I will keep pink as the main skin color, tying this design together with the adult alien, and create new palettes by introducing other colors throughout the character's limbs and visible internal organs.

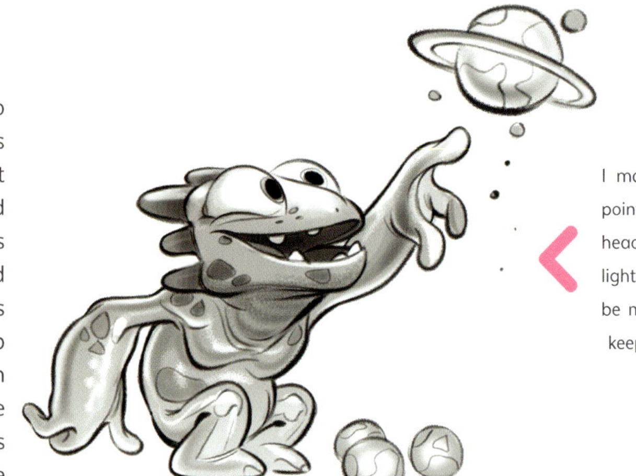

I make sure to keep the highest points of contrast towards the head. Lower in the body, the tones lighten – I imagine his lower body to be more translucent than the top, keeping the character's face clear.

I start experimenting with a split complementary color scheme of aqua, pink, and yellow. This works well to show how the character's see-through body reflects and refracts many different colors, and keeps the original design's vibrant sense of fun. I will use this palette for the final design.

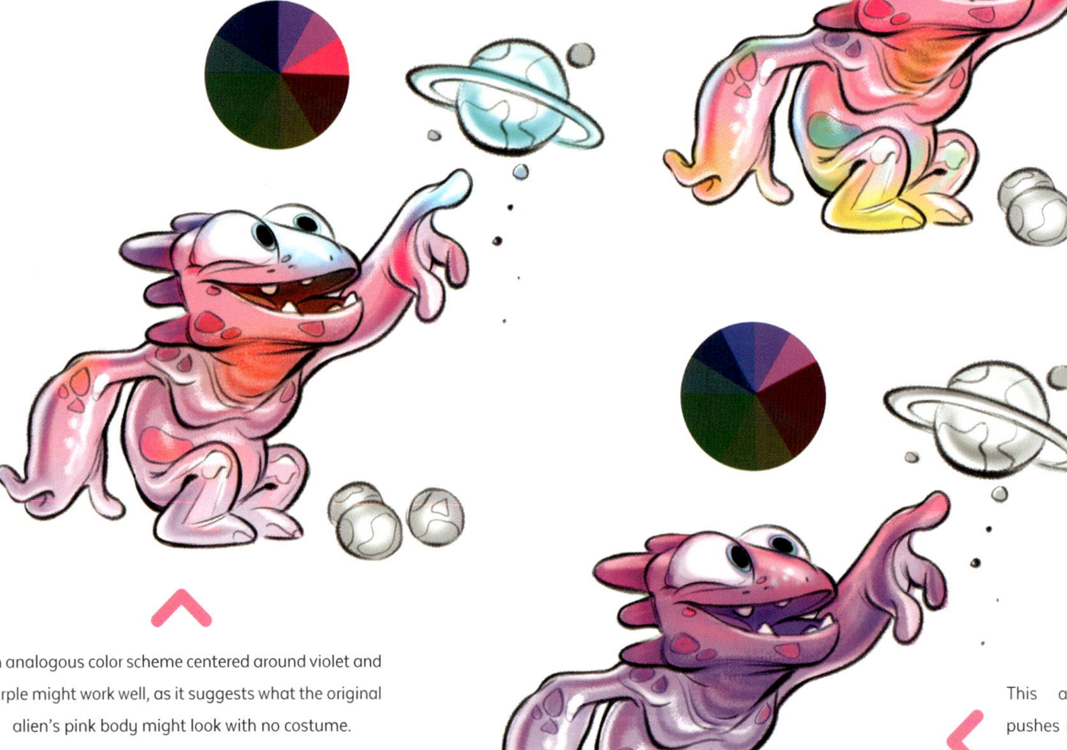

An analogous color scheme centered around violet and purple might work well, as it suggests what the original alien's pink body might look with no costume.

This analogous color scheme pushes more towards purple. I am less keen on this, as it's too different from the adult version.

FINAL DESIGN

This version succeeds in showing a younger, less physically developed version of the original main design. The softer forms, translucent skin, and lack of a costume suggest a child or baby. However, enough common elements remain to tie this in with the original design: we can see the same hands and general body shape, the similar face, and the hints of the spikes that will develop as he ages. The glowing spheres create a narrative between the two versions and maintain the sci-fi aspect of the character.

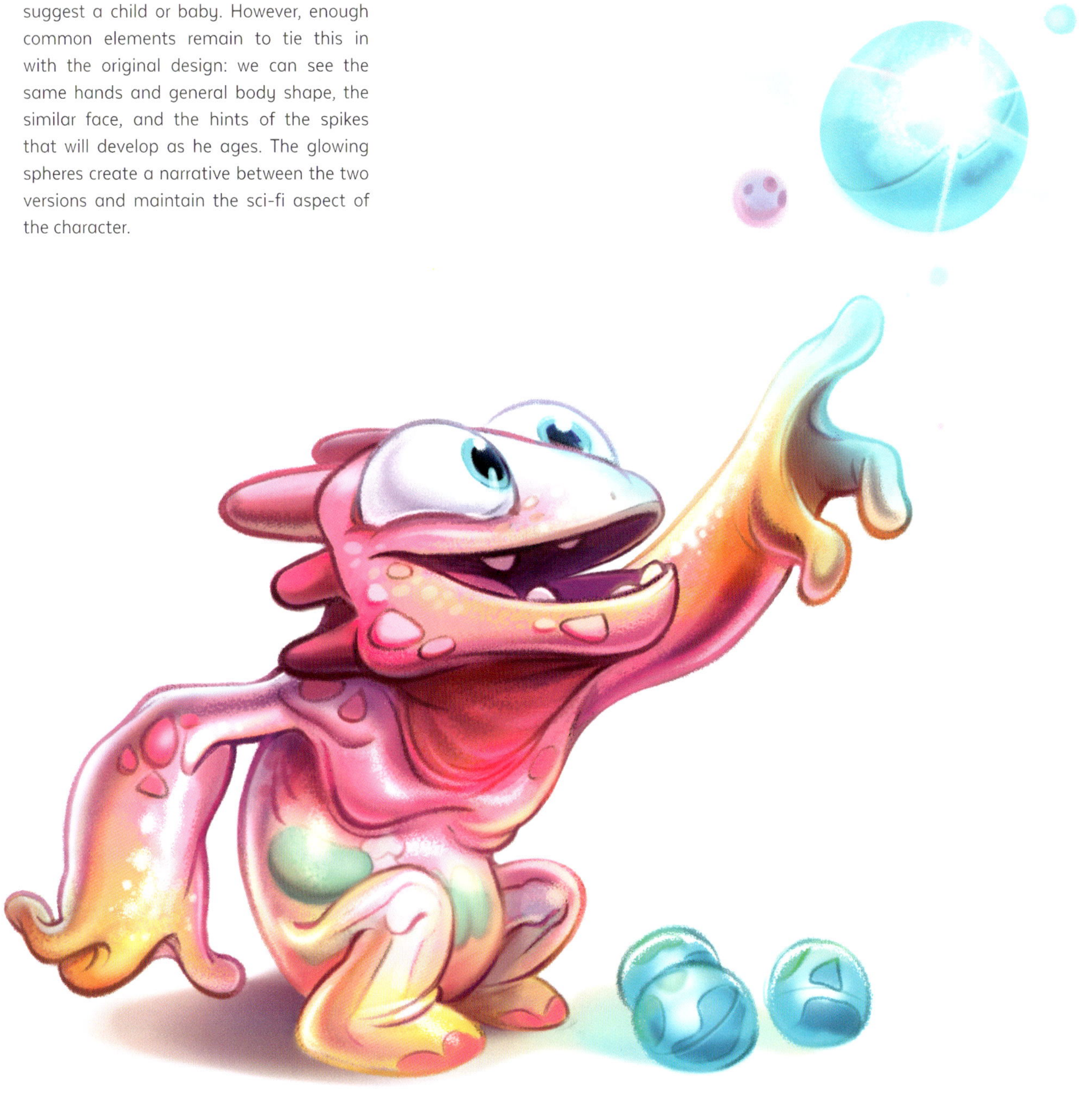

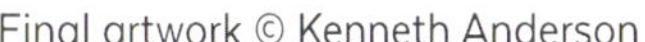

Final artwork © Kenneth Anderson

VARIATION 2:
DISGUISED VISITOR

IDEAS & RESEARCH

For this version of the character, I want to remove the character from a futuristic alien setting and place him on Earth, where he is trying to pass as a human. I need to explore ideas which fit this brief, while finding a unique way of approaching the narrative. I imagine I *am* the character – maybe I would find a garbage bag full of mismatched, unwanted clothes? Maybe I would disguise myself as a dinosaur mascot to hide my face? I consider what kinds of clothes would look ridiculous on the character, as I am now aiming for humor and want the design to read as a comedic rather than overly futuristic one.

I sketch out a random collection of clothes. A large wedding hat would obscure the character's face, as would a scarf, and a classic trench coat. A combination of all three would be on the right track, humor-wise.

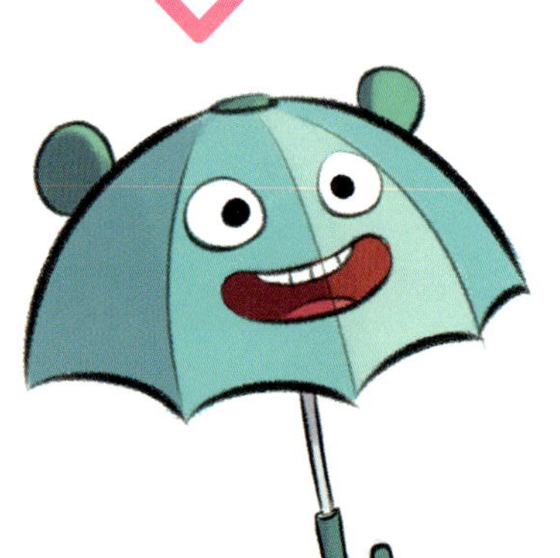

Maybe the character could hold a fun umbrella to hide his face? The printed umbrella face adds a bit of comedy.

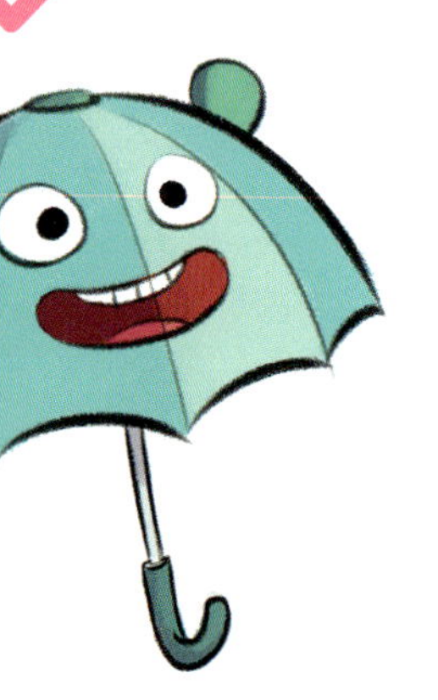

A dinosaur costume would be fun and offer many possible scenarios. Has he ended up at a costume party? Maybe it's a sports mascot, or someone handing out flyers for a dinosaur-themed restaurant? Either way, I like this idea, and it's a more unexpected angle.

The character could be dressed in a typical tourist style, wearing sunglasses and taking photos, though I am not sure this would be the best solution for a character trying to disguise himself.

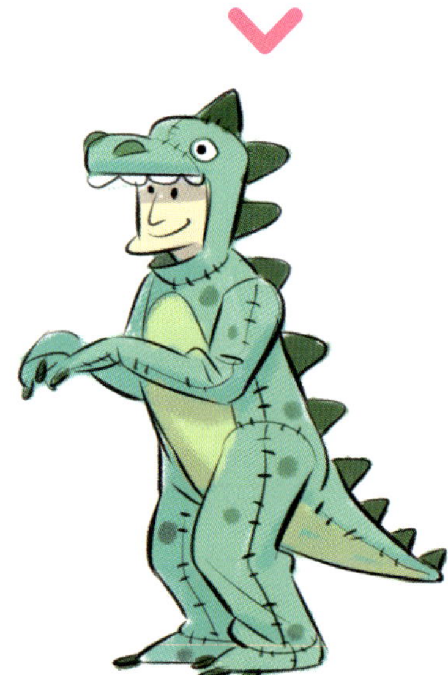

Large glasses would add a comical look, and could be combined with other elements to distract from his obvious non-human nature.

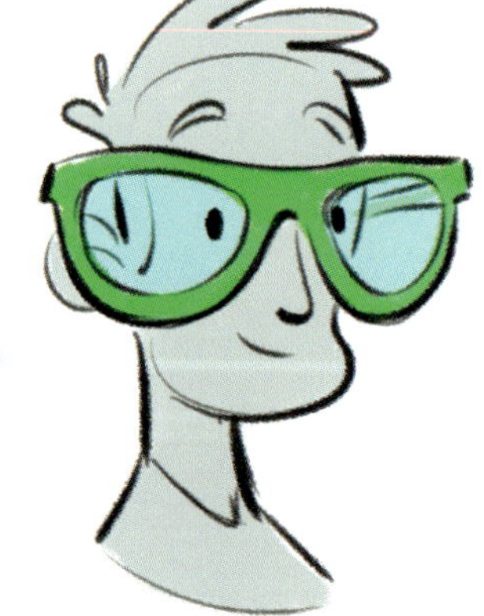

Being Scottish, I thought it might be fun to throw a kilt in there! Looking at the character's anatomy, I think that a kilt, or even a skirt or dress, might be a practical way to hide those amphibian legs.

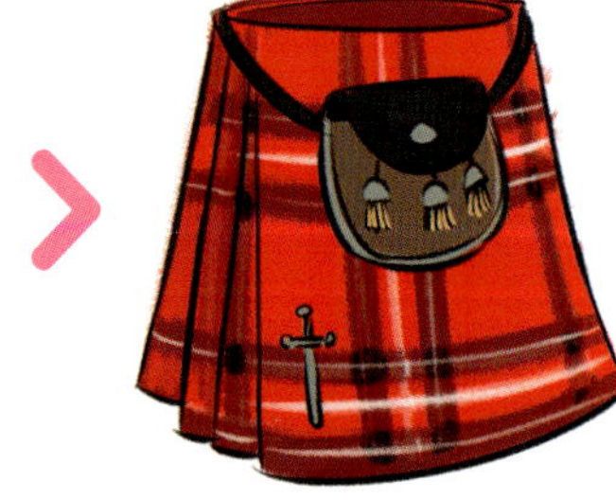

CHANGES

This character modification is all about the costume. I need to think of ways in which the character might disguise his features, in a manner which fits his personality and can be justified in a sort of mini-story scenario. I need to think not only about *why* he might wear something – for example, to hide a particularly obvious part of his alien anatomy – but *how* he acquired it in the first place. The single biggest change will be the loss of his futuristic suit, which will be hidden under his new disguise.

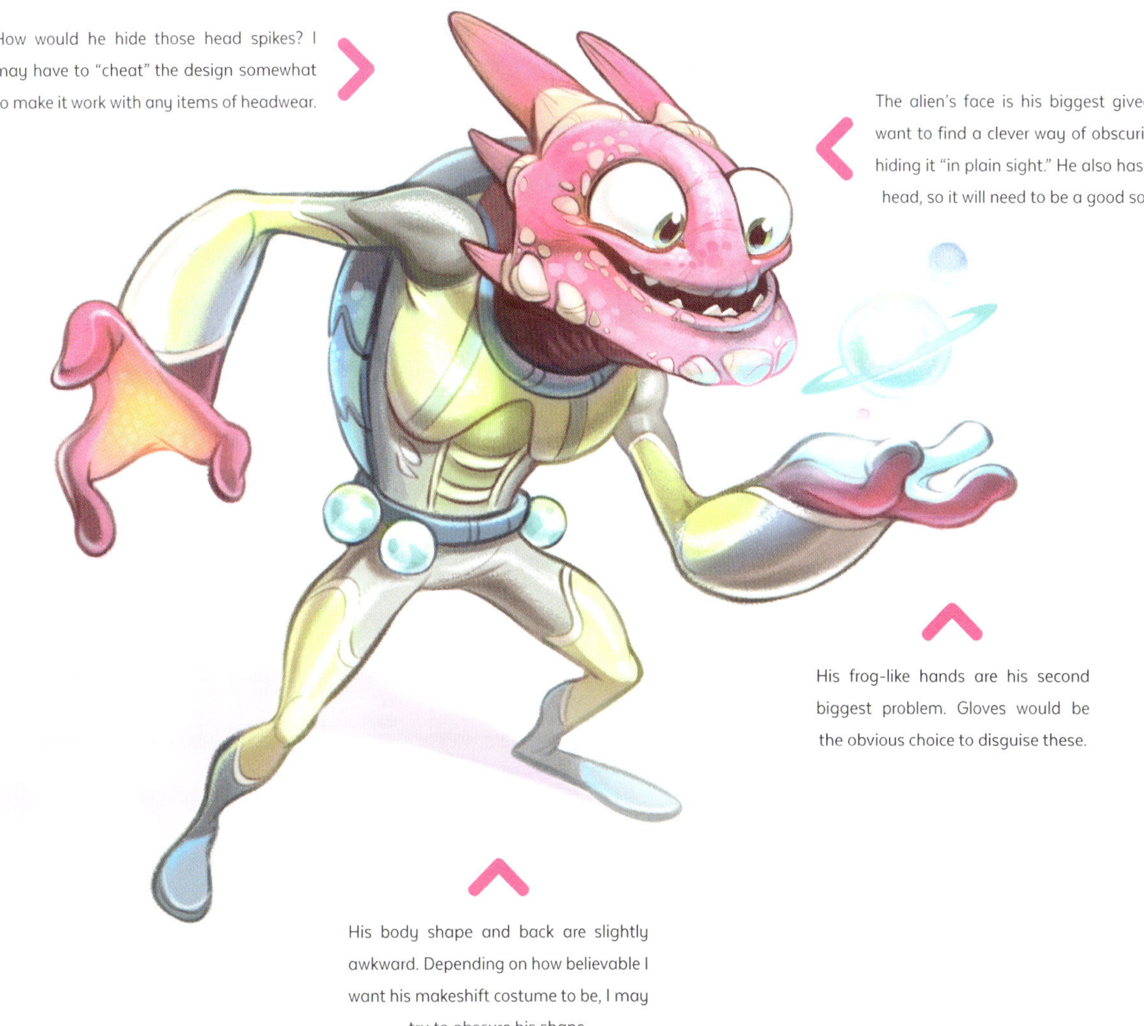

How would he hide those head spikes? I may have to "cheat" the design somewhat to make it work with any items of headwear.

The alien's face is his biggest giveaway. I want to find a clever way of obscuring it or hiding it "in plain sight." He also has a large head, so it will need to be a good solution!

His frog-like hands are his second biggest problem. Gloves would be the obvious choice to disguise these.

His body shape and back are slightly awkward. Depending on how believable I want his makeshift costume to be, I may try to obscure his shape.

THUMBNAILS

I explore most of the ideas I had at the research stage, translating them into the character's design. The mismatched costume ideas are fun, but I decide the most successful ones are the dinosaur costume and the umbrella disguise, as they seem the most unique and humorous. I also think the character is a clever creature – he knows he would easily be spotted in just a scarf and a hat. I choose to pursue the dinosaur idea as it has a clearer sense of setting, and there is an innate humor in a reptilian/amphibian character hiding inside a dinosaur suit.

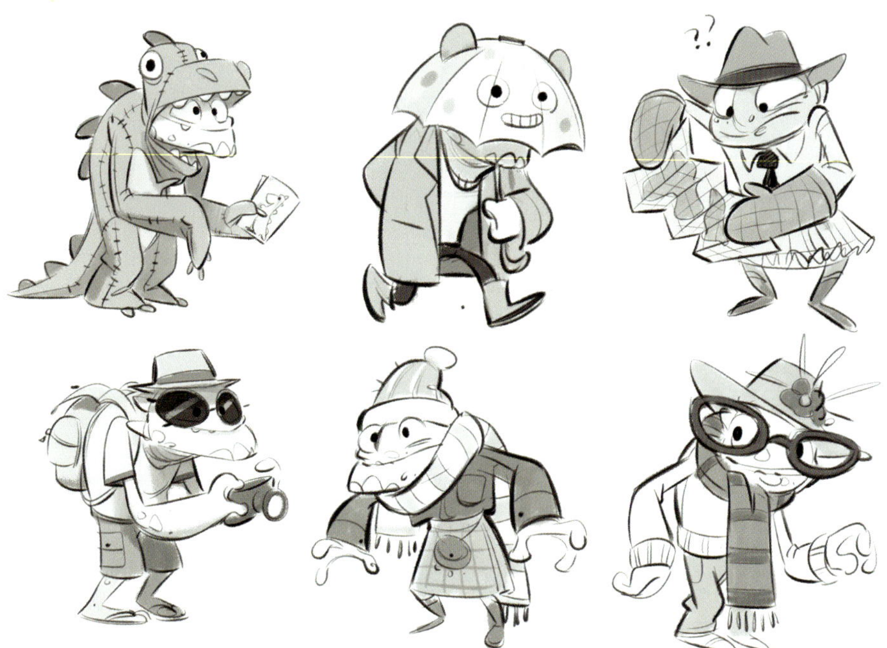

BASIC SHAPES

The dinosaur suit adds a whole new element to the character that needs a shape language of its own. In this case, I will make the costume more square and angular, giving the sense of a large suit that fits a little clumsily over the alien's more rounded body. Emphasizing this boxiness adds to the awkward feel of his disguise. The line of stumpy spikes on the dinosaur's back is a fun detail that creates something in common with the alien's own reptilian horns, though his horns are hidden from view here.

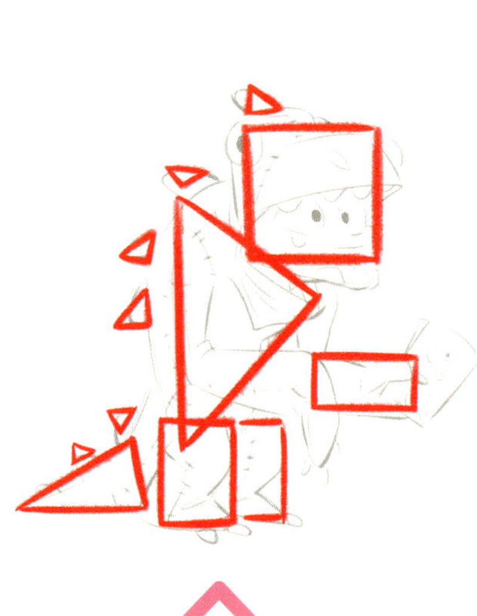

The basic shapes for this version are similar to the original design, but more square; I want to suggest that the costume is hiding his forms, so he is not as rounded or organic.

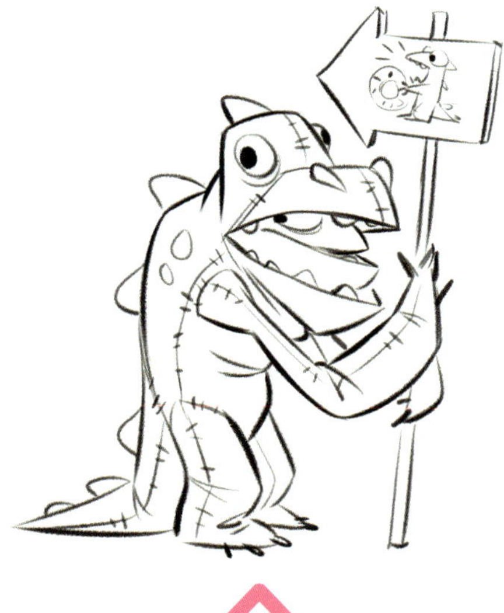

I think about how to fit the character's body inside what is essentially a big sack. Giving him a signpost to hold adds a straight, structured element that contrasts with the baggy suit. It adds visual balance and an extra narrative element.

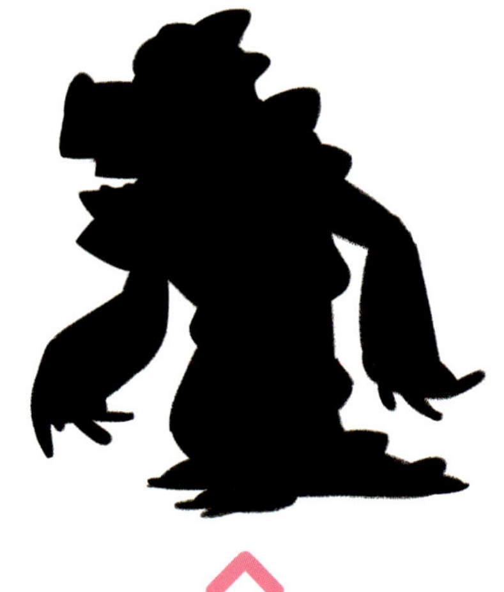

The silhouette reads as some kind of crocodile or dinosaur, effectively disguising the character's body shape. Its stance even looks a bit awkward, which I think is good, as it fits the narrative of the character trying comically to hide himself.

DETAILS

I want this costume to be believable as a human prop, so I add little details to suggest what it is made of, such as stitches, fluff, and folds in the fabric. I make sure that the costume is detailed enough to look like what it is meant to be, while not distracting too much from the character's face (though I do not want his head to be too obvious either, as he is meant to be in disguise).

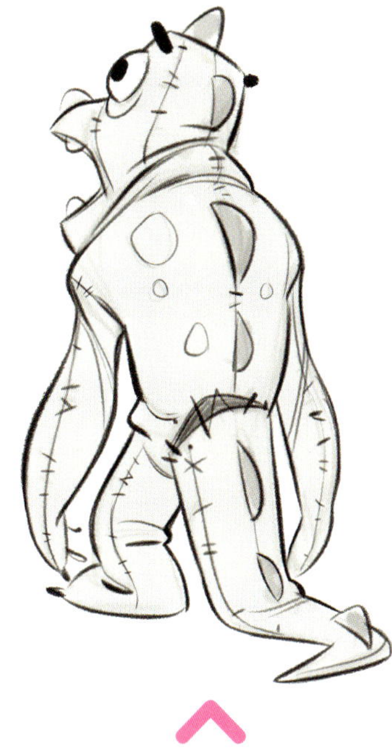

The character is holding a pole with an arrow pointing to a dinosaur-themed attraction – perhaps a donut stand. This gives the design a sense of place, as if he is in a busy tourist area on Earth. He is also holding his map upside down, unused to this primitive level of technology!

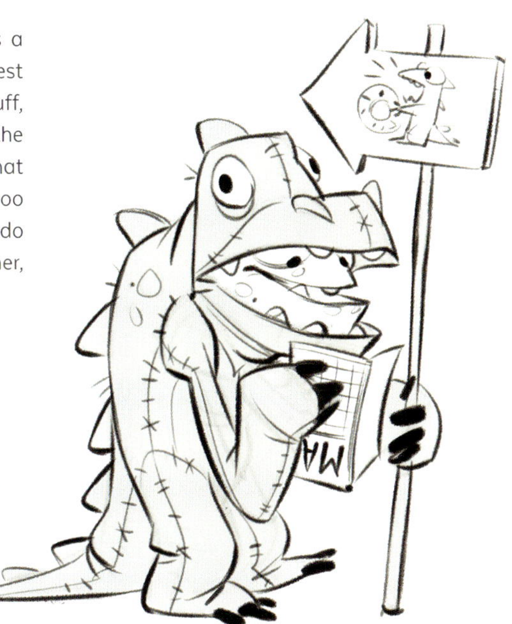

The costume's shabby stitching provides an element of tension and potential for a comedic mishap. Maybe, just maybe, those stitches will come undone, revealing our alien explorer?

EXPRESSIONS & POSING

To create poses, I imagine the character in possible scenarios. He would be conscious of the fact he is one mistake away from being discovered, so I want his body language to be sly and alert to reflect that. I also want the character to still seem like himself underneath it all – he should not be too human in his posing, even though he is trying to be.

I imagine, when no-one is looking, that he drops everything to study his map. Perhaps he is lost and trying to find his way back to his ship without being caught. This is a very expressive and alien pose, as well as being endearingly curious, but it obscures the bold silhouette of the dinosaur suit.

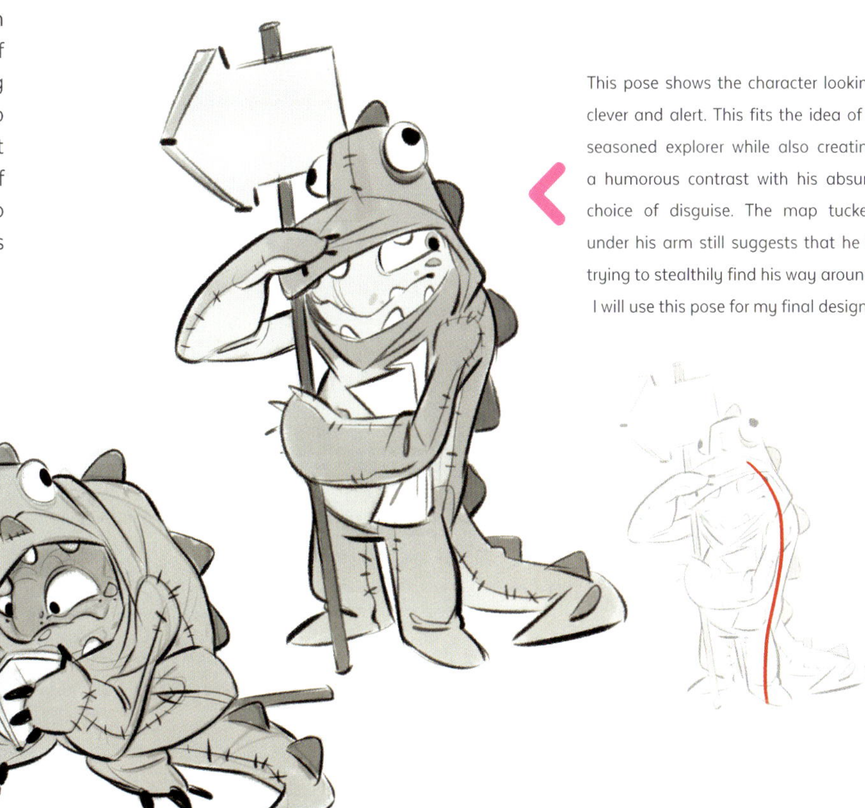

This pose shows the character looking clever and alert. This fits the idea of a seasoned explorer while also creating a humorous contrast with his absurd choice of disguise. The map tucked under his arm still suggests that he is trying to stealthily find his way around. I will use this pose for my final design.

VALUE & COLOR

My concern here is to make sure that the character's head still reads clearly within the costume. It will be quite easy for the head to become lost, which is good for an alien in disguise, but bad for a viewer of the character in action. This all comes down to contrast: I want the head to contrast with the surrounding costume, in both value and color, so it is readable. I want the costume color to be in harmony with my character's pink skin, while also standing apart from it, so that the design does not look flat.

This rough value structure keeps the head lighter than the costume so it stands out. With the exception of the costume's spines, the overall tone of the dinosaur suit is quite low in range, so as not to be too distracting.

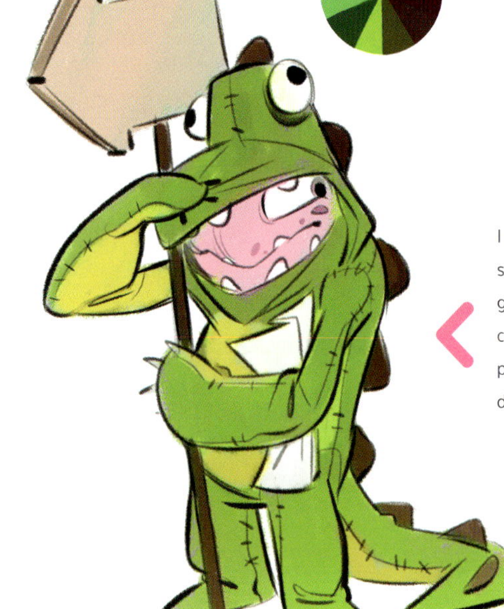

I play around with a split-complementary scheme using pink and two shades of green. The relatively muted colors of the costume make this a strong and legible palette, as the greens are sufficiently different from pink so as not to overwhelm the character's bright skin.

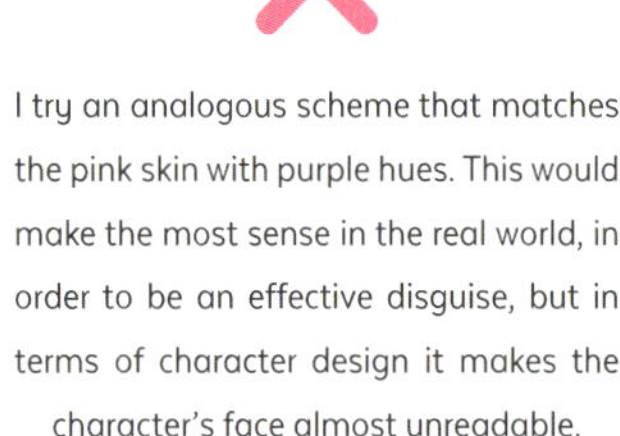

I try an analogous scheme that matches the pink skin with purple hues. This would make the most sense in the real world, in order to be an effective disguise, but in terms of character design it makes the character's face almost unreadable.

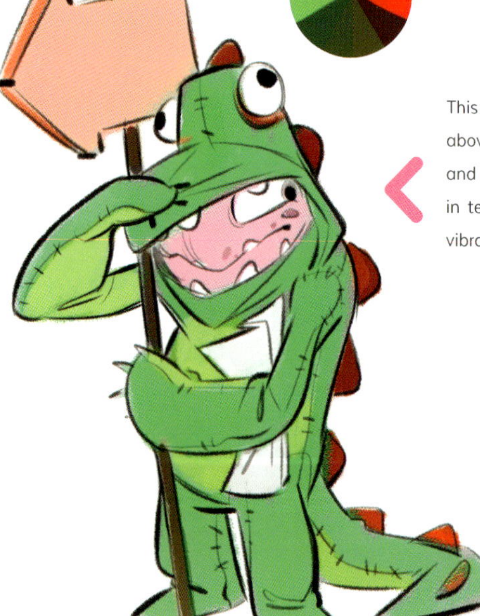

This is a variation of the green palette above, but shifts towards blue-green and a more saturated red. While it works in terms of color theory, I feel it is too vibrant for a dinosaur mascot costume, as well as for a disguise.

FINAL DESIGN

This design successfully removes all the obvious sci-fi elements from the character, while creating a humorous fish-out-of-water narrative that is still true to the character's existing role and personality. The dinosaur costume has enabled me to keep his underlying basic shape, while breaking his silhouette with drooping fabric and a long tail. If this design was used with the original as part of a story, this would still read as the same character, which is important in terms of an audience viewing and understanding what is happening.

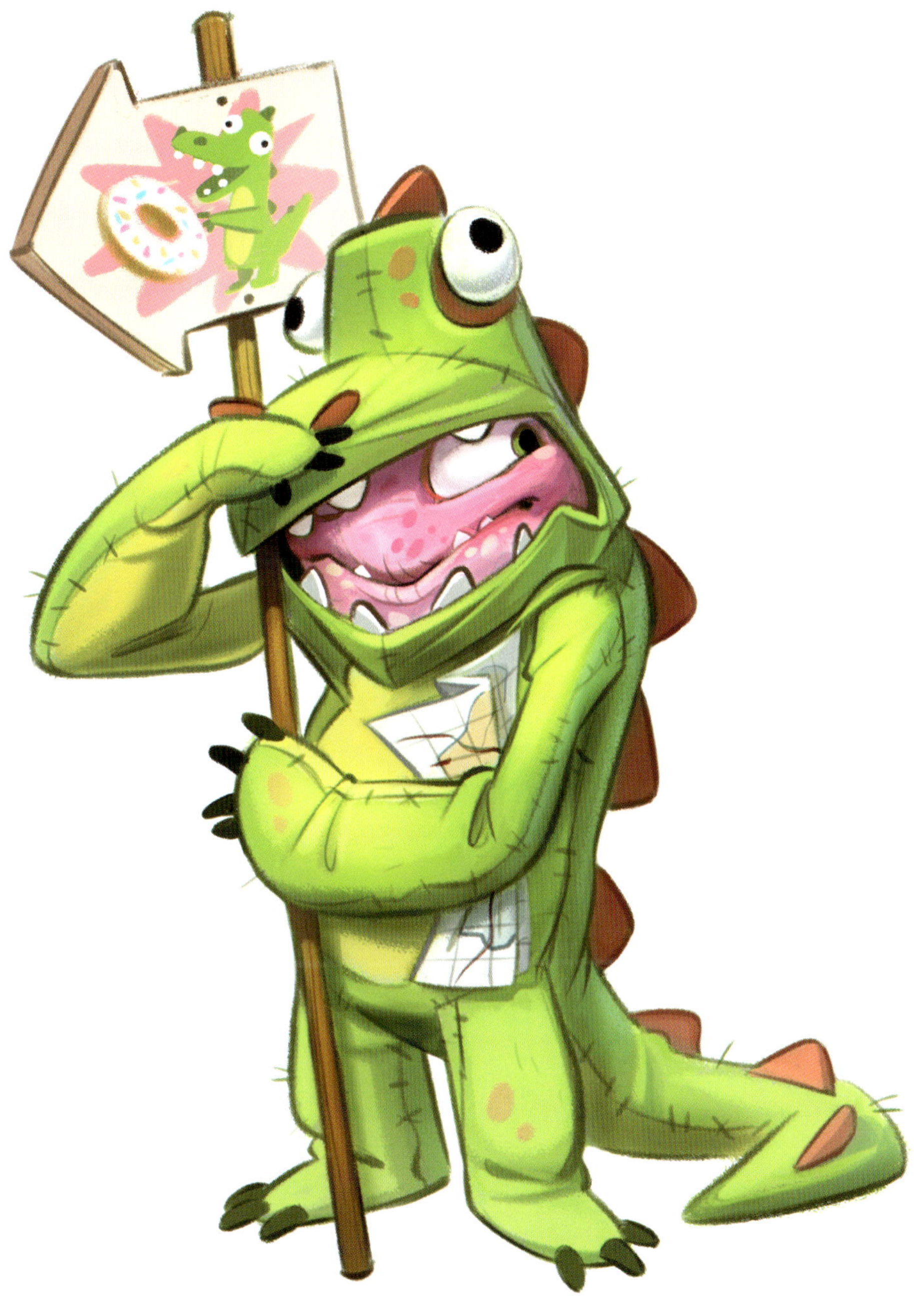

Final artwork © Kenneth Anderson

VARIATION 3:
QUADRUPED ALIEN

IDEAS & RESEARCH

For the final version of this character, I want to re-design the alien as a quadrupedal animal. This could be another part of his natural life cycle – an aged version that is more spiky and scaly than ever. The more wild nature of this creature leaves less ambiguity about how dangerous he might be. With this in mind, I return to lizards and crustaceans in my research, but also look for some more unusual animals for reference.

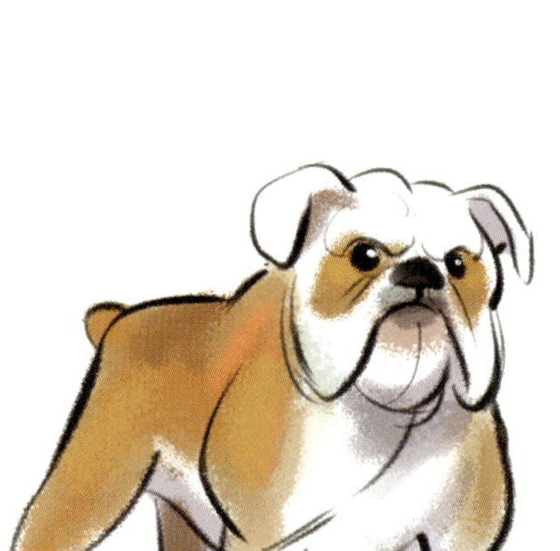

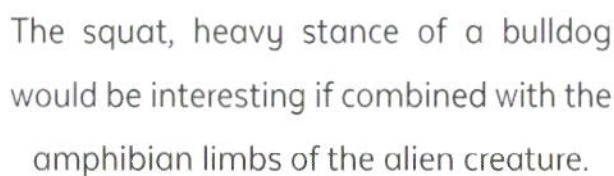

The pangolin has fascinating scales which make you wonder how it's even able to move. It may prove a useful reference for a more heavily scaled character.

The squat, heavy stance of a bulldog would be interesting if combined with the amphibian limbs of the alien creature.

In keeping with the original primate influence, I return to studying the posture and gait of chimps. This could be a useful influence for a lanky character that moves on all fours.

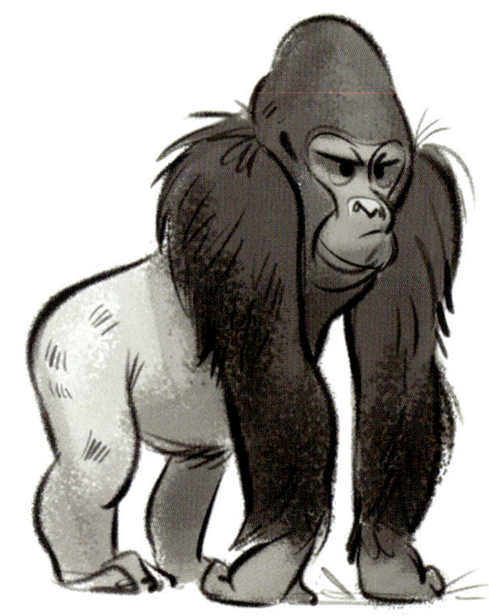

Gorillas move almost on all fours with their strong shoulders and arms. I like the idea of my character walking on all fours due to the weight of his arms and scales pulling him forward.

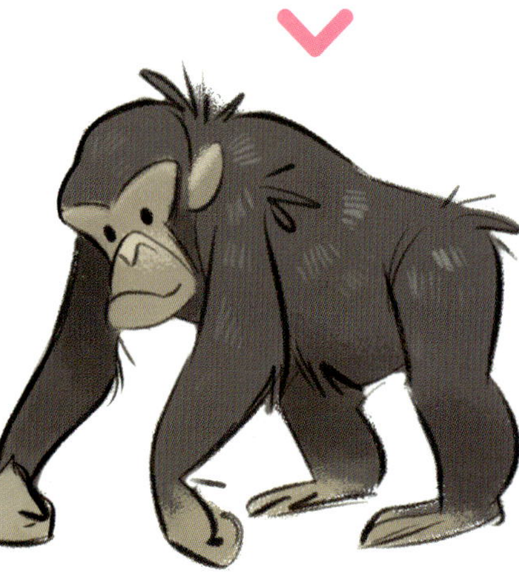

I continue to research lizards for this version, as I do not want to forget my original source material. While I have moved a fair way away from frogs and fish, I need the reptile influence to hold everything together through the character's different ages.

I return to researching crustaceans – this time more crusty and spiky than before. I like the texture of this unnamed species, as it looks like it has been around for a long time.

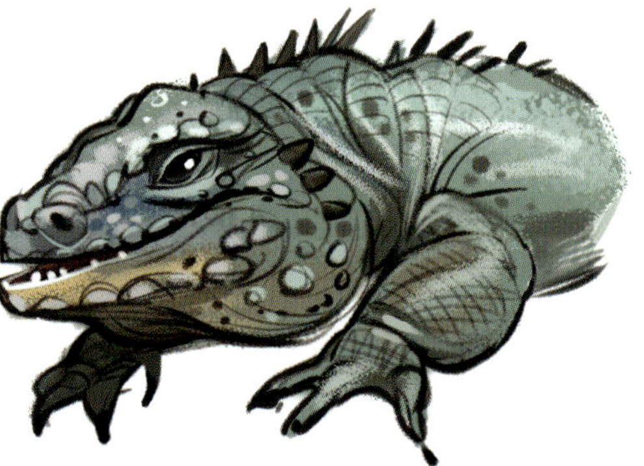

CHANGES

My concern here is to convey the design as the same character, while at the same time being totally different in posture and movement. Keeping some common features will help: the character's spines, frog-like arms, and overall body shape will be key to ensuring that he reads as the same creature – just with more spikes, scales, and a bad attitude.

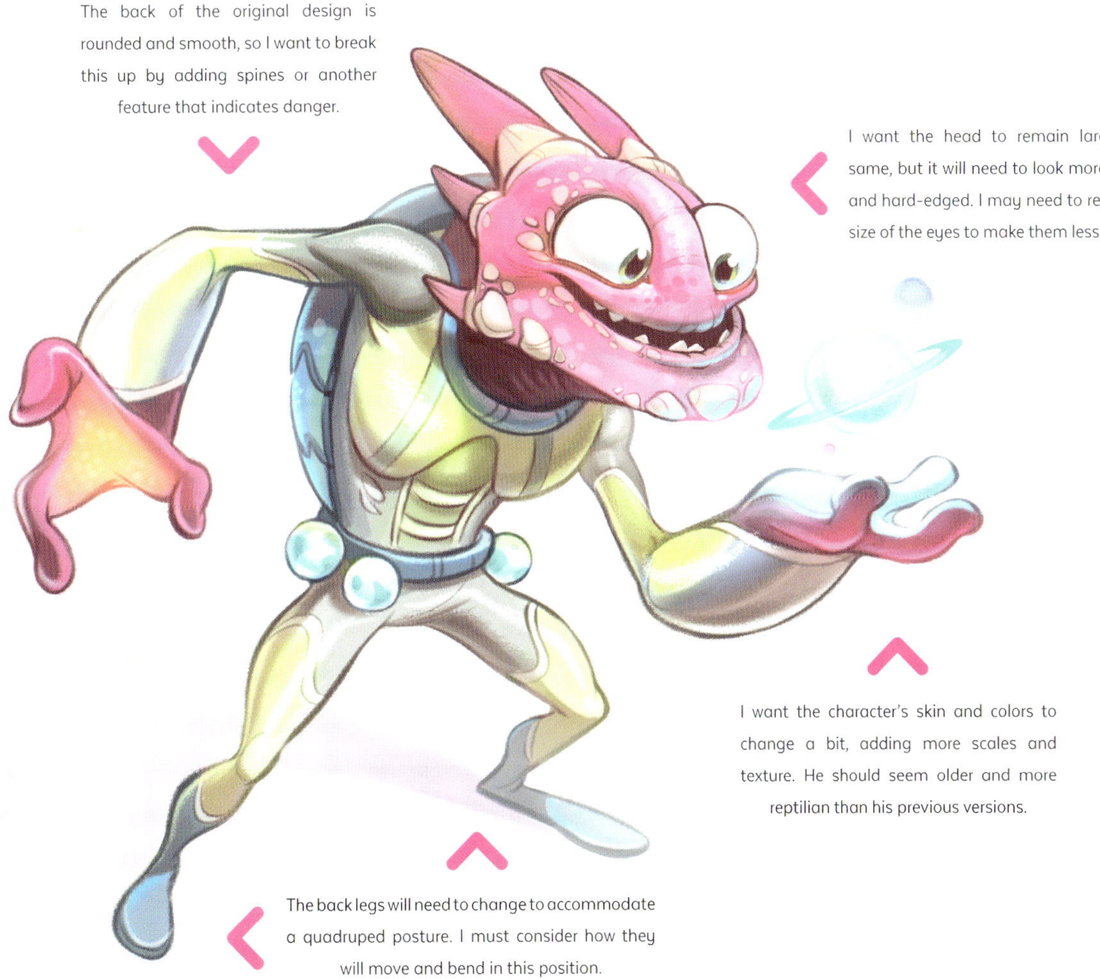

The back of the original design is rounded and smooth, so I want to break this up by adding spines or another feature that indicates danger.

I want the head to remain largely the same, but it will need to look more rugged and hard-edged. I may need to reduce the size of the eyes to make them less comical.

I want the character's skin and colors to change a bit, adding more scales and texture. He should seem older and more reptilian than his previous versions.

The back legs will need to change to accommodate a quadruped posture. I must consider how they will move and bend in this position.

THUMBNAILS

In my thumbnails, I aim for a shape that is dominated by strong shoulders or arms, or at least gives a sense of menace. I want to maintain some of the frog-like feel in the anatomy and posture, while also drawing influence from primates and bulldogs. I decide on the first thumbnail, as it has the potential to take forward while still looking like my original character. It is both spiky and frog-like, and looks cunning and agile.

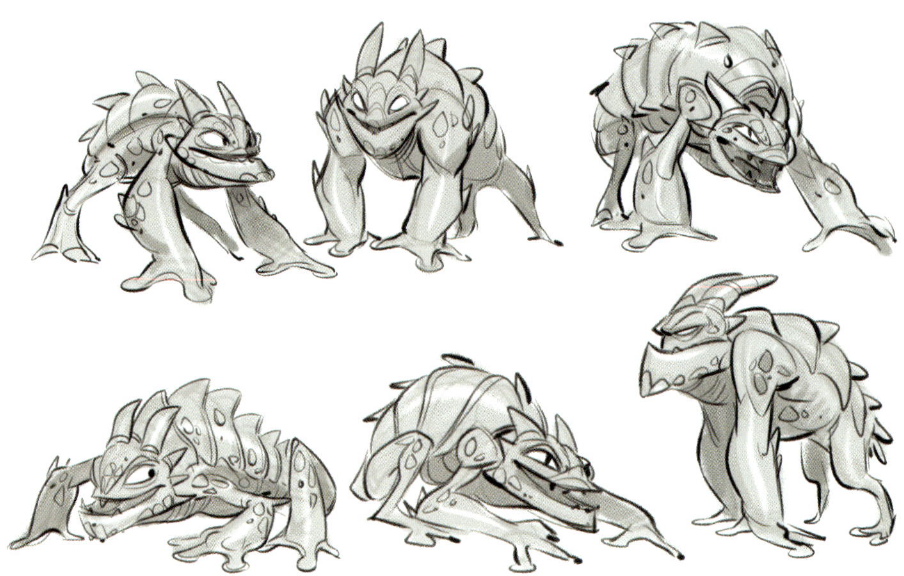

BASIC SHAPES

This creature is wild and dangerous compared to the original alien, so his underlying shapes must change accordingly to reflect this. Though he will still have the curved back and amphibian limbs that are common across all the previous designs, the immediate visual impression of this alien should be of a creature that is tough and unfriendly. Tapping into sharper, more angular shapes will be key to creating this sense of hostility.

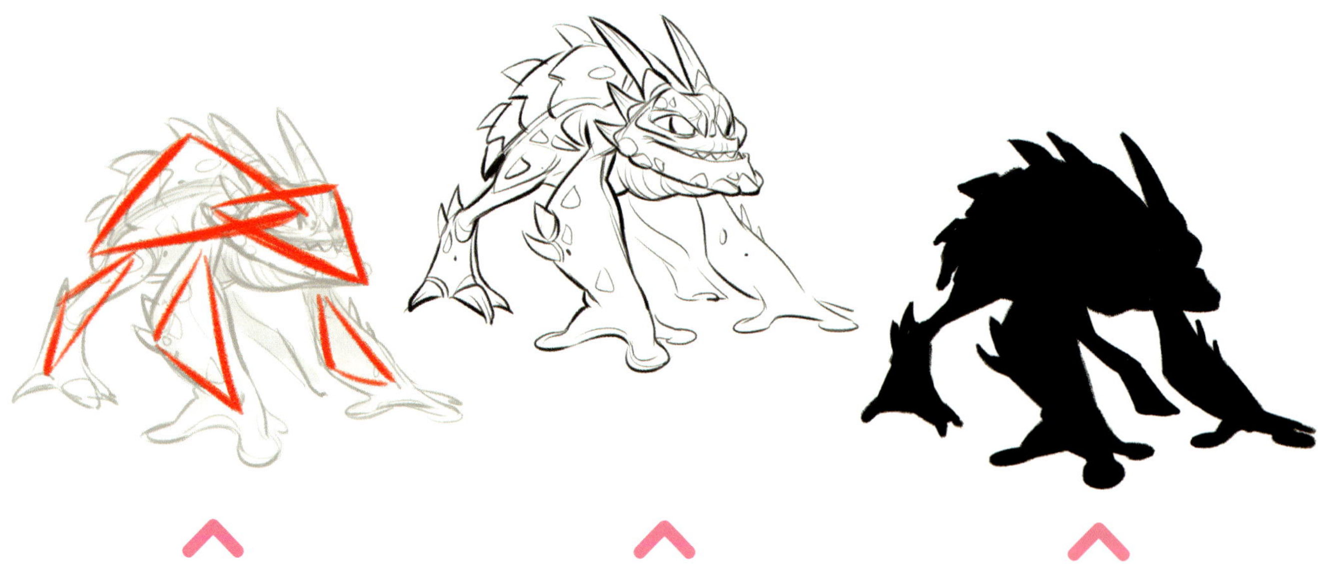

The design now entirely consists of triangles. Some of the smaller shapes in the hands will be rounded, but they will be dominated by large and small triangles which suggest danger and antagonism.

I try to find balance in the character's shapes. There are a lot of triangles present in the design, so I break them up into varying sizes for visual interest, and contrast them with the curves of the character's back and arms.

My new character's silhouette still reads as somewhat amphibian, but suggests that the previous design's soft body and friendly nature is no more.

DETAILS

Now I need to strike a balance between adding spikes and scales, and not going overboard. Too much detail will just confuse the design, especially for an organic, animalistic creature like this one. I want most of the detail to be in the face so the viewer's eye is focused there, but I need to be mindful of keeping the underlying design readable and reminiscent of the original character's face.

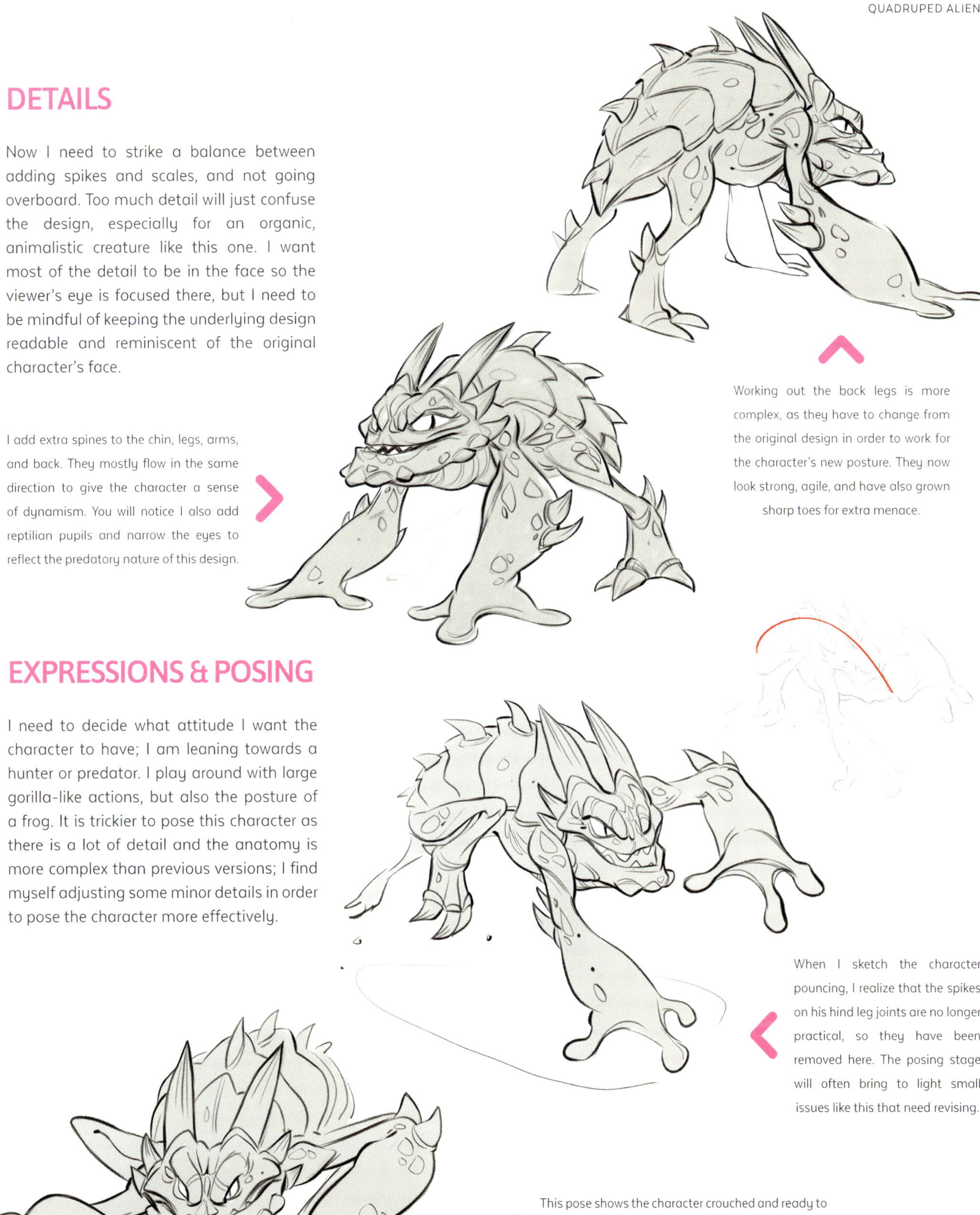

I add extra spines to the chin, legs, arms, and back. They mostly flow in the same direction to give the character a sense of dynamism. You will notice I also add reptilian pupils and narrow the eyes to reflect the predatory nature of this design.

Working out the back legs is more complex, as they have to change from the original design in order to work for the character's new posture. They now look strong, agile, and have also grown sharp toes for extra menace.

EXPRESSIONS & POSING

I need to decide what attitude I want the character to have; I am leaning towards a hunter or predator. I play around with large gorilla-like actions, but also the posture of a frog. It is trickier to pose this character as there is a lot of detail and the anatomy is more complex than previous versions; I find myself adjusting some minor details in order to pose the character more effectively.

When I sketch the character pouncing, I realize that the spikes on his hind leg joints are no longer practical, so they have been removed here. The posing stage will often bring to light small issues like this that need revising.

This pose shows the character crouched and ready to pounce. I want to keep the dynamism of my original character in here, clearly showing the amphibian inspiration that ties the different versions together.

VALUE & COLOR

I want the overall tonal pattern to be quite similar to my original design, with similar high contrast towards the head, created by the bright eyes and dark horns. However, I want to push the pattern of values and tones further, making them more varied and broken up to fit a more wild, natural creature. I also want the colors to recall the previous versions' colorful palettes.

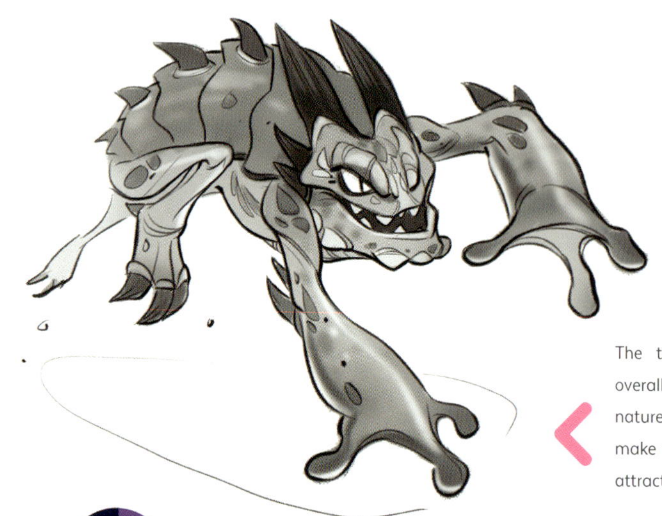

The tones in this design are overall a lot darker, fitting the nature of this new character. I make the spikes darker to really attract the eye and point out how sharp they are.

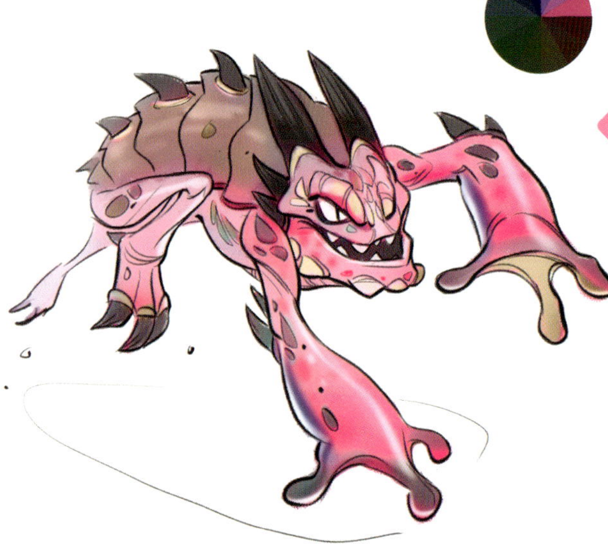

This analogous pink and purple color scheme works well to recall the original alien design. It is almost monochromatic, using different saturations and brightness of the main pinkish hue. However, it is a very bright color for a stealthy, predatory creature.

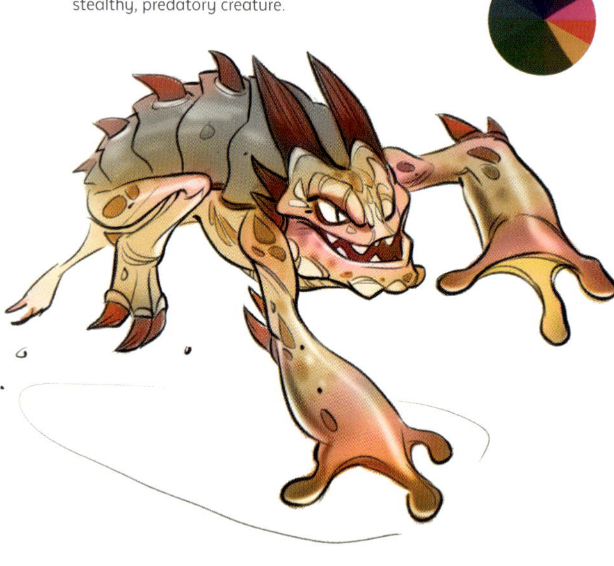

This analogous color scheme is focused on yellow and orange, leaning towards red. This suggests "danger" with every element, while recalling the varied colors of the original design. The earthy colors also create a more primal, camouflaged feel that suits a cunning predator. I will use this as a basis for my final design.

This triadic color scheme nods to the pinks of the original design, with the muted hues adding some visual tension. I have pushed some colors almost towards gray to make the character's back stand out, but this palette loses the vibrancy of the original.

FINAL DESIGN

The final design combines a new dominant shape theme – the pointy triangle – with an altered color scheme to convey a sense of danger and to contrast with the original design. I have kept a lot of elements similar (such as the face, horns, and amphibian limbs), so this version still reads as the same character, just older or mutated in some way. The posing is at its most dynamic and menacing to convey that he now has a completely different nature, no longer with any ambiguity to his design.

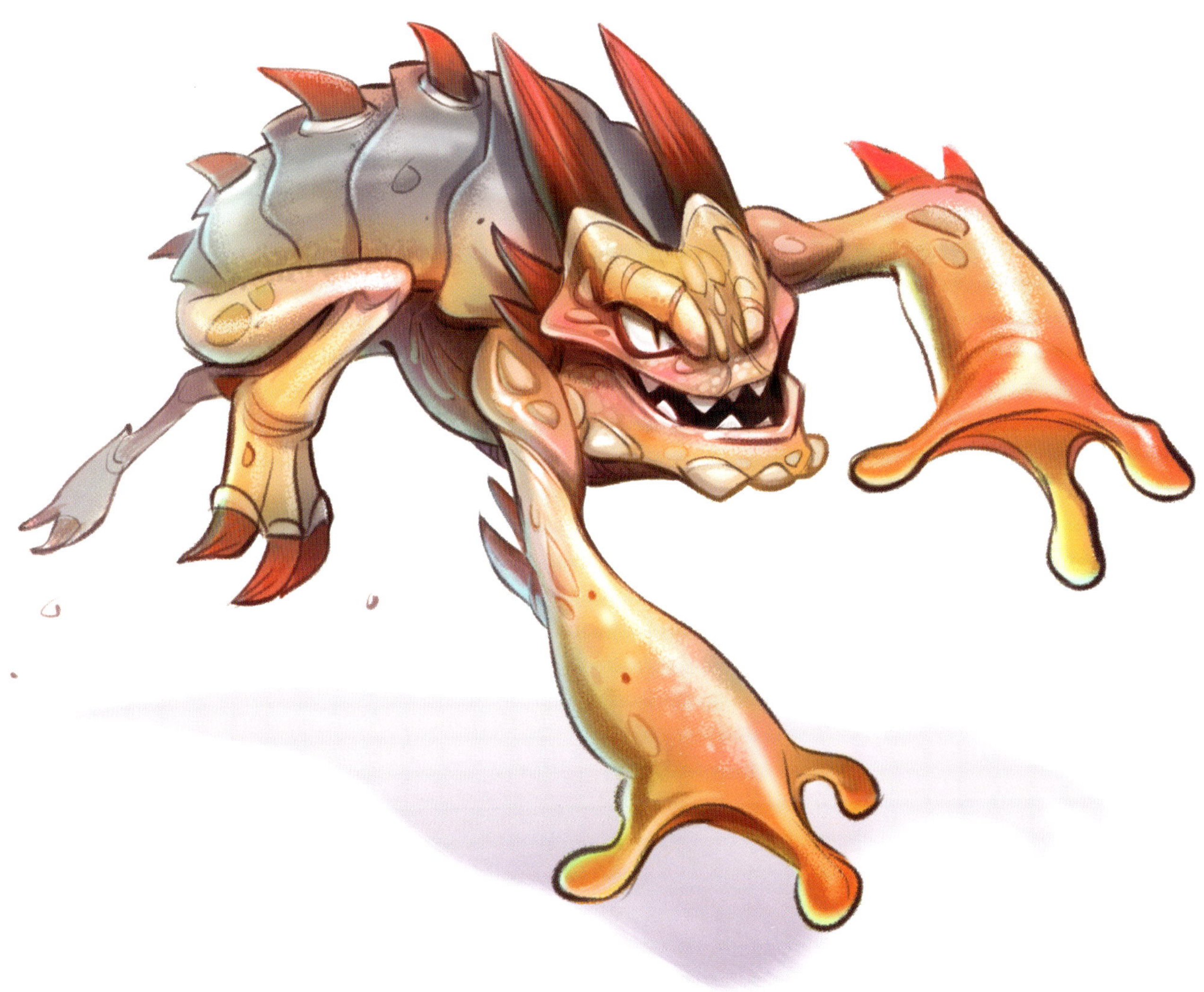

Final artwork © Kenneth Anderson

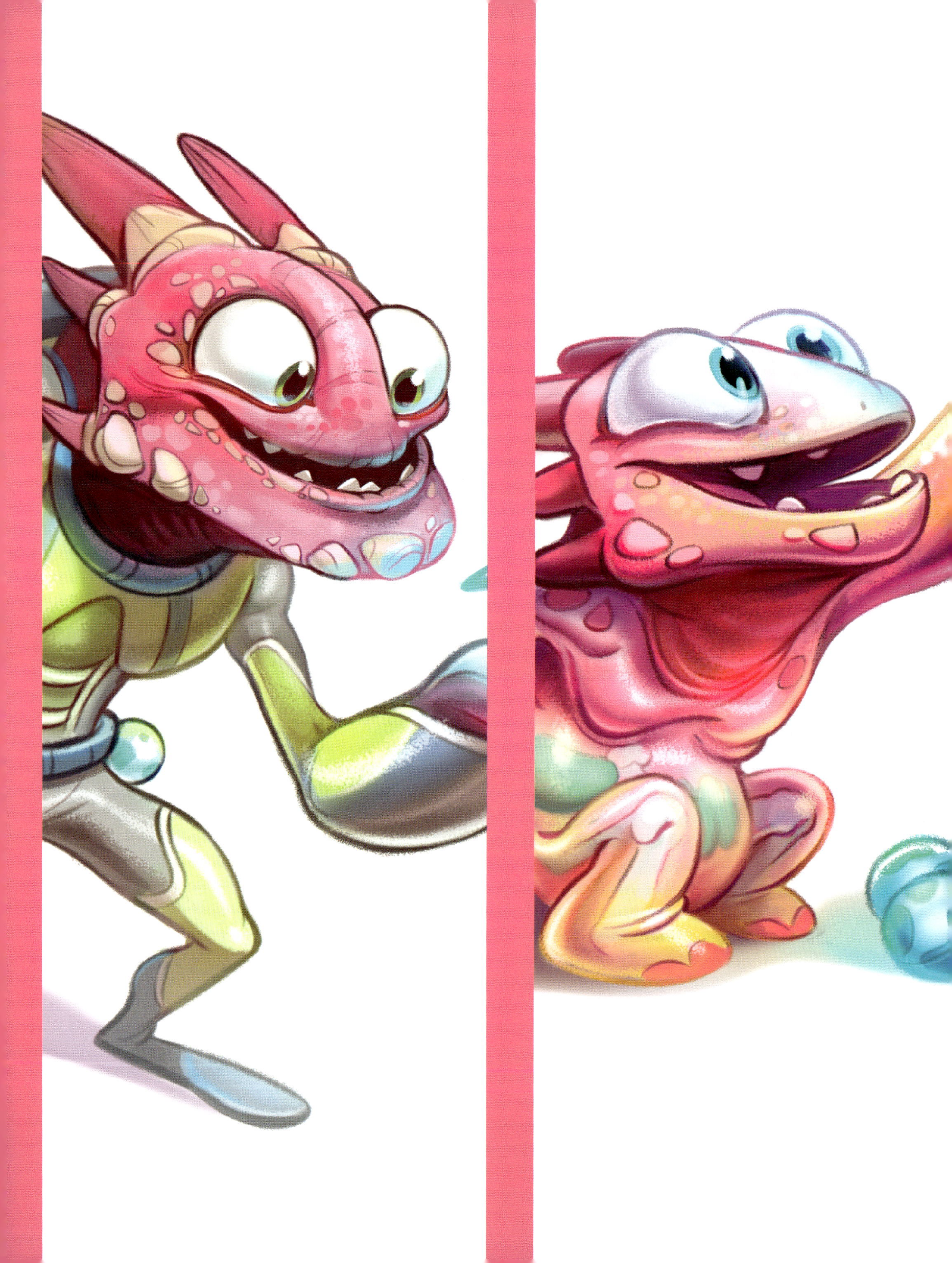

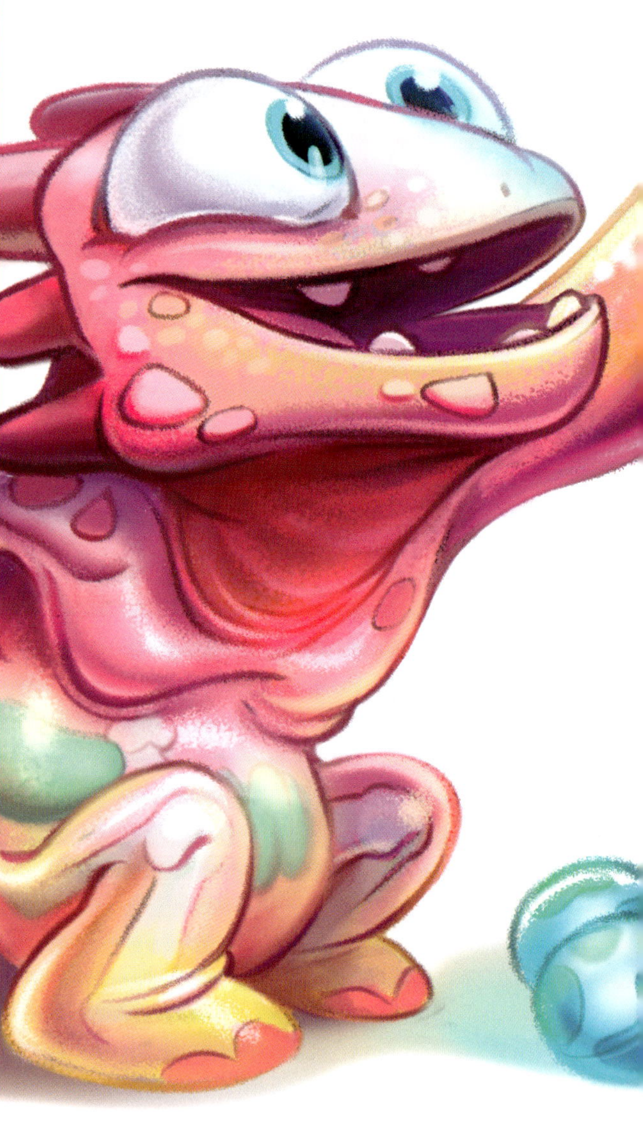

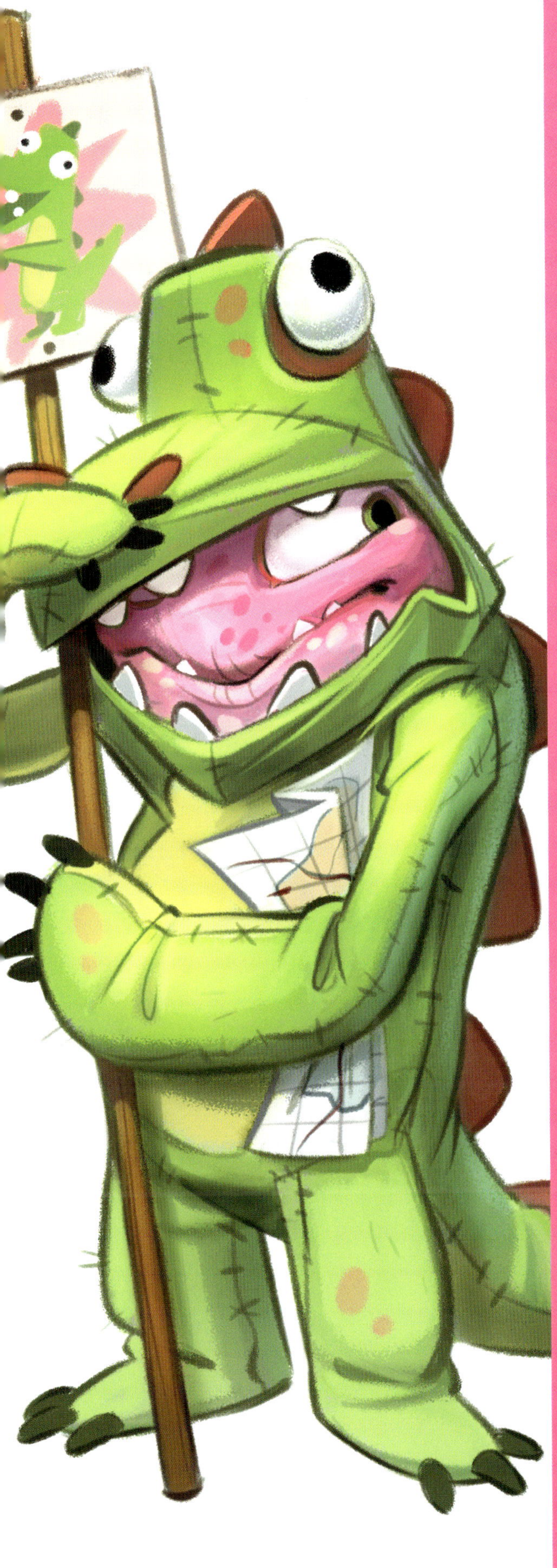

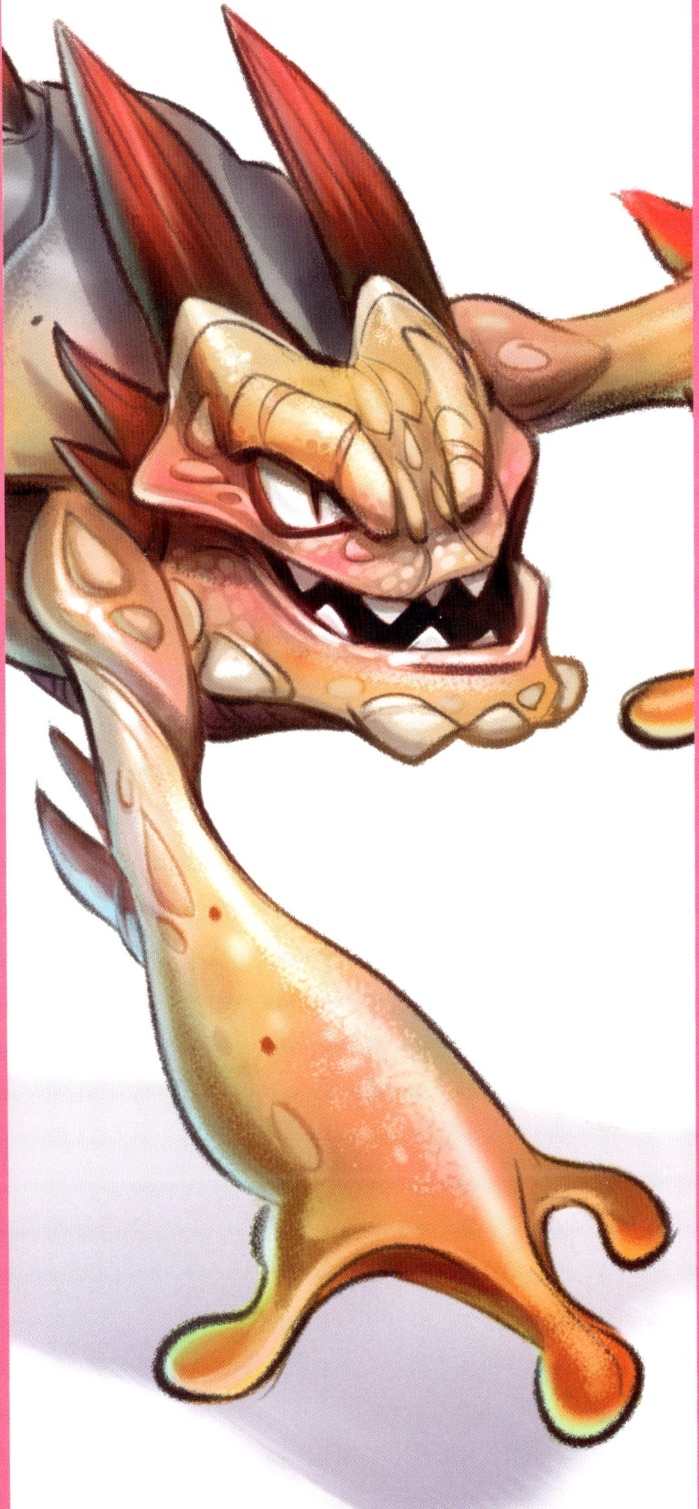

TEACHER

BY STEPHANIE RIZO GARCIA

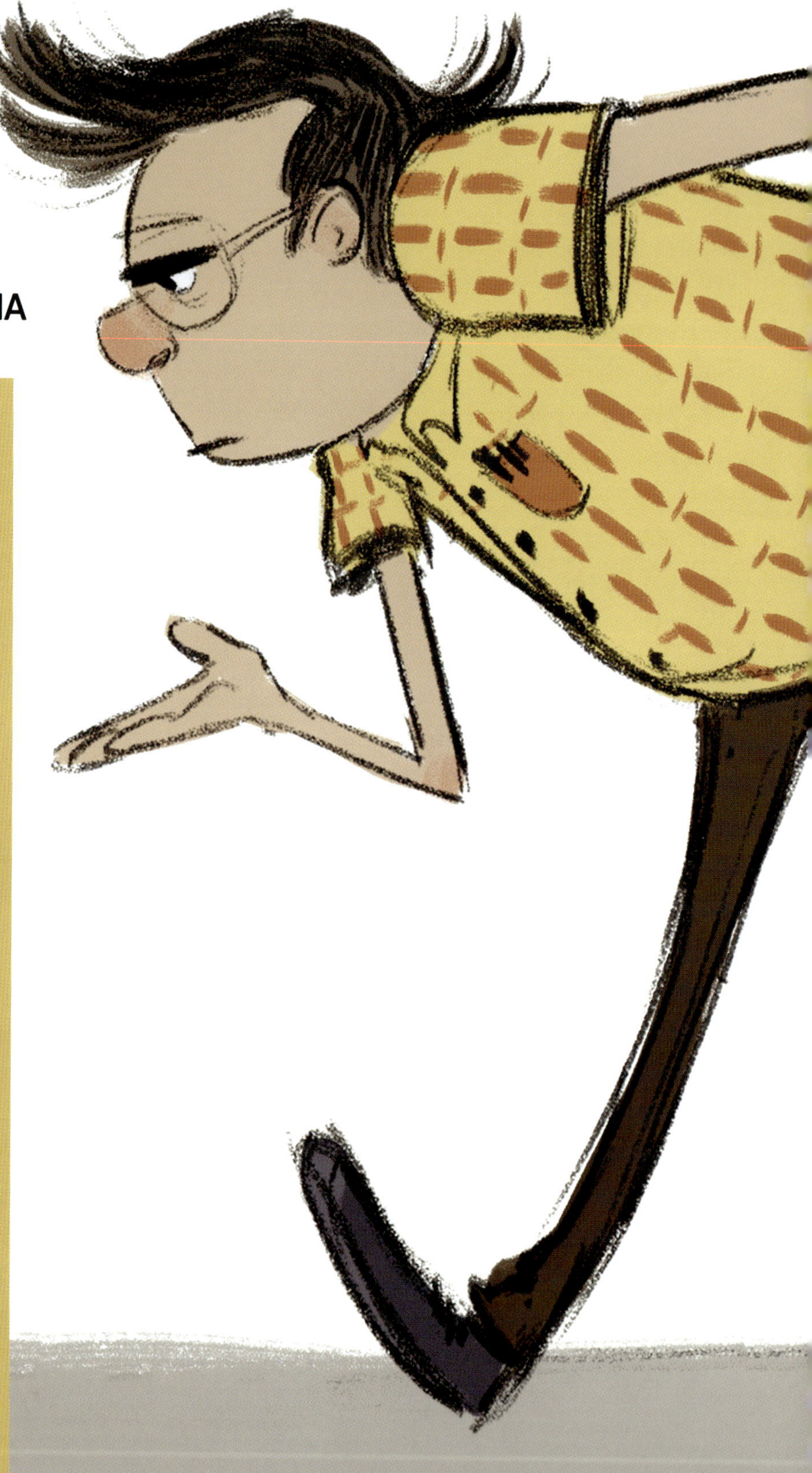

In this chapter, illustrator Stephanie Rizo Garcia designs a grumpy middle-aged schoolteacher who is stressed out by the demands of his job.

VARIATIONS

- SCHOOLBOY
- VICTORIAN SCHOOLMASTER
- ACADEMIC BAT

FOCUS

Stephanie's style focuses on contrasting shapes, expressive faces, and exaggerated poses that give her designs a sense of fun and energy.

Pay close attention to using varied shapes to convey your character's personality, and don't be afraid to heavily amplify their proportions and poses to create a more memorable design.

THE IDEA

In this project I will be designing a modern-day male schoolteacher. I start by asking myself who this character is, and developing a little backstory. Is he young, old, or middle-aged? Is he cheerful or grumpy, and why? Answering these questions will help me to decide what type of clothing, accessories, and shapes I might use in my design. Inspired by some of my own past teachers, I decide that I want the character to be slightly older, quite grumpy and strict, yet with a humble side. I like the idea of him wearing patterned shirts and sneakers to feel young and attempt to fit in with his modern times, but that he also feels upset and bitter for not having achieved the career he might have wanted when he was young.

Concept: A modern-day male schoolteacher

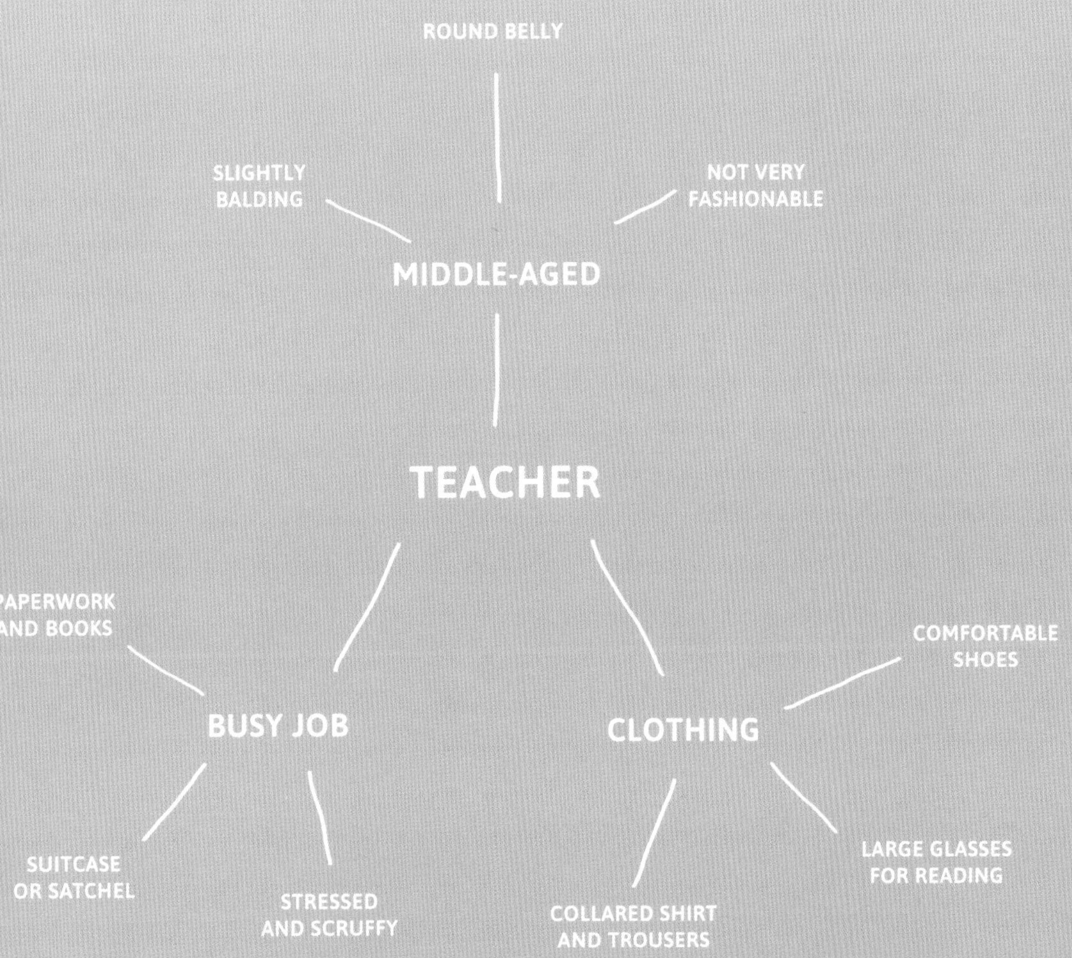

RESEARCH

To begin my research, I think back to some of my favorite teachers in high school. I had a history teacher who was extremely keen on history but was always grumpy; he didn't like that some of us might get ahead of him! I know that I want to add that personality into this character: a teacher who is passionate about his subject but is always severe with his students. The character must look somewhat modern and not completely old-fashioned, so I also draw inspiration from Jack Black's role in the movie *School of Rock*, as I like his character's patterned shirts and messy hair.

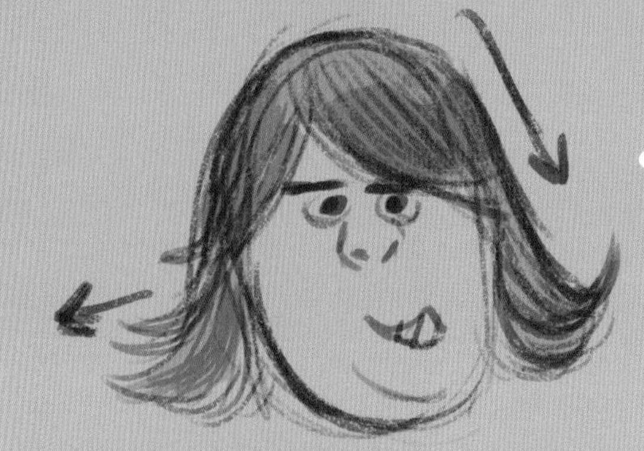

I research possible hairstyles for this character. I want him to have a messy but serious look, showing that he is strict but also has a comical side, even if he doesn't realize it.

This patterned shirt is something that my high-school teacher wore a lot, and his shirt and sleeves were always loose. This would make the character look both smart and somewhat untidy due to his busy job.

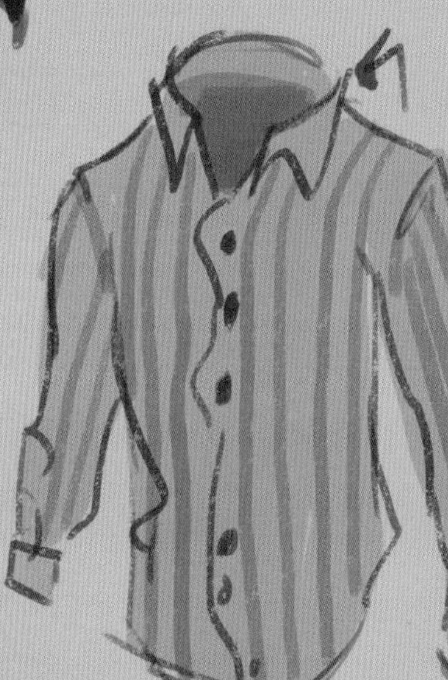

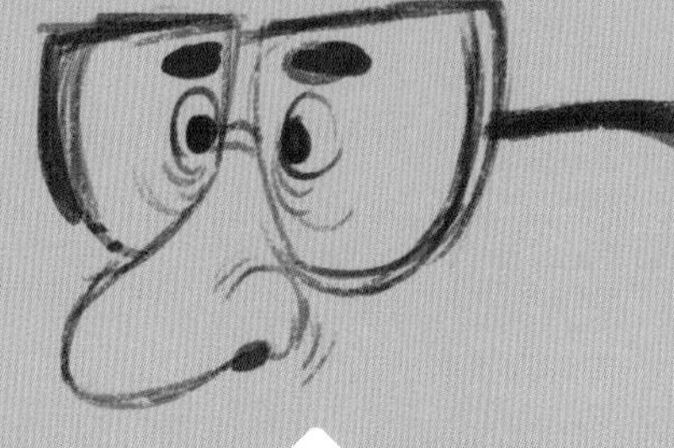

Glasses will help the character to look both intellectual and stern, so I research some different styles. Semi-circular frames could capture both of these qualities with their mix of round and straight edges.

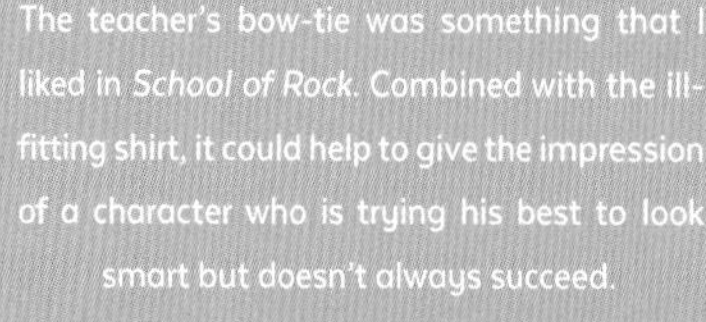

The teacher's bow-tie was something that I liked in *School of Rock*. Combined with the ill-fitting shirt, it could help to give the impression of a character who is trying his best to look smart but doesn't always succeed.

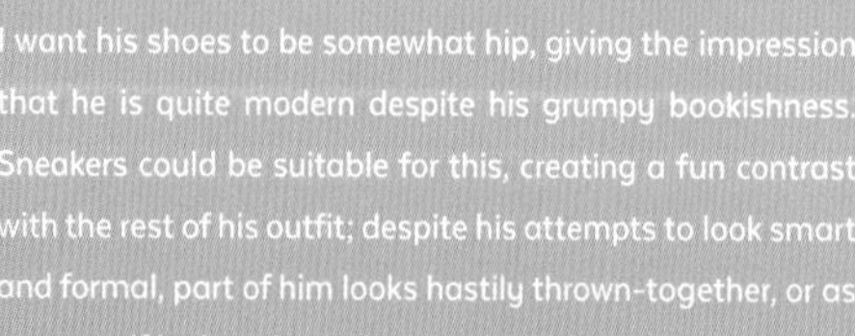

I want his shoes to be somewhat hip, giving the impression that he is quite modern despite his grumpy bookishness. Sneakers could be suitable for this, creating a fun contrast with the rest of his outfit; despite his attempts to look smart and formal, part of him looks hastily thrown-together, or as if he is trying to look cool and feel young.

I like the idea of the character's body shape being loosely inspired by objects you might find on a teacher's desk, like an apple or a ruler. I will explore different body shapes in more depth later.

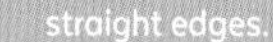

THUMBNAILS

As I start to create thumbnails for the character, I continue to ask myself who he is and what his backstory might be. I explore very different body shapes, inspired by the classroom objects I thought of in my research: tall and thin like rulers, short and round like apples, squat and rectangular like books, or a mix of these. I explore different shirts, haircuts, and accessories (such as a satchel and books) to see if they help to communicate his role and personality.

I like the first thumbnail because the overall shape is clear, and his stocky form gives him a lot of personality. The seventh thumbnail has strong shape balance, with long skinny legs holding all the weight of his body to create an appealingly contrasting look. I also like the tenth thumbnail, which is similar to the first but has a more oval body and long arms in comparison to his height. I will combine elements of these three thumbnails to create a concept I am happy to proceed with.

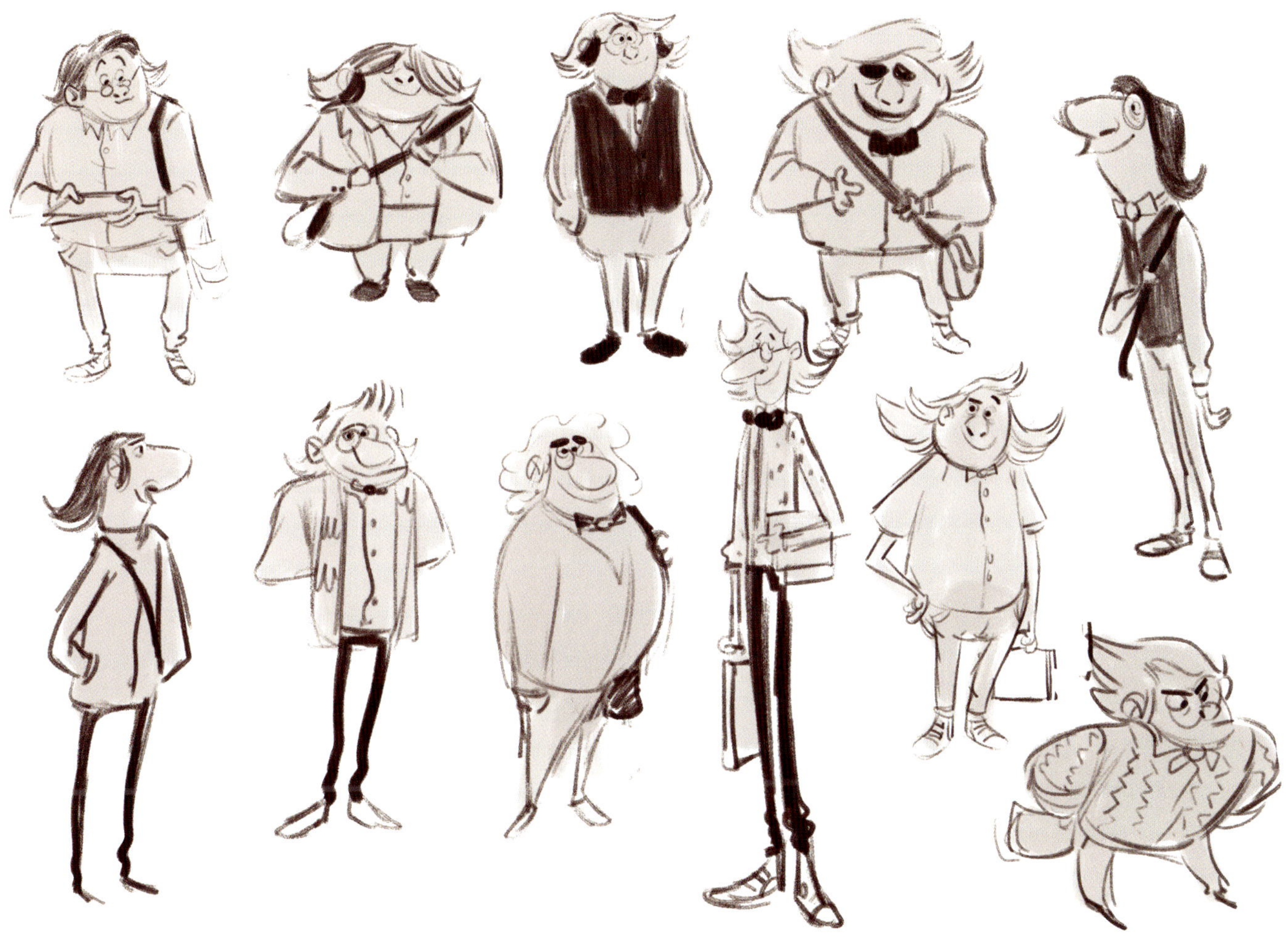

BASIC SHAPES

Choosing more than one strong thumbnail allows me to combine multiple good ideas to create one ideal design. In the case of the first, seventh, and tenth thumbnails that I chose on the previous page, their strengths are in their multiple contrasting elements. The combinations of stocky or round bodies with long, thin legs, or round heads with pointed hair, make those thumbnails compelling to look at.

After mixing these different elements together, my resulting design has a compact, oval torso with long, thin legs and a rounded head with hair that is almost triangular. These contrasts will guide the viewer around the design and ensure that their eye remains interested.

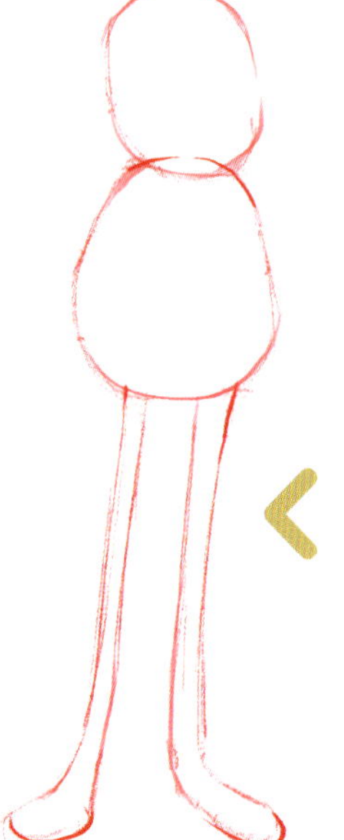

The combination of different shapes (straight and round, short and long) will immediately give eye-catching appeal to the design. The extreme contrast between the shapes of his head and legs will make him come across as quite comical, whether he intends it or not.

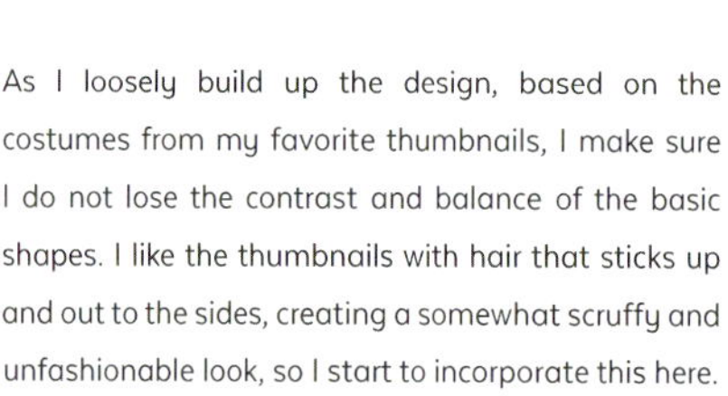

As I loosely build up the design, based on the costumes from my favorite thumbnails, I make sure I do not lose the contrast and balance of the basic shapes. I like the thumbnails with hair that sticks up and out to the sides, creating a somewhat scruffy and unfashionable look, so I start to incorporate this here.

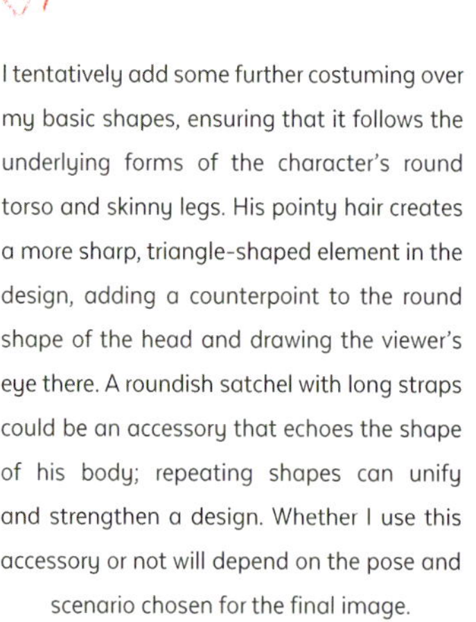

I tentatively add some further costuming over my basic shapes, ensuring that it follows the underlying forms of the character's round torso and skinny legs. His pointy hair creates a more sharp, triangle-shaped element in the design, adding a counterpoint to the round shape of the head and drawing the viewer's eye there. A roundish satchel with long straps could be an accessory that echoes the shape of his body; repeating shapes can unify and strengthen a design. Whether I use this accessory or not will depend on the pose and scenario chosen for the final image.

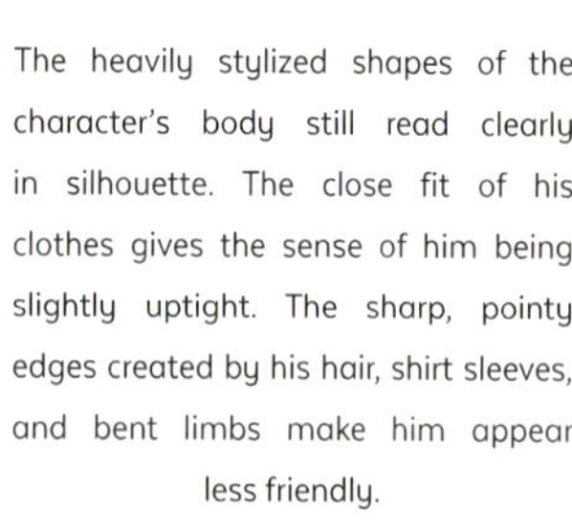

The heavily stylized shapes of the character's body still read clearly in silhouette. The close fit of his clothes gives the sense of him being slightly uptight. The sharp, pointy edges created by his hair, shirt sleeves, and bent limbs make him appear less friendly.

DETAILS

Now I can start to add the extra objects that help to define the character. We know that he is a grumpy teacher who is always busy grading papers and bossing kids around in his class. Drawing him with textbooks and paper in one hand and a mug of coffee in the other helps to convey how busy and stressed he is. I add some wrinkles to his face to indicate his age, but I am careful not to add too many, because I also add more detail to his hair and don't want the two elements to look too busy. I try to create similar contrast with his clothes, balancing out his striped shirt with plain jeans and very simple shoes.

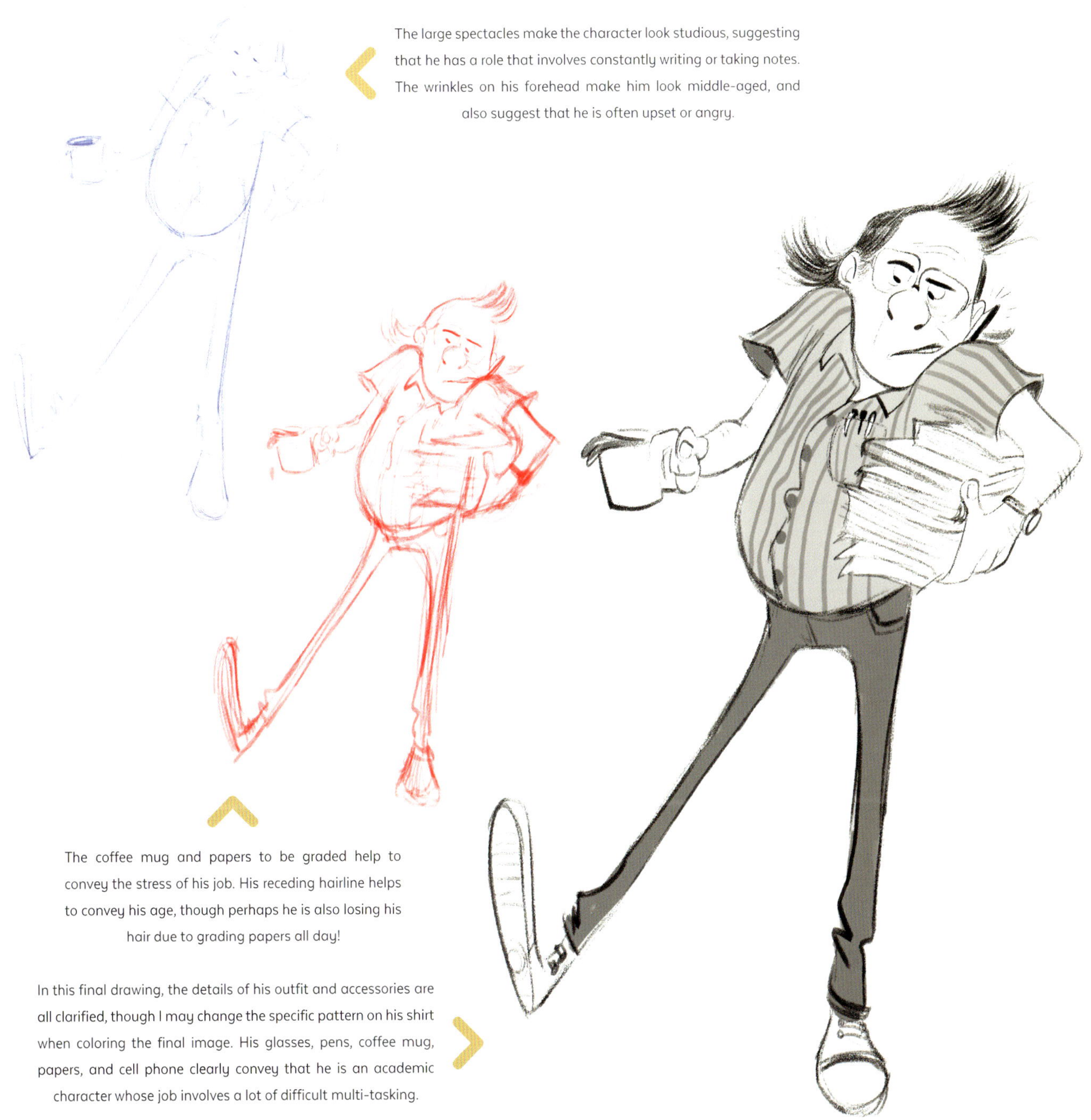

The large spectacles make the character look studious, suggesting that he has a role that involves constantly writing or taking notes. The wrinkles on his forehead make him look middle-aged, and also suggest that he is often upset or angry.

The coffee mug and papers to be graded help to convey the stress of his job. His receding hairline helps to convey his age, though perhaps he is also losing his hair due to grading papers all day!

In this final drawing, the details of his outfit and accessories are all clarified, though I may change the specific pattern on his shirt when coloring the final image. His glasses, pens, coffee mug, papers, and cell phone clearly convey that he is an academic character whose job involves a lot of difficult multi-tasking.

FACIAL EXPRESSIONS

When I explore the character's facial expressions, knowing what I have established of his personality, I try to find ways to communicate the different aspects of his temperament. Lowering his eyebrows, raising his shoulders, and giving him an exaggerated frown makes him look tense and irritable. Relaxing his brow and mouth makes him look more kindly and approachable.

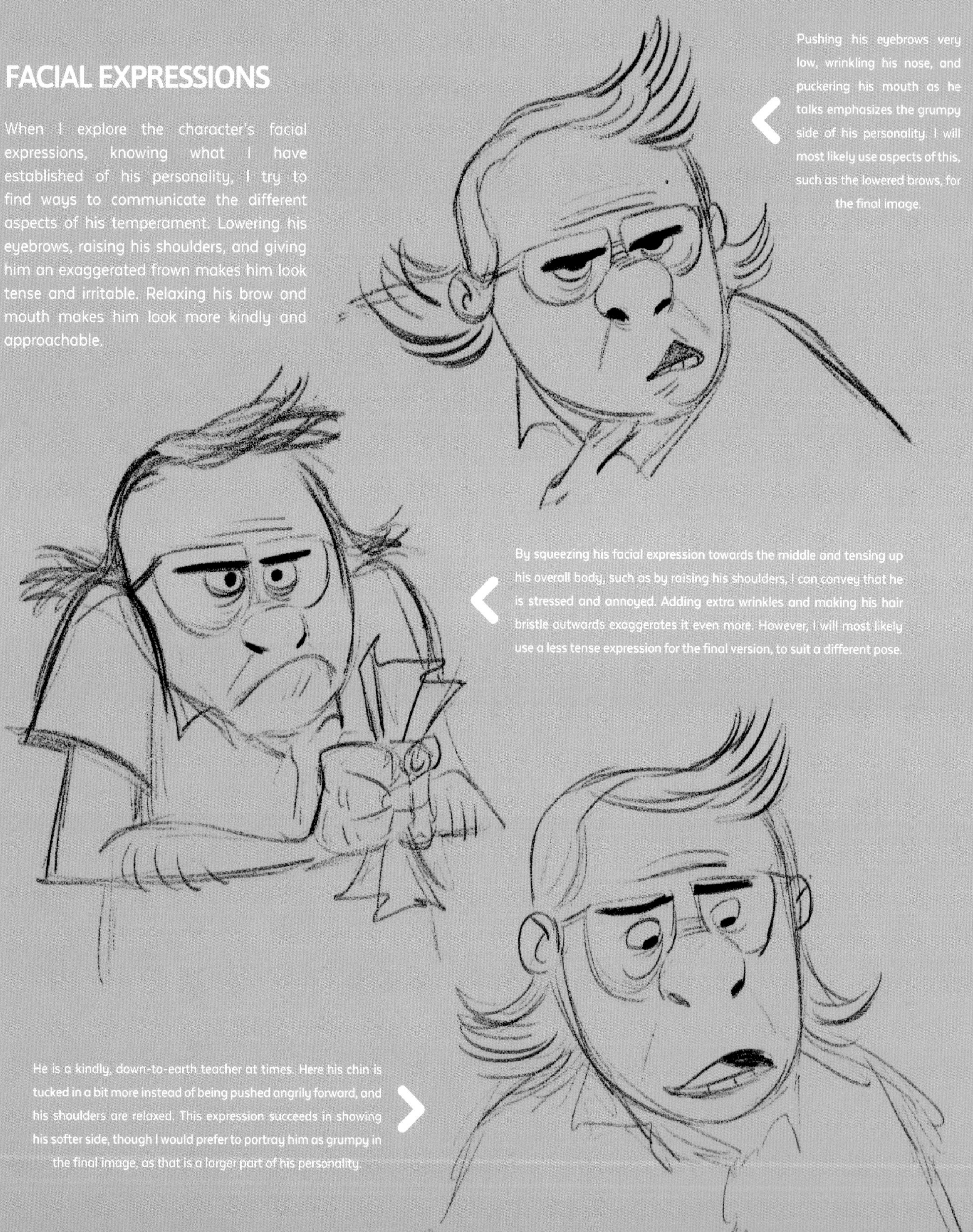

Pushing his eyebrows very low, wrinkling his nose, and puckering his mouth as he talks emphasizes the grumpy side of his personality. I will most likely use aspects of this, such as the lowered brows, for the final image.

By squeezing his facial expression towards the middle and tensing up his overall body, such as by raising his shoulders, I can convey that he is stressed and annoyed. Adding extra wrinkles and making his hair bristle outwards exaggerates it even more. However, I will most likely use a less tense expression for the final version, to suit a different pose.

He is a kindly, down-to-earth teacher at times. Here his chin is tucked in a bit more instead of being pushed angrily forward, and his shoulders are relaxed. This expression succeeds in showing his softer side, though I would prefer to portray him as grumpy in the final image, as that is a larger part of his personality.

POSING

I always aim to tell a story when creating poses, even if there is no background scene. As this character is a teacher, I sketch out poses and situations that fit a classroom setting, including some props to bring the scenes to life. I make sure to use his whole body to convey his personality and help each pose to read clearly. The character's skinny limbs are a key part of his visual impact, so I try to find poses that use his long arms and legs in the most expressive ways possible.

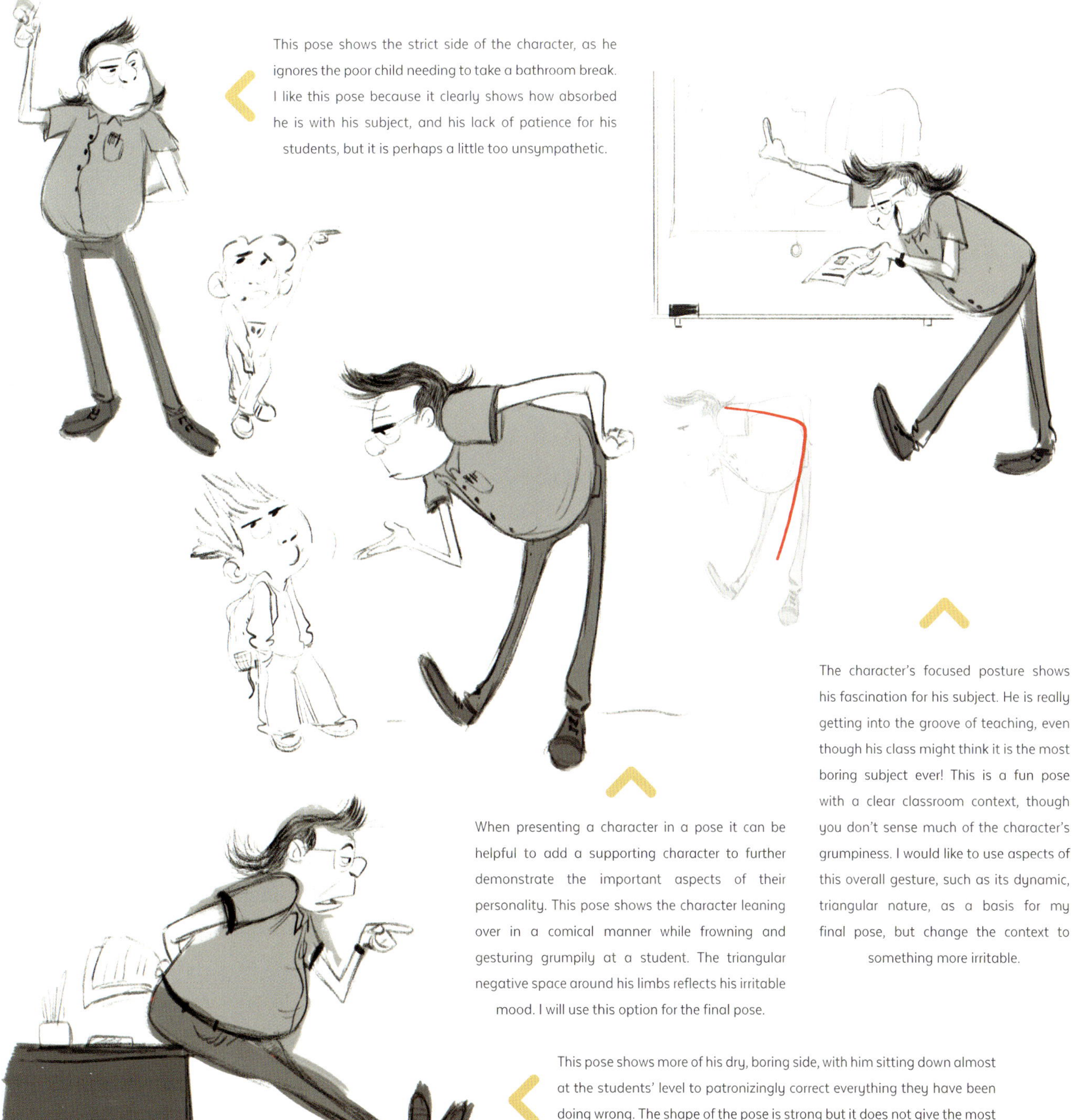

This pose shows the strict side of the character, as he ignores the poor child needing to take a bathroom break. I like this pose because it clearly shows how absorbed he is with his subject, and his lack of patience for his students, but it is perhaps a little too unsympathetic.

The character's focused posture shows his fascination for his subject. He is really getting into the groove of teaching, even though his class might think it is the most boring subject ever! This is a fun pose with a clear classroom context, though you don't sense much of the character's grumpiness. I would like to use aspects of this overall gesture, such as its dynamic, triangular nature, as a basis for my final pose, but change the context to something more irritable.

When presenting a character in a pose it can be helpful to add a supporting character to further demonstrate the important aspects of their personality. This pose shows the character leaning over in a comical manner while frowning and gesturing grumpily at a student. The triangular negative space around his limbs reflects his irritable mood. I will use this option for the final pose.

This pose shows more of his dry, boring side, with him sitting down almost at the students' level to patronizingly correct everything they have been doing wrong. The shape of the pose is strong but it does not give the most exciting and active impression of the character's personality.

VALUES & COLOR

When playing around with values and colors, I bear in mind the character's personality and the time he lives in or grew up in. He is middle-aged, fairly humble and ordinary to look at, and is considered somewhat boring by others. To express this, I pick colors for his clothes that are not too vibrant or adventurous. Colors can be challenging, so I like to pick one or two colors and create different values within those hues, giving me a narrower starting point from which to create a color scheme.

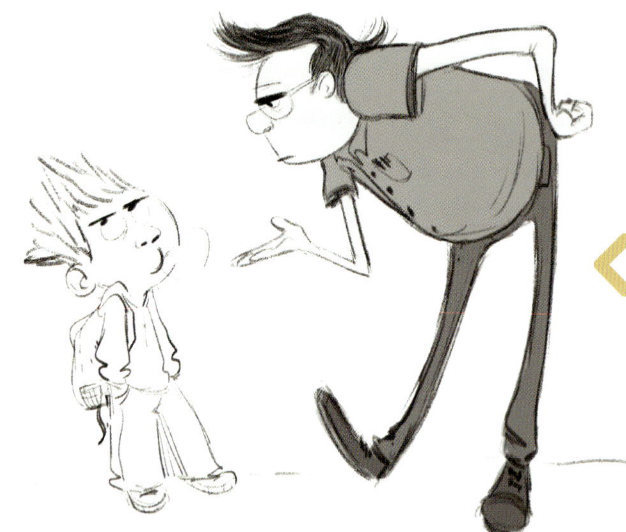

I use grayscale values to see which are the most important focal points of the design. I want to keep his skin tones and the whites of his eyes lighter compared to his shirt, pants, and shoes, which I imagine being muted and earthy colors, so the overall tone is not too dark.

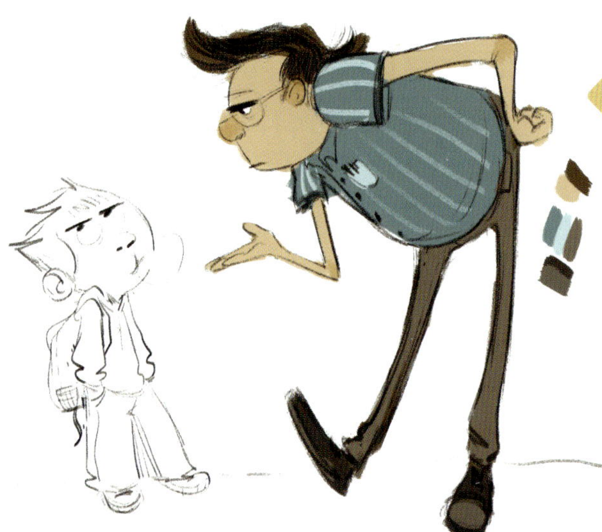

This color palette matches brown trousers with a blue shirt: a color pairing that is simple, classic, and ordinary in a way that fits the character. I like how the stripes of the shirt add some brightness to the design, but they are also slightly distracting.

I move on from blue to another earthy color combination, this time with a green shirt, dark jeans, and hints of gray for the shoes. However, this overall palette feels a little too dark.

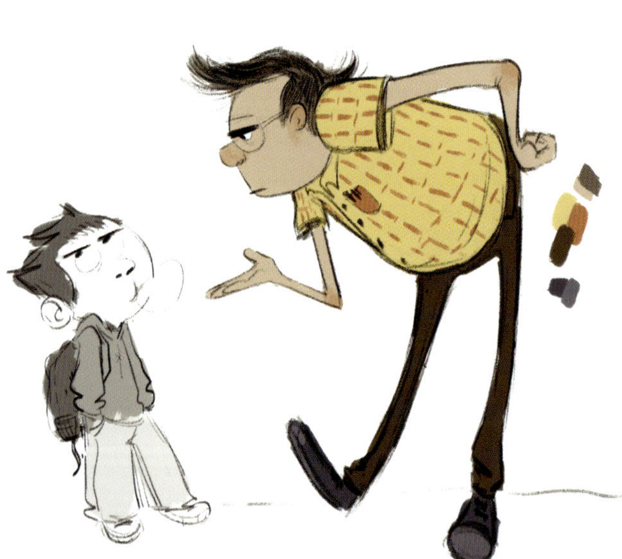

This yellow and brown color palette works the best for me. It is still earthy, but more desert-inspired, which suits his dry personality. The brown trousers and patterned shirt convey both the plain, boring side of his character and the side that tries to be young and hip. Yellow is often a happy, optimistic color, which creates even more of a fun contrast with his bad temper.

FINAL DESIGN

This final design clearly shows the character's personality and role, while also telling a story about something that might occur in his everyday life. His long legs give him the sense of impressive height, though he clearly fails to exert any authority in this scene! His large glasses and pocket full of pens are more subtle indicators of his academic role. The detail and texture in his hair gives it a frizzy look that makes him look even more bristly and irritable. I have made sure to leave his trousers and shoes plainer and less detailed than his shirt, to avoid distracting from the overall design. The bunching up of his brow and nose emphasizes his grumpy demeanor.

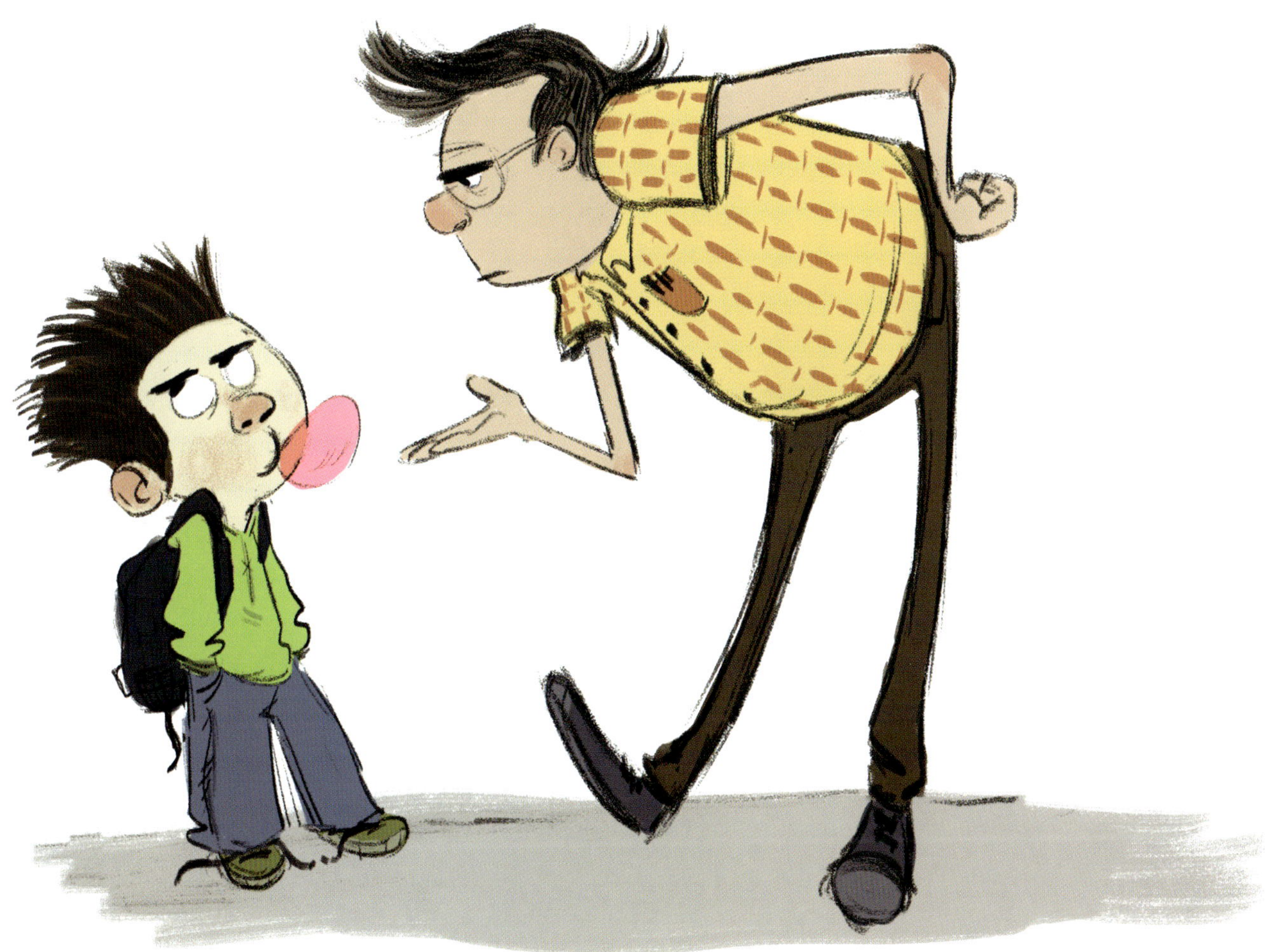

Final artwork © Stephanie Rizo Garcia

VARIATION 1:
SCHOOLBOY

IDEAS & RESEARCH

For this variation of the character, I want to design the same person as a young schoolboy. I already know what the main character's backstory is as an adult, but now I have to think about who he was as a child, and what he would have been like at school. I think it would be a fun twist if he was a rowdy young troublemaker at school, in total contrast to his strict, uptight older self.

I will take a small liberty with the adult character's timeline and imagine that he grew up around the nineties, rather than much earlier, because the clothing styles would be perfect for capturing his new personality. My research mainly looks at this new time period, helping me to understand how I might design a wardrobe and haircut that will suit his age and attitude.

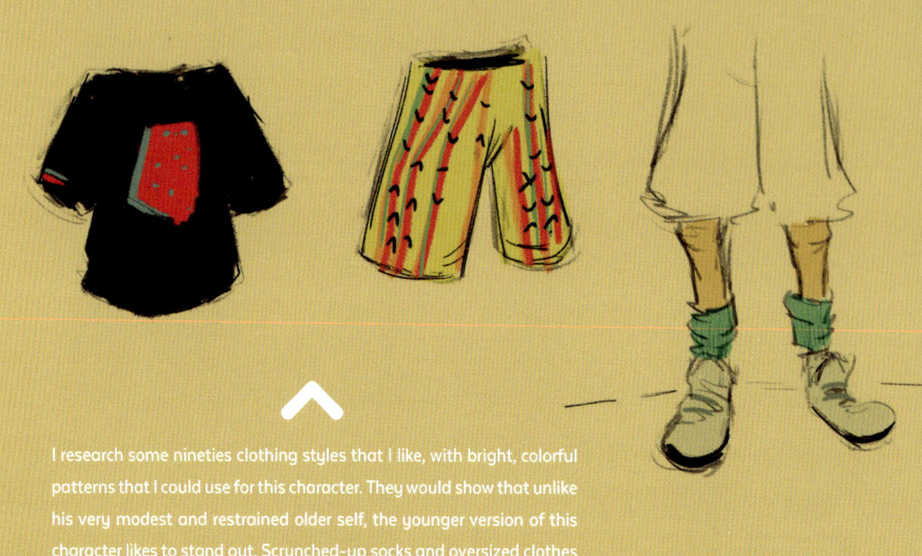

I research some nineties clothing styles that I like, with bright, colorful patterns that I could use for this character. They would show that unlike his very modest and restrained older self, the younger version of this character likes to stand out. Scrunched-up socks and oversized clothes would fit the era and show that he is a casual, laid-back person.

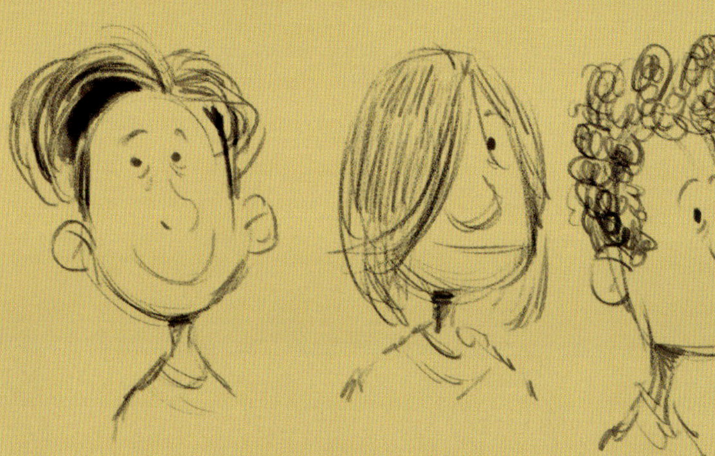

I research haircuts that would be appropriate to the time period, ranging from short to long hair. The adult character's hair is quite long, so I like the idea of this version having even longer hair to make him look unkempt. It would also tie the design in with the original character.

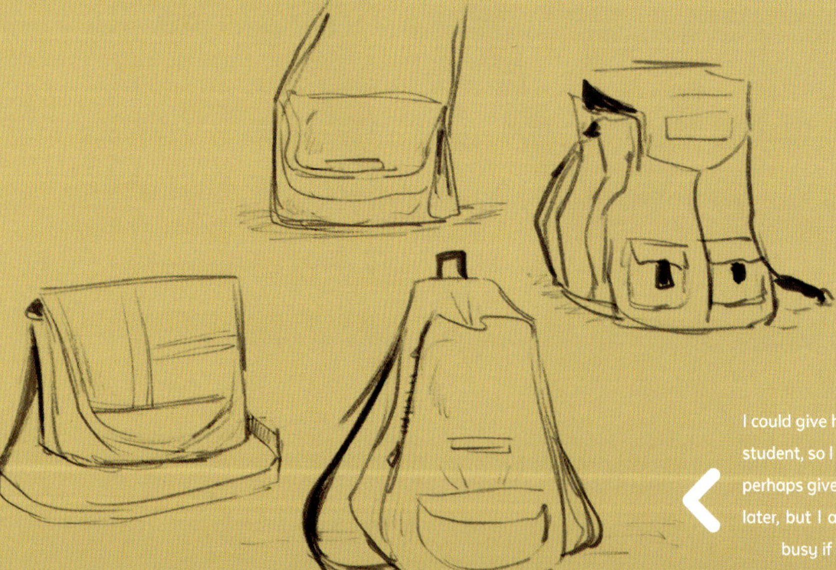

I could give him a backpack or satchel to clarify that he is a student, so I study a few different shapes and styles. I could perhaps give the bag some keychains and extra accessories later, but I also don't want to make his overall design too busy if his other clothes are patterned or colorful.

CHANGES

Many elements of the previous design will need to change to emphasize this new character's much younger age and different attitude, but I must also retain some details that will keep this design true to the original, clearly showing that he is the same person. With the research and sketches I have done, I know that his hairstyle, clothing, and accessories will have to change, but I must also think about ways in which I can "age down" the character's figure and give him younger proportions.

I want to change the character's hairstyle, giving him longer hair that will help to express his rebellious younger personality, creating contrast with the original design.

Making the character's nose and ears larger will help to show how much younger he is, though I will keep them the same general shape. I could also add a missing tooth to show that he is still growing up. This version of the character will also not have glasses, as if he doesn't need them until he is much older.

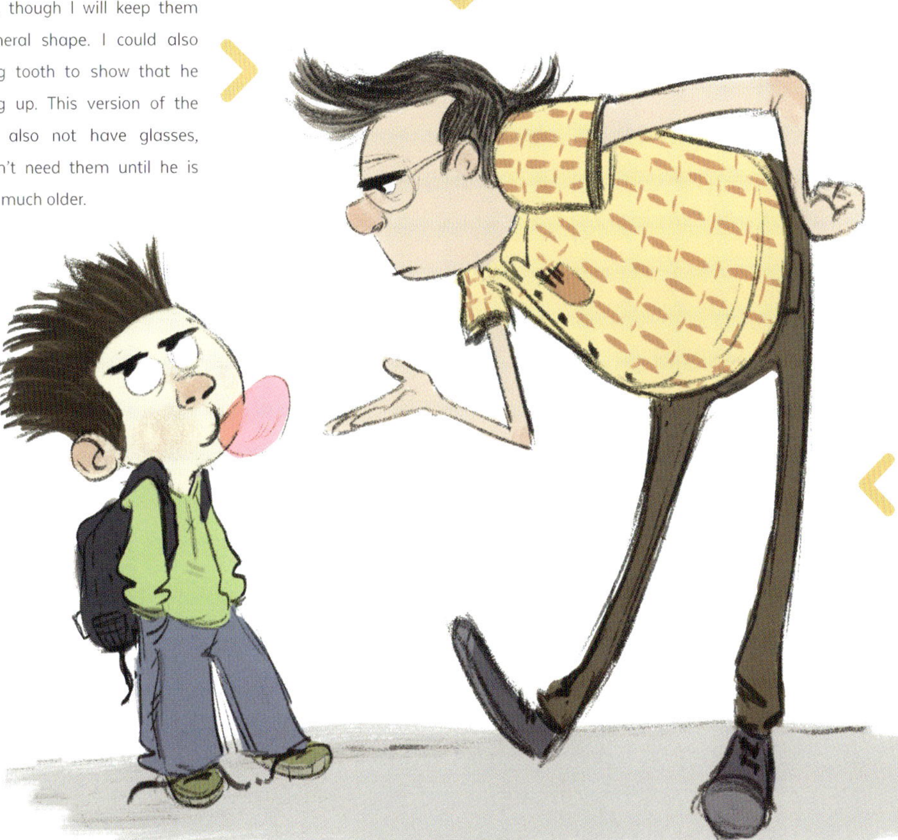

Because this version of the character is so much younger, his overall proportions will have to change. He will have a much larger head and more slender body, though his long, skinny limbs could be similar across both versions.

The character's clothing style will be quite different, showing how he is growing up in a different era. Giving him an oversized shirt and loose shorts would help to emphasize his youth and carefree attitude, compared to when he is older and his clothes are muted and tight to fit his uptight personality.

THUMBNAILS

Giving the character a bigger head and ears will help to indicate his younger age, while his large nose will be a common feature between the young and adult versions. I play around with different hairstyles, referencing the research I carried out into retro fashions. I also sketch various styles of clothing, exploring their different shapes and potential poses, trying to capture a scruffy look with oversized garments and a rebellious attitude. I decide that the third thumbnail captures the right sense of rebelliousness while also maintaining a resemblance to the adult version.

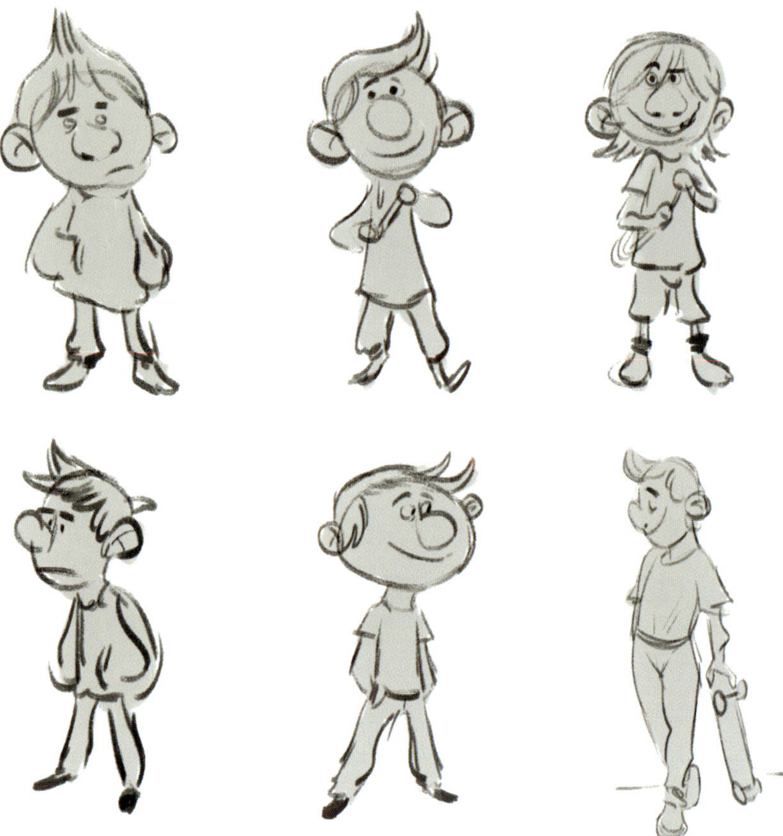

BASIC SHAPES

Though this version of the character has very different proportions from the original, his underlying shape language is quite similar. His head is round, creating contrast with his thin body and limbs, and though his hairstyle has changed, the pointed ends of his hair will help to make his face the focal point of the design in the same way as before. The body and legs create a triangle that points to his face while the extra large ears protruding from the core shape are comical and endearing.

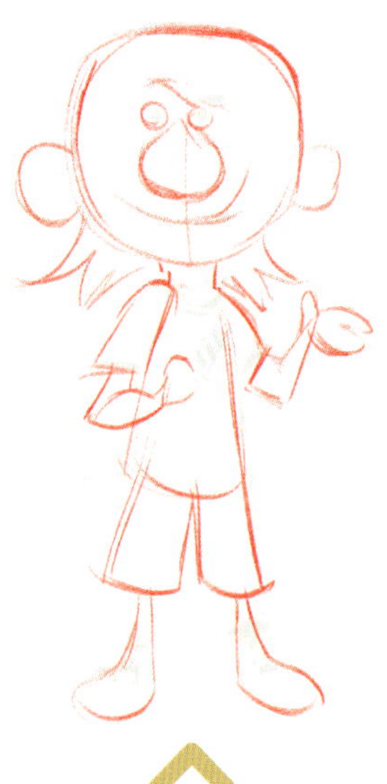

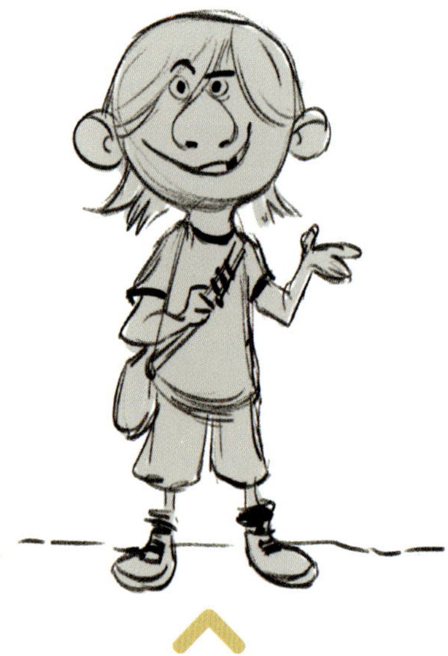

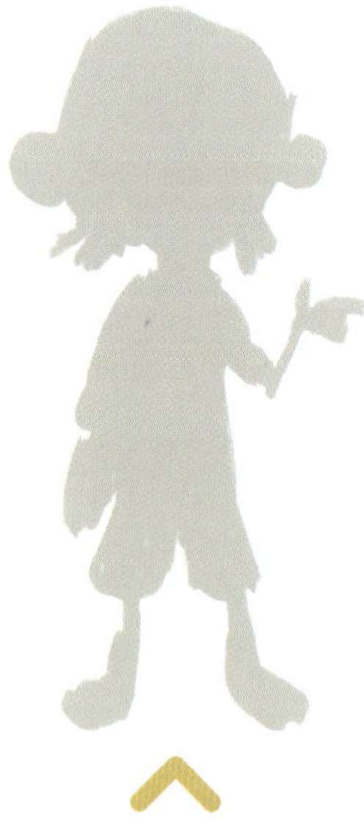

The character's head will now be the biggest shape compared to his overall body, as children always have proportionally larger heads. His skinny legs are carried over from the adult version, though he is clearly much shorter in height now.

I lightly sketch over the shapes to define more of his design and start to add some accessories that he might have for the final design, such as a backpack and pens. These will help to indicate his place in a school setting.

When the character is viewed in silhouette, his ears and hair create a distinct negative space shape around his head. This makes the design more clear and appealing to the viewer's eyes.

DETAILS

I have made sure to include some key details from the adult version, such as his large nose, sneakers, and long hair. Though his hair has a similar texture to his adult self, and will have a similar color, in this version it covers his face and eyes more. This makes him look more scruffy, and contrasts with the big forehead and receding hairline of the original character.

The character's long shirt, baggy shorts, and scrunched-up socks fit his overall scruffy, carefree look, and help to emphasize his age and smaller stature.

A skateboard is a great accessory for this character, making him feel more confident and cool, and fitting with his youthful retro style. It may not be used for his final pose, but it is a detail worth considering.

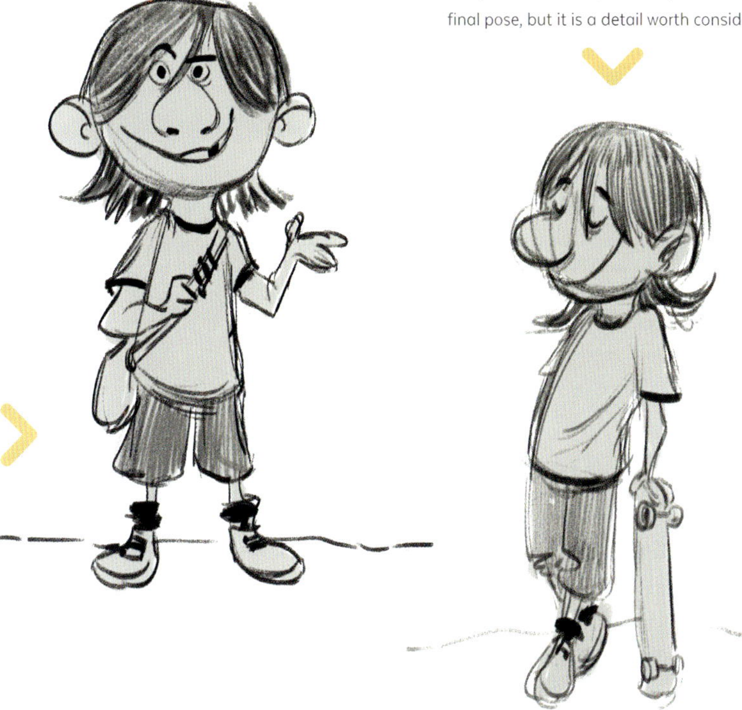

EXPRESSIONS & POSING

I know that this character is carefree and a troublemaker, so I want his poses to explore ideas of how he behaves in class, and how he acts when he is caught doing something wrong at school. I don't just think about the character's gesture and mood, but also think about how I can tell an interesting story or create an intriguing scenario with each pose. As I did with the schoolteacher, adding small props can help with this.

This is a strong pose for conveying the character's personality. Tipping his chair back on two legs, resting his feet on the desk, and blowing a spitball across the room all indicate that he is an unruly student who doesn't care about the class. Adding his jacket on the floor shows that he's scruffy and disorganized. I will use this pose for my final design.

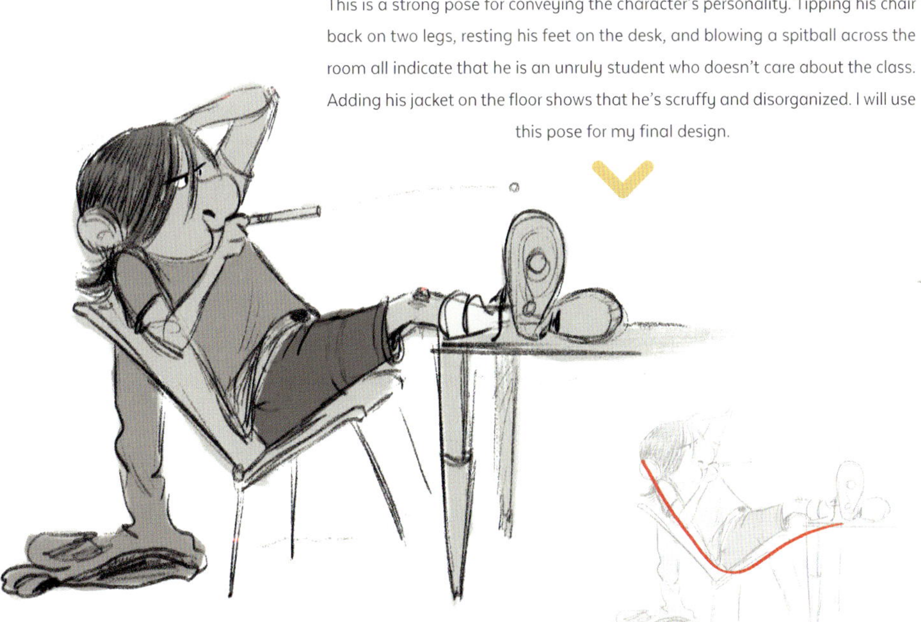

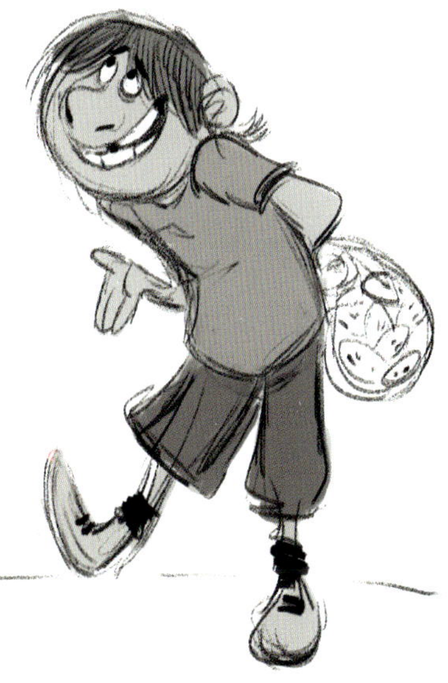

I like this pose because it shows him clearly as a wily troublemaker, having stolen some cookies from the teachers' lounge. This gesture shows his personality well, but the sense of setting is not specific enough; I would prefer to suggest that he is in a classroom environment.

VALUE & COLOR

I want to change the color scheme from the adult version, except for his skin and hair color, which should be similar to indicate that this is the same person. I use some bright colors inspired by my research into retro fashions, and make them slightly mismatched to show that this character is quite an untidy and careless dresser. These brighter pops of color are balanced out by the more neutral colors elsewhere in each palette, such as the colors of his shorts, skin, and hair.

The strongest contrast is around the character's head and face, drawing the viewer's attention to his expression; the dark tone of his shorts will balance out the brighter tones of his shirt and socks.

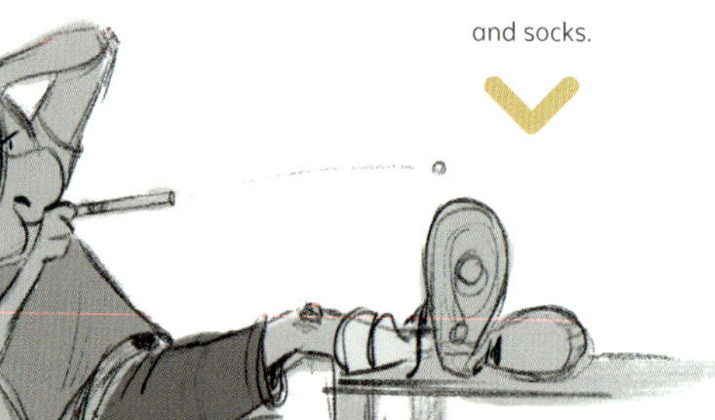

This color scheme balances both bright and neutral colors, which I think makes it strong and eye-catching. The colors of his shirt and socks pop out the most, adding a lot of fun to the design, while his jacket, shorts, and hair are more dark and neutral for balance. I will use this palette for my final design.

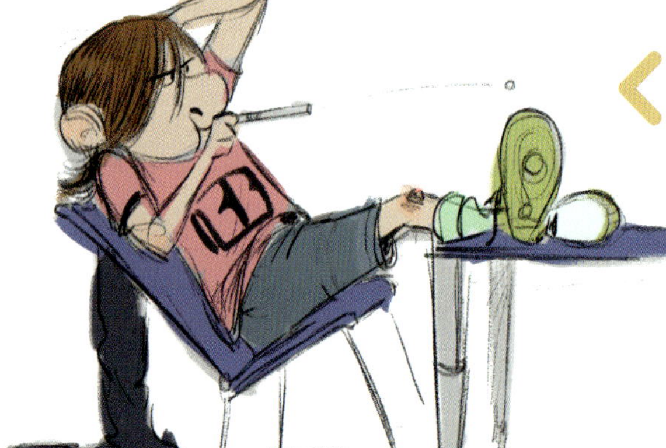

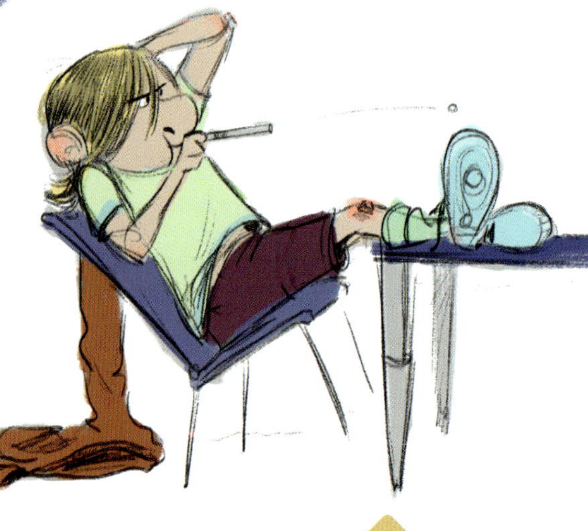

I try a palette with lighter hair, as it's not uncommon for people to have fairer hair when they are younger. However, this seems slightly too far removed from the adult design, and might confuse the viewer unnecessarily. It is important to repeat key information across designs if the audience is to understand the connection.

This color palette doesn't have the same fun, mismatched look, but the muted colors make him look more moody and sullen, like a grumpy teenager. The colors and pattern on his shirt are visually pleasing, but this scheme perhaps isn't bright and young enough to enhance his mischievous attitude.

FINAL DESIGN

This final version of the character works well because we still get a sense of the older character's physical features, despite the drastic changes in proportion and clothing. His long brown hair, large nose, and classroom environment carry over from the previous design, but his clothing, posture, and color scheme indicate a younger, more laid-back personality. The extreme horizontal brow is reminiscent of the grumpy face in the original design. The sharp bend of his gesture, which almost creates an L-shape or triangle, reflects his rebellious, challenging personality and laid-back attitude. This shape is also very similar to that of the original design.

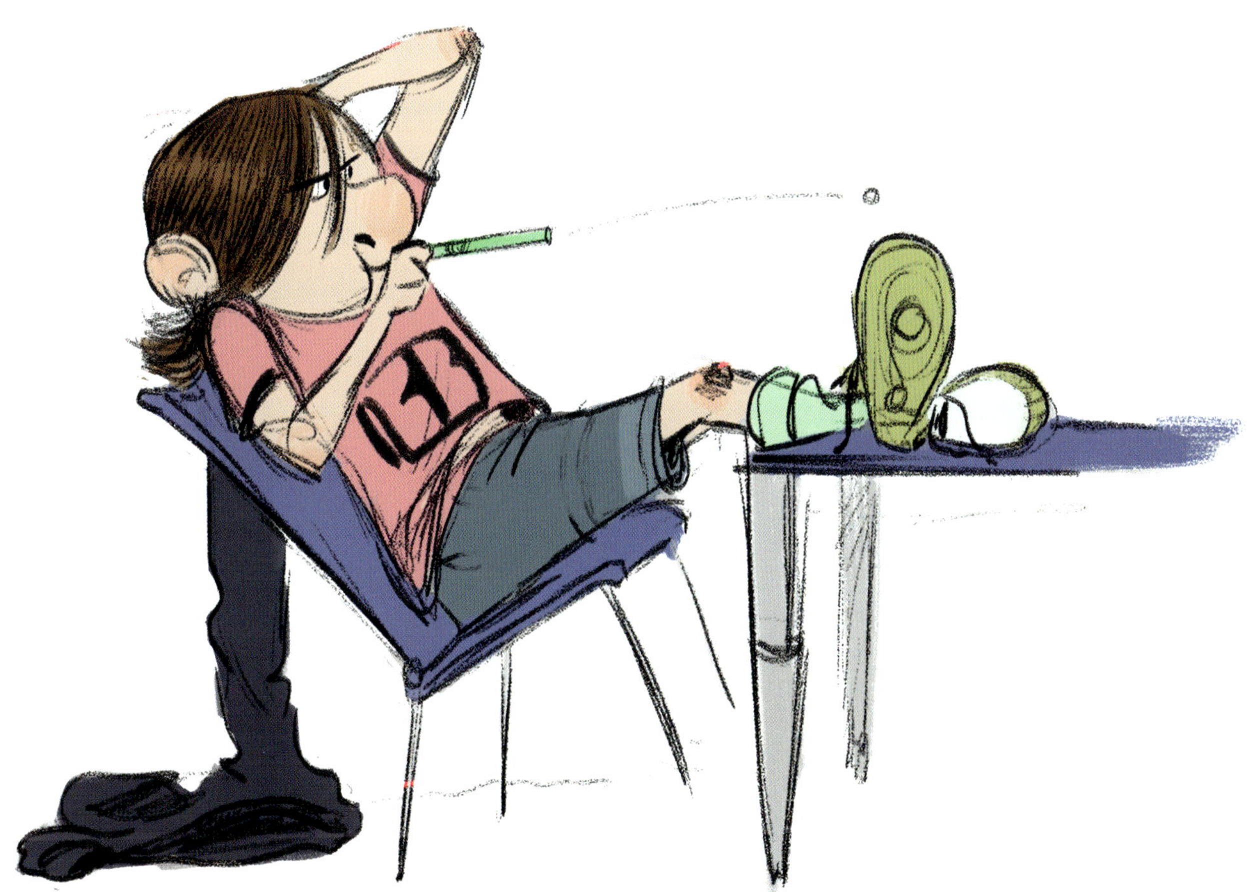

Final artwork © Stephanie Rizo Garcia

VARIATION 2:
VICTORIAN SCHOOLMASTER

IDEAS & RESEARCH

This variation of the schoolteacher character will be translated into a historical context, becoming a strict Victorian schoolmaster. I don't want to change too much of his original physical appearance, so that the characters have a clear resemblance, but this new design will require an entirely new costume.

In my research, I find that many teachers from this period were older and pale-looking; they were sometimes overweight, or looked physically imposing in their layers of formal clothes, or both. Research into the caps and gowns from that time will be key in shaping the overall design of this character, as they add large new visual elements that the modern-day teacher did not have.

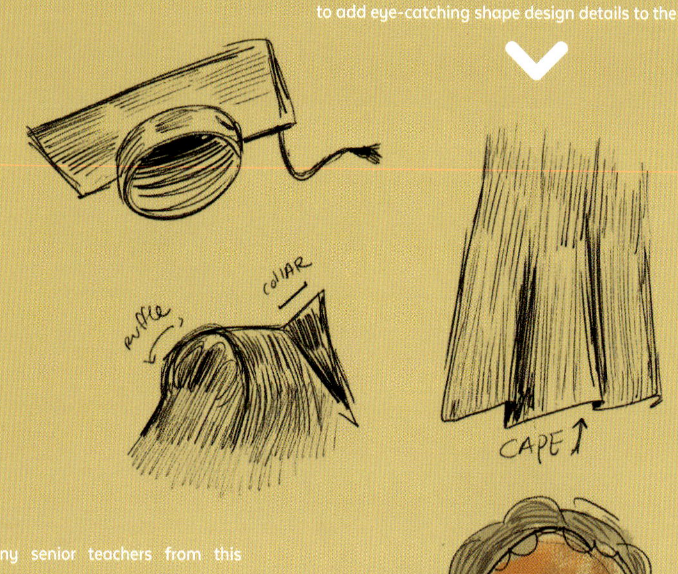

Caps and gowns of the time did not often have much detail on them, but the gowns sometimes had interesting folds around the shoulders and at the bottom. The caps have a great combination of small, wide, round, and square shapes. These details could help me to add eye-catching shape design details to the character.

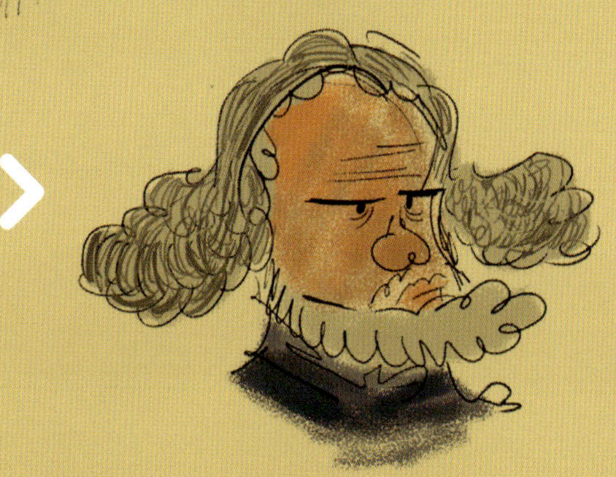

Many senior teachers from this time period seemed to be older, with white or gray hair. I want to incorporate this into my new design to indicate that this character is far older than the original version.

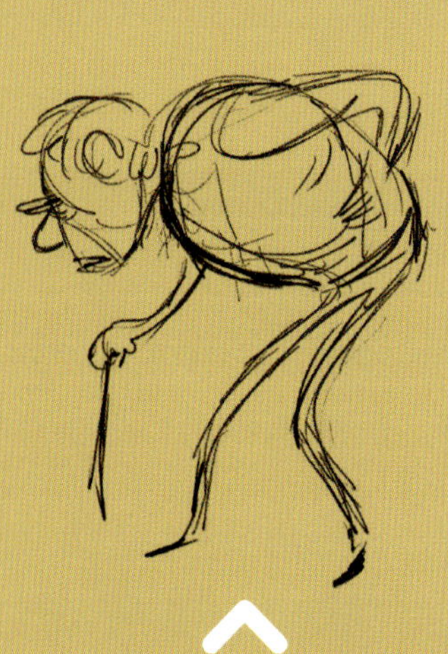

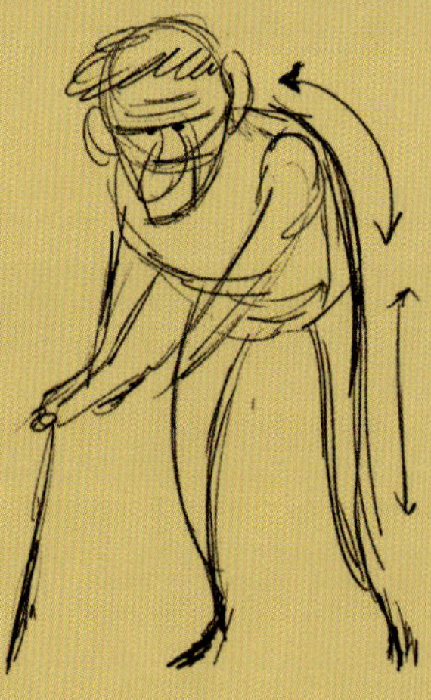

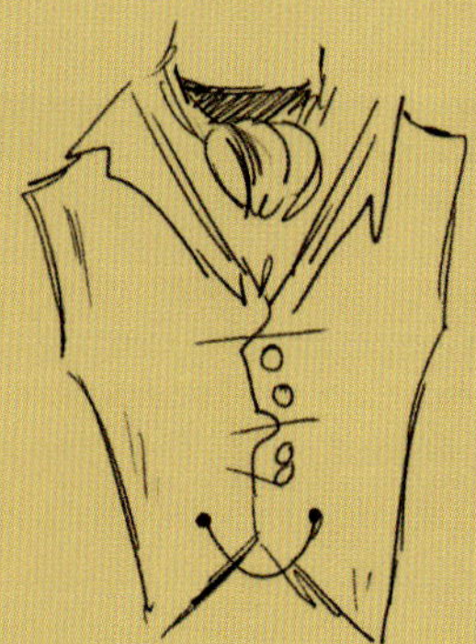

Changing the posture to a stoop would be another way to help make the Victorian version feel older than the original. I sketch some gestures that might help me when creating my thumbnails later.

Clothing from this time period often featured a lot of layers. This teacher might wear a buttoned shirt with a tight vest, an ascot tucked in the front, and other accessories such as a pocket watch and pins. These would help to clearly indicate the historical era. They could also enhance his stuffiness.

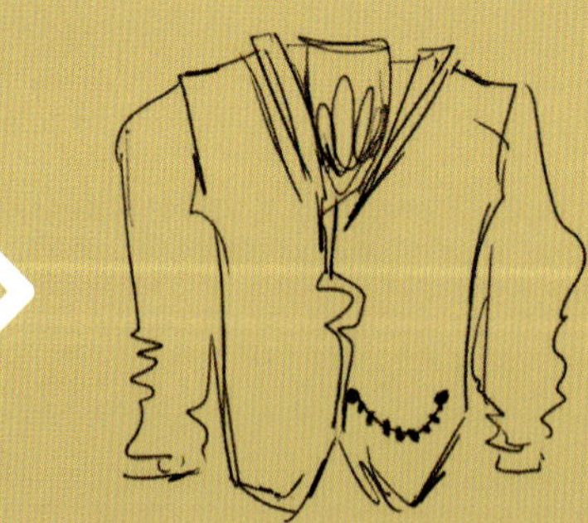

CHANGES

I want the character to show the same personality and have some physical features in common with the original teacher, but I will need to adjust many elements of his design and costume based on the research I have done. I may also need to change his body shape to balance out the new costuming, and change elements such as his hair and props to suit the era. The color palette may also have to change in order to make it more appropriate for the historical setting.

I do not want to change the character's hairstyle completely, but I will give his hair a trim to better suit the look and feel of a severe Victorian-era schoolmaster.

Increasing the character's age could give a greater sense of authority, so I will "age up" my original design by giving him a larger belly, white hair, and more facial wrinkles. People's noses often seem to get bigger with age, so that is another detail I could change.

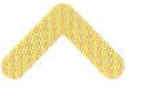

The character's new costume will likely involve a long cape, so I need to change his body shape slightly to keep his overall proportions in balance. I could achieve this balance by shortening his legs.

I need to replace many of the clothes and accessories based on my research. Giving him a cap and gown will convey his role clearly, and an old-fashioned pocket watch could replace his pocket full of pens as an accessory.

THUMBNAILS

Victorian schoolmasters wore a lot of layers: shirts, suits, caps, and gowns. In my thumbnails, I explore different variations of his body shape to see whether a stocky or tall character would carry all of these costume details effectively.

I focus on rounded shapes that will make him seem large and impressive, contrasting with the long, severe lines created by his cape and cane. I find myself leaning towards the second thumbnail, as his stockier overall shape gives him the most sense of commanding gravitas.

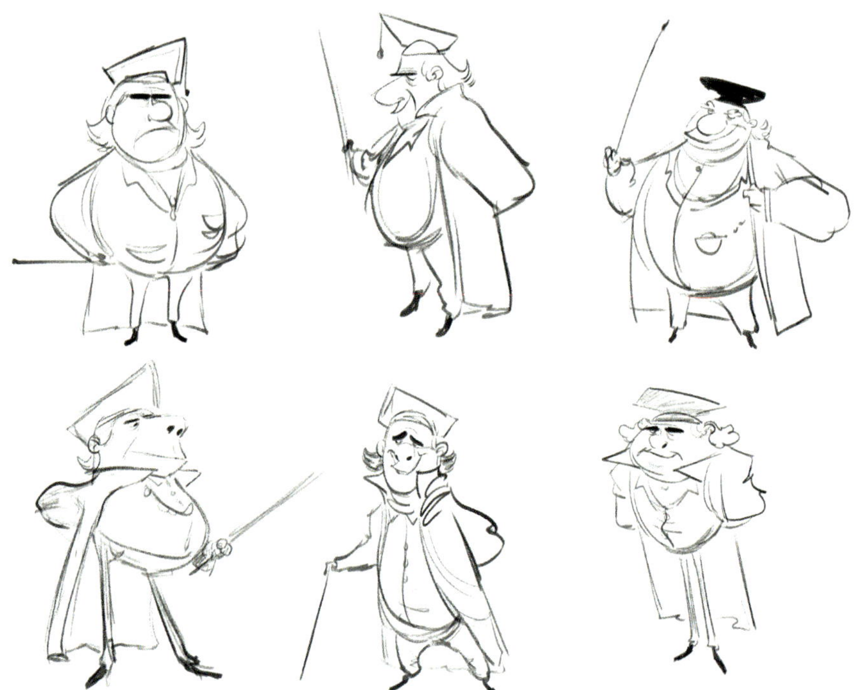

BASIC SHAPES

The Victorian schoolmaster will still have some shapes in common with the original character design, such as a round head, round body, and relatively skinny legs. However, the angular forms of his cap and gown give his overall shape a completely different feel, making him appear more bulky and authoritative. His legs are also shorter so that his cape does not become overly long.

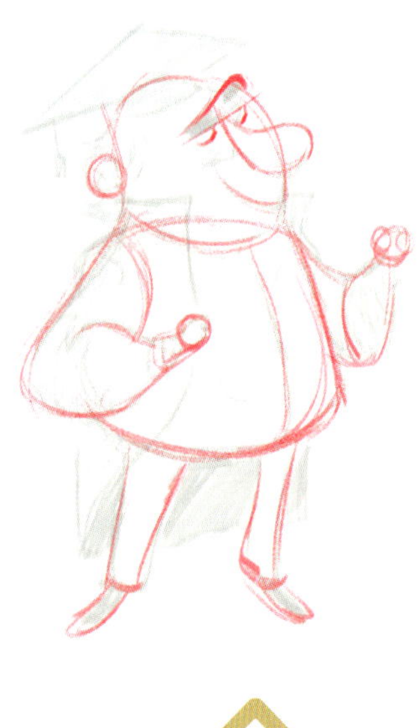

To add to the age and gravitas of the character, I use rounded, heavy shapes. Balancing his round belly with thinner legs creates a strong visual contrast that is still very relatable to the original design.

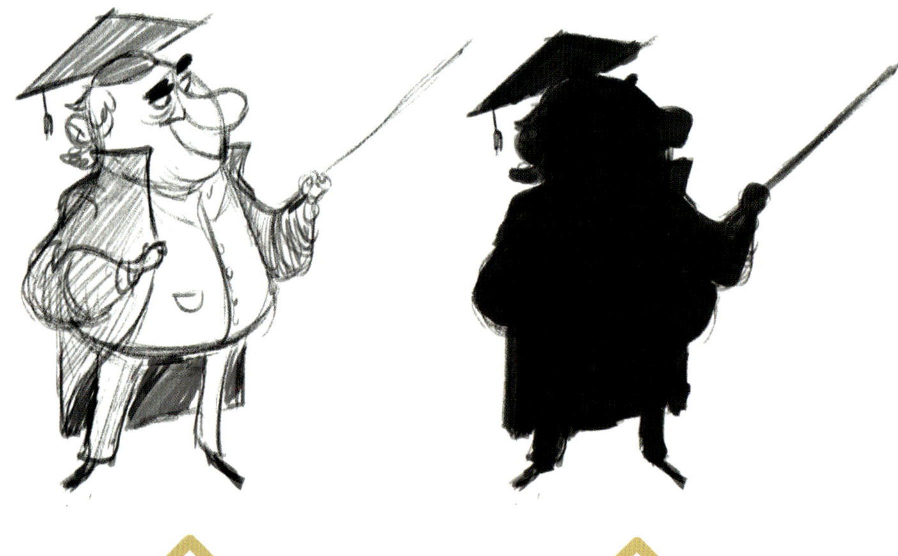

This rough pass builds up all the elements I would like to add to his costume. His tightly buttoned shirt will make him look appropriately uptight and reserved, and also helps to clearly show the curved form of his body.

I check that the gown doesn't overpower his whole design. It helps that the gown ends before it touches the ground, and that he has an angular cap and long cane; these elements keep his outline distinct.

DETAILS

I want to make sure that even though I have changed the time he lives in, the character's personality has not been lost. He is still the same boring, strict teacher as he was in the present-day version, which is communicated by his formal appearance, frowning brows, and severe mouth. Adding more wrinkles around his eyes and face help to show that this character is also much older.

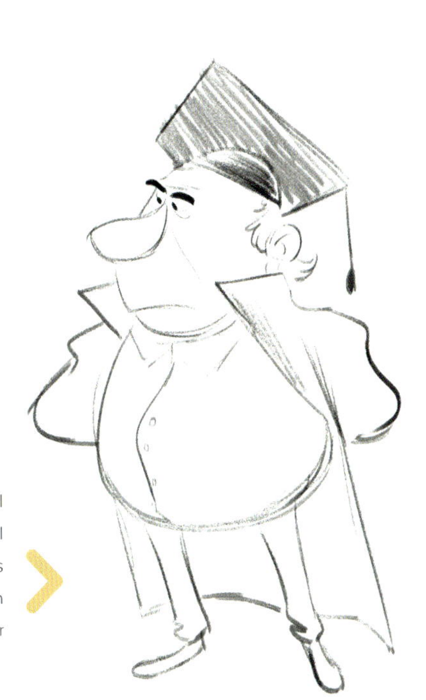

I make sure that the character still has several facial features in common with the original designs, such as his expressive black eyebrows and the wrinkles around his mouth. Though much of his head is concealed by the cap, his visible hair is also similar between the two versions.

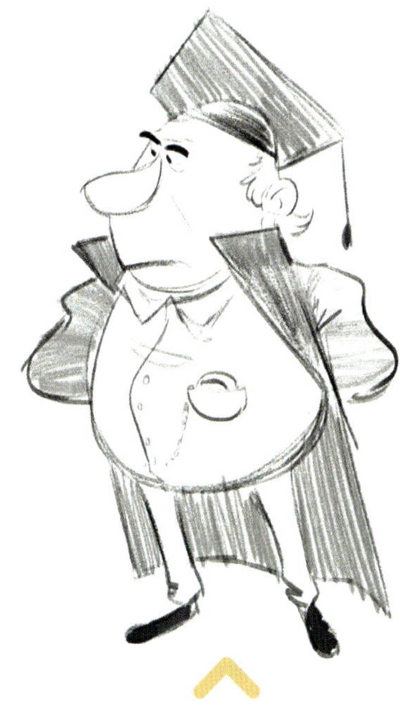

A pocket watch on a chain is an old-fashioned and practical accessory that helps to convey the time period, while also updating the original version's pocket detail to something more Victorian.

EXPRESSIONS & POSING

I want the pose and expression to convey the character's strict, stuffy personality. His posture needs to look more stiff and less dynamic than the original version, showing his age, but still with similar manner-isms. The cap and gown provide additional tools for showing the mood and action of each pose.

This pose shows the character leaning forward to his students' eye level, giving him a sense of authority. It is reminiscent of the final pose from the original design, but the change of costume and proportions makes him seem much more overbearing and superior. I will use this pose for the final image.

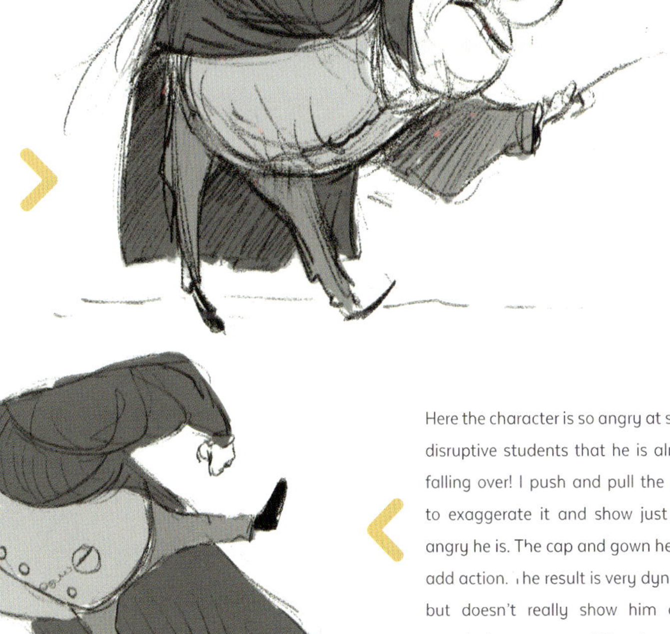

Here the character is so angry at some disruptive students that he is almost falling over! I push and pull the pose to exaggerate it and show just how angry he is. The cap and gown help to add action. The result is very dynamic but doesn't really show him as a boring, grumpy old teacher.

VALUE & COLOR

I refer back to my research to choose appropriate colors and values for a Victorian character. I will use colors that are much less saturated, fitting the fashions of that era, as well as fitting his severe personality. His overall color palette and values will be much darker in tone, though his skin tone remains similar to his modern-day counterpart.

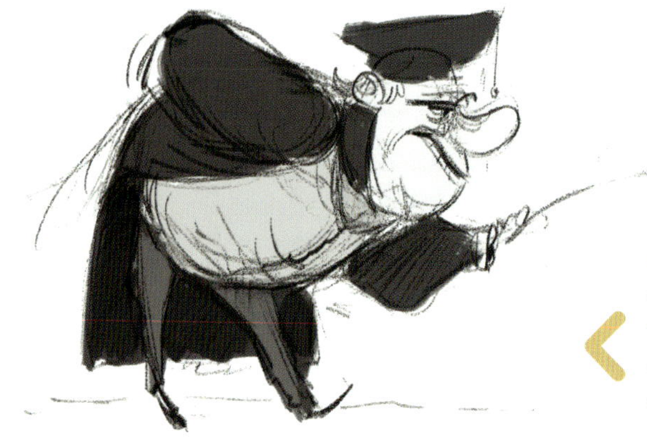

I want to keep a balance of light and dark areas, with quite sharp contrasts to emphasize the severity of the character. His skin is pale and his gown and cap are dark, so I create balance between them with a lighter shirt.

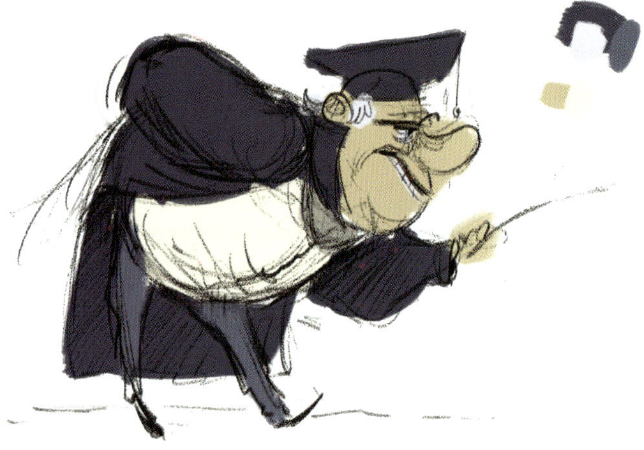

This palette uses shades of blue with a warmer skin tone, but the overall temperature is a little too warm. I would like the hues to be feel colder and more severe.

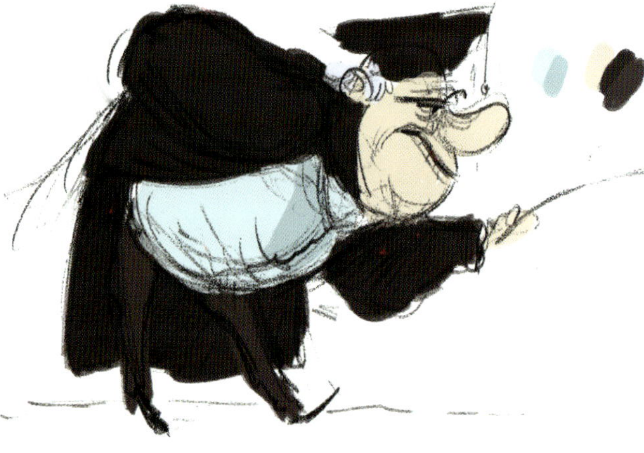

A more brown-gray robe is a strong complement for the pastel blue shirt, but the general impression is somewhat too monochrome, and some elements of his body, such as the legs, are easily lost.

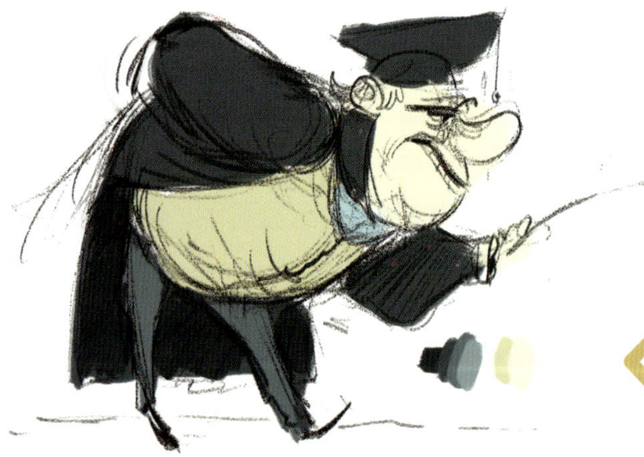

This is the color scheme I will use for the final design, as it captures both the time period and the character's moody personality very well. A typical gown would be pure black, but in order to show the details, I use cold green and keep the trousers lighter. Beige and light blue for his shirt and undershirt add a pop of restrained color without looking too bright and cheerful for the character.

FINAL DESIGN

The final version of the character works well in translating the original design into a historical setting. Even though his body shape and clothing style have changed, the viewer still gets a sense of his original hairstyle, facial features, gestures, and general temperament. His pale skin and wrinkles emphasize his age, with a hint of blush around his nose and cheeks to add a warm accent, drawing attention to his face. His cap and gown create a strong impact both in terms of contrast and shape, giving him a bold silhouette in which his profession is instantly recognizable. The sharp angles of his arms, legs, hat, and collar enhance his severity.

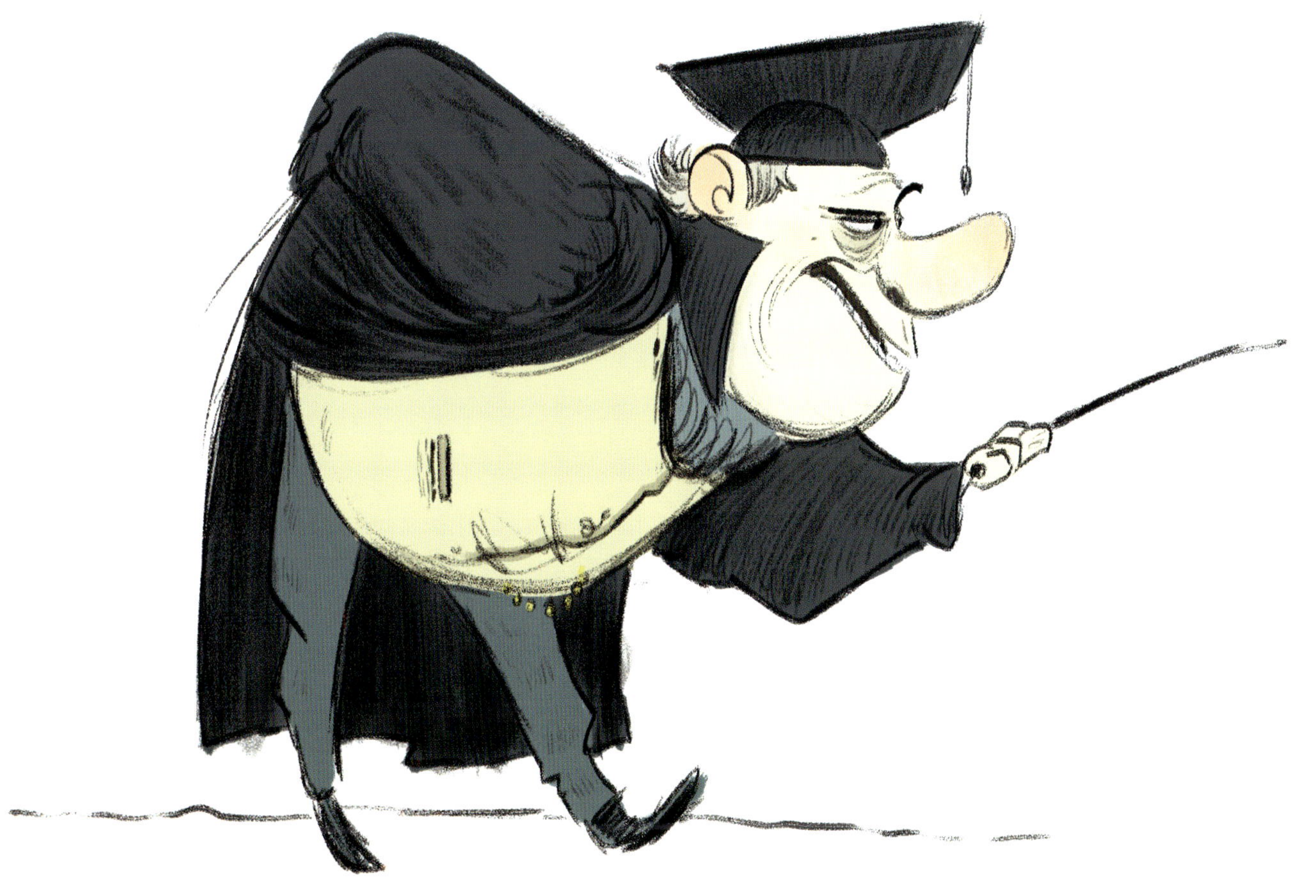

Final artwork © Stephanie Rizo Garcia

VARIATION 3:
ACADEMIC BAT

IDEAS & RESEARCH

When translating the schoolteacher into a different species, I start by considering which animal would best represent his personality. I decide I like the idea of him as a bat: something small, grumpy-looking, and very intelligent. A design with a small round body and long ears is almost a fun inversion of the human character's round torso and long legs, allowing me to explore some interesting proportions without losing some of the shape language of the original design. In my research, I explore different types of bats, and elements of their bodies that I can incorporate into this new design.

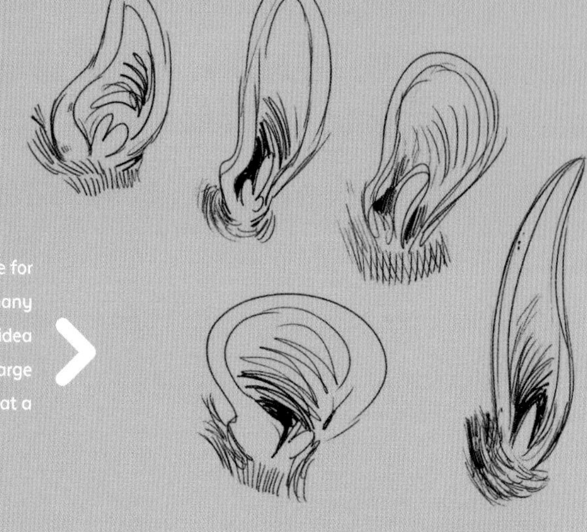

Large ears will be a key feature for a bat character, so I study as many variations as I can. I like the idea of the character using his large ears to catch any little noise that a student might be making.

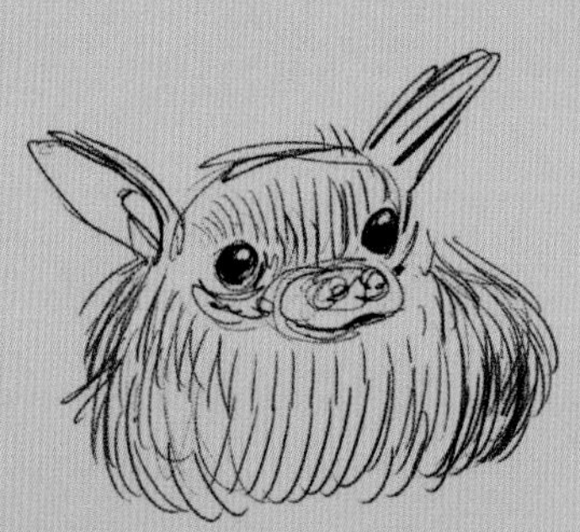

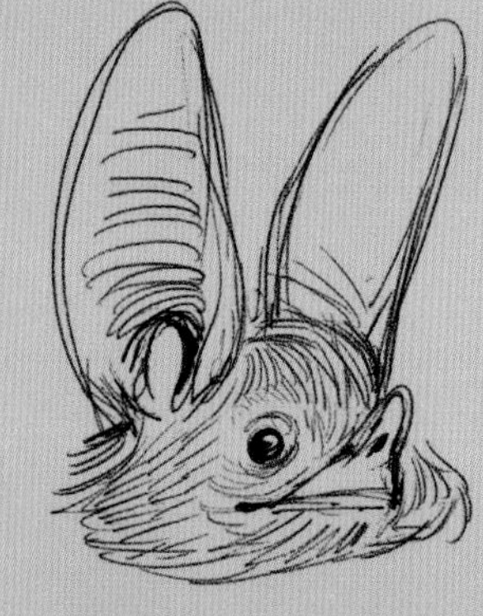

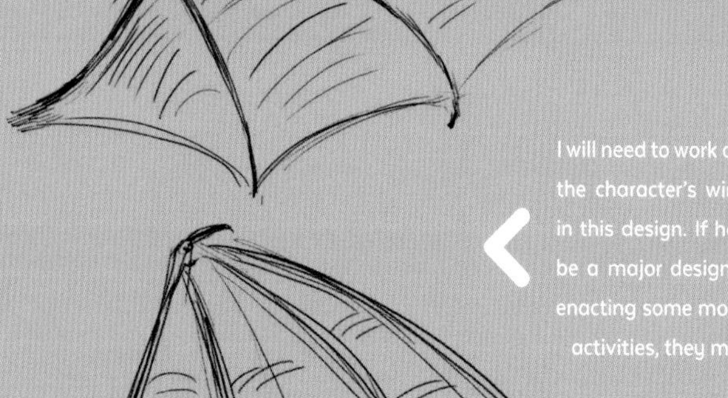

I will need to work out the degree to which the character's wings will be noticeable in this design. If he is flying, they would be a major design element, but if he is enacting some more "human" classroom activities, they might be folded away.

One of the prominent features of the human version was the hairstyle, but this bat would not have hair designed in the same way. I like the puffy mane and facial fur that some bats have, so I could use those as a substitute hair element.

I like the idea of the character wearing a little vest or waistcoat, making him look smart while accommodating his wings. Details such as a pocket watch or pin would fit well on a vest and relate the design back to previous versions. I play with the idea of a decorative moth-shaped pin; bats often hunt moths, so a moth pin would be something that this character might personally enjoy and relate to.

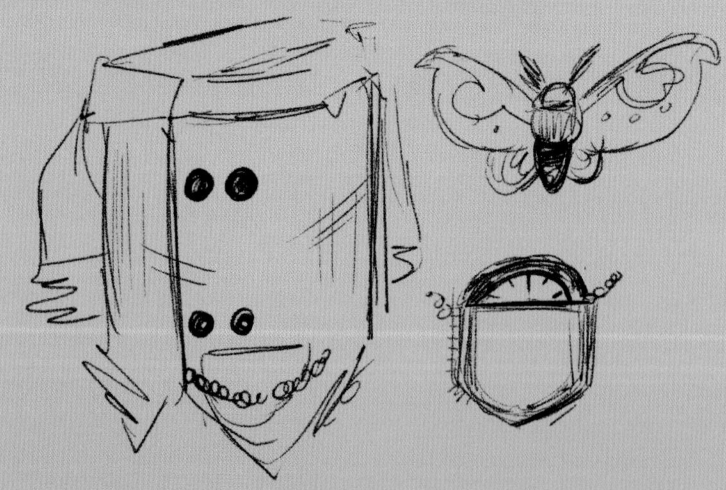

CHANGES

Following my research, I know that the character's overall body shape, hairstyle, and elements of his costume will have to change in order to portray him as an animal. However, there are still some design elements that I want to keep from the human version, as they are true to his personality.

As the character is now an animal, I have to think of a way to adapt the distinctive hairstyle to his new body. Some bats have mane-like fur, and I like the idea of using this as a way to give him "hair."

The character's face will have to change completely, but some features will lend themselves well to his bat form, such as small eyes and a pronounced nose.

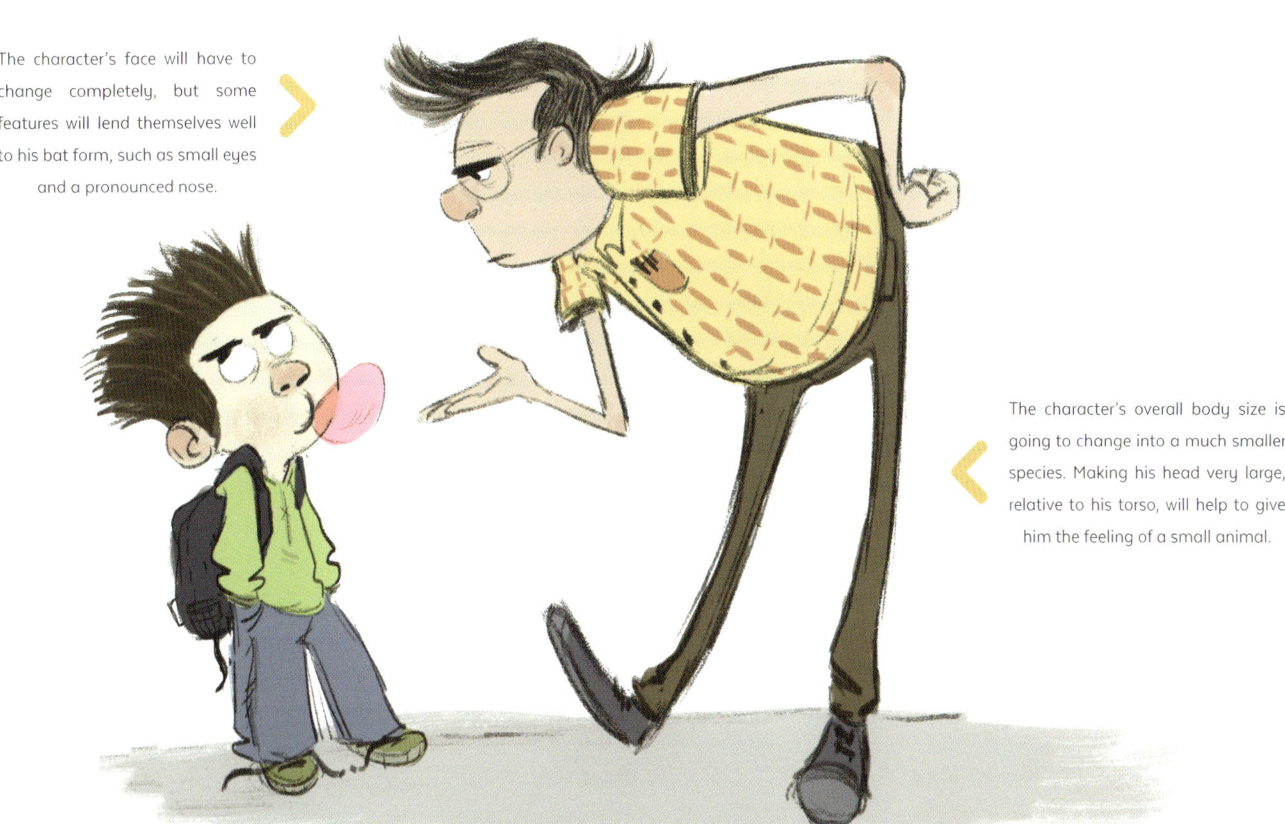

The character's overall body size is going to change into a much smaller species. Making his head very large, relative to his torso, will help to give him the feeling of a small animal.

The character's outfit will change completely to fit his bat body. It may be necessary to limit the number of garments he wears and accessories he is able to carry, as he will now be small and winged.

THUMBNAILS

Looking back through my research and references, some bats have rounded ears, some have long ears, and some have more or less fur than others. These ideas give me material for some very different variations of body shapes in my thumbnails.

I know that I want to keep the character's body short and round, like that of his human counterpart. I find myself favoring the third and fifth thumbnails, as he has suitably rounded, stocky proportions that are balanced out with comically large bat ears. This contrast makes the design fun to look at, and conveys the idea that he is a very small creature.

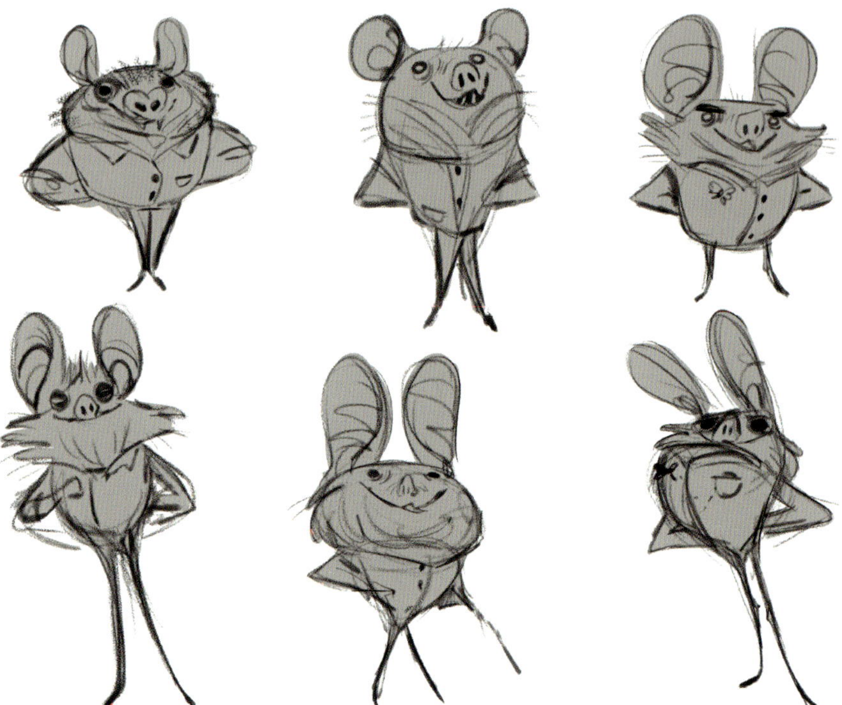

BASIC SHAPES

The most notable new element of this design is the character's large ears. They help to give him a more commanding air, as the original design's long, thin legs did, while also emphasizing the character's small size by making his head even larger. His legs are a much less prominent feature, as they are not a notable part of a bat's anatomy and I want to keep the focus on his face.

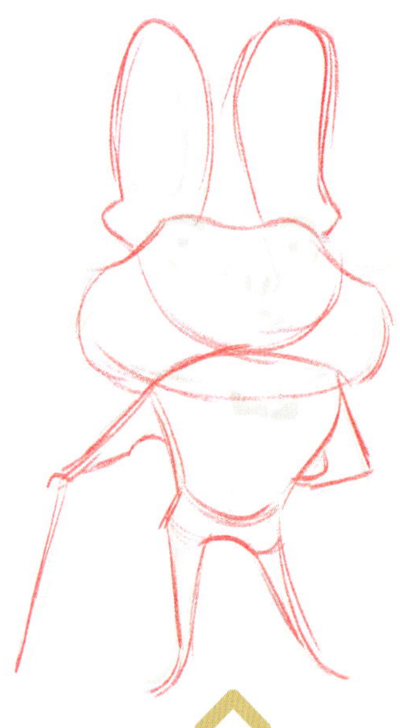

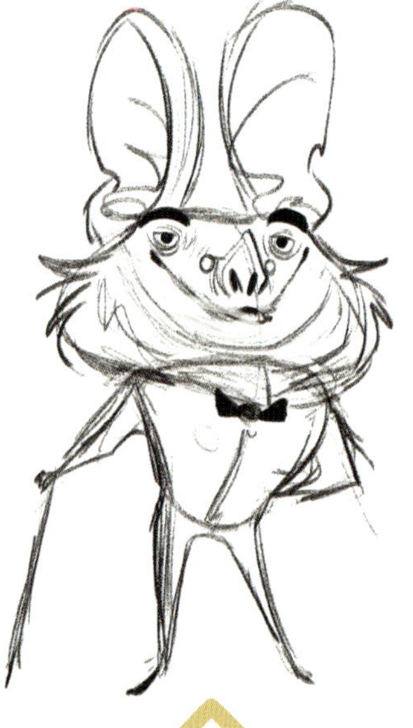

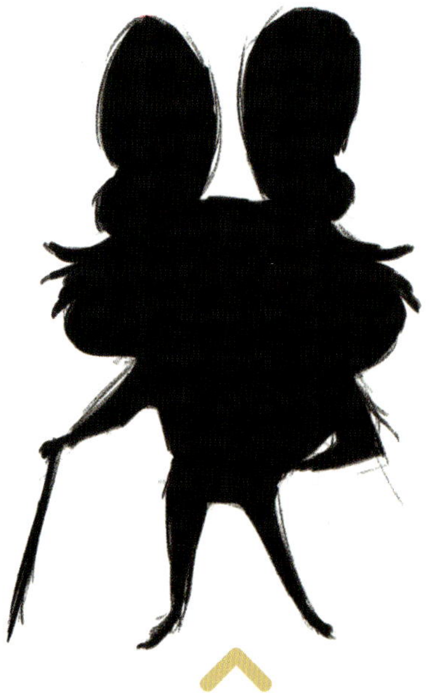

Ovals, circles, and triangles are key to the shape language of the character's bat form. Giving him a large, round head is a reference to the original design, and his legs are similarly thin but downplayed here to keep the attention on his more bat-like features.

I lightly sketch over the shapes to define them, building up the forms inspired by the original design, such as the round chest and skinny legs. The fur on his cheeks is flicked outwards, recalling the haircut of the earlier human versions.

The resulting silhouette is strong because it has a distinct negative space shape around the character, with a few furry areas that clearly indicate his animal nature. The balance of large, medium, and small shapes gives the silhouette a clear visual appeal.

DETAILS

Like his human version, this bat has thick eyebrows and small eyes, with some wrinkles around the eyes to indicate that he is tired and not especially young. His eyebrows will be great for creating poses and expressions later, whether he is smirking and self-important, or stern and frowning. His tightly buttoned vest is reminiscent of the original character's shirt, while being a simpler garment so as not to distract from his large head and furry neck.

Bats have poor vision, so it makes sense for the character to have spectacles. Their round shape creates an interesting counterpoint to the large triangular nose, and adds to the prim academic look. Like previous incarnations of the character, he has a small pocket, which could be used to carry a pocket watch like the Victorian version; this would suit the old-fashioned style created by his vest and spectacles.

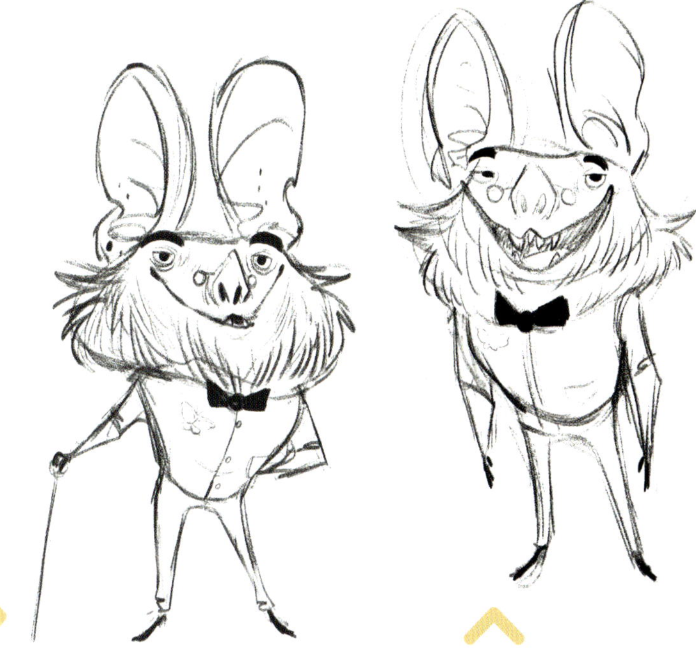

Bats are nocturnal and often hunt for moths, so I like the idea of him wearing a moth pin, indicating that it is his favorite insect. Along with the bow-tie, and similar to the casual sneakers in the original version, this eccentric personal touch suggests that he sometimes tries to be fun – at least in his own mind!

EXPRESSIONS & POSING

I want the character's poses to express his core personality as a stuffy teacher, though now I also need to incorporate bat-like movements or behavior into his actions. As bats are nocturnal animals, I decide it would be fun and appropriate for him to be teaching astronomy to his class.

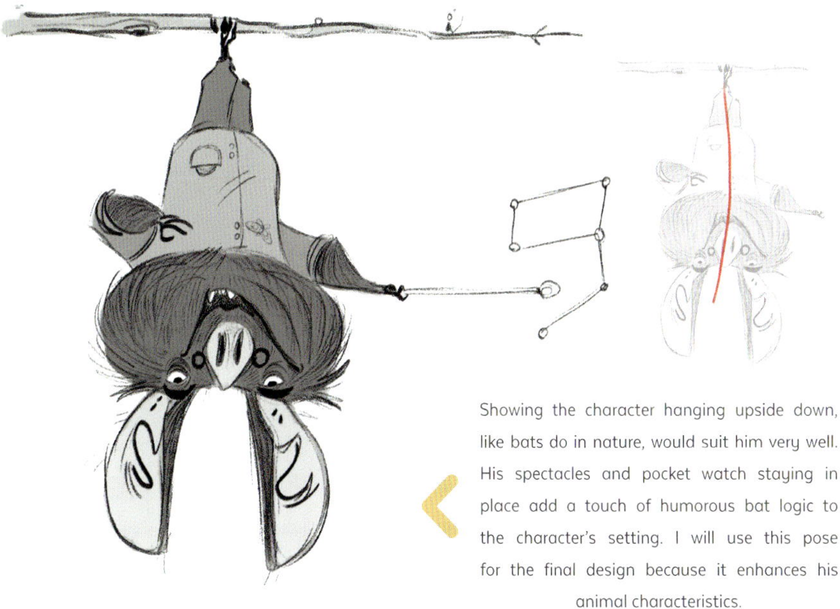

Showing the character hanging upside down, like bats do in nature, would suit him very well. His spectacles and pocket watch staying in place add a touch of humorous bat logic to the character's setting. I will use this pose for the final design because it enhances his animal characteristics.

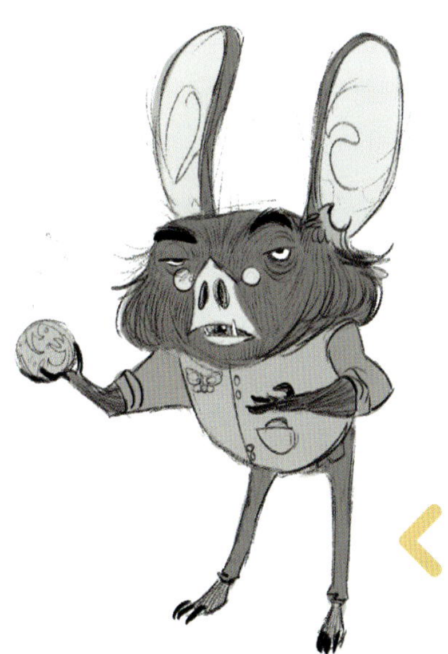

This pose is more directly reminiscent of the character's human self, standing upright and showing how bored and annoyed he is with teaching an inattentive class. His lowered eyelids and wrinkles underneath his eyes show how weary he is. However, this pose is slightly too human and doesn't make the most of his nature as a bat.

VALUE & COLOR

I know that the character, being a bat, will have darker values overall. However, I still want to explore different options and ensure that the character does not become too dark. I want to incorporate more natural hues, fitting his animal form, and maintain some yellowish or earthy colors that recall the original design. Eventually I settle on a purple color scheme because it represents an earthy night-time feel without being too cold and dark.

His overall tone is quite dark, fitting a bat that is mostly active at night. However, I make sure not to lose important features such as the face, where lighter tones on his nose and ears balance the design and draw the viewer's eye.

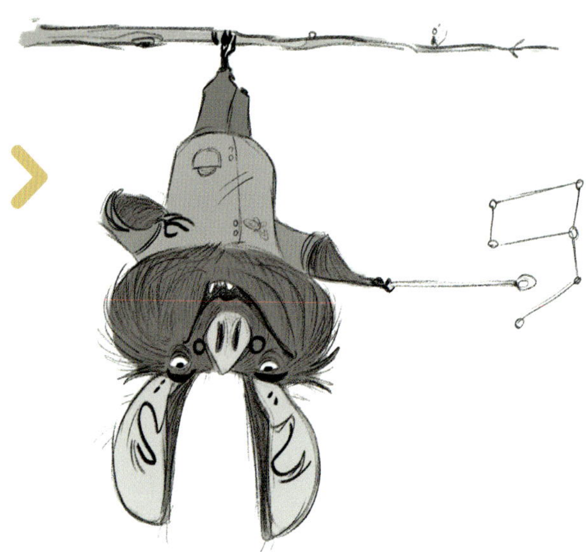

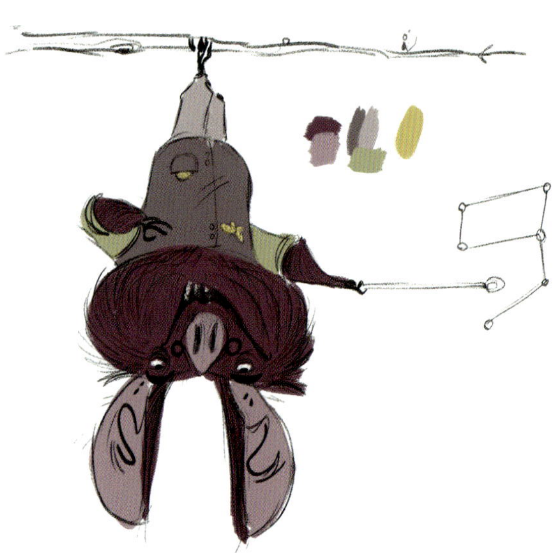

This purple-gray palette is low-key and earthy without being dull. The green sleeves and yellow accessories add complementary accents, and the more neutral colors of the vest and trousers keep the palette from being too busy. I will use this palette for my final version of the design.

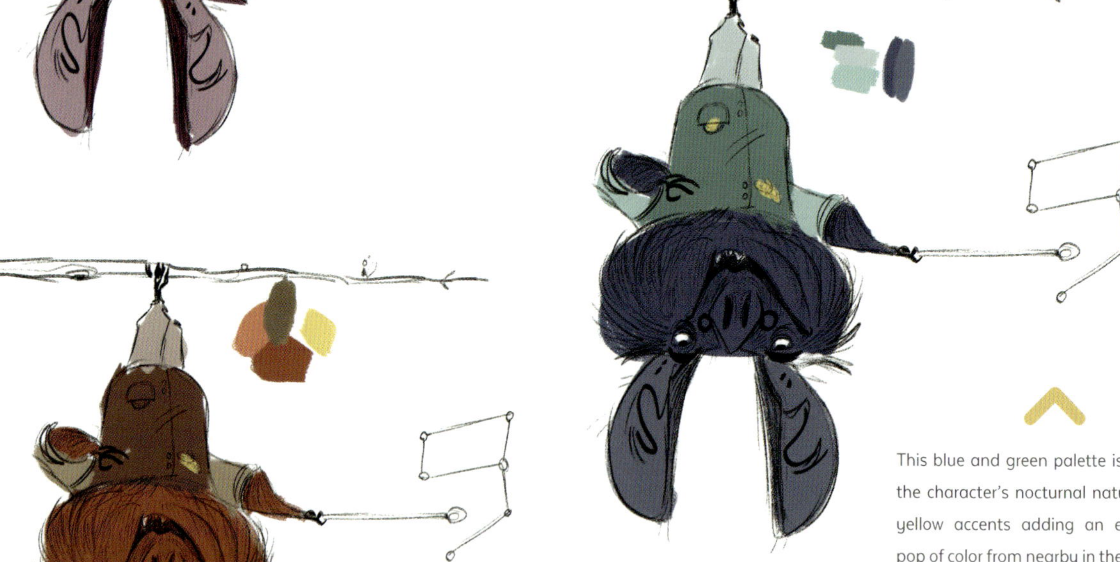

This warm, earthy palette is the closest in hue to the original human design, but perhaps doesn't give the strongest impression of him as a nocturnal creature with a morose temperament.

This blue and green palette is inspired by the character's nocturnal nature, with the yellow accents adding an eye-catching pop of color from nearby in the color wheel. However, the blue is very far removed from the original version of the character, as well as from the color of bats.

FINAL DESIGN

Changing this character into an animal was a challenge, but with the help of research and references, I feel I have made a strong design that stays true to the original character. Elements such as the contrasting body shapes, hair texture, and facial features help to capture the essence of his human form, while his new animal form creates the opportunity for fun, appealing shapes and poses that catch the viewer's attention. The character's smile shows his interest in the subject he is teaching, while his tired eyes and dark color palette help to convey the gloomier side of his personality.

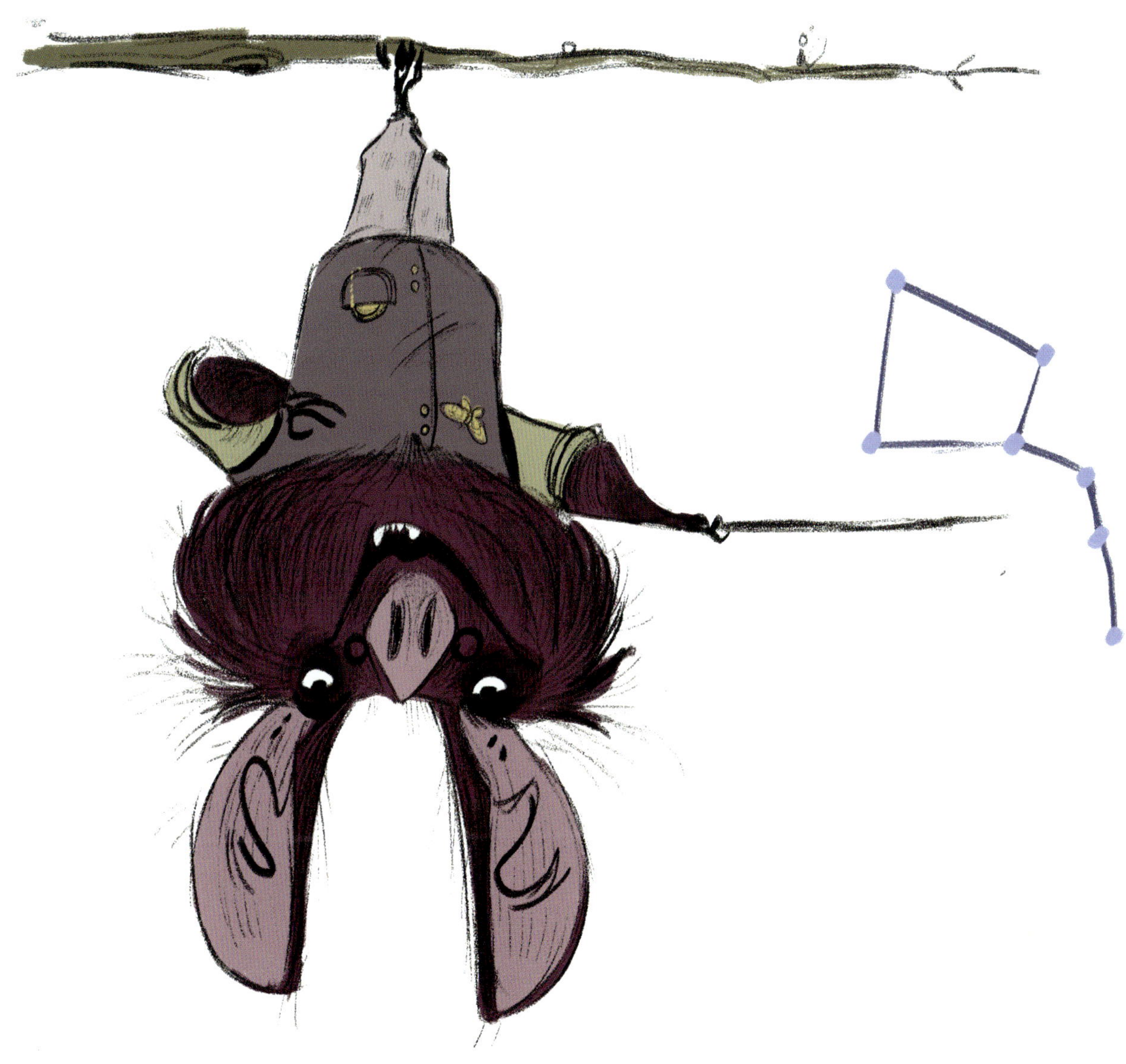

Final artwork © Stephanie Rizo Garcia

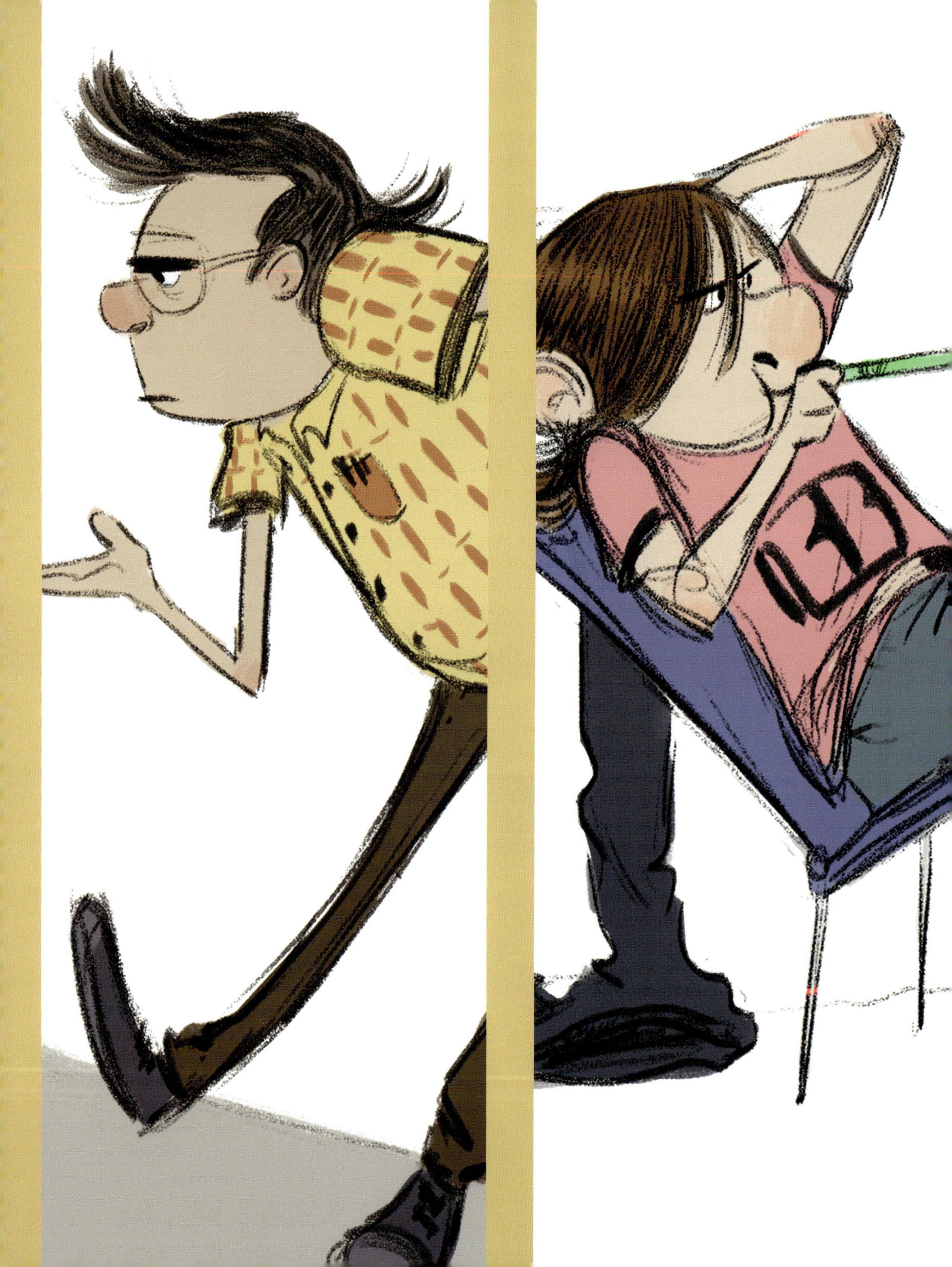

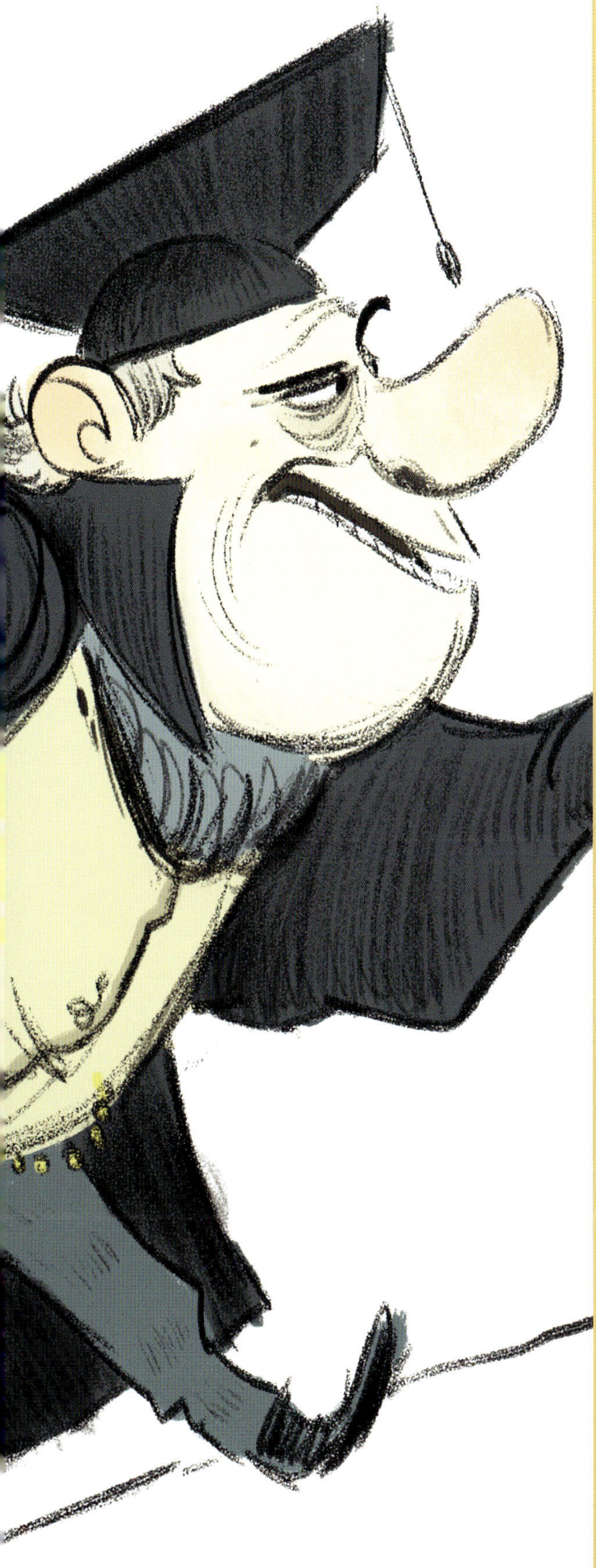

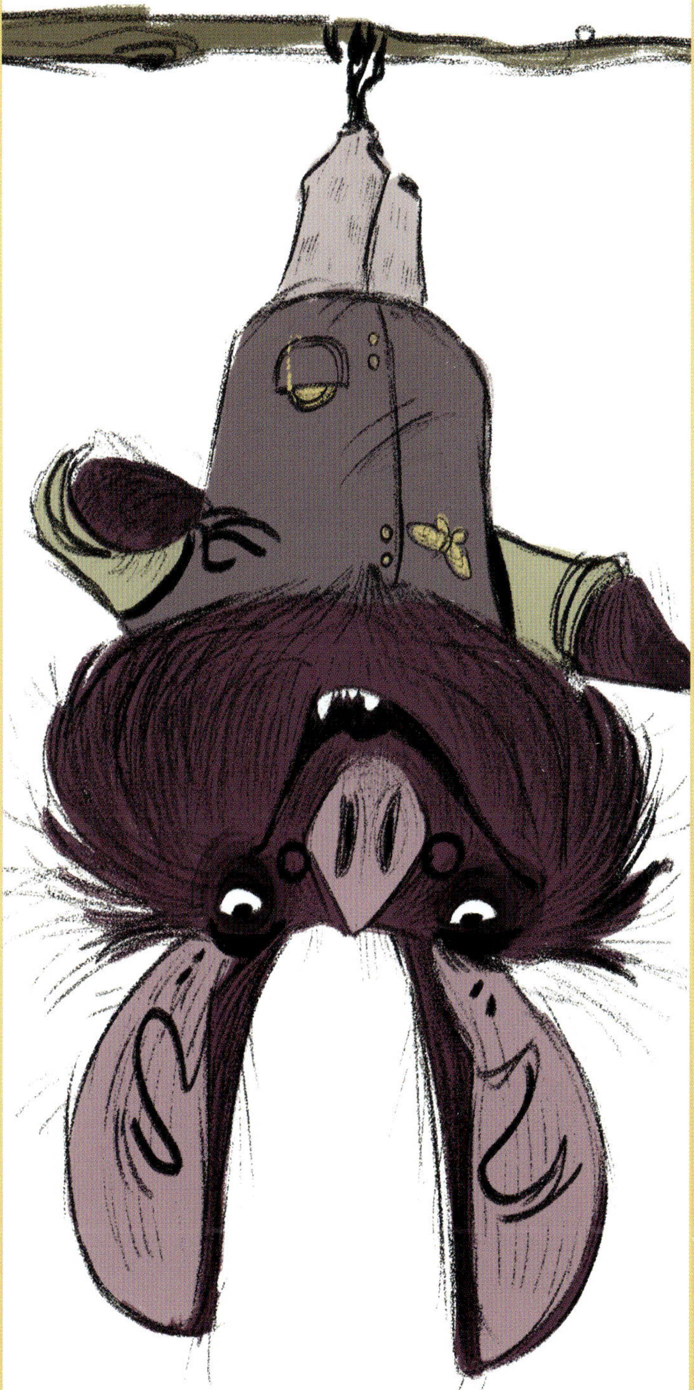

HEROIC SPACEMAN

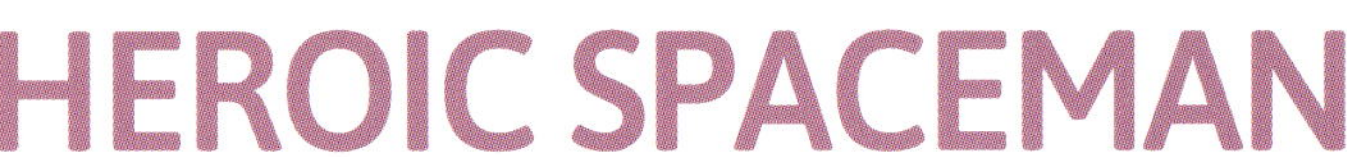

BY LUIS GADEA

In this chapter, animator Luis Gadea creates a heroic space adventurer with costuming inspired by retro sci-fi.

VARIATIONS

- AGED SPACEMAN
- FANTASY ADVENTURER
- SPACE MONKEY

FOCUS

Luis' style uses clean geometric shapes and bold silhouettes to create dynamic characters with features that pop. This approach is perfectly suited to 2D animation and designing for comics.

Pay close attention to the use of shape and color, keeping your choices simple and efficient, and don't shy away from revising areas until you achieve the strongest overall shape language.

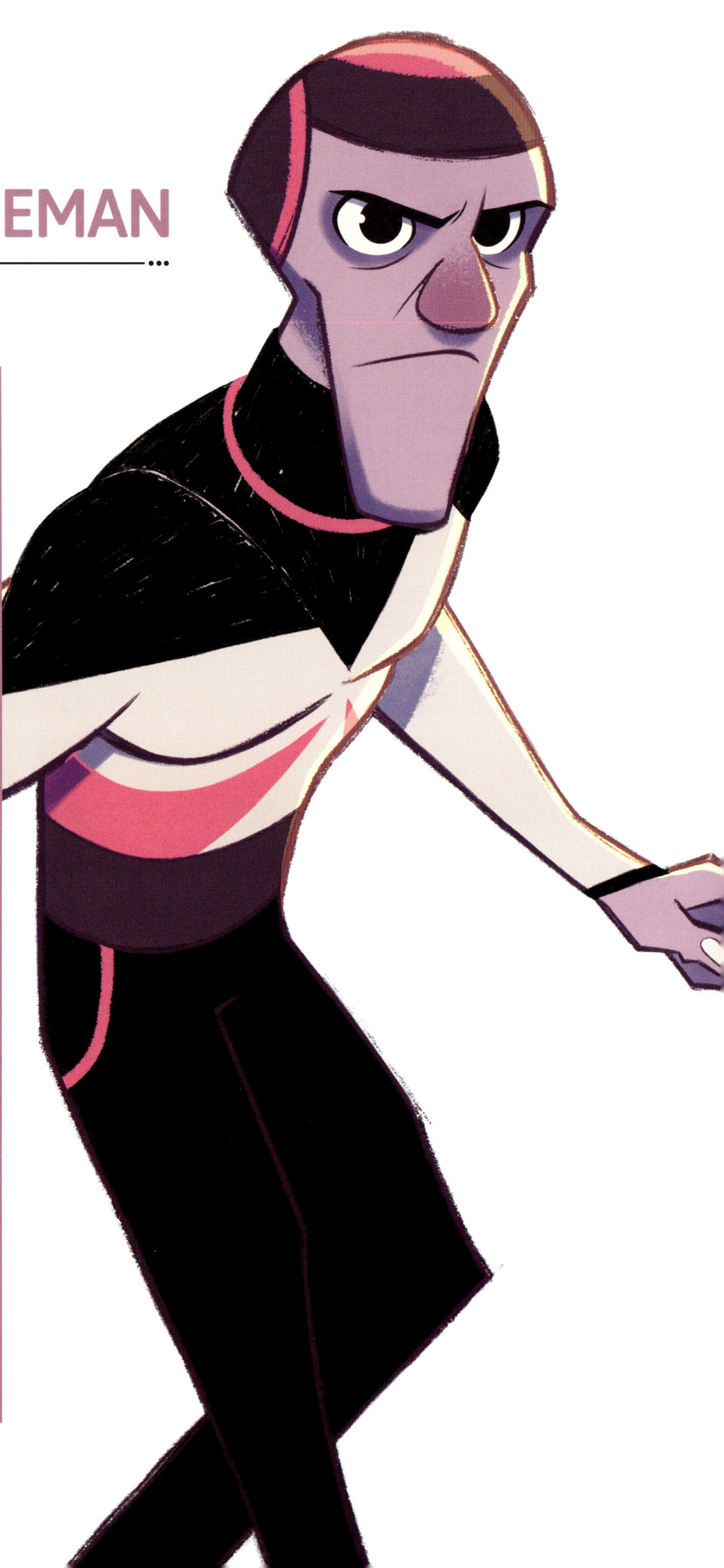

THE IDEA

When I start to plan my ideas, I mentally separate the concept into two halves that I need to consider: the "sci-fi" side and the "character" side. For the sci-fi side, I know I can look straight into references from comics, cartoons, movies, and books. I think about sci-fi aspects of the character's background. What is his planet of origin? Is he a human, a creature, a robot? This leads me into considering the "character" side of him: his role and personality. What kind of temperament could he have? What is his age, and how might it affect him, if it does? These are all questions I ask myself while I map out my ideas. I decide the character will be a brave human adventurer with a sleek costume inspired by retro sci-fi styles.

Concept: A human male space explorer or adventurer

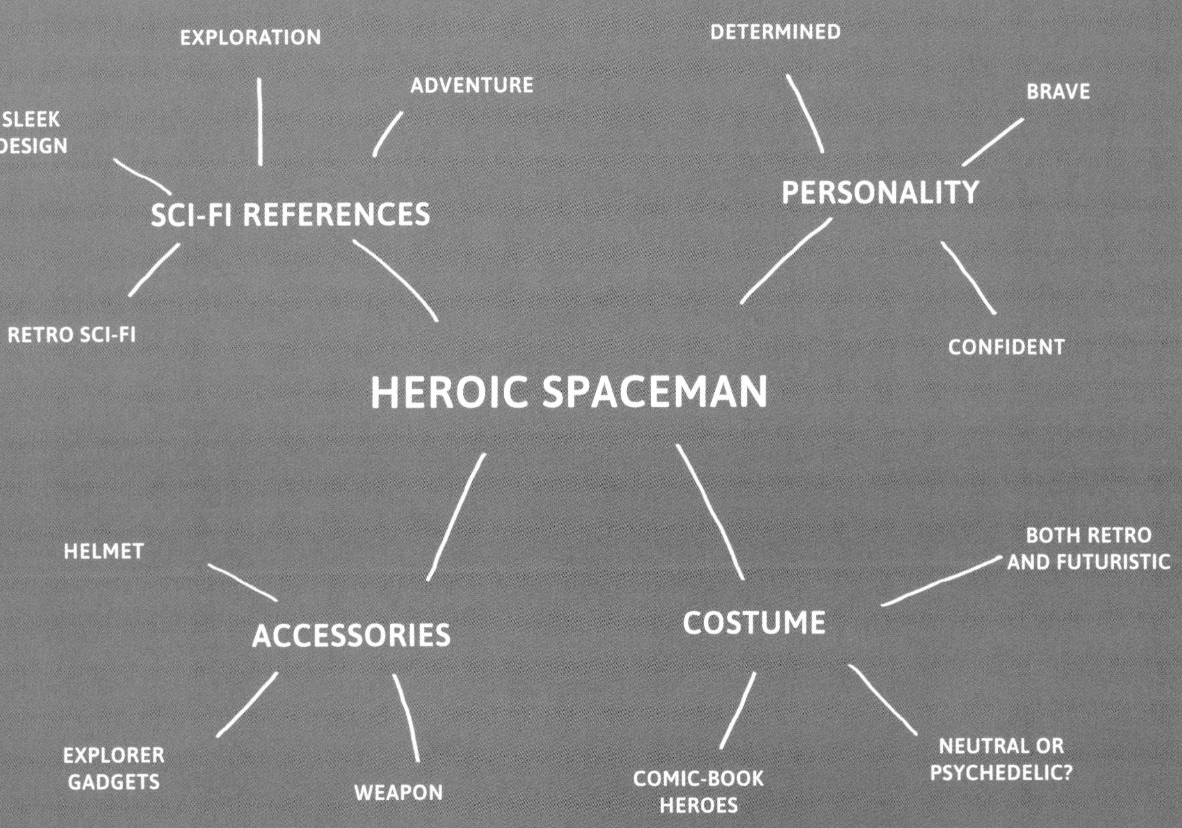

RESEARCH

I begin to search for and sketch real-life references, observing how I can simplify or stylize them to fit this character. I want him to have a futuristic suit and his own weapon, and the research will help me to decide whether I will keep his costume very clean and conservative, or more full-on psychedelic in a fun, retro fashion. The choice of style would affect both his suit and his props; I find myself leaning towards more simple, streamlined ideas that are still inspired by vintage sci-fi styles. I also research potential helmets and headgear that a character might wear in space, though my final rendition of him may not be wearing a helmet.

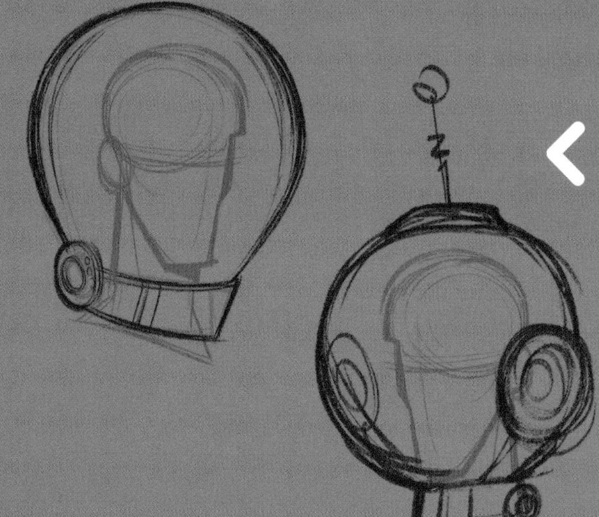

My first thought is of space helmets and old-fashioned diving helmets. I am a fan of big clean shapes with fewer details, as they create more visual impact, so I would prefer to have a simple round shape as a helmet. This will be important to enhancing the retro feel.

I want him to have a classic weapon that's very retro sci-fi, in the style of characters such as Marvin the Martian or Flash Gordon. These weapons use round and clean shapes just like the helmets.

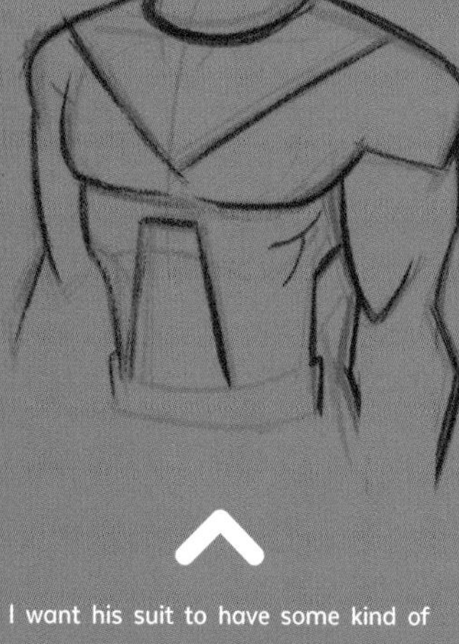

I want his suit to have some kind of mark on the chest, in order to draw attention to his head area. It would also give him a hint of vintage comic-book hero styling. Some very fine details like stitches or fine stripes on the arms will give it a futuristic feeling.

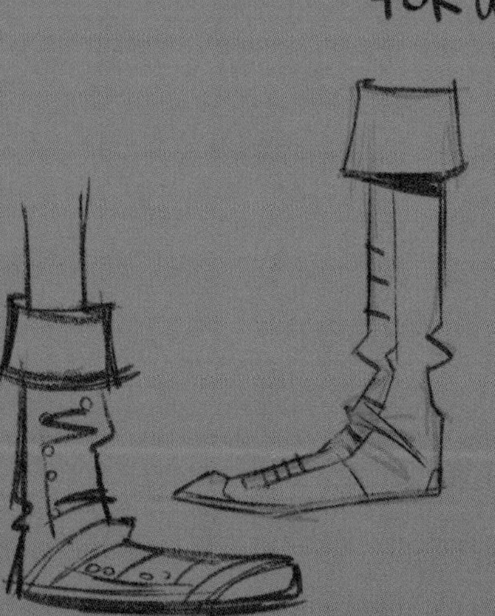

Like other vintage sci-fi characters, the spaceman could have retro-styled boots. Adding wrinkles to the material will give them subtle detail. Again, simple shapes rather than complex, mechanical design will help with the retro style.

THUMBNAILS

I come from a background in 2D animation, so I learned to start sketching quick ideas without worrying about details – not even the character's face. When making my thumbnails, I "break" the body into uneven parts to make the proportions more stylized and interesting than a realistic human body: for example, a wide torso with a small head, or a short torso with long legs. Not all these thumbnails are successful, as I don't want him to be a typical "super strong" hero character. Rather than a thumbnail with large shoulders and legs, I lean towards a slimmer design with long legs and big, expressive hands. This will help to sell the sleek sci-fi look I am aiming for. The long legs will help to express the adventurer aspect of the character, making him look agile and alert; the large hands will create a visually interesting contrast with his skinny limbs, as well as helping the character to emote.

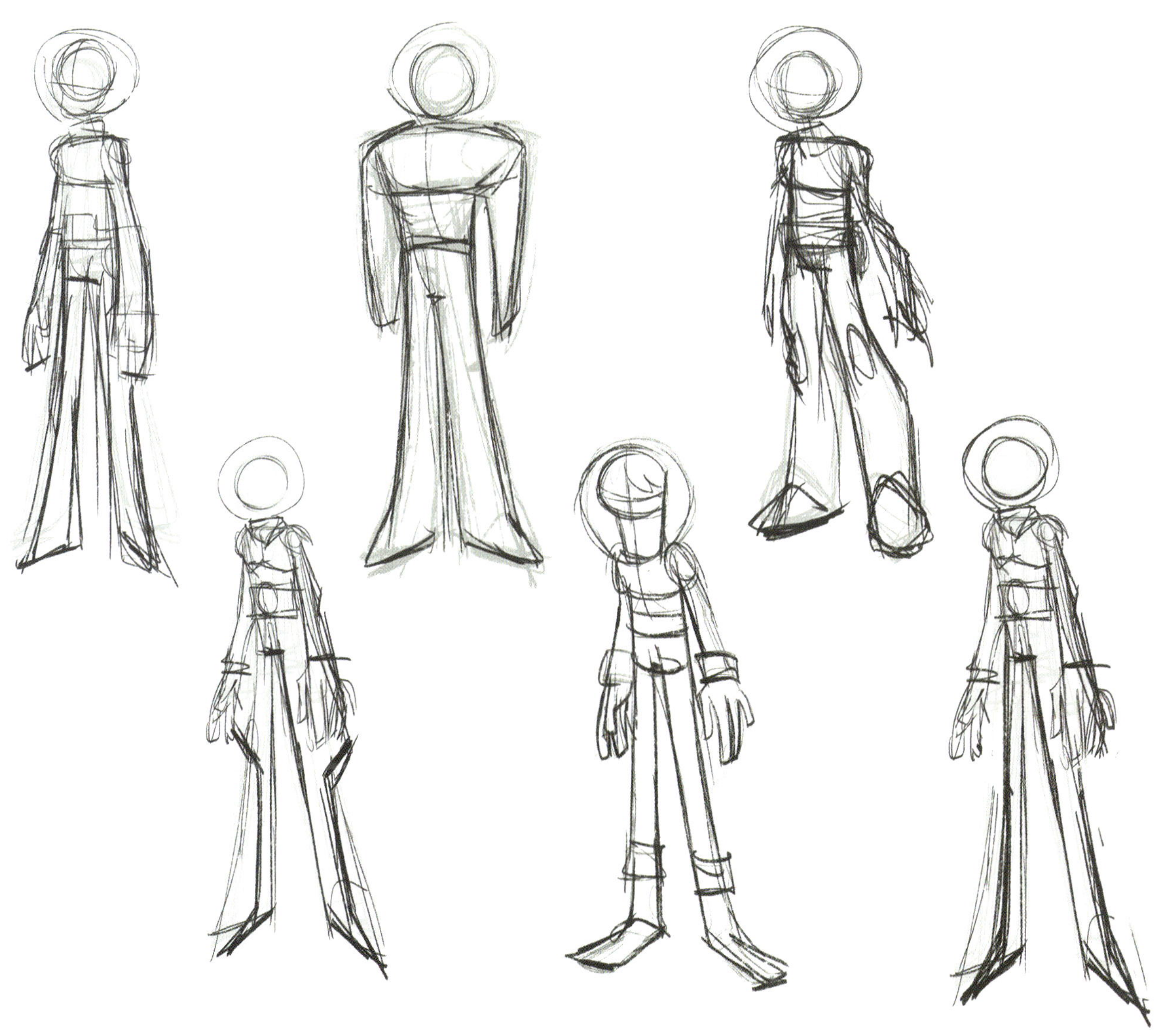

BASIC SHAPES

I start to build up the character using elements from the slimmer thumbnails. He has an overall triangular form, as it's a dynamic shape that is appropriate for a dynamic character. I spend some time finding a face shape that fits best on his body; I cut, paste, and redraw new heads, and stretch or squash parts until I arrive at the best solution.

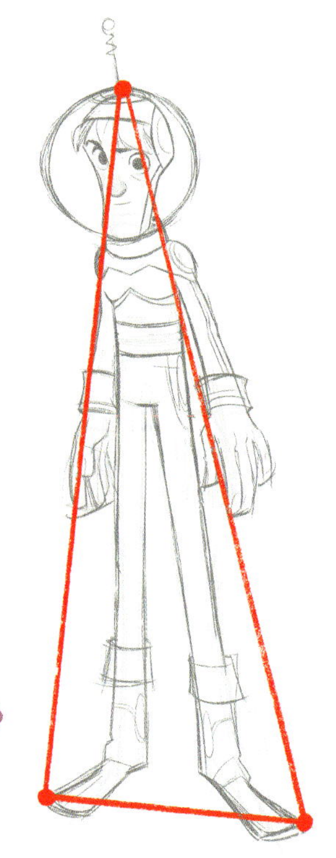

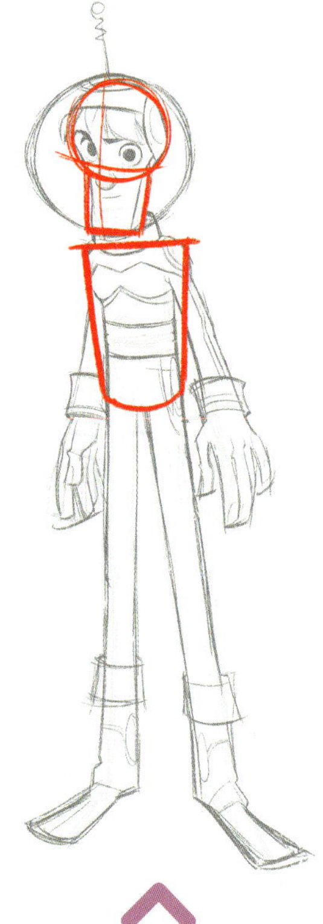

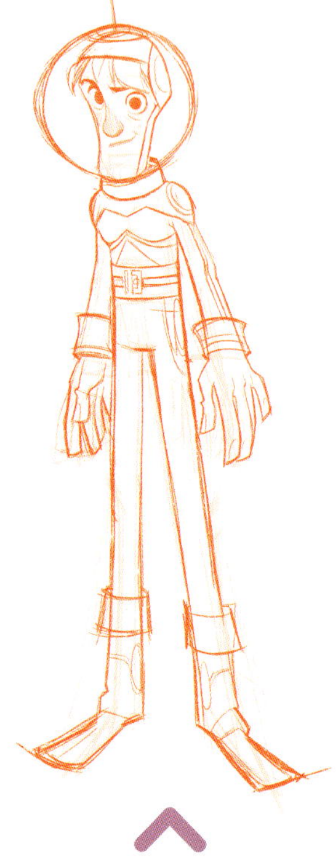

I want to keep the overall triangular shape that I found in my thumbnails. This will make him look like less typical heroic characters who normally have an inverted triangular shape with a wide upper body. Speed, determination, and intellect are his strengths rather than brute force.

For this sketch the face is just built with a circle and a square as the jaw, and the torso is simply a box.

Though the character has long legs, I want to keep the viewer's attention on the head and upper body by giving the character a very noticeable face and large hands, as they express more about the character. I "break" the silhouette by separating the smallest finger from the other fingers, which makes the shape of his hand more interesting and easier to interpret.

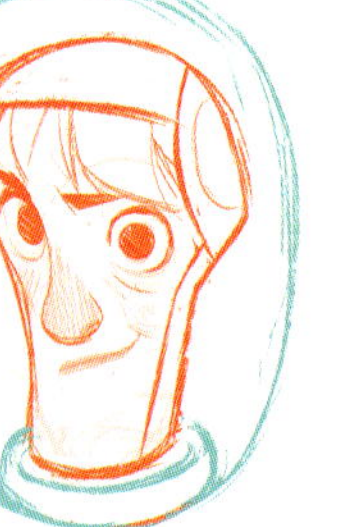

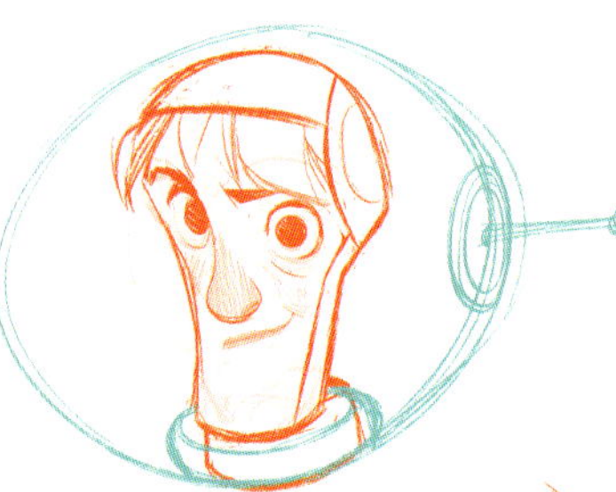

I explore more possibilities for the character's face. I keep the basic construction similar, but play with different proportions to find the most appropriate look for the character. I settle on a simpler shape for the head, and remove the helmet as the new head is already a sleek shape without it.

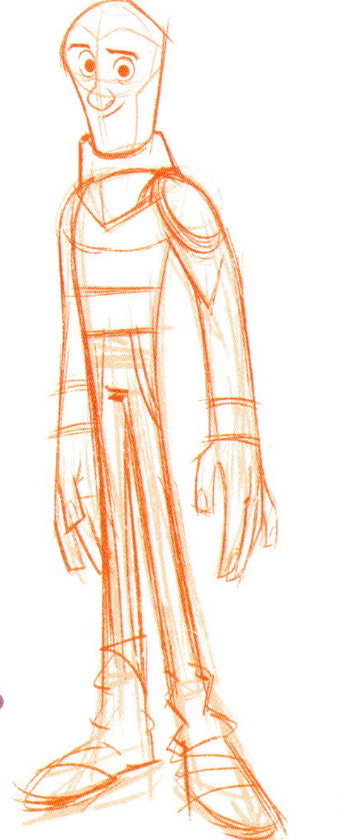

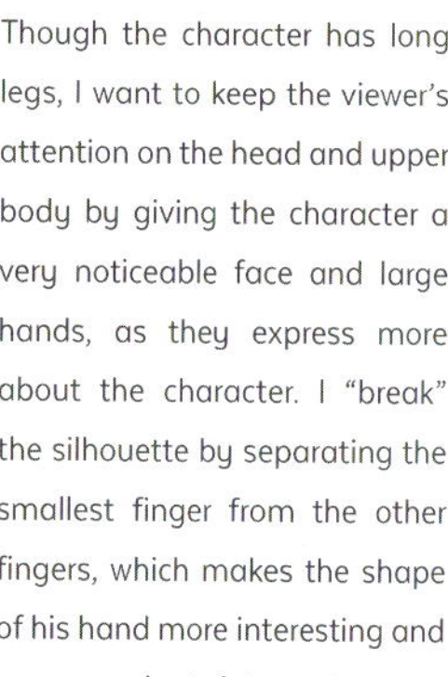

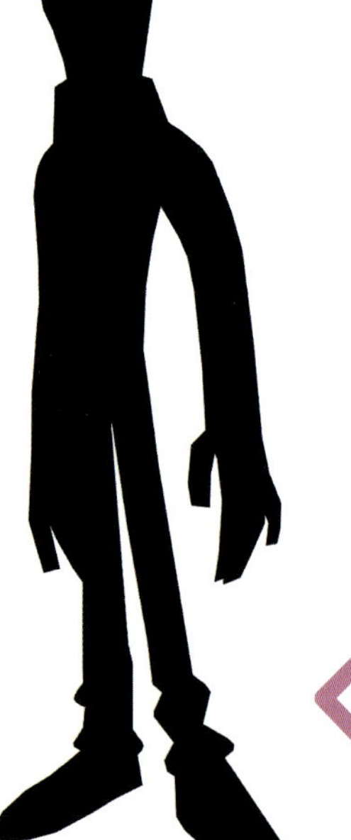

I refine the shape and style of other parts of the body to fit the new head. I make the arms longer to create a more agile, athletic look than the sketches I started out with, while still keeping his physique quite light.

In the resulting silhouette, you can easily make out the clean shapes of the character, and the strong visual contrast between rounded and angular shapes to keep the viewer's eye interested.

DETAILS

I start making final decisions and fleshing out the character, changing details around until I narrow down everything I like about the design. As you can see, I make the design simpler and simpler in terms of silhouette and costume detail; this all depends on the style you want to create, but in this case I want a very smooth, uncluttered shape that makes the character look futuristic and streamlined. To help with this, I tighten up the collar of his suit, and fill it in to create an eye-catching shoulder detail that's reminiscent of classic comics I researched earlier.

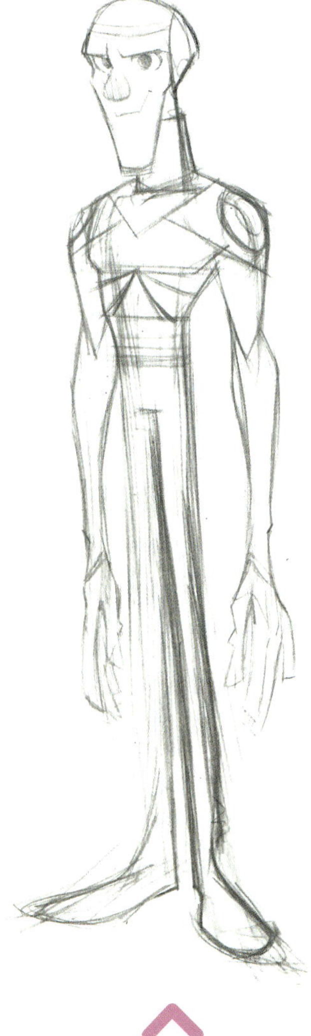

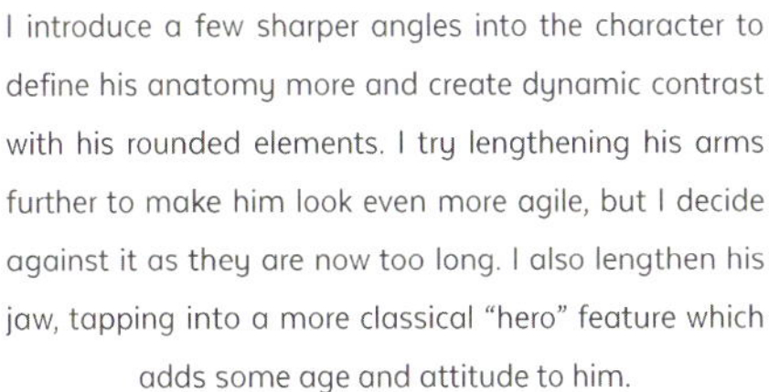

I introduce a few sharper angles into the character to define his anatomy more and create dynamic contrast with his rounded elements. I try lengthening his arms further to make him look even more agile, but I decide against it as they are now too long. I also lengthen his jaw, tapping into a more classical "hero" feature which adds some age and attitude to him.

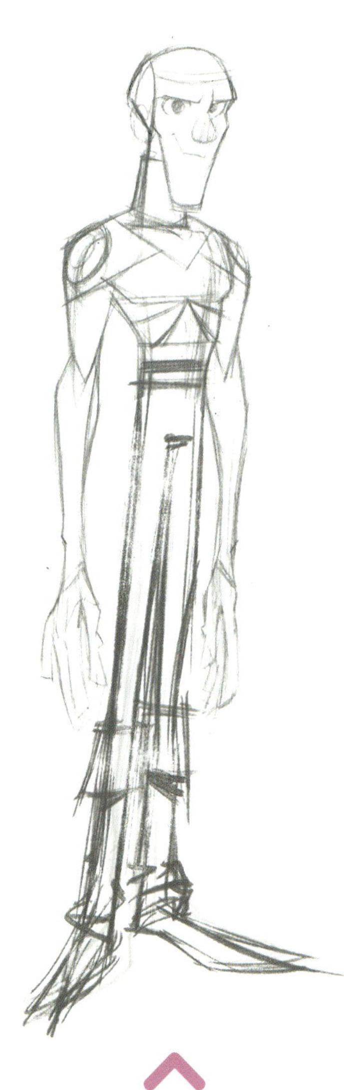

Flipping the sketch allows me to check my design choices with fresh eyes. I wonder whether to emphasize the flaps on his boots and bring back some sharper edges to his feet, which look more exciting than rounded shapes, but they seem too sharp and aggressive-looking.

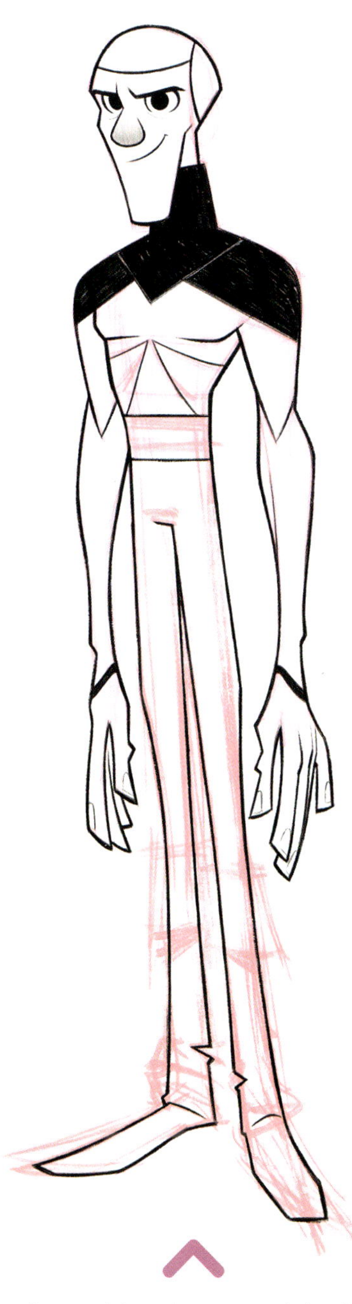

I settle on a balance between rounded and sharp boots, using an angular shape with no flaps and a few creases for interest. This prevents the design from looking too busy in the area around his hands, as they are already detailed. Finally, I draw attention to his chest and head with triangular shapes that echo his earlier silhouette.

FACIAL EXPRESSIONS

This character is keen to travel the universe and has seen many exciting things, so I want to make him seem confident, brave, and optimistic. His large eyes and strong eyebrows are ideal features for expressing this side of his personality. They are also perfect for capturing moments when he is scared or startled, though I will not use such an expression in my final image of him. I decide to tweak his concerned brow into more of a frown, and depict him with a closed mouth to make him look determined.

In this fearful expression I want to see how far I can exaggerate his open mouth. I stylize his teeth so that his back teeth aren't visible; sometimes little touches like this are necessary to keep the design simple and readable. It is not the brave, heroic face I would like for my final image, but by closing the mouth and tweaking the worried brows into a frown, I could create a braver expression that has the same striking contrast between the round eyes and straight, lowered eyebrows.

This captures the character perfectly, showing him as a positive, confident explorer, always ready for the next adventure and unconcerned by any trouble he might run into. It's important to add asymmetry to expressions to make them more exciting and believable. However, I would like to show him looking tougher.

Here he looks a little reckless and complacent, as if he is showing off a new specimen he has captured, thinking he has everything under control. Little does he know that the situation might turn on him! This expression shows his personality well, but I would like to show his open eyes in the final version of the character, to give a clearer view of his whole design.

POSING

When working on the poses, I explore two specific qualities. First, on a technical level, I want to see how the character's body reacts to specific movements after some of the stylization decisions I have made. Second, on an emotional level, I want to express two sides of him: the adventurous character who is focused on his mission, and the friendly, welcoming hero he is also capable of being.

Here I wanted to show the character in a bending pose to test the stylization of his shapes when moving. Sometimes, especially in animation, it's necessary to "cheat" on specific poses to solve a visual problem; in this case, you can see how his knee changes from an angular shape to a flat one, so it looks "right" when touching the ground. Here he's investigating some dirt on a planet's surface, but I would like the final pose to be more upright and action-oriented.

This character is a brave adventurer who might confront incredible creatures out there on other planets, so I want to convey his fearless and determined side. This pose shows him ready for action or combat, with his weapon drawn and feet planted firmly apart, in an angular stance that recalls his underlying triangle shape. I will use this pose for my final image.

This pose shows the character's friendly side. His big smile shows all his teeth and his arms are open in a welcoming manner, as if he is ready to hug somebody. Though this is true to his personality, I would like to depict him in a more heroic action stance.

VALUES & COLOR

I try out some very different options for the character's color palette, such as a commonly used palette that people can relate more immediately to, and a palette with colors that are less obvious. I look back to my research into comics, movies, and television, thinking about the emotions I want the palette to show. I want to depict a character with mature, minimalistic colors that suit his clean, streamlined shapes. Keeping the legs almost silhouette-like will help to make his pose pop and to keep the viewer's attention focused on his expressive upper body and face.

I want his colors and values to fit with the clean and minimal design, with the shape of every color reading clearly. The high contrast and detail around his head and upper body immediately draw the viewer's attention towards his head and face.

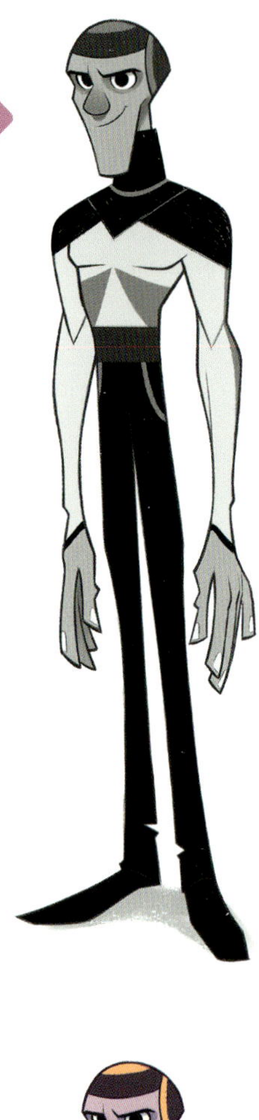

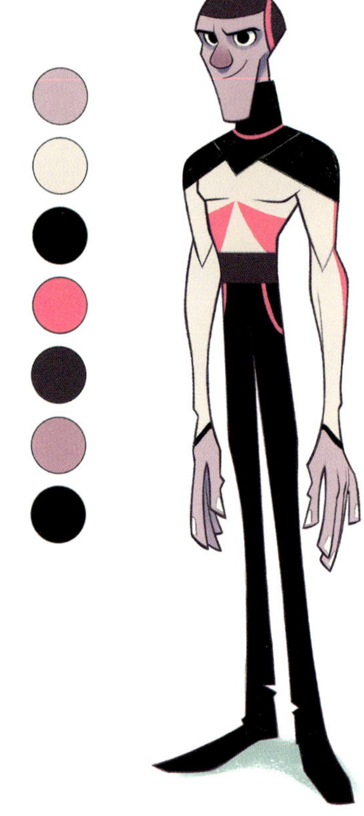

This mostly neutral palette uses a sort of "bone-white" color, black, and a few hints of pink and desaturated purple. These colors make the design look clean and mature, creating a focal point around the upper body by leaving the legs almost as silhouettes. This is the palette I will use for my final version.

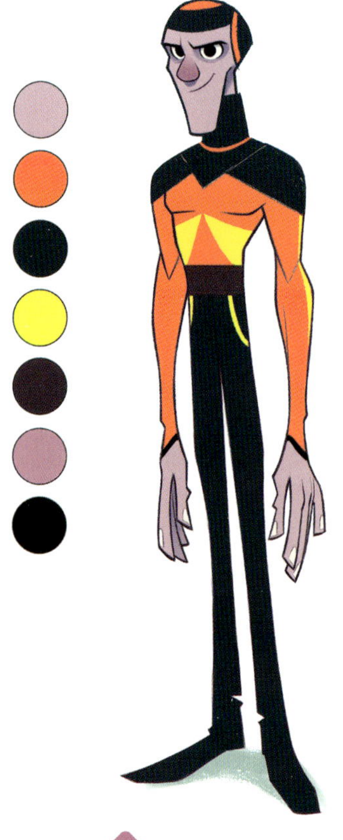

I try a more vivid, colorful palette that the viewer might be more used to seeing, as turquoise and orange is a popular complementary palette, especially in sci-fi properties. I like this palette a lot, but it's a bit too commonplace for my tastes.

This is another palette with more atypical colors, using hues halfway between the other two color schemes. However, I don't think it's very successful, as the bold "superhero" shapes of the character's outfit do not come across clearly enough.

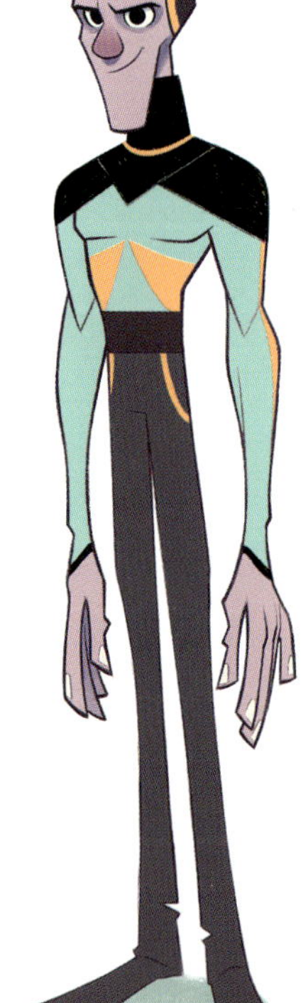

FINAL DESIGN

I am very happy with the evolution of the final character; I feel the design became stronger and more mature with each decision I made. Many of my original ideas from the beginning are still here, such as the strong triangular body shape, which also carries through the costume and pose. The simple face shape is intact, but giving the character a stronger jaw adds years of experience to him. The restrained color choices keep his retro-styled uniform from looking garish or predictable. His weapon is reminiscent of old sci-fi comics and cartoons, helping to place him in a context of exciting galactic adventure, and uses similar colors as his suit so it is not distracting. The big, expressive hands enhance the character's bold pose and personality. The smallest finger of the hand holding the weapon breaks the silhouette, just like in the basic shape sketches, to add extra flow and interest to the pose.

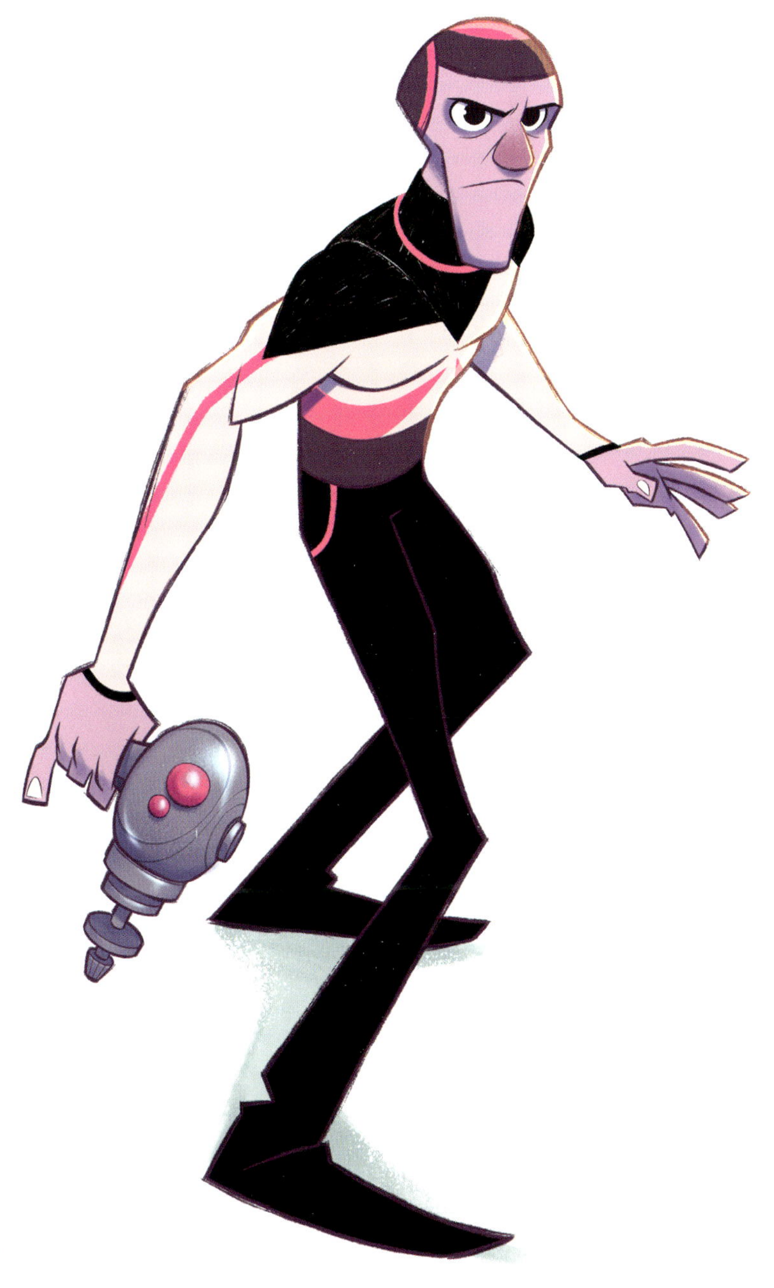

Final artwork © Luis Gadea

VARIATION 1:
AGED SPACEMAN

IDEAS & RESEARCH

This version of the character will be older, looking like a hero past his prime, but with the same sense of toughness and determination. I focus my research on three main elements which I want this version to explore: the eyes, which will be drooping with age, the wrinkles around his jaw and mouth, and the fabric textures of his old suit. As time passes, things start happening to your face; in my family, we develop wrinkles on our foreheads, which I've begun to get now! All these minor details are important to take into consideration to capture a believable sense of older age.

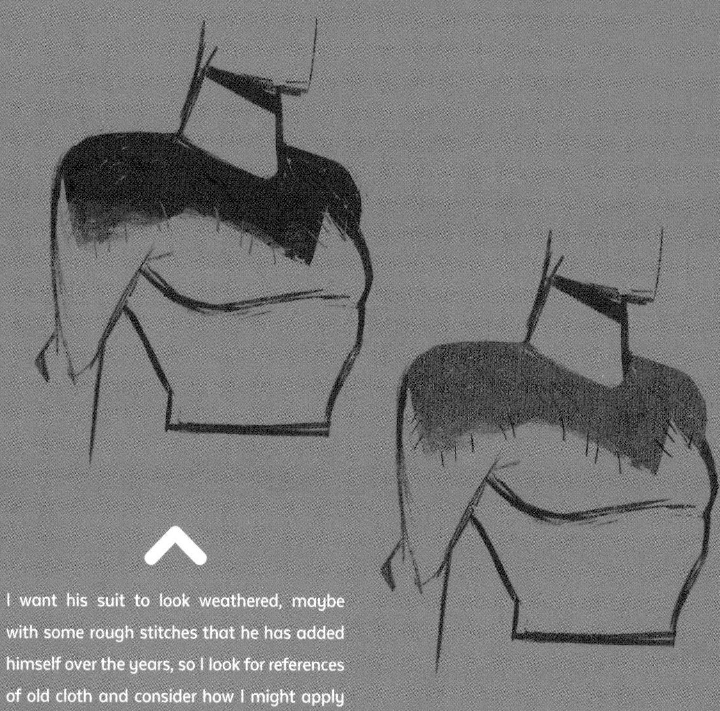

I want his suit to look weathered, maybe with some rough stitches that he has added himself over the years, so I look for references of old cloth and consider how I might apply these to the costume.

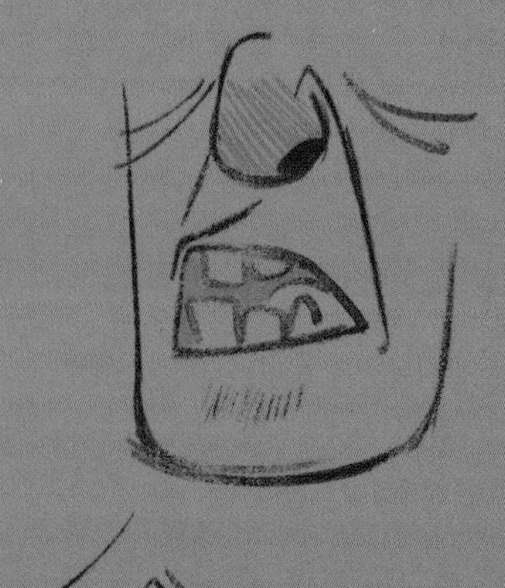

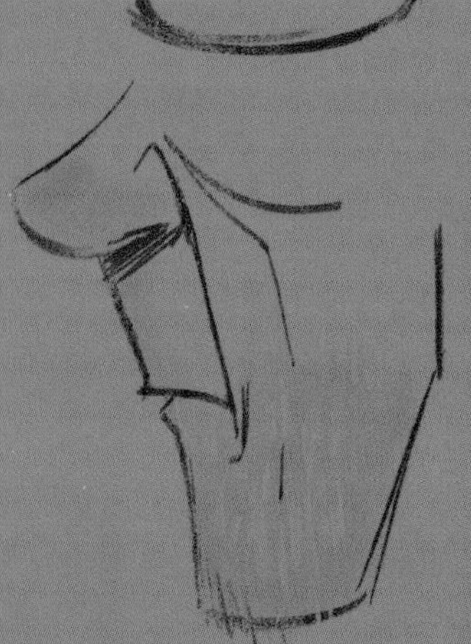

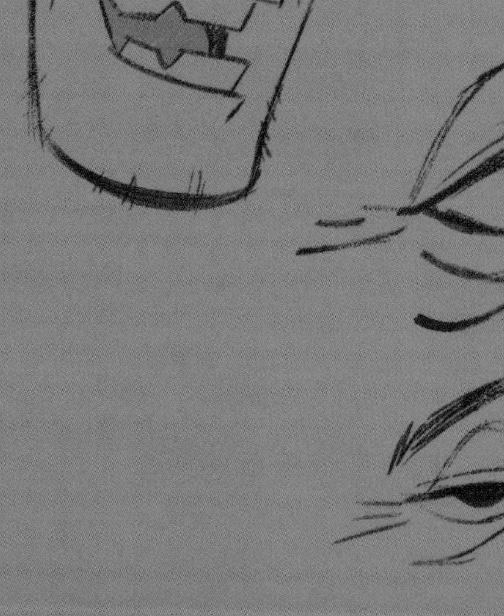

The character's jaw is quite a prominent feature on his younger face, so I look for references of wrinkles around the mouth and jaw areas. These will help me to convey his older age through a feature that the viewer will definitely notice. Whiskers could also be added.

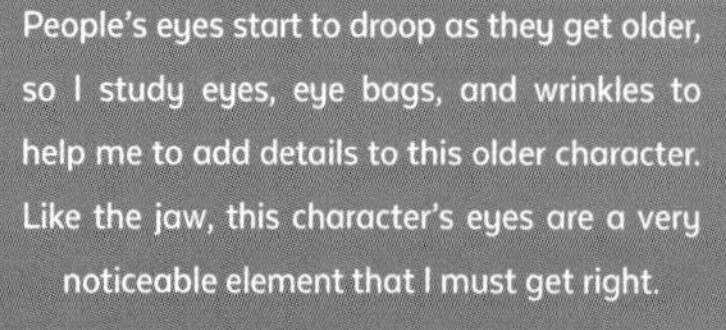

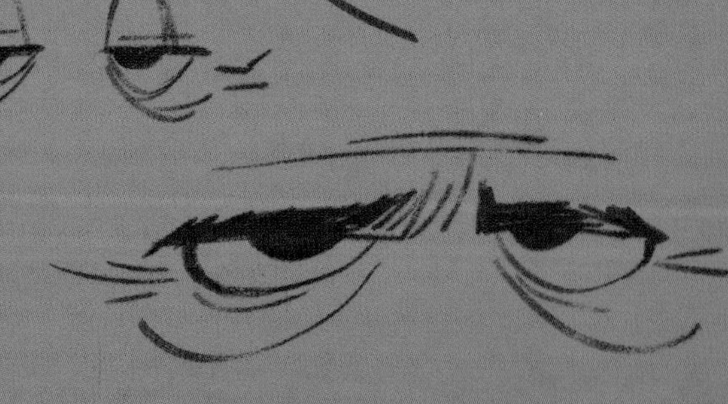

People's eyes start to droop as they get older, so I study eyes, eye bags, and wrinkles to help me to add details to this older character. Like the jaw, this character's eyes are a very noticeable element that I must get right.

CHANGES

To make the original character older, I want to keep the same overall look and feeling, but show how some features have reacted to the passing of time. When working out what to change, I think a lot about my grandfather, as he has a similar nose shape, and the character's eyes remind me a lot of him. This will help me to make authentic choices when changing my character.

His eyes will have become smaller, with dark bags and wrinkles appearing around them. However, I feel like the deep-set, sharp eyes are an iconic feature of his younger version, so I want to maintain some of that look.

As time passes, people's noses grow bigger; in this case, the character's nose might grow bigger in width. To balance this out, I may also need to increase the size of his jaw, making it wider too.

As my grandfather ages, I've noticed that he keeps his overall slim physique, except for his belly which increases. I could borrow this detail for the character and emphasize it with the tight waist of his suit. The tight neck of his suit might also create fleshy rolls around his neck.

I like the design of the suit itself and want to keep it for the old version of the character, but it would be dusty, dirty, and in need of stitches, having been with him through all his adventures.

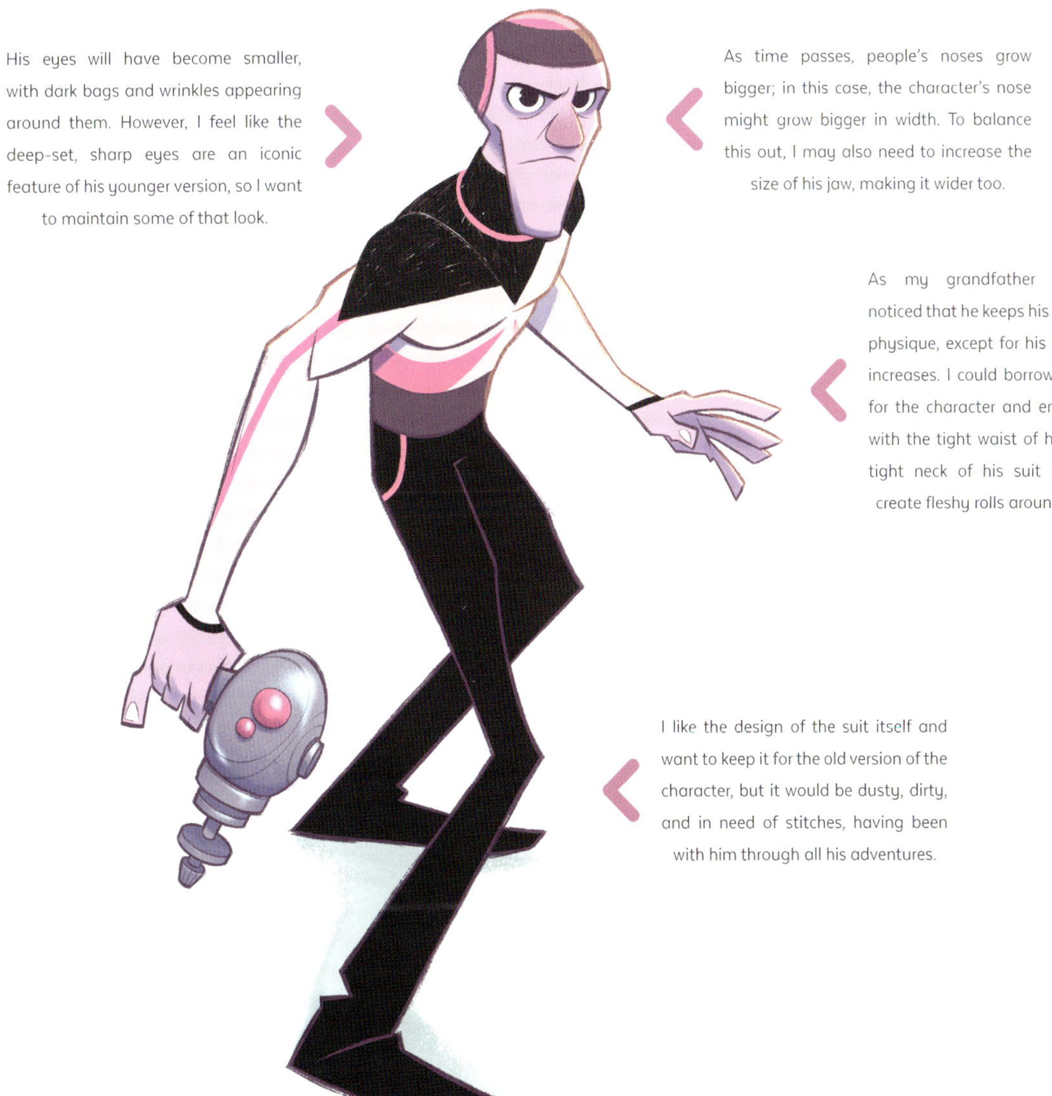

THUMBNAILS

I base my thumbnails on the proportions of the original character, always keeping in mind that he is the same person, just older. A few key features must stay the same so that this is immediately apparent to the viewer, such as his long limbs.

I decide to gather and combine ideas from all of these thumbnails: the larger nose, the height slightly reduced with age, and an overall scruffy, unshaven look.

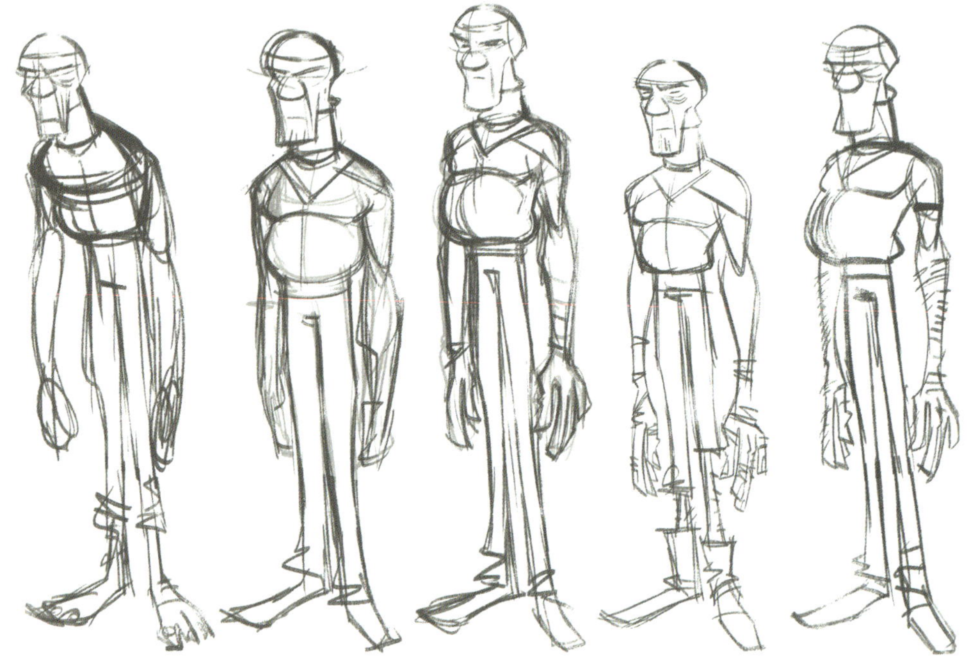

BASIC SHAPES

This character will be almost identical to his younger self in his underlying shape structure, as he is still upright and active, but I will make some changes to his surface forms and silhouette to suggest his changes in age and weight.

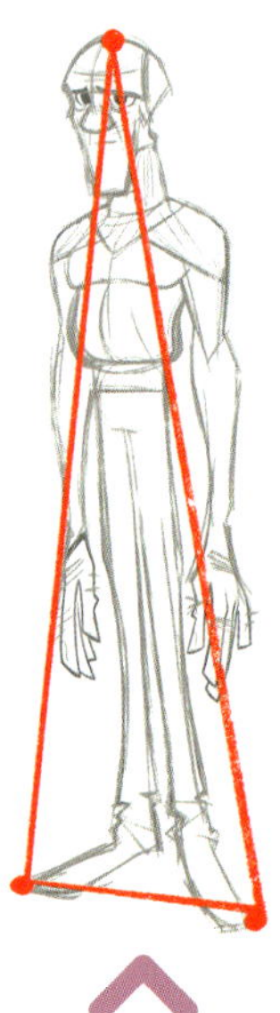

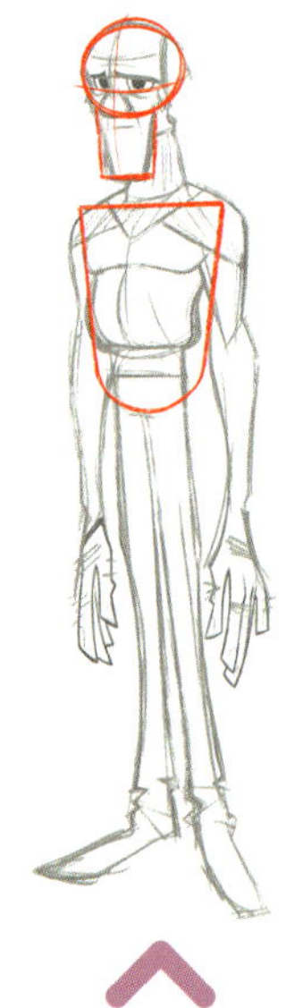

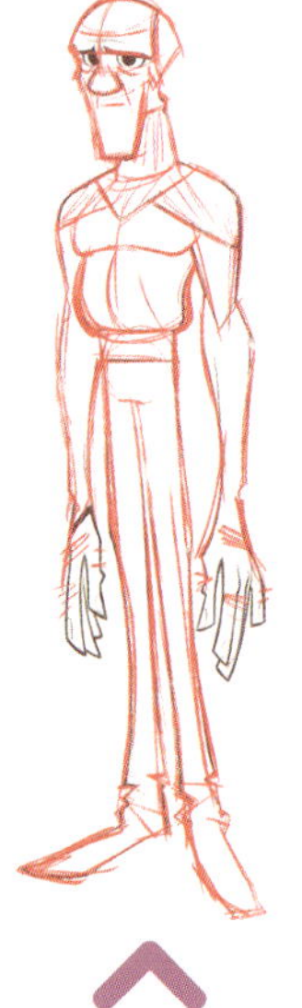

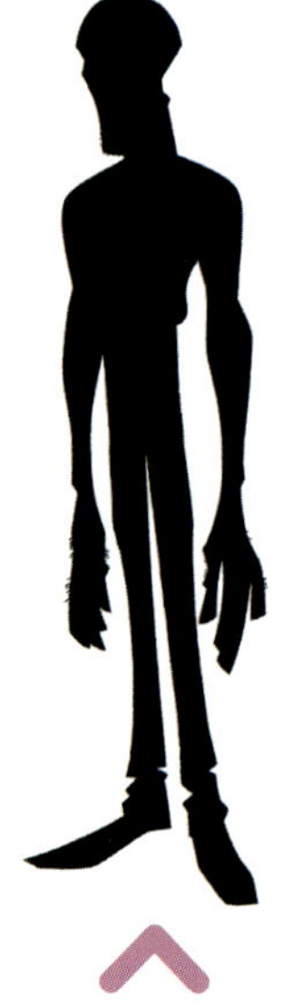

I want to keep the triangular shape of the original character, as this version's proportions have not changed drastically, and it's important that he is still recognizable.

I want to keep the construction of the face and body very similar, using a mix of round and rectangular shapes. This keeps the character's physique in line with the original, though his belly is now larger and rounder within that shape.

Here you can see more clearly how I have taken the strongest aspects of the thumbnails and combined them, and also kept some aspects the same as the original character, such as the hands and feet.

The silhouette looks like the same person, though with subtle but definite signs of aging, such as the paunchy shape of his torso and the fuzzy hairs breaking the character's outline.

DETAILS

I continue piecing together aspects of the younger version with ideas for aged features, aiming to keep a strong physical resemblance and the same spirit as the original design.

The fact that the character is still wearing the same uniform gives the impression that he has been stranded on a planet for a while, or has been on the same mission for a very long time, suggesting a little narrative that the viewer can interpret.

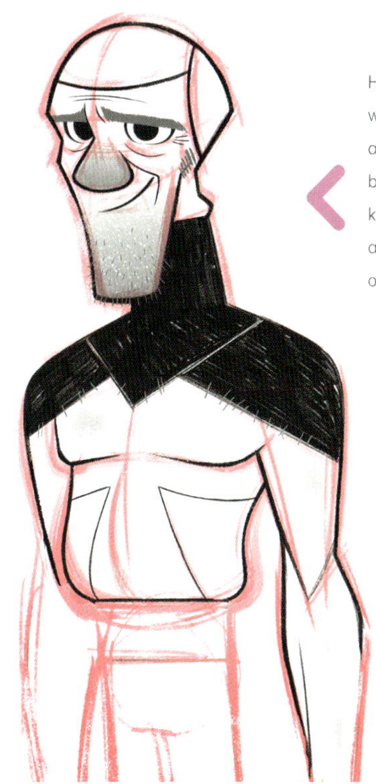

His nose and jaw are bigger and wider, having spread a bit with age. His eye area is now more baggy and wrinkly, but the eyes keep some of the same depth and alertness as his younger self. His overall look is slightly sadder, as if he has been through a lot.

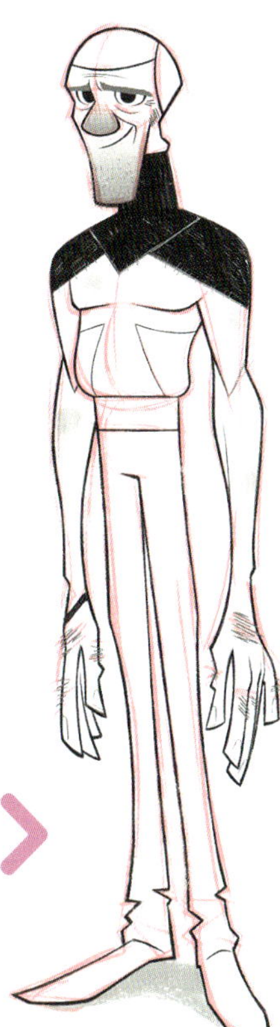

I keep the same arms and feet as the original design, creating contrast with his round belly. His hands are now hairier than before, and his suit is dirtier and a bit baggy compared to the younger version, with a torn sleeve adding to his unkempt look.

EXPRESSIONS & POSING

I want the character's poses to convey that he is still a brave adventurer. He may be older and a little paunchy, but he is not weak; he is still going out on missions and taking on some tough creatures. His long arms and legs allow me to create poses that are still quite exaggerated and dynamic, like his younger self.

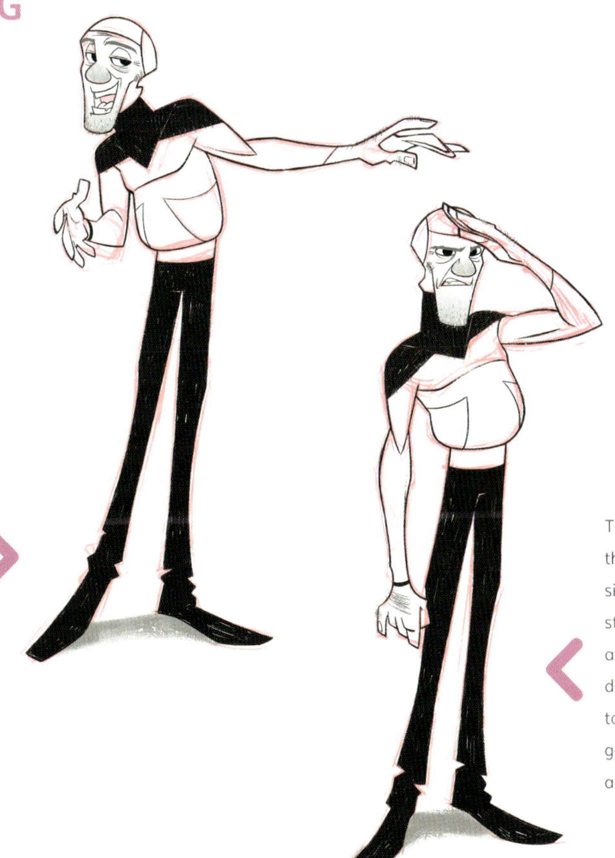

This pose represents the "cool" side of the character, and allows me to emphasize features like his expressive hands and the rolls on his neck. He is older now, full of jokes and stories, and knows how to get out of a situation with a funny one-liner. However, this pose doesn't give much sense of him being an adventurer.

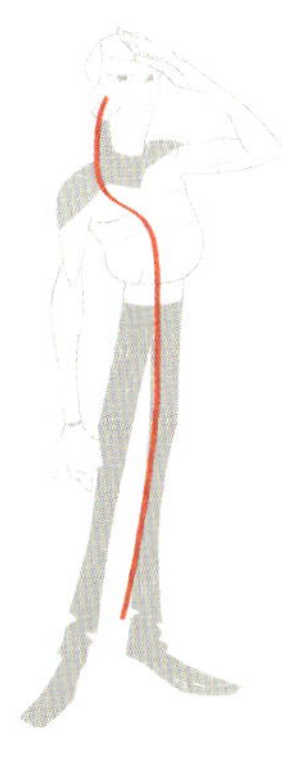

This brave salute shows more of the character's tough, determined side, demonstrating that he is still in action, receiving orders and completing missions. I even draw his belly a little larger here to emphasize the proud forward gesture of his pose, as I felt it looked a little shy. This is the pose I will use for the final design.

VALUE & COLOR

I do not want to change the character's suit itself, because its similarity to the original design suggests an interesting possible backstory between the two versions. However, I do need to age and weather it somewhat to distinguish this character as an older version. While the young hero was very sleek and clean, this version is enhanced by textures: the gray dust on his suit, the "five o'clock shadow" on his face, and the pink detailing now worn-out and imperfect. All of this will retain the same clean "read" as the original version if I keep the color palette similarly limited.

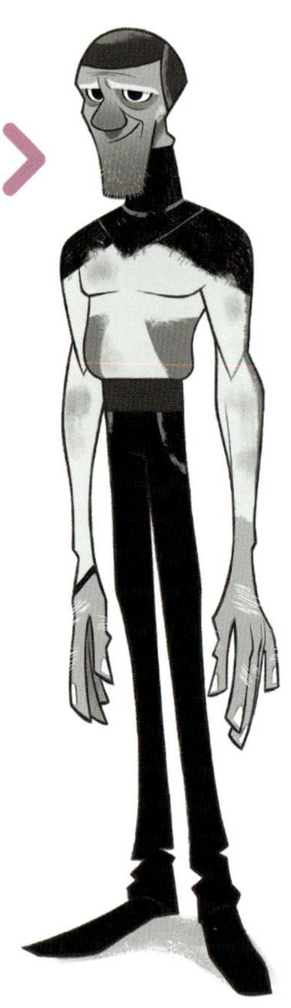

The values of the character read very clearly, with an even balance of dark, light, and medium tones. His eyebrows are now white, adding a subtle aging detail that is just light enough to stand out against his skin.

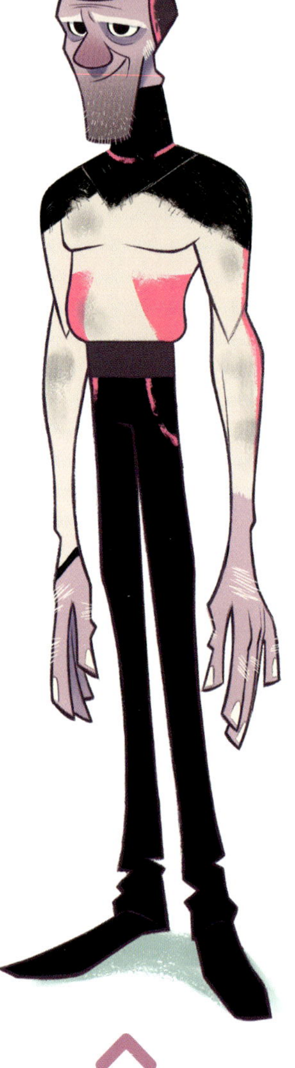

This palette uses the exact same colors for his suit as the original version, but I find that it's too vibrant for this context and does not put across an "aged" feeling enough.

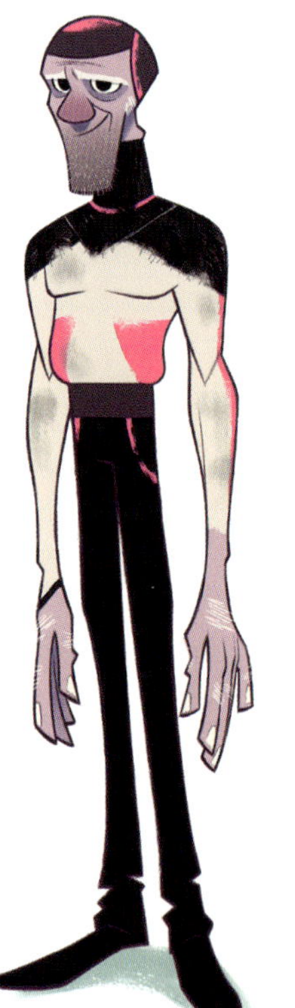

I think this is the most successful color palette, keeping the iconic bright pink, but lightening the black to more of a gray-purple. This lower contrast makes the design feel older and more weathered without losing its overall impact.

In this version, I try to wash out the bright, punchy pink details on his suit. This succeeds in making him look older, but the pink is now quite close to his skin color, which might just confuse the viewer at first glance.

FINAL DESIGN

My final design represents what I wanted to capture for this brief: an older adventurer with a bit of extra weight around his middle, who is still determined to take the next great mission into outer space. The worn-out suit helps to tell a lot of this story and keeps him recognizable as the same character I began with. Keeping his proportions and overall anatomy very similar to his younger self also goes a long way in creating continuity between the two versions, enriching both designs by sowing the seeds of a possible narrative in the viewer's mind.

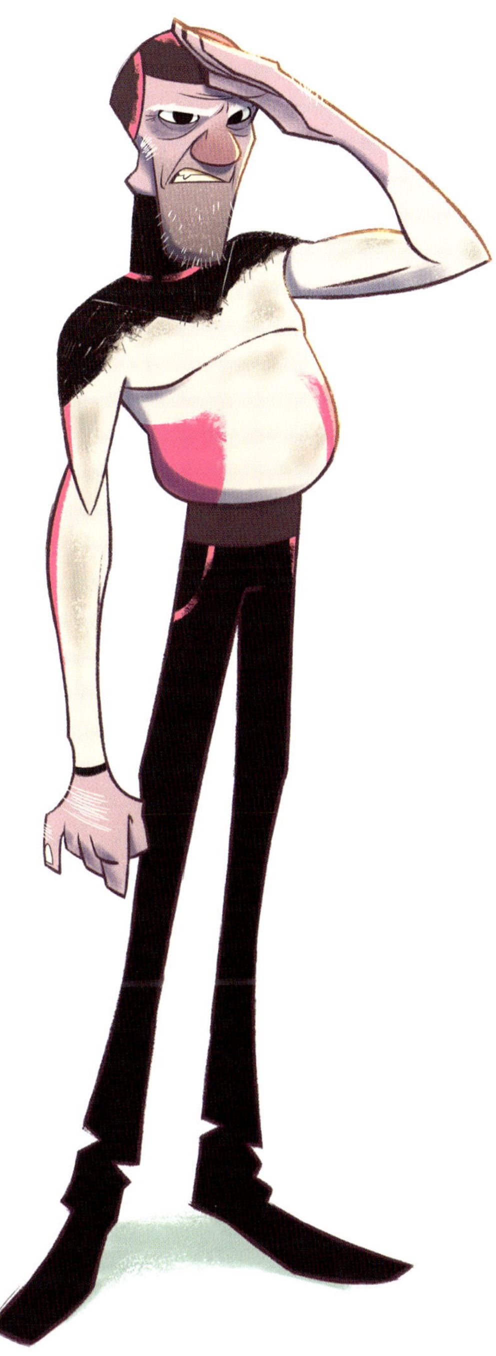

Final artwork © Luis Gadea

VARIATION 2:
FANTASY ADVENTURER

IDEAS & RESEARCH

For this fantasy variation of the character, I want to set myself a challenge by translating the design into new proportions, weight, and height. I want to create a dwarf warrior, which will push me to come up with very different design solutions from the previous two versions. He will almost look like the opposite of his sci-fi version, but with enough features in common that he seems like the same hardy adventurer. The character's overall style will change a lot from sleek, simplified sci-fi shapes to a fantasy design with finer details and more materials and textures. I start by researching ideas for his costume and props, even if I do not intend to use them all.

I study a few very basic swords that the character might wield in lieu of a ray gun. If the sword becomes a prominent part of the design, I may give it more attention and customize it, but it might just stay as a basic prop.

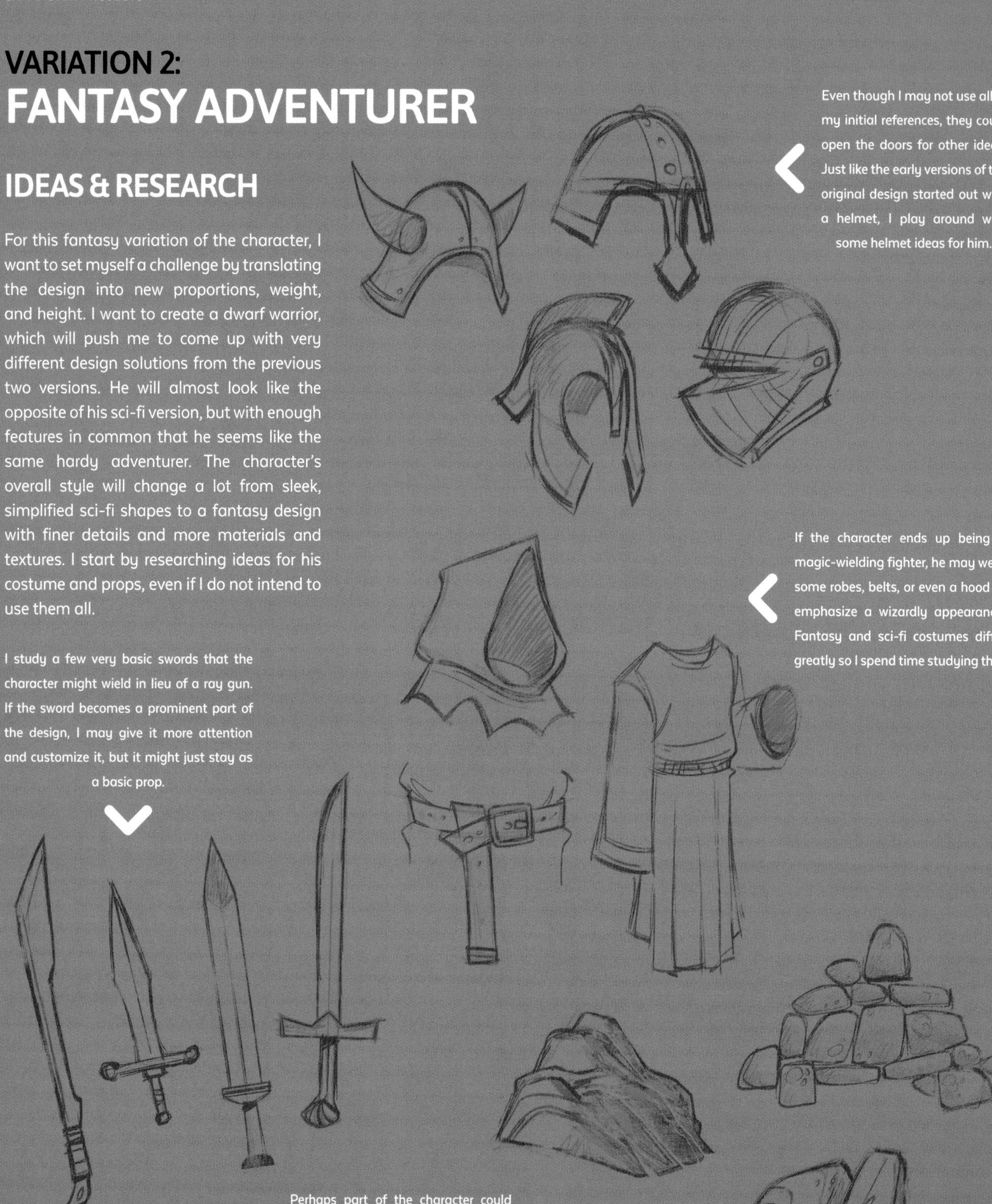

Even though I may not use all of my initial references, they could open the doors for other ideas. Just like the early versions of the original design started out with a helmet, I play around with some helmet ideas for him.

If the character ends up being a magic-wielding fighter, he may wear some robes, belts, or even a hood to emphasize a wizardly appearance. Fantasy and sci-fi costumes differ greatly so I spend time studying this.

Perhaps part of the character could resemble rocks, or be made out of rocks, emphasizing his dwarvish background. This could be an interesting way to add eye-catching asymmetry and texture to the character.

CHANGES

Now that the character lives in a fantasy world, I will need to drastically change some aspects of him, yet keep enough features to allow the viewer to relate this design to the original. While the sci-fi version is slim and light, with a minimal, futuristic suit, this fantasy dwarf will be heavyset and dressed for adventuring in a fantasy setting.

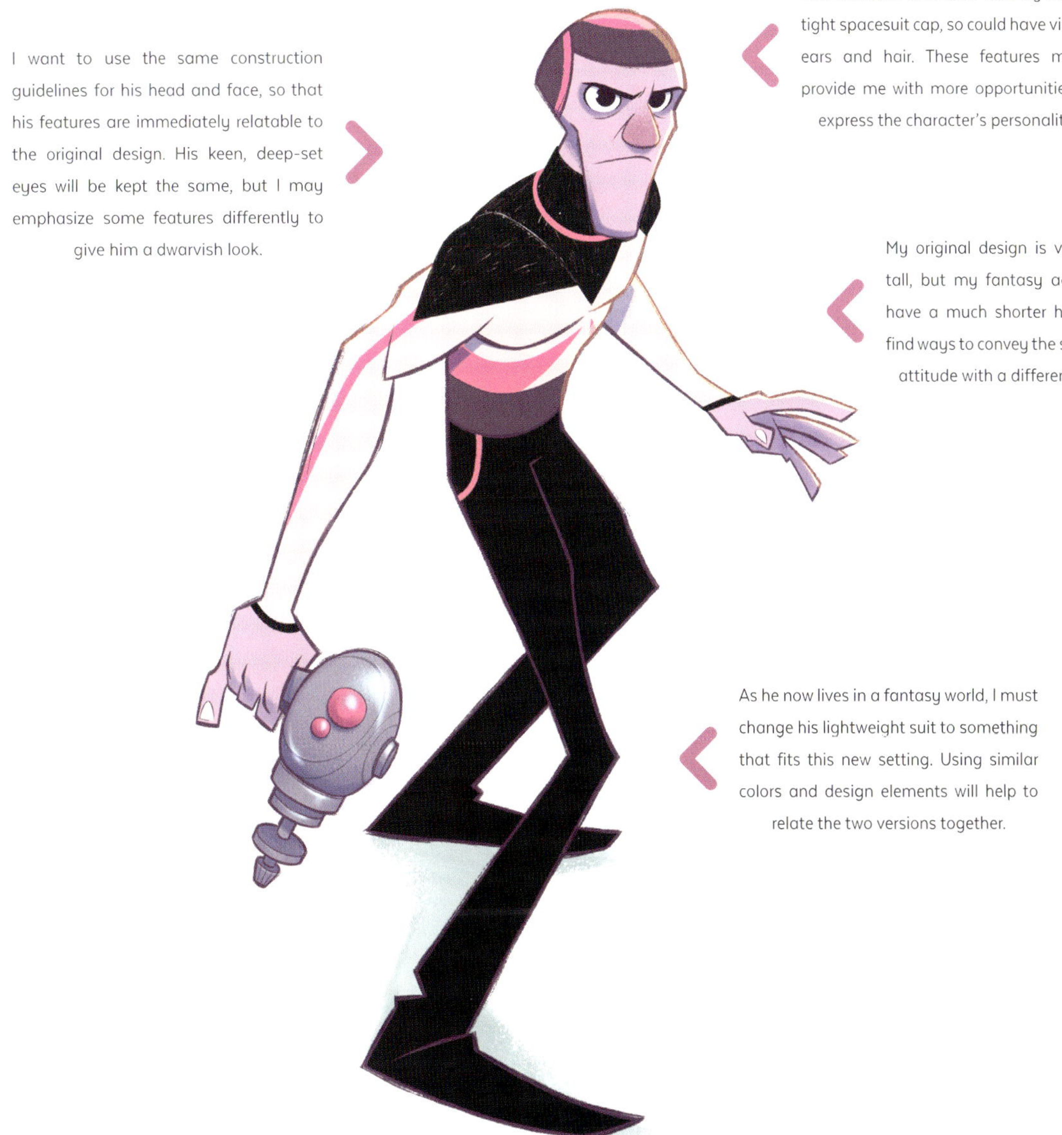

I want to use the same construction guidelines for his head and face, so that his features are immediately relatable to the original design. His keen, deep-set eyes will be kept the same, but I may emphasize some features differently to give him a dwarvish look.

This character will not be wearing a skin-tight spacesuit cap, so could have visible ears and hair. These features might provide me with more opportunities to express the character's personality.

My original design is very long and tall, but my fantasy adventurer will have a much shorter height. I must find ways to convey the same role and attitude with a different physique.

As he now lives in a fantasy world, I must change his lightweight suit to something that fits this new setting. Using similar colors and design elements will help to relate the two versions together.

THUMBNAILS

When I make my quick thumbnails, I use the original character's head as a base for my new ideas. The face is the one part of the character that will remain very similar across both versions, so this will help me to stay true to his original features.

The character's physique is very different now, but some subtle elements such as the cloak and boots recall features like the shoulders and legs of the sci-fi versions. My final choice is the third thumbnail, but I will remove the helmet so that it does not distract from the rest of the costume.

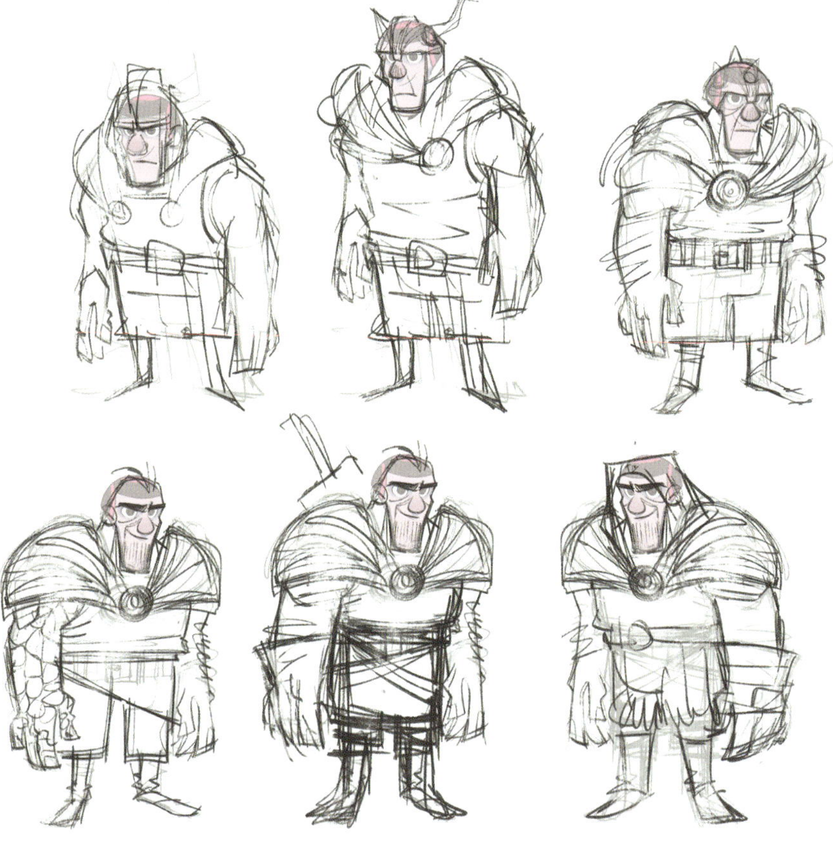

BASIC SHAPES

To emphasize this character's dwarven stature and more brawny warrior's physique, his underlying shapes will lean away from the tall, thin triangle of the original version. Giving him a square body with short legs will make him feel solid and closer to the ground.

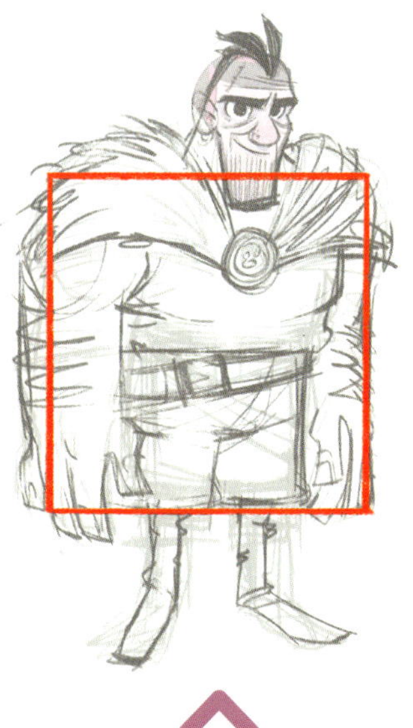

The character's overall body shape is now a square rather than a tall, dynamic triangle. This will give him a strong, solid feel that fits a heavyset dwarf warrior. While the visible legs are short, they remain lean as in the original design.

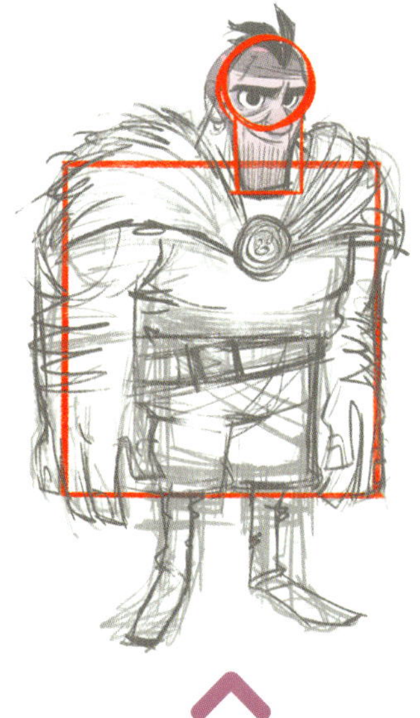

Keeping the same construction guides for the character's head will ensure that he looks similar despite his very different body shape. Features like the original design's strong rectangular jaw will translate well to this new context.

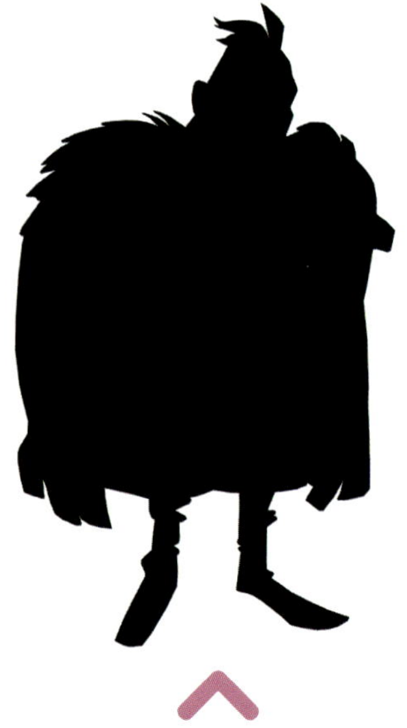

Here you can see how the silhouette feels like a big heavy block with two thin legs for contrast, which is the impression I want to create. Like with the original version, the viewer's attention will be drawn towards the upper body, while the legs give a sense of agility.

DETAILS

I start to make final decisions on the elements of the costume I like the most, and those that I don't. I still want the character to seem mobile and agile despite his short stature; adding a flowing robe and longer cape will give me more opportunities for exciting poses, so I opt for a robe over the short trousers I drew initially. I also use the cape as an opportunity to break up the silhouette, moving away from the streamlined shape language of the sci-fi character.

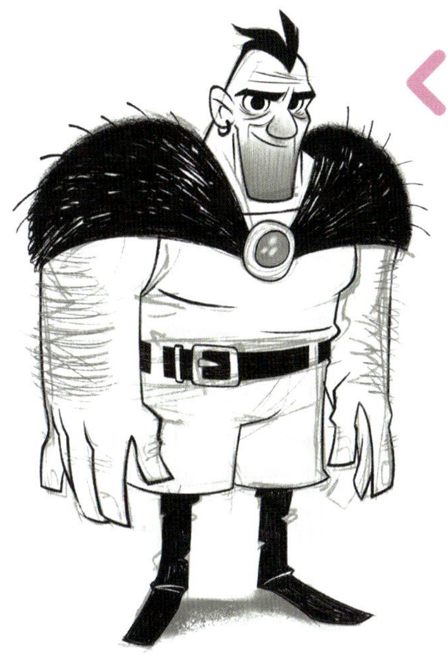

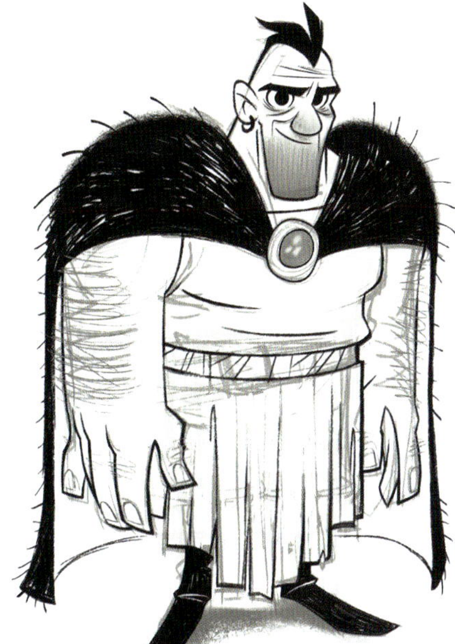

The character's spiky hairline and cloak recall the sharp black shapes on the original suit, while the earring adds a roguish charm that fits his overall demeanor. Adding more hair enhances the dwarvish appearance.

Giving him a robe and a more noticeable fur cape creates a slightly more mystic touch, as if he is a versatile fighter who is also capable of using magic. I like this addition because it makes him less of a straightforward hero, which is also what I wanted for the original design.

EXPRESSIONS & POSING

I want the character's pose to still capture the essence of the main character: someone tough, daring, curious, and ready for anything. The addition of the long cloak gives me a totally new element with which to create a dynamic pose. Though the character is equally at home wielding magic or a sword, I opt to show him with a sword – the additional long prop adds extra flow to the design.

This pose shows the character using his magic powers. This emphasizes his large, expressive hands, and is also both different and similar to the sci-fi version: he doesn't need a ranged weapon, like a ray gun, but can still fight effectively from a distance. However, this pose does not make the most of his cloak as a dynamic design element.

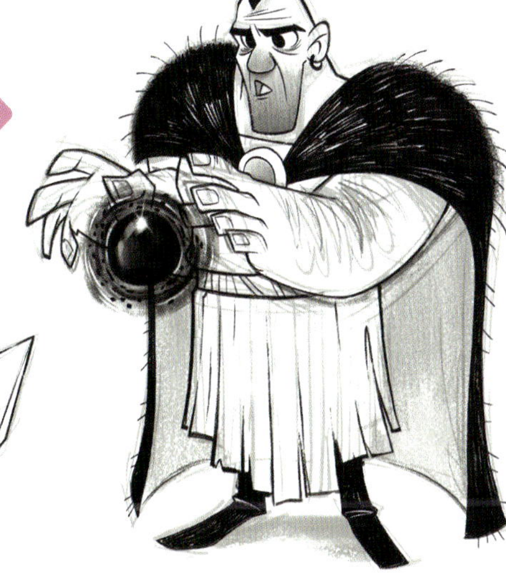

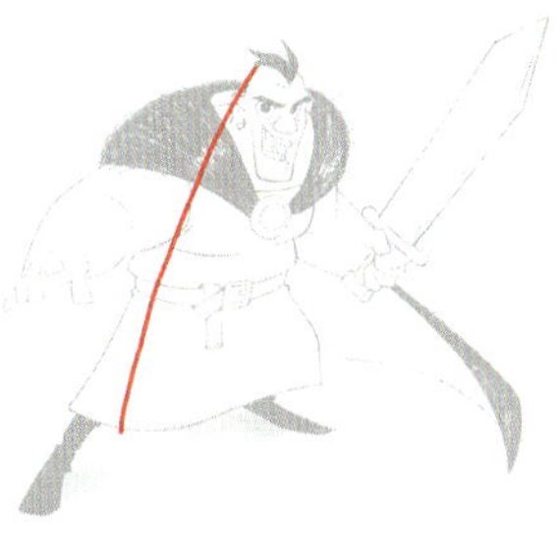

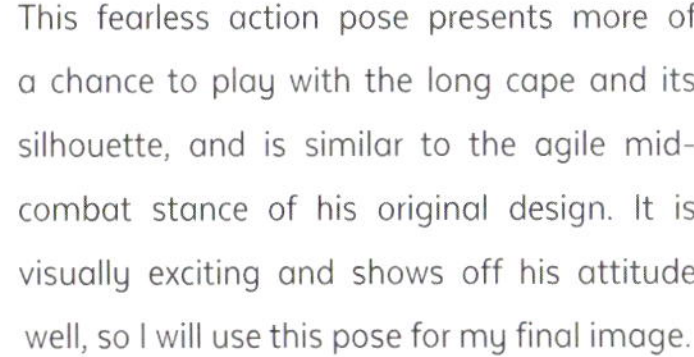

This fearless action pose presents more of a chance to play with the long cape and its silhouette, and is similar to the agile mid-combat stance of his original design. It is visually exciting and shows off his attitude well, so I will use this pose for my final image.

VALUE & COLOR

I want the color palette of the character to stay the same, relating him back to the original design, but I will play around with the distribution of colors to suit this new character. Enforcing this restriction on myself encourages me to be smarter and more resourceful in how I use my limited color palette.

This value distribution will be the ideal one to aim for, as it keeps the elements of the character distinct from each other. The light value of his belt keeps the darker value of his robe from looking too dark and flat.

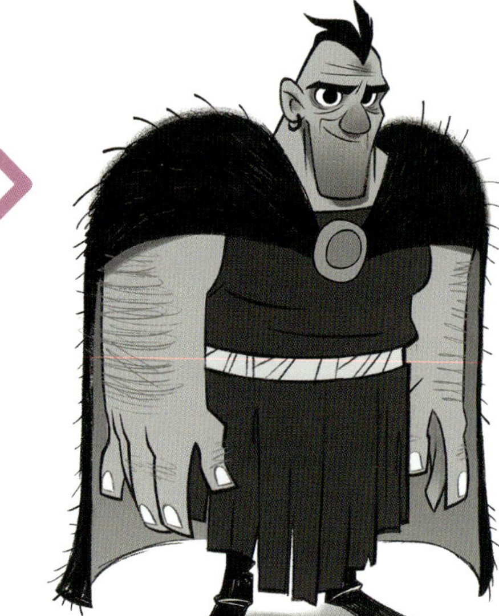

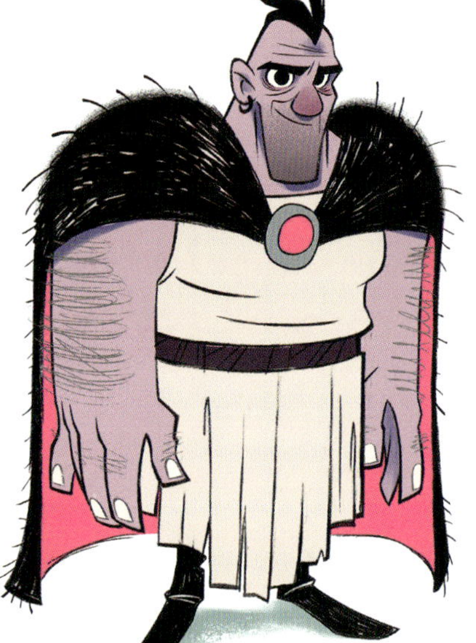

This color palette relies heavily on the bone-white color that was prominent in the sci-fi version's suit. However, the values are too light overall, and it doesn't give the impression of a rugged adventurer; he seems more like a priest or cleric.

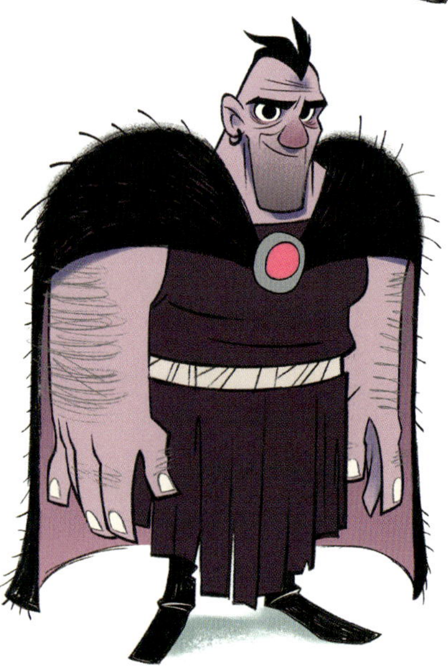

The palette has a strong balance of dark and light colors. The bright pink accent is now limited to the jewel in his cloak, and the black cloak and boots hark back to the original design without being too obvious. I will use this color scheme for my final design. The extra purple also hints at his potential mystical abilities.

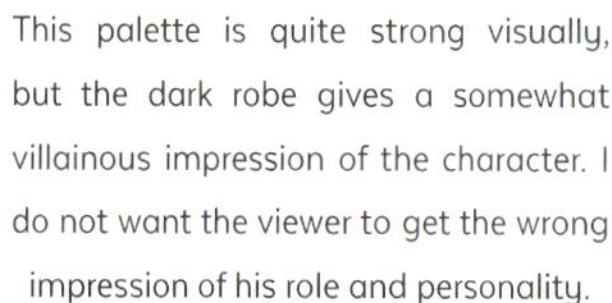

This palette is quite strong visually, but the dark robe gives a somewhat villainous impression of the character. I do not want the viewer to get the wrong impression of his role and personality.

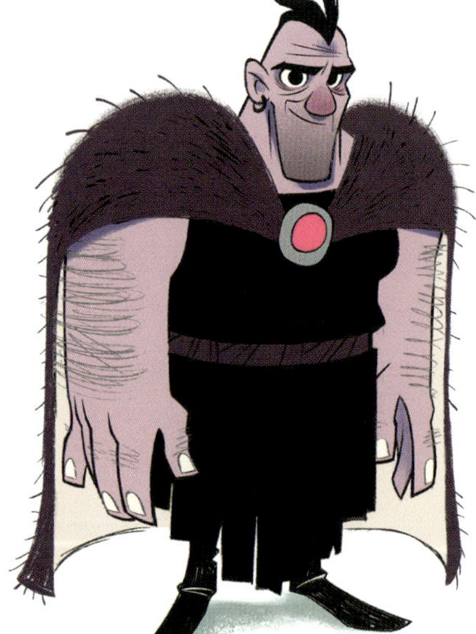

FINAL DESIGN

This final design succeeds in translating the character into a different setting, genre, and even body shape. His face is still very much relatable to the original design, and this is reinforced by the character's whole pose and attitude, as well as the more subtle cues in his costume design and color palette, such as the black collar of his cloak. The long cloak and sword are dynamic new elements that enhance his pose and make him seem physically impressive despite his smaller height, paralleling how the original character's attitude and tall height made him seem impressive despite his lack of typical heroic strength. The massive arms further convey his power. Adding some ragged edges to his robe is a finishing touch that suits his role as a tough adventurer.

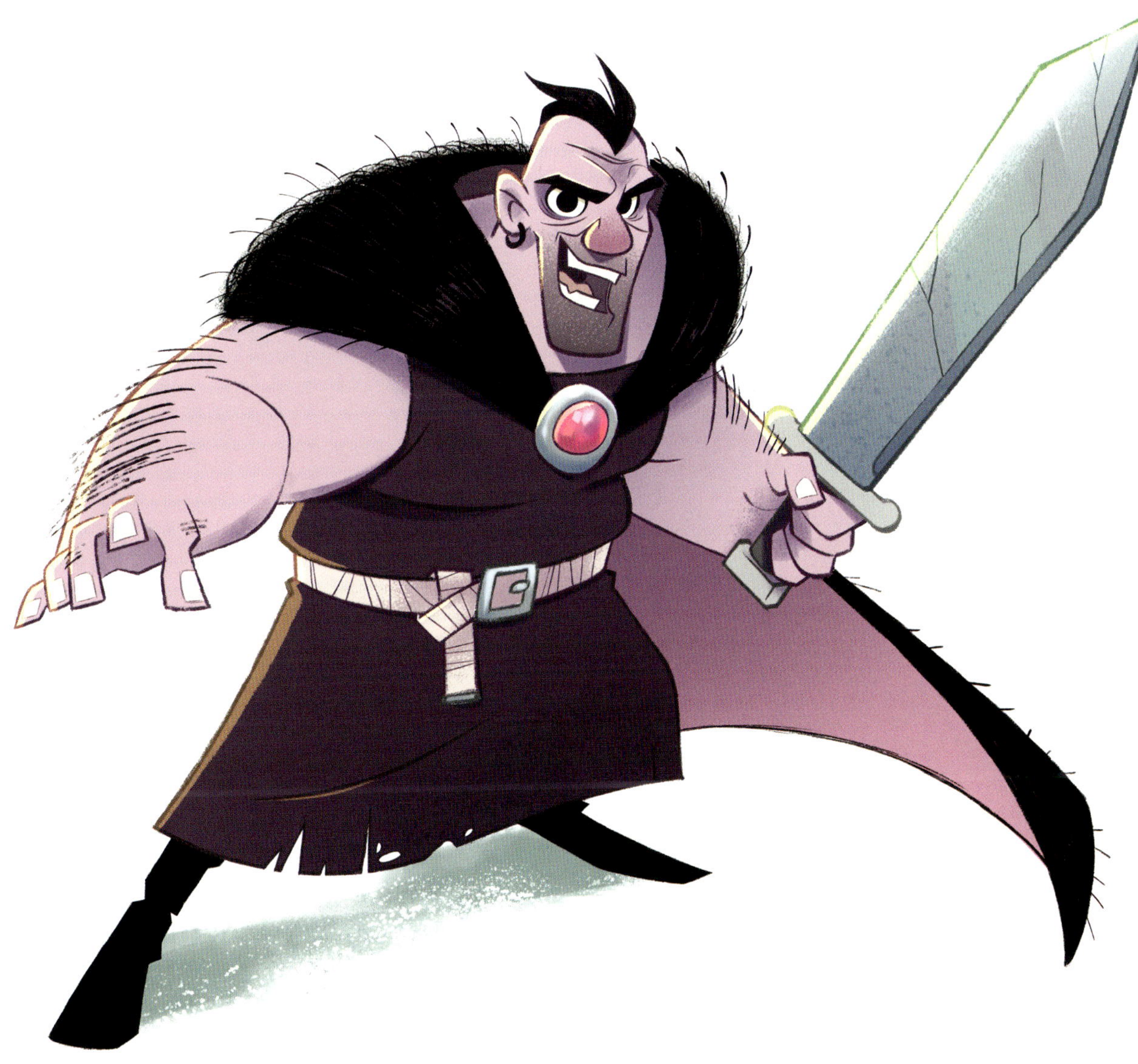

Final artwork © Luis Gadea

VARIATION 3:
SPACE MONKEY

IDEAS & RESEARCH

For this variation I will transform the human spaceman into an animal, in this case a monkey. The imagery ties in with real-world history of apes and monkeys being sent into orbit by space programs, and even with sci-fi properties like *Planet of the Apes*, creating an association for the viewer that is immediately familiar and relevant. I want to keep my research very simple, focusing on three main aspects which are the monkey face, hands, and feet. I would like the body to stay very similar to the original design, as the human character's exaggerated proportions and long arms already seem appropriate for an anthropomorphized monkey.

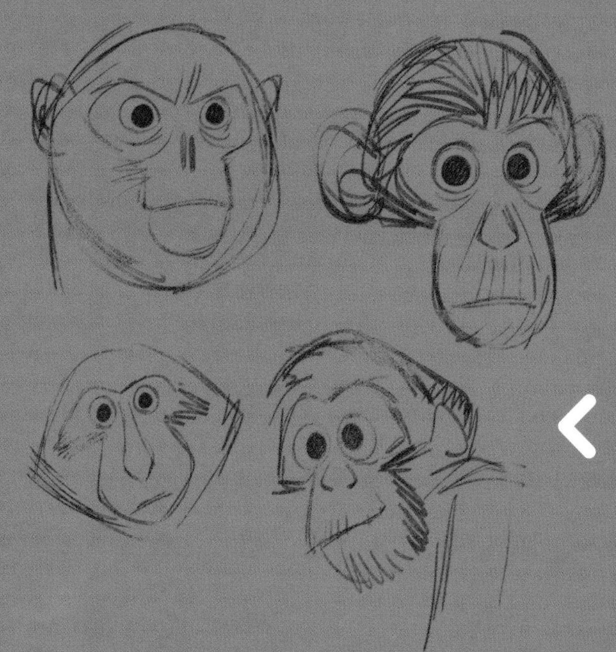

As with the previous versions, I want to make the face the focal point of the design, so head shapes and different solutions for noses are key to this. I research some different species of monkey with very varied features, looking for something that will capture the personality of the original character. Expressive eyes and strong contrast around the brow area will be key to achieving this.

I research and study some references for the monkey's hands. The human character has big hands already, and I think I can enhance this feature in the monkey version by adding wrinkles to his hands and making them hairy.

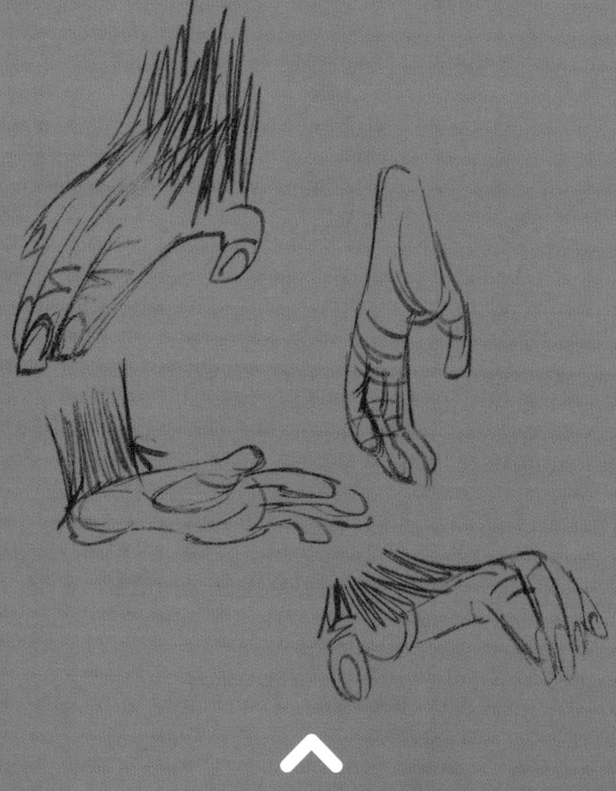

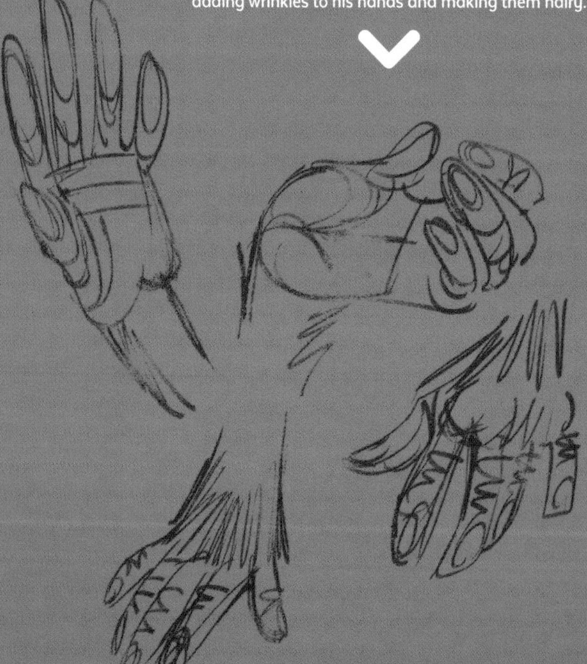

I could possibly make the character barefoot to show off his prehensile monkey feet. In this case, as with the hands, I study some references to get a better understanding of the feet's construction.

CHANGES

I need to find a balance between keeping the original character's body shapes and changing the design to capture the look of a monkey. One of the challenges will be to keep the monkey recognizably "in character," making him relatable and expressive, not losing the personality and main reference points of his human counterpart. I start by pinpointing the key design choices of the original design, in order to judge what will translate to this new species.

The biggest change in this character will be the design of his face and head. His accessories may change to fit his simian head shape, so I must find ways to ensure that his design still has similarities with the human original. For example, the shape of the monkey's fur could resemble the human's cap.

I want to keep the same feeling and style for the monkey's suit as I had in the original character, as portraying the monkey as technologically advanced is key to the design still being sci-fi. However, I don't want it to look completely identical, so I could try to combine the same colors in a different way.

The eyes are a key feature of the human character's face, expressing much of his personality. It will be very important to translate the eyes to this new character without losing their deep, perceptive look, so I will pay special attention to them.

Like the original character, I want the focus of the design to be on the upper body and head. Maintaining a similar silhouette will help with this aspect.

THUMBNAILS

For the thumbnail process, as with the other designs, I do not necessarily choose one specific thumbnail. Instead I gather the strongest ideas from all of them and take them to the next stage. In this case I want clear-cut shapes with most of the attention on the upper body, keeping the limbs simple and lanky in a way that suits a monkey and is true to the original design. I feel the first and fourth thumbnails capture this especially well.

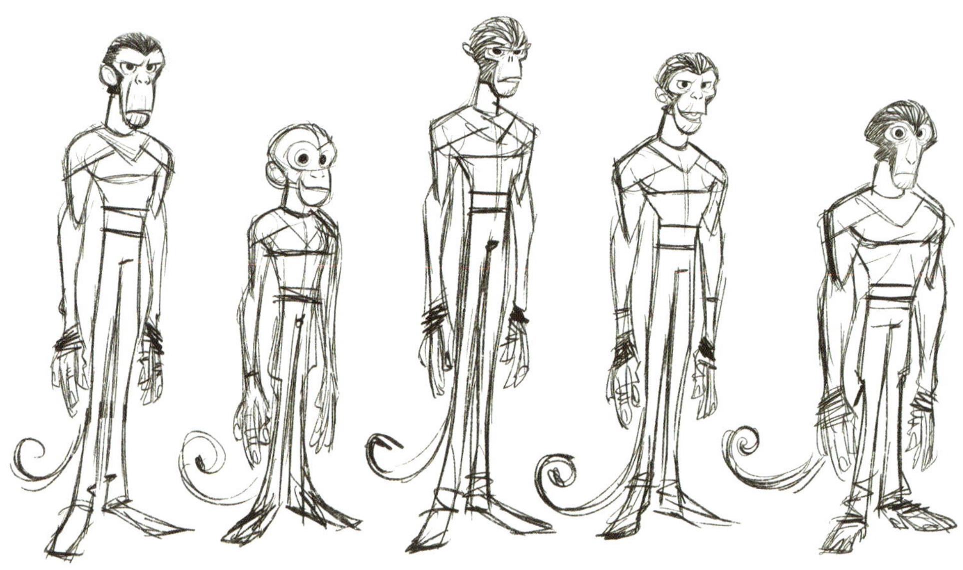

BASIC SHAPES

The space monkey's core body and limbs will not deviate far from the original character, who by chance was already rather agile and simian in his proportions! Instead I will focus on emphasizing the monkey features that are visible outside his suit, such as a large head and distinct tail. Exaggerating these features will ensure that his species is clear despite his other more human aspects.

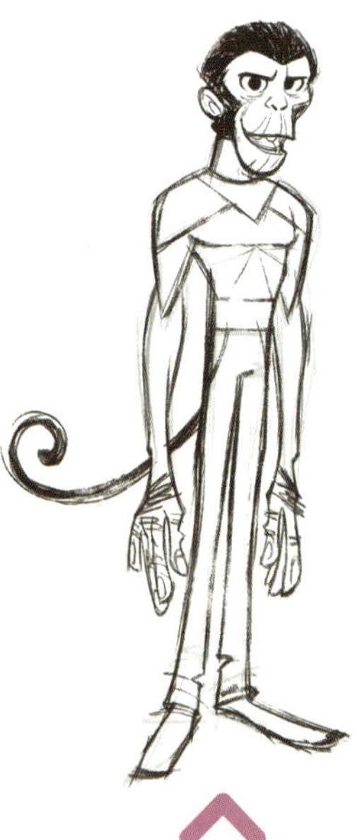

I combine the best ideas from my thumbnails, choosing one of the higher-contrast heads framed by sharp fur to make a strong focal point. I discard the idea of the character being barefoot, as I want him to seem like an advanced, futuristic monkey, rather than a regular Earth monkey who is wearing a spacesuit by chance.

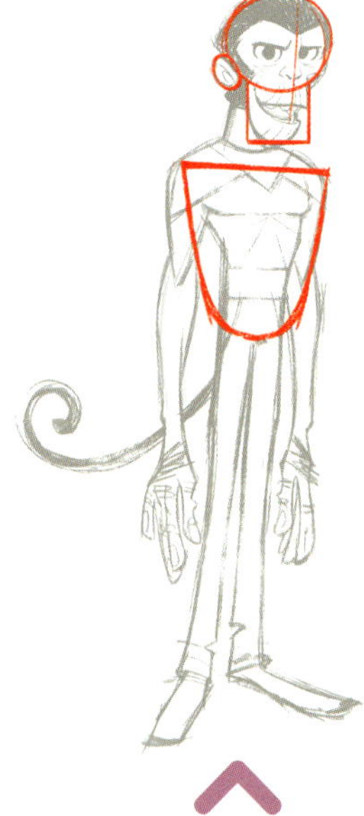

You can see how I am trying to use the same basic shapes and construction guides as I did for the human character. This will ensure that the two versions have a similar final structure. However, I make the character's head slightly large relative to his body, so that he is still clearly monkey-like and not too human.

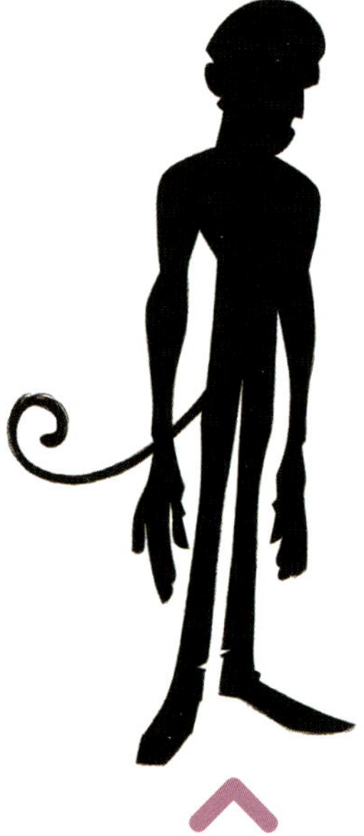

The silhouette is very similar to the original human version, but the clear shape of the tail conveys that he is definitely not a human. The proportionally larger head also gives the impression that this character is not as tall as the original.

DETAILS

During this stage I clarify which of my earlier ideas will make it through to the final piece. I decide on a head with strong eyebrows that will allow me to create very "human" facial expressions. The black fur on his head is drawn close around his face, like the original character's spacesuit hood, while also echoing the black triangular pattern of his suit. I join the fur and collar detail almost together, creating a solid, striking black shape that is the emphatic focal point of the design.

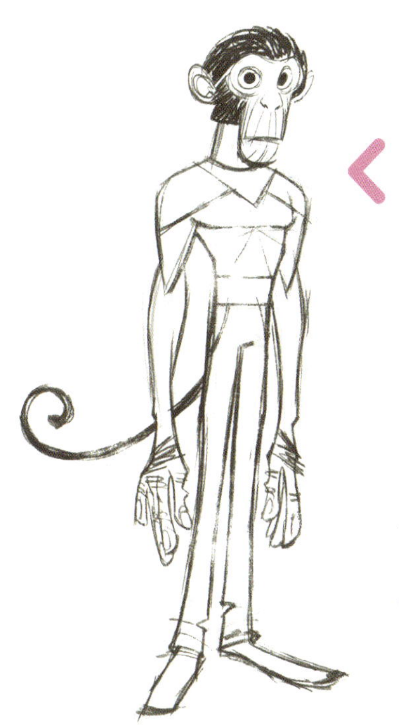

As I opted against showing the monkey's feet, his hairy hands and tail must be enough to sell the animal aspect of the design. The contrast created by these details must also complement my final choices for values and colors later.

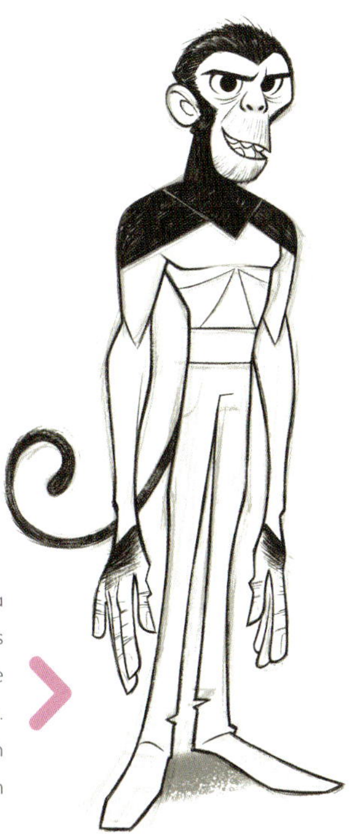

This mischievous expression is a perfect fit, with the deep-set eyes and confident smile recalling the personality of the original character. Making his face hairier enhances both his roguish charisma and his simian appearance.

EXPRESSIONS & POSING

For the posing stage, I want to convey the same energy and positive personality of the human version, using upright stances that are more relatably human than animal.

This pose is very lighthearted and monkey-ish, giving an impression of him as a spontaneous and fun character. However, it doesn't clearly communicate his role as a space hero.

This pose more accurately portrays the character as a space adventurer, with his weapon drawn and his attention focused on his mission. The animal snarl keeps his expression from looking too human. I will use this pose for my final image.

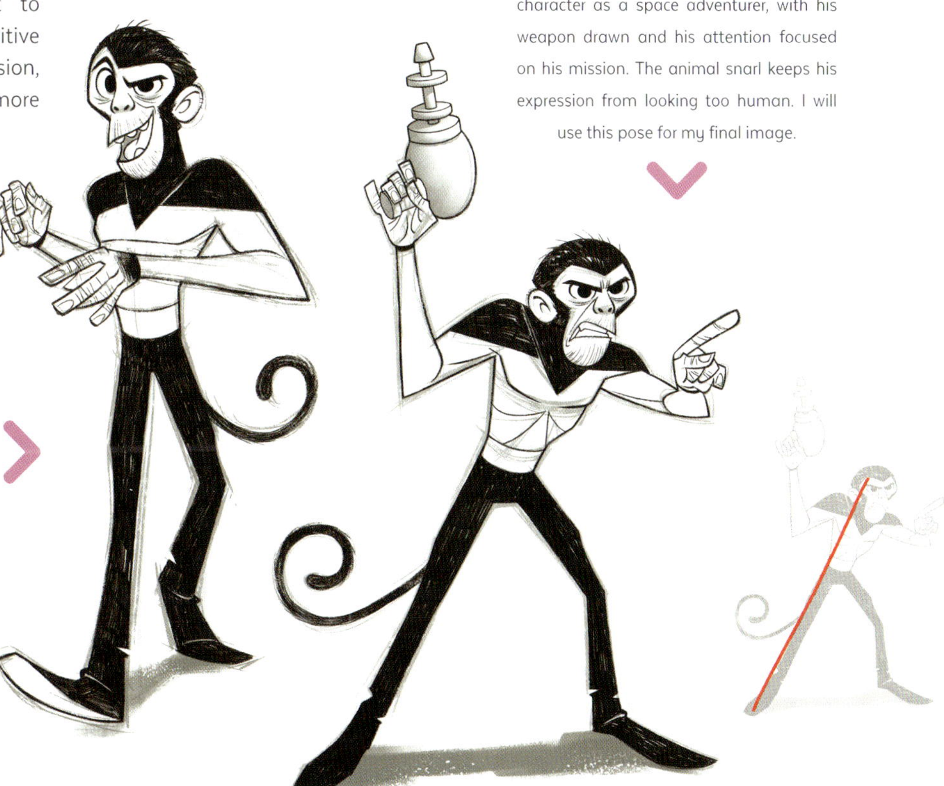

VALUE & COLOR

Like I said before, I want to keep the character clearly the same in role and personality, but now simply a monkey rather than a human. However, I do not want the designs to be completely the same; I need to re-evaluate the color palette to account for the monkey's different values and contrasts. Using the original design's simple, sophisticated-feeling colors as a starting point, I try to find a new distribution of colors that will fit this character.

Like with the human version, I make the character's legs almost a silhouette, and this time I also darken the values of his upper body. This makes his face pop even more vividly. I really want to emphasize the dark, severe brow from my simian research.

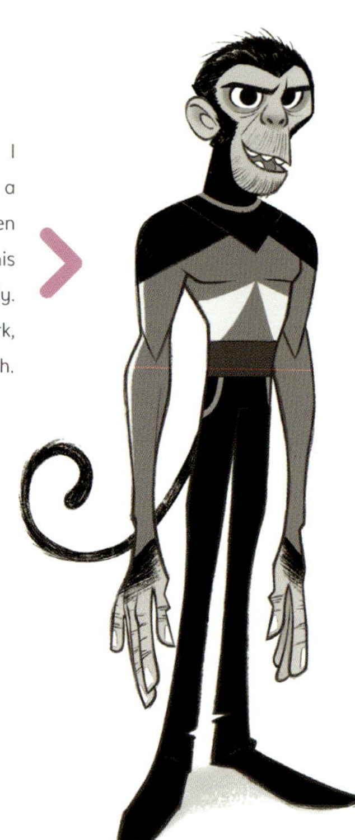

This palette prioritizes the dark purple color, which makes the face pop but does not contrast so well with the rest of his suit. The bold black shapes of his shoulders are not very legible against this color.

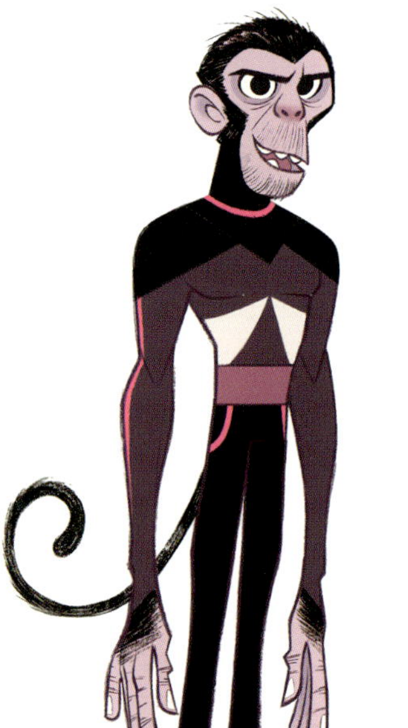

Using this muted pink as the main color makes the design fun and colorful without being excessive. Unlike the other palettes, it provides a sufficient level of contrast between both the character's face and the dark details on his suit, being neutral rather than too light or too dark. I will use this for my final design.

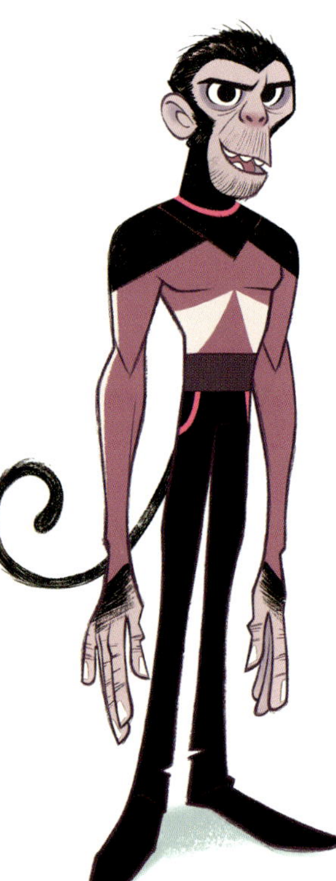

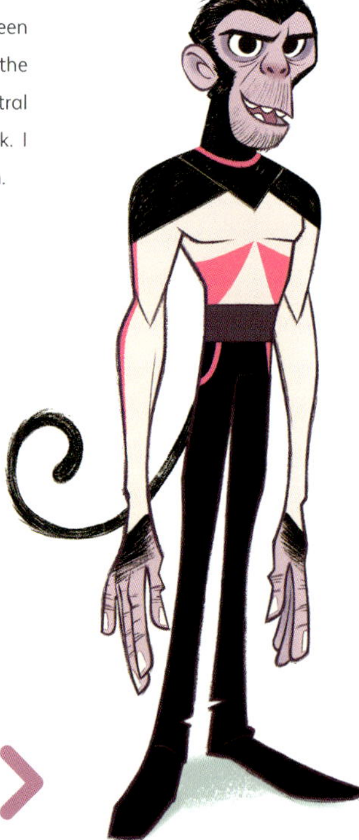

I try using the colors as they were in the original character palette, as it could suggest a bit of backstory if the monkey and human wear the same uniform. However, as I thought, the light colors draw attention away from his face. The design would be stronger if the monkey's suit was more his own.

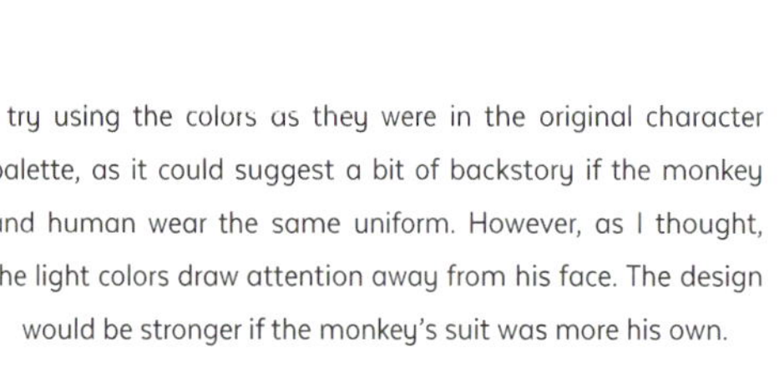

FINAL DESIGN

My final version of the space monkey succeeds in relating a new species back to the original design. His determined pose and expressive eyes capture the same sense of the character being a brave adventurer, and the color palette is relatable to the original design despite the emphasis on a different color. His large head, when paired with such skinny limbs, gives the subtle impression of the character being smaller than a human, and is further played up by the relatively large size of the ray gun. As before, his legs are just silhouettes that support the focal areas of the character rather than drawing any attention away. The long, curly tail adds a sense of flow and fun that keeps the design appealingly light-hearted, even in a tense action scenario.

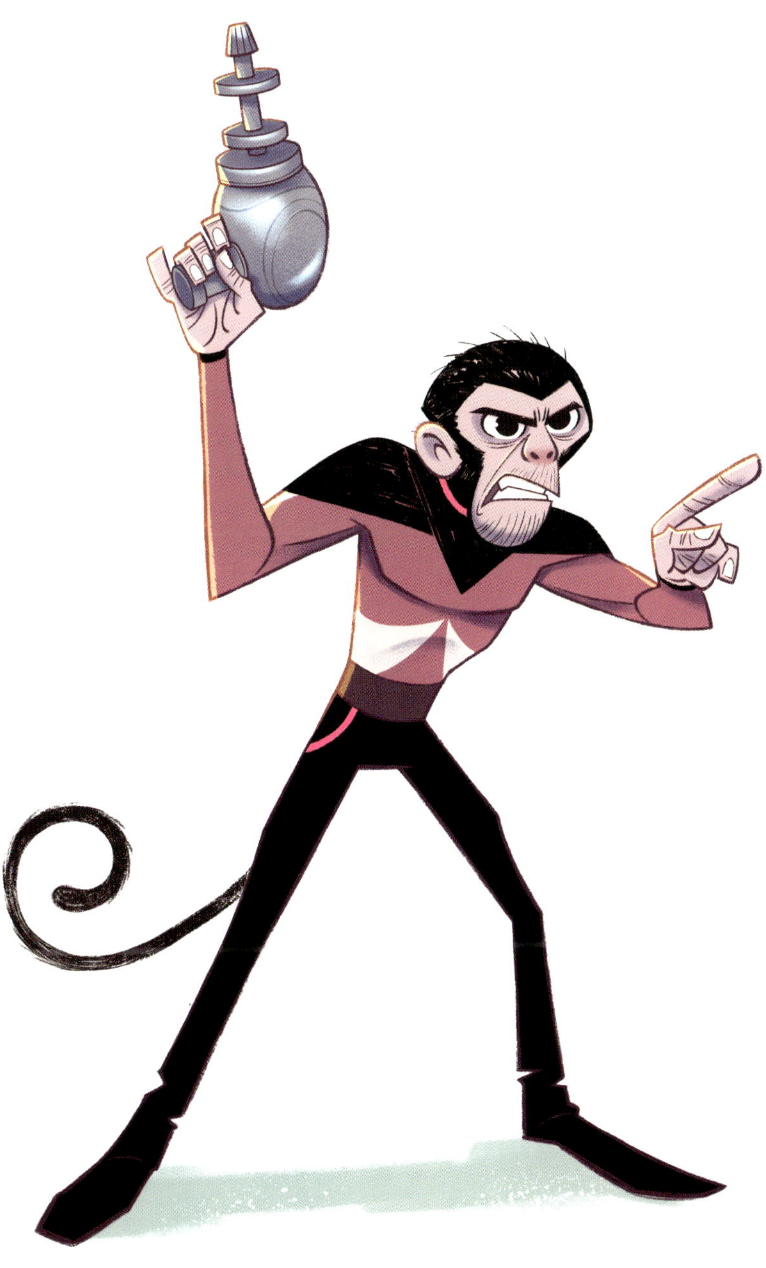

Final artwork © Luis Gadea

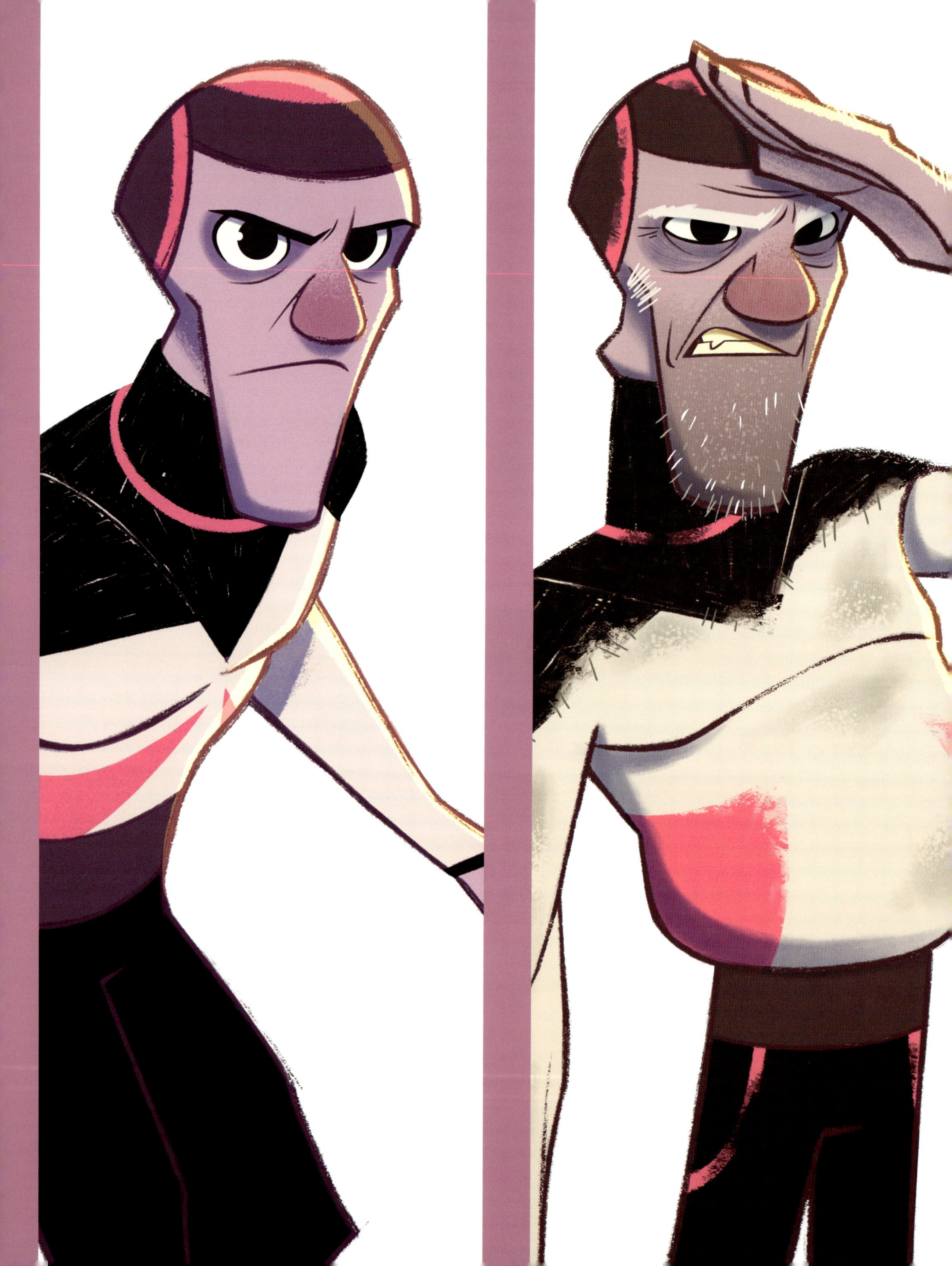

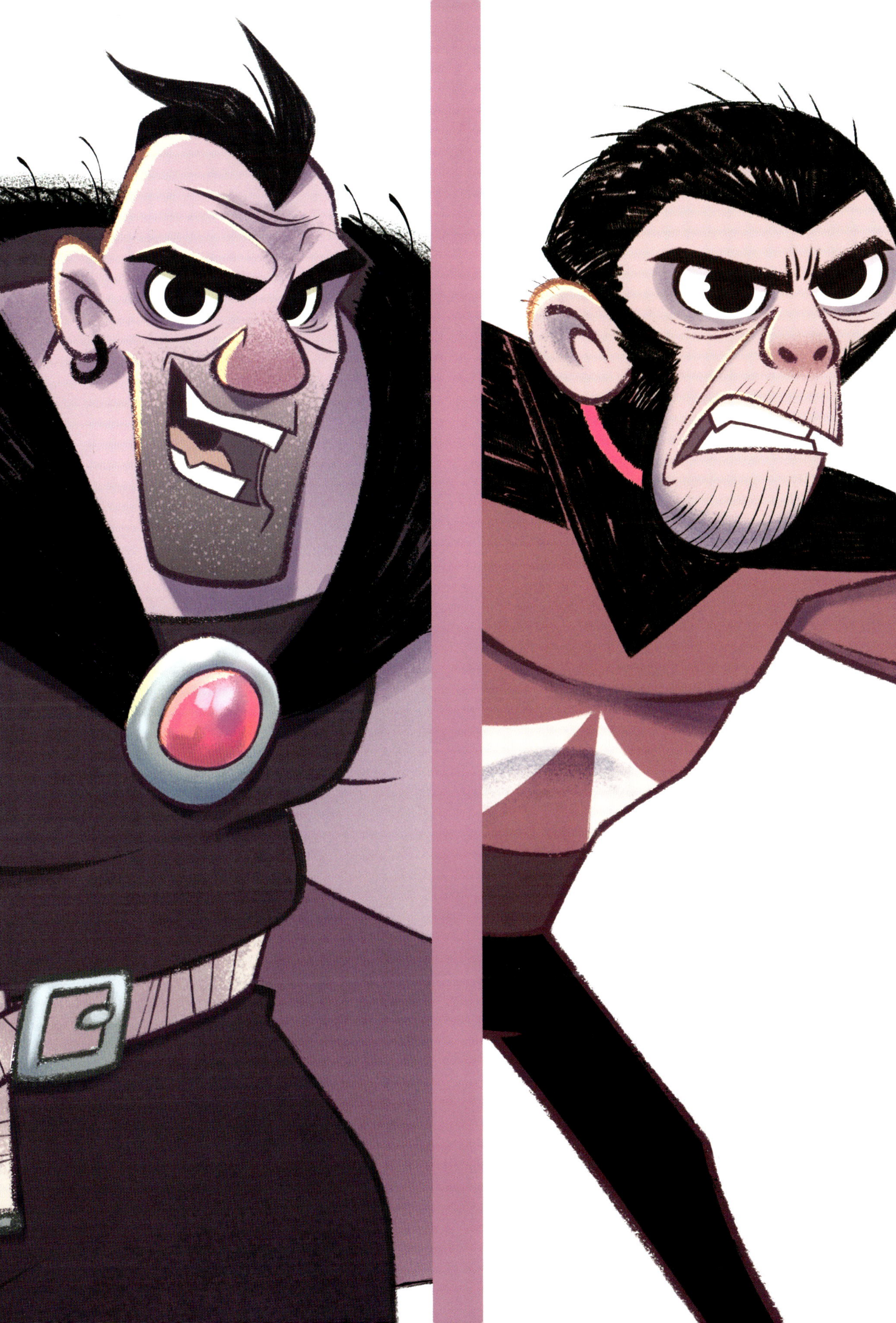

FANTASY WARRIOR

BY ENRIQUE FERNÁNDEZ

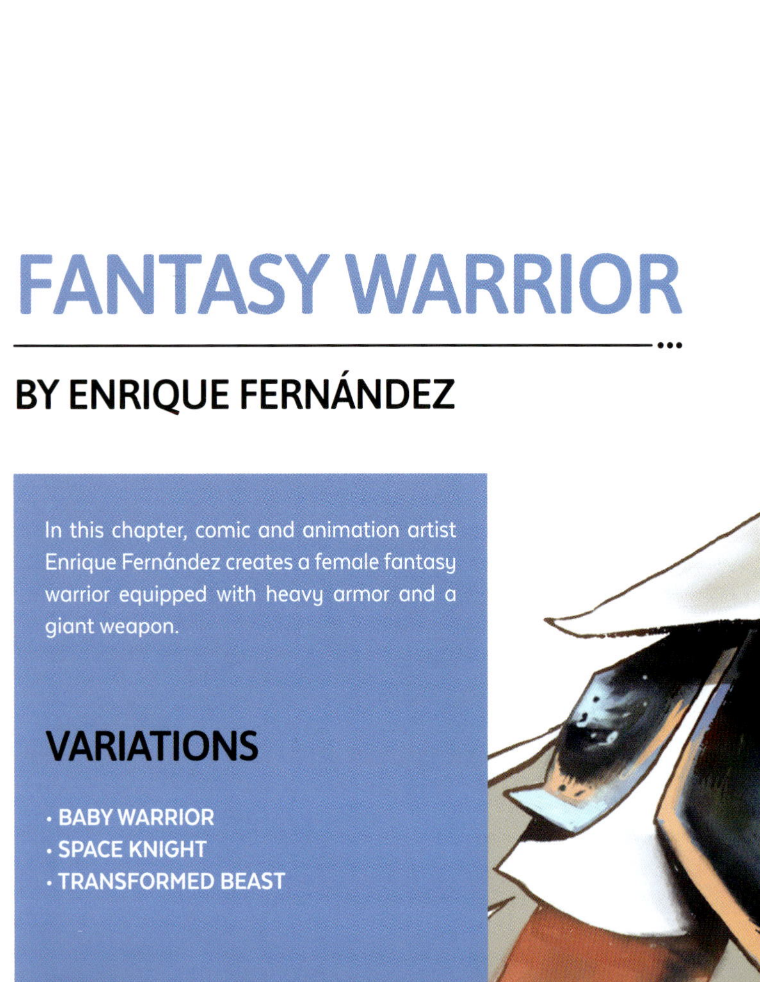

In this chapter, comic and animation artist Enrique Fernández creates a female fantasy warrior equipped with heavy armor and a giant weapon.

VARIATIONS

- BABY WARRIOR
- SPACE KNIGHT
- TRANSFORMED BEAST

FOCUS

Enrique's style makes use of strong geometric forms, material textures, and a painterly finish. This approach would be perfectly suited to a comic or graphic novel.

Pay special attention to creating bold recurring shapes and patterns, and how these can be used to create a sense of continuity and story across very different-looking versions of a character.

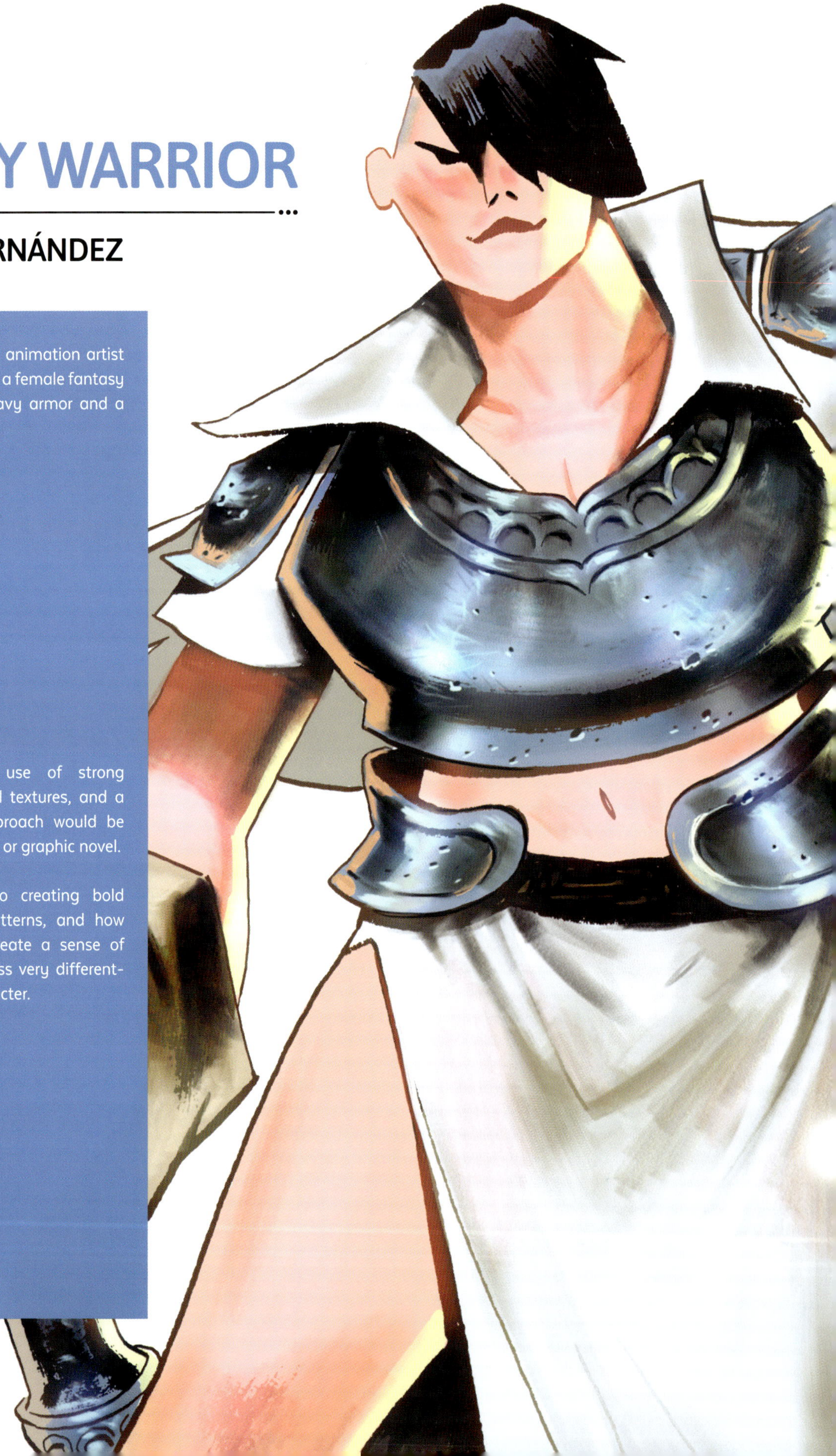

THE IDEA

In this project, I am going to depict a female warrior from a medieval or fantasy setting. I want to avoid the modern "industry" standards of beauty when figuring out the appearance and proportions of the character. I would like her to look strong and fast, and also charismatic and quite feminine. However, though she might be attractive both physically and in attitude, I don't want to depict her as a fashion model instead of a fighter, or she wouldn't last long on the battlefield! I will focus on large, clear shapes, and on the contrast between materials when creating the final version - such as rough textures for her armor and soft textures for her clothes - as this will make her more dynamic.

Concept: A female warrior with armor and a heavy weapon

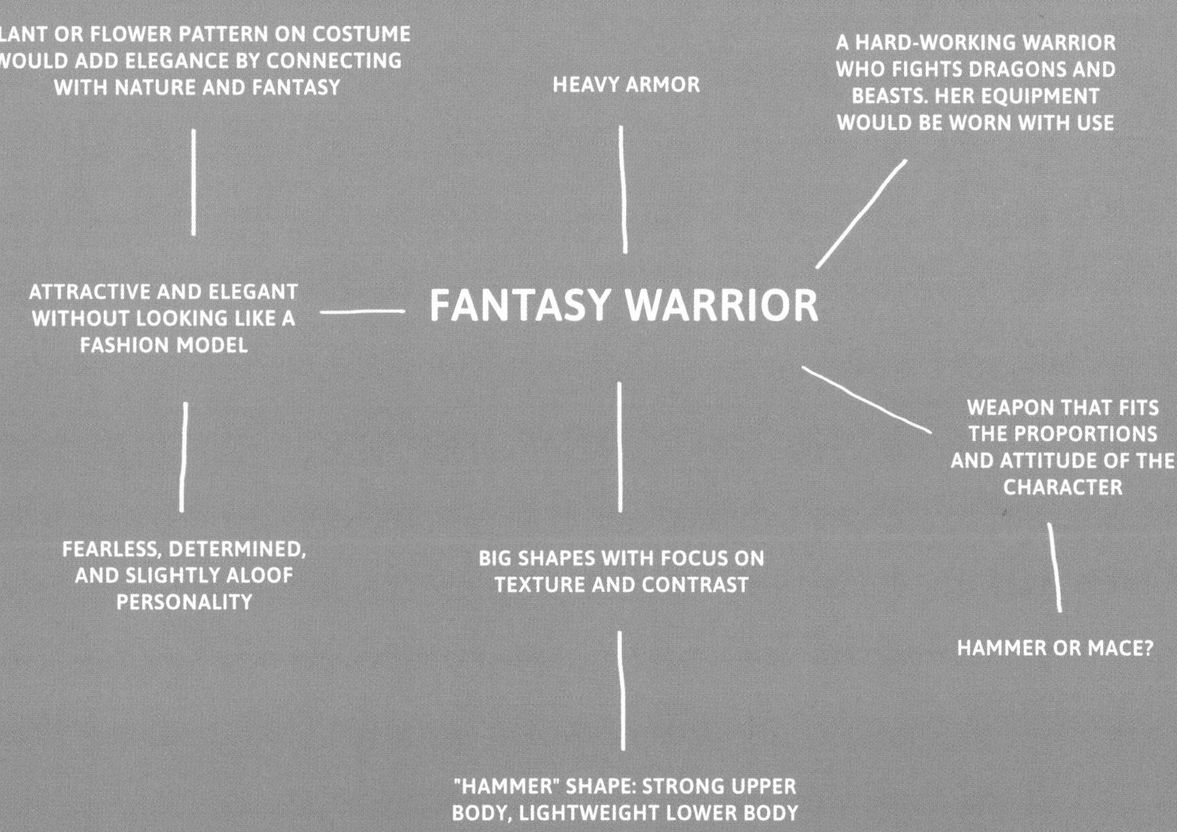

RESEARCH

The first thing I look for in my research is a basic "shape" for the character. I want to be sure that the design is clear and has internal coherence, using just one or very few basic shapes. I think further about my idea of hammer-like proportions for the character: top-heavy with a lighter lower body, recalling the shape of a hammer with a strong upper part held up by a lightweight handle. This would be a strong shape, and means she would be powerful when hitting things, conveying her strength as a warrior.

I also need to think about how to depict the character's fantasy aspect. Her armor could feature references to animals, plants, or imaginary beasts to add a fantasy element, but these should be subtle to avoid drawing too much visual attention.

Using flowers and plants as a reference for the armor designs will add a natural element and give the character elegance.

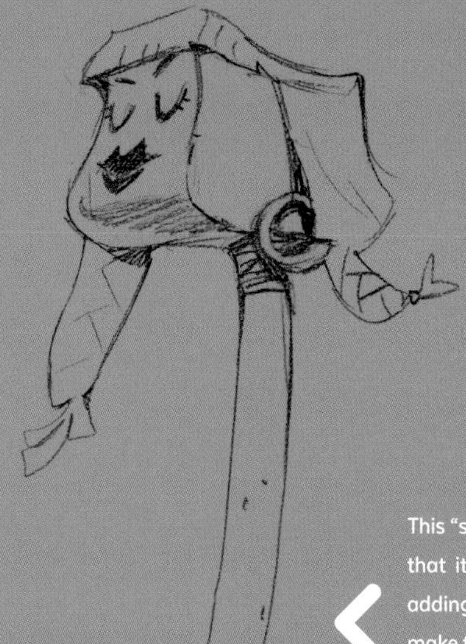

This "sexy hammer" is a reminder that it won't be as easy as just adding lipstick and eyelashes to make the design more "feminine." I have to find better and more subtle ways to achieve this.

I like the idea of the character having "hammer" proportions, but should she be square or rounded? Rounded shapes will add femininity to the concept.

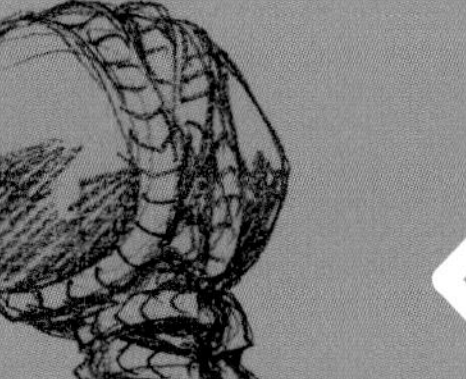

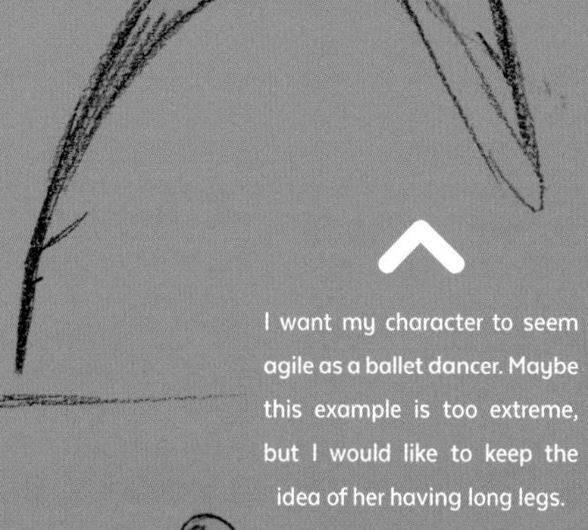

I want my character to seem agile as a ballet dancer. Maybe this example is too extreme, but I would like to keep the idea of her having long legs.

I look at references of beasts, animals, and dragons, and even some samurai helmets which have fierce faces like demons.

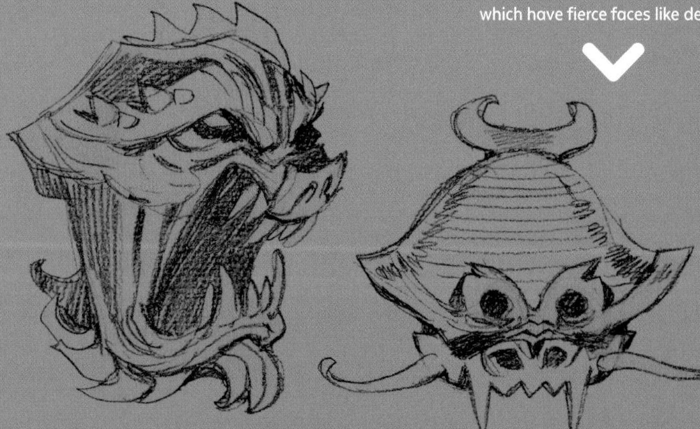

This gauntlet captures the idea of using contrasting textures: soft on the skin, and hard on the metal parts used in combat.

THUMBNAILS

I begin playing with the basic idea of a top-heavy character, inspired by that hammer motif: broad shoulders and arms, with long, slim legs. I try rounded shapes and angular shapes, stretching and squashing the proportions to find each concept's limits. I add elements that I know won't be included in the final design, such as long hair, dresses, and ornate armor, just to test them and work out which parts are not necessary. Some thumbnails do not capture the broad, long-legged proportions I am looking for. I try some bladed weapons, but they also do not fit my core shape idea. I decide that I like the simple heavy armor and clothing of the top row of thumbnails, but adding a flowing fabric element shown on some of the others will add grace to the design.

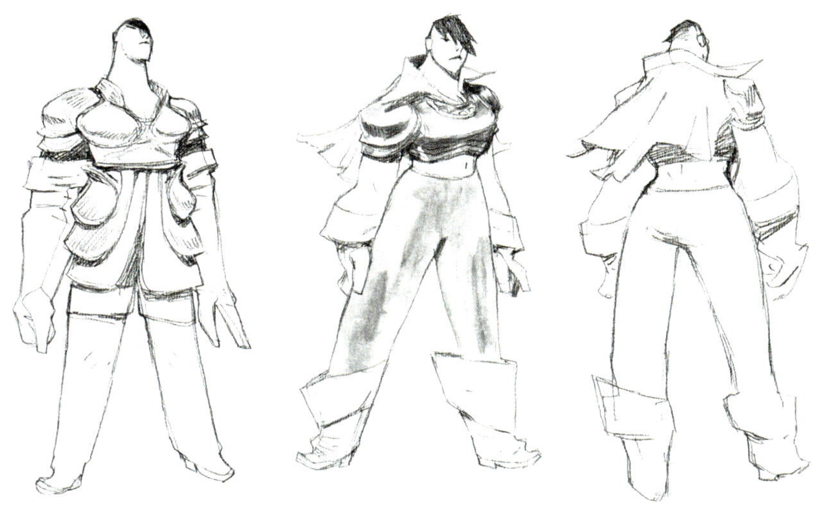

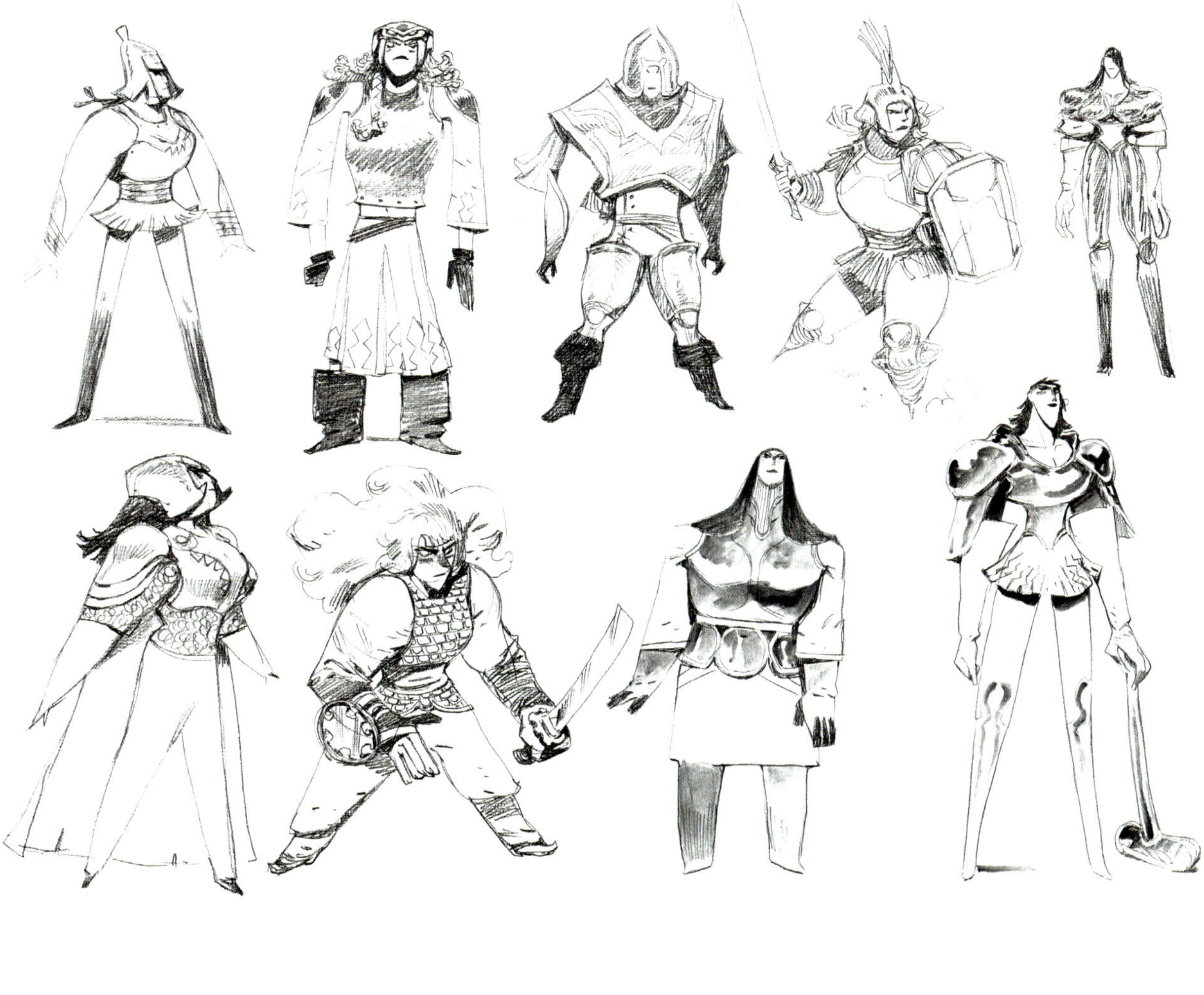

BASIC SHAPES

Now I combine the strongest elements of the thumbnails I mentioned on the previous page. The character's over-sized armor will draw a lot of attention when reading the character at first sight, and her short hair, shirt collar, and cape will add interest to the area around it.

The strong legs will make a powerful visual impact, with tiny, agile feet that work well to suggest that the character can jump and run with no effort. The narrow upper arms with large, gloved forearms and hands will also create visual contrast, ensuring that the design ties in with the hammer-like proportions I discussed earlier.

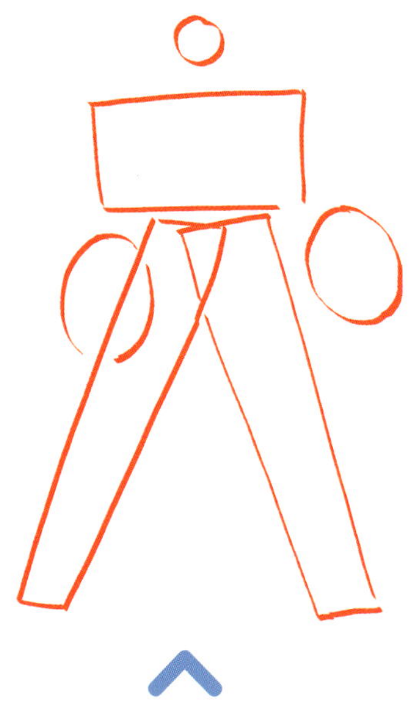

These basic shapes are representative of the initial hammer idea. I start with a square torso, even if the final shapes will be more rounded due to the overlying anatomy.

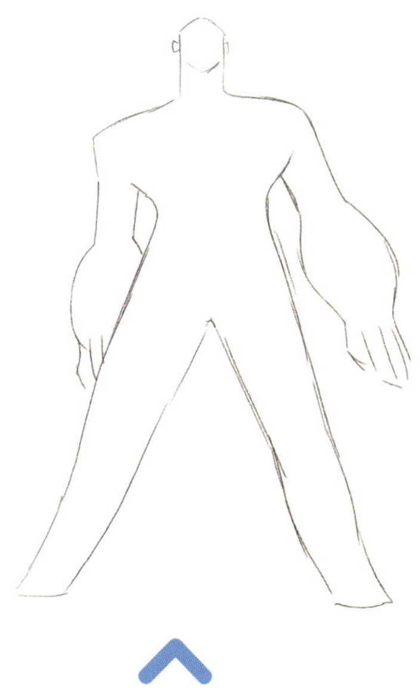

I begin outlining the shapes, making them more subtle and elegant, rounding off some corners while keeping the proportions. I start defining the parts of the body here.

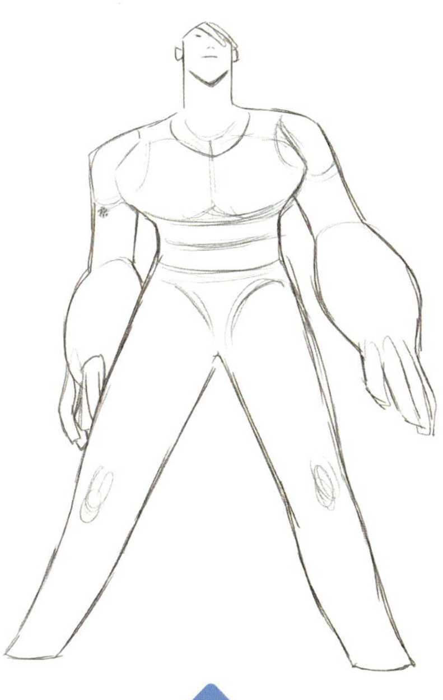

I ensure that I understand the volumes by defining the connections between the parts and highlighting some anatomical landmarks. You can see the character's strong physique becoming more defined.

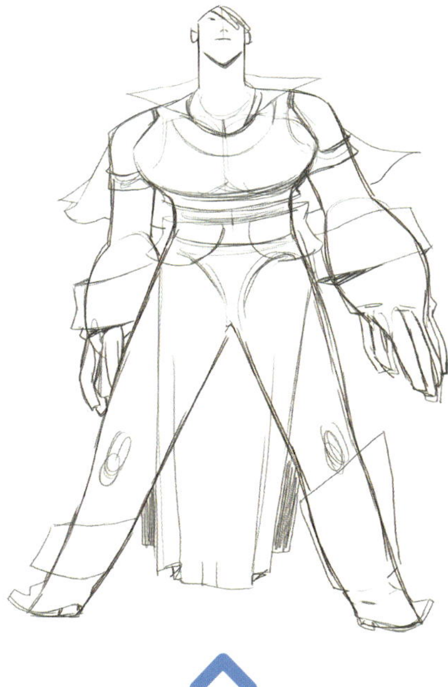

I add more elements and details, dressing the character. Angular shapes (such as the collar and boots) contrast with the more rounded forms (such as the arms and shoulders) to make the design dynamic.

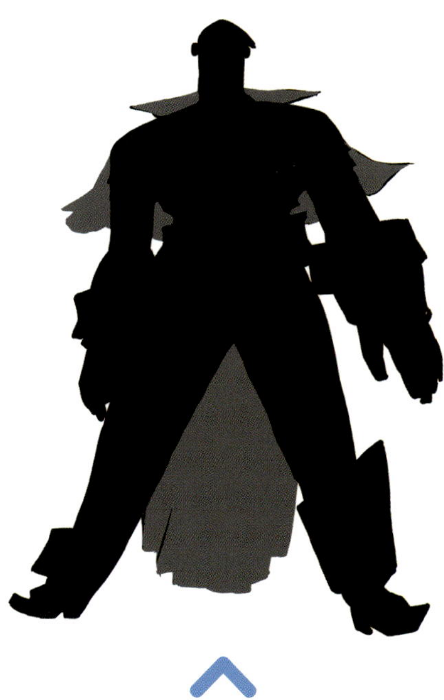

A black silhouette helps me to figure out if the character's main shape is recognizable. In this case, there are some fabrics that have a lot of movement. I have indicated these in gray because they won't determine the lines of the main body when it is posed.

DETAILS

I start to "dress" the character with details. I keep the cape short, so that it does not break the bulky shape of the upper body, and to make the whole character feel more mobile.

Small details like the design on her armor will add interest and contrast against the main armor texture, as well as introducing a kind of floral pattern that makes the whole design more elegant.

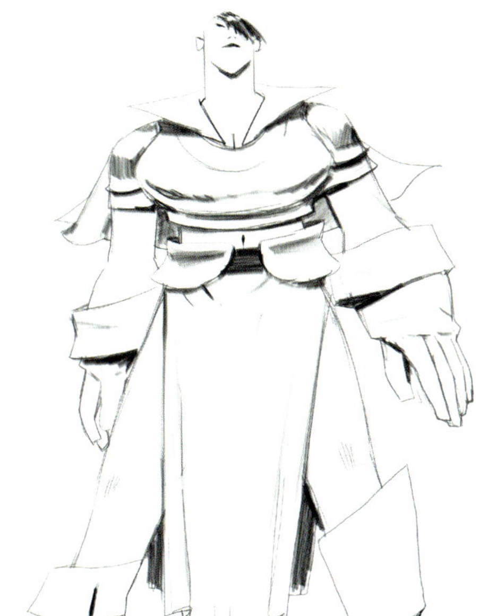

I start blocking in the shadows to better understand the character's volume. This is especially useful on a character with large forms such as this one. Her collar draws attention to her face, and her asymmetrical boots add flow to the costume, ensuring she doesn't look too blocky.

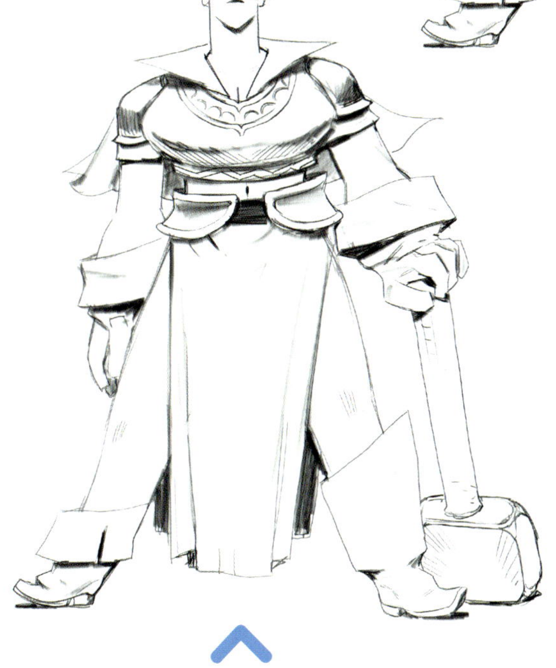

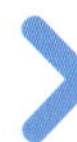

I add more textures to help describe the materials of the clothes and armor. At this point I add the initial design of her weapon (a hammer) and the ornamentation on her armor inspired by my research into floral designs. Her short haircut is tough-looking and covers one eye which, along with her long neck, makes her somewhat aloof and distant.

I change the hammer to more of a club or mace, to avoid being too repetitive with the character concept. The shape of it is still coherent with the rest of the character, echoing the shapes of her arms and legs.

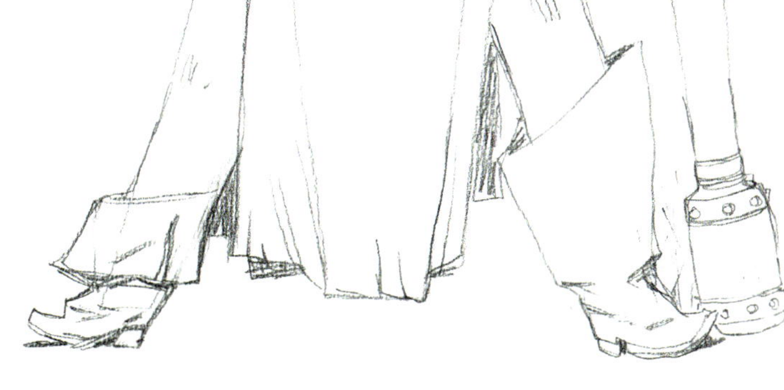

FACIAL EXPRESSIONS

It's time to make the character feel alive, giving her attitude and expression. Even without writing a single word on paper, I try to create stories to help me understand the background of the character, how they might react to situations, and how their usual facial expressions might be. We all have our own way of laughing – it is useful to think about the little things that make all of us different. Her angular facial features already help to indicate that she is a tough character, but her expressions must also convey her determination and confidence.

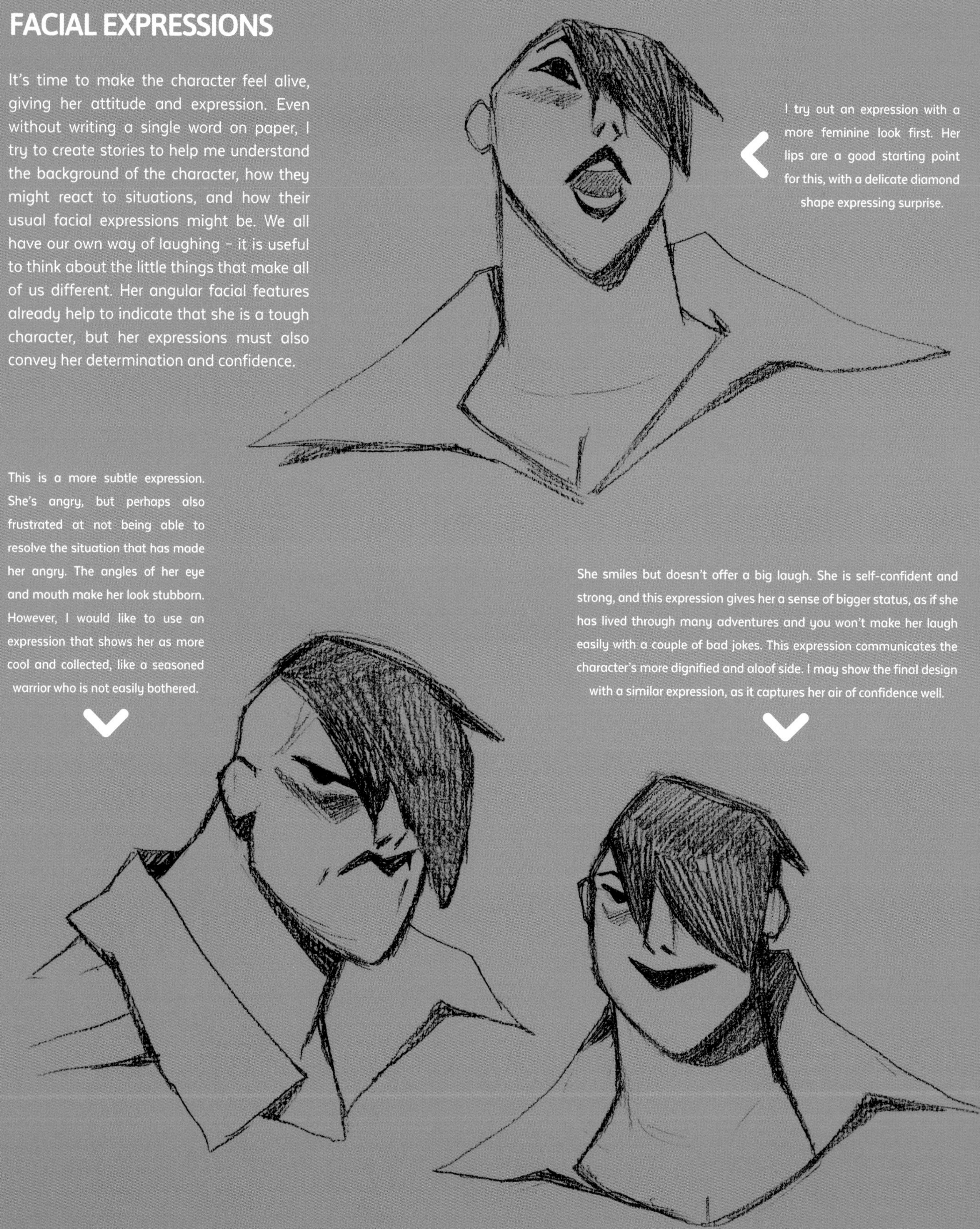

I try out an expression with a more feminine look first. Her lips are a good starting point for this, with a delicate diamond shape expressing surprise.

This is a more subtle expression. She's angry, but perhaps also frustrated at not being able to resolve the situation that has made her angry. The angles of her eye and mouth make her look stubborn. However, I would like to use an expression that shows her as more cool and collected, like a seasoned warrior who is not easily bothered.

She smiles but doesn't offer a big laugh. She is self-confident and strong, and this expression gives her a sense of bigger status, as if she has lived through many adventures and you won't make her laugh easily with a couple of bad jokes. This expression communicates the character's more dignified and aloof side. I may show the final design with a similar expression, as it captures her air of confidence well.

POSING

Posing the character will help me to understand the volumes and movement of the design. I want to try out poses that are both relaxed and in action, to see the behavior of the character in different situations. I need the pose to describe as much as possible about her attitude, showing that she is a warrior, fighting or preparing to fight. Her posture must show her broad, powerful physique – ideally with the sense of elegance and agility I defined in my research and thumbnails – and clearly project her confident personality.

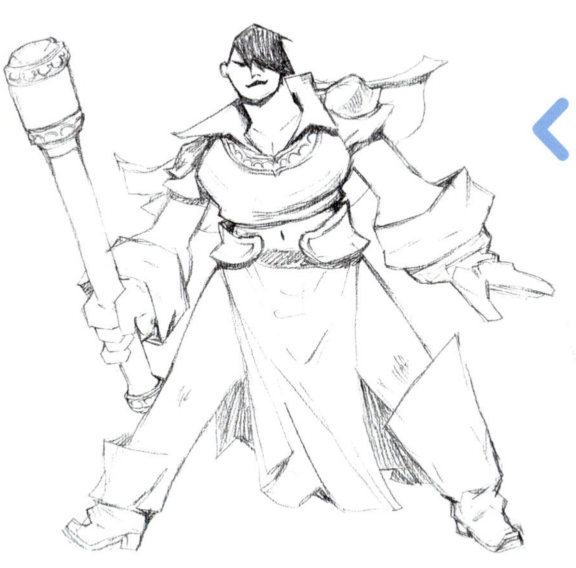

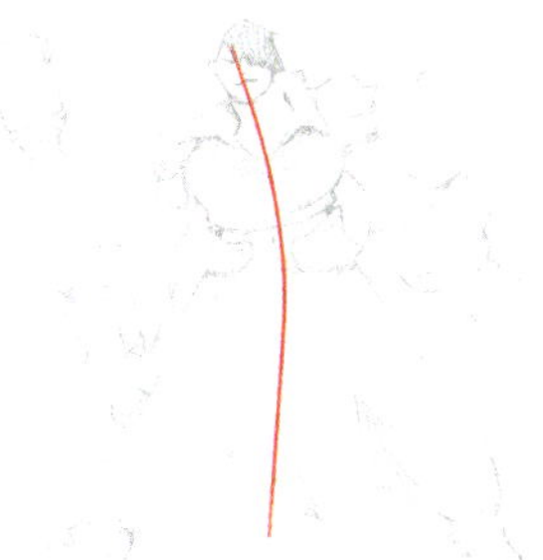

This pose is a good combination of an action pose and one that clearly describes all the elements of the character. We can see every piece of the design here, and her stance seems both steady and light-footed, suggesting a graceful sense of strength.

This pose reflects her natural behavior when relaxed. She stands with a strong vertical line that shows her self-confidence, even in a casual pose, and also conveys a sense of elegant poise. However, it does not show her weapon, which is a key part of her design.

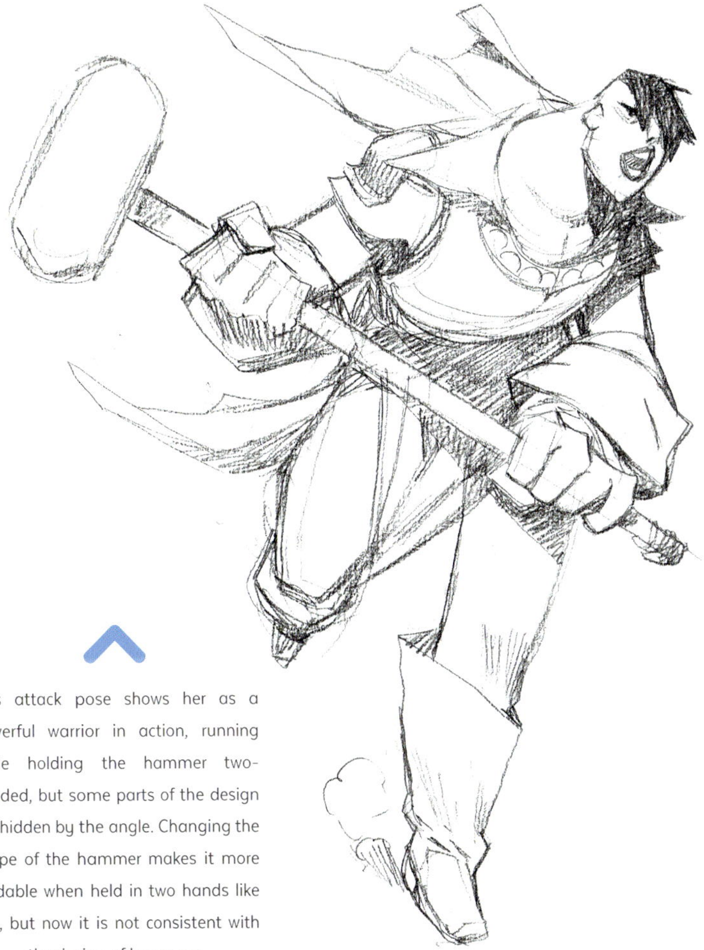

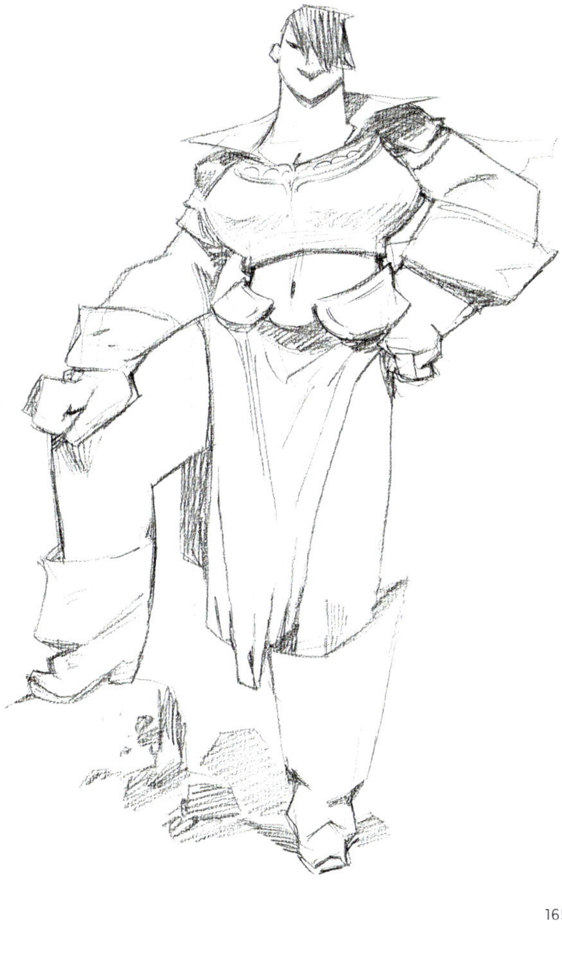

This attack pose shows her as a powerful warrior in action, running while holding the hammer two-handed, but some parts of the design are hidden by the angle. Changing the shape of the hammer makes it more readable when held in two hands like this, but now it is not consistent with the design of her armor.

VALUES & COLOR

For my final pose, I choose the wide, confident stance on the top right of the previous page, which shows her ready for combat, with all aspects of the design clearly visible. Now it is time to give the character more personality using color. It helps to think of the palette as just dots of colors that would make the character recognizable even without the rest of the design: for example, we all know that blue and red make Superman! I want to use colors that convey both her cool determination and her fierce warrior's attitude, so I test out cooler colors such as green and blue, and warmer shades of red, until I find a balance.

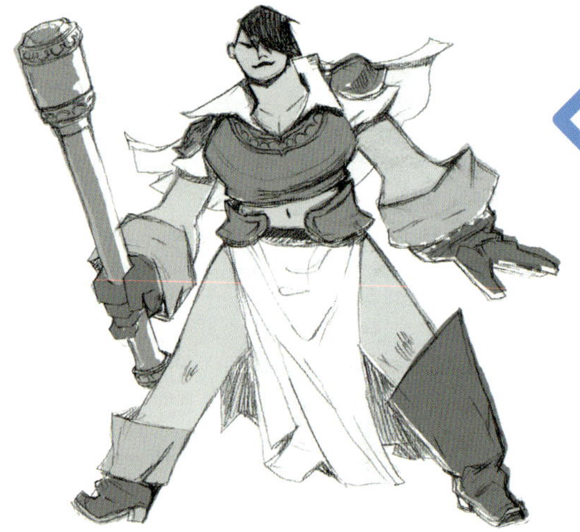

This value scheme is well balanced overall, with darker details on important areas such as her hands, feet, and armor, balanced out by the loose, light cloth areas, which are secondary elements for creating flow.

I try using bright reds to make her more aggressive looking, as if she likes to attract attention to her strongest elements, the ones that she use to fight: her fists, feet, and armor. However, this lacks variety in tone and color.

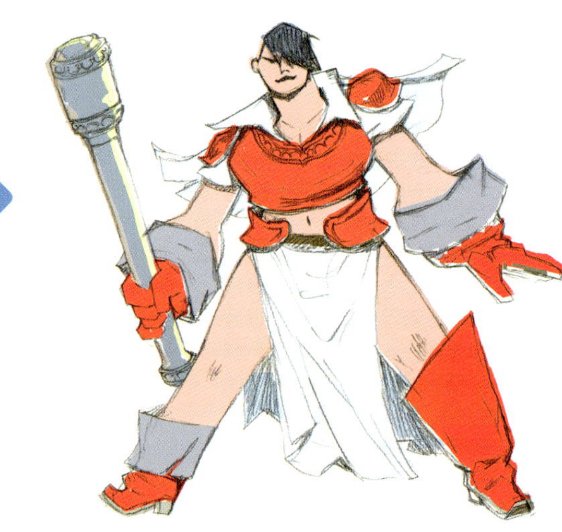

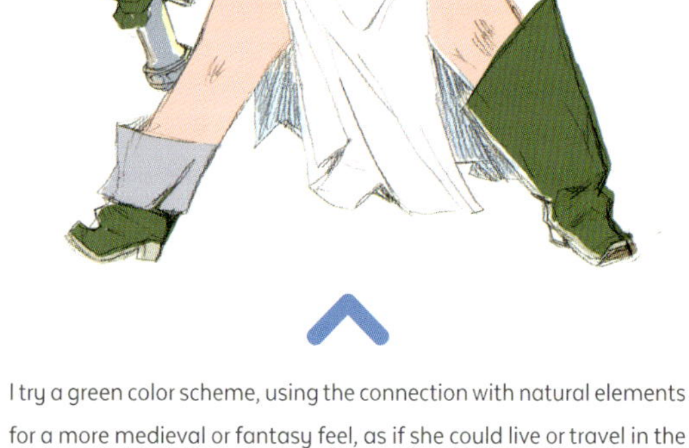

I try a green color scheme, using the connection with natural elements for a more medieval or fantasy feel, as if she could live or travel in the forest. However, it is not a very aggressive color.

In this version I have found a good balance of colors and values. The tones are softer, better conveying the material of every piece. The red on her fists and feet is less aggressive than the previous version, complemented by the calm, steely blue of her armor, which makes her seem more cool and restrained.

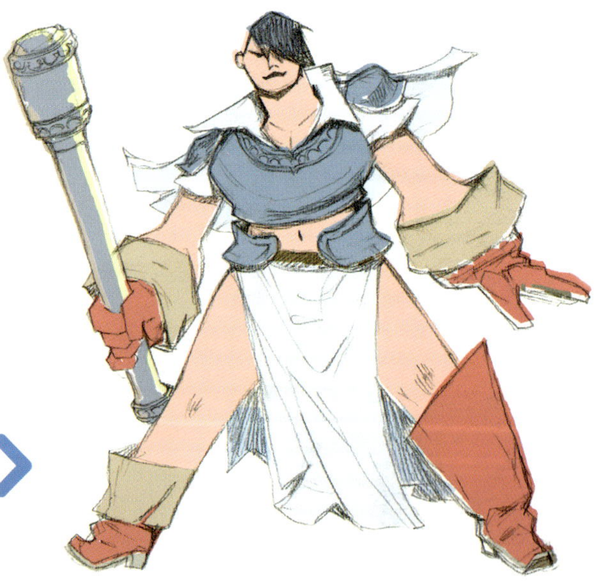

FINAL DESIGN

The design is now finished. The character has a good balance and contrast of textures between the hard, rough surfaces of the metal armor, and the soft material of her clothes, which reflects the different sides of her personality and attitude. The angular lines of her hands, feet, and head contrast with her arms and legs, which are softer and rounder but still massive and powerful,

creating variety in her silhouette. The yellow highlights of my final image help to describe the volumes.

There is a matching pattern on her armor and weapon, so the viewer might imagine that she usually wears these items together. They are well worn from everyday use, which suggests her role in the world as a hard-

working fighter. The shirt, skirt, and cape are elements that give a feeling of elegance and movement. She could be dressed this way both on the battlefield or at the king's hall. Her short haircut adds to her attitude, summing up all the previous ideas: a warrior who is aggressive but elegant.

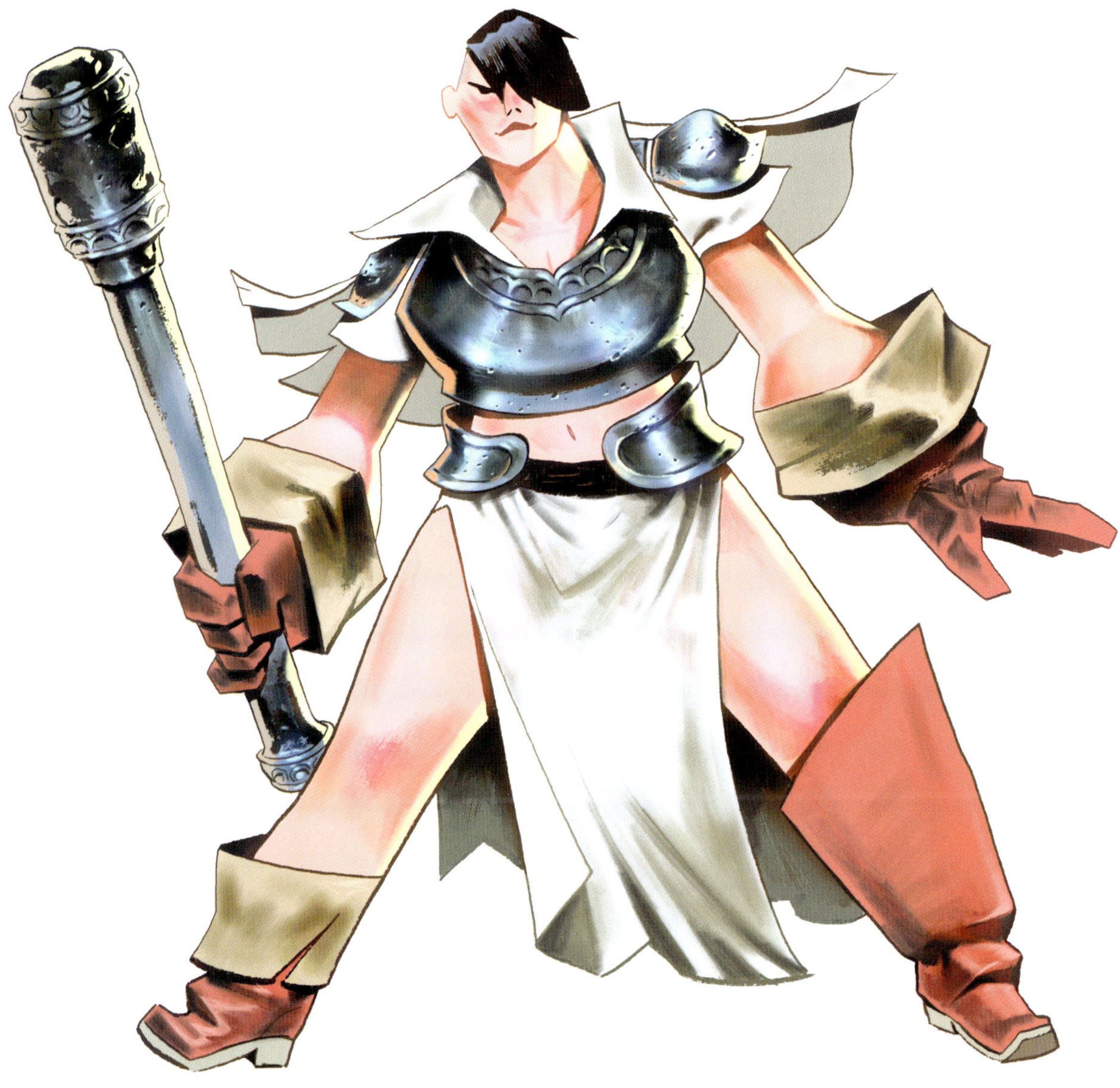

Final artwork © Enrique Fernández

VARIATION 1:
BABY WARRIOR

IDEAS & RESEARCH

For this variation, I will redesign the character as a cute little girl who wants to be a brave warrior from a very early age. All her behavior and attitude is focused on this goal, creating a fun contrast between the innocence of childhood and the pretense of being an adult warrior. I imagine her asking everyone around for weapons and armor, and even epic quests to accomplish! She won't stop asking about it, and the adults eventually surrender to her cuteness by making a suit of armor that barely fits her.

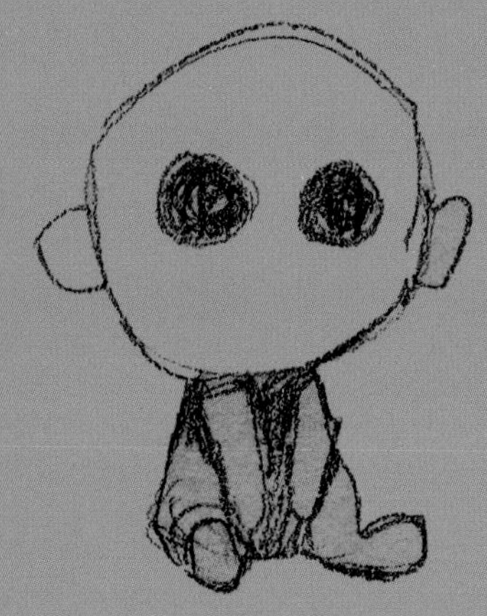

When conveying the proportions of a child character, it is key to note the large size of the head relative to the body. I will make the head as big as possible. This will enhance the character's cuteness.

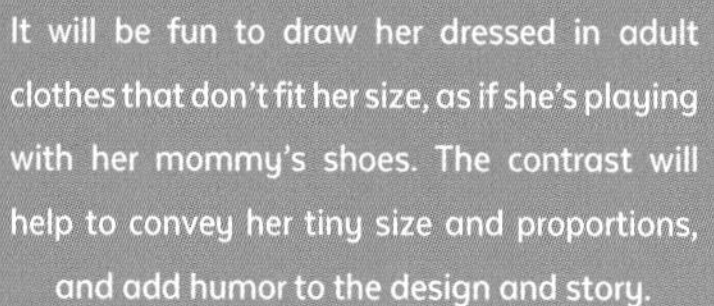

It will be fun to draw her dressed in adult clothes that don't fit her size, as if she's playing with her mommy's shoes. The contrast will help to convey her tiny size and proportions, and add humor to the design and story.

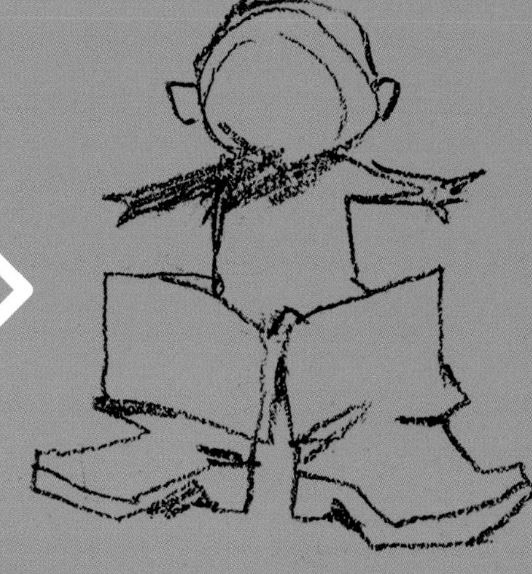

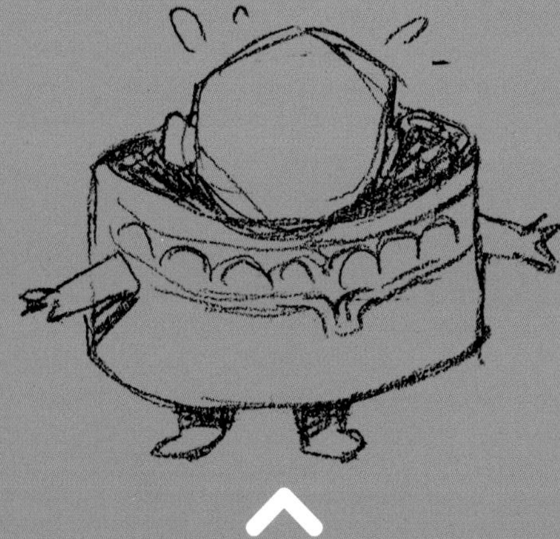

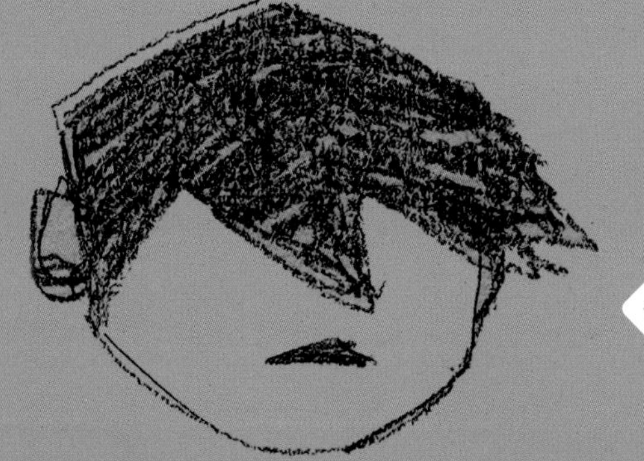

I want her to seem like an active child, and also create a parallel with her adult self, so she will have short hair, maybe in a bad or messy haircut.

Even though she asked for some armor, the suit she gets will not be the right size. It will be fun to see her carrying around an annoying piece of metal, pretending she is okay with it, and it will add to her short, round proportions which are also important indicators of her age.

She won't play with dolls, except if they need to be rescued from dangerous situations! Instead, she has a taste for toy weapons, and she will carry a big one. However, it will only be made from wood.

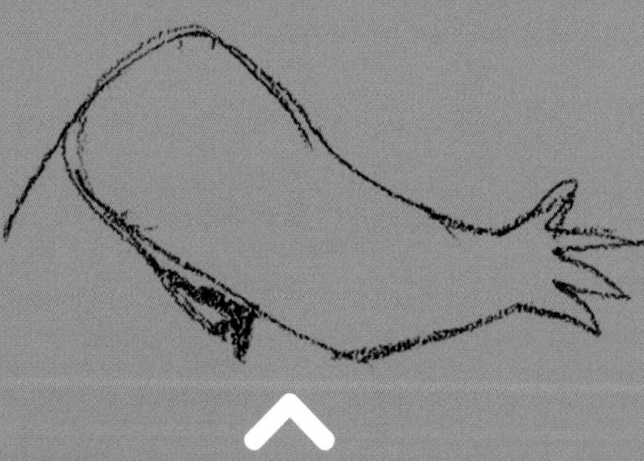

Babies and children have tiny hands with small fingers, so her hands will have completely different proportions from her body, compared with the adult design where the character has an enormous warrior's hands.

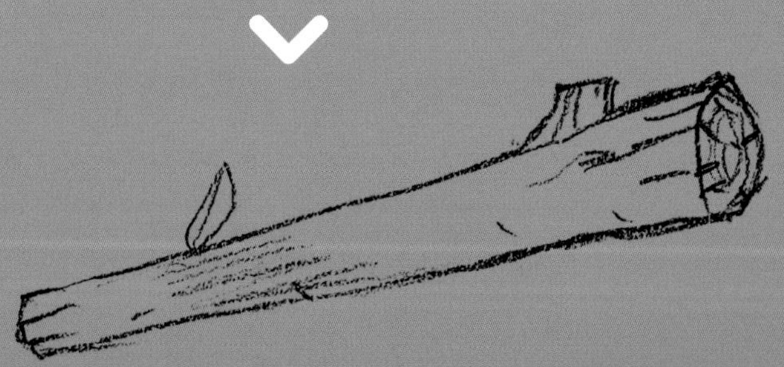

CHANGES

I want to keep as many elements as possible of the initial design, to make the character easy to recognize. For the adult design, I played around with the idea of a character with top-heavy proportions, like a hammer, but now that I am making a small, cute concept, I want to adjust the proportions to make the character round and simple, almost like a baby toy.

The haircut contributed a lot of personality to the original design, so I'll maintain its basic shape. The character's head will be proportionally larger, giving the hair more visual importance.

The length of the neck was fitting for the adult version, but I want to play with the size of the head now, so the neck will be reduced and barely noticeable.

I will keep the design of the armor and the dress, even if they are different in proportion. It will almost look like she's been temporarily shrunk with a magic beam, which adds humor to the design!

Another feature of the original design was her strength, and even though for this version she will be a child, I want her to seem like she is capable of a good fight or of lifting a heavy weight. She will only have small hands, but perhaps she could still be carrying a large weapon.

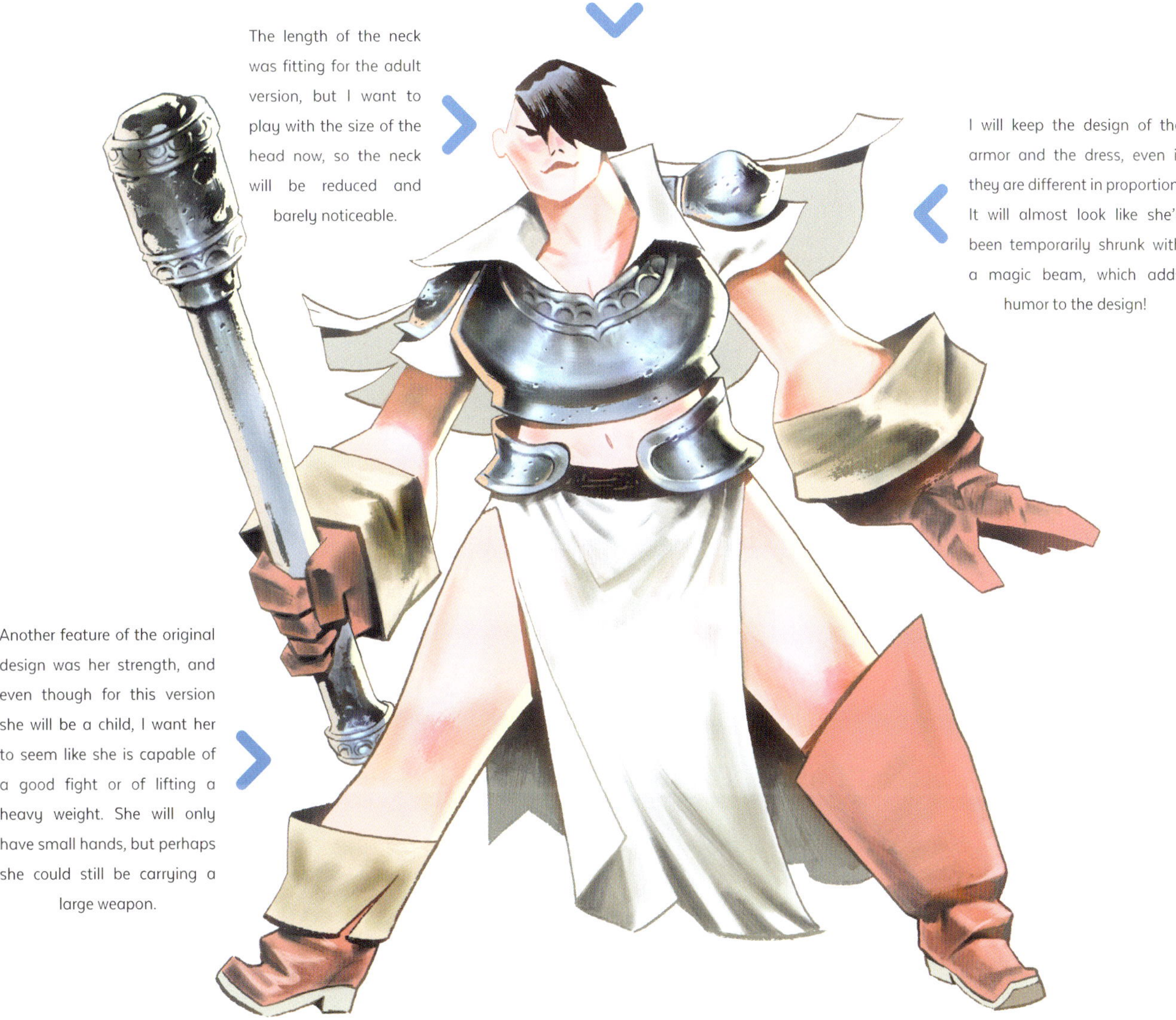

THUMBNAILS

In my thumbnails, I search for a character that shows determination, pretending to be an adult. She doesn't realize how cute she is, and even if she did, she wouldn't care at all. She is absolutely focused on being a warrior, always carrying around her weapon and armor, and it requires all her energy and strength of will. I decide on the bottom middle design, as it shows an ideal balance of combined cuteness and strength.

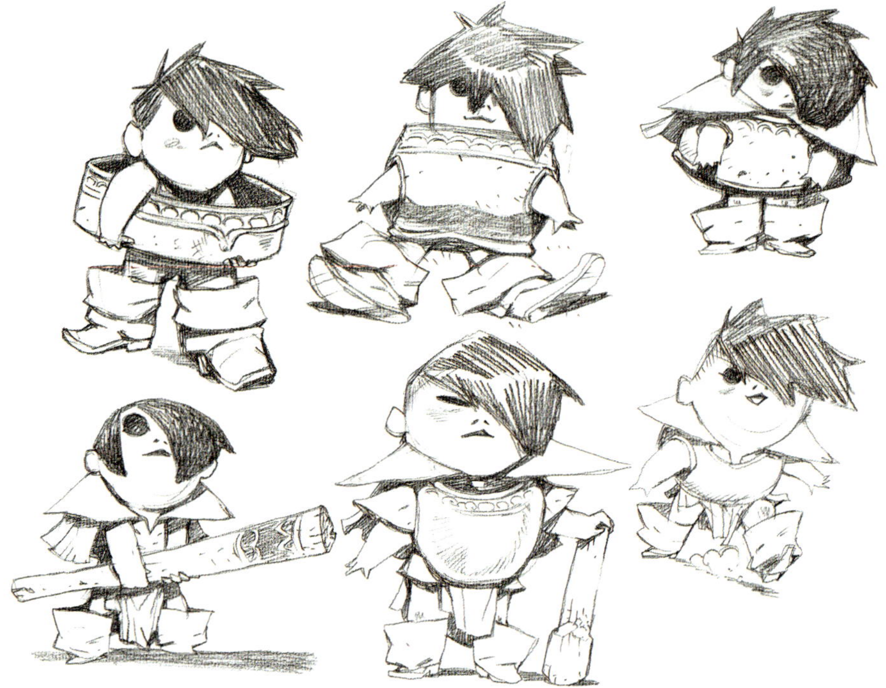

BASIC SHAPES

The overall proportions will be the biggest difference between this version of the character and the original, as they are what will clearly communicate her much younger age and smaller size. She will now have a proportionally huge head, as babies do, and the other forms of her body and outfit will be secondary to this focal point. The facial features, costume, and limbs of the adult character are not overly complex, so will scale down easily to fit the baby warrior while still being very recognizable.

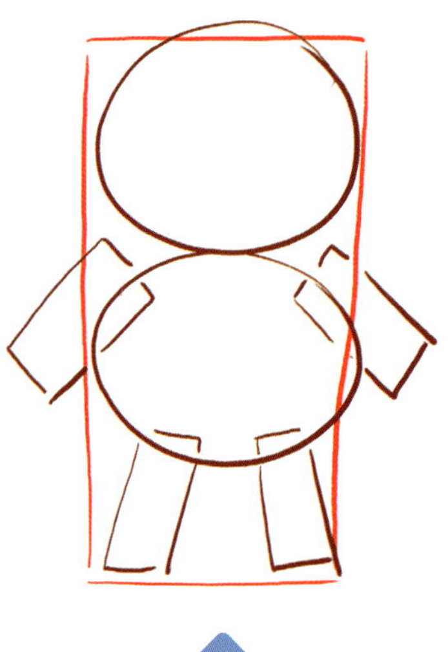

This time the basic shape starts with a solid block (lighter red), the square shape giving the impression of determination and strength. The main volumes of the head and armor will be in equal size. The arms and legs will be small compared to her body, as decided in my research.

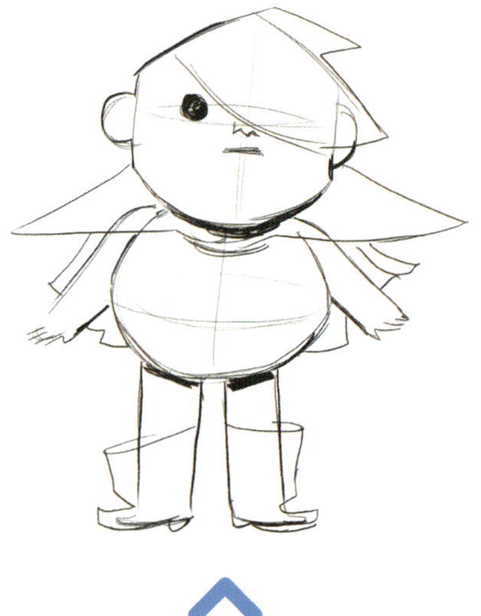

I start to define the proportion and relative size of elements, and to sketch out her outfit. The large triangular collar will again help to direct attention to her head and face.

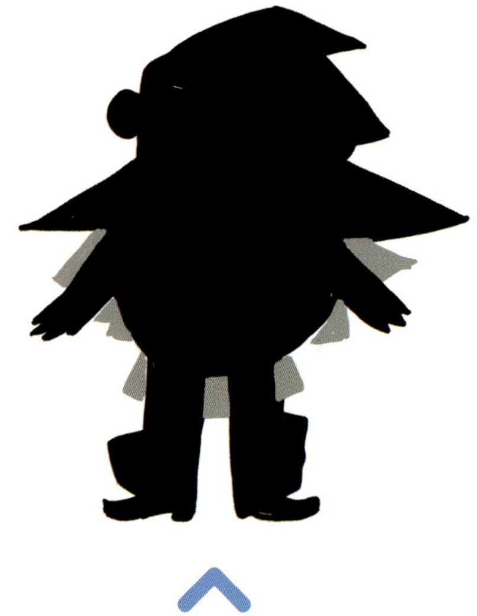

The black silhouette confirms that each part of the character is clearly readable. Again, I separate the loose cape from the main figure, as it will probably be shown in motion.

DETAILS

I start to dress the character with details translated from the original design. The design and patterns of the armor and weapon help a lot with this continuity. The shirt with a big collar makes her outfit seem even more oversized. The different heights of her boots match the original design while also helping to add motion to her short legs, and prevent the design from becoming too symmetrical.

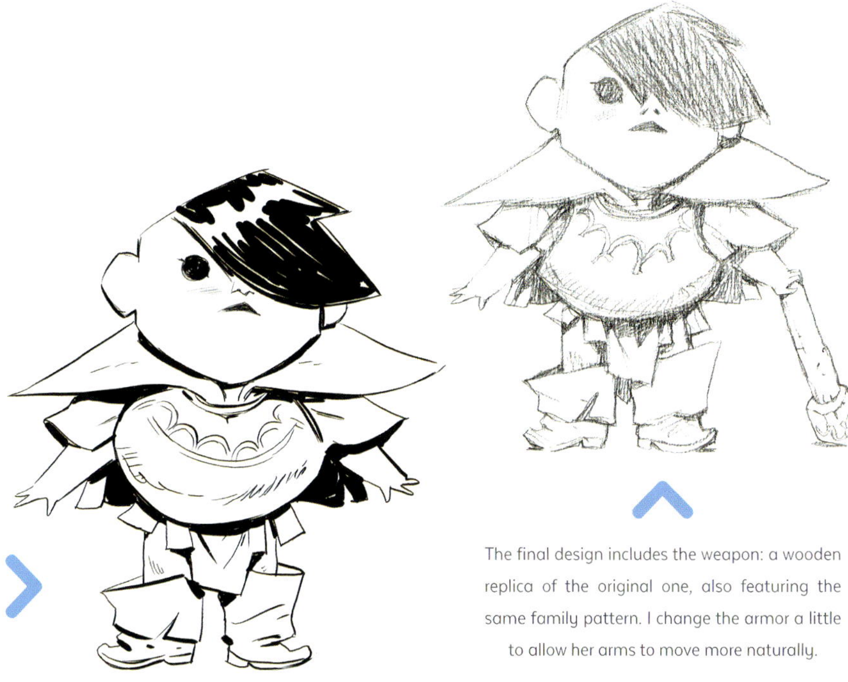

The big round eye gives a sense of innocence to the character. The armor features the same organic detail as the original design - perhaps it's a family pattern, which works well in terms of adding backstory to both versions of the character.

The final design includes the weapon: a wooden replica of the original one, also featuring the same family pattern. I change the armor a little to allow her arms to move more naturally.

EXPRESSIONS & POSING

I want to find a pose that conveys the character's energy and strong will, but I also want to keep it cute. I do not want her to look aggressive, even if I like the idea of her being powerful enough for that! I want the audience to smile when seeing the contrast of this young character pretending to do something grown-up.

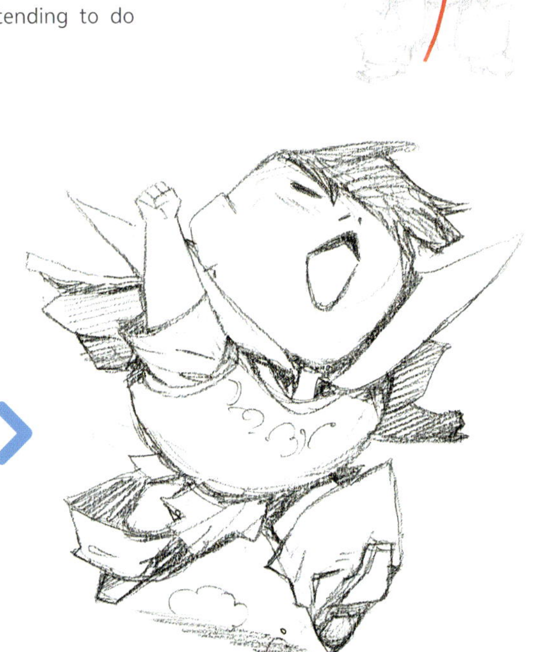

She is an active character who can move her round body with great energy. Her tiny fist and short arm add cuteness and humor to the strength of the pose - she could barely hit anyone if she tried to! This pose is fun and dynamic but I would prefer a pose that includes her weapon.

She is carrying an oversized weapon, clearly using her whole body in the effort - you can see how she has to rotate her upper body and balance with her free arm. At the same time, she feels happy, powerful, and confident when she's holding it. You could imagine that she has just received this weapon as a birthday present, and is posing proudly with her new "toy." Her slightly lopsided, crouched stance gives a sense of her wild energy.

VALUE & COLOR

I choose the pose with the weapon positioned over her shoulder for the final design. Rather than deviating from the original design, I want to use a similar color scheme, giving the impression of a miniature version of the same character. This creates a narrative between the two images: seeing the character as a child helps the viewer to better understand her as an adult. However, I try some variations anyway, to see how different distributions of red and blue would look.

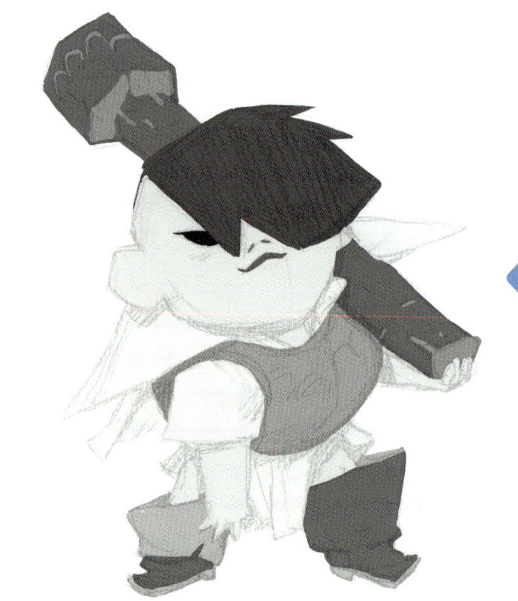

The character has fewer accessories as a child; I limit the darkest tones to her weapon, hair, and boots, so they do not look overpowering.

I try balancing out her bluish hair with shades of red for her armor and boots, but this seems too muted and earthy for such a fun, young character.

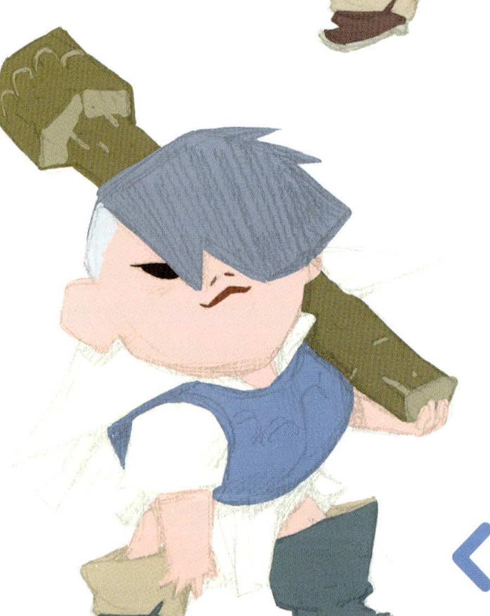

This color distribution is the same as for the adult version. It is good to play with different combinations, but in this case, being true to the original design will add meaning to this one.

I try a blue-only color scheme, that might make her seem softer and younger, as it has no overtly aggressive red, but it is rather too blue.

FINAL DESIGN

The final design clearly shows the wooden material of her weapon, which she's barely able to carry, but which foreshadows the real weapon she will carry as an adult. It is carved with the same pattern that appears on the original version, and the pattern is also painted simply on her armor, perhaps by herself. These elements give a sense of childhood scrappiness and make-believe, but also create continuity between the two versions of the character, suggesting a backstory which is satisfying for the viewer who notices it. She looks determined that she will be a warrior some day soon, and the viewer only has to see her self-confidence to smile!

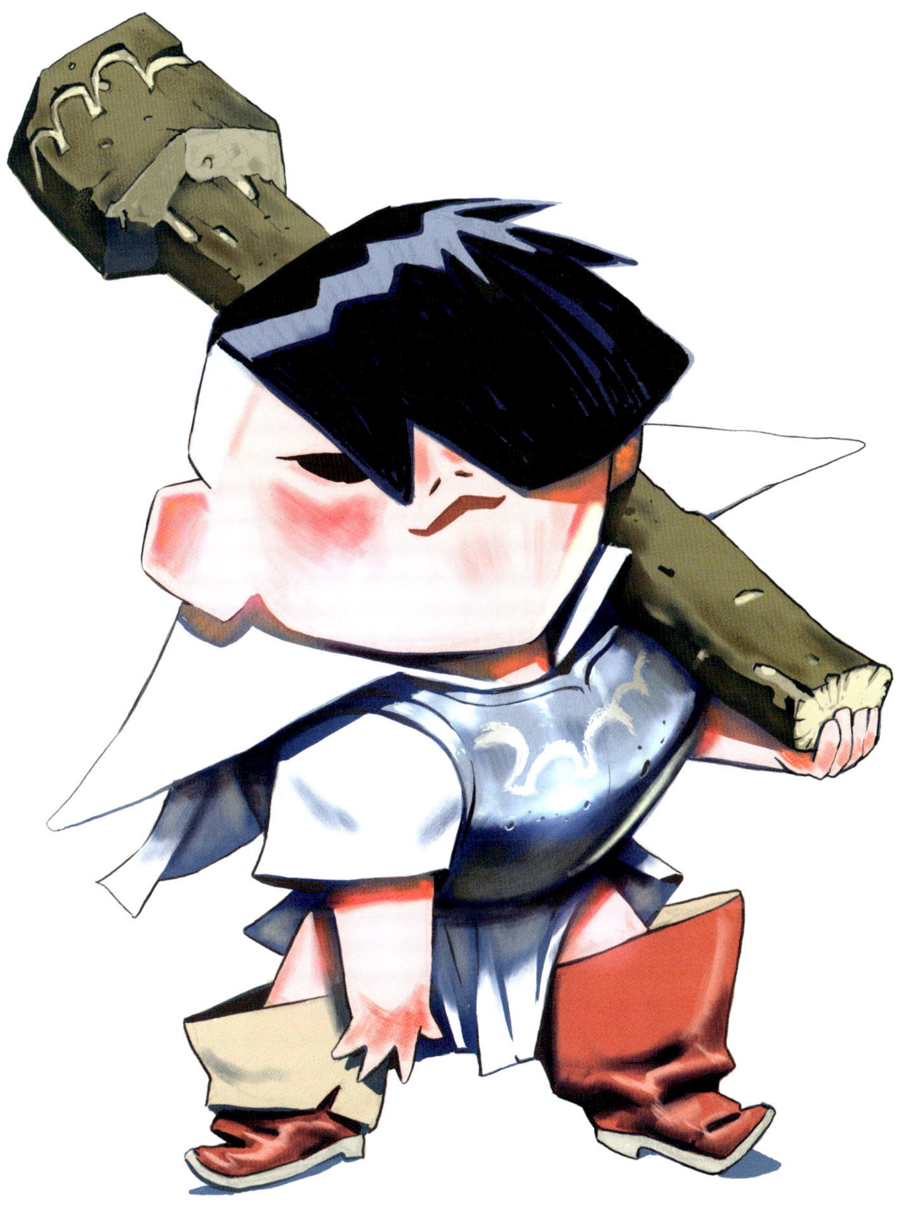

Final artwork © Enrique Fernández

VARIATION 2:
SPACE KNIGHT

IDEAS & RESEARCH

This variation will be a kind of sci-fi knight, maybe an explorer of the unknown. The design will need to show some futuristic technology, but I would like to keep a vintage look that recalls the textures and materials of the original version. I love to be surprised by the designs in sci-fi stories, so I want to show some elements that the viewer won't recognize immediately, such as a weapon that we wouldn't know how to use. I would also like to show her as a more gentle warrior, not as tough and fierce as the original, who lived in a more hostile medieval setting. The whole design could be more rounded and elegant to convey this.

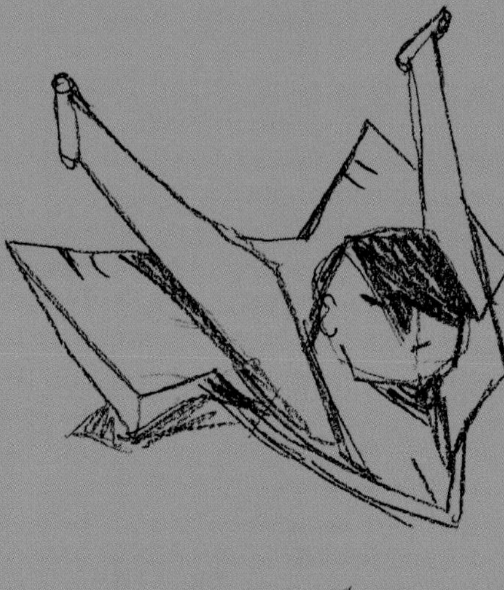

If she is able to fly, I could adapt the shirt design of the original version into a pair of wings to help her balance in flight.

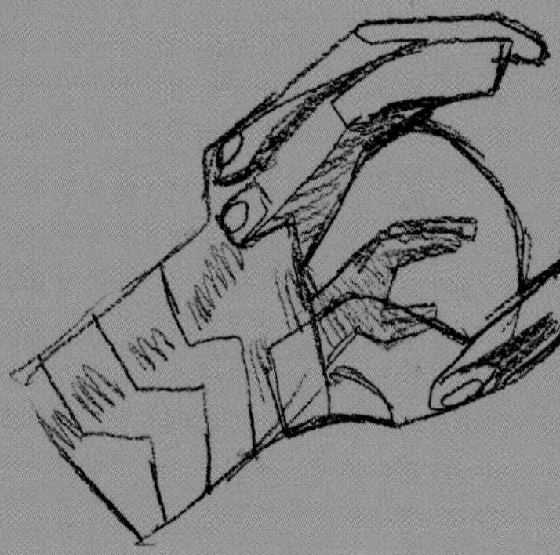

I definitely want to add some technologically advanced gauntlets to the design. I want the hands to be big and powerful, not just real-sized gloves.

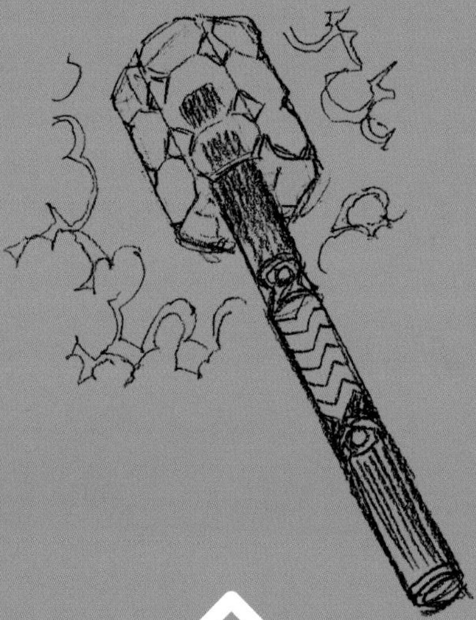

The design of the weapon will be more focused on light beams or energy sparks, not just a piece of metal for bashing things. I consider how to capture these effects.

Of course, she will need new armor – the intergalactic kind! Researching retro sci-fi suits is a good starting point.

Like the hands, I want the feet to be visually strong, and useful on any terrain. This could be achieved by giving her boots with rugged soles.

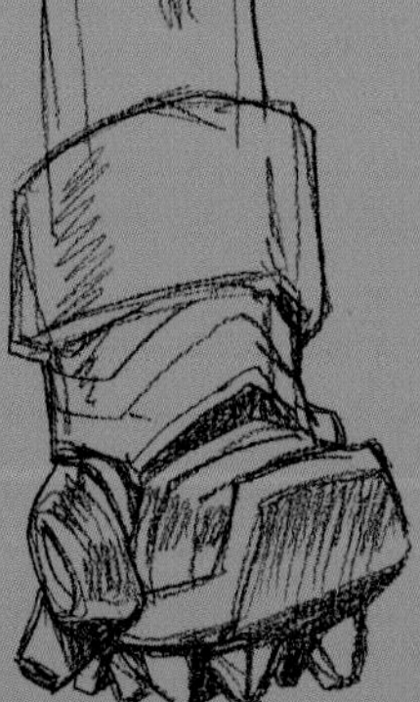

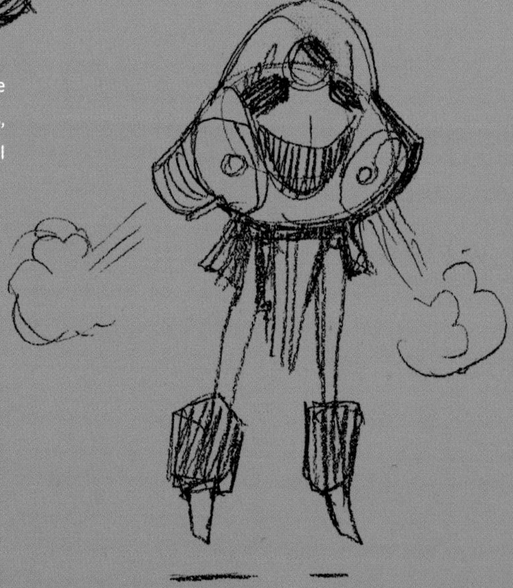

Maybe the final version wouldn't have rockets on her back like this, but she should be able to fly for sure, and to do it with style!

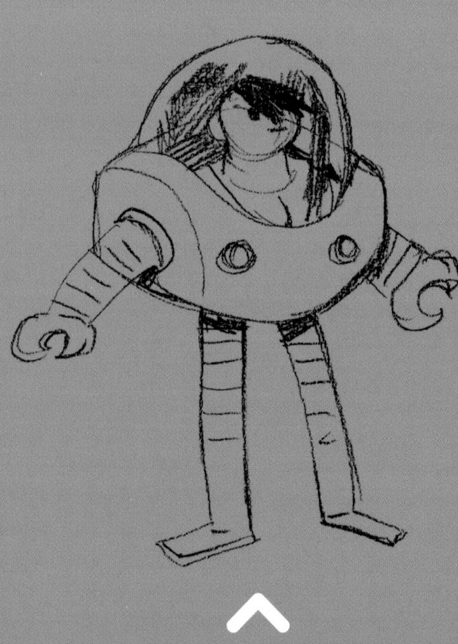

CHANGES

There are a lot of options and sci-fi topics to play with here – almost everything is possible! To keep things simple, I will stick to some ideas that made the original character a good design. Other ideas will evolve naturally to adapt to the sci-fi genre, and I would like for the two final designs to be coherent when shown together.

I want the outfit to have a feminine style, maybe with a texture that reminds the viewer of those great vintage designs from 1960s sci-fi movies. This will require changing the metal and cloth materials of her previous outfit.

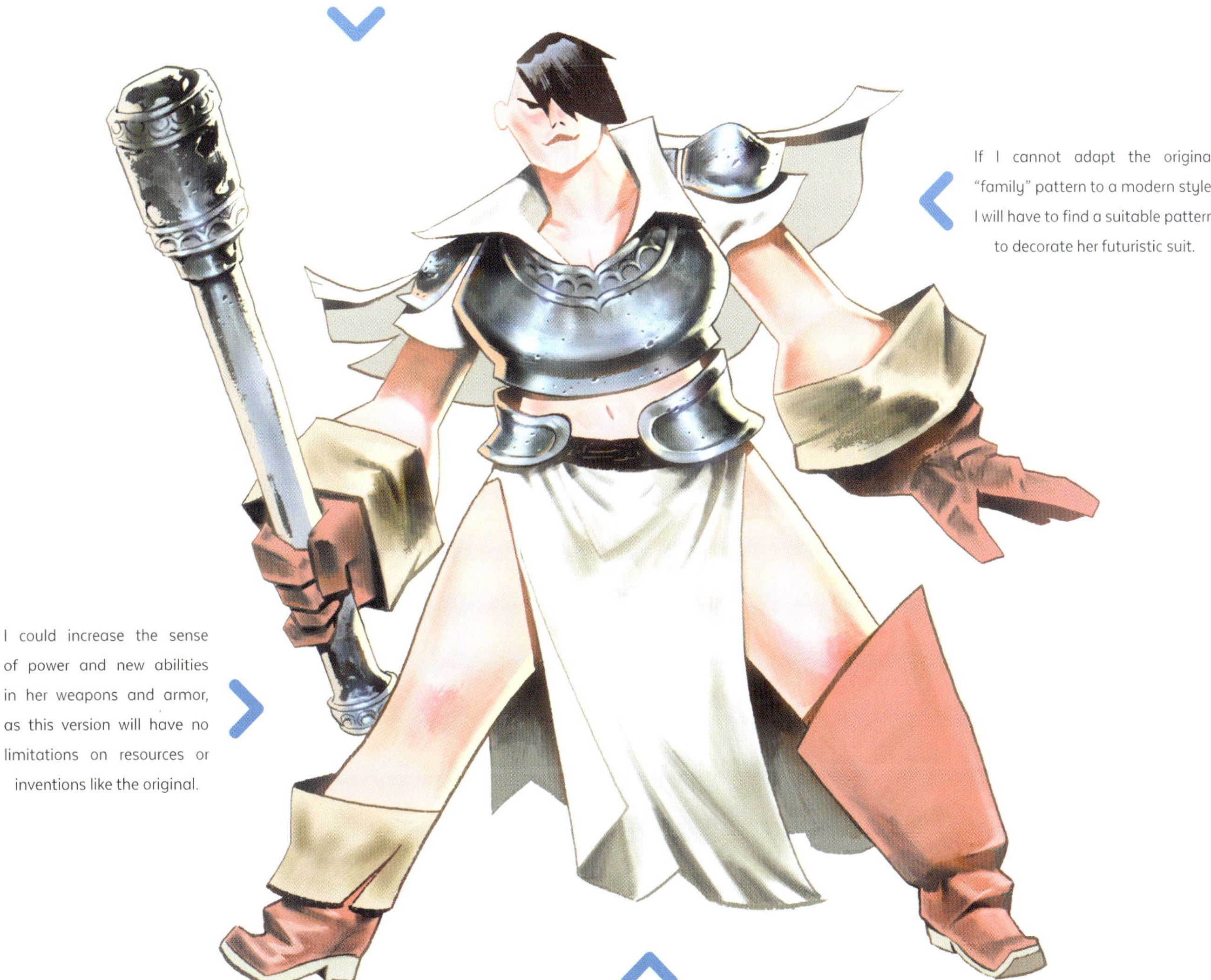

If I cannot adapt the original "family" pattern to a modern style, I will have to find a suitable pattern to decorate her futuristic suit.

I could increase the sense of power and new abilities in her weapons and armor, as this version will have no limitations on resources or inventions like the original.

The hammer-inspired body shape was a good feature, and I would like to keep it as much as possible. But to make it different, I could almost invert the concept. I could make the large upper part of the body seem less heavy than the rest, perhaps by using a lighter material or color.

THUMBNAILS

There are a few common elements that I explore in my thumbnails. I want the armor to be like a spacesuit, which she can breathe inside of like an astronaut. The arms are powerful like the original design, and show advanced technology, but with a vintage sci-fi feel. I choose the bottom middle thumbnail because I like the more organic design of the armor. It is not metal or crystal, but could be a futuristic new material that is both very strong and able to adapt to the wearer's body movements. It could be slightly translucent to show the character inside.

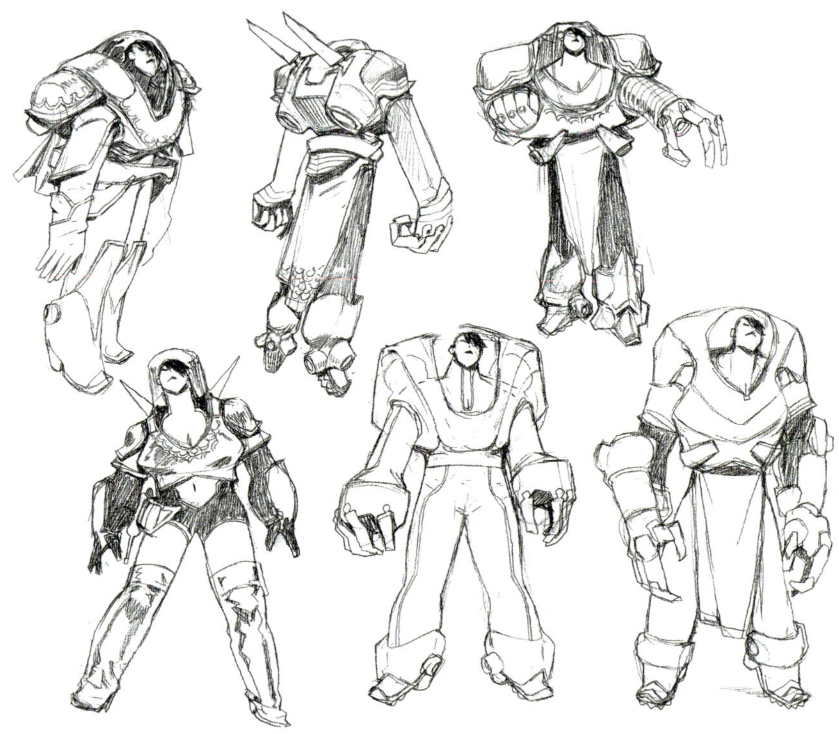

BASIC SHAPES

In this version of the character, the focal point will still be around her general head area, though the attention will be not only on her face but on her sci-fi armor. Its impressive shape and size, and later its unusual texture and color, will help to draw the viewer's gaze to it, and then to the character herself inside. The shapes of her arms and legs will be relatively simple so they do not detract from this aim. The armor's squared-off forms will give it a sense of being strong and robust.

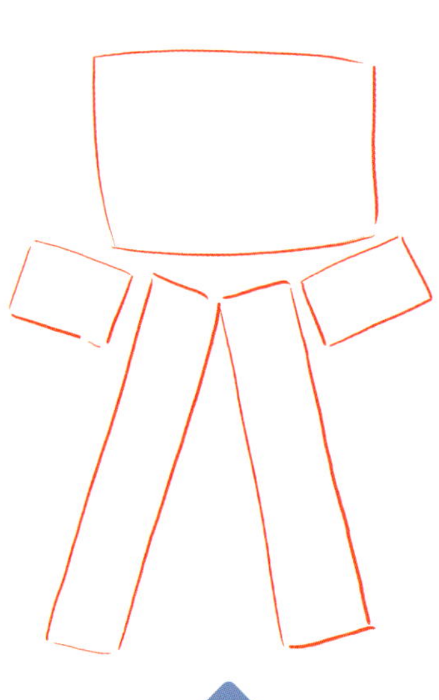

I continue using the hammer-shaped design structure, this time making it even bigger and heavier. Unlike the original version, the upper part of the design is now a complete square.

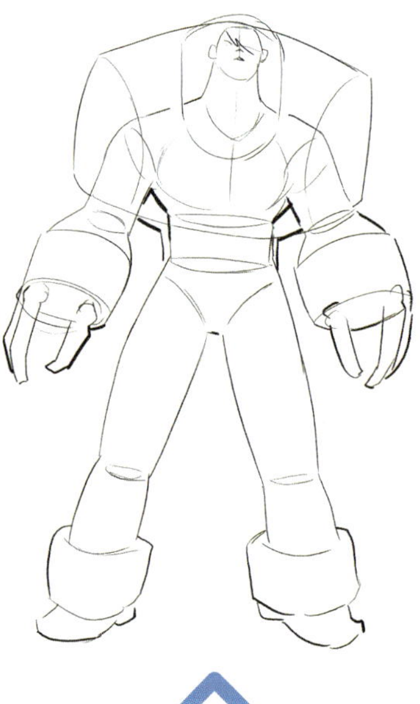

I define the volumes of each element, making the overall shape language more curved and rounded. There are some details that will be defined more clearly later, such as the hands.

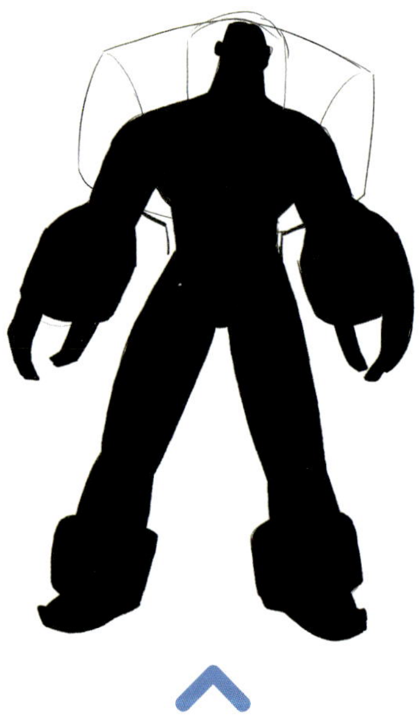

The solid silhouette of her figure is clear and powerful, though I leave the upper armor structure translucent for now, so that we can clearly distinguish the shape of the character inside.

DETAILS

Most of the character is simple to define in terms of lines, as the final design will be more oriented towards color and texture. The translucent armor is something that will be conveyed more clearly in the color stage as well, but for now I would like to polish the other details, adding more clarity to the design of the hands and shoes.

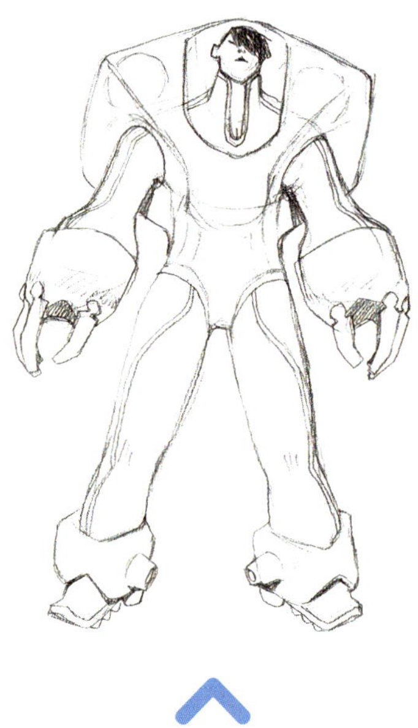

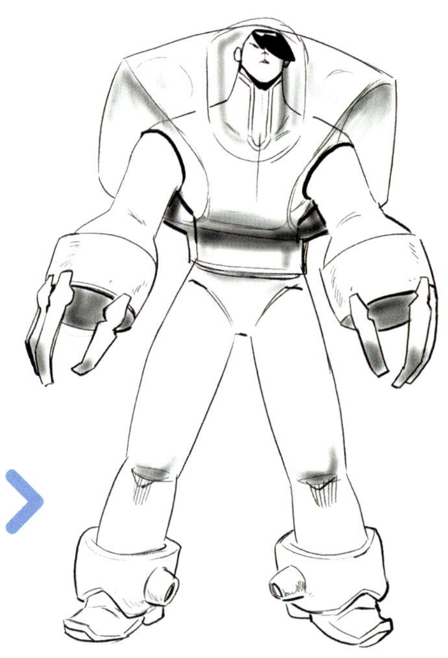

There's more elegance in the flow of the armor now, making it more dynamic. Her "fingers" are almost flat surfaces, just simple metal pieces with little volume.

I add some decorative lines that help to describe the volumes of the body. The shoes have been shaped better to add rugged soles based on my research, and more angles to add movement, while keeping a strong visual structure.

EXPRESSIONS & POSING

The character's armored suit is flexible to some degree, but appears rigid to the eye. I need her final pose to show that she is unhindered by this strange unknown material, letting the viewer imagine what it is capable of. I want a pose that shows as much of the whole design as possible, as well as showing the character's attitude and capabilities in action.

This is a clear pose that will help me to show the full design, and adding a weapon gives an extra element to the narrative. Similar to how her heavy armor is translucent to subvert the top-heavy "hammer" motif, the head of her new weapon is not made of metal, but of light or energy. Her stance is fearless and recalls the pose of her original design.

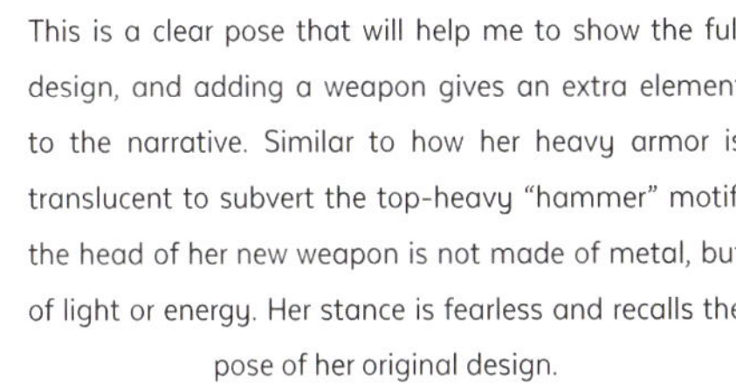

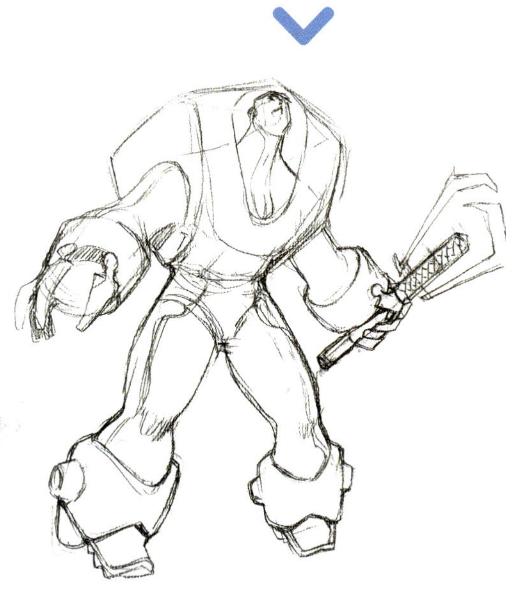

She can fly using some kind of energy that comes from her boots and gloves. This pose is good for showing that she can easily lift her own weight into the air, but does not really convey that she's a warrior.

VALUE & COLOR

I choose the second pose for the final version of the character. I test out color schemes that are similar to the original design's blue and red palette, but I want the colors to have evolved in intensity, using brighter hues which will be suitable for a shiny, futuristic finish. They should give this version of the character her own distinct sci-fi identity.

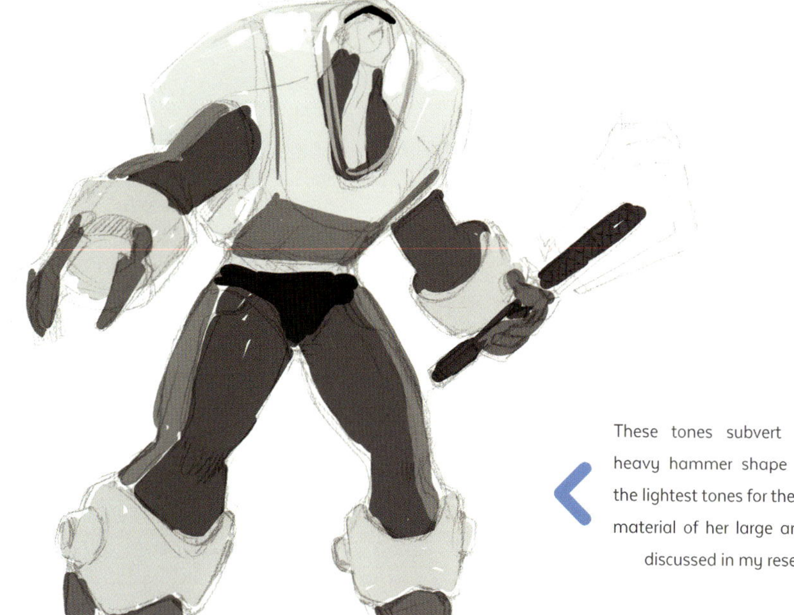

These tones subvert the top-heavy hammer shape by using the lightest tones for the futuristic material of her large armor, as I discussed in my research.

Light aqua and aggressive red are not far away from the color scheme of the original version, but do not give the impression of the same character; the reds are too prominent.

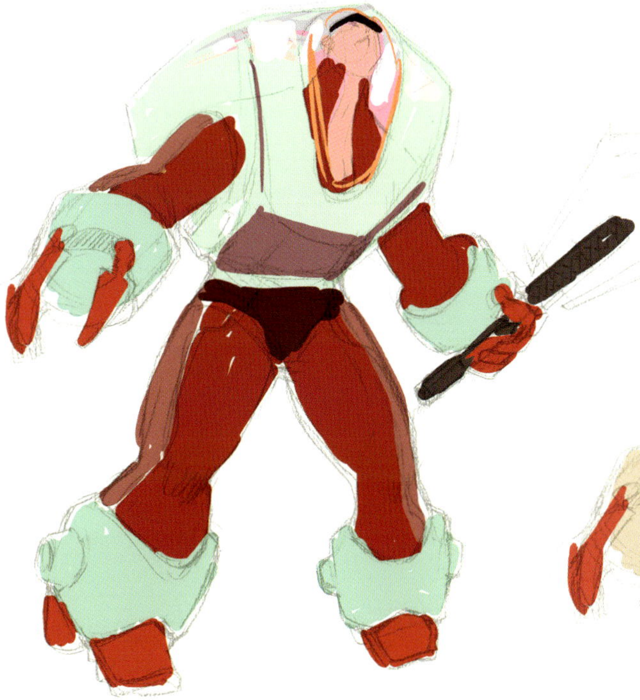

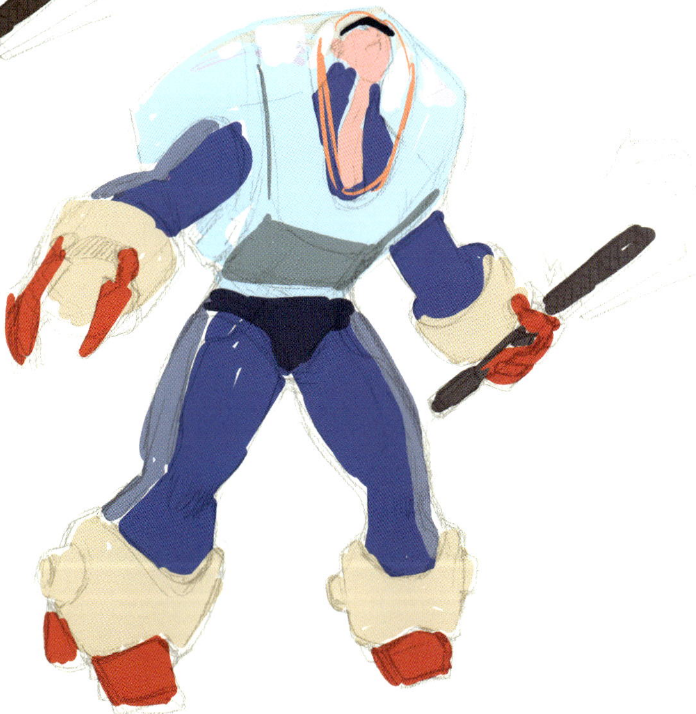

This color scheme shows more saturation and respects the relative position of the colors I have in the original one, but will be translated to a whole new set of textures.

FINAL DESIGN

With this variation I have discarded two major aspects of the original design: the organic pattern on the armor, and the long, flowing clothes. The pattern would have drawn too much attention and distracted the eye on such a sleek design, and the loose fabric doesn't make sense with a spacesuit! I use different textures on her suit to give the impression of unusual, futuristic materials. I have still depicted the same determined, powerful character, with plenty of energy, and prepared for action. The lines are more elegant and the shapes are softened, but her face, gloves, boots, and overall physique strongly recall the original design.

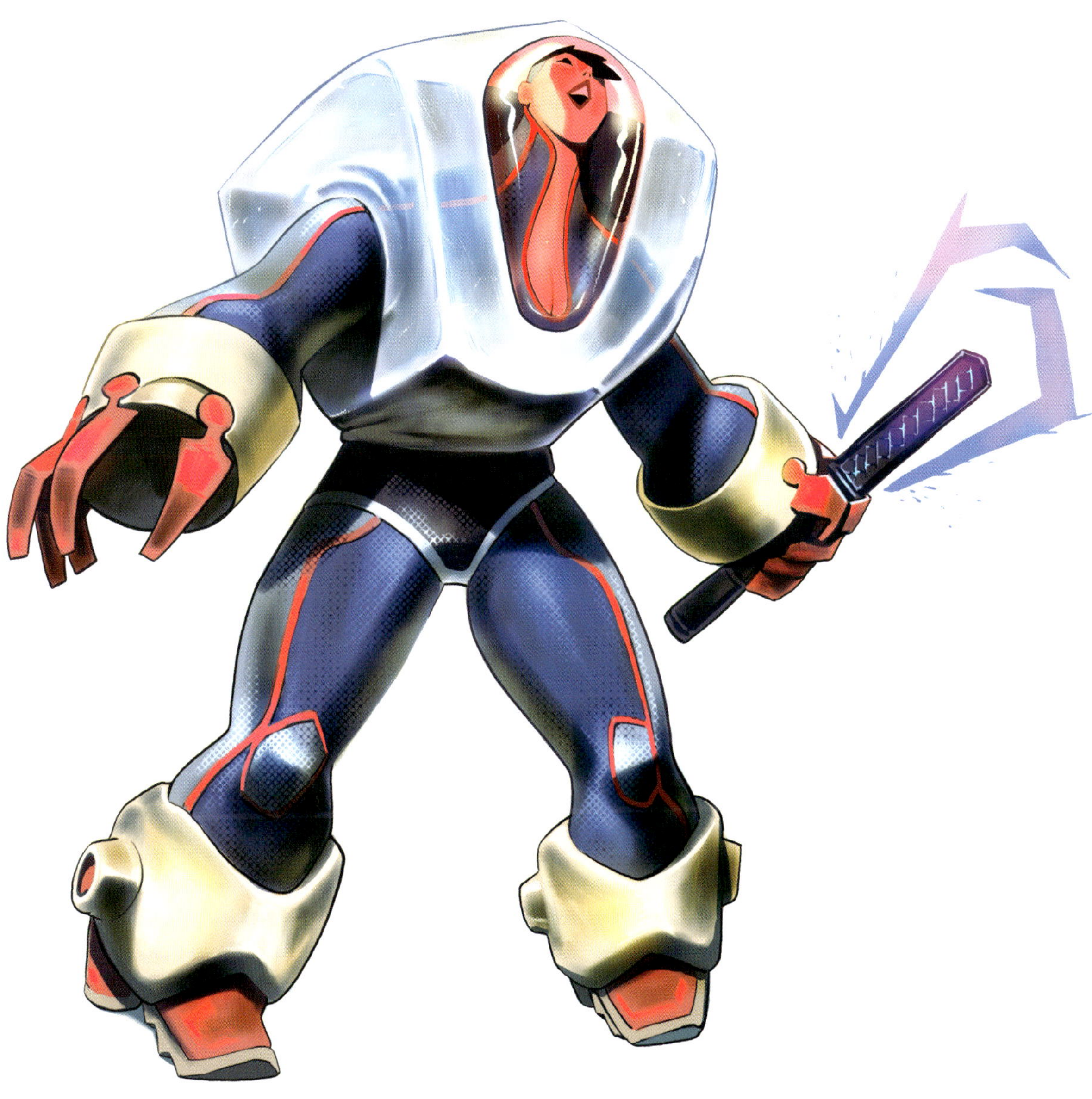

Final artwork © Enrique Fernández

VARIATION 3:
TRANSFORMED BEAST

IDEAS & RESEARCH

For the animal variation of the character, I have chosen a mix of a wolf and something feline, to convey fierceness and agility. Perhaps our warrior has been doomed to transform into a beast! What would she look like, and how would she behave after her transformation? I imagine her clothes would tear, and her attitude would be more aggressive and primal, but at the same time she could keep some of the elegant feminine qualities of her human form. And she would have more hair – a full body of it!

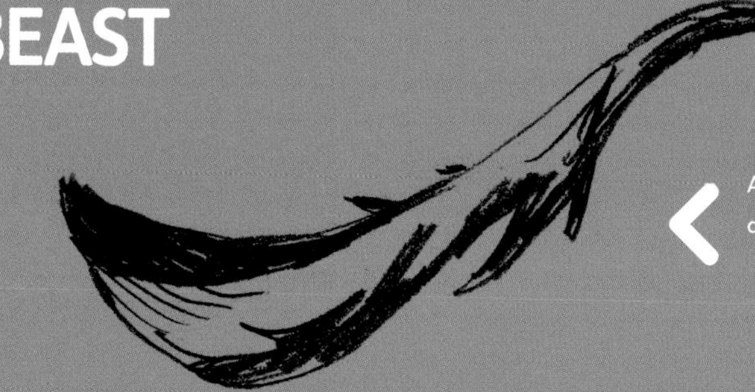

A tail will help to emphasize her animal appearance. There's no doubt about including it!

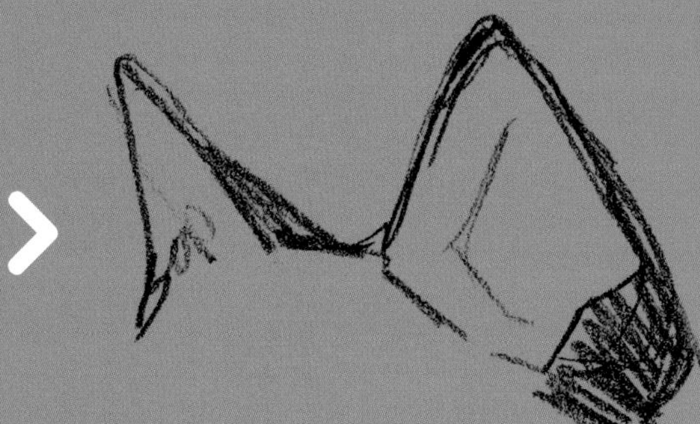

The ears could keep a rhomboidal shape, similar to both a wolf's ears and the original design, using shape language to add continuity.

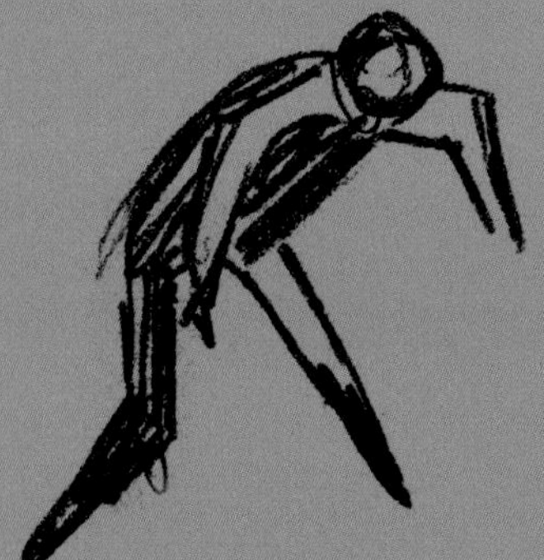

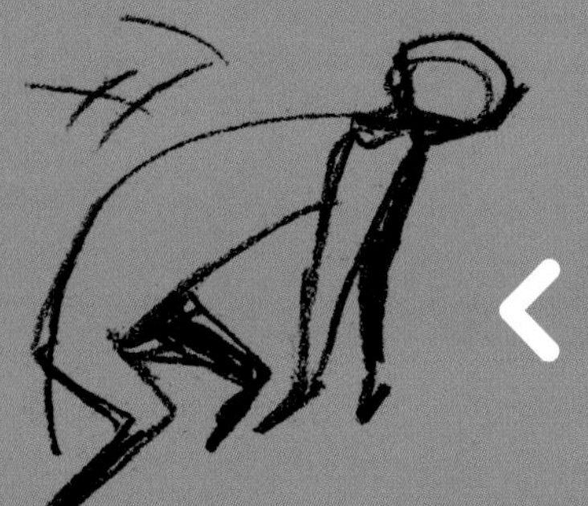

The attitude of the character will be more like an aggressive predatory animal; I study poses of creatures hunting and sneaking around.

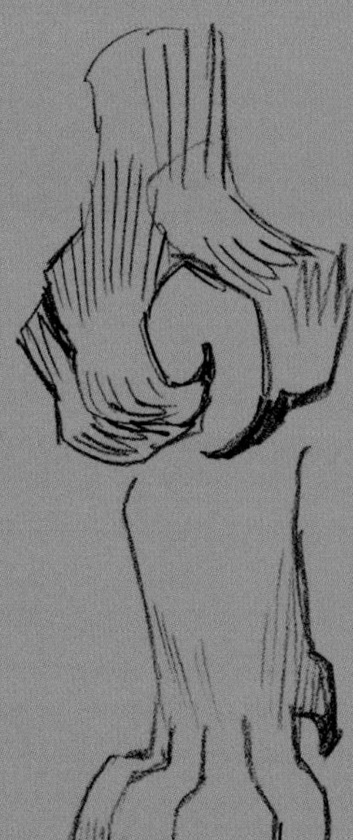

I study wolves' noses and mouths to help me depict the character's savage muzzle. This will completely change the character's face and make her unmistakably feral.

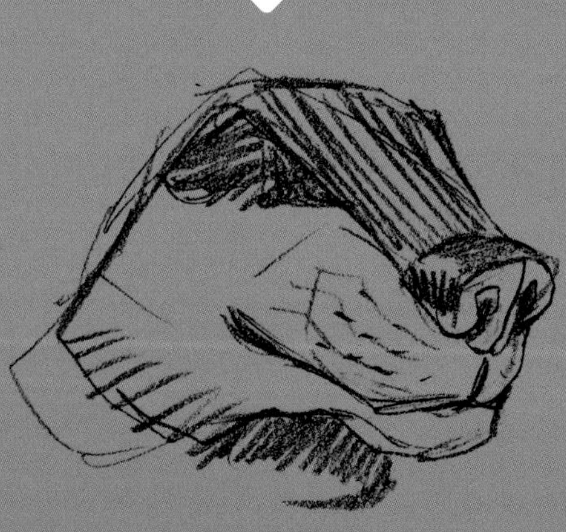

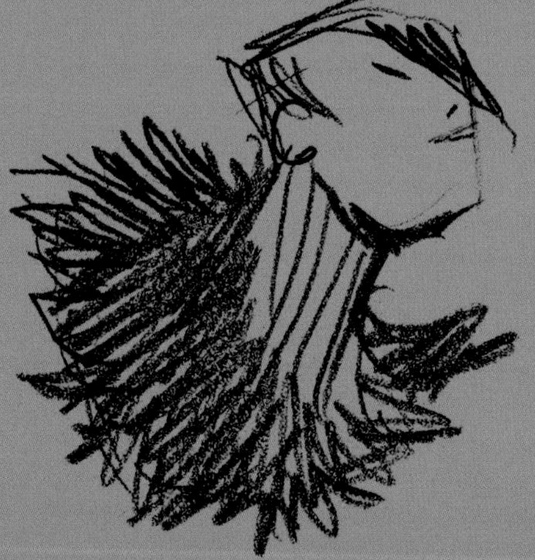

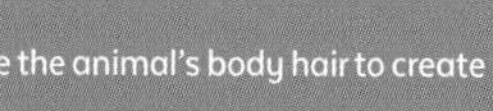

I could use the animal's body hair to create an elegant effect similar to a fur coat.

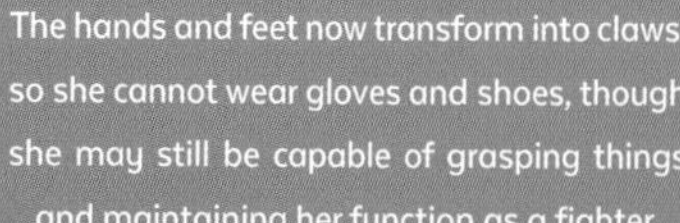

The hands and feet now transform into claws, so she cannot wear gloves and shoes, though she may still be capable of grasping things and maintaining her function as a fighter.

CHANGES

The changes in this version will be more evident, reflecting the loss of many elements of the original design. This time I am not evolving the character's clothes and accessories, but going a step backwards to a more primal situation. Despite the character losing her gloves, shoes, and weapon, I still want to keep some of the old clothes and armor to create a sense of narrative about her animal form.

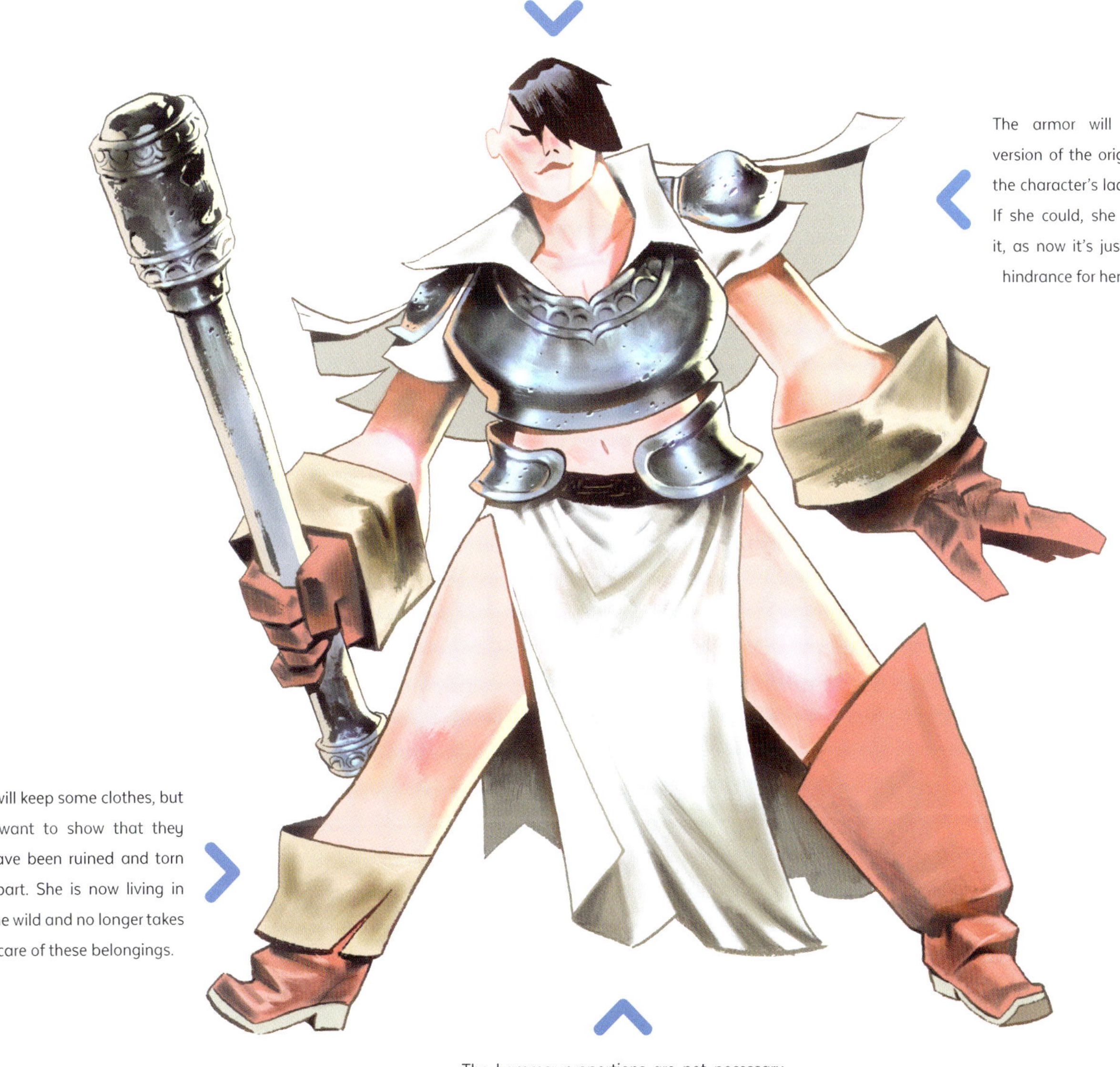

I will keep her human haircut as a reminder of the original design, but because the character already has a hairy body, this reference will need to be made very clear.

The armor will be a rusted version of the original, to reflect the character's lack of care for it. If she could, she would remove it, as now it's just an annoying hindrance for her animal form.

I will keep some clothes, but I want to show that they have been ruined and torn apart. She is now living in the wild and no longer takes care of these belongings.

The hammer proportions are not necessary now, as the overall pose of the character will change to a more curved and hunched shape.

THUMBNAILS

In my thumbnails, I search for ways to translate her human physique and rounded shapes to this new design. Making the mouth thin and pointed will help, similar to her human face. I explore some feline aspects as well, introducing different shapes to the overall idea. The rest of the body, with the oversized hands and feet, is already reminiscent of the original.

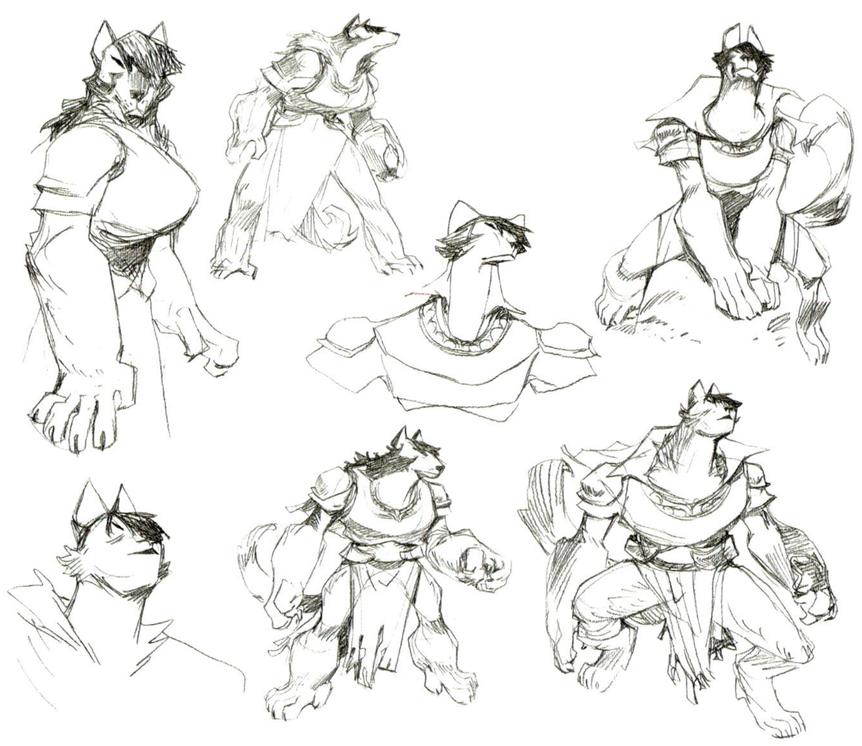

BASIC SHAPES

The basic shapes and proportions of this animal character still largely resemble those of her human counterpart, but her shapes are more organic and less supported by armor and clothing. Instead of large gloves and boots, for example, she has thick, powerful paws. This character will most likely not walk upright, so any long clothes she wears might be obscured, but her bushy tail is a new element that could provide interesting opportunities for posing and composition instead.

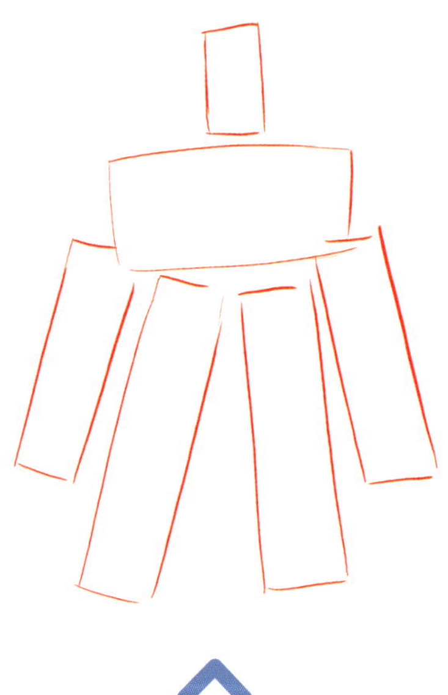

A neutral "A"-pose is a bit tricky for this character, as she would not naturally do it, or be capable of doing it, but here you can see how her shapes and proportions are still similar to her human body.

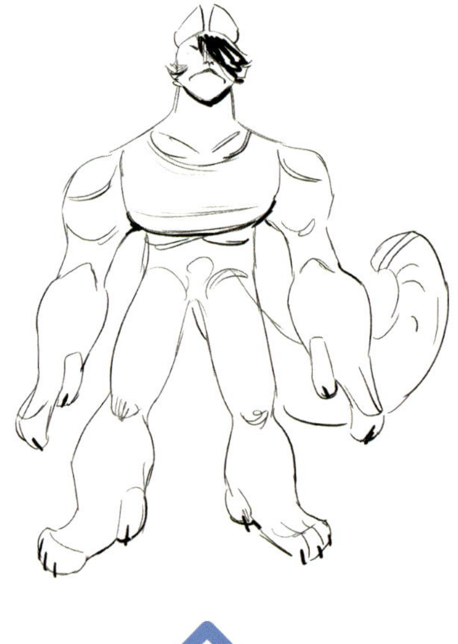

Notice how the ears have changed position on the head, but I have made them almost the same rhomboidal "human" shape.

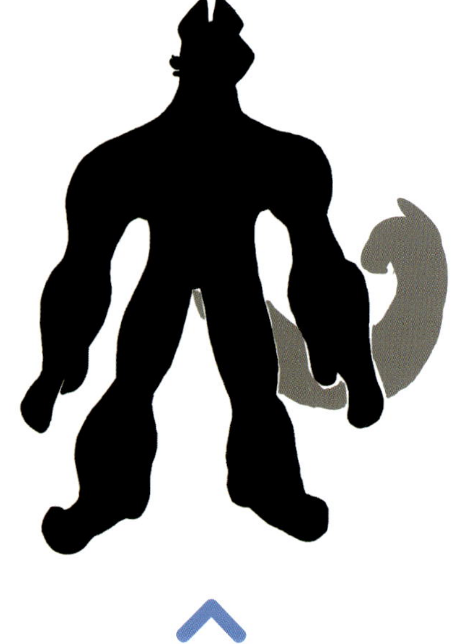

The black silhouette shows a clear human-like character, but with changes in proportion, especially the length of the arms, and the shape of the hands and feet.

DETAILS

Most of the accessories for this design are direct translations of the original character, but there are still some new considerations to make, such as the patterns of her hair and fur. The fur and tail give me opportunities to add details that were lacking now that the character has no gloves, boots, or weapon.

The hair on her head is designed around the neck and face in a way that clearly separates her human haircut, even when using only two values.

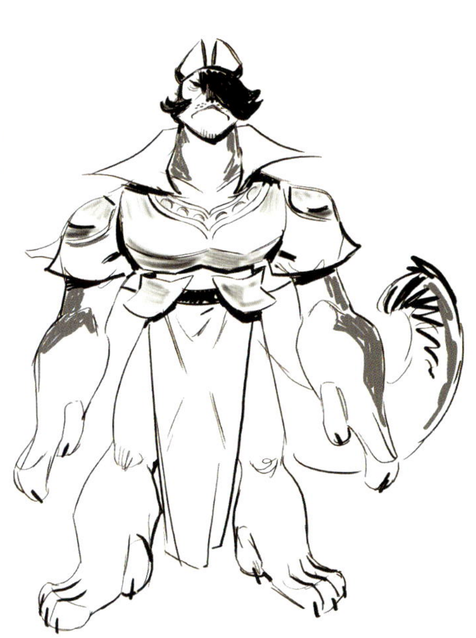

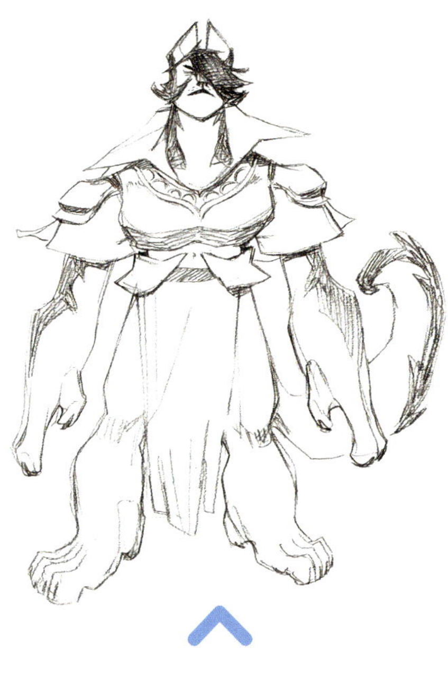

I define the paws and claws, and add the character's full outfit, though it will not be fully visible in her natural stance. Her paws recall the large hands of her human form, and make her look like a dangerous fighter.

EXPRESSIONS & POSING

I initially want to show the character in an aggressive pose, but on further consideration, I want to make her more menacing than violent. She is a human transformed into a beast, and doesn't want anyone to get close to her; it's not a wild aggression that would make her attack anyone nearby, but more of a defensive stance. She hates being transformed, and is angry and ashamed. Like a real lone wolf, she is a solitary being.

This will work as a pose to show some leg movement, and for action scenes. I could even widen her stance more to make the line of action stronger, but it's not what I am looking for to describe the character, as it is outright aggressive rather than threatening.

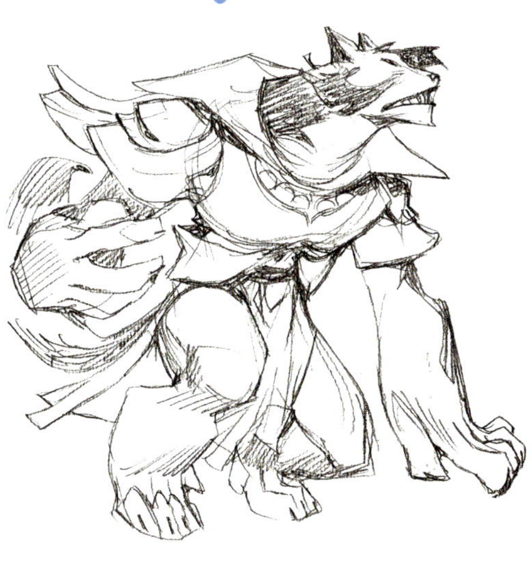

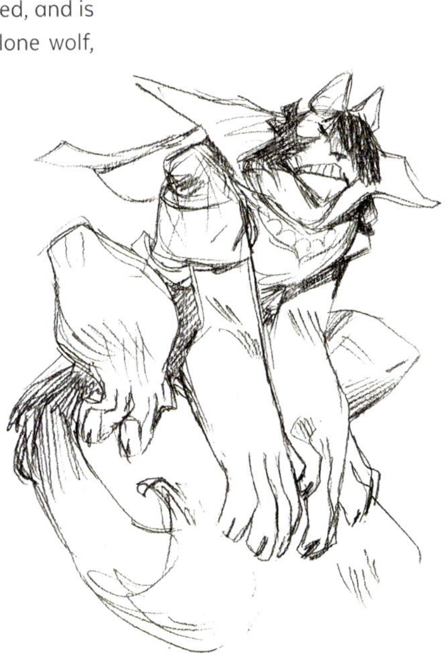

This is more like the idea I had in mind. She is defending her personal space, like a wild animal, and protecting her weaker points. She is not pursuing you, but menacing you for trespassing into her territory.

VALUE & COLOR

As the character has been transformed, I think it would be a good idea to also invert the color palette, making her seem different, but not totally removed from the original. The blue colors of the armor are now the fur color, similar to the gray coat of a real wolf, and the skin tone is now the red color of the rusted armor. The metallic blue tones of the fur also give a feeling of coldness and hardness, like the wilderness in which she might be living.

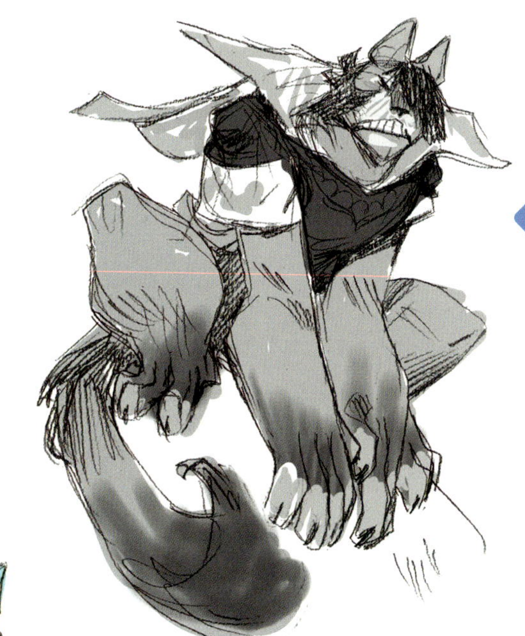

I choose tones that are quite naturalistic for a wolf-like creature, and instead limit the highest contrasts to the remnants of her clothes and armor.

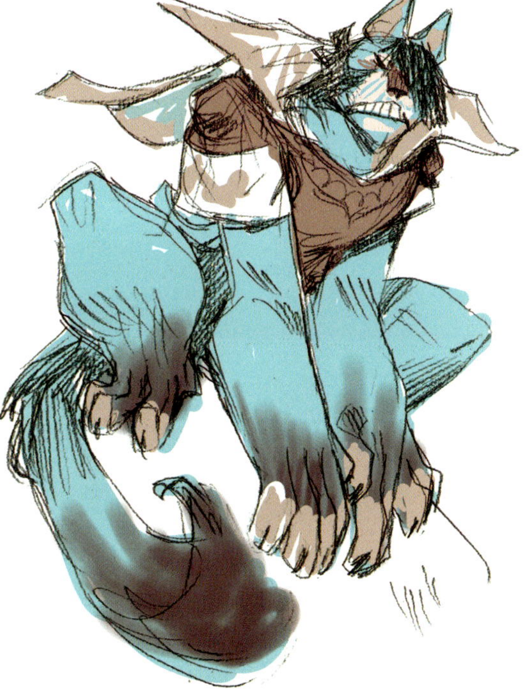

I revisit the aqua color I touched upon in the sci-fi version, but it does not recall enough of the original fantasy version of the character, which would share the same setting as this one.

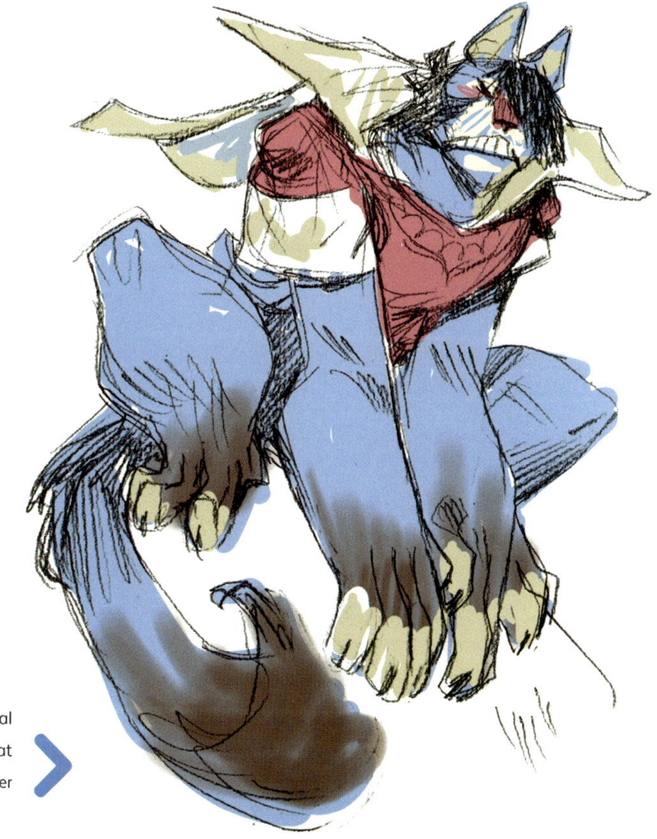

I choose a palette that preserves the colors of the original design. The clothes are dirty, as are the claws, showing that she has been living in the wild. The reddish brown on her claws also balances out the cool blue color of her fur.

FINAL DESIGN

The character's furry body and lack of clothes give a real sense of wildness. She could be standing on a rock above our heads, following our movements like a hunting predator. Like her human counterpart, she feels capable of moving very fast, jumping with those powerful limbs, and the armor doesn't seem like a heavy weight for her. The armor still bears the same pattern as the original character, which works well from a narrative standpoint, creating an anchor to her human past.

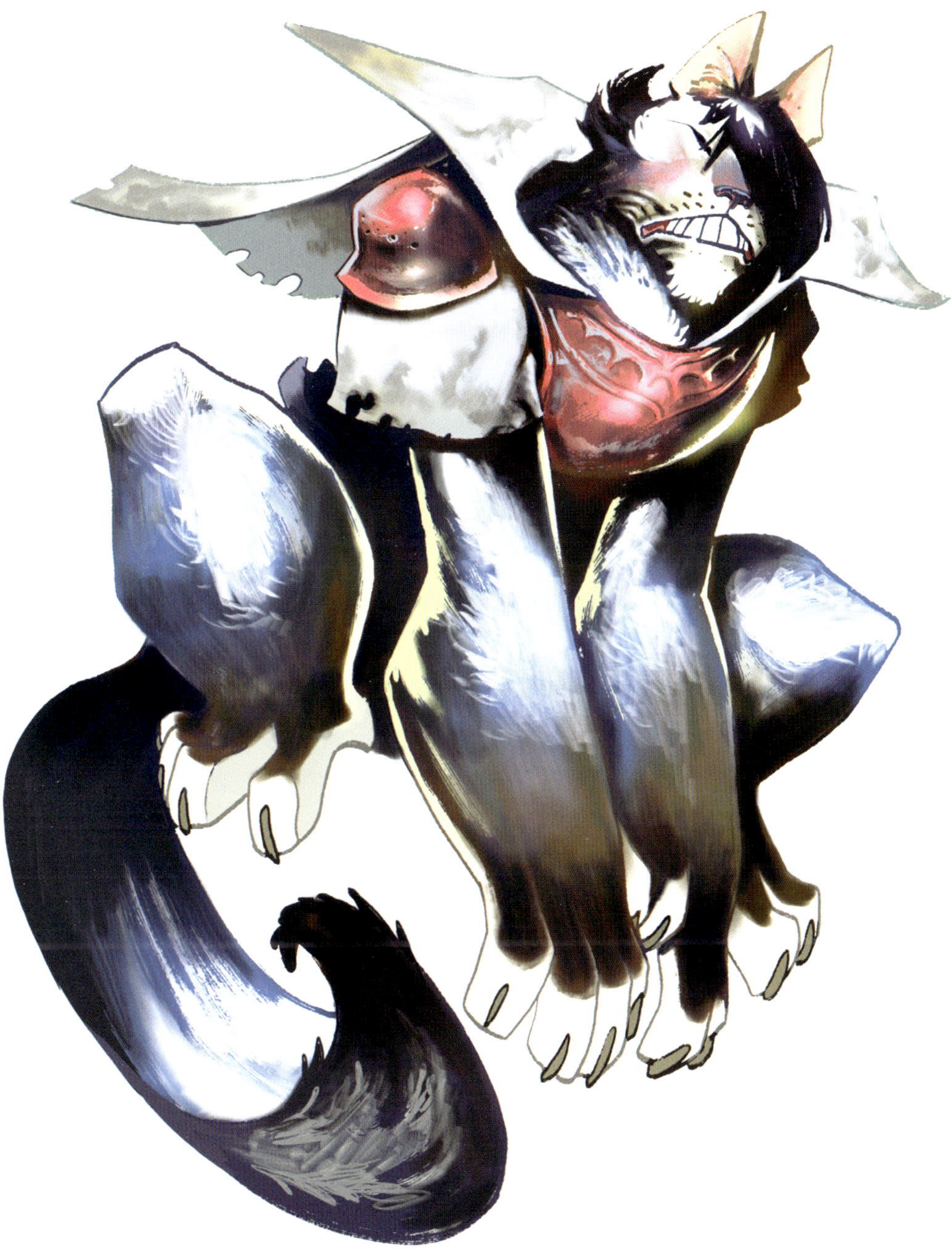

Final artwork © Enrique Fernández

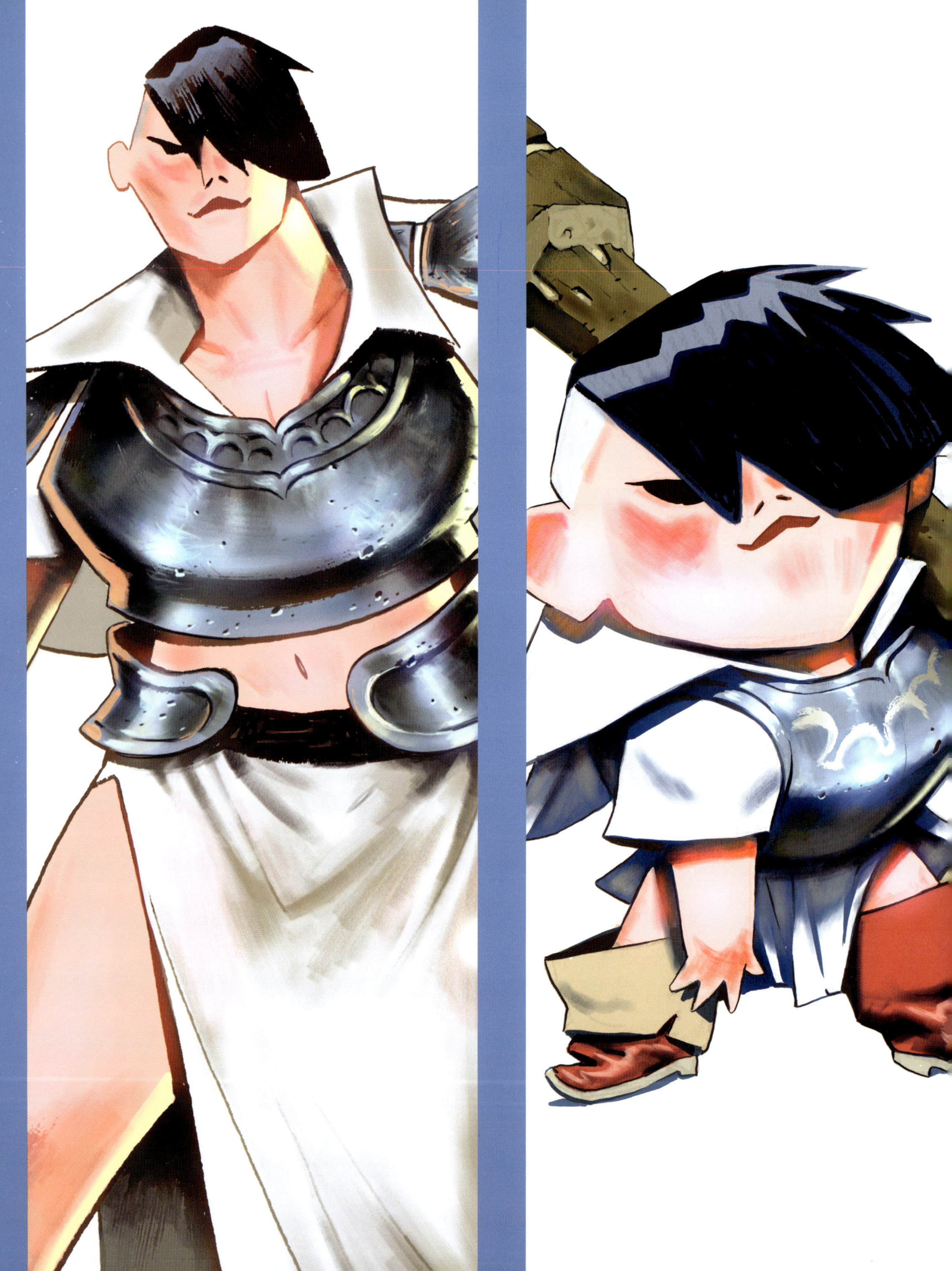

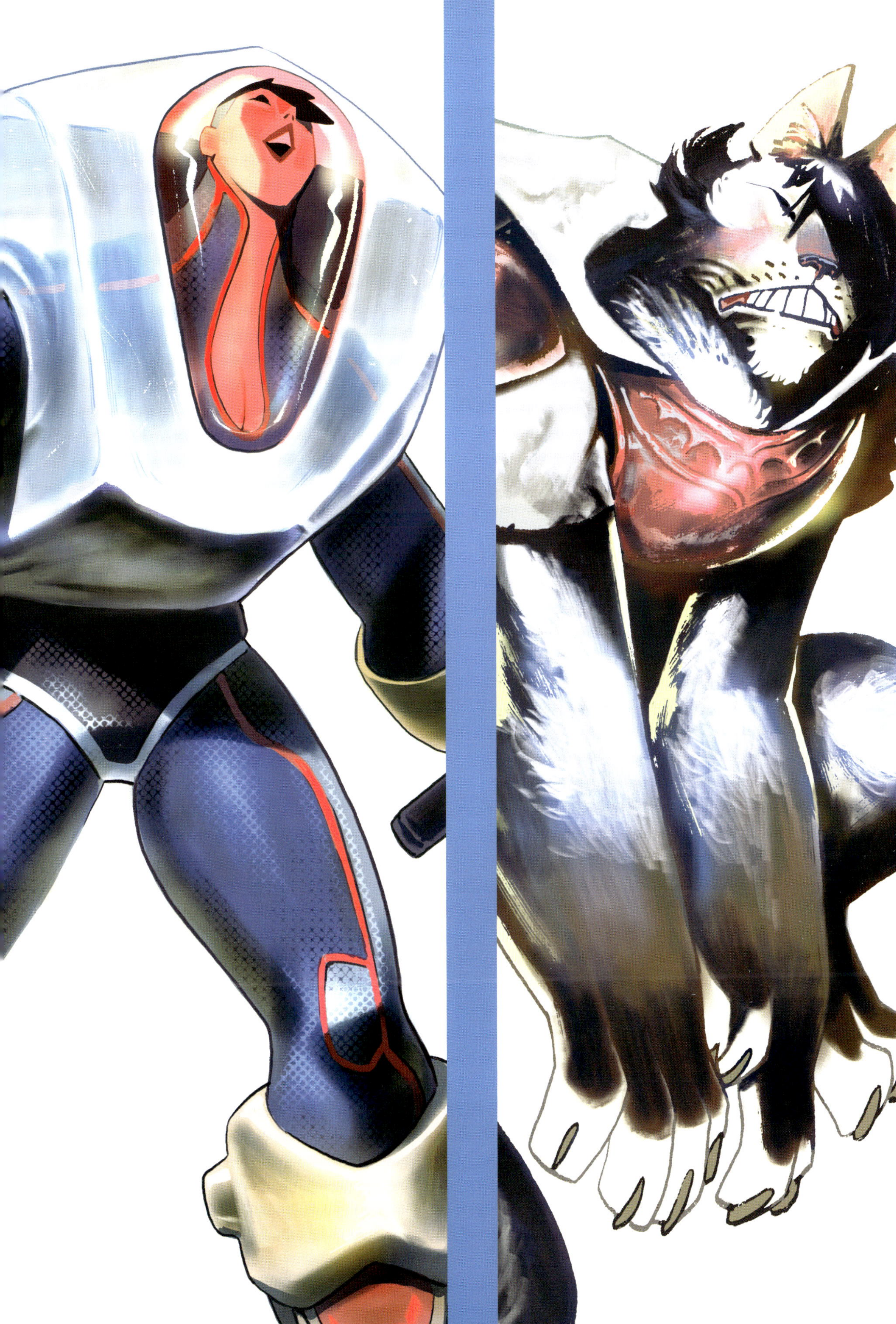

CABIN BOY CAT

BY SHAUN BRYANT

In this chapter, character designer Shaun Bryant designs a plucky cabin boy from a crew of pirate cats and explores different angles for depicting anthropomorphized animals.

VARIATIONS

- SALTY SEA CAT
- GHOSTLY CAPTAIN
- SHIPWRECKED BOY

FOCUS

Shaun's style focuses on developing strong shapes and silhouettes, and creating distinctive, colorful costumes that are tailored to reflect the character's backstory.

Put plenty of thought into the overall shape of your character, and consider how you can use clothing and accessories to make your design more fully realized and unique.

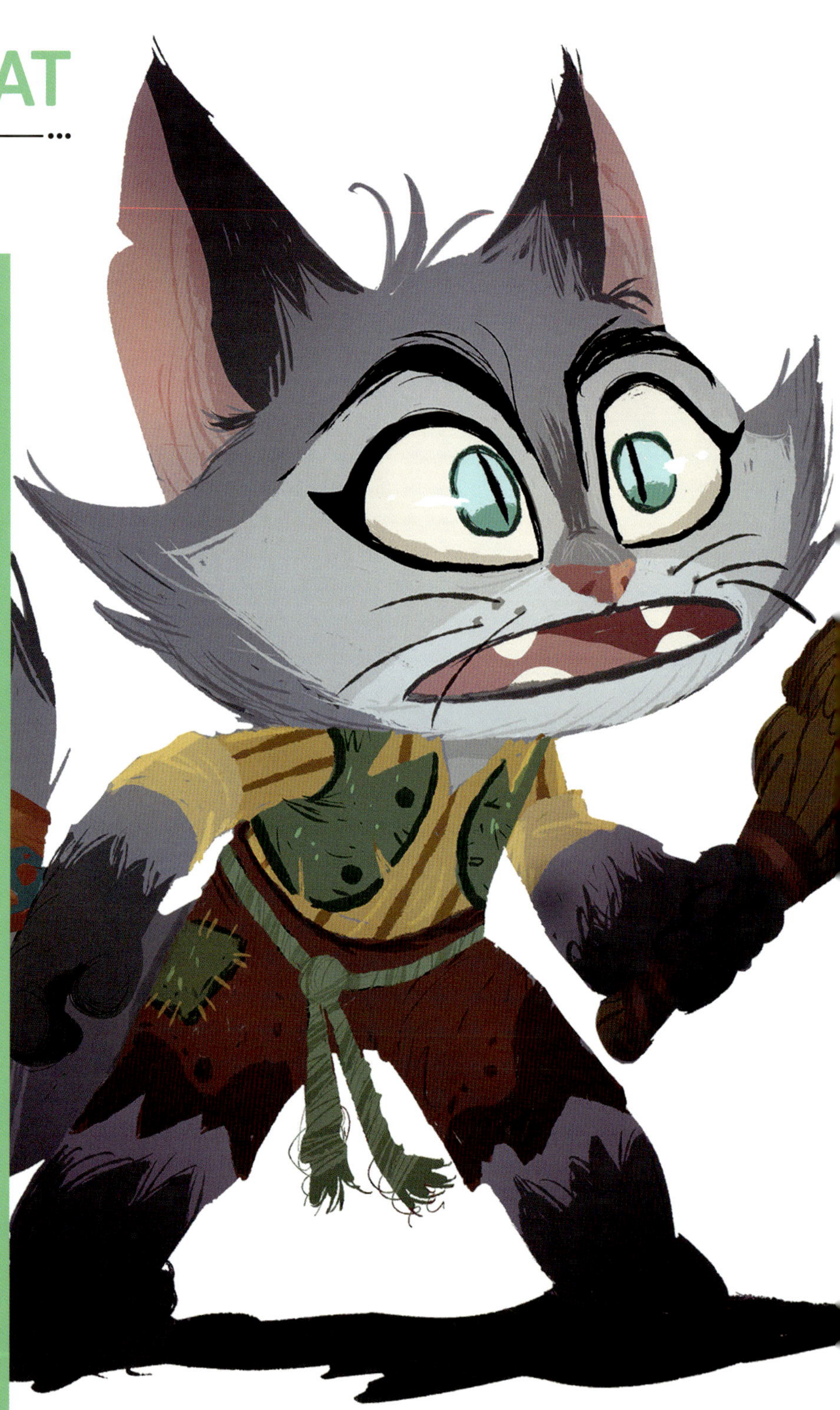

THE IDEA

In this chapter I will be creating a pirate-themed cat character. Creating characters without a story leads to flat, uninteresting designs, so I begin by penning down a rough outline of a backstory. I decide my character will be a young cabin boy on board the ship *The Whiskered Wisp*. He joined the freebooting pirate crew for adventure and riches; he may be a bit wild, but he is good at heart.

Concept: A cat who is a young member of a pirate crew

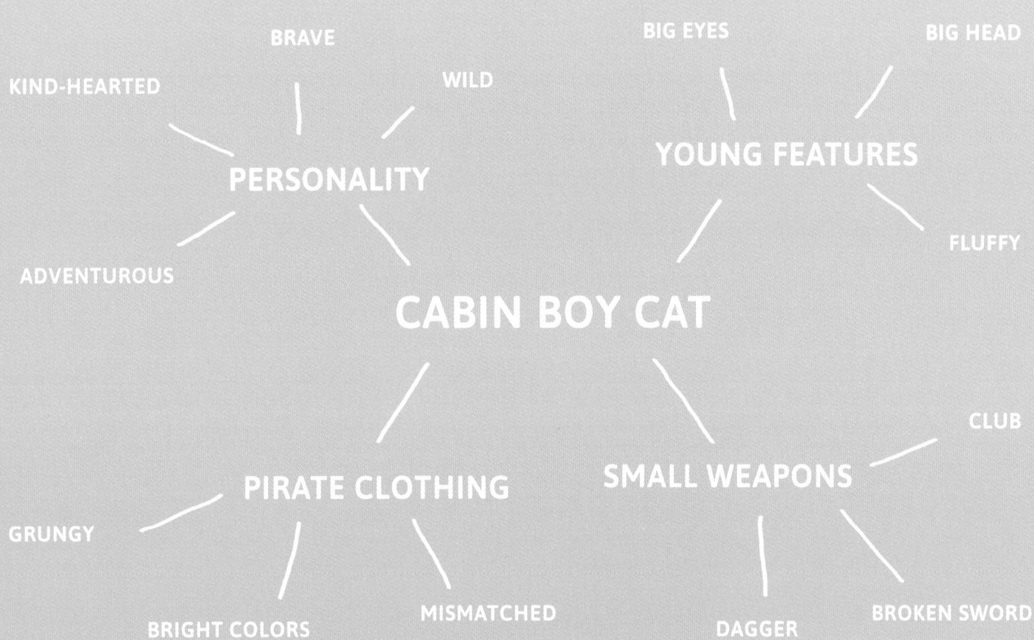

RESEARCH

I start researching some key items that I can use to build a base for the character. Large eyes and stubby paws would fit the character's feline nature and help to convey his young age. He would also need clothing, accessories, and a weapon suitable for a pirate, so I sketch out as many different possibilities as I can.

The cat's eyes will be a key feature for expressing his personality and age, so I spend some time playing around with different shapes to work out what will be most appealing. Some of these are overtly feline and others rather more human. I would like a relatable mix of both.

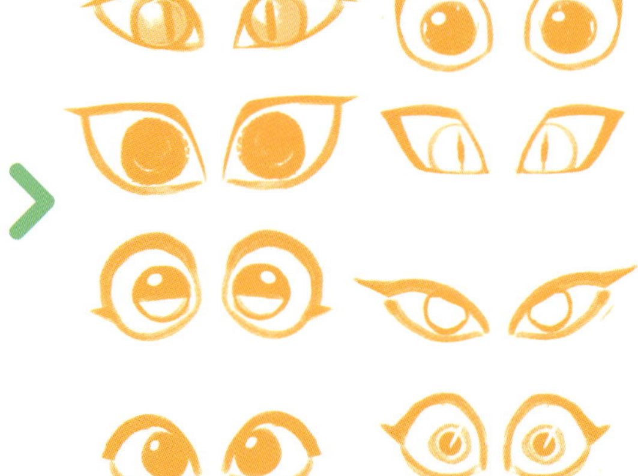

Simplifying and stylizing the hands is an important step for this cat character; when mixing human and animal anatomy, it is key to find similarities between their shapes. This cat could have fingers and thumbs for holding items, but shorter and fewer fingers to maintain a paw-like appearance.

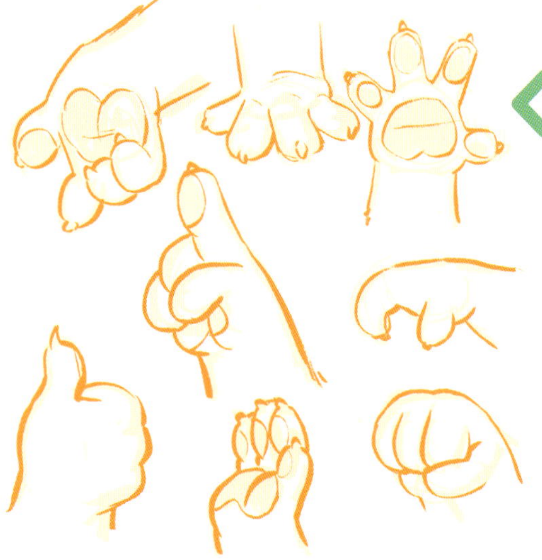

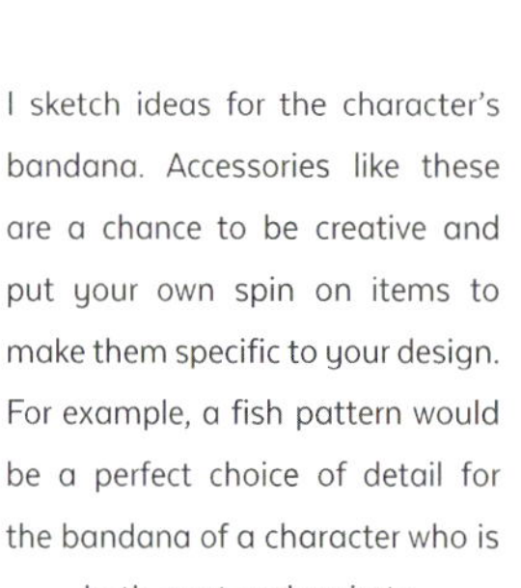

I sketch ideas for the character's bandana. Accessories like these are a chance to be creative and put your own spin on items to make them specific to your design. For example, a fish pattern would be a perfect choice of detail for the bandana of a character who is both a cat and a pirate.

As I watch pirate movies as part of my costume research, I make pages of these quick sketches as notes for costume ideas.

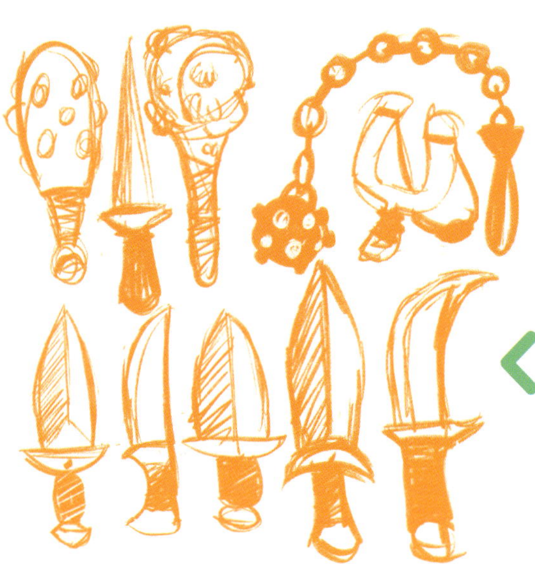

Here are some of the early weapon ideas I come up with in my research. They are all choices that might fit a small, agile character, or one who is quite low in the pirate ranks and doesn't have an elaborate weapon.

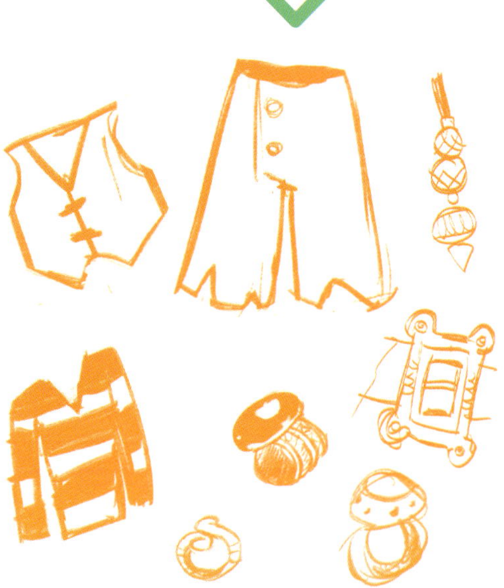

THUMBNAILS

I start sketching in symmetry so that I can quickly make decisions about shape and indicate some costume ideas; I like to work loosely and layer in more details until I come up with something cohesive. I want the character to feel child- or kitten-like, to convey his young age. I look towards cat breeds that are fluffy and have big eyes, as these are endearing features. I make his head larger while keeping his shoulders and hips a similar width so they don't feel too developed and muscular. I keep the eyes and ears large in comparison with the muzzle, to give him an alert, adolescent look. With each iteration of the character, I try to emphasize a different feature or make a slightly different choice, such as the eye shapes and costumes, so that I can see what is the most appealing and interesting. Some of these thumbnails look a little too mature and well-dressed. I lean towards the fourth thumbnail as it has the most young-looking proportions, reinforced by upward-facing shapes that make the character look endearing, and a more scrappy costume befitting a low-ranking pirate with a wild personality and adventurous lifestyle.

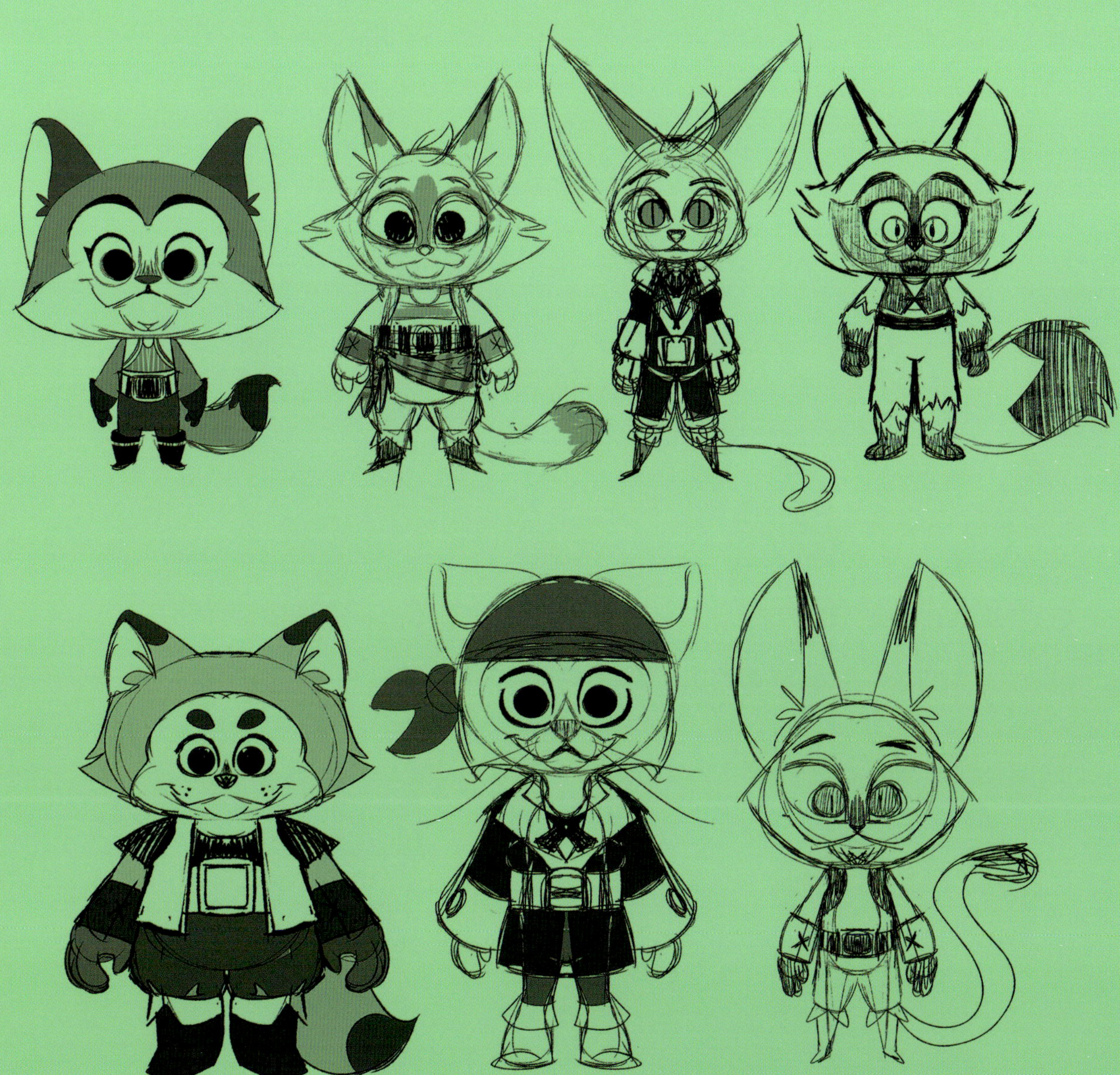

BASIC SHAPES

As I clean up the fourth thumbnail, I try to use circular forms at the ends of the arms and legs to suggest a sense of weight. The ratio between head and body size is really important in younger characters; by lengthening the limbs and body shape, you "age up" the character, and vice versa. Studying classic comic shape language, such as in the work of Paul Coker Jr. and Bill Keane, will give you a great idea of children's cartoon proportions.

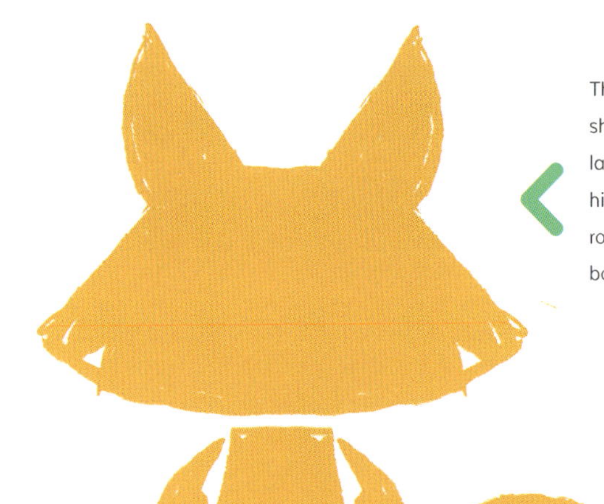

These basic shapes show the overall kitten-like shape of the character, with a proportionately large head and short limbs that really highlight his young age and small size. Using a mix of round and sharp shapes will help to convey both his age and friendliness, and his fierce, scrappy pirate's attitude.

Here you can see how the basic shapes correspond with the thumbnail I have chosen as my base. The sketch fleshes out areas like his neck, tail, and ears, but the overall proportions are still very clear.

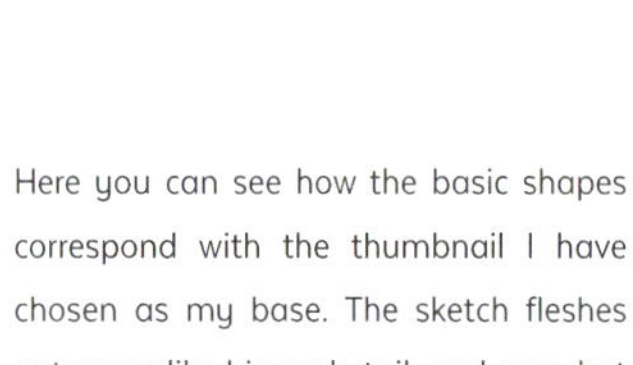

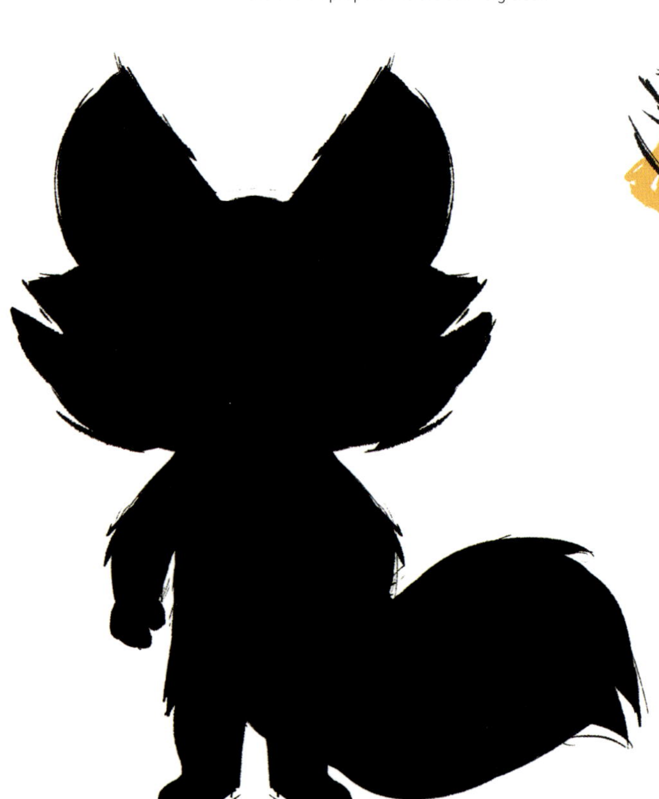

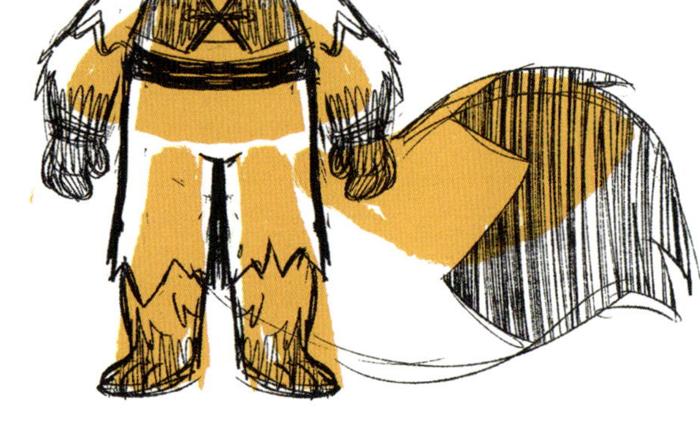

I check that the silhouette reads clearly and still has the impactful positive and negative space that I liked so much in my initial thumbnail. In this case, the character is clearly recognizable as a cat-like animal with quite young proportions.

DETAILS

The thumbnail for this character was already quite developed, but I want the final design to have a slightly less threadbare costume. I want to give the impression that he has lost and added various items articles of clothing during his adventures at sea. Giving him a rope belt adds a scrappy, nautical feel because that item would be readily available to him on deck. His clothes are weathered and patched except for the fun, patterned bandana around his tail, which suggests that even a cabin boy reaps some rewards on *The Whiskered Wisp*'s adventures.

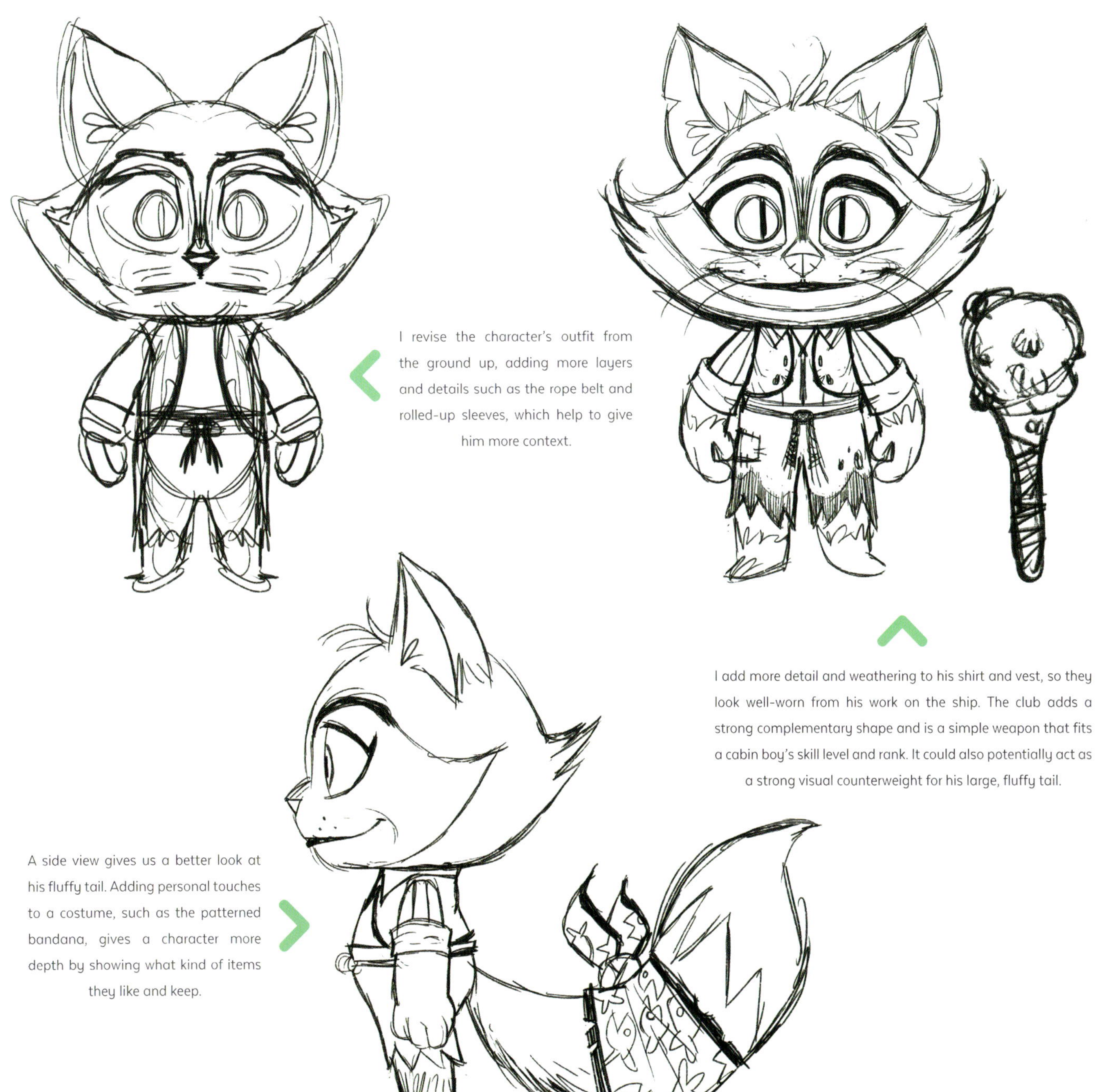

I revise the character's outfit from the ground up, adding more layers and details such as the rope belt and rolled-up sleeves, which help to give him more context.

I add more detail and weathering to his shirt and vest, so they look well-worn from his work on the ship. The club adds a strong complementary shape and is a simple weapon that fits a cabin boy's skill level and rank. It could also potentially act as a strong visual counterweight for his large, fluffy tail.

A side view gives us a better look at his fluffy tail. Adding personal touches to a costume, such as the patterned bandana, gives a character more depth by showing what kind of items they like and keep.

FACIAL EXPRESSIONS

I find it useful to take selfies or capture screencaps from films to make my expressions more authentic, isolating the basic shapes of an expression and then applying it to the character I am creating. In this case, I watch everything from *Pirates of the Caribbean* to *The Pirates of Penzance* to gather ideas for this character's expressions. I decide to mix elements of the three faces shown here for my final image, which will look alert and ready for a fight.

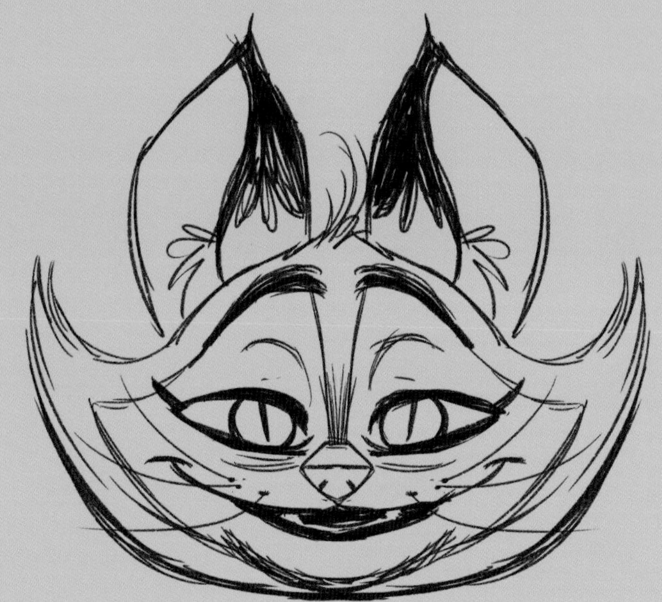

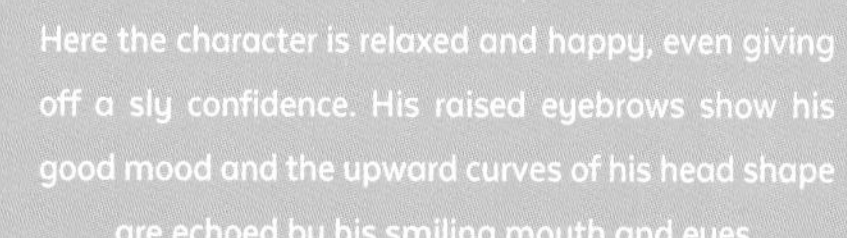

Here the character is relaxed and happy, even giving off a sly confidence. His raised eyebrows show his good mood and the upward curves of his head shape are echoed by his smiling mouth and eyes.

The lowered ears, surprised mouth, and shrunken irises indicate that the character is shocked or afraid, which fits the idea that he is a relatively young, small, and inexperienced pirate compared to the rest of his crew. His whole head shape seems to droop, along with his whiskers, while the fur on the top of his head is standing up straight in fear. I would like the final pose to be less fearful than this, as he is overall a tough little cat, but I will use elements of the large, startled eyes to convey his relative innocence in contrast to his pirate crew members.

Here the cat's brows are lowered and teeth bared in a snarl, and his fur and whiskers are bristling upwards in anger, reflecting the wild side of the character that I touched on in the mind map. I would like the final portrayal to look brave but less furious and scary than this, so I will use a slight frown with wide eyes and perked-up ears for the final design.

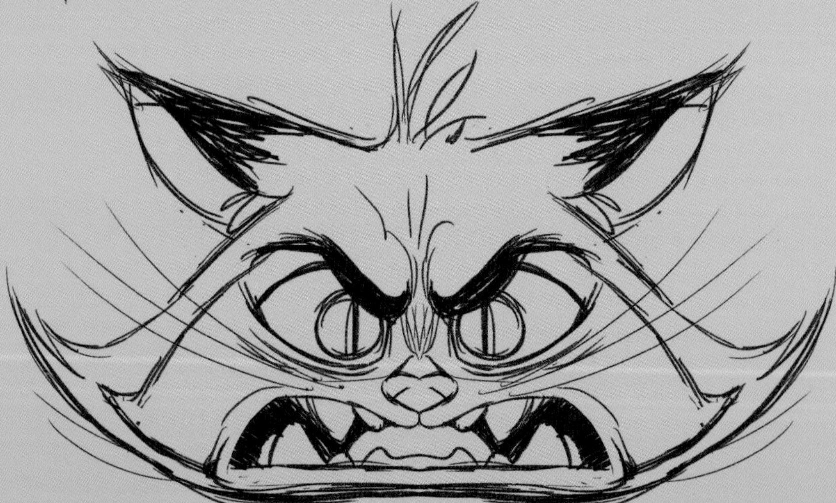

POSING

I try to imagine the character's exact reactions to the events in his story. He might be surprised but ready for action, so a fairly open pose with a shocked expression could work well. Perhaps his tail would be extra puffy, as cats' tails are when they want to look more intimidating, and he would have his club at the ready. As with creating expressions, photographing myself in a pose can really help me to understand the weight of the character.

As well as making sure the individual body parts work well together, I always try to ensure that the whole figure has a coherent sense of shape and direction; in the case of the top-right pose, the overall flow of the character is a dynamic, upward-pointing triangle. This shape language is reinforced by the negative space created around the character, such as the triangular gaps formed between his ears and feet. This stance makes the character look brave and dynamic, with arms tensed and his feet planted firmly apart. His face shows a combination of surprise and fierceness, blending elements of the expressions I explored previously.

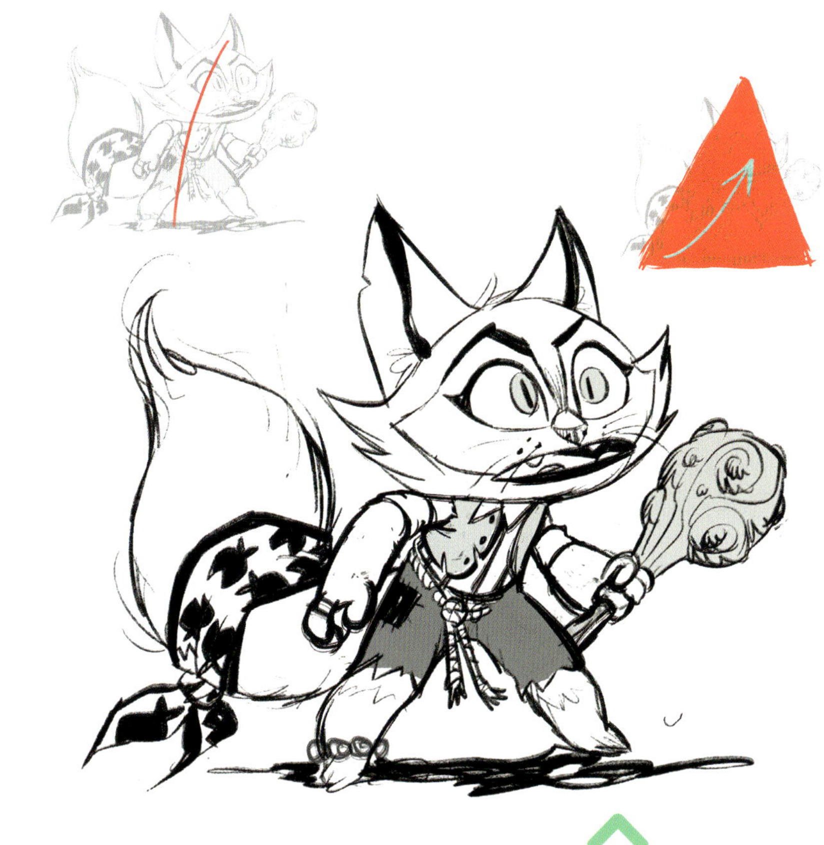

I want to imbue my character's basic geometry with more natural flow, so I imagine a large impactful shape to act as a guide. In this case it's a triangle – a dynamic shape that gives characters a sense of weight around their feet. All the character's basic shapes, from his tail to his facial fur and ears, flow upwards to reinforce this energetic shape.

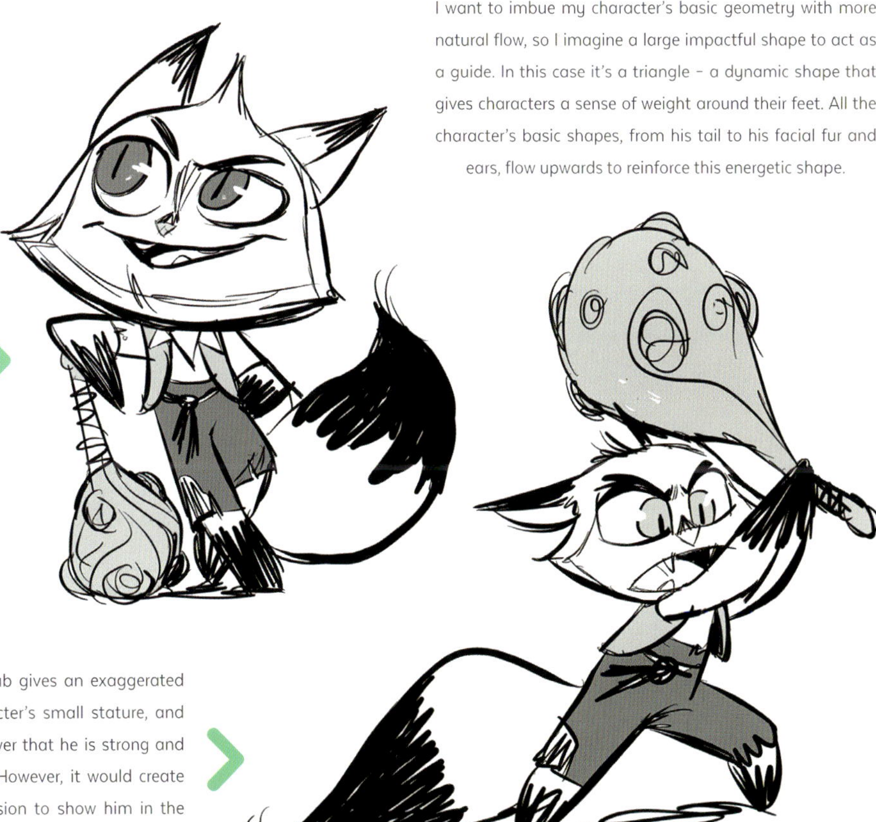

This is a more everyday pose that gives a sense of this young cat's brash pirate swagger, with a cheeky smirk and relaxed, casual stance. The club becomes a useful prop to lean the his weight on, adding to his attitude. However, I would like a more action-packed pose for my final design.

The large raised club gives an exaggerated sense of the character's small stature, and also shows the viewer that he is strong and tough for his size. However, it would create more narrative tension to show him in the moments before a fight instead.

VALUES & COLOR

I want the eyes and face to be the focal point of this design, as these features are what make a character easy for the audience to relate to. I can achieve this by giving him white eyes surrounded by pure black, making the eyes the highest point of contrast in the design.

I choose a neutral grayish hue for the body because I want the eyes to pop with color. The colors of the clothing are also low in saturation, adding to the weathered adventurer look and keeping the emphasis on the character's face.

Adding some pops of bright color to his tail bandana harmonizes the whole color scheme and serves as a counterpoint to the saturated eyes.

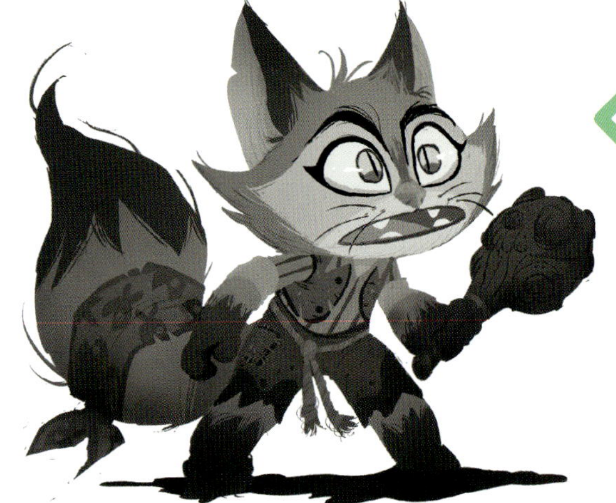

Radiating out from the eyes, I make a gradient of values that concludes with the hands and feet having the body's darkest values. This value structure creates a sort of "bullseye" that leads the viewer's eye to the character's face.

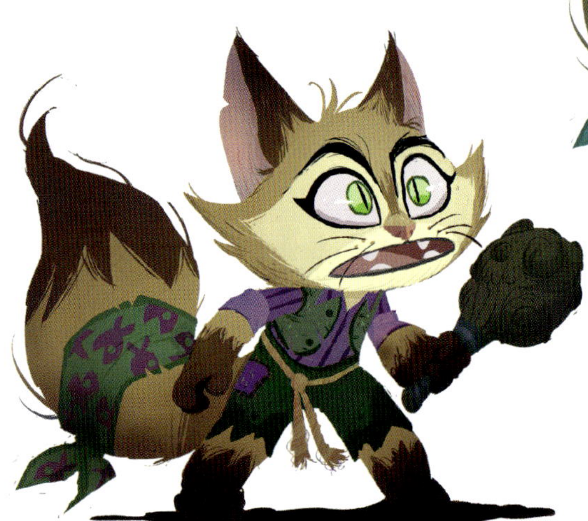

This neutral gray-brown palette is simple and appealing, with appropriately nautical blue accents. It perhaps feels a little too earthy and plain, but I would like the final palette to be similar to this.

I try saturating the fur more, but the focus doesn't feel right; the fur is now too bright and takes away from the focal point of the character's eyes.

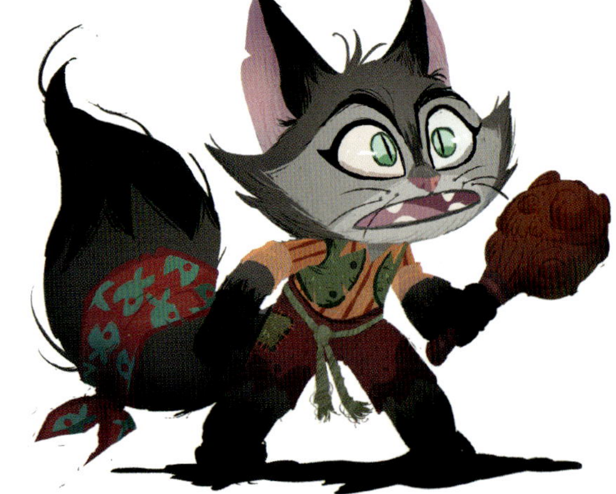

The fur feels too dark and lifeless here, and the high contrast again takes too much away from the eyes. However, the bright sea-colored eyes are a striking feature, complemented by the more earthy costume. Combining aspects of this palette with the other gray-brown palette shown above should create an ideal balance of colors for the final design.

FINAL DESIGN

The little cabin cat is finished and ready for his adventure on the high seas! Having a strong understanding of a character's backstory is essential for creating a design; when I was working on this character, I tried to layer in elements and details that would make the viewer imagine how he has reached where he is in life. For example, his simple, makeshift clothes indicate his lower status in the crew, while the bandana adds a colorful bit of individuality, as if enjoys the pirate lifestyle. Making sure that everything you add to a character is essential to the story will take your design from being a bland image to one that will evoke a sense of storytelling. In this case, every aspect of the character gives the viewer a strong sense of his youth, attitude, and nautical setting.

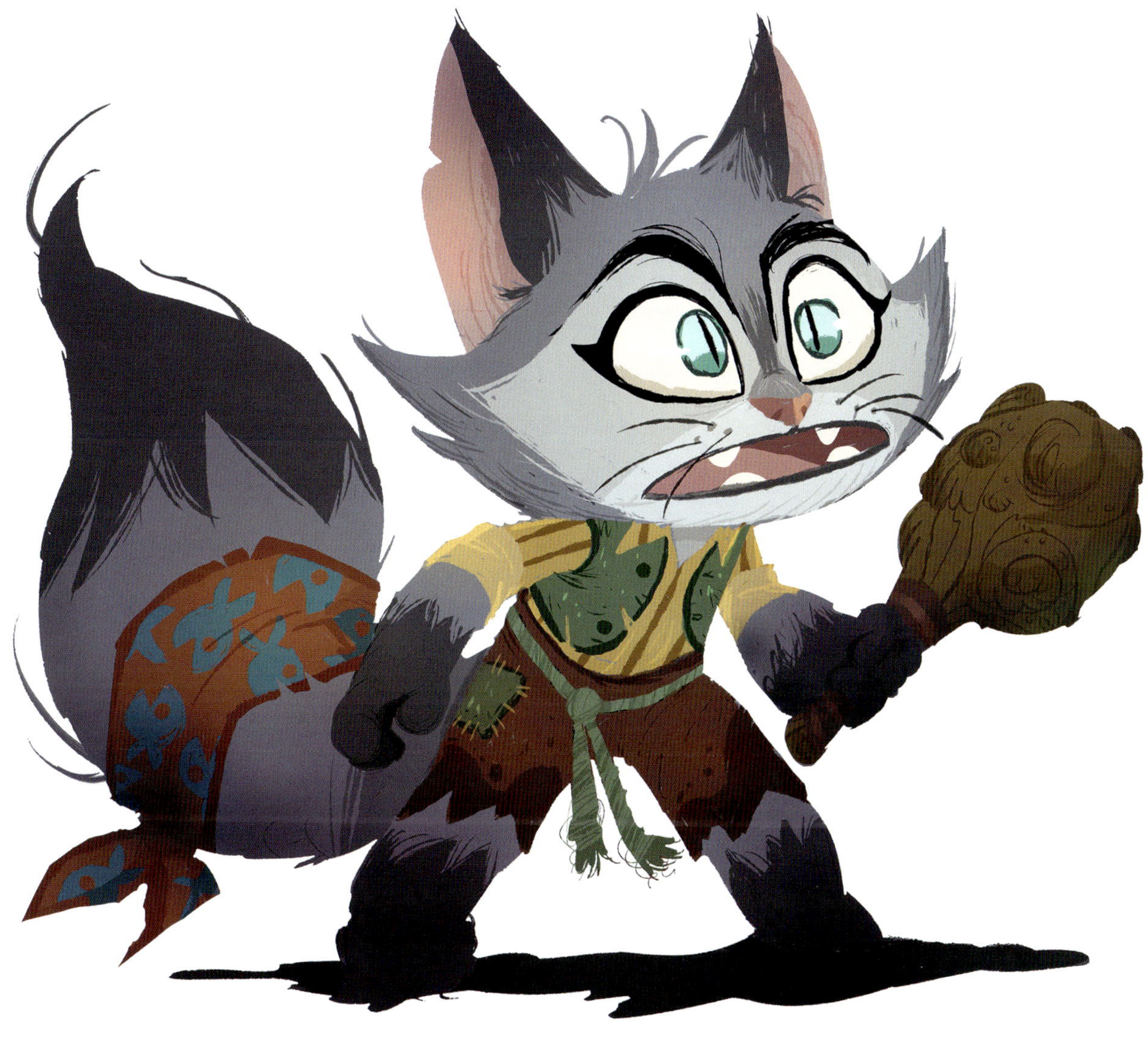

Final artwork © Shaun Bryant

VARIATION 1:
SALTY SEA CAT

IDEAS & RESEARCH

For this variation of the character, I am creating a salty old "sea dog" cat – or a salty old "sea cat." I still have plenty of research in reserve, but now I need to layer in more items and look for elements that will raise the age, rank, and experience of the character. I will change his features and costume, add in some treasure, and maybe some scars to show that he has earned his stripes. This sly cat has seen and been through a lot, but he still has a heart of gold – it's just buried in a chest on a desert island somewhere.

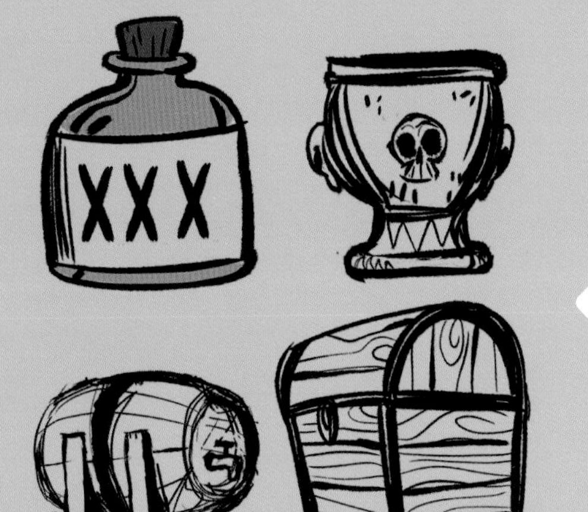

Props can help identify a character's relationship with the world. Items such as a treasure chest or a bottle of grog will help to convey this old sea cat's role and lifestyle.

Giving the character a pipe to smoke would add a lot to his sense of age and gravitas, as it is rather an old-fashioned habit. I explore some fittingly cat- and fish-related decorations which would make the pipe more individual.

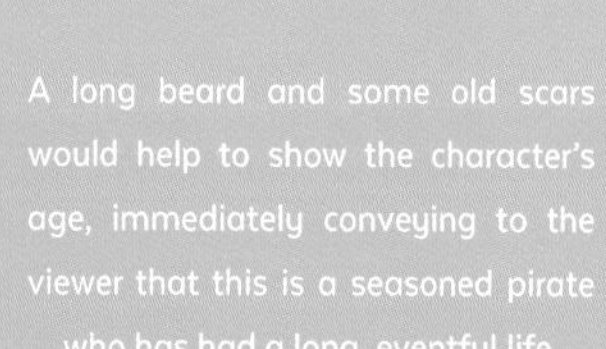

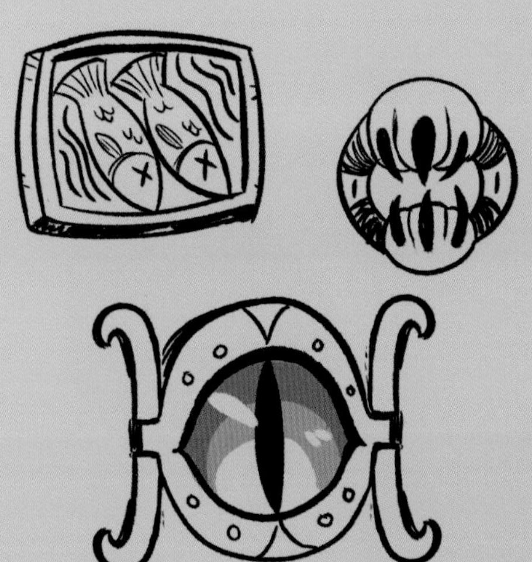

I sketch out ideas for decorative details that might suit the character's accessories or pieces of loot, based around cat-like or fishy themes.

It can be helpful to sketch out a full garment and work out how it might be distressed and torn up. I like the idea of the character wearing a historical uniform jacket with many buttons, perhaps something taken from a fallen enemy.

A long beard and some old scars would help to show the character's age, immediately conveying to the viewer that this is a seasoned pirate who has had a long, eventful life.

It would make sense for this seasoned pirate to carry a dangerous weapon. A heavy sword would give him a greater sense of menace than the cabin boy's wooden club.

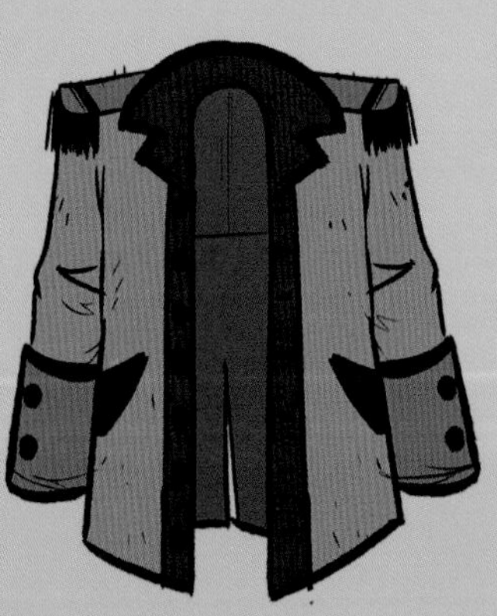

CHANGES

I will need to make many changes to the proportions, physique, and costume of the original character. This version will be an adult cat, so will have a head more equally proportioned to his body, more evenly-sized facial features, and a thicker body that has seen a few adventures. After spending years at sea, I imagine him to have a gruff, sly personality, reflecting his greater experience on the high seas compared to the wide-eyed, childlike attitude of the young cabin boy version.

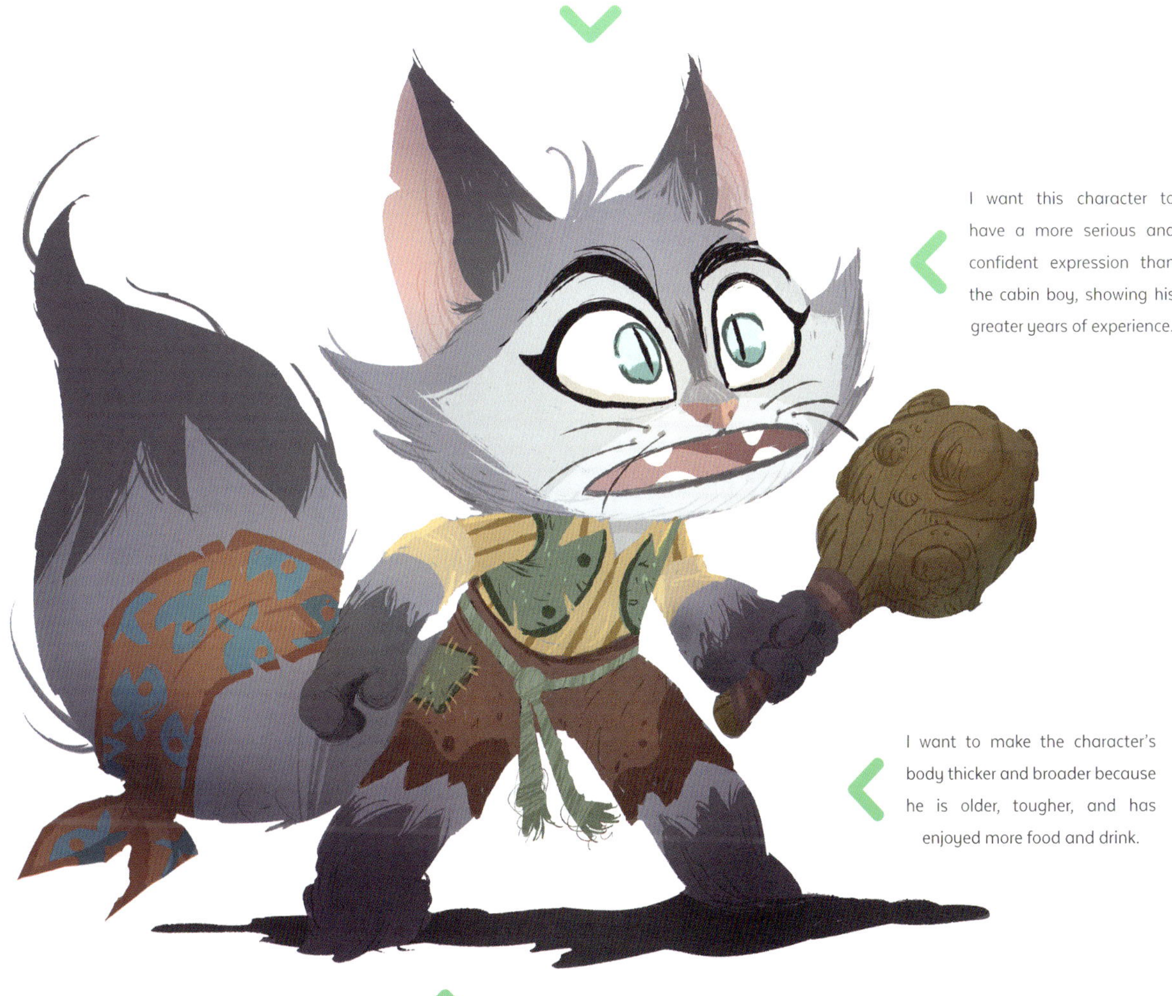

Adding small details such as scars or an eyepatch would help to show the tough road this cat has traveled.

I want this character to have a more serious and confident expression than the cabin boy, showing his greater years of experience.

I want to make the character's body thicker and broader because he is older, tougher, and has enjoyed more food and drink.

Giving the character layers of clothes and jewelry will represent the many adventures he has tackled and the riches he has won.

THUMBNAILS

I like the idea of this character becoming a bit thicker in the waist as he gets older, so I start by thumbnailing some rounder, stouter shapes for the body. I think of characters like Gibbs from the *Pirates of the Caribbean* films, and Han Solo from *Star Wars*, and incorporate a bit of their swagger into him.

I try layering in more items like bandanas, hats, belts, and jewelry to distinguish each design. Where the cabin boy was more fluffy and youthful, I want this old cat to seem more weathered and frayed. As I mentioned on page 192, longer limbs and a longer body will help to "age up" the design. Smaller, squinted eyes from years at sea, some scars, and maybe some missing limbs would help to tell the story of a cat who has lost a few of his nine lives along the way.

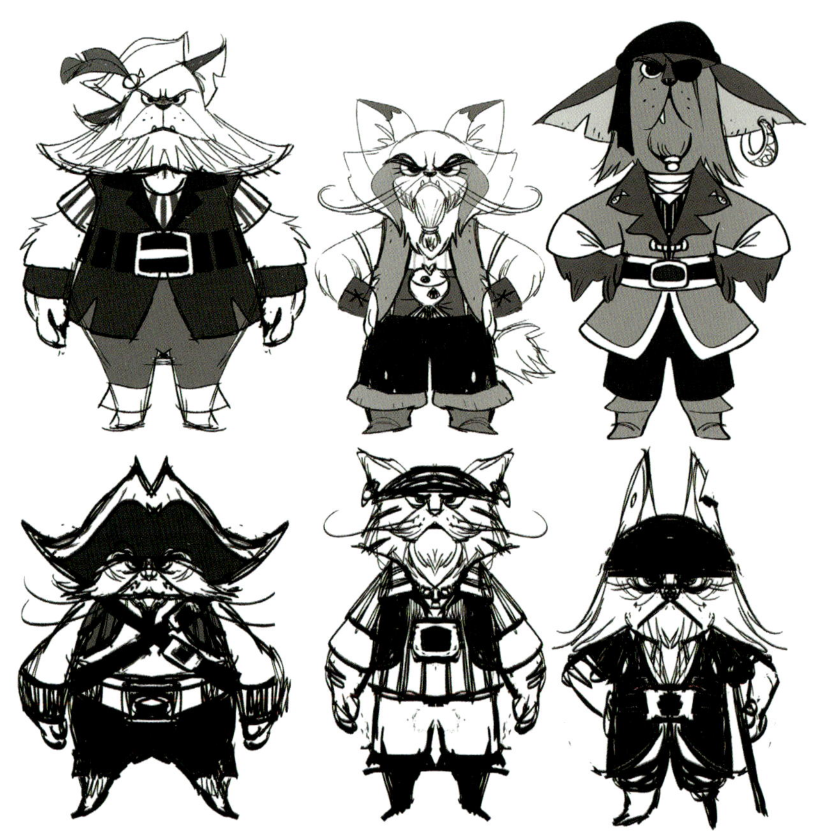

BASIC SHAPES

The second and fourth thumbnails have the most appeal for me, with twirled whiskery mustaches that convey the character as a cunning old rogue. I create an amalgamation of the strongest elements of both, combining the stocky body of the second thumbnail with the more intimidating head shape of the fourth. I want to move away from the sharper, downturned shapes shown in some of the thumbnails to rounder, upturned shapes that make the character look confident and assertive, harking back to the upturned shapes of the cabin boy design. This helps to lighten the mood of the character slightly, so he has some swashbuckling charm, while still keeping him gruff.

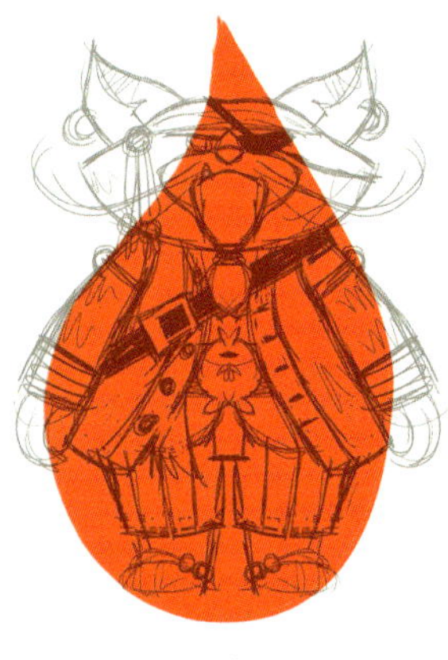

I like the idea of a nautical character having a fluid shape, almost thinking of him as a water balloon. This round, bottom-heavy shape will give his broad body more weight.

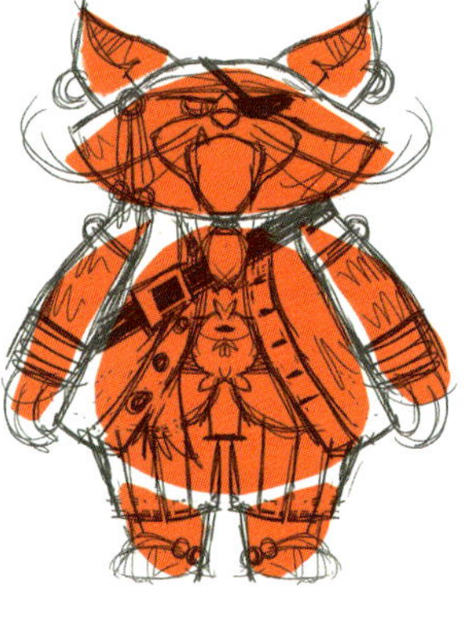

I flesh out the character's body while keeping in mind his overall teardrop shape. The wide lower body gradually narrows towards his neck in a way that directs the viewer to his face, which is a similar shape to the original.

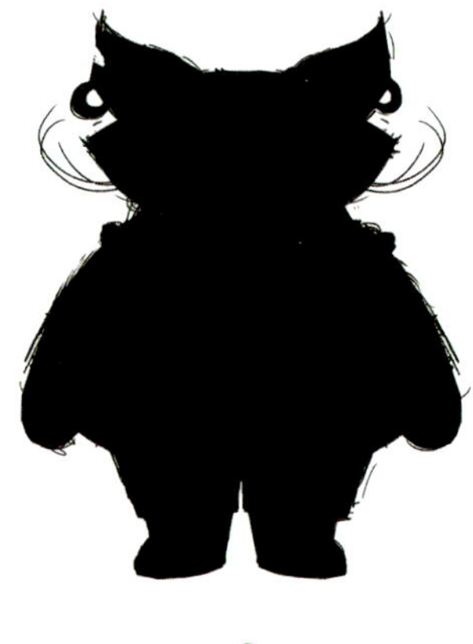

In this silhouette view, you can see how elements such as his earrings and whiskers help to break up the character's outline, ensuring that his very thick, solid shape is still interesting to the viewer.

DETAILS

I want this character's costume to be heavy with trinkets and jewelry, as if he has won many items in battle during his long career as a pirate. His chipped ears and eyepatch suggest that his life has been full of peril and adventure, and his fancy jacket, large belt buckles, and long beard show that he is a cat with more clout than the low-ranking cabin boy.

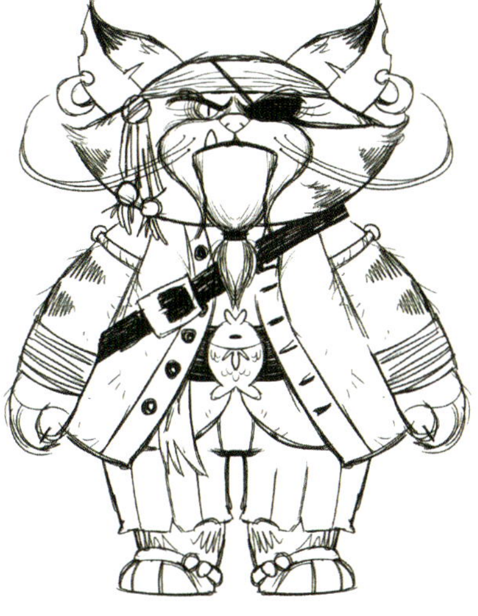

I am designing this character as if for media with young viewers in mind, so I add pieces of whimsy that add to the personality of the character and keep him from looking overly grim, such as his dramatic whiskers and slightly comical fish buckle.

This character's tail is much less prominent than the young cabin cat's; he is already bulky and doesn't need a large tail to make him look fierce. It's likely he lost some of it in battle.

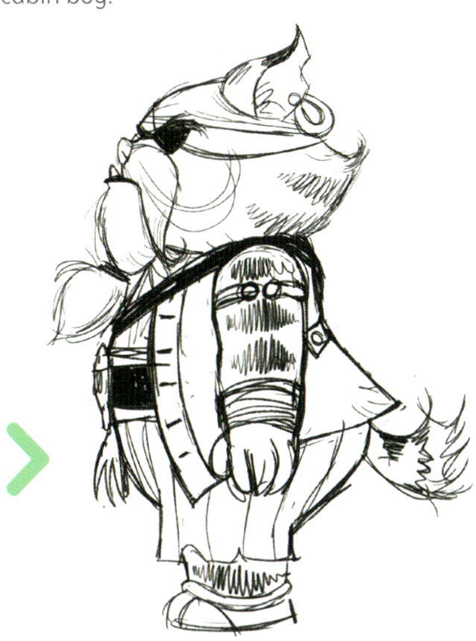

EXPRESSIONS & POSING

I want this character to look competent and confident in his skills, with his mature age and broad physique lending weight to how he carries himself. His costume features many accessories and details, and I would like to show him posing with a prop that tells us about his story, so I must consider how to show all these elements clearly to the viewer in his pose.

I start with more of a "power pose" that shows him confidently brandishing his sword, but quickly realize that this is too heroic a pose. I would like to portray him as more heavy and stern.

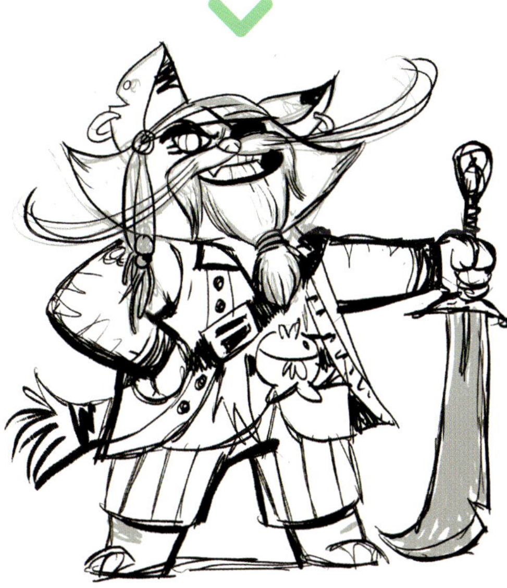

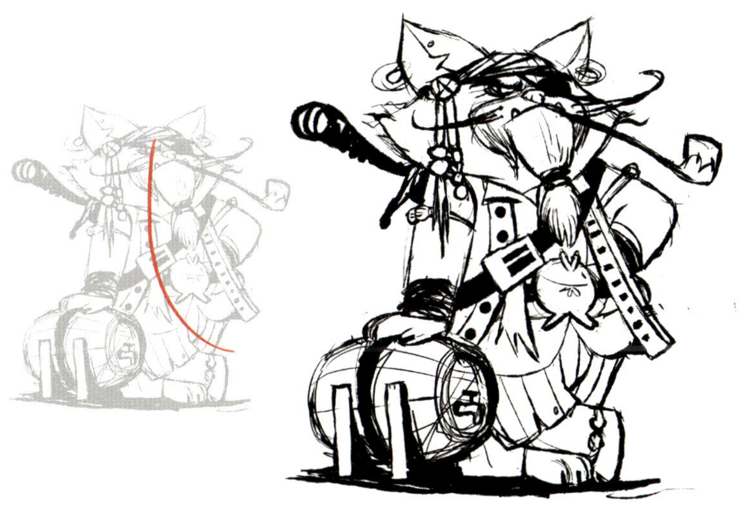

This serious but relaxed pose still holds the confidence needed for this character's story. His posture is slouchy and lower, in keeping with the bottom-heavy droplet shape I established earlier. One paw leans on a looted barrel of rum, creating interesting asymmetry in the pose and giving the impression that he's not a cat to be messed with.

VALUE & COLOR

After testing several color palette ideas, I decide that I want this version of the character to be an orange tabby. It is a color that will suit his gruff, roguish appearance without him looking overly gloomy or too villainous, and is a natural color for a cat, like the cabin boy's gray fur.

A medium orange hue will not overpower the design, and the tabby pattern will create some value changes that add variety. His face and the paw leaning on the barrel are important narrative features of this pose, conveying the most about his attitude, so I want those areas to have higher contrast. Using pops of blues and greens will complement the orange fur and help to lead the viewer's eye around the design.

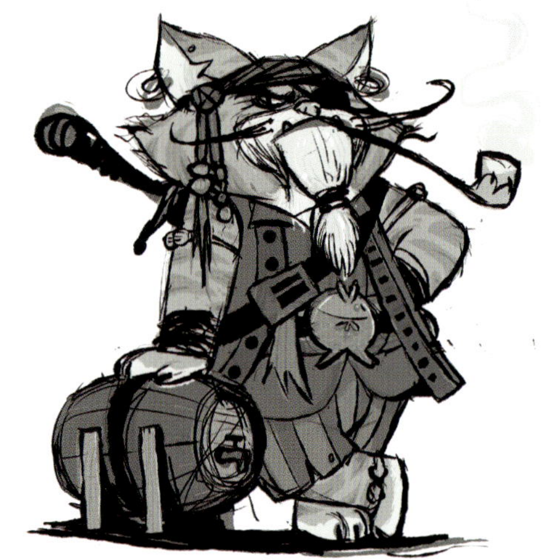

The character's tabby pattern will help to create contrast in important areas of the design. For example, the darker ears and lighter beard help to focus the viewer on the center of his face.

This color palette is almost sea-green, befitting a seafaring character, with some warmer browns and reds for contrast. The character's gray beard stands out in a way that emphasizes his age, which is a strong feature, but the overall impression is a little too cold.

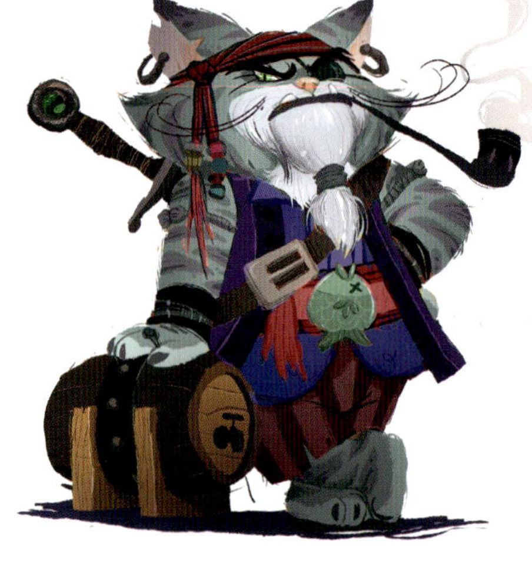

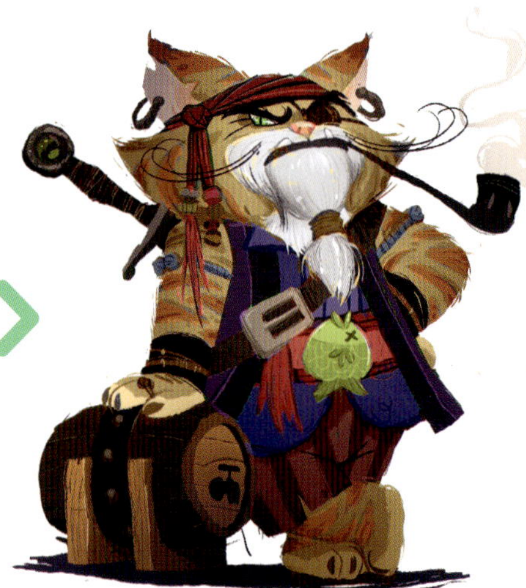

This ginger tabby color palette is close to what I want, giving the character more of a warm, fiery look that suits his grumpy temper. However, I could emphasize the oranges and yellows even further in the final version to make him more vibrant, and borrow some of the blue and teal elements from the other palettes to complement his orange fur.

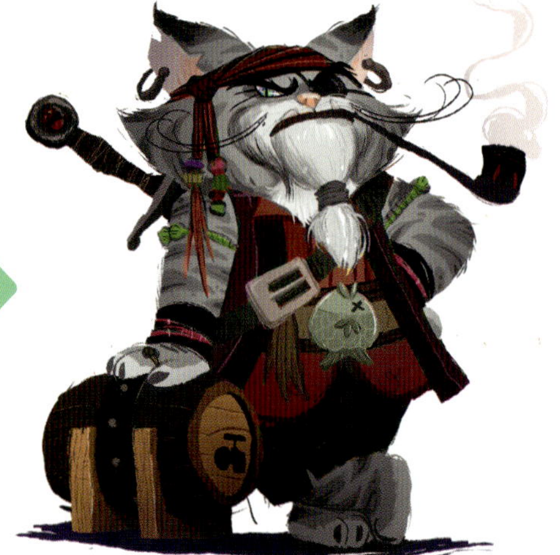

This more neutral gray palette is very subdued, and the use of deep reds and greens suggests a much more villainous personality. It is a visually strong palette, but perhaps a little too dark and villainous for a character who is more of a straightforward scrappy rogue.

FINAL DESIGN

This character really came together through analyzing the story and considering attributes that would fit a wily old sea cat. The final design succeeds in creating an older character who is suitably haggard and battle-scarred, with many accessories that show off his accumulated loot and riches. His warm ginger tabby palette gives him a fierce look, suitable for a character who is experienced and gruff, but not so cold and antagonistic that his younger crewmates can't turn to him for help. The design's subtle value changes, along with the line of his pipe, direct the viewer straight to the focal point of his single frowning eye.

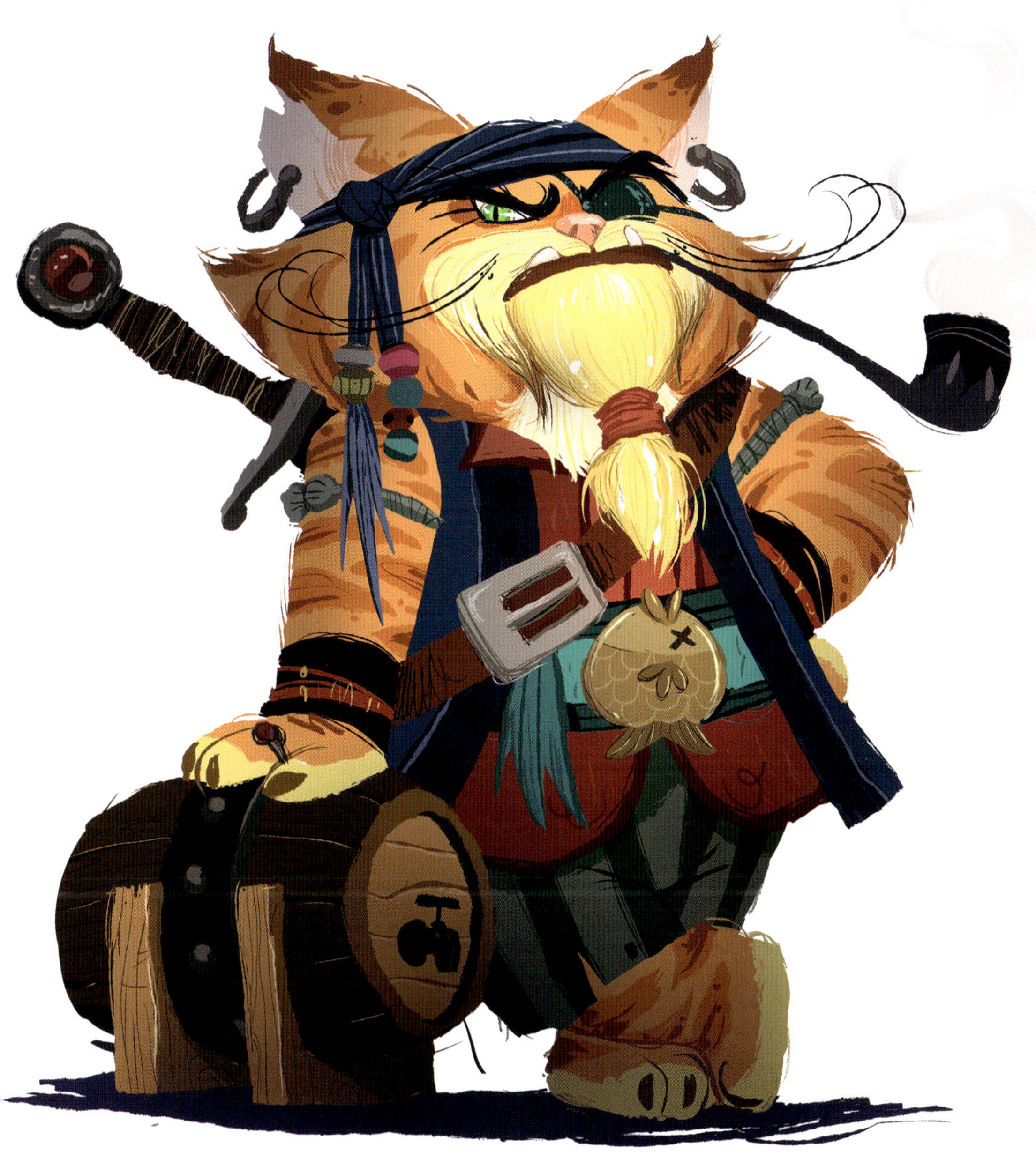

Final artwork © Shaun Bryant

VARIATION 2:
GHOSTLY CAPTAIN

IDEAS & RESEARCH

This variation of the pirate cat will draw more influence from supernatural and horror sources such as *Ghostbusters* and *The Frighteners* to set the desired tone. I want to create a villainous character who would be a frightening sight floating above the waves: a ghostly captain searching the high seas for souls to add to his spectral crew. However, like the previous designs, I would like him to be heavily stylized and fun rather than outright scary, as if geared towards a young audience.

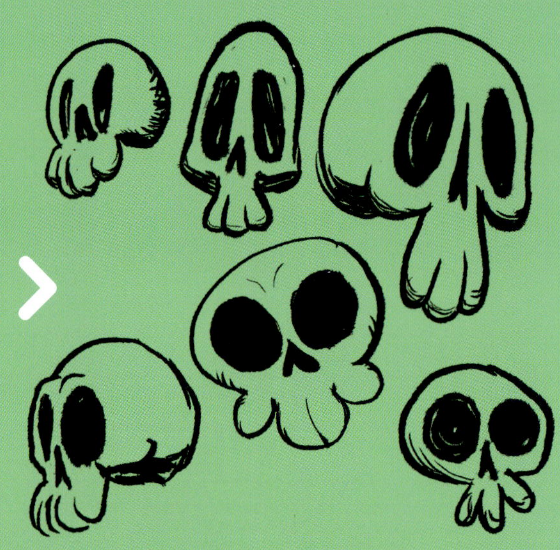

I test out some stylized skull baubles for the character's foggy beard. They will make him more dangerous and intimidating, but a very simplified, exaggerated style of skull will also keep the design fun.

I research some possible weapons for the character. A heavy sword with some spooky personalized details seems like the best fit for a pirate captain.

I test out and stylize some different breeds of cat to see what features might suit this character. Scowling, grumpy cats with small eyes and short noses have a strong attitude and older look that I really want to capture.

I want the character to appear in a cloud of swirling, spooky effects, so I sketch out some possibilities for different special effects that would help to convey his spectral essence.

CHANGES

This version will incorporate more costume items than the design we began with, and perhaps hair and a beard full of other details and ornaments, as these aspects will help me to represent the character's high rank and sinister nature. I want it to be immediately apparent to the viewer that this character belongs to the same heritage as the previous designs, but with a supernatural twist that sets him apart, so I must consider how this could be done through my use of details and colors.

The previous designs had fairly neutral or natural fur colors, but I want to really emphasize that this version is a supernatural horror. Instead of grays and browns, he should have a spooky, unnatural color.

I want the character to glow with the inner light of souls he has captured on the high seas. This will give me a chance to explore new value ideas, different from the cabin boy version, where the only bright values are focused on his face.

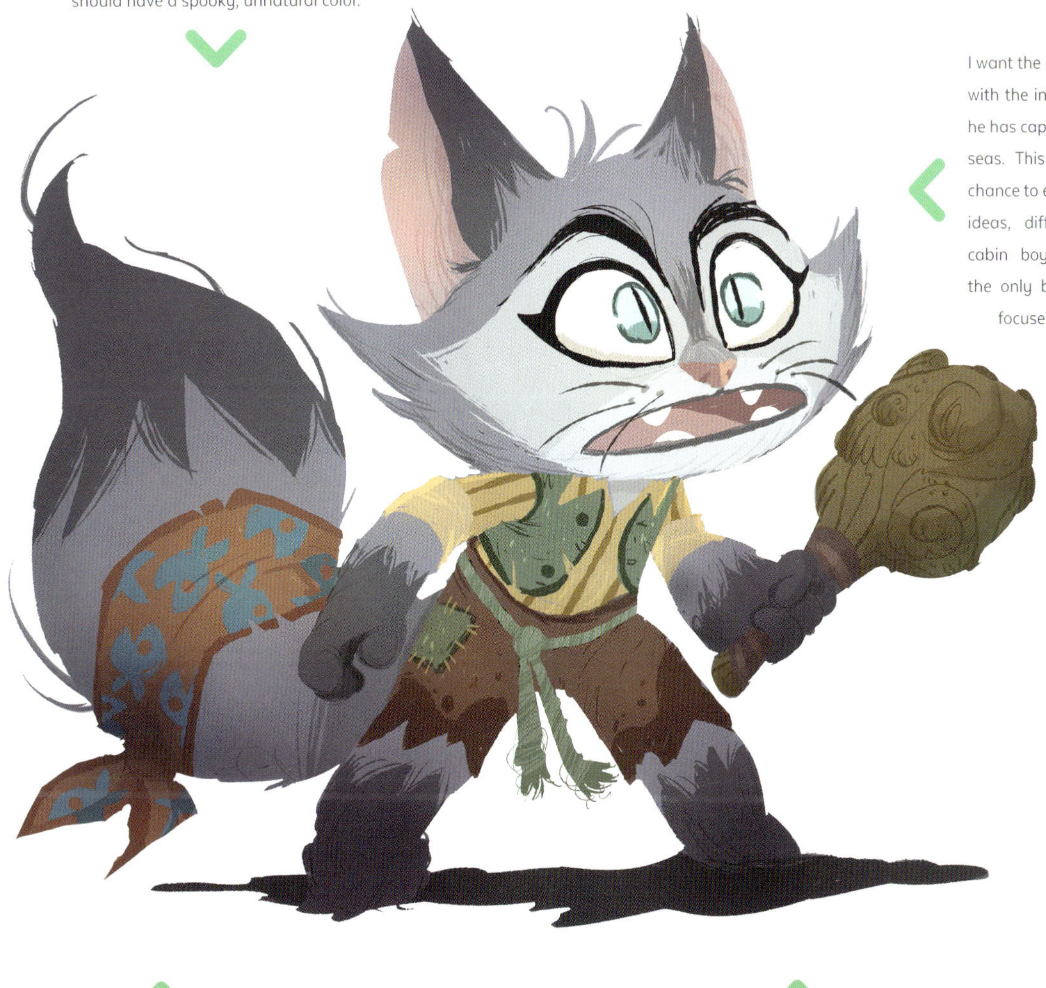

Each of the versions so far has a key prop or accessory that adds an extra sense of their personality or role, such as the cabin boy's bandana and the old sea cat's stolen rum. This design's key item could be an impressive captain's hat.

I want this design to be older and more villainous, but elements of his appearance still need to tie him in with the original character. Giving him elements like a patterned shirt or ragged belt would be consistent with the previous versions.

THUMBNAILS

At first I play with the idea of the character using a musical instrument to lure human souls. It is a good idea from a narrative standpoint, but after a few sketches I decide it adds too complicated an element for the viewer to immediately understand.

My thumbnails then turn in a direction that tries to make the character look more intimidating, harking back to the broad, menacing look of the salty sea cat. A huge captain's hat will add to the impression of his size and rank.

I lean towards the fourth thumbnail, with a stocky body and feet surrounded by ghostly vapor, though I will change his hat and beard from triangular to rounded shapes to give it a more exaggerated size.

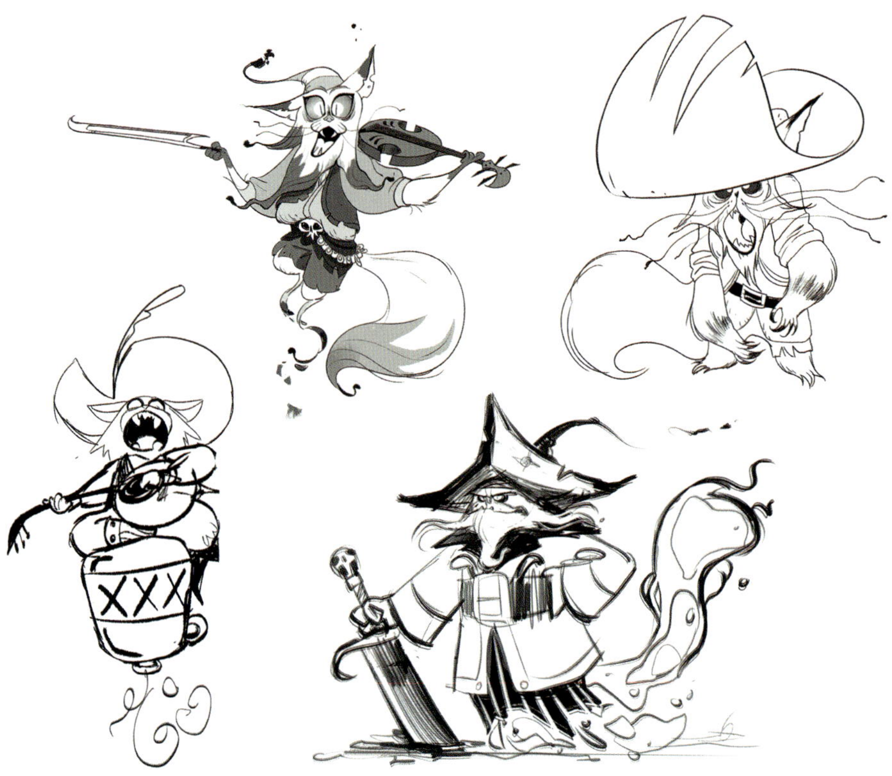

BASIC SHAPES

The shapes will be a bit different for this version because I am aiming for something more physically nebulous than the previous designs. Even though his body mass has a similar teardrop shape to the old sea cat, the weight of this area will be less visible when his feet are concealed by fog. Instead I focus on the dominant shape created by his hat, which is almost an inverted triangle that flows down to his feet. When creating my final rendition of the character, the boldest details will be focused around the top end of the triangle to make a strong, flowing design.

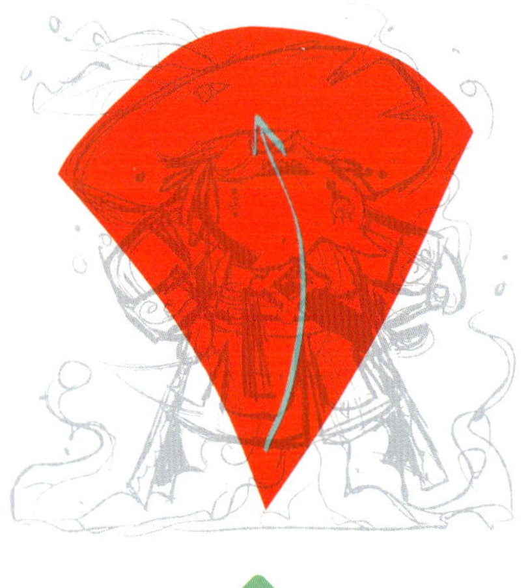

I take the triangular or teardrop-like shape that I used for the previous designs, but invert it this time. Now the captain's hat will be the prominent feature, while his lower body fades away into smoke.

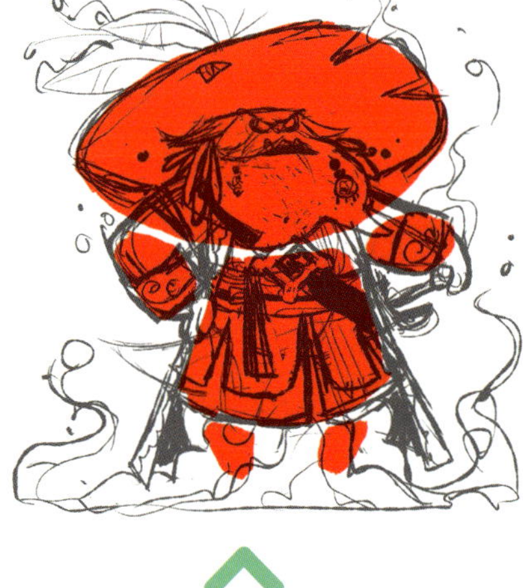

I make sure I clearly define the underlying form of the character before I add any ghostly effects later. A strong base is key for pulling off a design that will heavily use special effects.

I make the captain feel incorporeal and ethereal by using ragged edges to break up the solid outline of his silhouette. This will make him seem more like an evil spirit whose body is not fully of this world.

DETAILS

This character is an infamous and powerful pirate captain, so it would be appropriate for him to have a bigger, more elaborate jacket, embroidered clothes, and a fancy hat that all distinguish his rank from the previous designs. I add small items and ornaments that he could have won in his conquests, such as an extravagant belt buckle and the skulls and beads in his beard.

At this stage I leave out the foggy effects, which will obscure his lower body in the final version, focusing instead on the concrete details of his design. This will ensure that the final version still has a strong underlying design, and is not unintentionally shapeless.

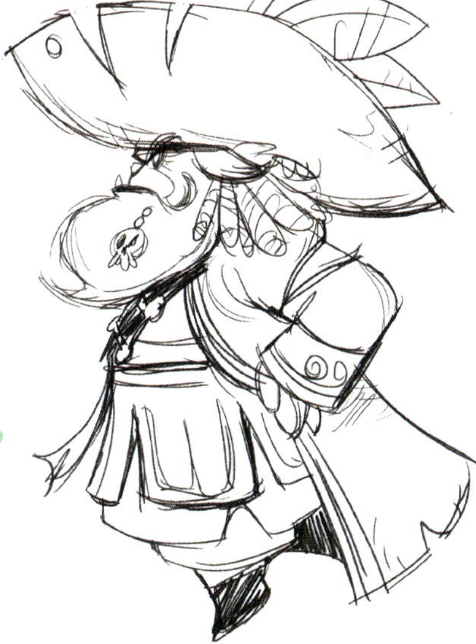

The character's huge beard and hat give him a commanding presence and frame the focal point of his face. The feathers on his hat add an appealing asymmetrical touch, making the costume more interesting to look at.

The pirate's snub nose and exaggerated underbite with bared fangs give him a tough, fierce look, especially coupled with his broad body and the skull ornaments in his beard.

EXPRESSIONS & POSING

The character's pose must capture both his commanding, villainous personality, and his ghostly, undead nature. A simple pose will work best – something that will not overwhelm the design when all the foggy effects are added later. For my final pose, I decide I will combine elements from both of the poses shown here, to make a confident, maniacally laughing pose that will keep the tone spooky but still quite light.

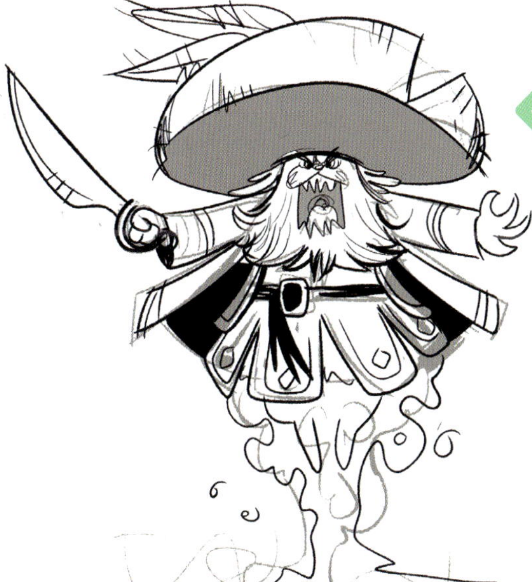

I start with an idea of him flying upwards and screaming, but it makes him seem too deranged; I want him to look more evil and commanding.

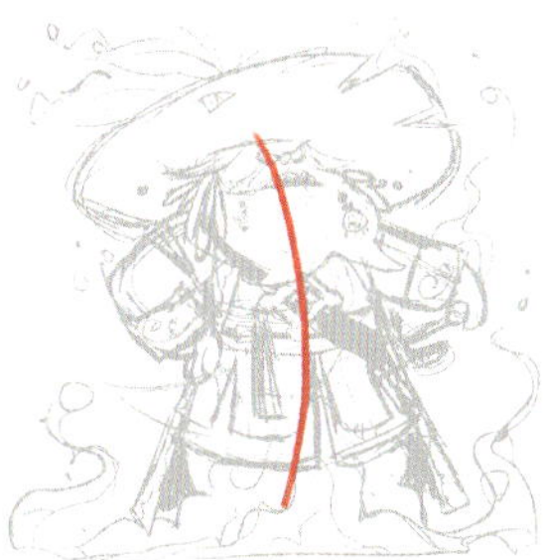

This pose is more simple and confident, and I think it shows the character's personality better. However, I decide to borrow the idea of the wide-open mouth from the other pose, as I would like the final image to have a malevolent laugh rather than looking merely grumpy.

VALUE & COLOR

I want to use an analogous color palette to describe the ghostly nature of this character, so that his colors are intentionally monochromatic and less "alive." I test various colors that are vividly different and unnatural compared to the colors of the previous designs, ranging from yellow to a spooky blue-green. I try to evoke an otherworldly feeling while creating contrast around his face and weapon to make them feel the most dangerous and corporeal.

I want to use a monochromatic color palette for this, but some parts of the character still need to be distinct. Here you can see how his face, hat, and sword pop with high contrast, while his legs fade out into low-contrast fog.

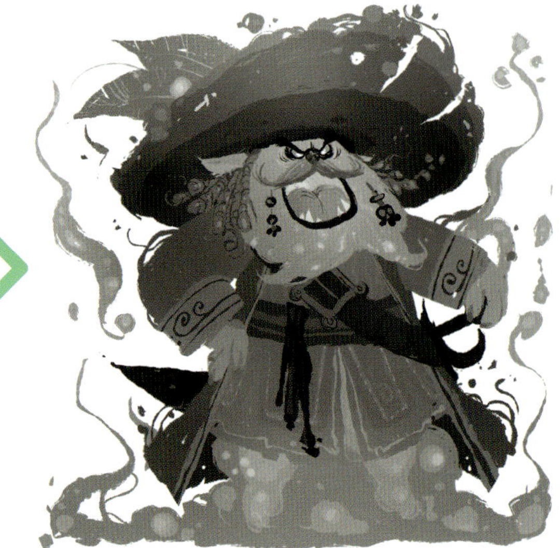

This bright, demonic pink and purple palette is striking but is perhaps not a color palette that is instantly relatable to an undead character.

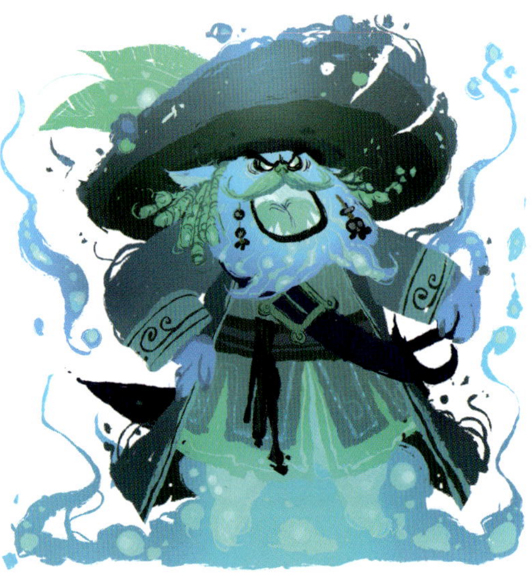

A cold blue and aqua palette is more ghostly and has an aquatic feel that fits the character's setting, but it is also slightly too obvious for a nautical phantom.

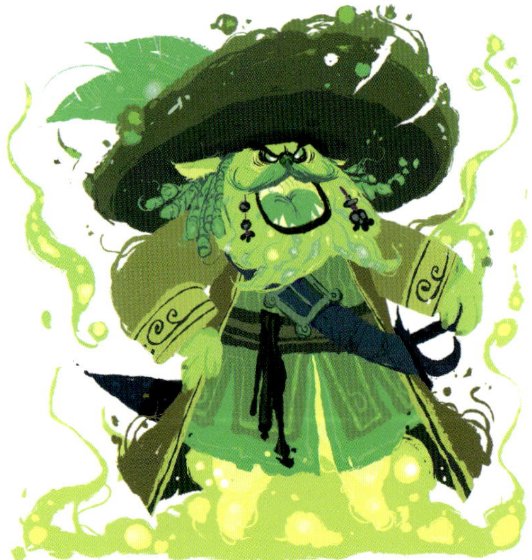

This yellow-green palette is eye-catching and has a grotesque sense of fun, reminiscent of classic characters like Slimer from *Ghostbusters*. It is eerie and supernatural without being as obvious as the blue palette, so I will use this for my final design.

FINAL DESIGN

This phantom character really came to life during the coloring phase. The gloopy spirit smoke and glowing green spectral light in his face are spooky and appealing at the same time, creating paths for the viewer's eyes to follow. The ragged edges of his silhouette add to the sense of him being partly incorporeal. Despite his otherworldly colors and more frightening demeanor, the character's shape language and accessories tie him in successfully with the previous designs, such as the salty sea cat's broad, intimidating physique, and the cabin boy's tattered, patterned clothing. The contrast of the tiny nose and enormous jaw emphasizes his intimidating character in a humorous way.

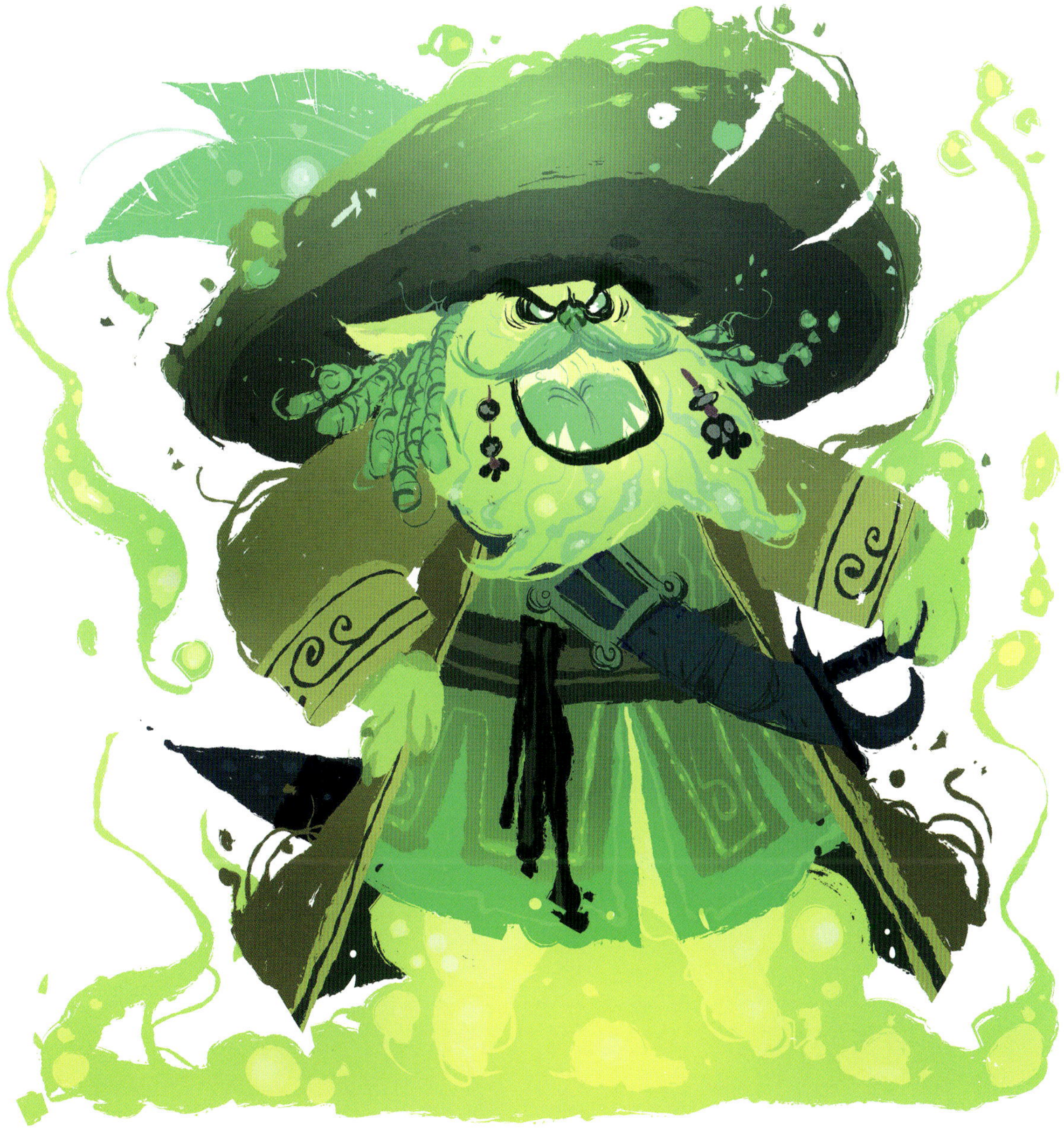

Final artwork © Shaun Bryant

VARIATION 3:
SHIPWRECKED BOY

IDEAS & RESEARCH

This variation will be a young human boy, providing me with a good opportunity to revisit some of the research and ideas from the cabin boy cat. However, this character will not be a pirate, but a stowaway or shipwreck survivor that the pirate crew encounters. I want him to seem like he belongs to a family or crew that he needs to get back to, and had an ordinary everyday life before he landed in such unfortunate circumstances. This will make him feel like less of a background prop, rather than just being a waif-like prisoner character.

This character will need a proportionally large head to indicate his young age, similar to the cabin boy cat's shape, so I make some studies of potential body shapes and proportions.

I want this character to have a special little item that holds a bit of meaning and mystery for the character. It could be an heirloom, adding to the idea that he has a home and family to get back to.

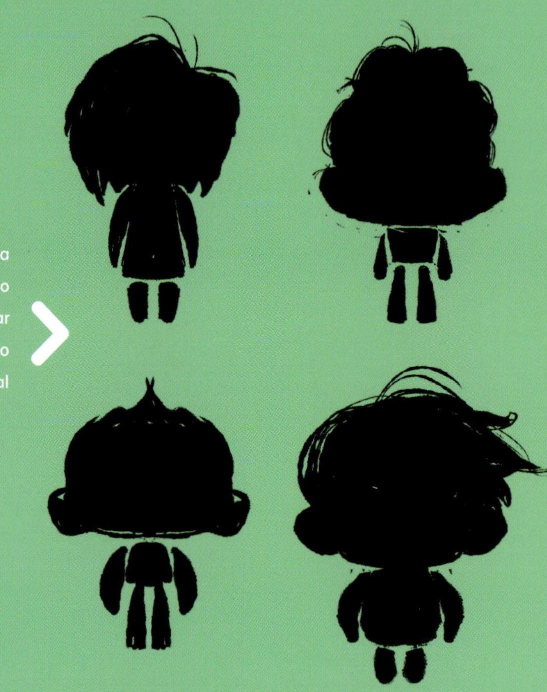

This character might carry a weapon, but I want it to be very small and have an almost leaf-like shape, to make it nonthreatening. He is not an experienced fighter like the pirates, so this would emphasize his vulnerability.

None of *The Whiskered Wisp*'s feline crew wore shoes, probably being more comfortable without, but for this human character I take a stab at different boot designs. Some are workmanlike and others are more ornate. I lean more towards the simple, everyday-looking boots.

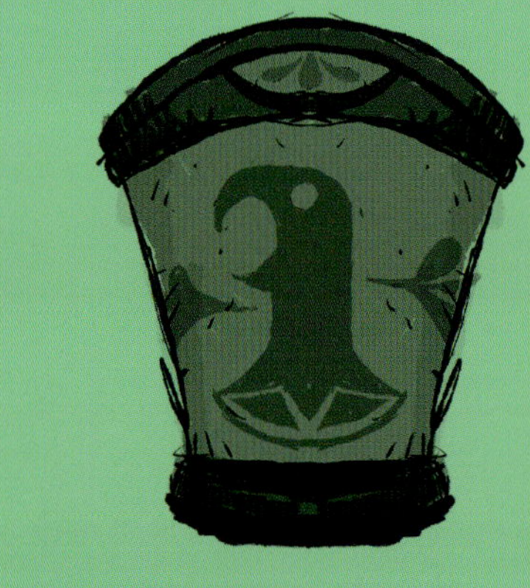

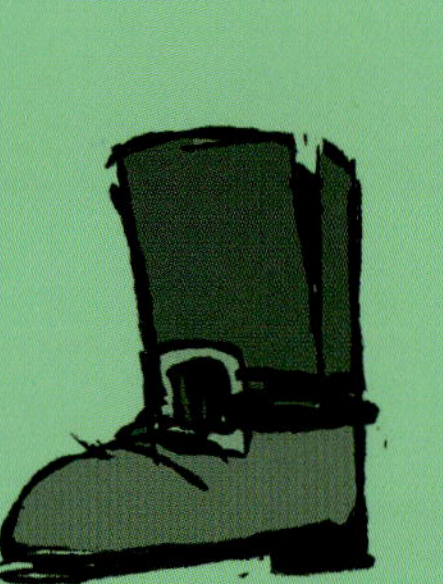

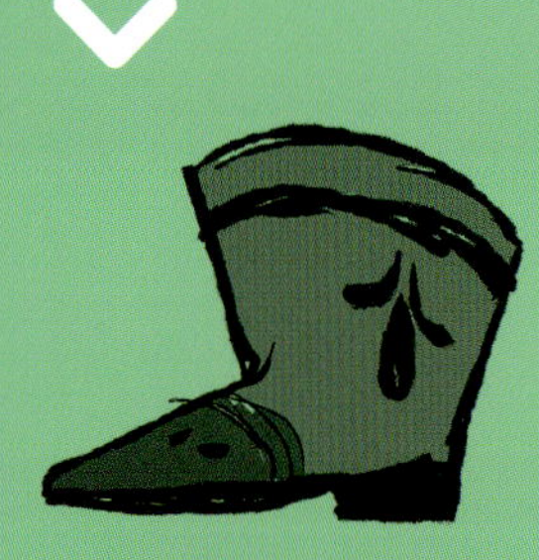

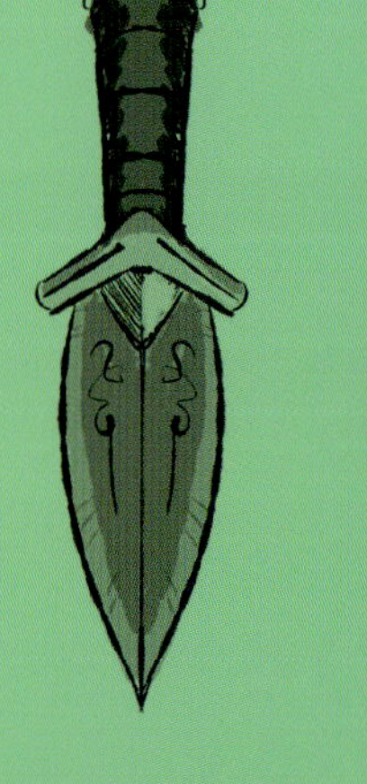

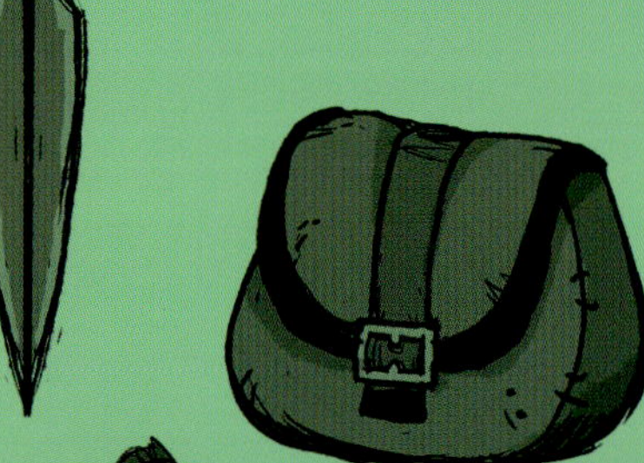

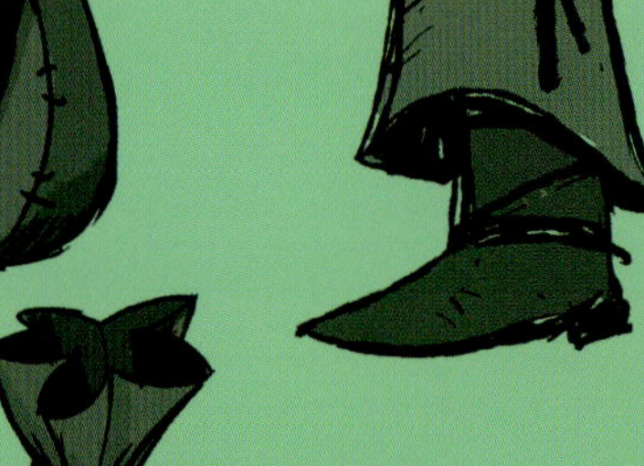

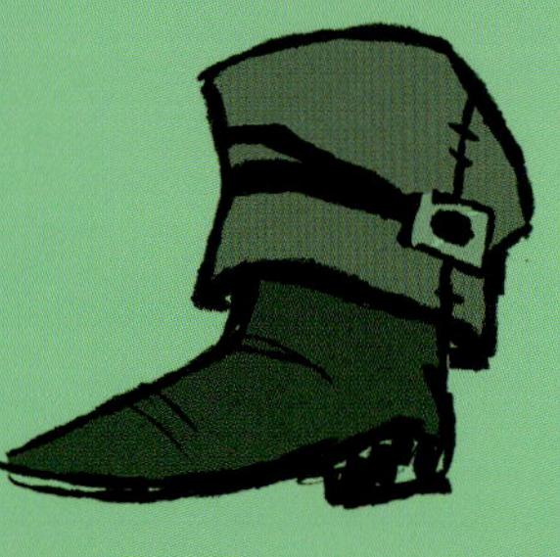

Pouches and bags can be a standard and generic accessory, so I spend some time researching and designing something more unique and personal to the character. This would add more interest and individuality to his costume.

CHANGES

This version will follow a similar pattern of shapes and proportions as the original character, but he should feel less like a pirate and more like a lost child. I want his clothes to look respectable despite his current circumstances, without any real excess or jewelry to speak of, to contrast his design and personality with the pirates and their wild, freebooting lifestyle.

Unlike the young cat character, this version will have human hair as an extra design element to play with. I want his hair to feel like a wave just hit him, creating a distressed, dynamic shape.

I will keep close to the original character's proportions, but place even more emphasis on round, childlike features. This will make the human boy seem more vulnerable than his scrappy feline counterpart.

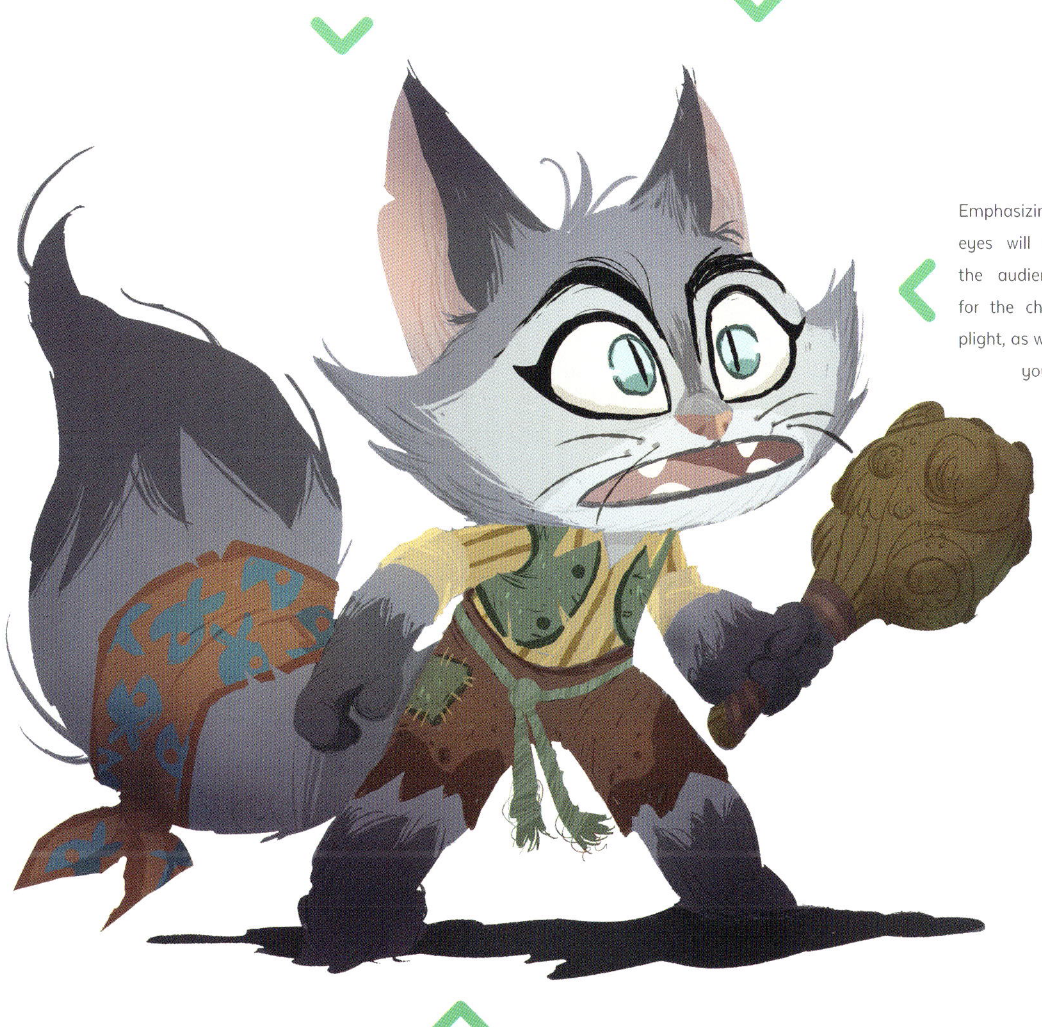

Emphasizing his big, sad eyes will help to garner the audience's sympathy for the character and his plight, as well as convey his young age.

The clothes could feel a few levels above the original character's in quality, but somewhat worn from the shipwreck. Plain, practical clothes such as sturdy boots, a leather tunic, and thick wool trousers would make the character look modest and working-class compared to the pirates' tattered, mismatched clothes and stolen jewelry.

THUMBNAILS

During the thumbnail phase, I definitely lean towards making the character more of a lost traveler than a captive, as it gives him more of his own context and backstory.

I like the shapes of the thumbnails with narrow bodies and contrasting oval heads, and long scruffy hair, as they come across as small, harmless, and unkempt. I will combine these options into one design with which to go forward.

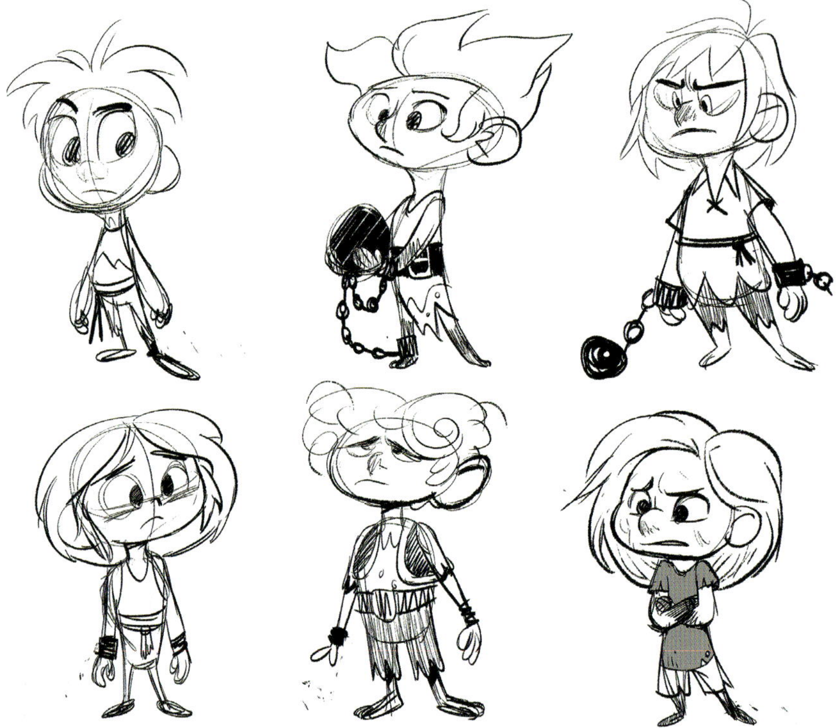

BASIC SHAPES

A challenge of this stage is taking a character of a very similar age and build to the cabin boy cat version, but portraying him completely differently in terms of personality and demeanor. Though he has a large head and small body, this human boy noticeably lacks the sharp edges and points of the tough young cat, which immediately changes how he feels to the viewer.

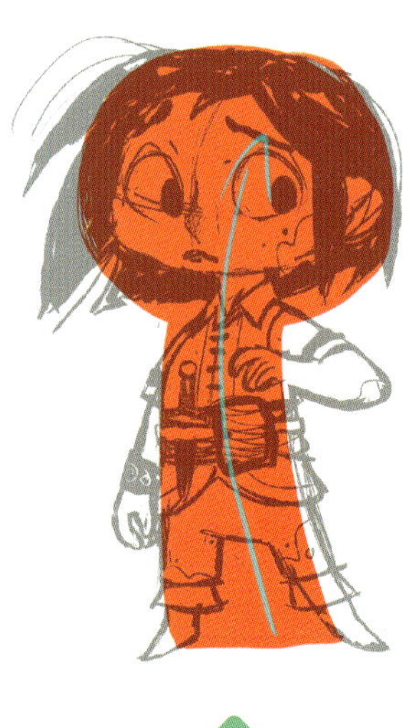

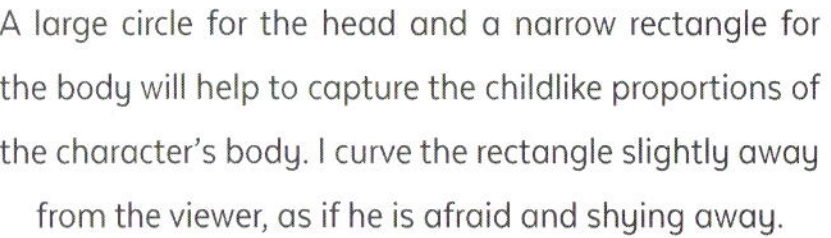

A large circle for the head and a narrow rectangle for the body will help to capture the childlike proportions of the character's body. I curve the rectangle slightly away from the viewer, as if he is afraid and shying away.

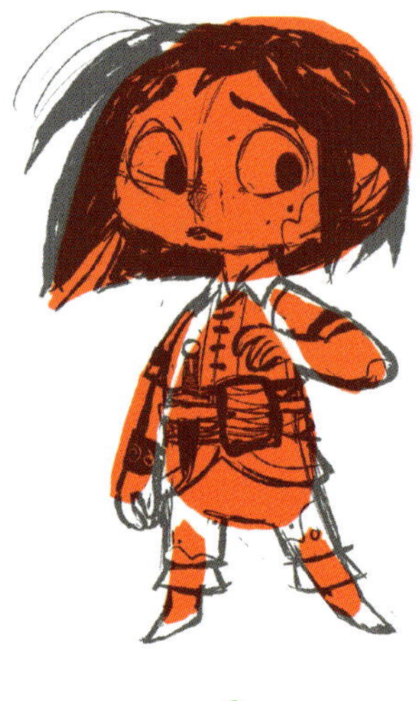

I like the idea that the character is lost and an outsider, which leads me to the idea of a teardrop shape for the composition of his hair and body. He has a very thick droplet shape to his core body, and even his arms have an aspect of it. Embedding this icon into his design gives the character a sad and sympathetic feel.

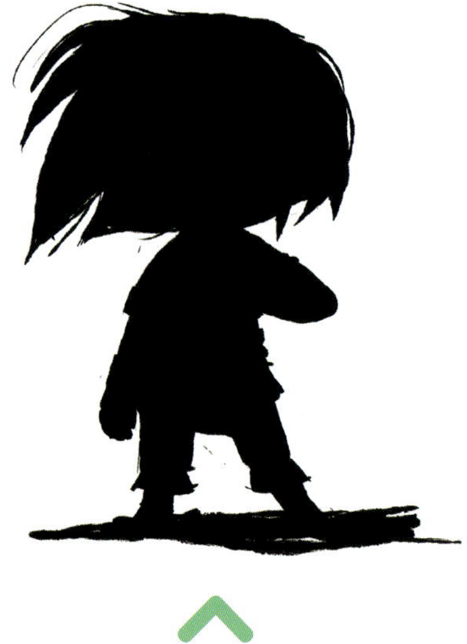

The character's lost and forlorn feeling comes across even in his silhouette. His messy hair adds a more angular, dynamic shape and flow to the outline, and though his proportions are almost identical to the cat boy's, he is clearly readable as a human.

DETAILS

I want this character to seem like he comes from a more steady life than the cabin boy version. His clothes are more well-kept and respectable; they have some subtle decoration, but overall are more generic and workmanlike than the pirates' idiosyncratic outfits. He should seem like a lost child who is impressed with the pirates' lifestyle and riches, but is out of his element and looking for home.

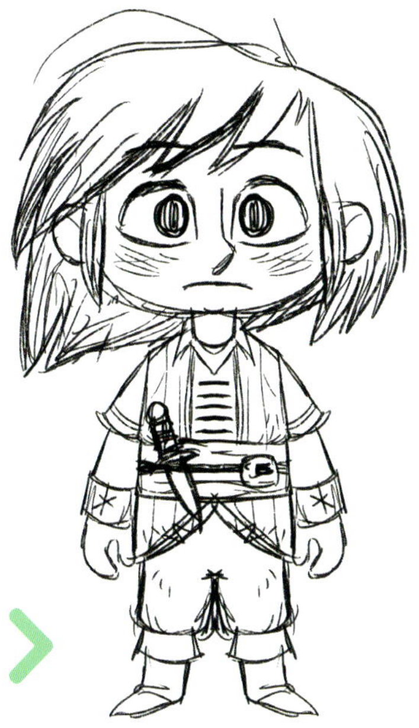

Here you can see how the teardrop shape of his body is carried through the windswept shape of his hair, just at a different angle. His overall rounded shapes and large eyes make him instantly sympathetic. His clothes are modestly tailored, making him seem like an ordinary boy rather than a pirate.

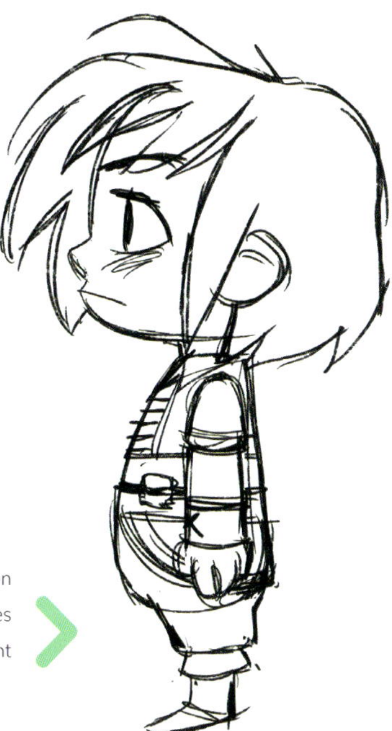

The boy's head and body are similar in proportion to the young cat's, but the down-turned shapes of his hair and features give him a very different sense of personality.

EXPRESSIONS & POSING

I would like the pose for this character to be fairly neutral rather than overly action-driven. A lot of his emotion should be communicated through his expression, rather than a very dynamic pose that seems less appropriate for his backstory and personality. I decide on a pose that shows him looking wary and unsure of his new situation, with wide eyes and one arm raised, as if to ward off danger.

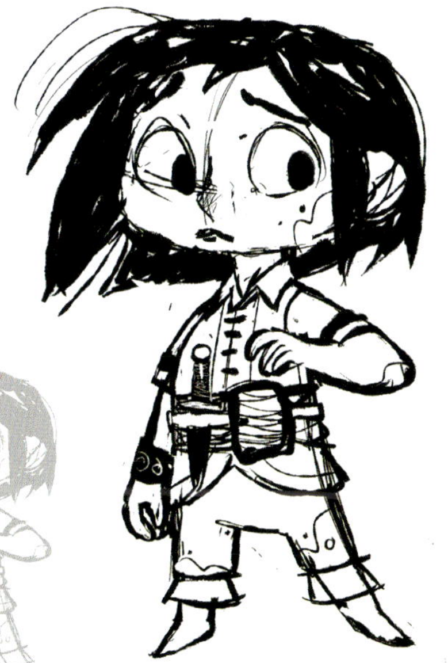

This pose gives a strong sense of the character: he feels out of place and uncomfortable, with his limbs in a slightly protective posture that helps to sell his story. I will use this pose for my final design.

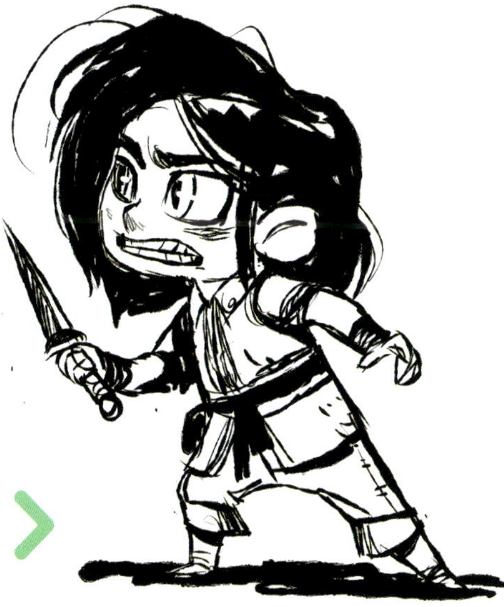

This pose shows him wielding his dagger, but is far too aggressive for the personality I want to show. His snarl and dilated pupils almost make him look cat-like, which is an interesting throwback to the original character. Perhaps he has spent too much time with the pirates?

VALUE & COLOR

After trying some lighter color palettes, I settle on a darker scheme that frames the brighter values of his face with dark hair that is almost a stormy, muted purple-black. I frame his bright, wide eyes with dark eyelashes so the high contrast really grabs the viewer's attention. I base the rest of his split-complementary color scheme on this hair color, which makes the orangey-pink skin pop and his costume feel unified and not ostentatious.

As with his young cat counterpart, I make sure the boy's head and face are the areas of the highest contrast, while the rest of his body and costume is closer together in tone.

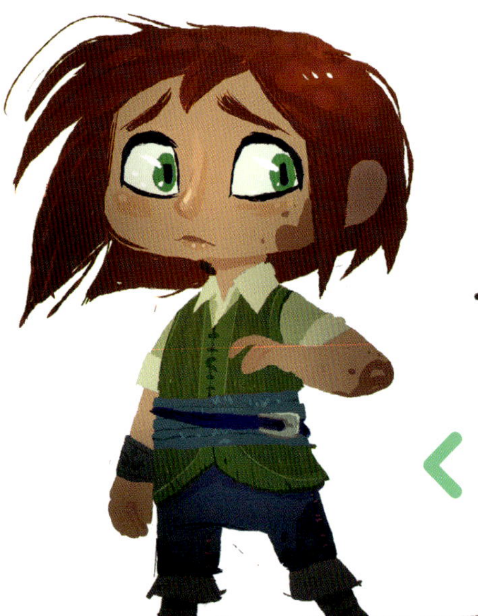

This is a classic earthy palette of red-orange with complementary green and blue. However, I think using browns or more muted hues for his costume will make him seem more ordinary and workmanlike.

This complementary yellow and purple color scheme is very visually striking, but again, does not perfectly embody the humble background I have for the character, as the colors are too showy and vivid.

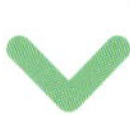

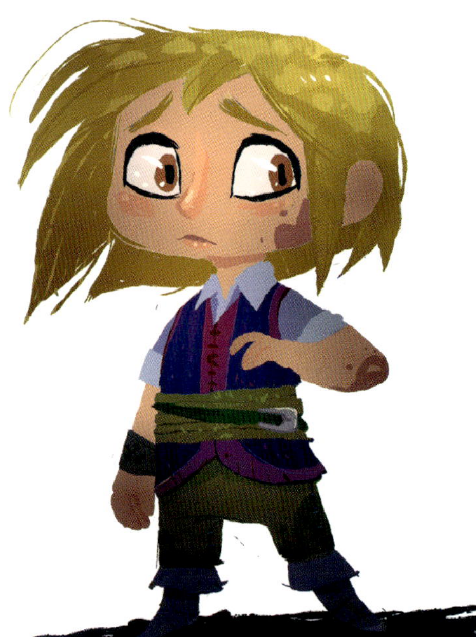

I settle on this palette for my final design, with a darker complexion and darker hair that makes his forms pop. The desaturated palette of his costume keeps the focus on the character's face, as well as making him feel a bit more waterlogged. The bright focal point of his eyes is made extra striking by his unusual irises.

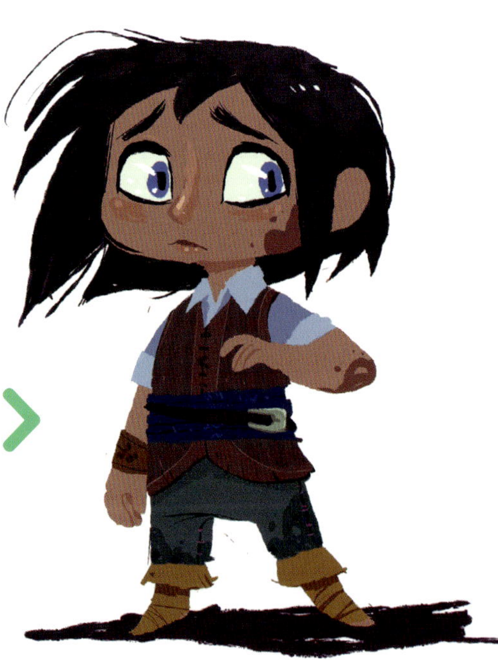

FINAL DESIGN

The shipwrecked boy is now finished, and I think he makes a strong addition to the crew. His design succeeds in taking the familiar shapes and proportions of the original character and translating them to a version with a completely different species, personality, and backstory. His pose and large eyes make him look lost, bewildered, and more than a little frightened, while the mud and water on his face and clothes help to explain his situation. I like that the design is interesting enough to hold the viewer's attention on its own, but also leaves room for the character to grow as he adventures with the crew of *The Whiskered Wisp*.

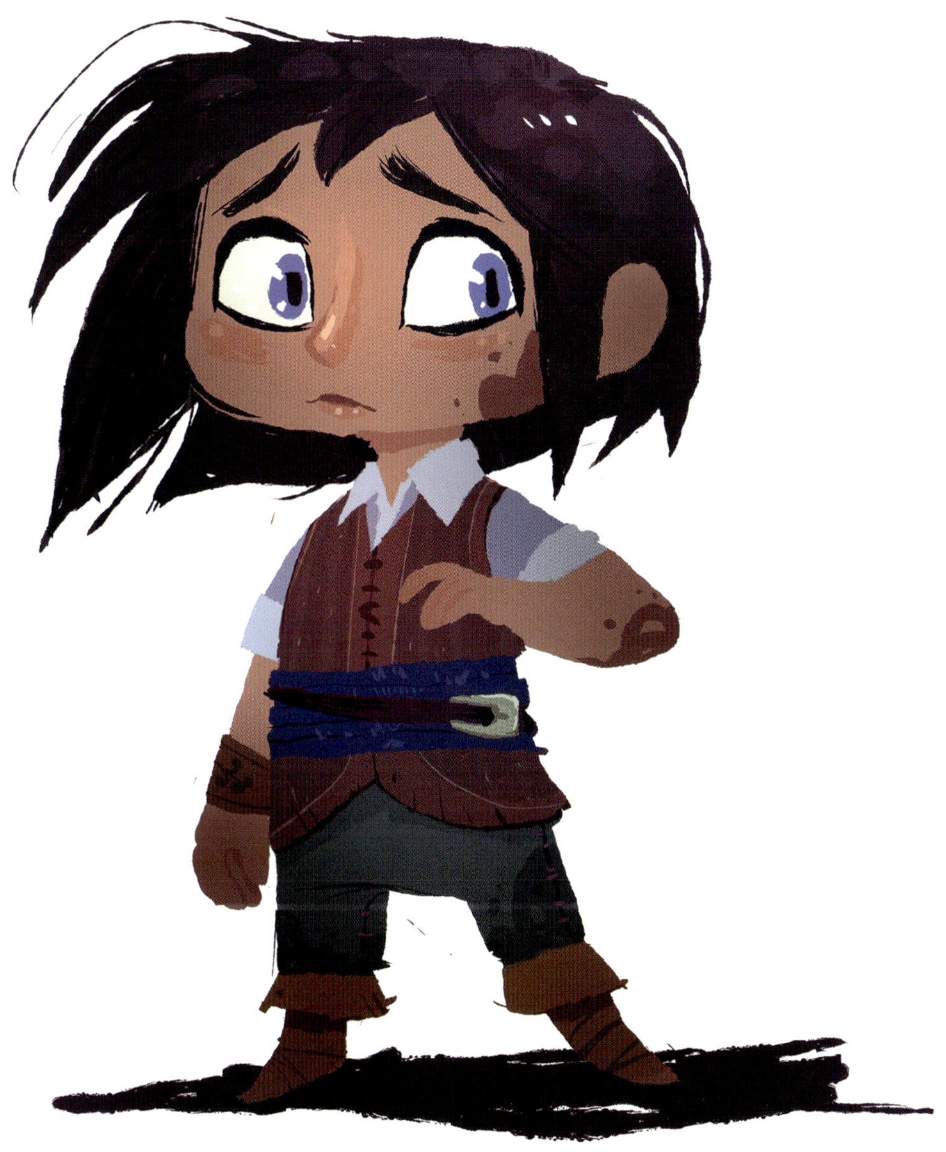

Final artwork © Shaun Bryant

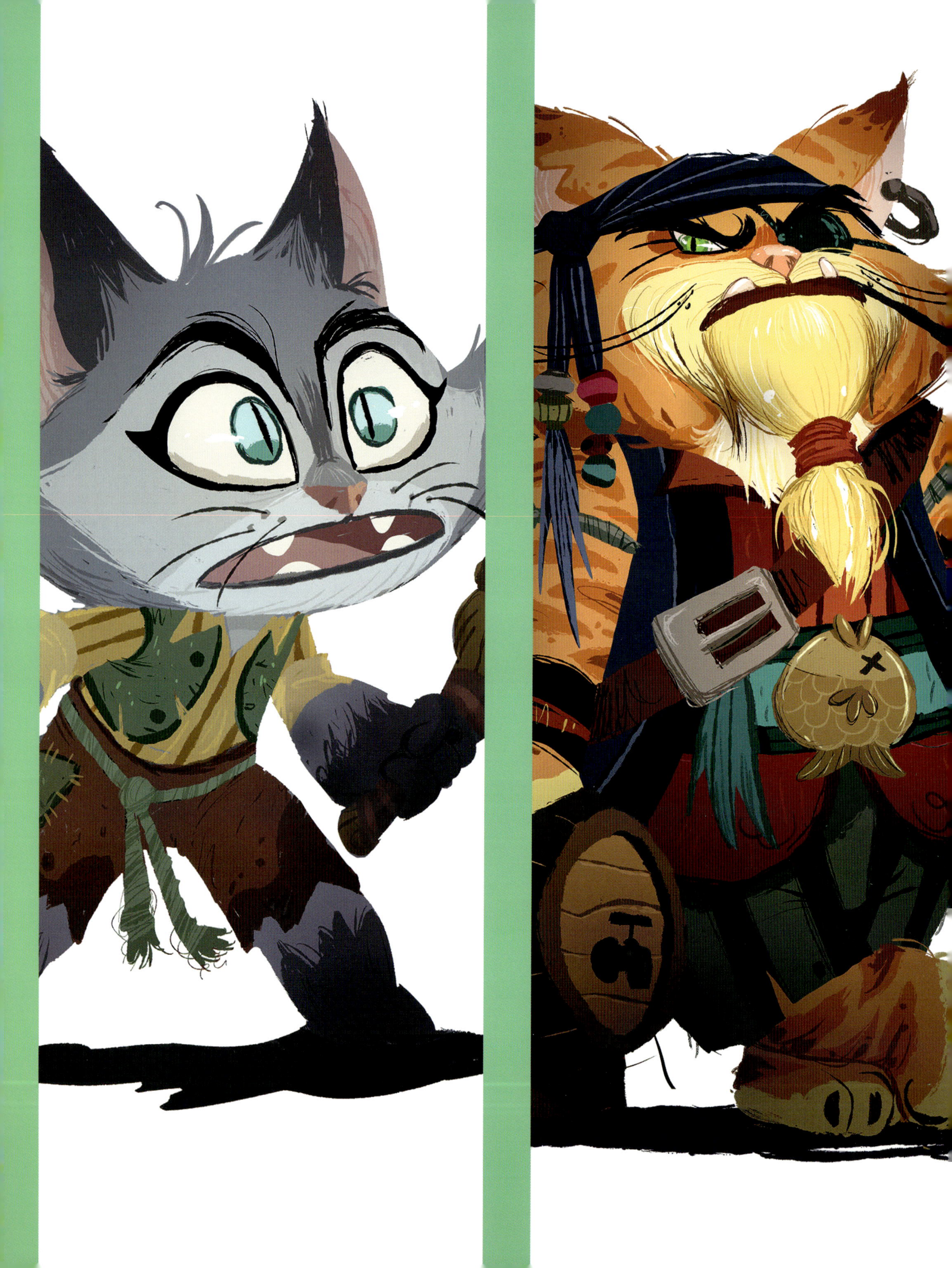

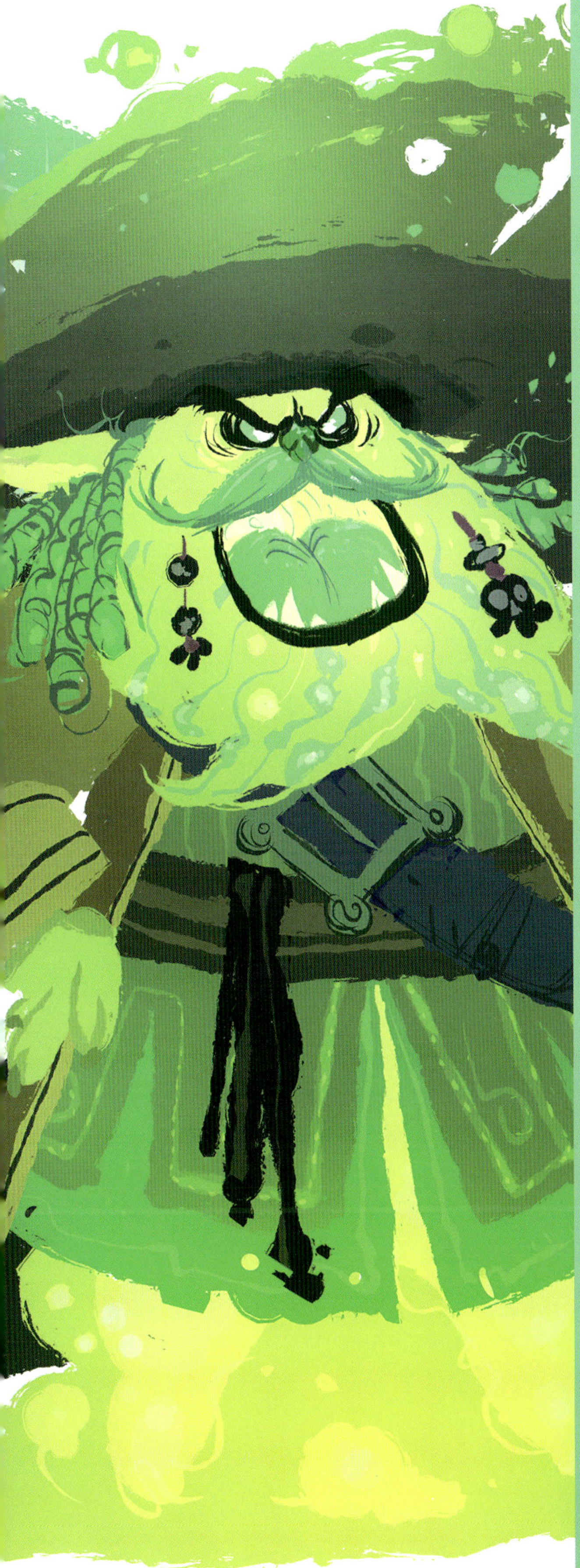

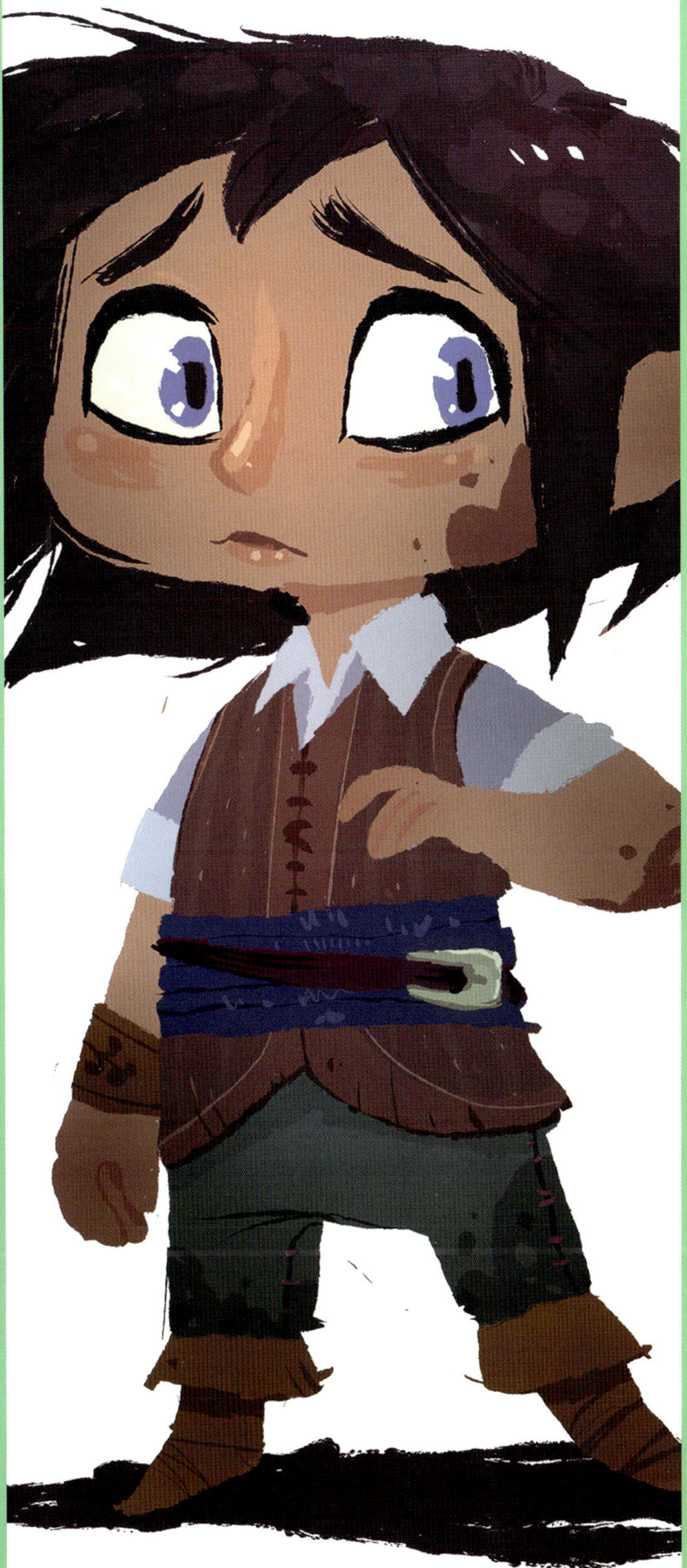

ALIEN ROYALTY

BY MAX GRECKE

In this chapter, illustrator Max Grecke creates a high-ranking alien villain equipped with a protective armored suit.

VARIATIONS

- BABY ALIEN
- FERAL MUTANT
- HUMAN VILLAIN

FOCUS

Max's style uses dynamic, fluid poses to create a sense of action and personality, even when the character is standing still. This approach would work well for illustrating a comic or designing for animation.

Pay close attention to using recurring details, patterns, and forms, and using research into real-life sources to create consistency across characters of different shapes and sizes.

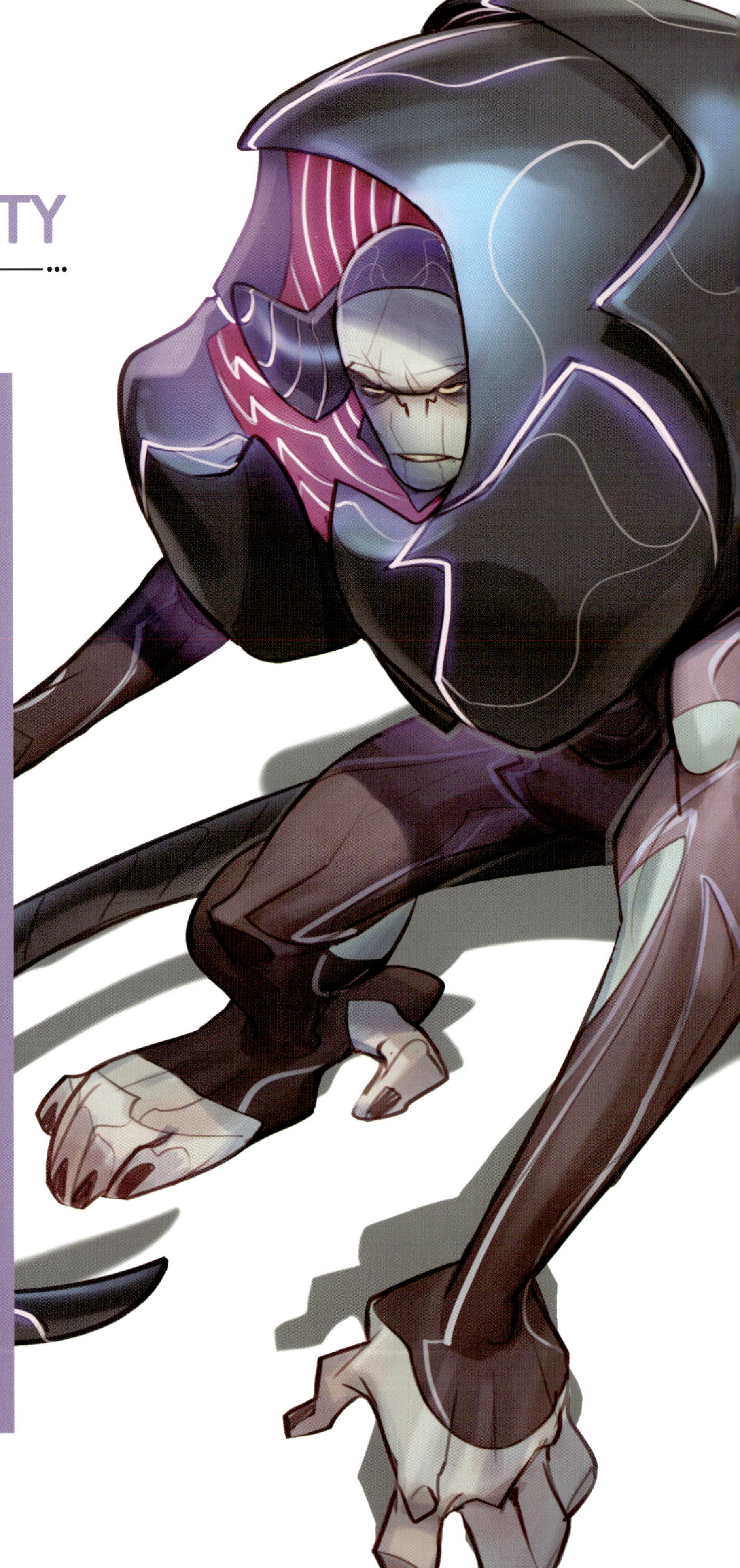

THE IDEA

"Alien royalty" are the keywords I start to work from. This character should be someone recognizably an alien from another planet, with elements of technology or materials that are not from Earth. I want this character to be a villain: tall, dignified, and lanky to make the design more creepy and alien. A member of royalty doesn't have to be the ruler; creating a character of lower standing within a royal family could be more interesting. I think about what attitude and personality this character could have, and decide he is a prince or relative to the highest royalty on his planet. He has less responsibility, so he's something of a rebel and doesn't want to be perfectly behaved all the time, but still has access to the best and finest equipment his race has to offer.

Concept: A sci-fi character who is royalty in an alien race

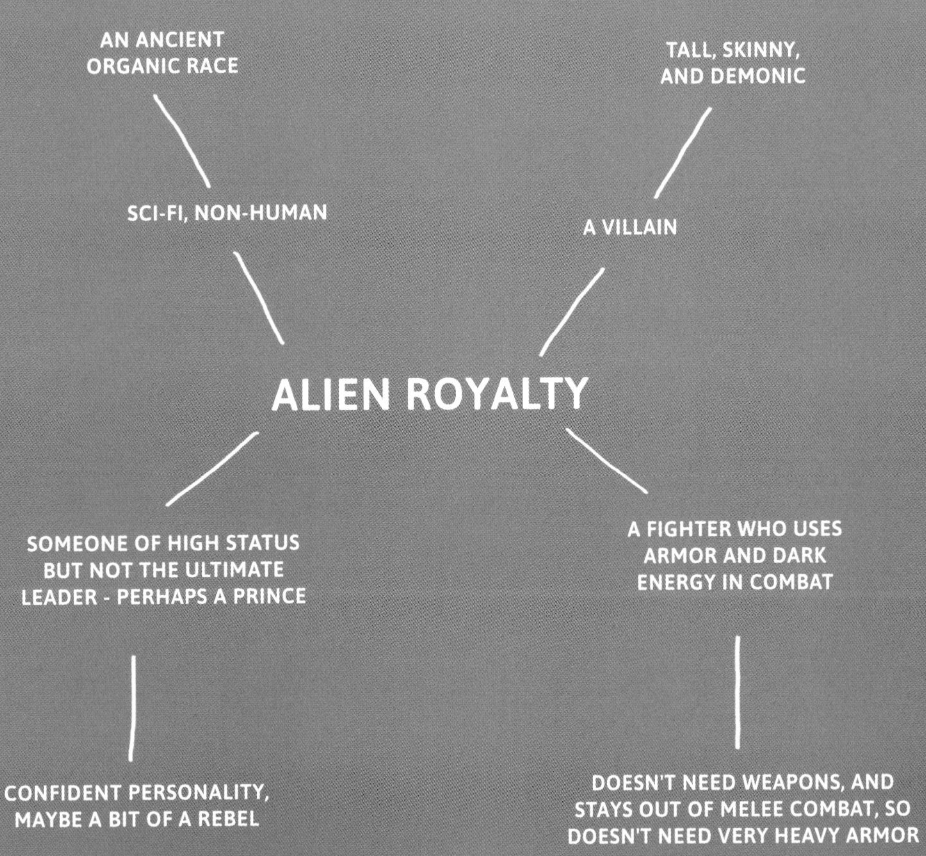

RESEARCH

One challenge of designing an alien character is to make the design believable, with elements that the viewer can relate to, yet still clearly of an *alien* race. This is perhaps why alien designs often lean towards being animal-like, in addition to having a lot of humanoid elements. Studying some of these more recognizable elements, such as primate anatomy and animal talons, will enable me to make the most effective design choices.

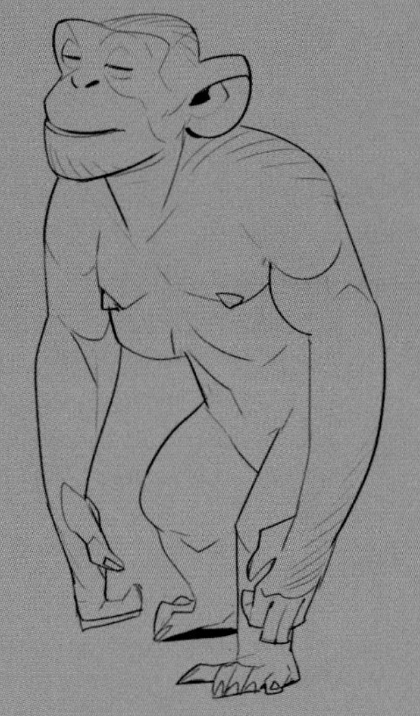

Apes are very humanoid and have a lot of traits that I can exaggerate to make them "alien," such as long, powerful arms and feet with opposable grasping toes. This could form an interesting basis for the alien's anatomy.

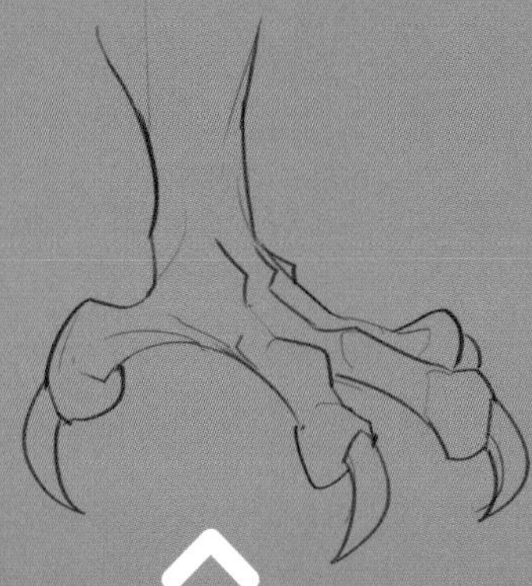

The character should look and feel evil and villainous. Bringing in jagged and sharp design elements help to sell this idea easily, so adding some sharp claws might work well.

A younger ape fits a lot more with the tall and lanky proportions I want to use for this character. In this study, I try to explore the shapes of the wiry arms and hunched body to get a feel for how an ape works.

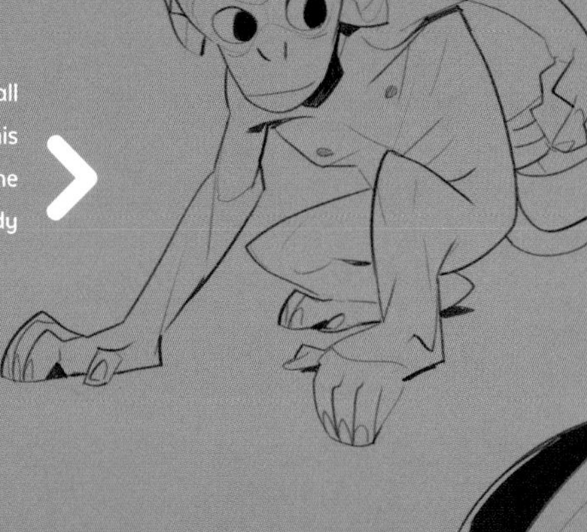

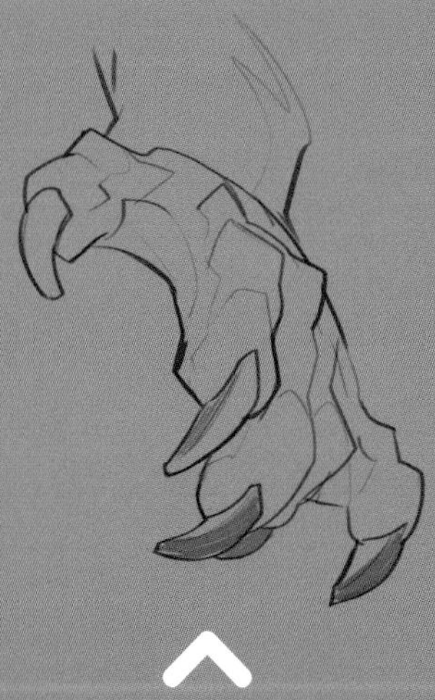

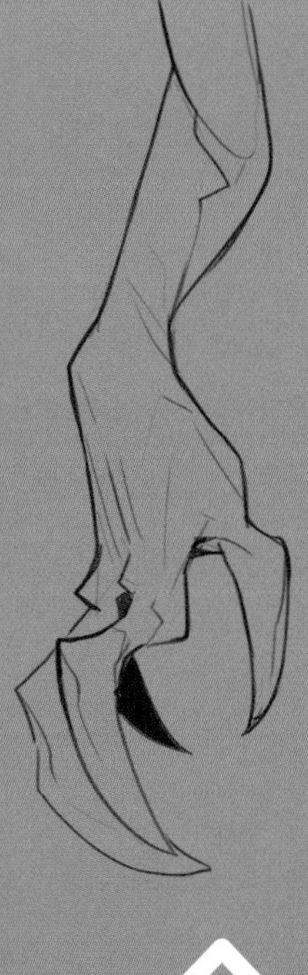

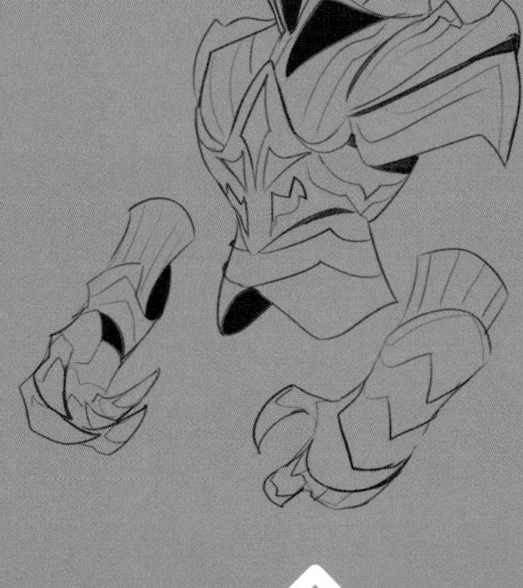

Here I am exploring a sort of monster hand which I really like, and that might fit very well for the character. It has some relatable human elements but is still very primal.

This has more of a "creature" feel to it, but the long palm of the hand gives a strong flow to the arm which would strengthen a design with exaggerated limbs. However, the very long claws might not fit a more sophisticated, civilized alien race.

I really want parts of this character to have armor, indicating his role as a fighter, but not anything recognizable as armor from Earth. Nonetheless, I study how our armor is built, as this will give me a foundation from which I can start to think outside the box.

THUMBNAILS

I imagine the character as tall but somewhat hunched over, adding an animalistic touch, with long, lanky arms and legs. I use very broad marks and motions to capture this feel in my thumbnails, and try to mix sharp edges with long swoopy motions, especially for the limbs and big claw-like hands. Aim to get a wide variation in your thumbnails, even exploring some ideas that you're initially not sure you might want – you never know what might work out. A few of these thumbnails are too scrawny, too bulky, or lacking in armor, but I have highlighted the three thumbnails that I particularly like. They show a mix of animal and human shapes, with threatening, jagged armor and ape-like limbs and feet which will be a strong basis for this villain.

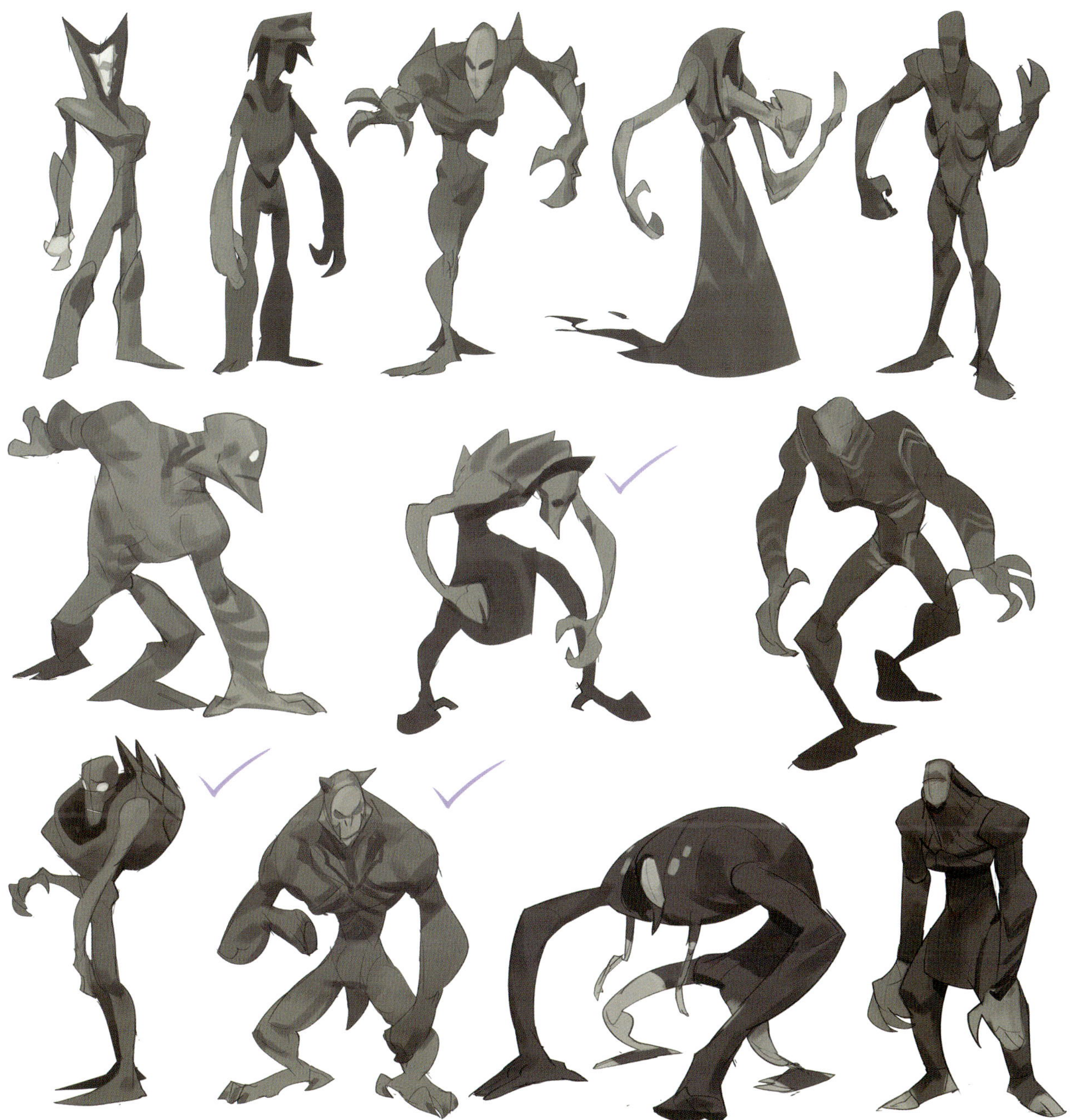

BASIC SHAPES

Now that I have chosen the strongest thumbnails, I can start to refine what I want from my final character by puzzling together the elements that I like the most. Basing his form around a large diamond shape will draw the viewer's eye to his head and armor, while his long limbs will add flow around it.

I like the idea of this alien race having a love for powerful armor and energy weapons, yet being quite vulnerable without their suits, and with relatively skinny limbs. This would also fit the idea of a rebellious prince, who is perhaps not a seasoned warrior, but compensates for it with a bad attitude and the most expensive equipment. The over-sized armor seems like a defensive threat display, making him look larger and tougher; I like this idea of the character having a vulnerable side without his armor, but with it, he is an imposing, evil being.

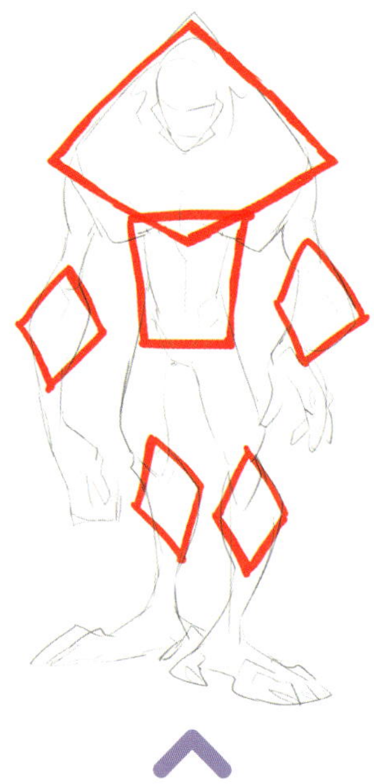

Starting with a strong core shape is important to make the character read well, to make the design dynamic, and to express his personality. I use a huge diamond shape, as it is pointed and villainous. This will be echoed through his limbs to create flow.

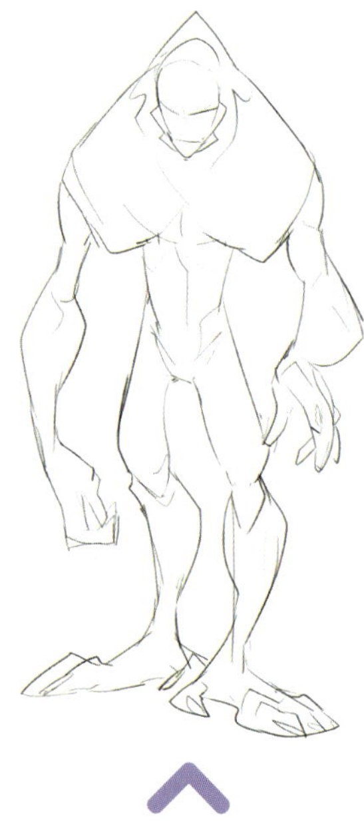

The character will wear large chest armor as his main core of power, with a tight spacesuit underneath. This will add to his ape-like but alien sense of proportion, with a hunched back and skinny limbs.

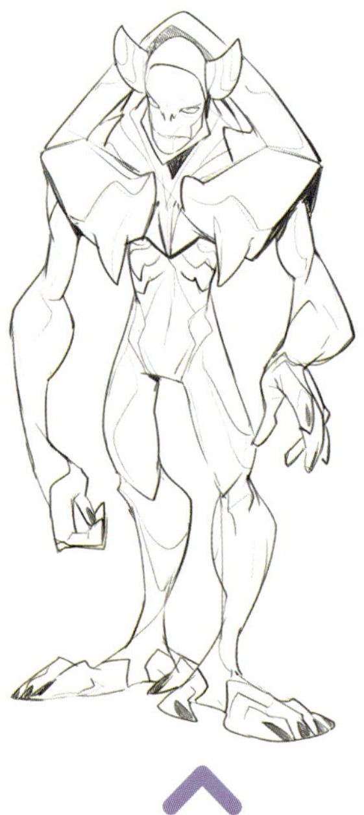

I fill in more details to get a better grasp of the character and finally give him a face. Adding horns to the hood of his suit makes him look menacing and evil, and almost gives him a regal crown which suggests his rank.

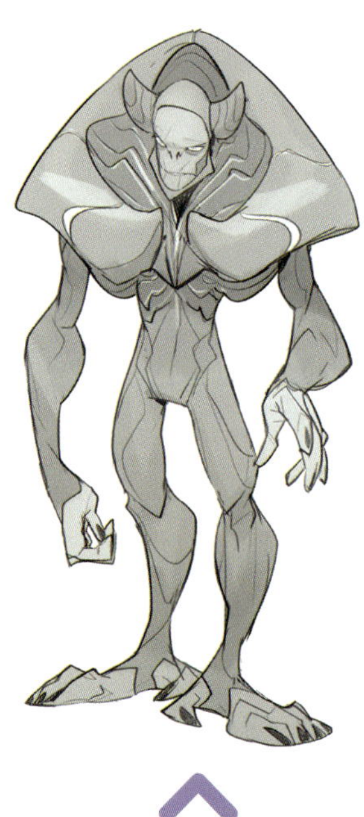

As the design develops, some of the weight and shapes of the torso start to get lost, so I revisit that area and enlarge it to recover the dramatic, over-sized proportions that I liked in the thumbnails. The muscular arms and legs are inspired my ape research, though I avoid making him too bulky, in keeping with the idea that these aliens rely heavily on their armor.

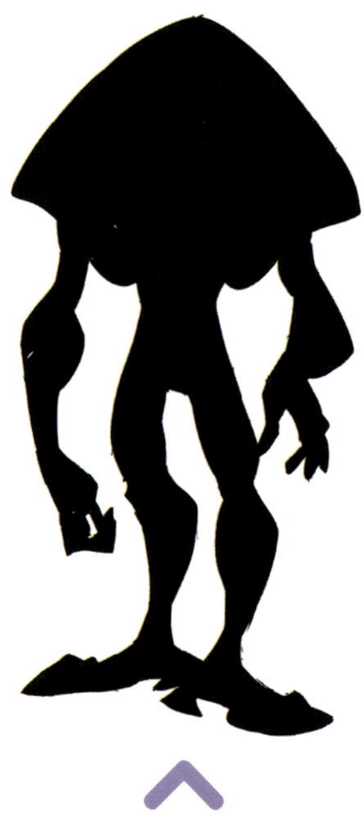

I check the silhouette to confirm that the upper body has kept a strong diamond shape, and that I have not lost the clarity I started out with. I would like to add a tail to the design, but I do not indicate it here to keep his silhouette clear from the front.

DETAILS

As I add details to the character, I want to show that he has advanced, fancy gear; this race values its energy armor highly, and with his royal connections, he would have the best armor there is. I therefore want to show that it is ornamented with lavish details; these ridges and lines clarify the hard, shell-like nature of the armor, as well as adding more flow to the design and drawing focus towards his head. In the final version, these patterns might glow with light or energy to add an extra sci-fi aspect. In the profile view, you can see that I've added a long armored "tail" piece to his suit, which will be mobile and add visual flow to his pose later. This also ties in with the contrast between the armor and the alien's thin, somewhat vulnerable body.

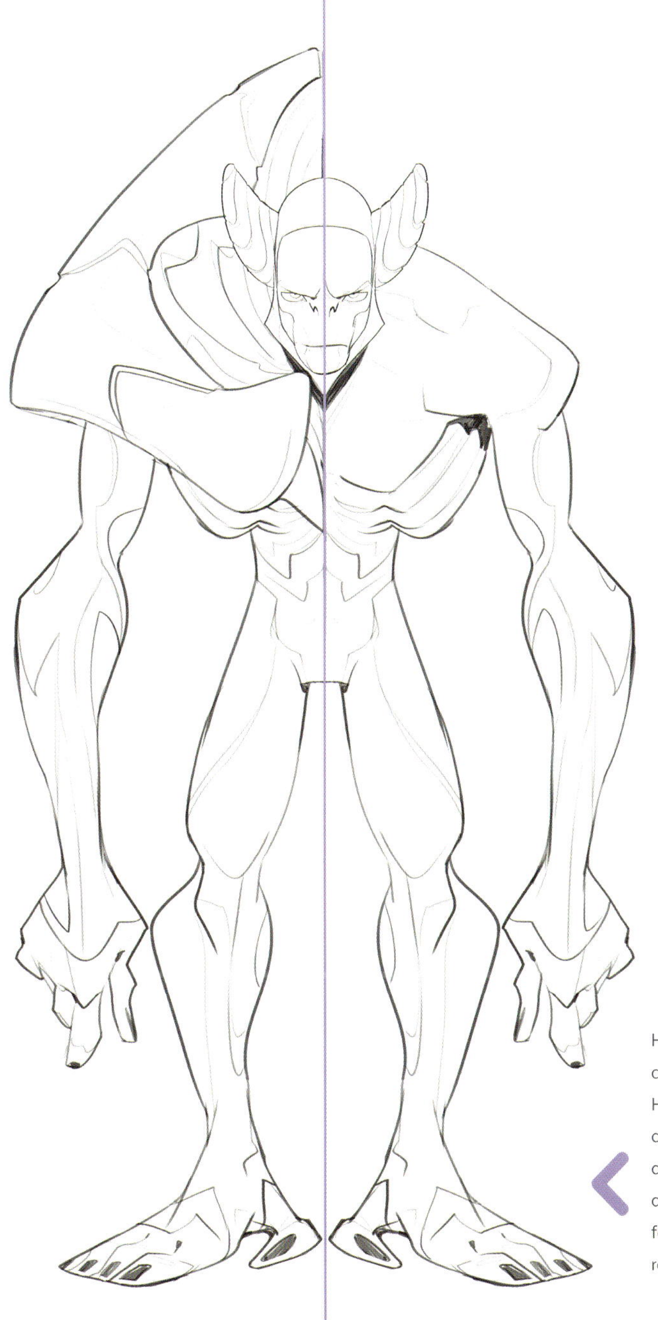

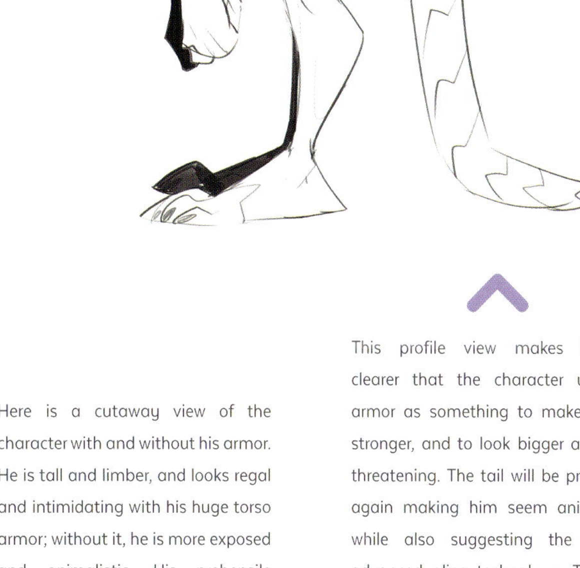

Here is a cutaway view of the character with and without his armor. He is tall and limber, and looks regal and intimidating with his huge torso armor; without it, he is more exposed and animalistic. His prehensile feet, based on my earlier research, reinforce his ape-like qualities and add a non-human strangeness.

This profile view makes it even clearer that the character uses his armor as something to make himself stronger, and to look bigger and more threatening. The tail will be prehensile, again making him seem animal-like, while also suggesting the armor's advanced alien technology. This view also shows more clearly that his regal horns are, in fact, part of his suit!

FACIAL EXPRESSIONS

There are many options I could explore with a character like this. The most obvious choices for a villain would be sneering and snarling expressions, but I also want to try a more fragile or confused face, suggesting that he's not always as tough as he appears. As his horns are only part of his suit, I do not include them when sketching his facial expressions. He essentially lacks a nose and eyebrows as secondary features to emote with, so his mouth, chin, eyes, and heavy brow ridges must be heavily emphasized.

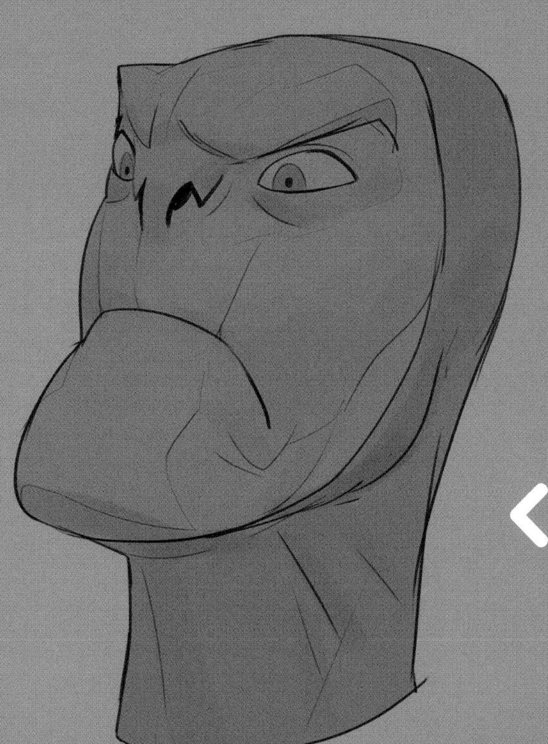

As a villain, his main expressions would be sinister and ill-intentioned, but I also feel like he would be arrogant and superior due to his rank and wealth. This haughty expression fits him well, with his chin up and nostrils flaring, but it does not show much of his animal side.

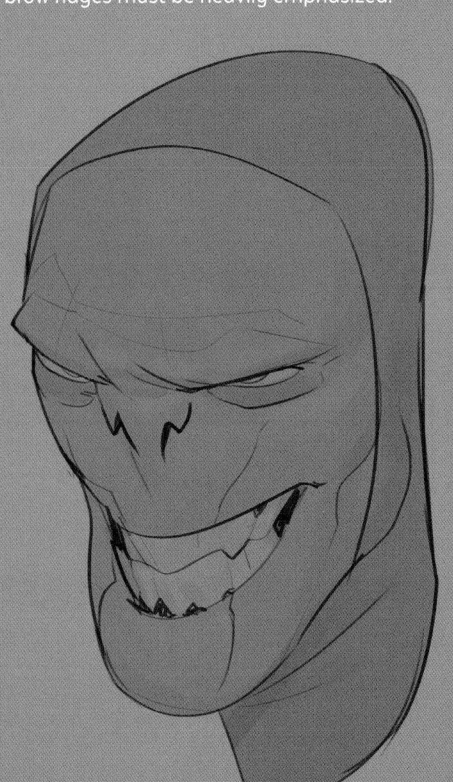

The character has very jagged teeth, so giving him a wide grin really shows off his dangerous fangs. Lowering the brow makes him appear feral and villainous, which is something I want to bear in mind for my final image.

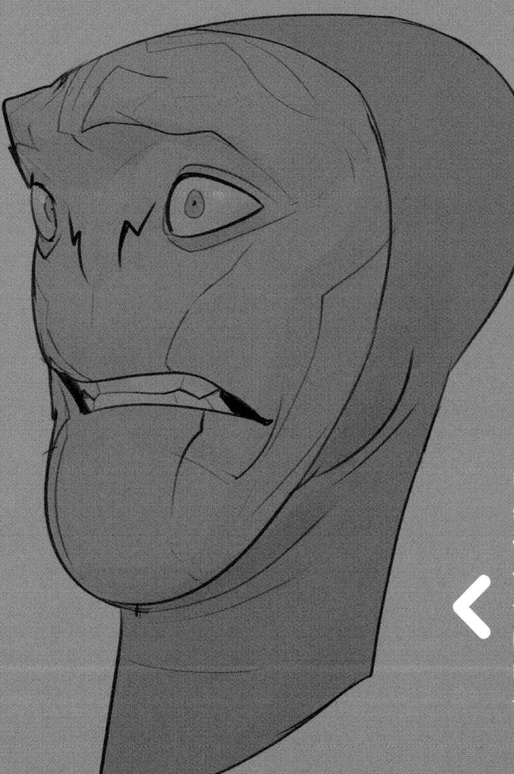

I also try a more surprised and stunned expression, consistent with the idea that this character is vulnerable without his armor, and that things might not always go as he has planned! This could help to invite the viewer's sympathy, but that may not be a quality that I want for a depiction of this wicked villain.

POSING

Posing a character wearing this sort of armor is a tricky part of the process, but I am able to create a lot of variety with his long limbs and tail. I really try to use all of the elements of his design to make him feel alive. I need a final pose that shows he is impressive, threatening, and capable in combat.

This fun pose utilizes every part of the character's design, and the posture of the arms and hands is alien and somewhat creepy. However, it doesn't indicate very much about his role and personality.

The armor is a big part of this character, and tells the viewer a lot about him. Showing him in a more defensive action stance, as if he is in battle, shows off how he might use it. The feral crouch reinforces his non-human nature, giving a clear view of his armored tail and strange feet. I will use this pose for my final design.

This pose is confident and relaxed, which is indicated by his whole body, such as his loosely hanging arm and long tail lying on the ground. He looks regal and imposing, but it's not particularly obvious that he is a fighter or a very active character.

VALUES & COLOR

Throughout the design process, I usually have an idea of how I want the final design to be colored, but it is important to explore other options besides the first one I have in mind. This ensures that I do not miss out on a better solution. When choosing colors for the design, I keep in mind that he is a villainous character, and that this must shine through in all my choices. I also want to create contrast between the skin and armor, so that the key parts of the design are shown clearly. The details of his armor will also give me an opportunity to add some lighting effects, creating visual interest and reinforcing the sci-fi setting he comes from.

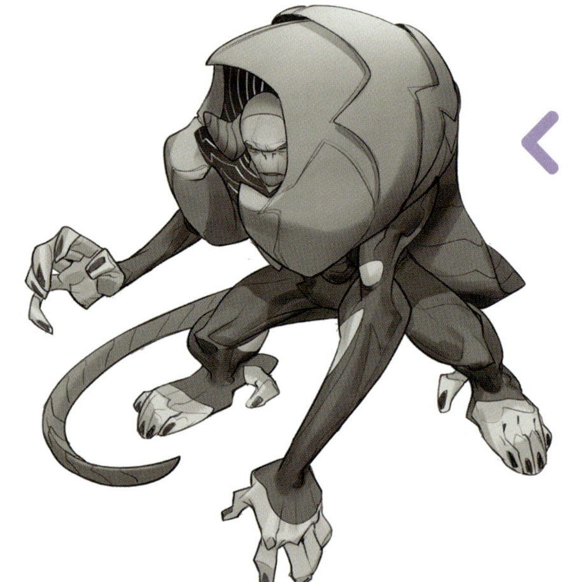

Applying grayscale values helps me to see the volume and shapes more clearly. You can see where I have created contrast between his suit and his skin, and between his pale face and the dark interior of his armor.

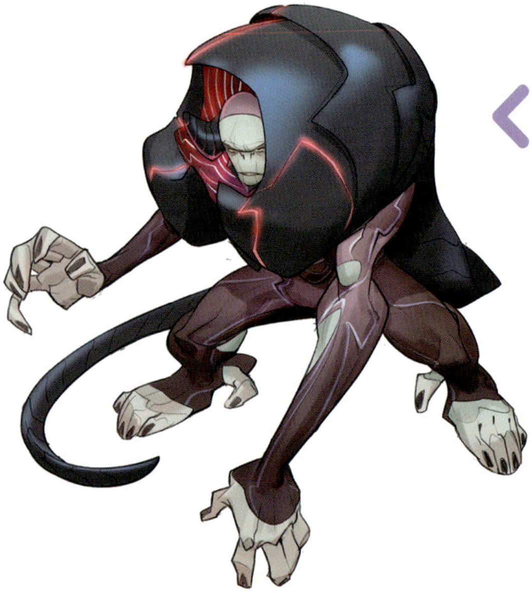

These are the colors I pictured for the character as I started working on him. They are quite desaturated, which makes the glowing red elements pop. Black and red is a classic villainous combination: dark, aggressive, with the high contrast giving a sense of danger.

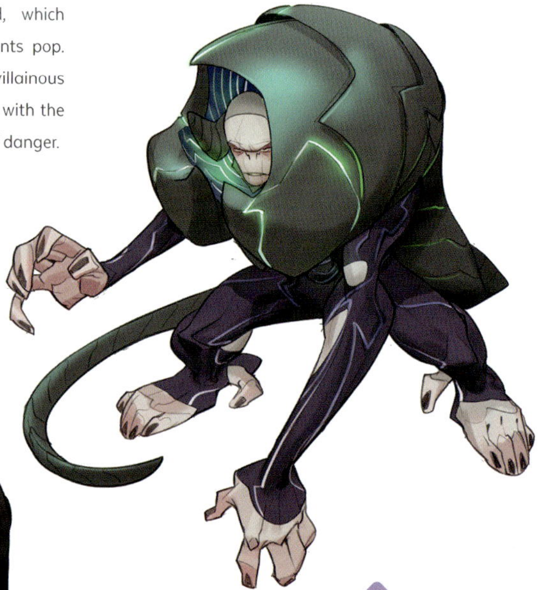

The character has an almost reptilian look to him, with his armored shell and long tail, so I try out a green-based color scheme. However, removing the striking reds also removes his aggressive edge.

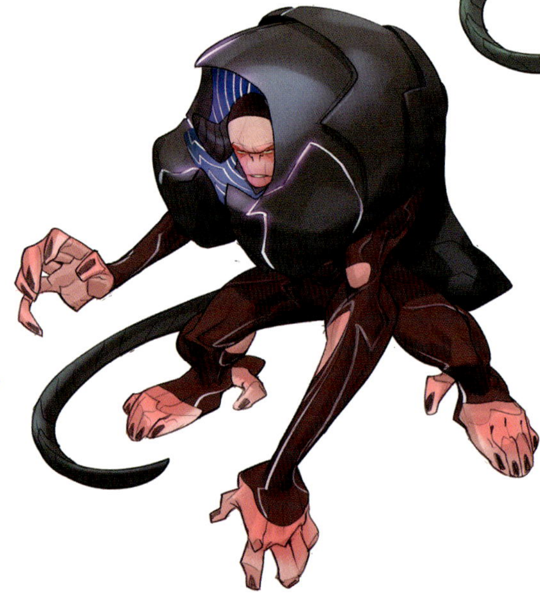

I want the character to look very pale, but I also like the reds I have used so far, so I try giving him bright red skin. Unfortunately, this distracts too much from his armor, but I like how the purple glow stands out against his armor; this could be something I can use for the final design, and is a less obvious choice than my initial red.

FINAL DESIGN

The final color scheme combines elements of my first and third ideas from the previous page, moving away from the classic black and red villain scheme to feature more pink and purple colors that add a sense of showiness to his armor. The overall look is still dark and threatening, further enhanced by his angular muscles and jagged armor, but the final palette does not rely on cliché colors, making it more interesting.

Designing an alien character is always tricky, because you may want to create something original, something that no one has seen before, but your design still needs to be something that the viewer can relate to. It can be difficult to convey a concept such as "alien royalty" without also showing what an average alien of this race looks like (see page 60, "Keep your cast in mind"), or drawing too much from our ideas of royalty on Earth, but I feel I succeeded in conveying this through his personality, pose, and looks.

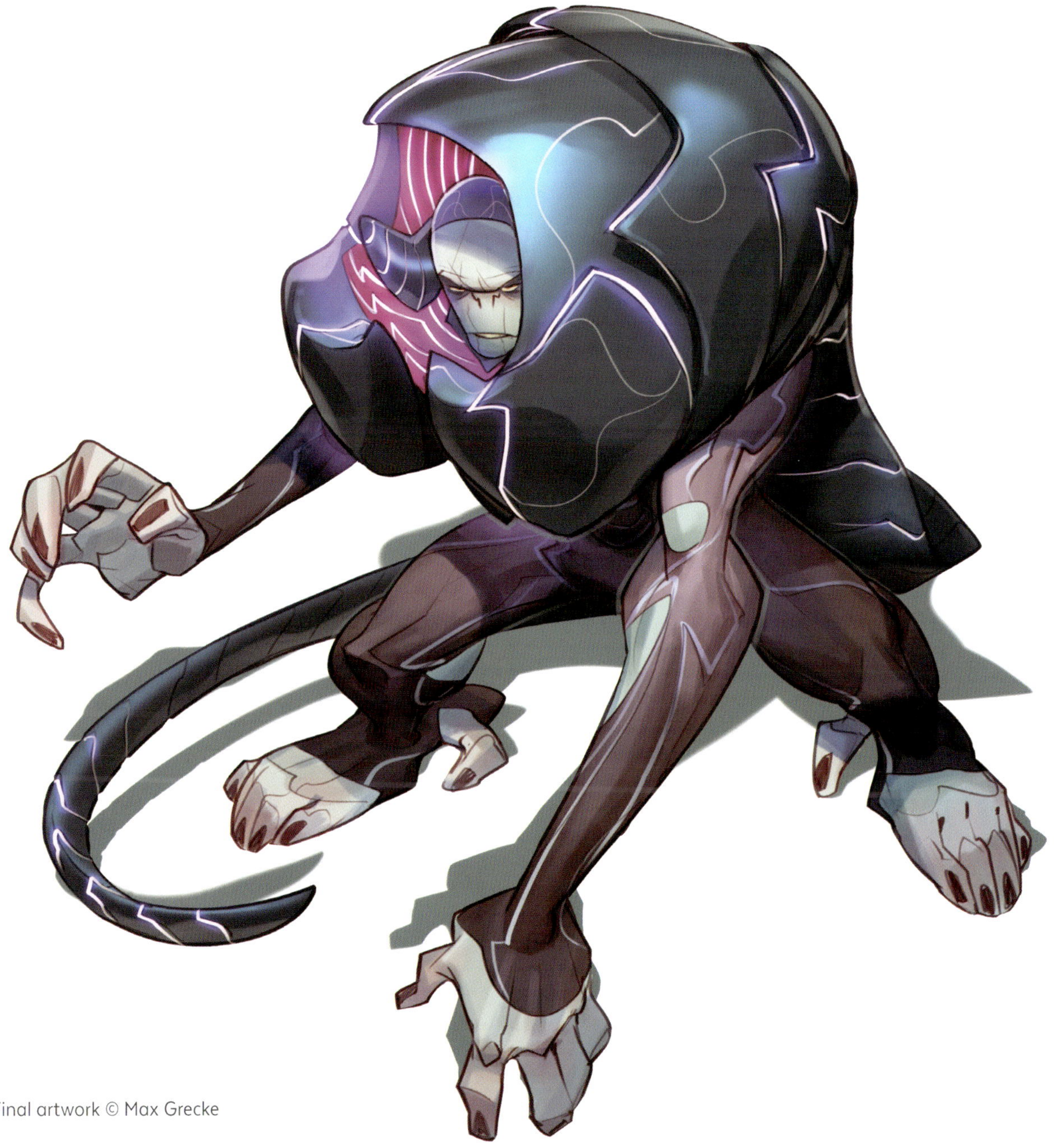

Final artwork © Max Grecke

VARIATION 1:
BABY ALIEN

IDEAS & RESEARCH

For this variation, I will design a baby alien, based on my established character and an understanding of how his race works. This means not just making a young alien version of that race, but actually making the same character younger and keeping as much of him recognizable as possible. The whole idea of this alien race already works well for designing a baby or infant; I imagine them using their shell-like armor as protection for their weak bodies, and perhaps they even grow into their suits in a way.

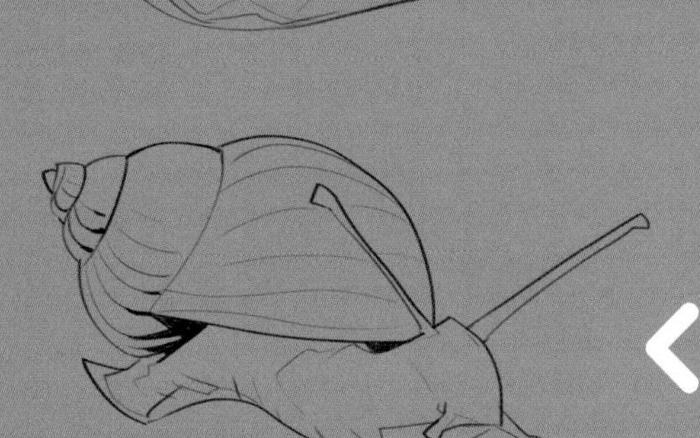

The original character's defensive armor gets me thinking about other creatures that use a shell or armor for a protection, such as snails.

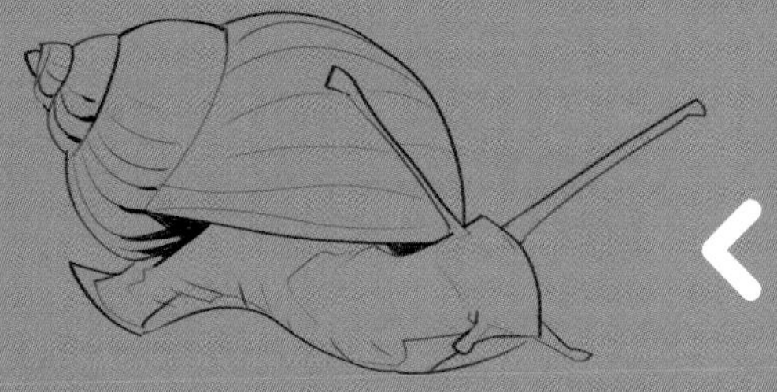

Snails' shells protect their vulnerable bodies exactly like I imagine my alien race's armor to do. Perhaps I could use a spiral element in this design, in reference to snails, similar to this angular shell.

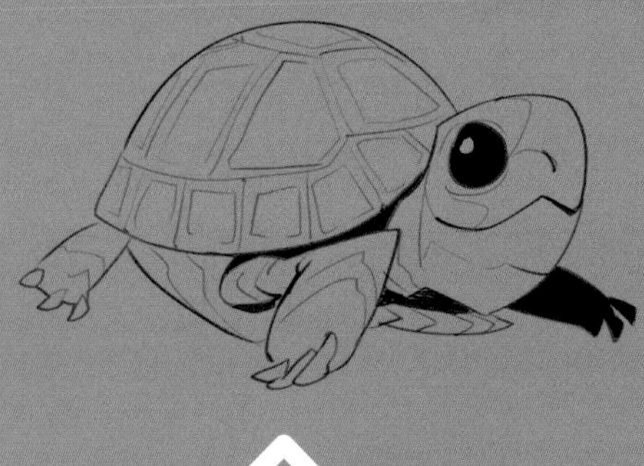

Baby tortoises and turtles might also have something in common with the snails I have looked at. I want to show how the alien's armor acts almost as a shell for his whole body. These baby creatures' large eyes are also a striking feature that would fit a character of this young age.

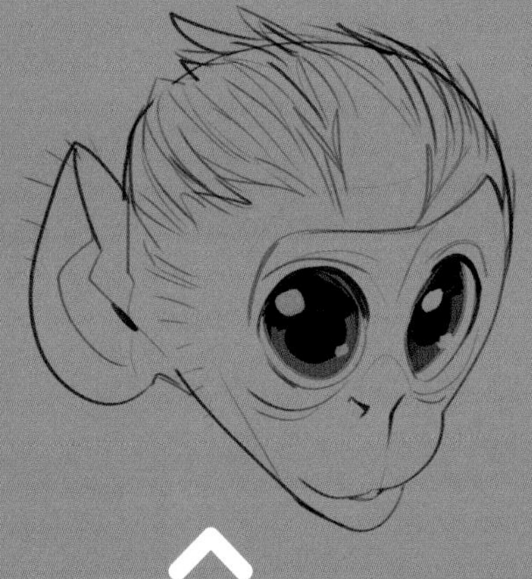

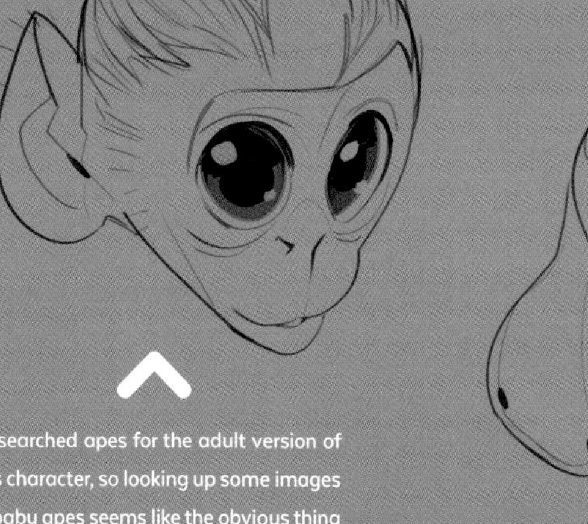

I researched apes for the adult version of this character, so looking up some images of baby apes seems like the obvious thing to do for this variation. This will help to ensure that the baby keeps a strong resemblance to his adult self. Baby apes' huge eyes and small, wrinkly faces would suit this design perfectly.

Baby apes have a lot of attributes that I can use for this infant creature, such as a large, bald head; big, round eyes; and much skinnier limbs than an adult ape, with proportionally large hands and feet.

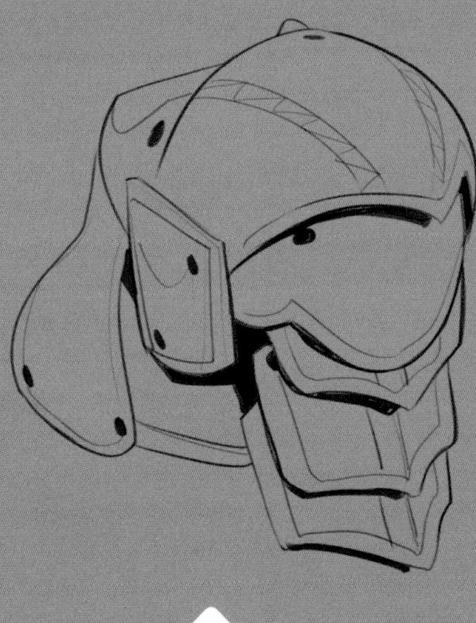

I make sure to research some further references for the armor, as that is what I want the baby to be wearing or held in. Like the adult version of the design, there may be some overlapping, pointed plates to retain a villainous edge.

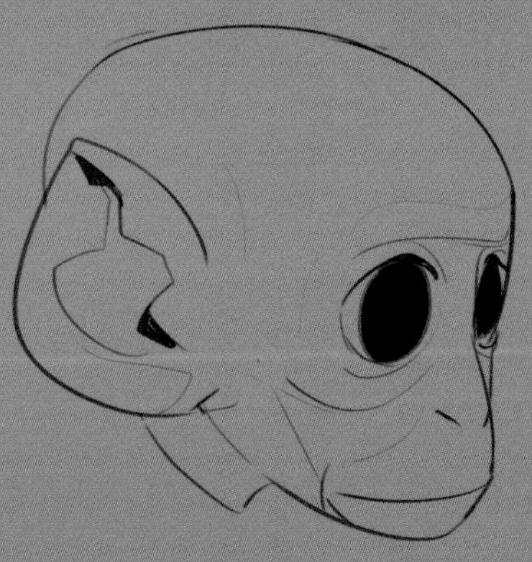

CHANGES

The most major changes to this version will be to his size and proportions, but I must make sure that he reads as the same character. The armor will be emphasized a lot more in this version, relative to the size of his body, so I may focus on that slightly more than the character's actual body.

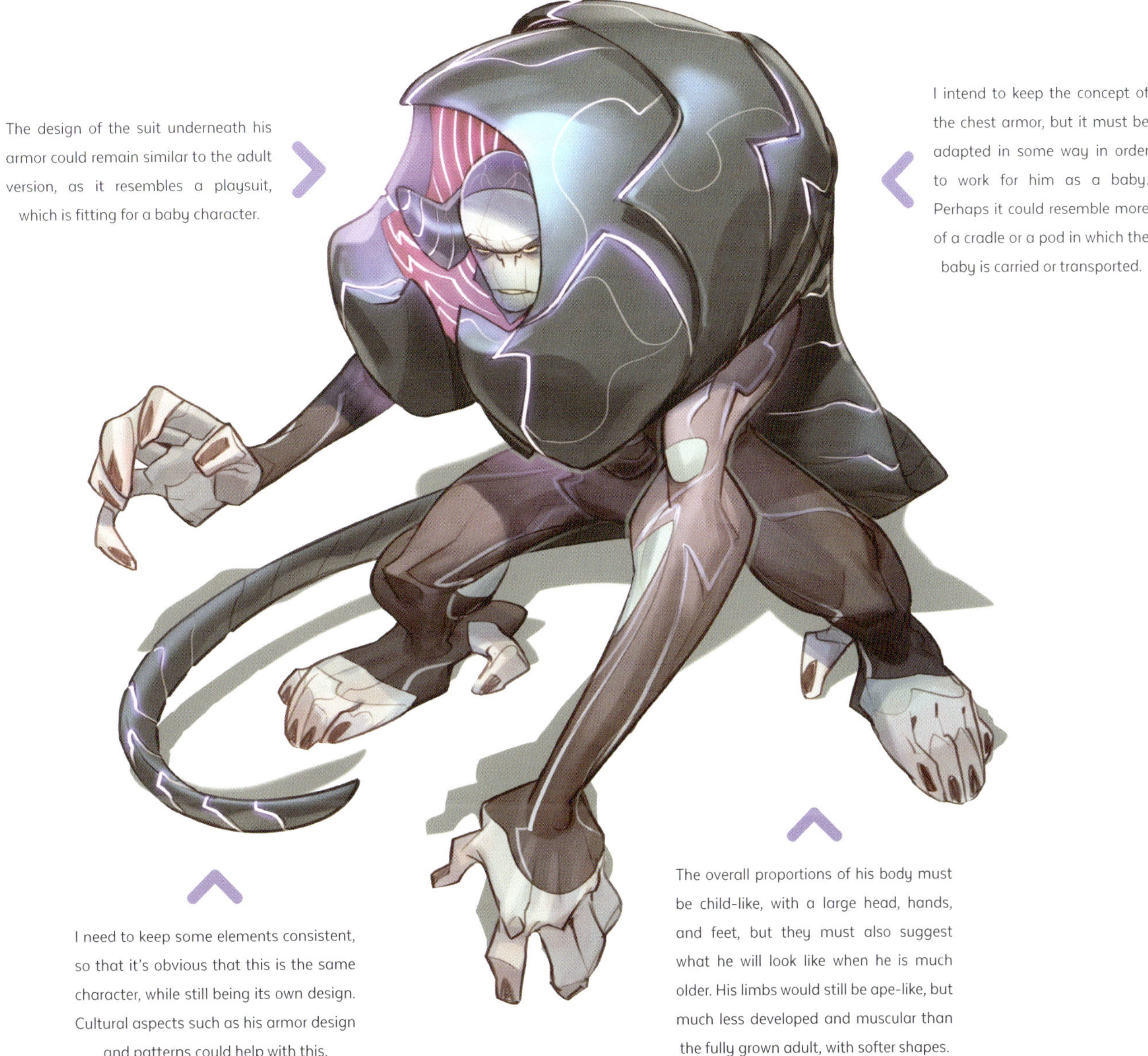

The design of the suit underneath his armor could remain similar to the adult version, as it resembles a playsuit, which is fitting for a baby character.

I intend to keep the concept of the chest armor, but it must be adapted in some way in order to work for him as a baby. Perhaps it could resemble more of a cradle or a pod in which the baby is carried or transported.

I need to keep some elements consistent, so that it's obvious that this is the same character, while still being its own design. Cultural aspects such as his armor design and patterns could help with this.

The overall proportions of his body must be child-like, with a large head, hands, and feet, but they must also suggest what he will look like when he is much older. His limbs would still be ape-like, but much less developed and muscular than the fully grown adult, with softer shapes.

THUMBNAILS

At first I imagined the character being carried around by his armored pod, but as I explore my thumbnails, I find it pays off to try ideas that I did not initially plan for. I much prefer the thumbnails where you can see his limbs, especially the one on the top right, as it creates proportions that are really quirky and more dynamic. This is the one I choose to work with.

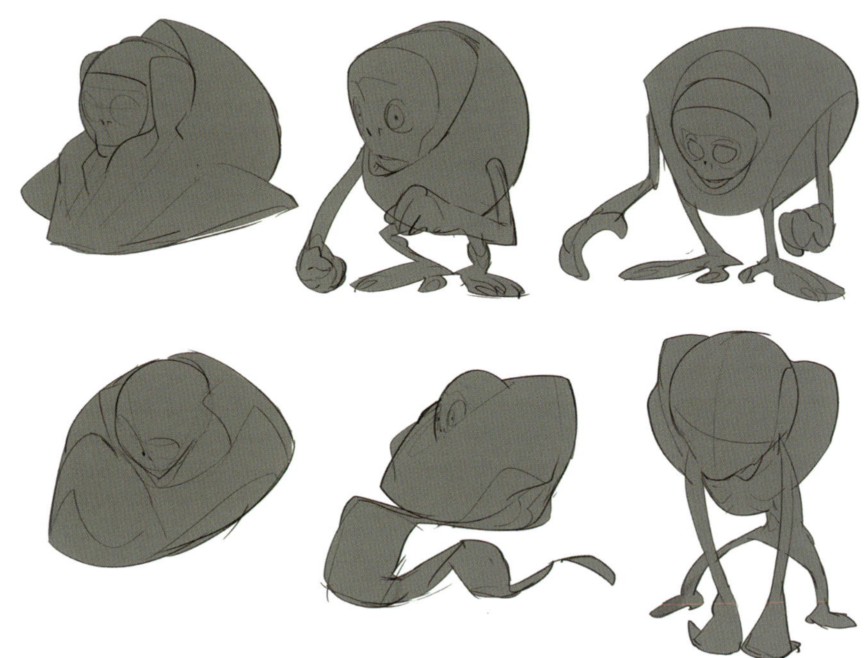

BASIC SHAPES

My chosen thumbnail features both a strong shell shape and distinct arms and legs that will allow me to create a wider range of poses. I want to use underlying shapes that are similar to those of the adult alien, but make concessions to the character's much younger age and more endearing proportions. I will make the edges more rounded and less angular, and also reduce the athletic bulk of his limbs, making them resemble the scrawny arms and legs of the baby apes I covered in my research. The relatively huge size of his hands and feet will also make him look younger, adding to his ungainly toddler's stature.

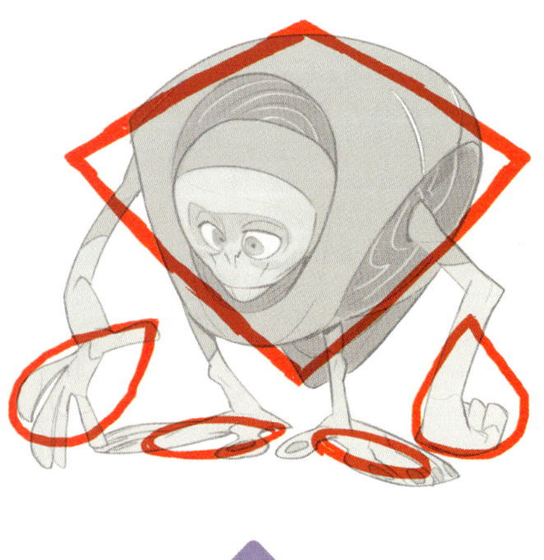

Keeping the shapes consistent from the adult version is important, but I give them a softer feel and more child-like proportions, with a large head and small limbs. The main body is still a diamond shape, but his hands and feet are now rounded.

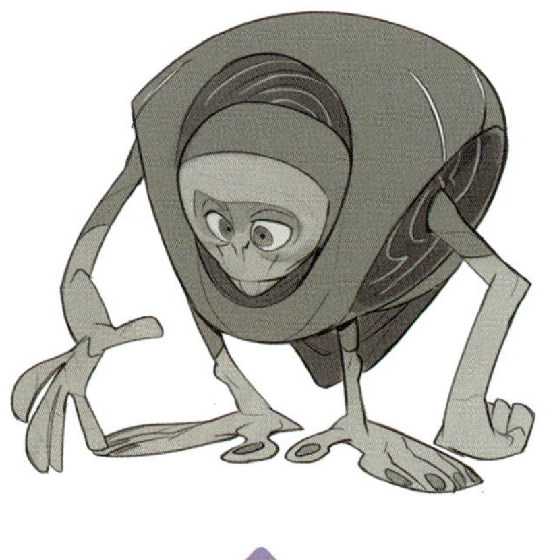

He now resembles a shrunken-down version of his adult self, with a diamond-shaped body and even a little tail, but the forms are more minimal and rounded to suggest his age. His arms and legs are also straighter and skinnier in shape, showing how he lacks muscle mass at this age.

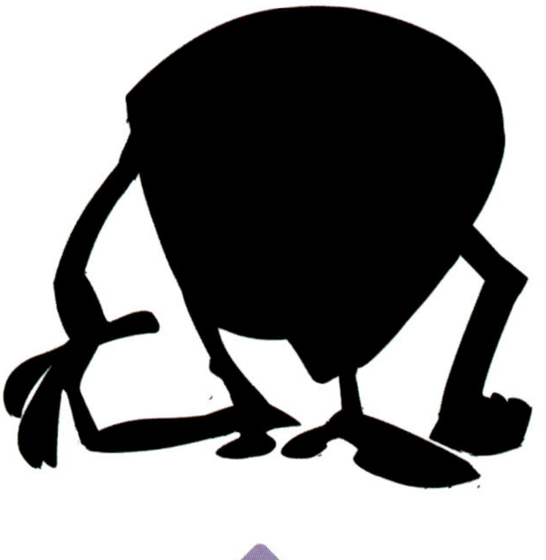

When I see the silhouette, I'm glad that I chose this approach to the character, compared to him just lying in a pod. The limbs add interest and more opportunities for posing.

DETAILS

This younger design leaves the character's face more exposed and readable, so I explore this further as I develop the character's details. During my research, it was interesting to see how the faces of apes and monkeys develop, with the babies being very wrinkly and thin, so I introduce those elements of my research to the design.

Compared to the adult character, this version can demonstrate a lot more emotion through his face and those big eyes. However, I don't want him to look too cute, as he is still a villainous character. My studies of baby monkeys help me to find a balance between looking childlike and slightly creepy and alien.

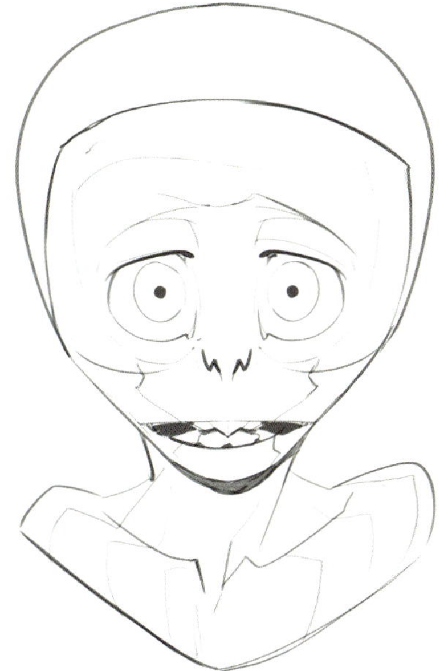

In this side view, you can see where I have brought in some of the snail shapes from my research, adding to the appearance of a swaddled baby while also suggesting the armor's protective shell-like qualities.

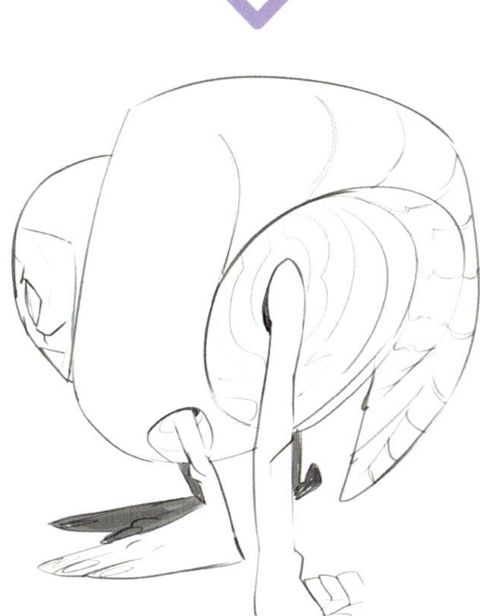

EXPRESSIONS & POSING

The thumbnail that I chose on the previous page went against my very first idea of having the armor as a pod that can both protect and transport the character, which worked out to my benefit. Now that the character has limbs, and can walk and stand, I can explore how he might interact with his armor and use it in different ways.

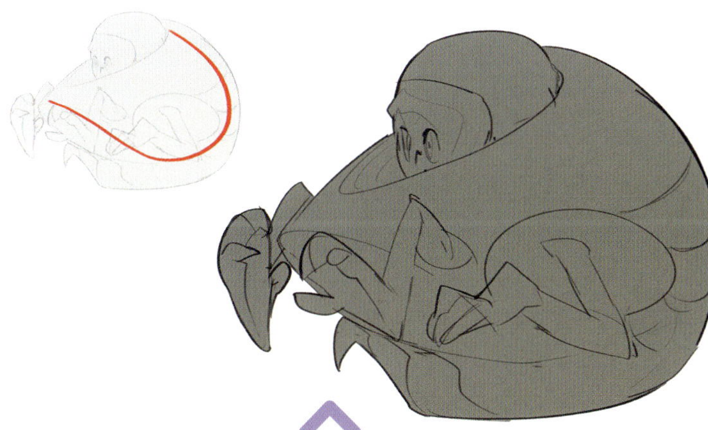

This harks back to my original idea of the baby being contained in a pod, but reinterpreted for this more dynamic character, showing him curling up defensively and pulling in his limbs. Presenting this tiny character protected by an over-sized shell also suggests that he is a baby of some importance, which is appropriate for his princely rank.

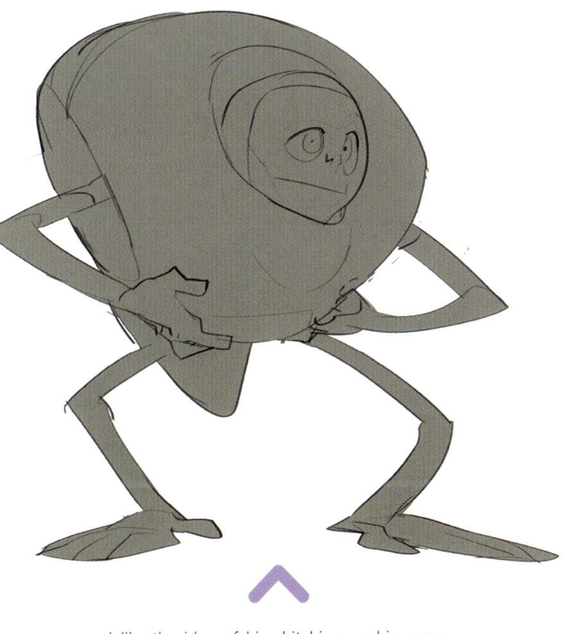

I like the idea of him hitching up his armor as if to get ready for running, but it's hard to immediately tell by the pose that he's pulling up the suit, so this does not really work.

VALUE & COLOR

The original character's color scheme was already a strong one. However, going back to my studies and seeing how different some baby animals look from adults of their species, I want to approach this version in a new way by adding some patterns like those that young animals often have. I also try out some brighter colors to make the character more playful, fitting his younger age, but I try to stay true to the original adult version.

The value distribution will be similar to the adult alien, with dark armor that makes the character's pale face stand out.

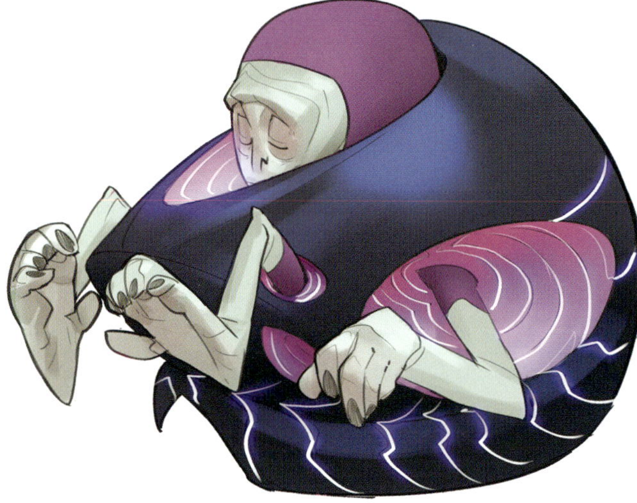

This palette is largely similar to the original, but slightly more colorful, with the pink being more prominent. This version forms my main basis for the final design, but I will mix in some features from the other palettes.

This palette features a lot of green, and has perhaps moved too far from the adult version's color. However, the greenish skin could be a great complement for a palette with more pink or warm colors, so I will adapt it into the final design.

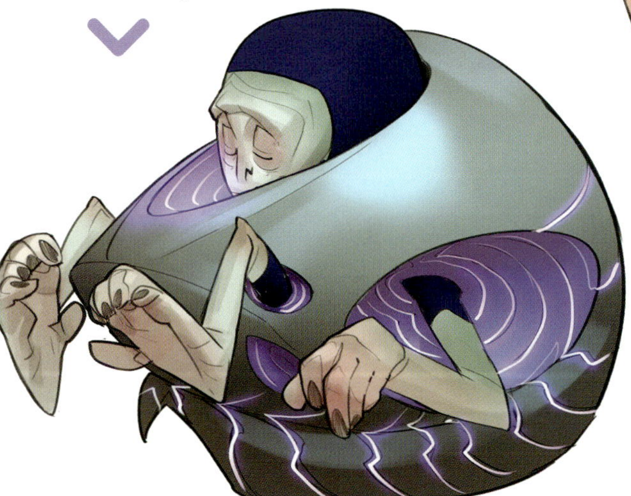

Baby animals often have spots or markings that they grow out of in adulthood, so I explore that concept here. It adds an interesting but subtle new pattern to the design, which I will use for the final version.

FINAL DESIGN

The final design uses a mix of the strongest ideas from each of the different color explorations: the brighter colors make him look younger, as does the freckled skin, while his green hue complements the pink and makes him appear fragile and alien. The design of his armor is different from the adult version, but still similar enough in color and design to suggest that this is the same character. The subtle, decorative patterns on his armor and suit add a touch of luxury that suggest his rank and importance. His sleeping eyes and curled-up hands and feet help to emphasize the more vulnerable nature of the alien at this young age.

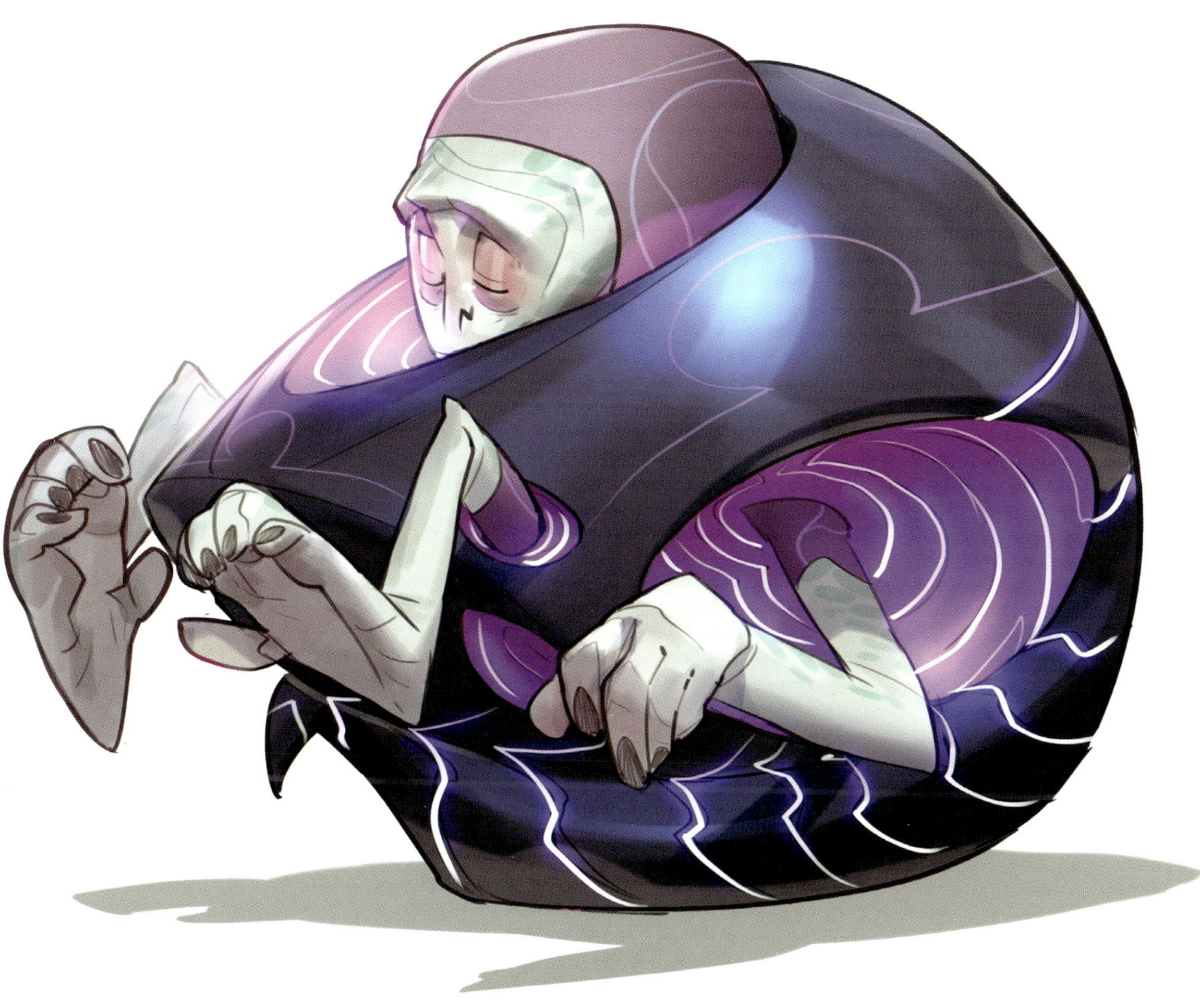

Final artwork © Max Grecke

VARIATION 2:
FERAL MUTANT

IDEAS & RESEARCH

So that I do not lose track of the very first original ideas for the character, I try to study within the same "field" of subjects that I used for reference before. This makes it much easier to come up with ideas early on, using the basis I have already built, but branching out into larger and fiercer creatures for inspiration.

I return to the ape kingdom for my research. For a bigger, scarier character, I study gorillas for inspiration. With their massive physiques and large teeth, they can be really fearsome.

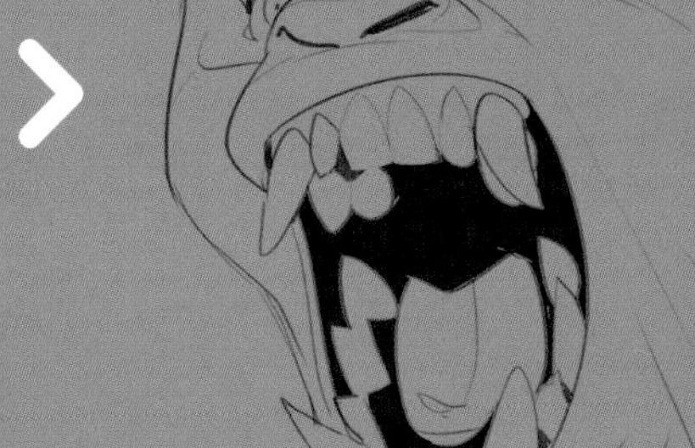

The gorilla's proportions are very striking, bulky, and different from the previous apes I studied. They could work well for this version.

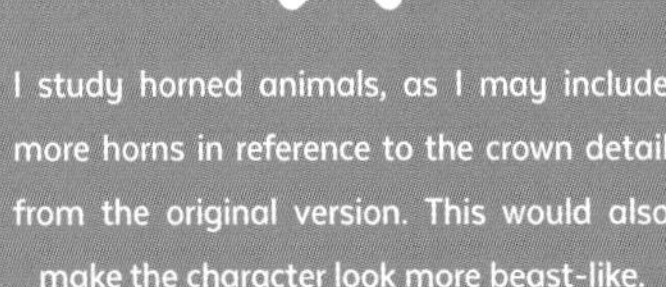

I study horned animals, as I may include more horns in reference to the crown detail from the original version. This would also make the character look more beast-like.

I did not really get to use my research into claws for the original character, but including it here fits the brief a lot better. They will be a striking feature that still keeps a similar essence of the original design.

CHANGES

My initial feel and idea for this variation is to make the character a big beast: massive compared to the previous version, with large, scary limbs, but still keeping the core ideas of contrast between forms. Many aspects will have to be dropped or changed, such as the clothing and armor, but I will aim to keep a similar sense of shape and color.

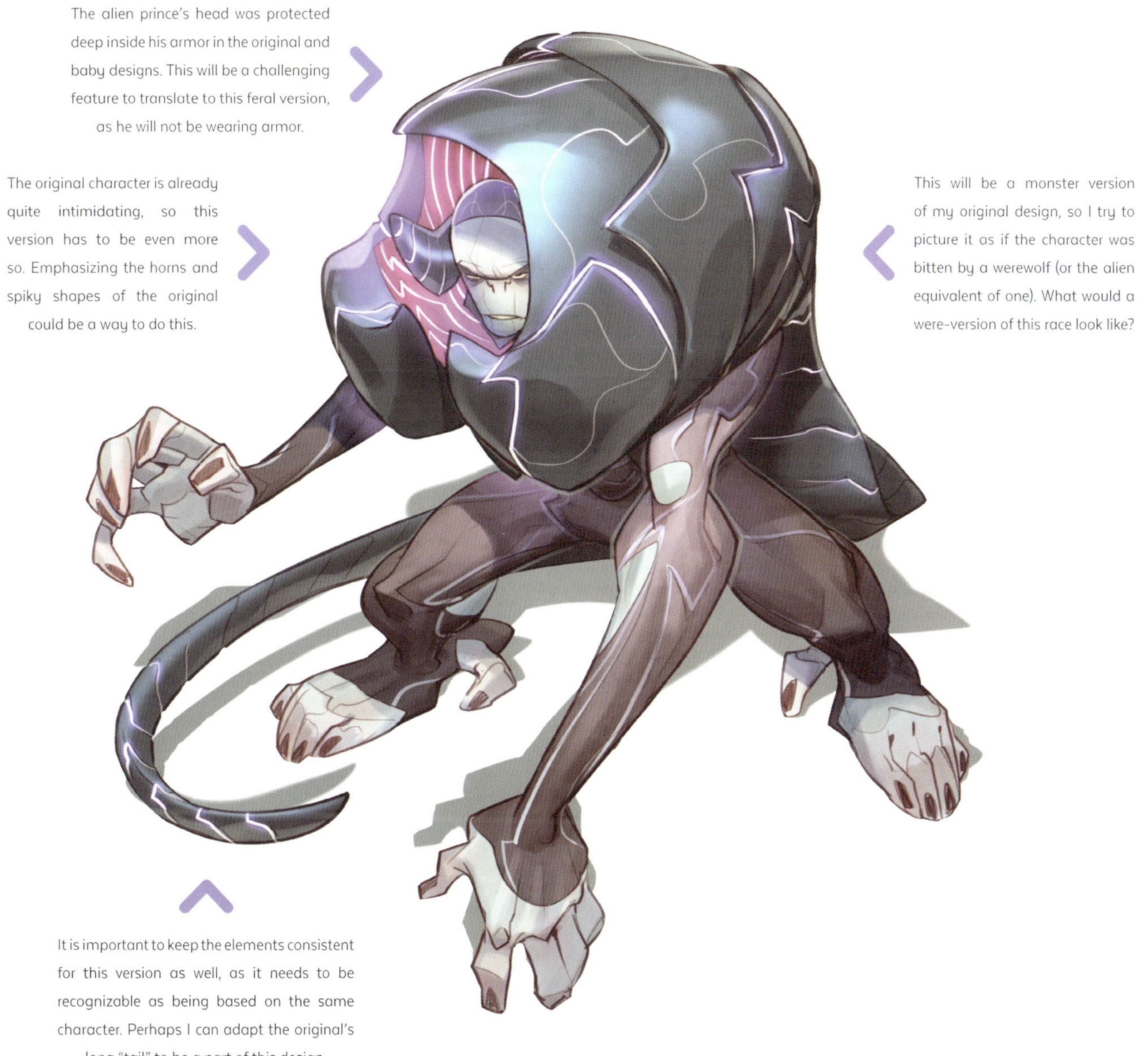

The alien prince's head was protected deep inside his armor in the original and baby designs. This will be a challenging feature to translate to this feral version, as he will not be wearing armor.

The original character is already quite intimidating, so this version has to be even more so. Emphasizing the horns and spiky shapes of the original could be a way to do this.

This will be a monster version of my original design, so I try to picture it as if the character was bitten by a werewolf (or the alien equivalent of one). What would a were-version of this race look like?

It is important to keep the elements consistent for this version as well, as it needs to be recognizable as being based on the same character. Perhaps I can adapt the original's long "tail" to be a part of this design.

THUMBNAILS

I want to keep the idea of a very heavy upper body with thinner limbs coming out of it, as that is the recognizable core shape of the original character. In my thumbnails, I focus on exploring different postures and how this creature's anatomy might work. Would he now be standing on two legs, or on all four? I lean towards a quadrupedal design as it suggests a more wild and feral nature. I mix varying amounts of gorilla-like bulk with the sharp, scrawny visual language of the original character. The head is tucked low between the shoulders like the apes in my research, also recalling the deep protective neck armor of the previous designs.

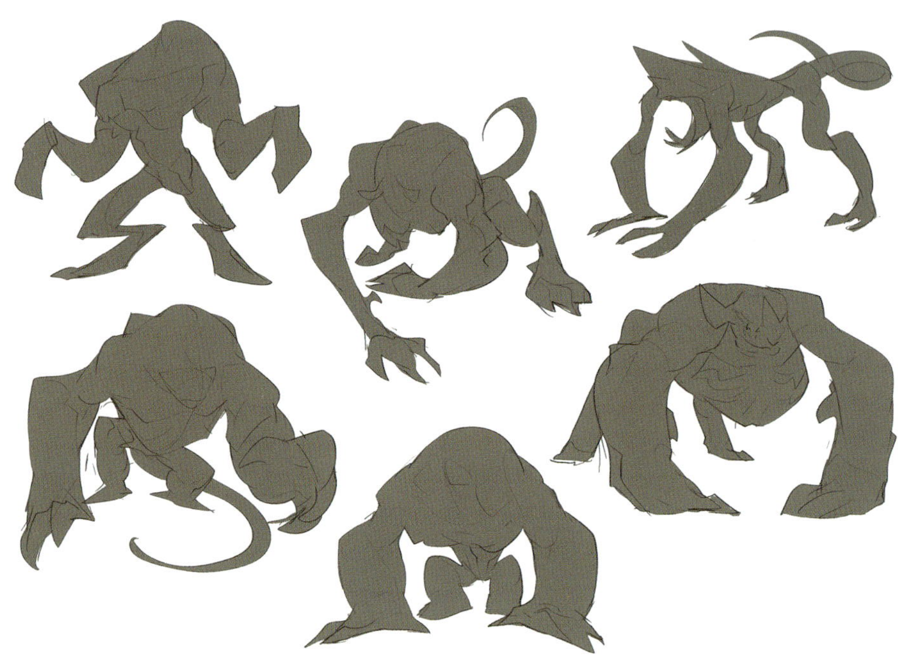

BASIC SHAPES

As with the previous versions of the character, the core body shape I use is a diamond. This creates a solid but dynamic sense of strength, sharper than a square but heavier than a triangle. In order to play up the impressive bulk and threatening nature of this character, triangular and diamond-shaped elements will recur throughout his body, framing his formidable muscles and sharp, tapered extremities.

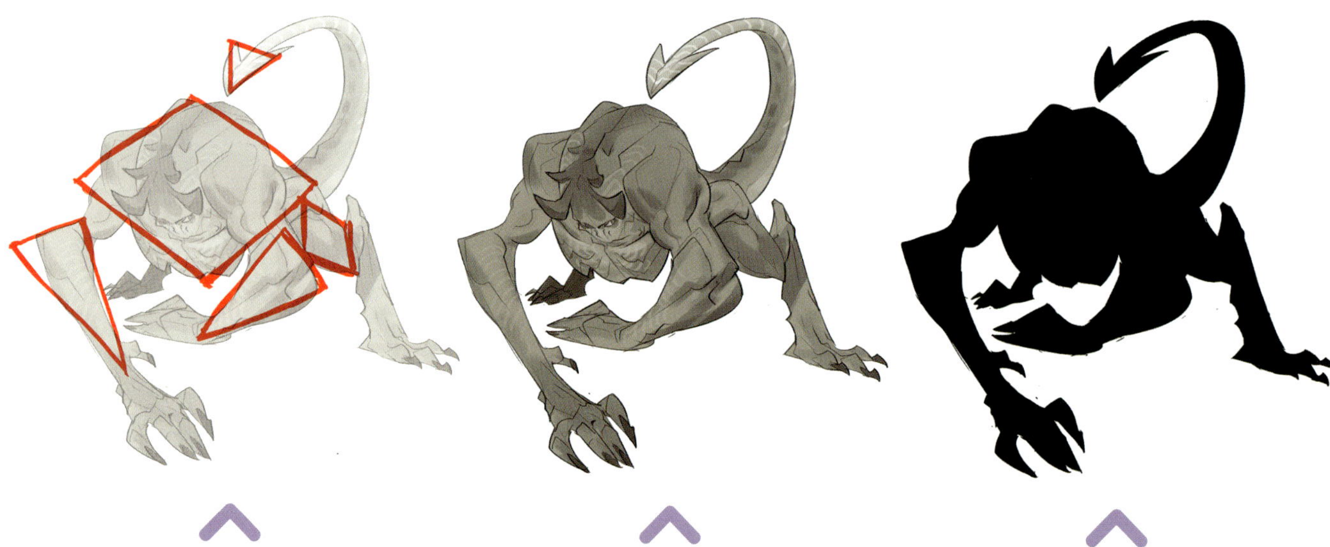

The core shape of the original character was a large diamond with curved limbs flowing out from it, which you can see carries through this new version as well.

As this character doesn't have any clothing or armor elements, I will need to bring more focus to the body shapes and patterns. For example, his horns and spiked tail have a similar shape, creating a visual rhythm which is also reminiscent of his original armor.

Seeing the silhouette confirms that the design comes across as creepy and dangerous, and has a strong flow to its shapes, so I consider it a success!

DETAILS

Now I can really push the similarities between the original alien and this mutant version. Here you can see the similarities in contrasting forms more clearly, balancing bulky shapes with skinny ones.

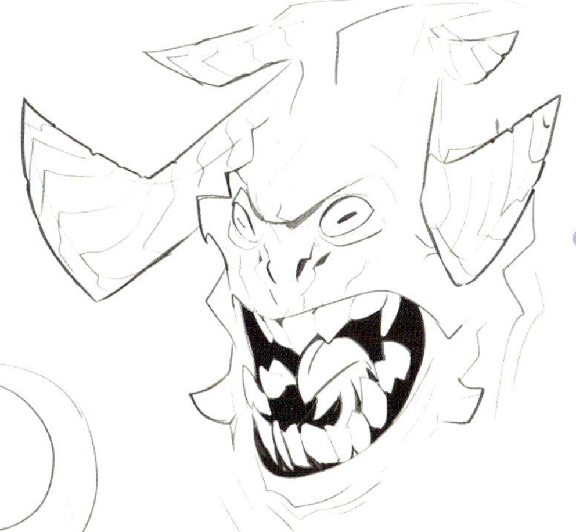

The face has not been a prominent part of the sketches so far, so I want to focus on it here, exploring how it works. I add more details to the horns, making them resemble the shapes and patterns of the original design more closely. The large fangs are inspired by my research into gorillas, and the overall sharp shape language of his tongue and teeth complements his spiky head.

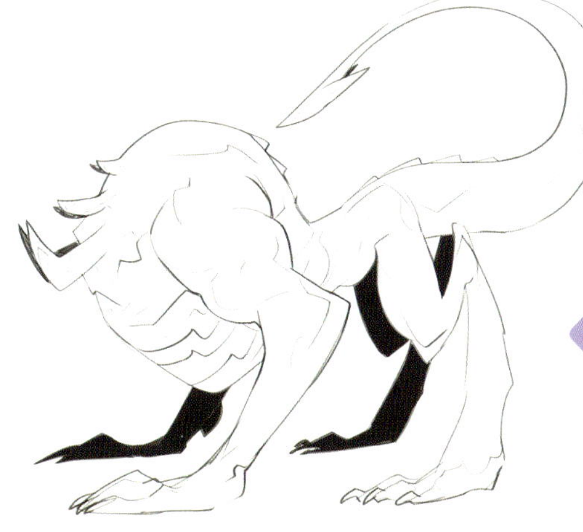

The profile view has more of an animalistic look which makes the character menacing. I really exaggerate the chest area, contrasting it with the thin waist, similar to the physique of the original design. The scales and ridges echo the original's ridged armor design, and the forked tail helps to tie the long tail in with the horns and spikes around his head.

EXPRESSIONS & POSING

This character should feel even more intimidating and scary compared to the original version. While the original was more defensive, wearing armor to protect himself, this mutant is highly aggressive and already has all the armor he needs! I try poses that emphasize his physical bulk and dangerous claws, and menacing, villainous character.

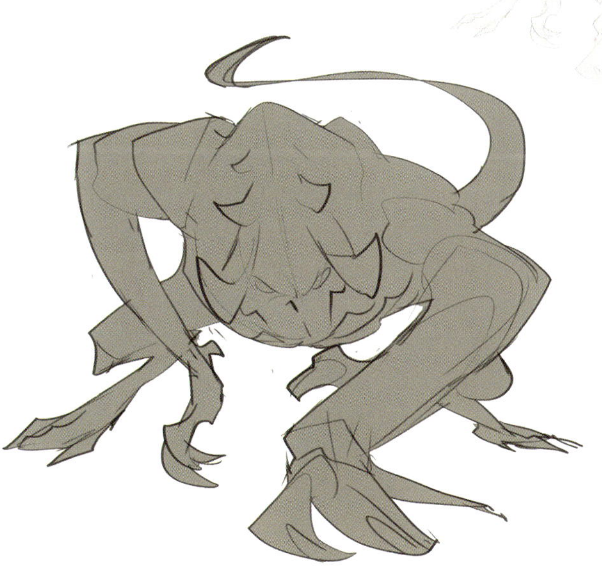

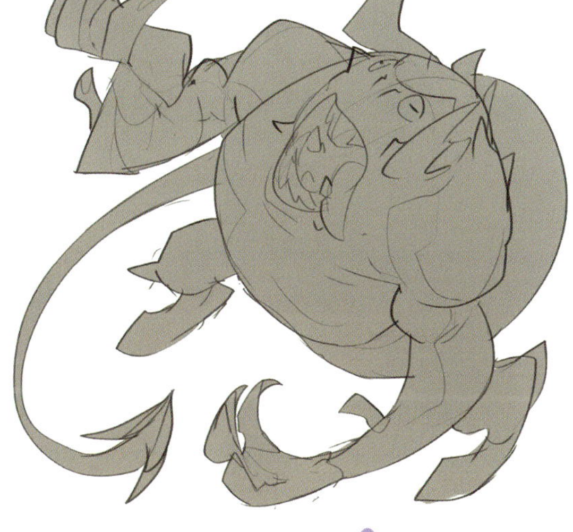

This pose is more stealthy, as if he is creeping up on his prey, which I feel captures the danger of the character more effectively. I will use this for the final pose.

I try a dramatic top-down angle to get more focus on the character's claws and face, but it doesn't give it the sinister feel I want to convey.

VALUE & COLOR

For the character's colors, I focus on defining the values and shapes to ensure the design reads well, because there are no elements such as clothes or armor to break it up, only the alien's own skin tones. Thus I try to keep the base tones simple and organic, while using gradients and patterns to create interest and definition.

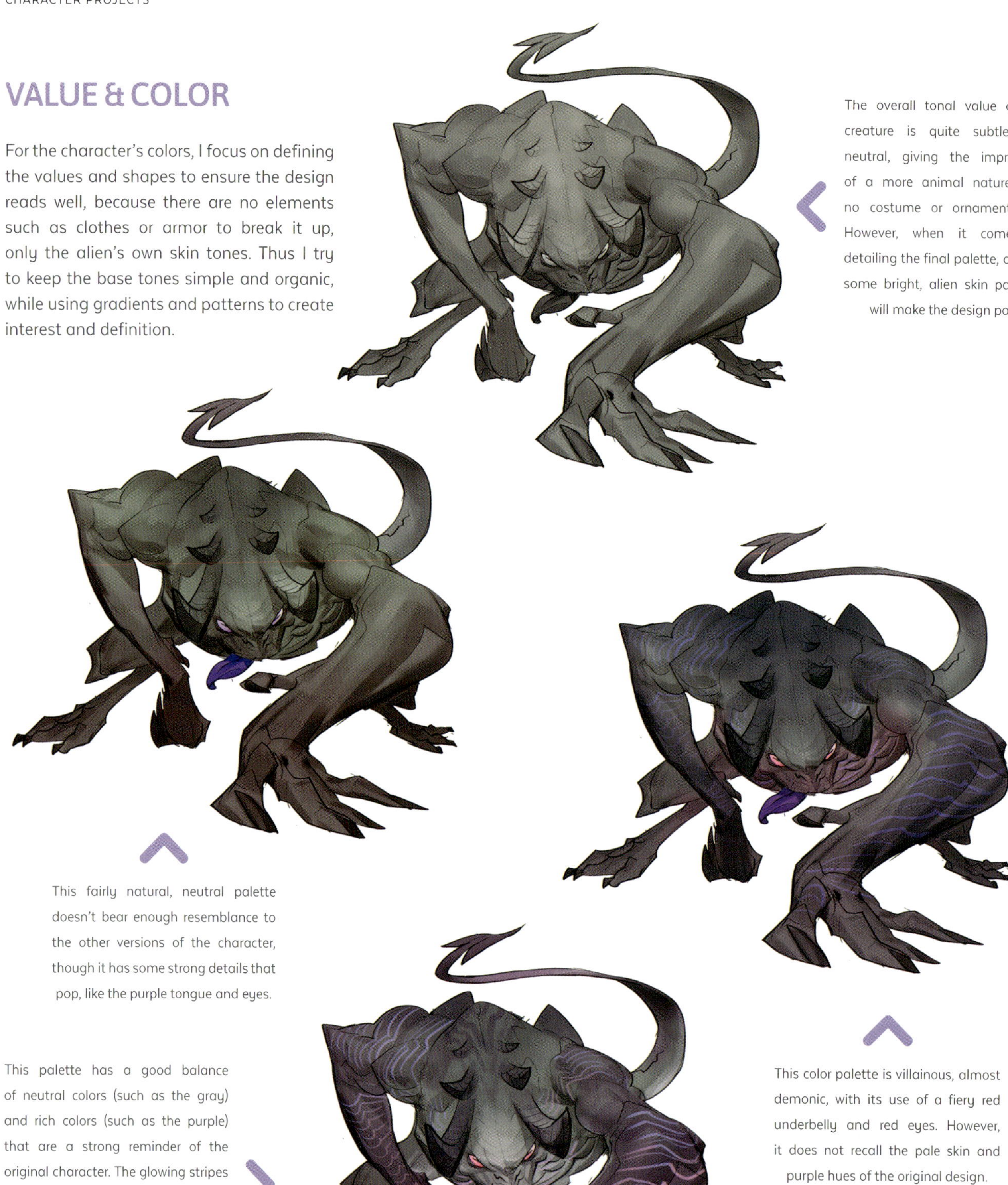

The overall tonal value of the creature is quite subtle and neutral, giving the impression of a more animal nature with no costume or ornamentation. However, when it comes to detailing the final palette, adding some bright, alien skin patterns will make the design pop.

This fairly natural, neutral palette doesn't bear enough resemblance to the other versions of the character, though it has some strong details that pop, like the purple tongue and eyes.

This palette has a good balance of neutral colors (such as the gray) and rich colors (such as the purple) that are a strong reminder of the original character. The glowing stripes and pale face are reminders of the previous designs, while also calling to mind dangerous real-world predators such as tigers. I will use this as a basis for the final version.

This color palette is villainous, almost demonic, with its use of a fiery red underbelly and red eyes. However, it does not recall the pale skin and purple hues of the original design.

FINAL DESIGN

The final version of the character succeeds in recalling the original design, while also presenting something new. Features such as the pale skin and purple palette bear a resemblance to the character's original version, as well as the stripes, tail, and horns, which are now integrated into the mutant's body for a more wild, organic appearance. The tense, predatory crouch and lolling tongue immediately convey that this is a dangerous feral beast on the hunt. Adding some specular highlights to the final design enhances the sense of an alien skin texture and muscular ape-like bulk. By playing close attention to the choices made earlier on in the process, it becomes easier to design without losing the spirit of the original character.

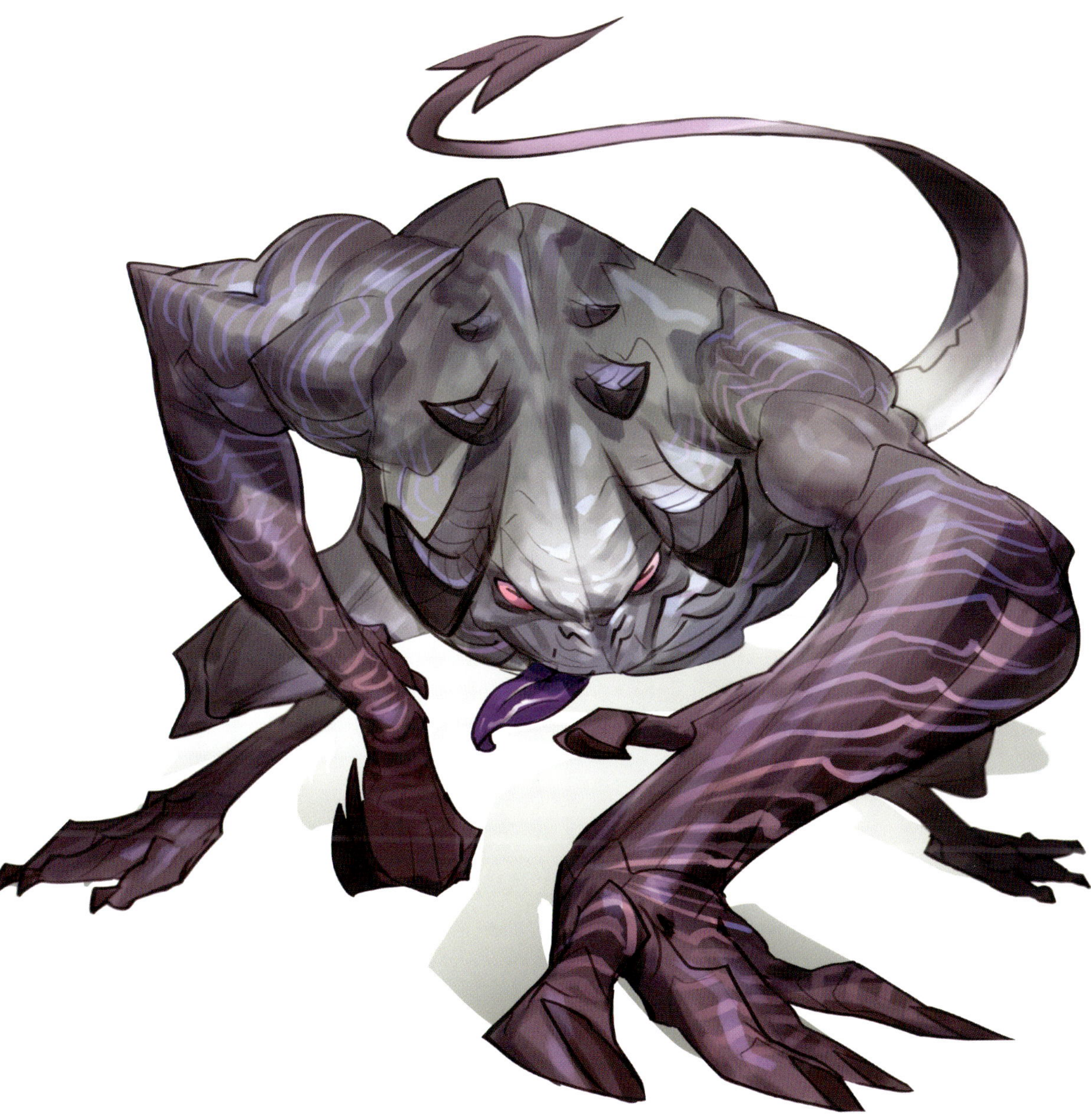

Final artwork © Max Grecke

VARIATION 3:
HUMAN VILLAIN

IDEAS & RESEARCH

Making a human version of an alien character is an interesting challenge to think about. I start by considering how it would work if the versions were created in the opposite order: what would the human look like if I had based that alien design on him? The original alien isn't extremely far from a human, but achieving a similar silhouette will be more of an obstacle; I want this human to be a present-day character, creating a challenge for myself, as he would not be wearing extravagant armor or anything overly fantastical or futuristic. In my research, I explore options for clothing and accessories that might help to convey the character's personality and capture aspects of his alien form in the context of a human.

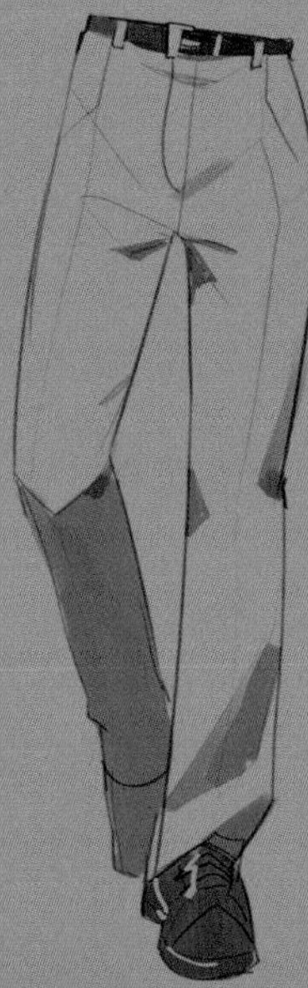

An elaborate royal jacket would definitely help to convey his rank and importance. The final version might not look like this, as it is too historical, but it would be a good idea to merge this with a more modern design.

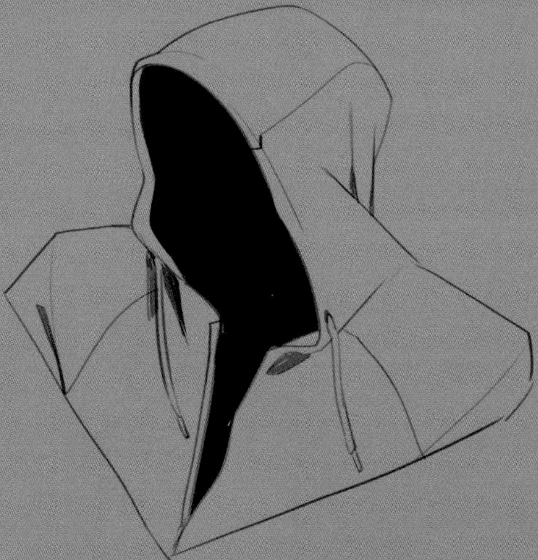

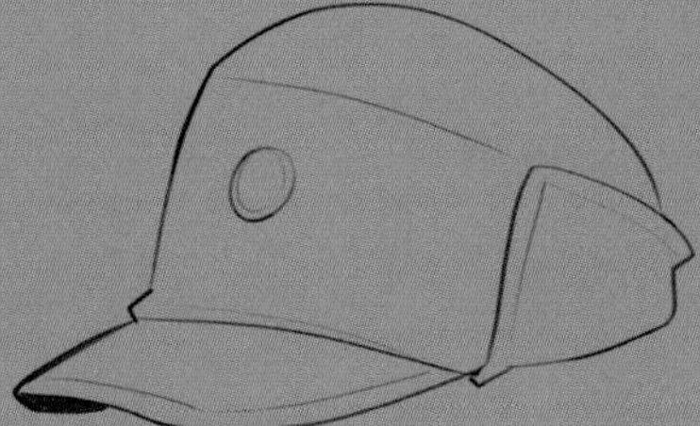

I also research inspiration for headgear that is not just a typical cap. This type of shape would give the character a more formal, military edge, consistent with the original alien design. Even if I don't use these specific elements, I can transfer the ideas to other items, such as the jacket.

A hat might help to convey the cocky attitude of this rebellious prince, and could also remind the viewer of the horns and headgear of the previous versions.

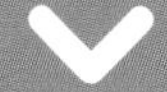

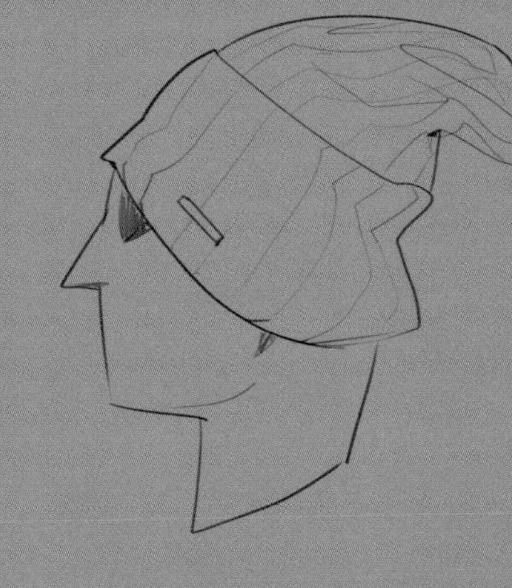

Smart dress shoes could give the design an elegant touch, as long as they don't make him look silly or clumsy with their size. Their pointed shape would also add to the angular, villainous shape language.

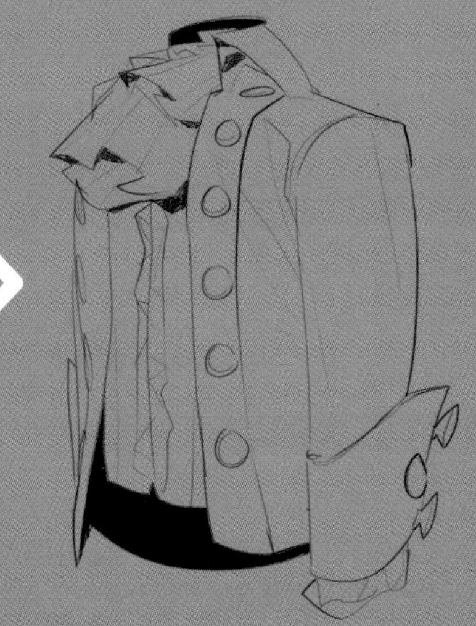

The human version should have expensive clothing suitable for a wealthy villain, so formal dress pants seem fitting for him.

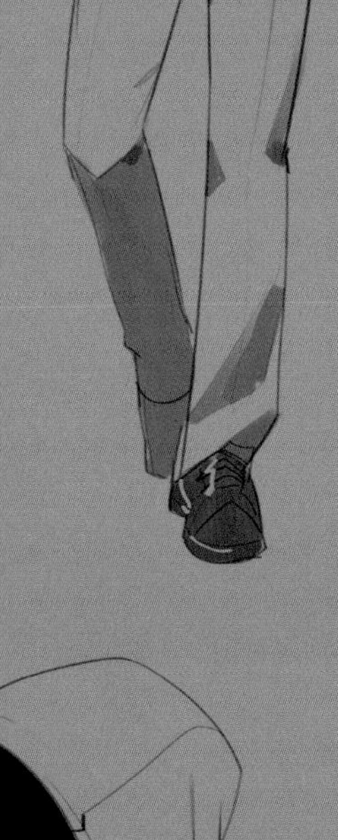

Alternatively, if the character doesn't have any headgear, perhaps he could wear a hood. This would suit the look of a more modern human, and successfully call back to the hooded suits and protective armored shells of the alien designs.

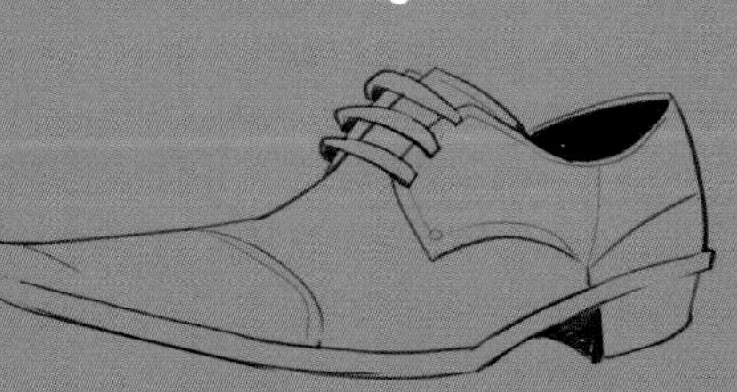

CHANGES

I want the human character to have the same personality and intentions as the alien character, but set on Earth instead of a sci-fi planet. Many of the overtly futuristic and alien elements will have to be changed, so I must find other, more human ways to capture the same personality and the almost demonic shape language.

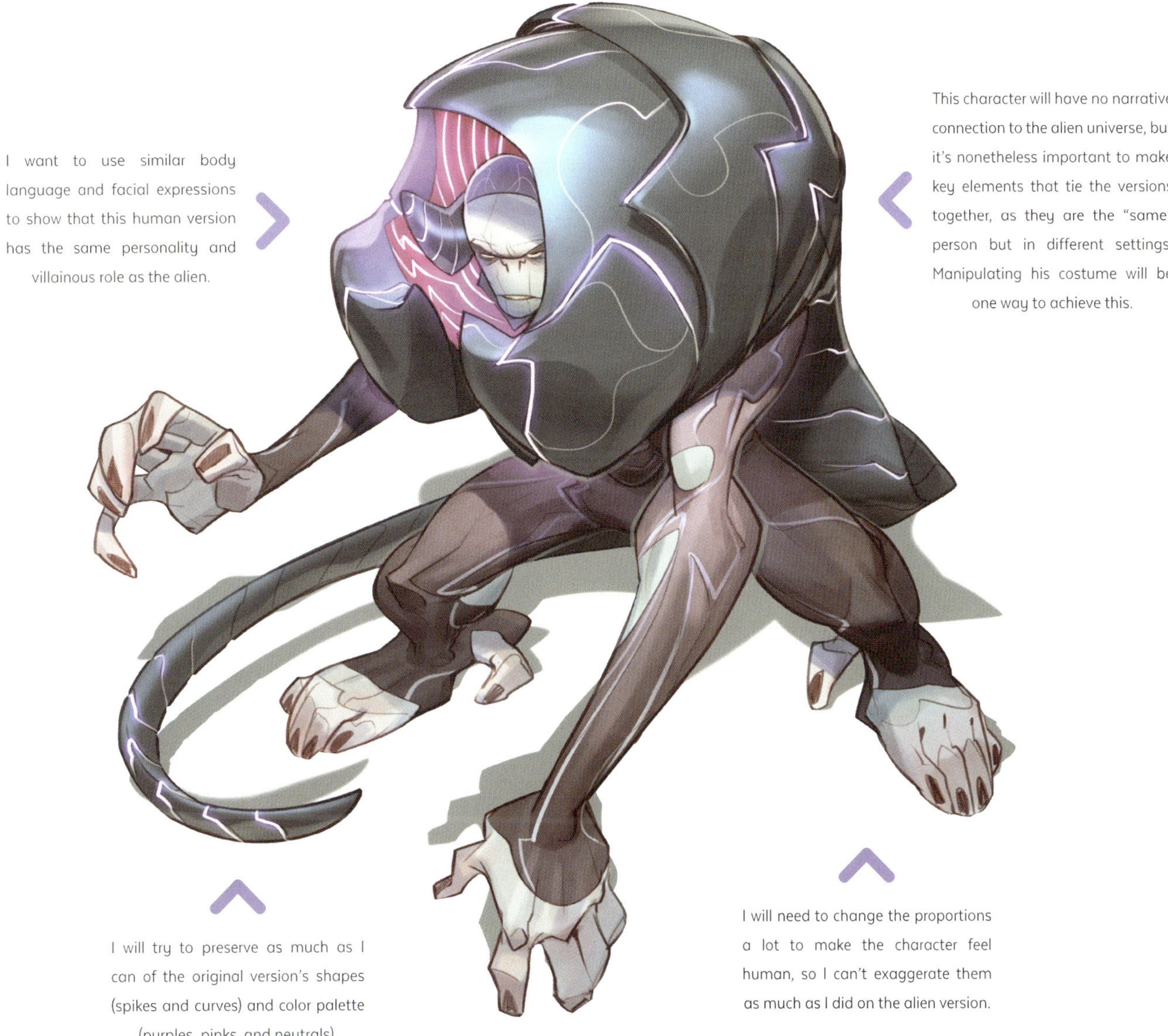

I want to use similar body language and facial expressions to show that this human version has the same personality and villainous role as the alien.

This character will have no narrative connection to the alien universe, but it's nonetheless important to make key elements that tie the versions together, as they are the "same" person but in different settings. Manipulating his costume will be one way to achieve this.

I will try to preserve as much as I can of the original version's shapes (spikes and curves) and color palette (purples, pinks, and neutrals).

I will need to change the proportions a lot to make the character feel human, so I can't exaggerate them as much as I did on the alien version.

THUMBNAILS

In my thumbnails, I play around with how regal and formal or rebellious and casual he might look. I explore different shapes for jacket collars or hoods, creating sharp angles or a strong diamond shape like basis of the original design. Using sharp, angular shapes helps to convey that he is a dangerous, untrustworthy character, so diamonds and triangles are a recurring element.

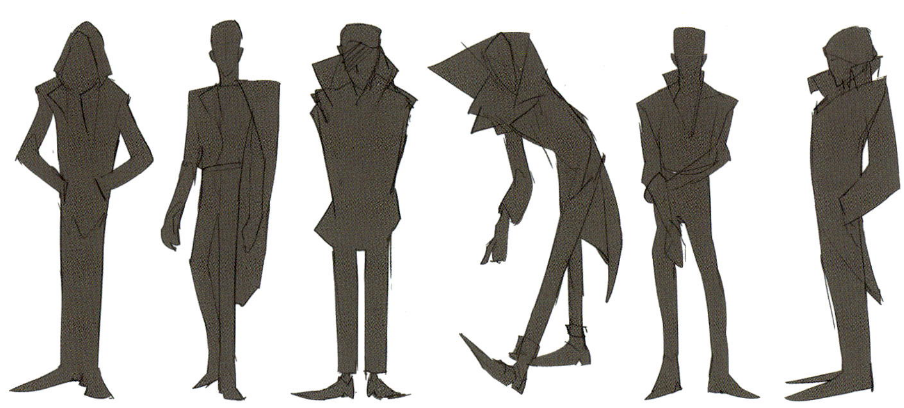

BASIC SHAPES

This character does not have the beastly bulk or heavy sci-fi armor of the previous designs. Instead, the villainous nature of this human is conveyed through recurring triangular shapes. His overall physique would be less ape-like and primal than a race of alien warriors; instead, he might be a villain that relies more on intellect and cunning than physical strength. The sharp, narrow triangles underlying his figure make him look menacing and severe, and his long, thin legs give him a sense of impressive height without bulking up his physique too much. The long shoes add another sharp triangular element that ties in with the horns, spikes, and pointed extremities of the previous alien designs.

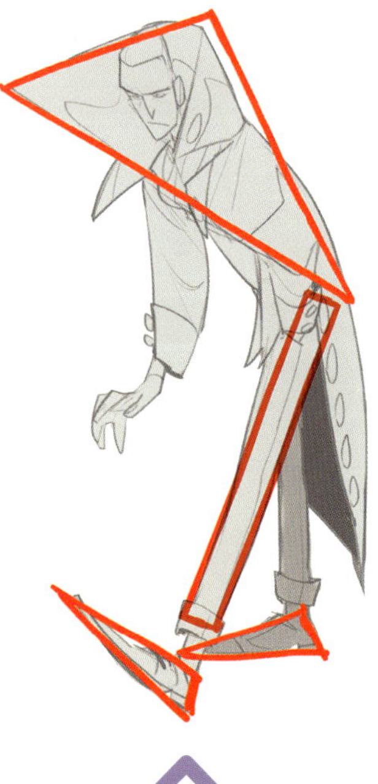

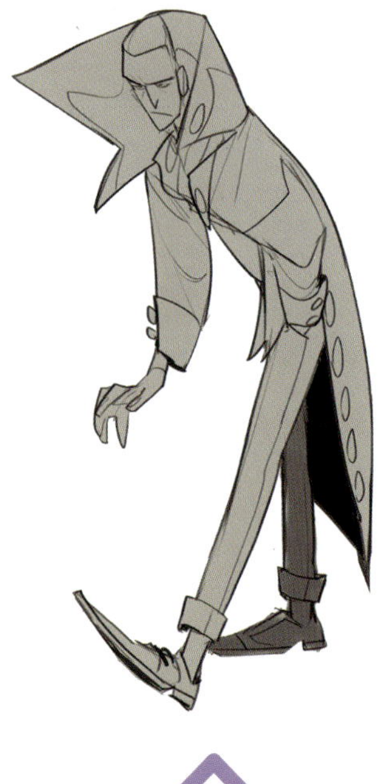

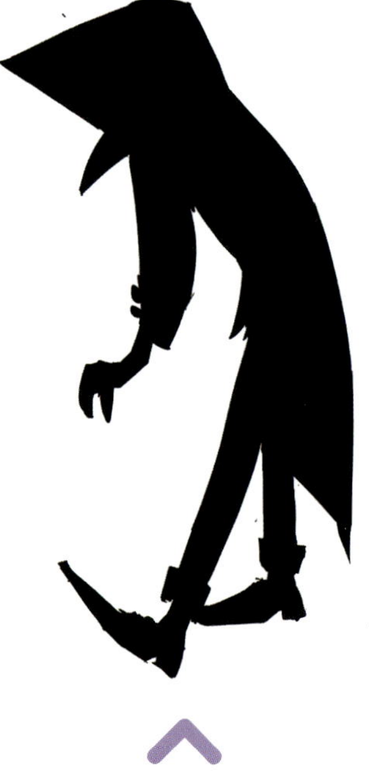

I choose to develop the thumbnail that's somewhat hunched and mysterious, as the high collar is a visual reminder of the original design's protective shell-like armor. The very triangular shape, with much narrower arms and legs, is also similar to the menacing top-heavy structure of the alien.

Having the very big collar works well, recalling how the armor pieces looked around the face of the alien version. His hair is cropped short around his head, like the hooded suit of the original design. His shoes look expensive and sinister, and echo the pointed shapes of his collar.

The silhouette clearly shows the strong balance of large and narrow shapes, angles, and curves. The large coat almost disguises his skinny human figure, making him look more menacing. The multiple sharp and pointed edges convey the villainous, dangerous aspect of the character.

DETAILS

In the detailing stage I really focus on the elements that will tie the human and alien versions of the character together, finalizing how the character's clothing looks and suggesting that it works in similar ways.

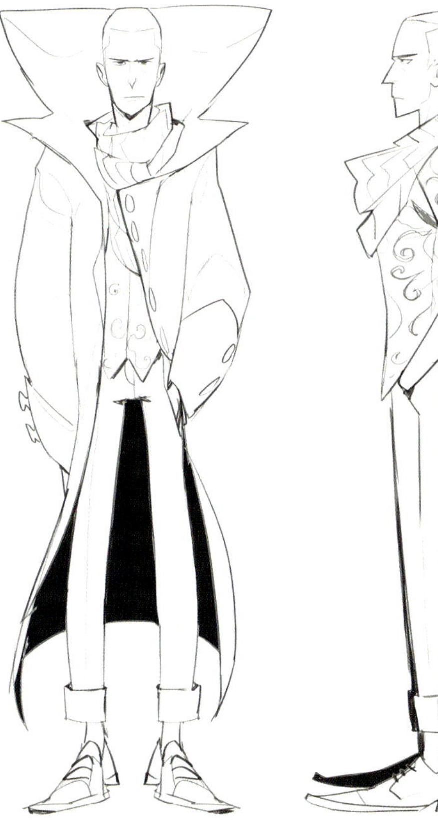

My initial sketch obscures the character somewhat, so this detailed front view shows all his clothing, and we get to see what's under the jacket as well. The textures and patterns of these elements will tie this character together with the alien version.

Here you can see his physique and costume more clearly, without the jacket. The loose, striped scarf is a reference to the neck of the alien's armor. The fancy patterns on his shirt are also similar to the glowing patterns of the sci-fi armor, while also making him look refined and wealthy.

EXPRESSIONS & POSING

I look back at some of the poses I drew for the alien version, and consider how I could translate some of them to this character – maybe even trying the exact same poses with a human figure. The tail on the alien design added a sense of motion which I can parallel with the long jacket.

This is a throwback to one of the unused alien poses, with a regal and arrogant bearing and simple angle that shows the character's posture and every aspect of his design clearly. I will use this pose for my final design.

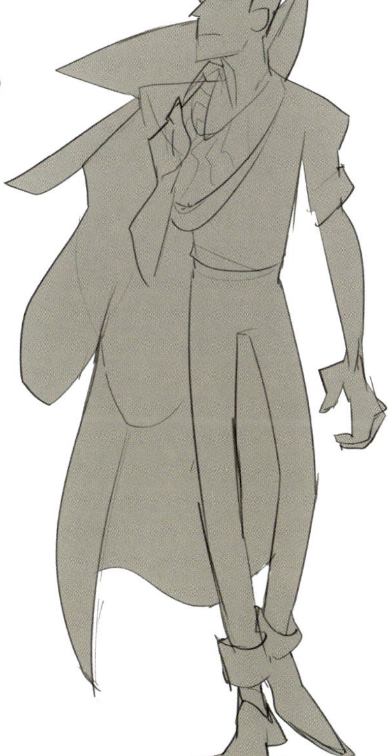

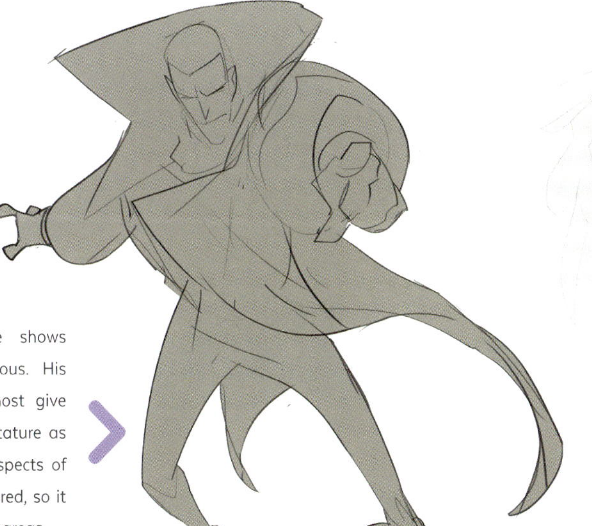

This action-oriented pose shows him as physically dangerous. His stance and long coat almost give him the same shape and stature as the alien. However, some aspects of his costume would be obscured, so it loses its similarity in other areas.

VALUE & COLOR

The color palette will really sell the similarity between the alien and human designs, with a dark outer shell and a brighter purple or pink inside. When exploring colors, I keep that core idea and branch out into different options from there, using the character's accessories and clothing patterns to add eye-catching pops of color inspired by his alien counterpart.

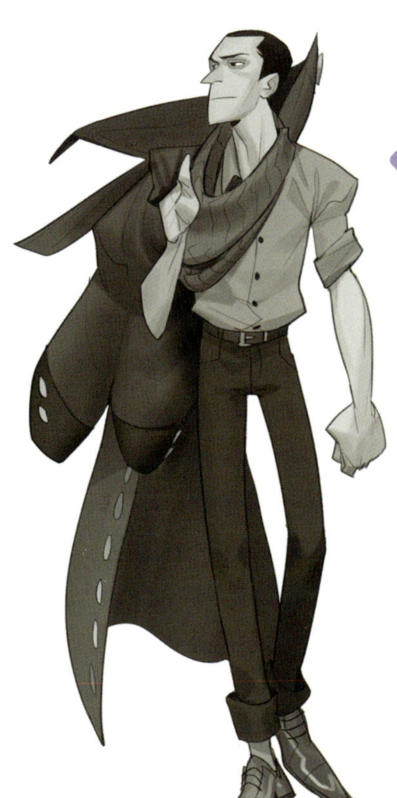

I use dark values for the character's pants and jacket, as I did for the original alien's suit and armor, and balance them with the lighter values of his shirt and pale skin.

This palette has a cooler feel overall, with a blue jacket that recalls the alien design, and a bright scarf that is very eye-catching against the neutral shirt color.

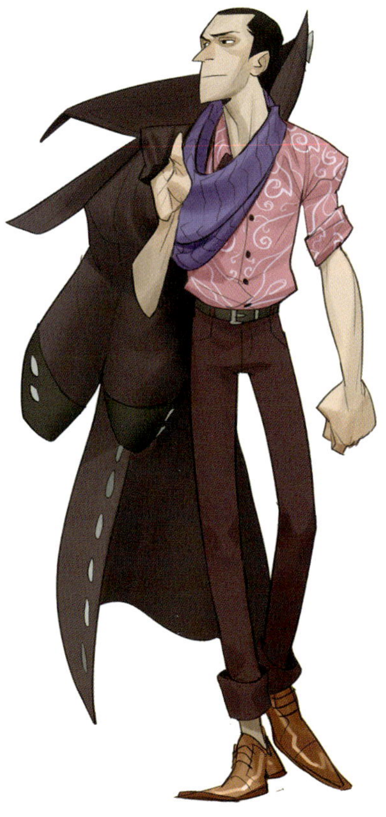

This version has eye-catching purple and pink hues, but the earthier tones of the coat and other accessories do not have a strong association with the original color palette.

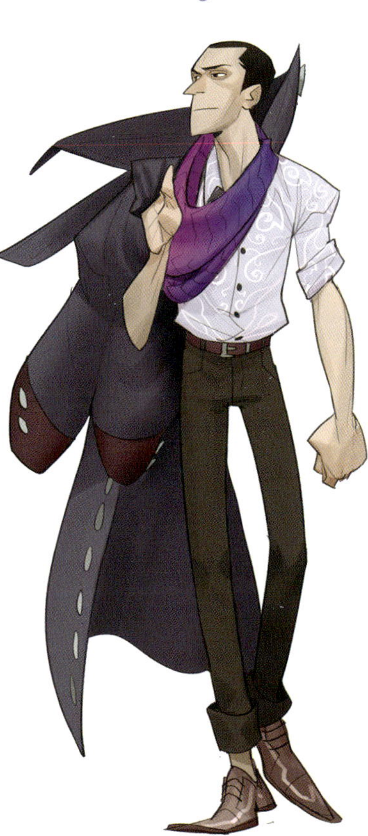

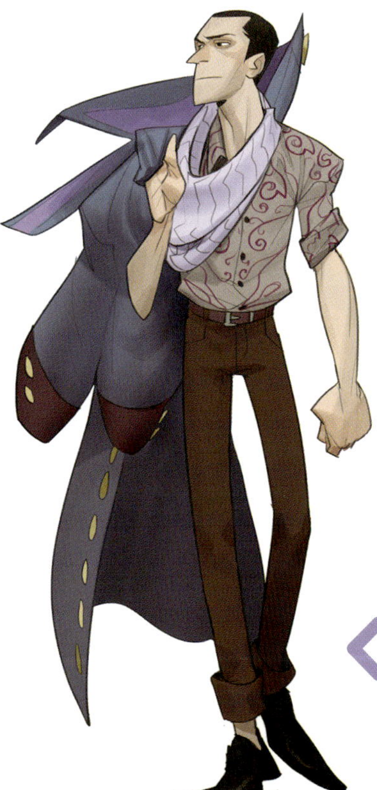

This palette shows a fine balance between the warm, dark colors of his shirt and trousers, and the cool blue of his jacket. The light-colored scarf stands out well against this shirt, but is no longer a vivid purple like the original design; I will use this overall palette as the basis for the final design, but incorporate ideas from the other scarves as well.

FINAL DESIGN

This final design is successful in transferring the attitude of a tall, impressive alien to a skinny, villainous human. Carrying across similar colors, patterns, and shape language between the designs plays a huge part in this, conveying the same cunning personality and sense of wealth and importance despite the characters' different species and settings. The dark blue overcoat, bright purple scarf, and ornate shirt are directly inspired by the alien's armor and glowing accents. The character's pointed, angular facial features and severe, arrogant demeanor help to communicate his villainous side, along with the sharp, dramatic shapes of his silhouette.

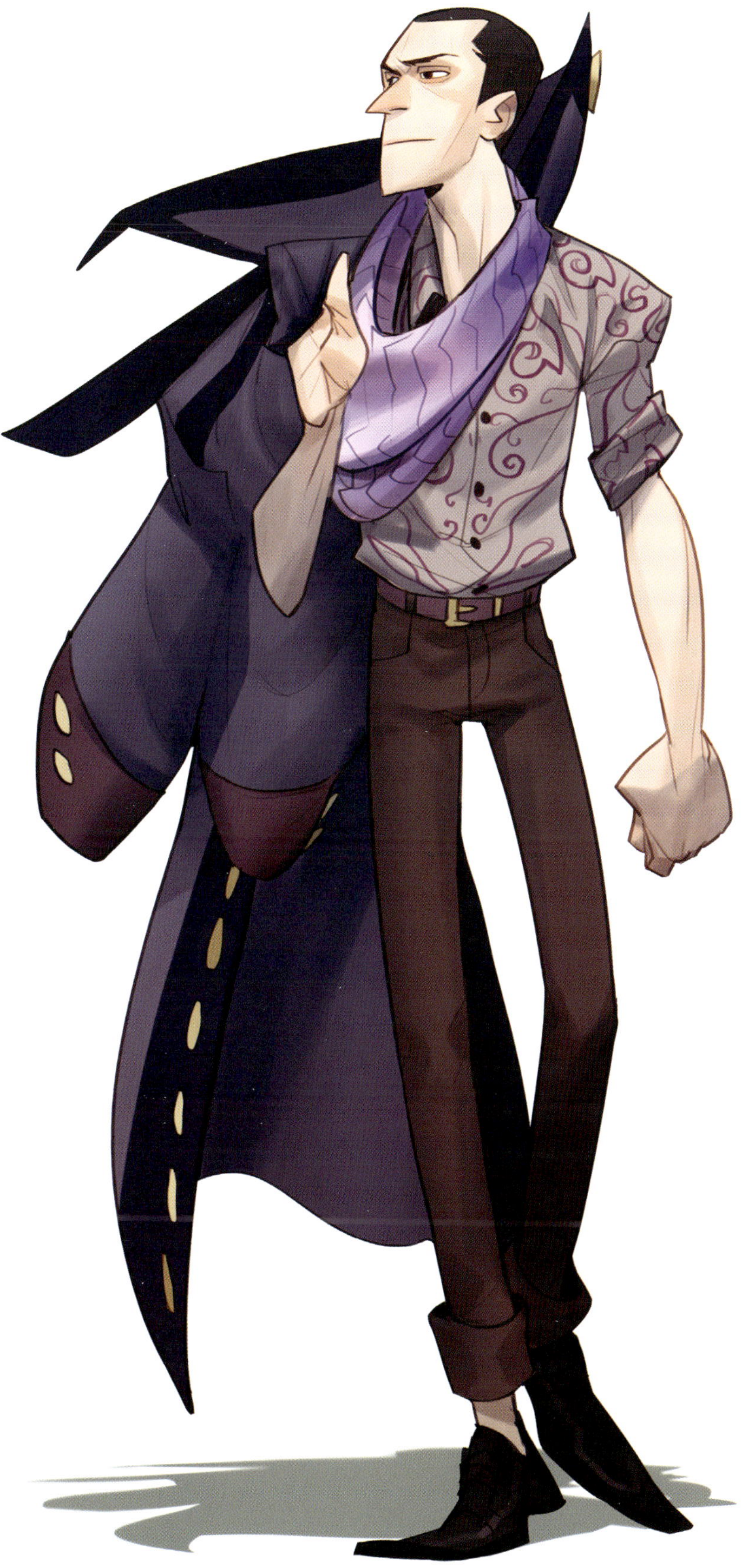

Final artwork © Max Grecke

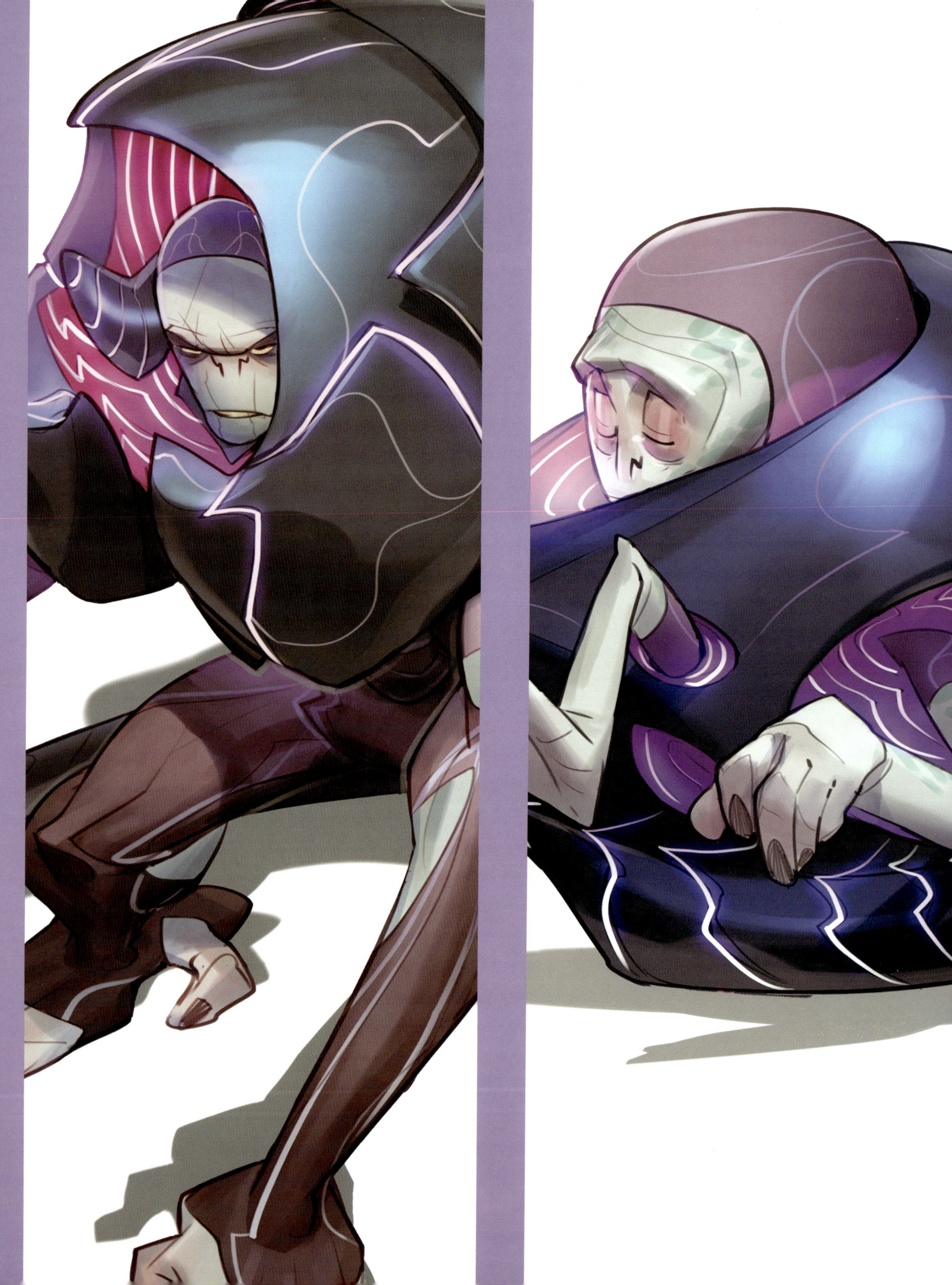

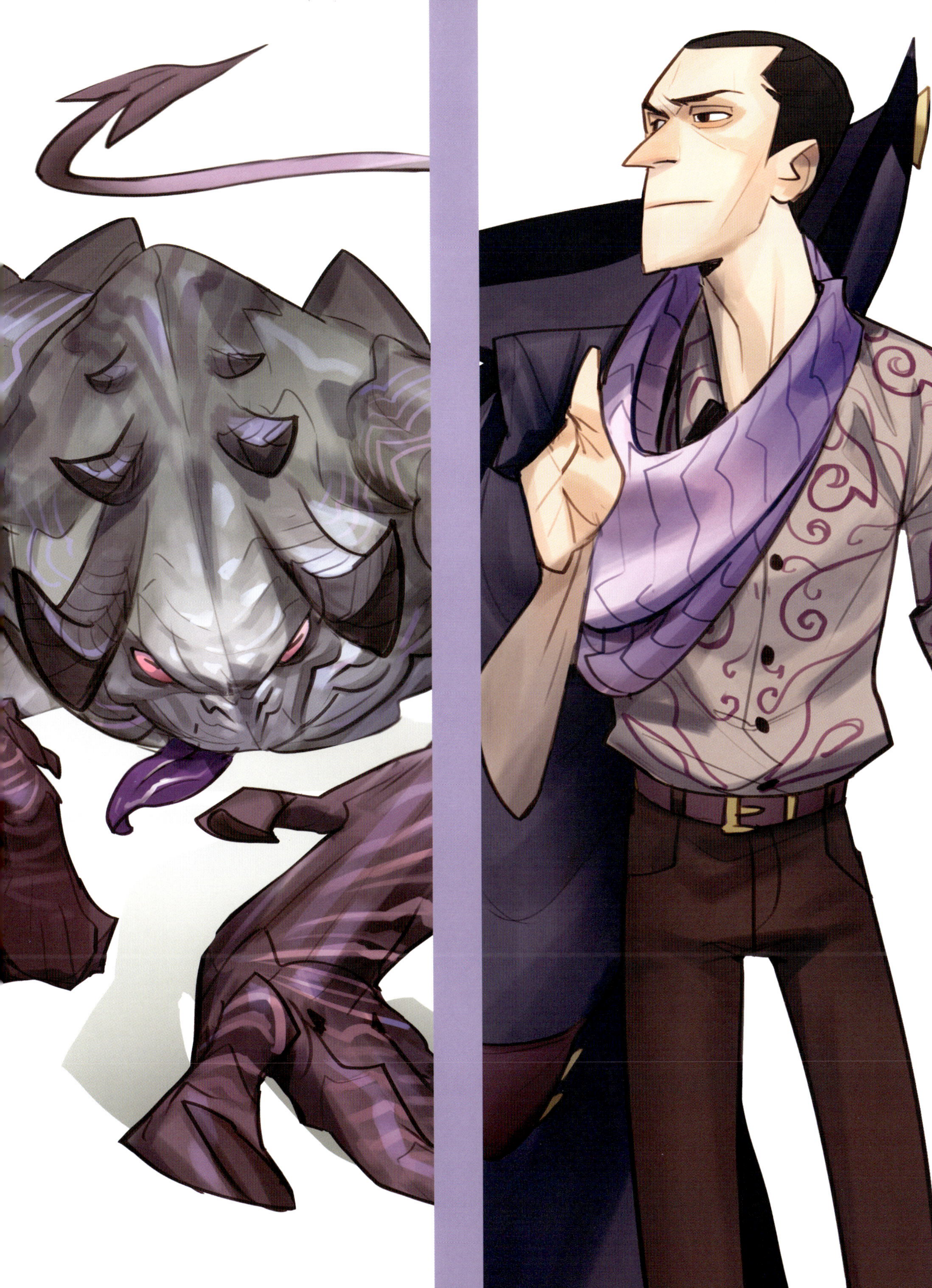

BREAKDOWN GALLERY

In this final section of the book we will explore the creative processes of several different artists, each with their own unique style, giving you some more ideas for development techniques and workflows that you can take forward with your future character designs.

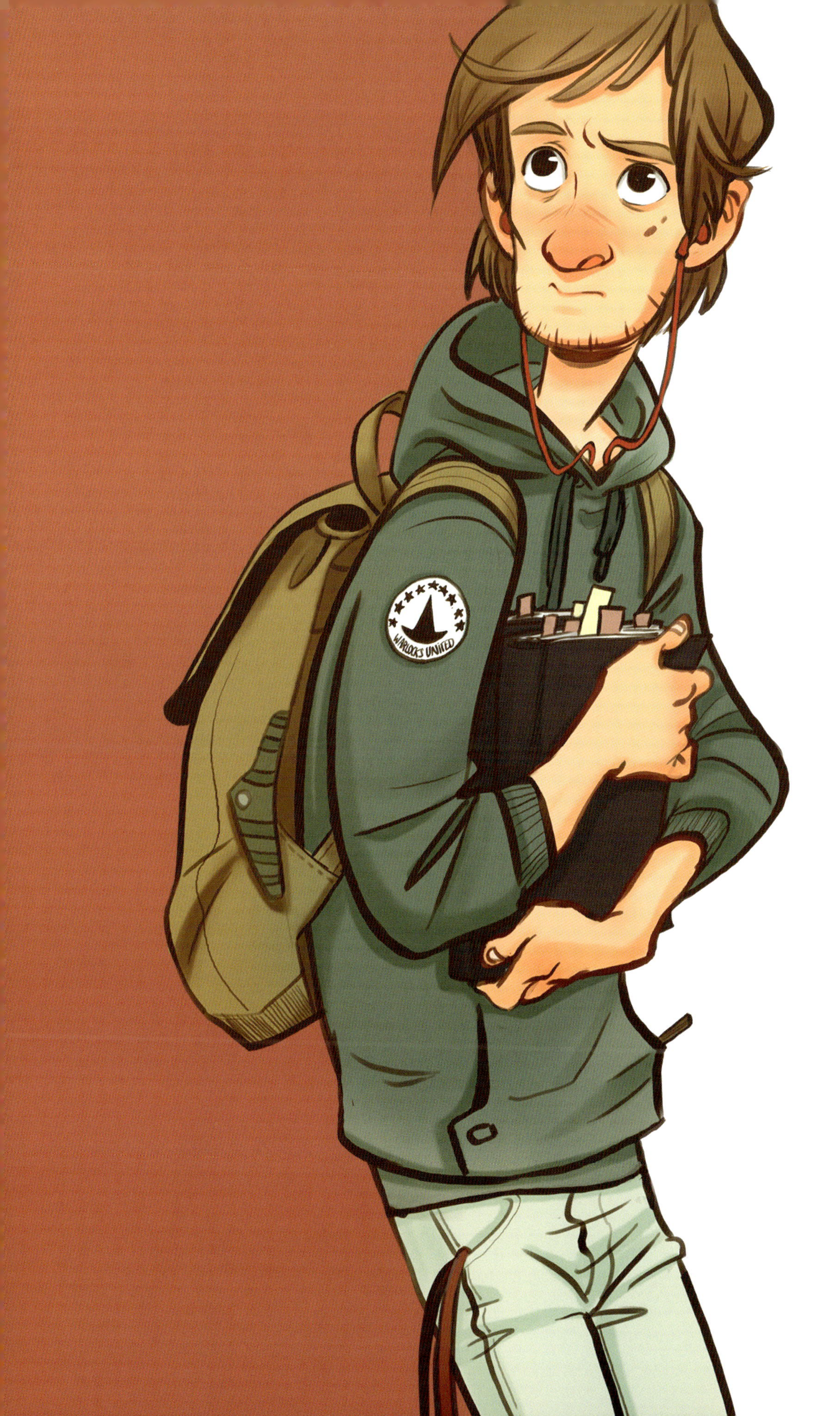
WARLOCKS UNITED

SORCERESS

BY MARIE THORHAUGE

My key aim for designing this sorceress is to make it clear she is a gothic character but not necessarily a villain. I want to touch on these elements but also try to challenge the concept by incorporating an extra spin into it: I would like to add an almost sci-fi touch to the character, which will come across in her outfit and colors.

When you think of "gothic," a black, gray, and red color palette often comes to mind. However, I choose to go with a pink, purple, and blue color scheme for interest. Her skin is very pale, and her hair has a gray tone, so my palette still has a melancholic gothic feel, but it is the less obvious choice.

When designing characters, it is always the easy solution to go with the stereotype; you can draw any character and give them a stereotypical personality by giving them a different outfit. For example, giving this character pale skin, a black robe, and a wand to create a gothic sorceress, or giving her blonde hair, a crucifix, and a stake to make a vampire slayer. Instead of doing this, my favorite part of designing is to re-think a concept and approach it from another angle. Then the success of my design is reliant on pure design theory and technique.

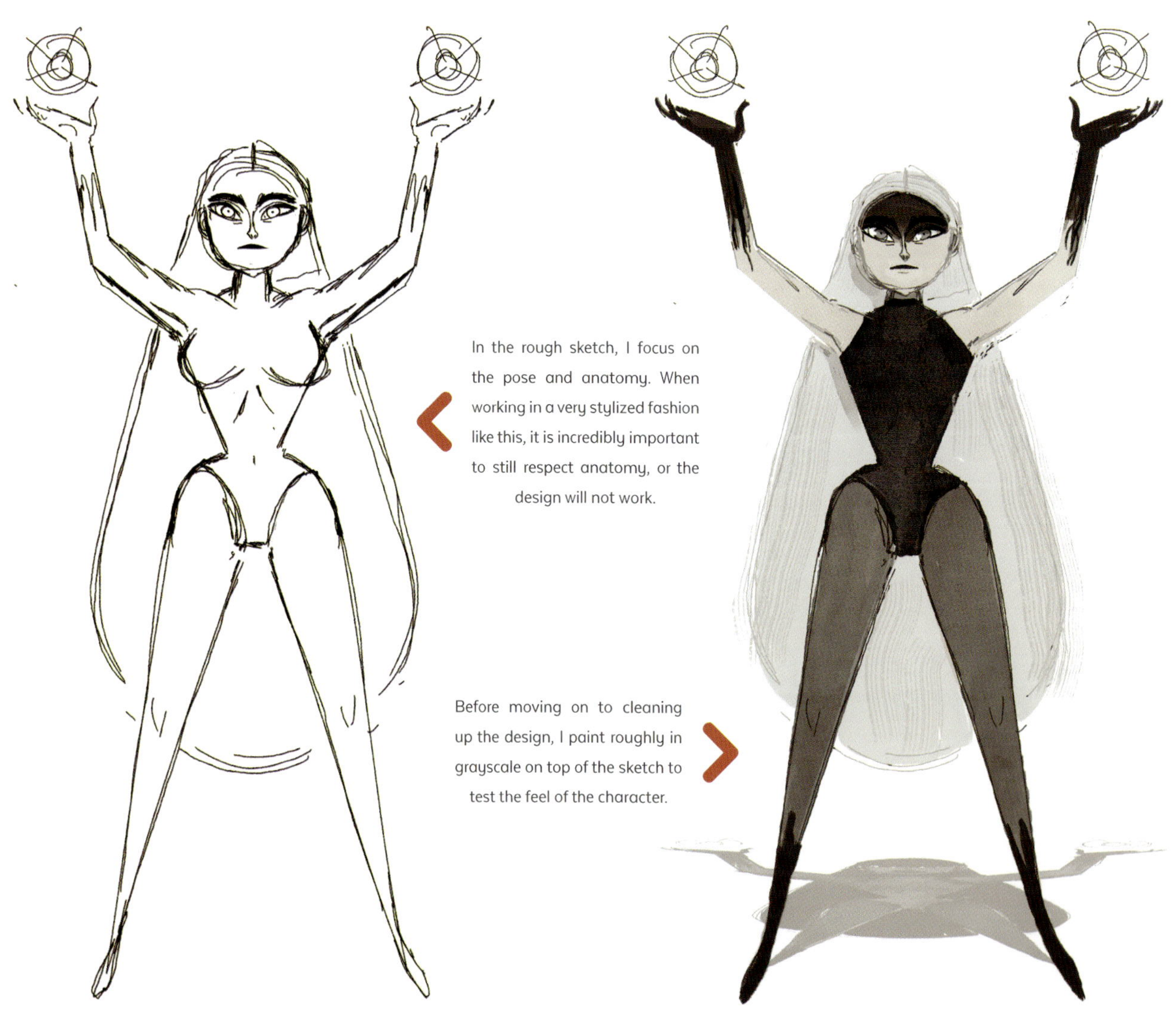

In the rough sketch, I focus on the pose and anatomy. When working in a very stylized fashion like this, it is incredibly important to still respect anatomy, or the design will not work.

Before moving on to cleaning up the design, I paint roughly in grayscale on top of the sketch to test the feel of the character.

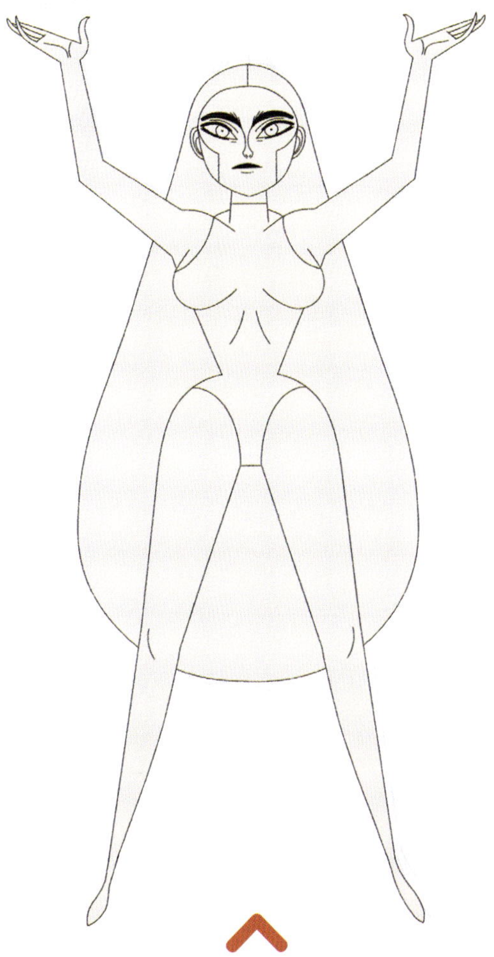

Now I make the final refinements to the shapes, lines, and details, such as the hands and facial features. As this design is so heavily stylized, I have chosen to draw it with a completely even line. A thin, flat line such as this requires a very tight, decisive pose and anatomy in the sketch, otherwise you run the risk of "killing" the design by stripping away the elements that make the sketch look appealing.

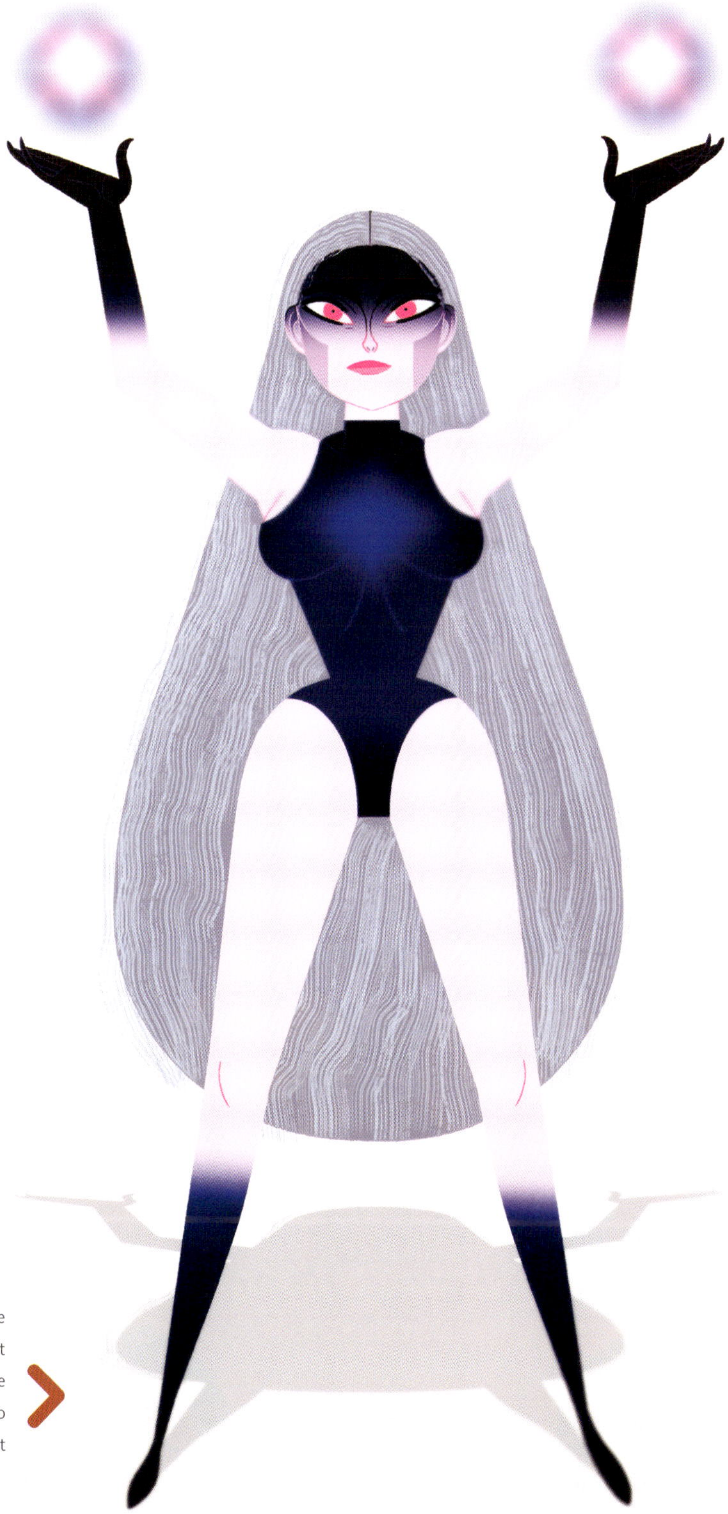

In this final image, I have chosen to only outline where the character's shapes overlap. This effect gives a more three-dimensional feel to an otherwise completely flat design. Adding texture to her hair also makes the design feel more organic, creating contrast with the very clean shapes and colors elsewhere.

Final artwork © Marie Thorhauge

COLLEGE STUDENT

BY SIMONE GRÜNEWALD

Here my aim is to design a college student character carrying a bag and books. I start by giving the character a backstory – nothing too detailed, but one that will help me to get to know the character. I envision him as a shy member of a group of college students who are the lucky few who have a magic course, as they have magical blood.

I start by looking for a pose and outfit that might be fitting. I consider adding a hat, but discard it quickly, as it would look too extreme on this mixed campus of wizards and non-wizards; instead he will be dressed like a regular student, but with a college jacket that carries the emblem of his group. My first version of the character seems confident, which I like, but I decide to try for a more awkward and nerdy look. I imagine he might secretly be in love with one of his fellow students, which helps me to make him more shy and expressive.

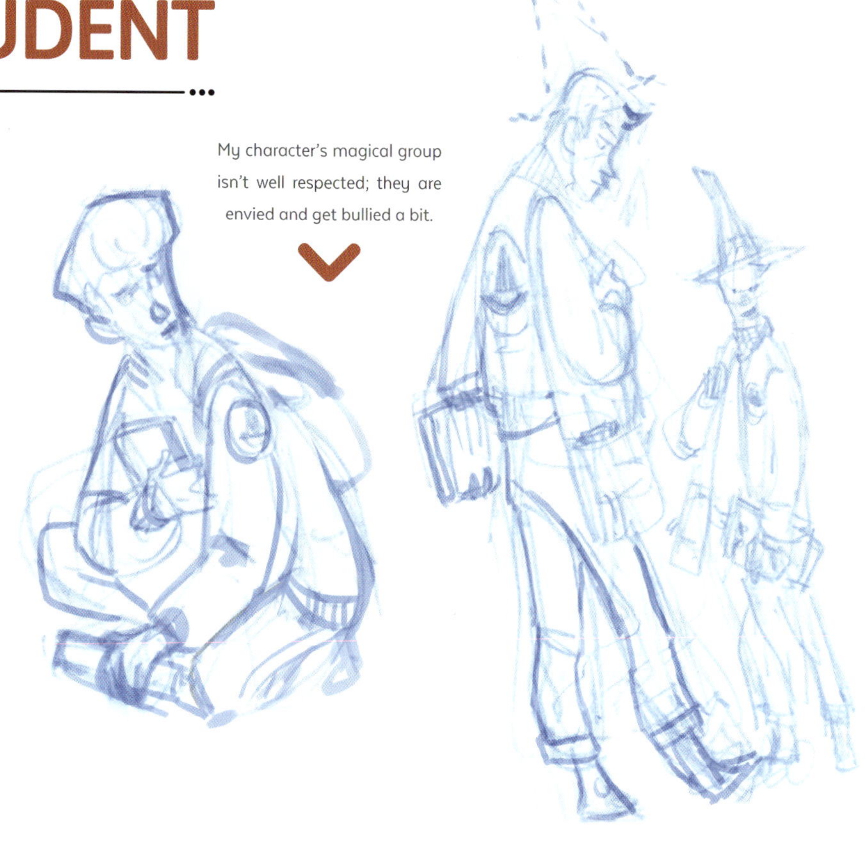

My character's magical group isn't well respected; they are envied and get bullied a bit.

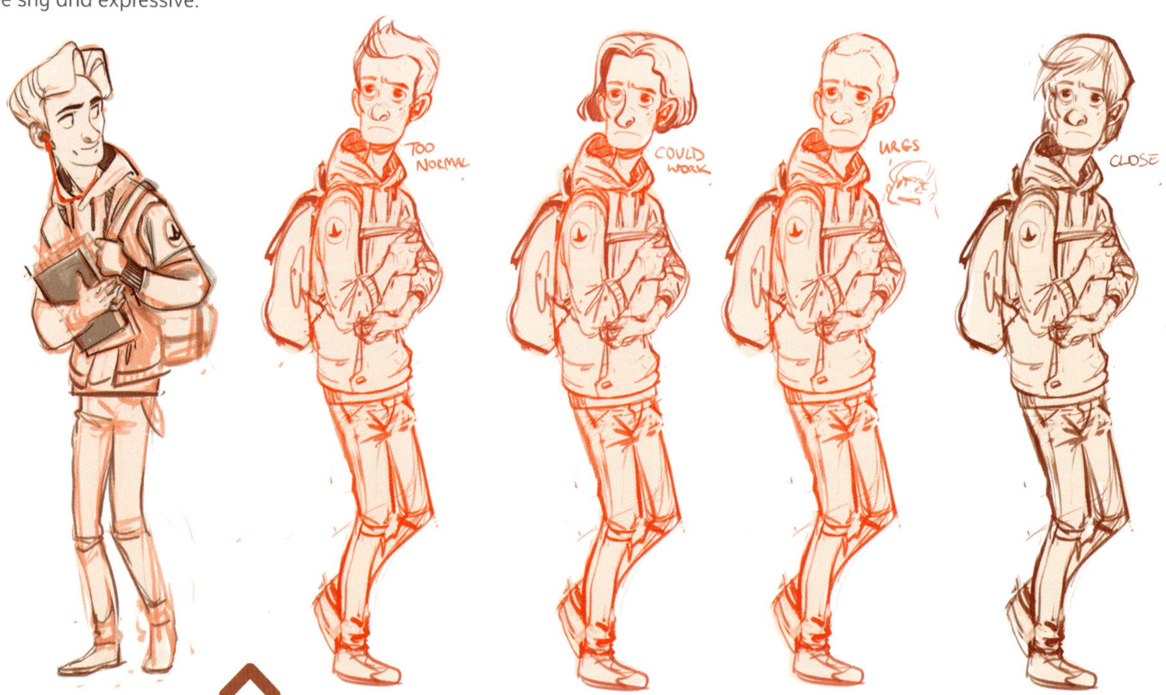

I want the character to tell a story with his stance, expression, and details. The last version (on the far right) is slightly too unhappy, but otherwise I am satisfied with the design.

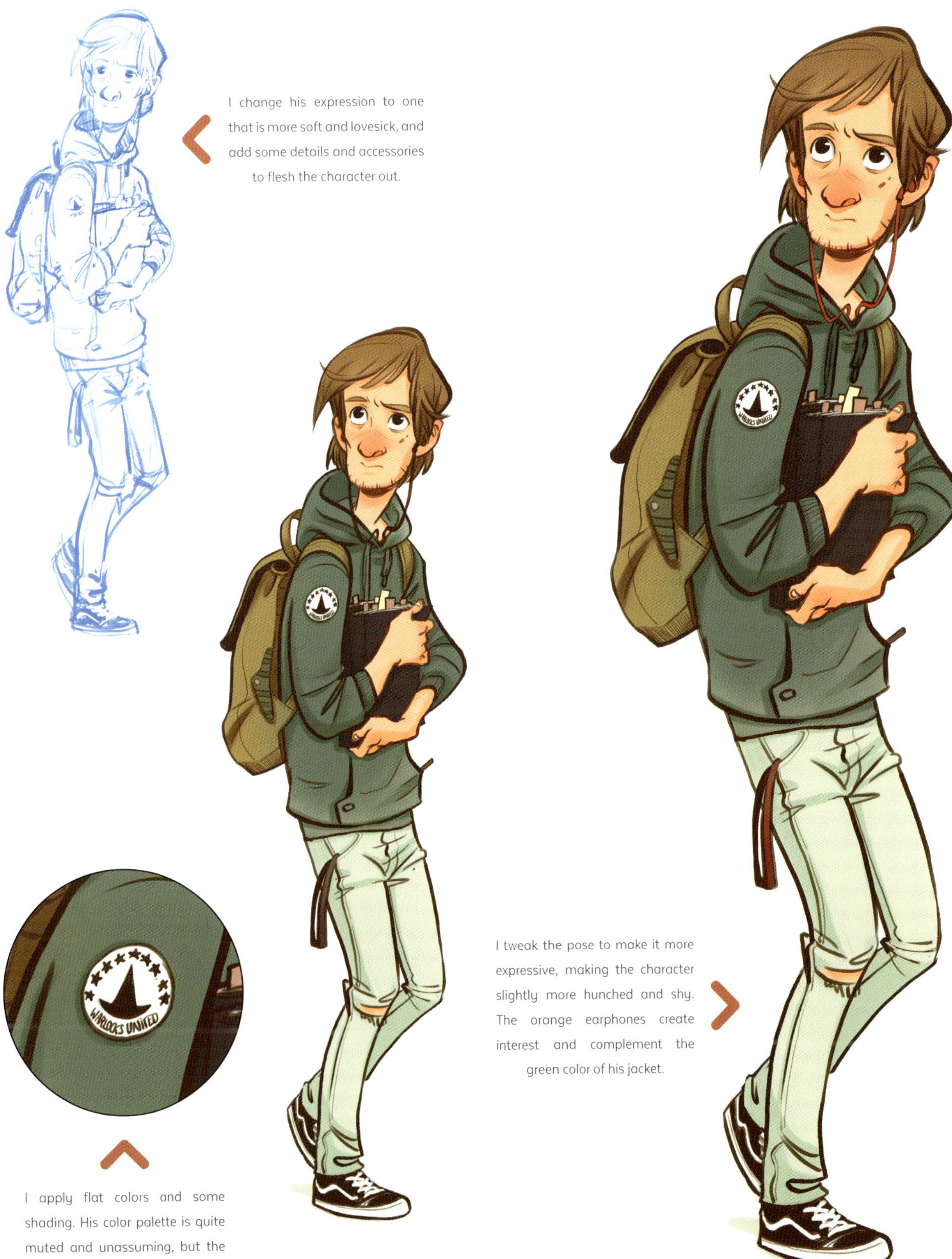

I change his expression to one that is more soft and lovesick, and add some details and accessories to flesh the character out.

I apply flat colors and some shading. His color palette is quite muted and unassuming, but the "Warlocks United" patch stands out and indicates his group.

I tweak the pose to make it more expressive, making the character slightly more hunched and shy. The orange earphones create interest and complement the green color of his jacket.

Final artwork © Simone Grünewald

SCI-FI ASSASSIN

BY ALEXANDRA FRANTSEVA

I have always been interested in character and costume design, so when designing this sci-fi assassin, I instantly start thinking about how I can convey the character's story through their clothing and accessories. I have to thank all my jobs in video games, where artists have to keep in mind the size of the characters on a screen, and be very careful not to overdo the details so that the whole figure remains readable.

This character was born and raised in a giant cyber metropolis; it's likely he would be biracial or mixed race. His costume would look not only futuristic, but allow him to blend in with his urban environment. He is quite young, with a youthful, agile physique, but giving him a mechanical arm would suggest that he has already been through a lot in his dangerous line of work. In order to emphasize the artificial nature of his arm, I leave some "bones" out in the open. Perhaps the limb is an unfinished high-tech project that assists him in his work.

It is important to keep balance between areas with lots of visual noise and areas where the viewer's eye can rest. This is why I leave the lower part of the character's figure with little detail compared to his face and upper body, which are the focal points of the design.

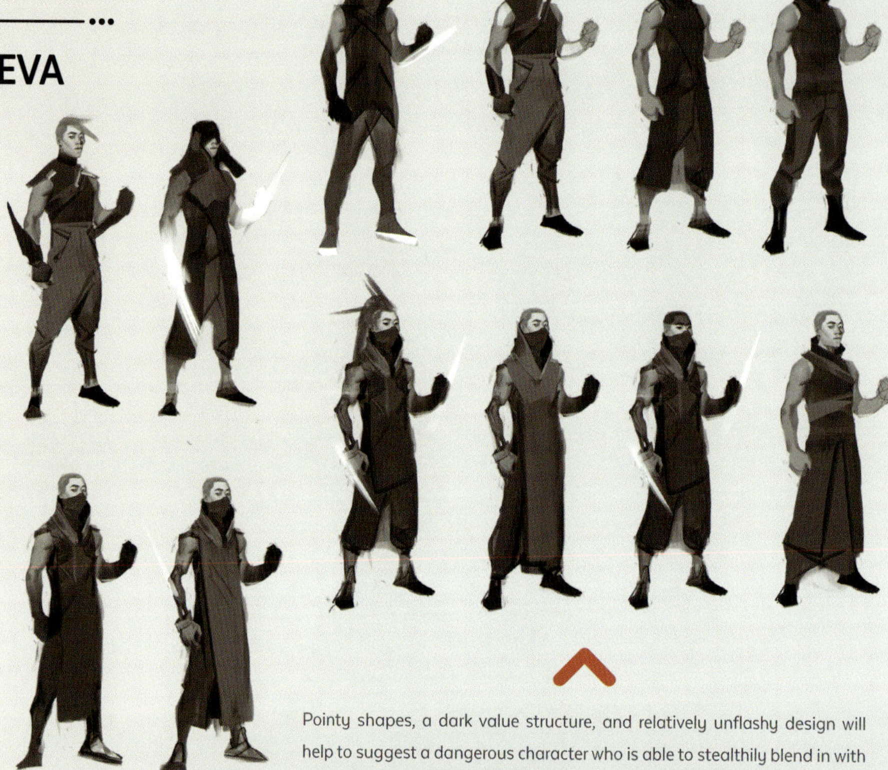

Pointy shapes, a dark value structure, and relatively unflashy design will help to suggest a dangerous character who is able to stealthily blend in with the crowd. His comfortable clothing is unburdened by decorative elements, so he would be able to move quickly.

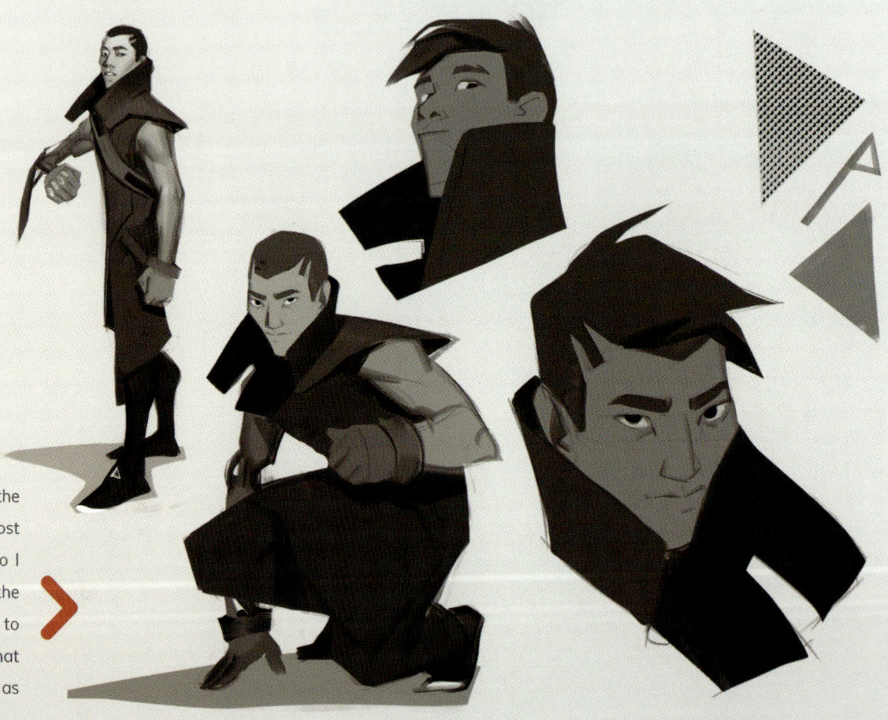

I test poses, details, and expressions for the character. Faces have always been the most important part of character design for me, so I want to draw the viewer's attention towards the assassin's head by adding most of the details to the upper part of the figure. I test out details that might be appropriate for his costume, such as sharp triangle patterns.

I experiment with values, colors, and contrasts for the design. Sci-fi designs tend toward colder palettes, so I test both a stereotypical blue palette and an unusual earthy palette. My favorite scheme has a strong contrast between the almost black color of his coat, blue and red accents, and the warmer color of his skin. This palette is striking and suggests a more vibrant futuristic setting than the others.

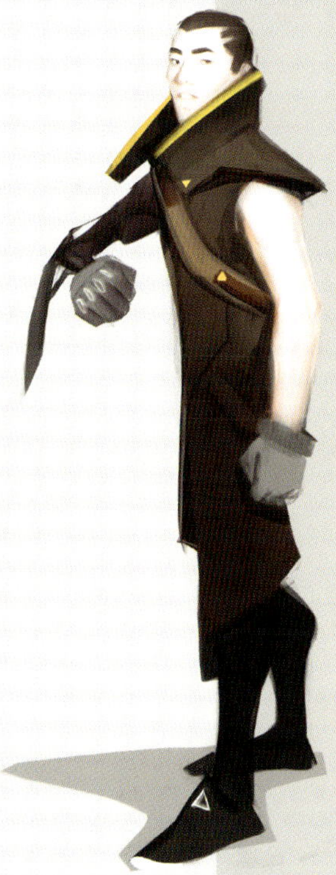

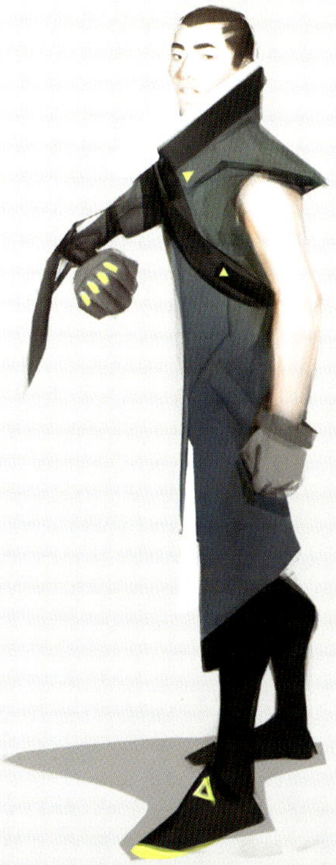

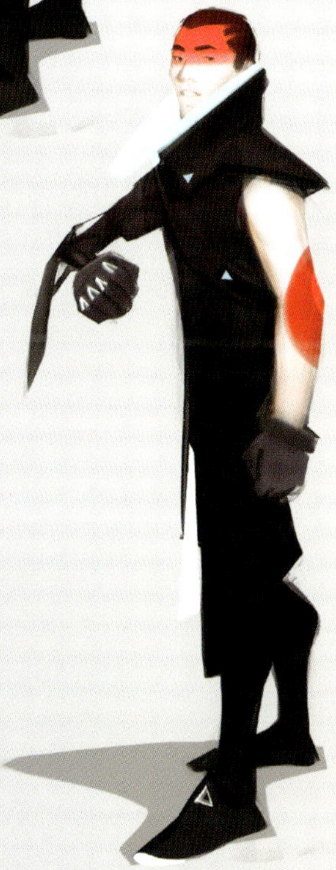

My final design represents my initial idea well, finding a balance between the dark, sharp parts of his outfit, and the lighter colors and warm tones of his face and human arm. The final pose conveys the character's personality well, showing him as proud and confident in himself and his abilities, and prepared for action.

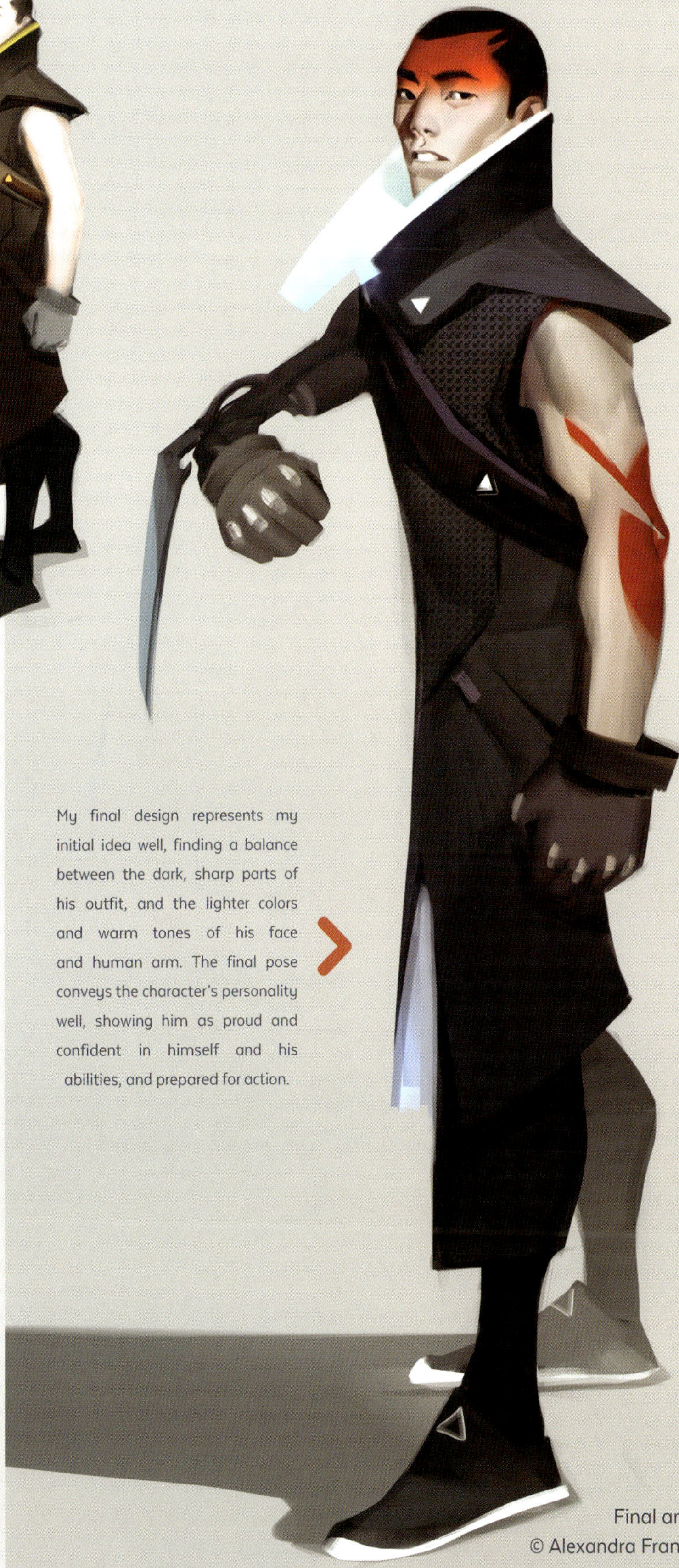

Final artwork
© Alexandra Frantseva

ALIEN MERMAID

BY LAURA "LAUMII" MÜLLER

When I start the character design process, I think of a story that I would enjoy illustrating. Here I want to draw a mermaid character, but one that is alien from a typical mermaid world. I begin by scribbling around, trying out different shapes, colors, gestures, and emotions. I do not worry so much about anatomy or perspective at first, and just go with the flow, producing what I call "spaghetti drawings." It is easy to change the design at this rough stage.

When I find a design that really feels right, I make a cleaner line drawing. In this case, I choose the design with lots of bubble eyes, which help her to spy on her surroundings; I imagine them wobbling around when she is moving, giving her an alien touch instead of normal flowing hair. This stage is also where I fix the character's anatomy and exaggerate the initial idea further. I try to convey some mermaid-like traits with the lines, aiming for fluidity and vividness. At

this stage I still change elements as I go, such as the mermaid's tail, which becomes a flatter, thinner shape to balance out the round mass of her hair.

When choosing colors, I stick with an underwater theme, using greens and blues with complementary earth tones and oranges. Giving her little fish companion an orange touch also adds to the contrast, making the main character stand out more.

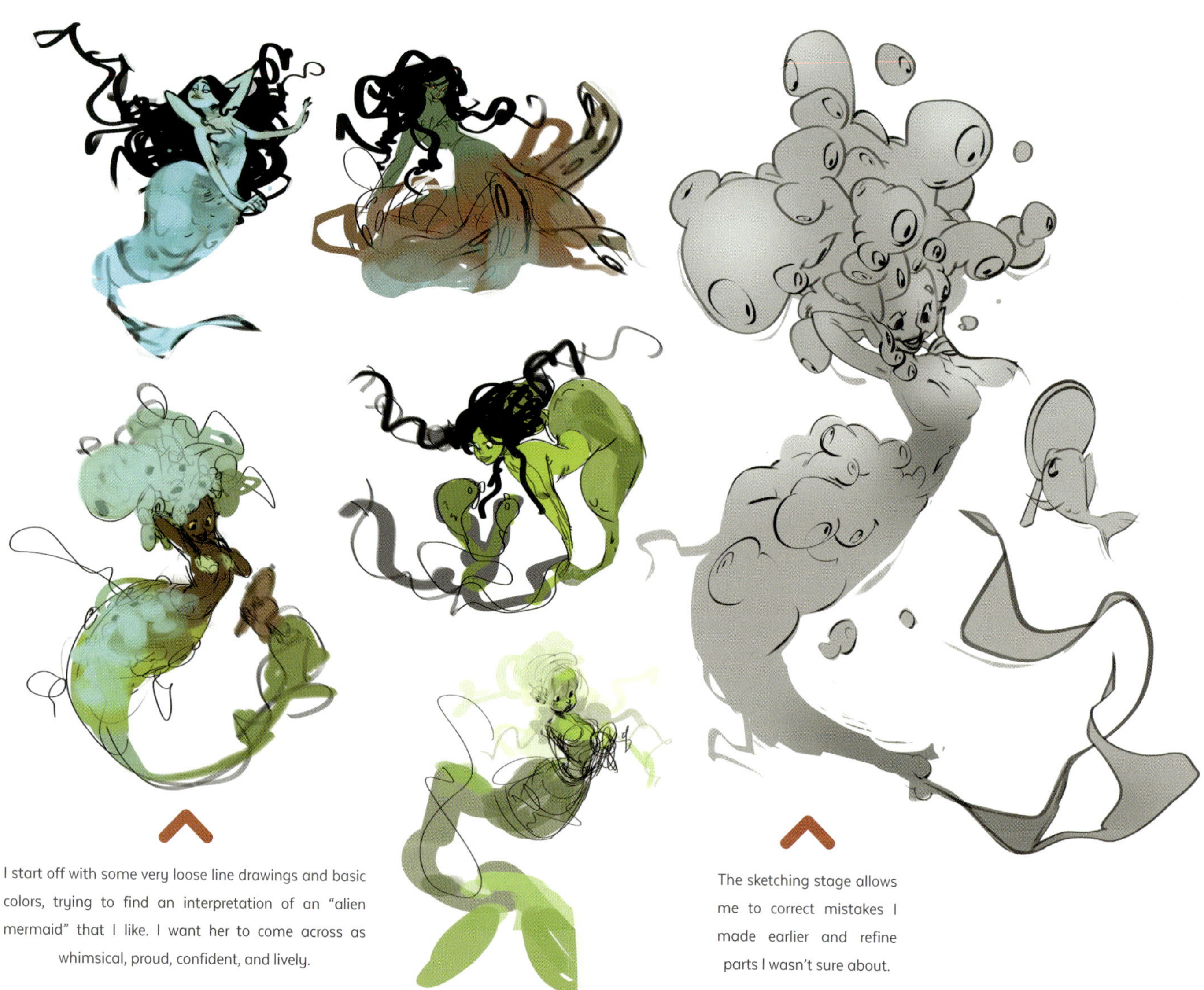

I start off with some very loose line drawings and basic colors, trying to find an interpretation of an "alien mermaid" that I like. I want her to come across as whimsical, proud, confident, and lively.

The sketching stage allows me to correct mistakes I made earlier and refine parts I wasn't sure about.

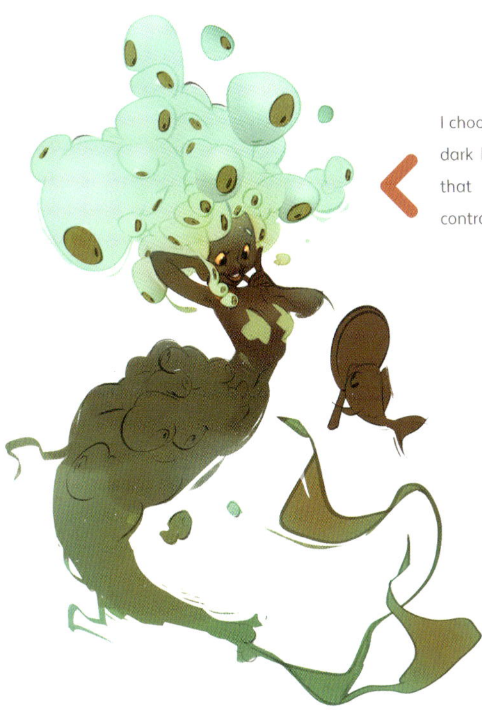

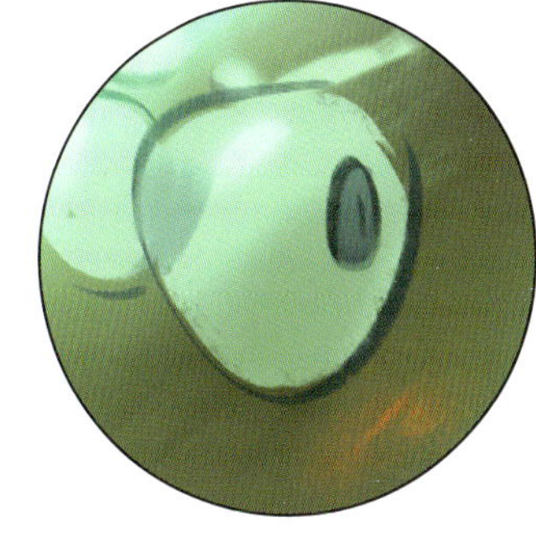

I choose a light green and dark brown color scheme that creates a value contrast between her skin color and hair.

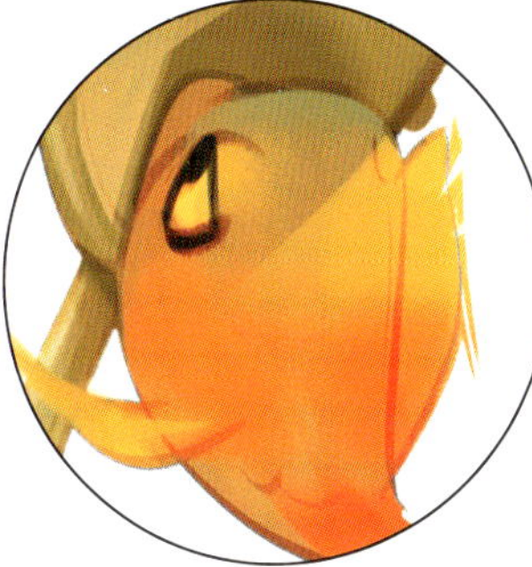

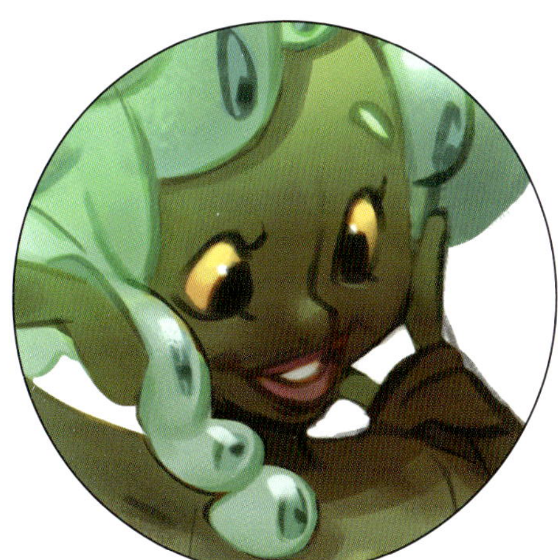

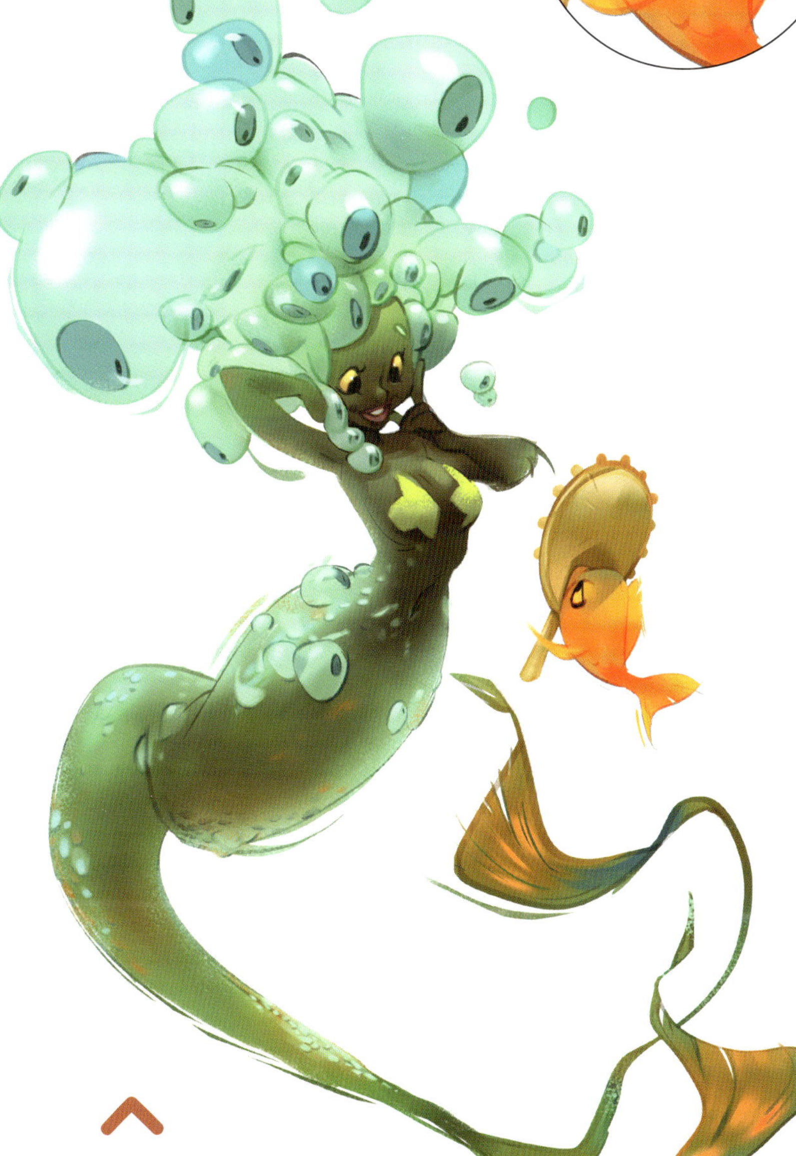

REMEMBER PERSONALITY

Don't get lost in just making a character look cool. Think of their innermost personality; give them a reason to exist and equip them with feelings and emotions. If you are struggling to find or convey a character's personality, try adding a little companion, sidekick, or environmental element, which will help to dictate how the character acts.

Here is the final alien mermaid. Adding the finishing details at the end is the most time-consuming part, but fun.

Final artwork © Laura "Laumii" Müller

ANIMAL SHERIFF

BY TATA CHE

For this project, I want to design a dog character who is a sheriff. He has survived in the Wild West for a long time, and despite his old age is still a danger to the bad guys. He is not necessarily a hero, but he is a good, trustworthy, silent character who you don't want to mess with. I research images of similar figures from history, such as real-life cowboys, scouts, and William "Buffalo Bill" Cody. I also draw some inspiration from cinema, such as Jeff Bridges' character in *True Grit*. These help me to convey the sheriff's personality and design his costume.

I choose a dog that looks middle-sized, not huge; the bad guys won't see him as a threat until they know him better! His tall white hat makes him look fancy and gives him authority, while his long black coat, inspired by research, makes him look more solid. The bright colors of his star and spurs really stand out, immediately conveying what role he plays and the setting he comes from. Using triangular shapes and parallel lines in his design and pose helps to make him look stable and severe.

I start by sketching different breeds of dog to test out their personalities and natural characteristics. A dog with a mustache and beard would work well for a Wild West character.

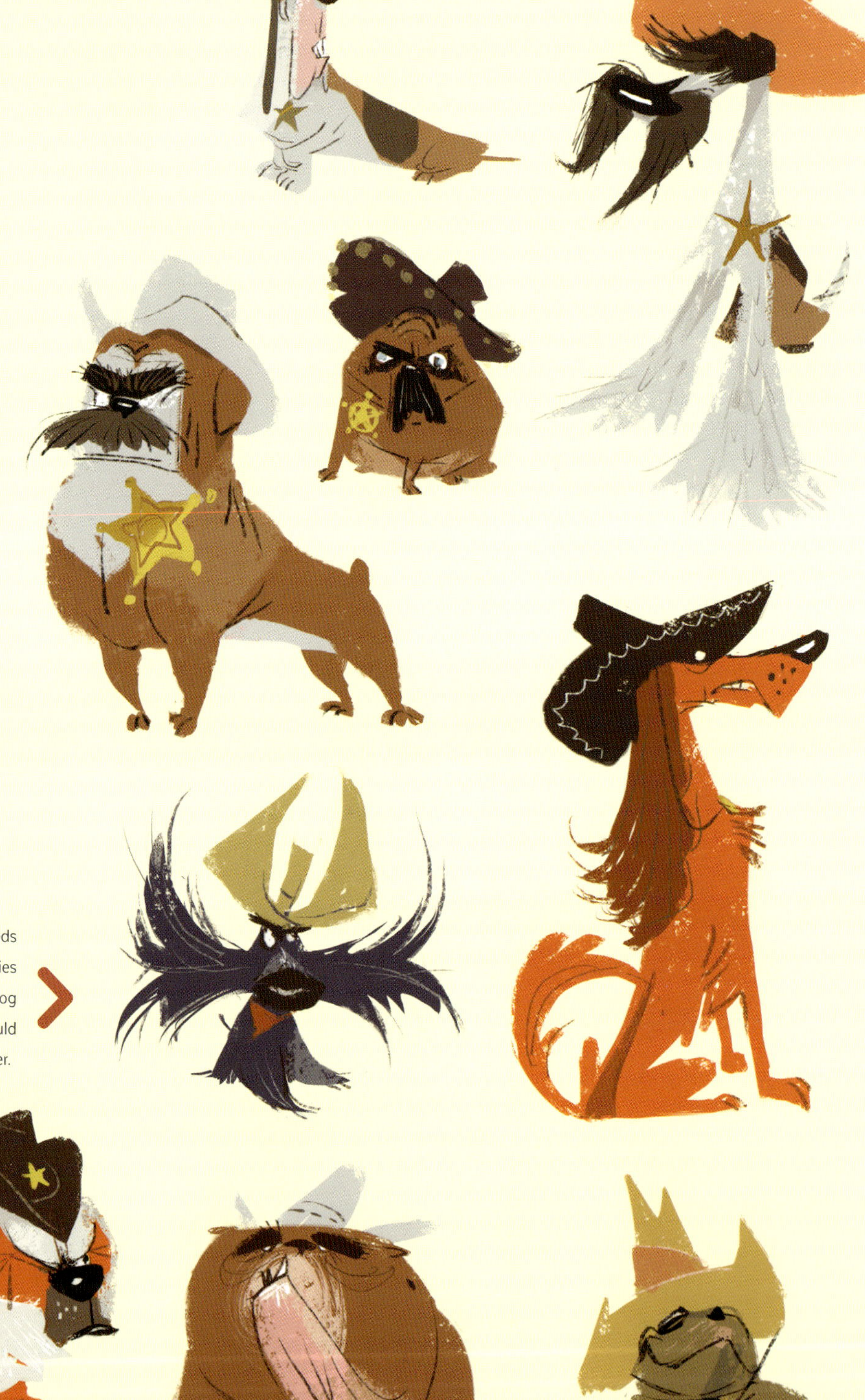

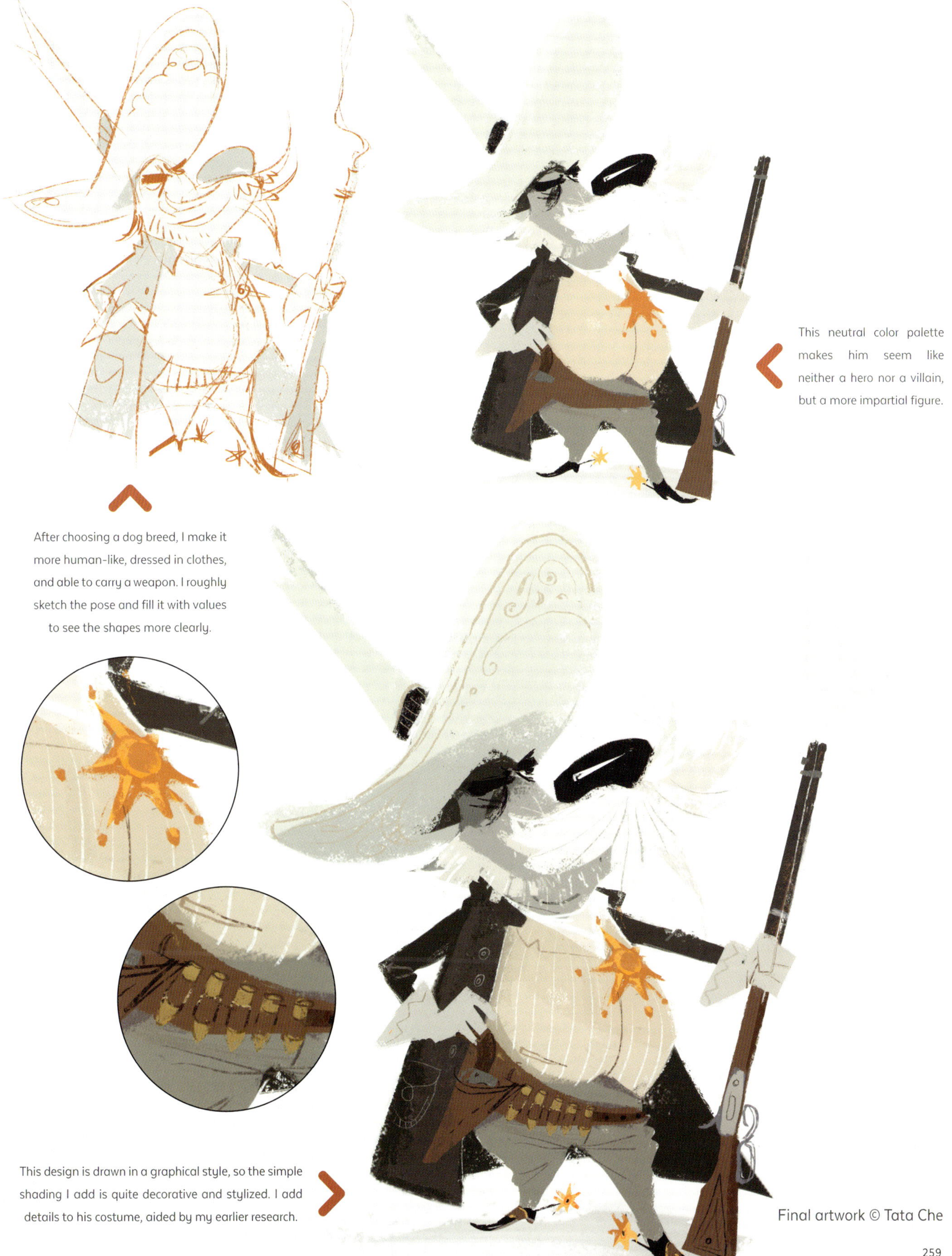

This neutral color palette makes him seem like neither a hero nor a villain, but a more impartial figure.

After choosing a dog breed, I make it more human-like, dressed in clothes, and able to carry a weapon. I roughly sketch the pose and fill it with values to see the shapes more clearly.

This design is drawn in a graphical style, so the simple shading I add is quite decorative and stylized. I add details to his costume, aided by my earlier research.

Final artwork © Tata Che

CONTRIBUTORS

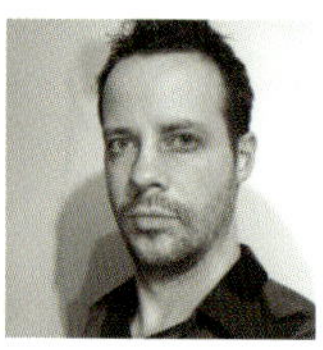

KENNETH ANDERSON

Kenneth Anderson is a character designer and illustrator from Scotland, currently working as a designer for children's television.

charactercube.com

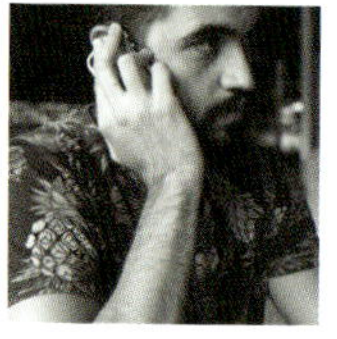

LUIS GADEA

Luis Gadea has worked on characters for *Angry Birds* and The Lego Movie sequel, and now works at Stellar Creative Lab on feature films and other animated projects.

luisgadea.com

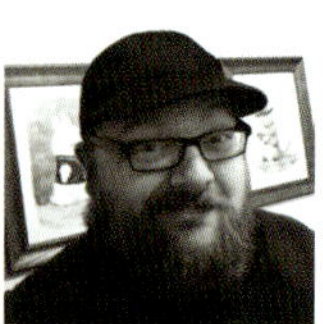

SHAUN BRYANT

Shaun Bryant is a visual development artist with credits including *Trolls: The Beat Goes On!* and Harvey Street Kids at DreamWorks Animation.

art-bomb.com

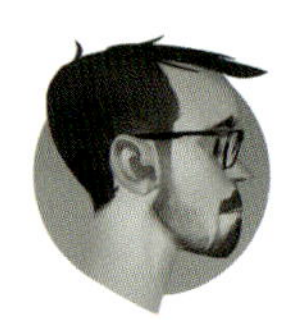

MAX GRECKE

Max Grecke is a freelance illustrator and concept artist based in Sweden.

instagram.com/maxgrecke

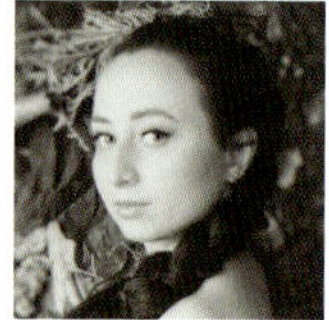

TATA CHE

Tata Che started her artistic career studying decorative art, but always had a passion for storytelling and animation. Now she works on worldwide animation projects.

tatacheart.com

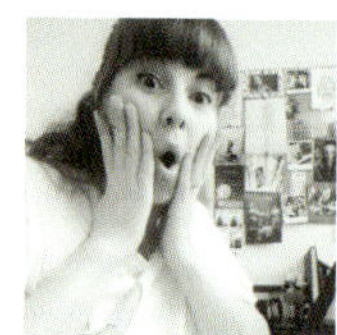

SIMONE GRÜNEWALD

Simone Grünewald started work at Hamburg games company Daedalic Entertainment after finishing her studies in 2008. She still loves working there, now as Head of Art.

instagram.com/schmoedraws

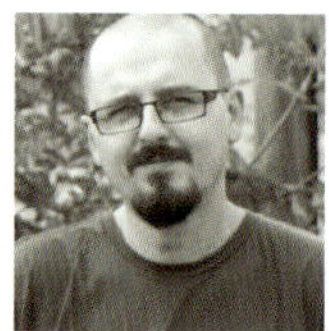

ENRIQUE FERNÁNDEZ

Enrique Fernández is an award-winning artist with over twenty years' industry experience as a character designer, art director, storyboard artist, and more.

enrique-fernandez.com

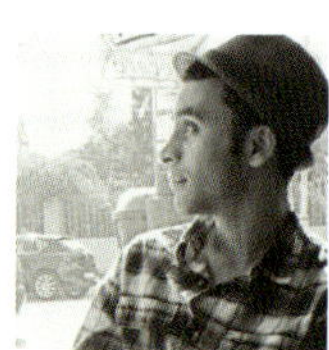

HICHAM HABCHI

Hicham Habchi is a concept artist and comic artist whose credits include projects with Blizzard Entertainment and Riot Games, such as *Overwatch* and *League of Legends*.

artstation.com/hichamhabchi1

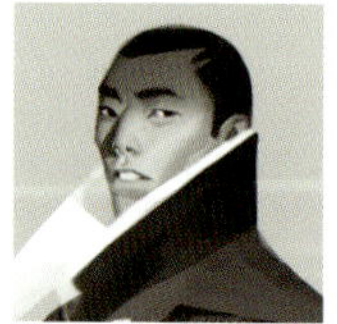

ALEXANDRA FRANTSEVA

Alexandra Frantseva is a concept artist for video games and animation based in Kiev, Ukraine.

artstation.com/alexfranz

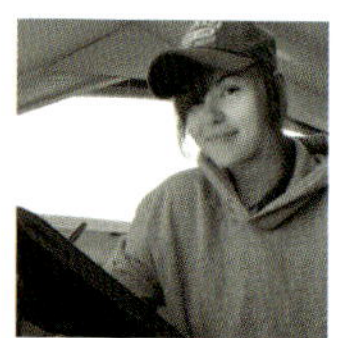

IDA HEM

Ida Hem is a character designer and visual storyteller working in the animation industry. She has worked for clients such as Nickelodeon, DreamWorksTV, and Universal.

idahem.com

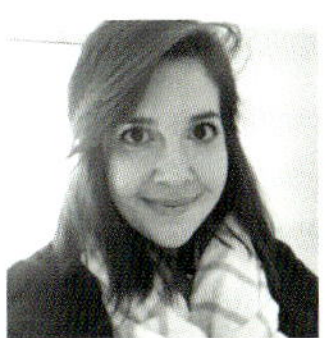

AMANDA JOLLY

Amanda Jolly is a character designer for animation, and has worked for companies such as Sony, Warner Brothers, and Disney. She watches too much TV.

instagram.com/amandajollylines

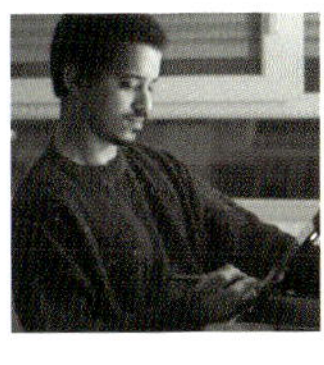

KÉVIN ROUALLAND

Kévin Roualland was born in Nice, France, and has drawn since his childhood. Kévin also loves cinema, something his mother passed on to him at a young age.

rouaroua.tumblr.com

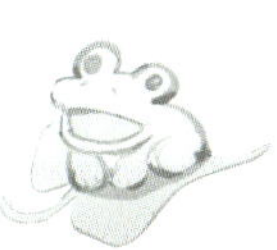

IRIS MUDDY

Iris Muddy is an illustrator, concept artist, and whimsical forest pond creature. Iris works in games and animation, and also enjoys photography, storytelling, and adventuring.

artstation.com/irismuddy

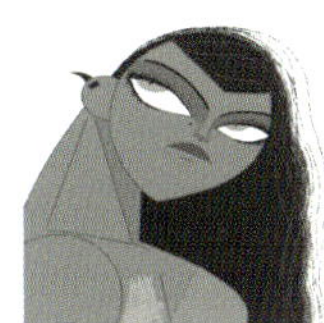

MARIE THORHAUGE

Marie Thorhauge is a character designer and visual development artist who was Head of Design at Cartoon Saloon before starting her own one-woman company in 2015.

mariethorhauge.com

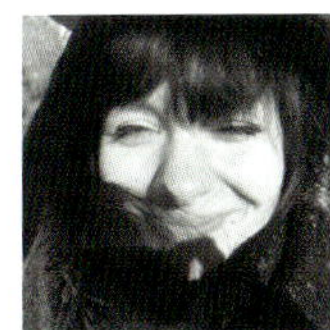
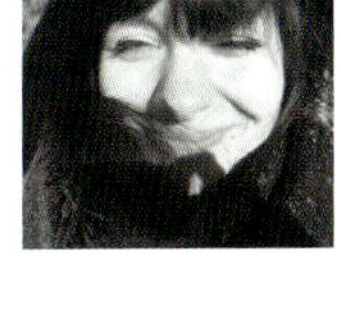

LAURA "LAUMII" MÜLLER

Laura "Laumii" Müller is a freelance illustrator and concept artist from Germany, with a passion for children's books, animation, and everything heartwarming and cheerful.

artstation.com/laumii

VARUN NAIR

Varun Nair is a freelance character designer and visual development artist currently based in Paris, France.

varunsartwork.tumblr.com

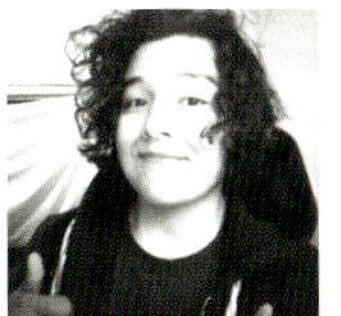

STEPHANIE RIZO GARCIA

Stephanie Rizo Garcia is a character designer based in Southern California. She has worked with clients such as Disney, Warner Bros. Animation, and Interscope Records.

stephanierizo.com

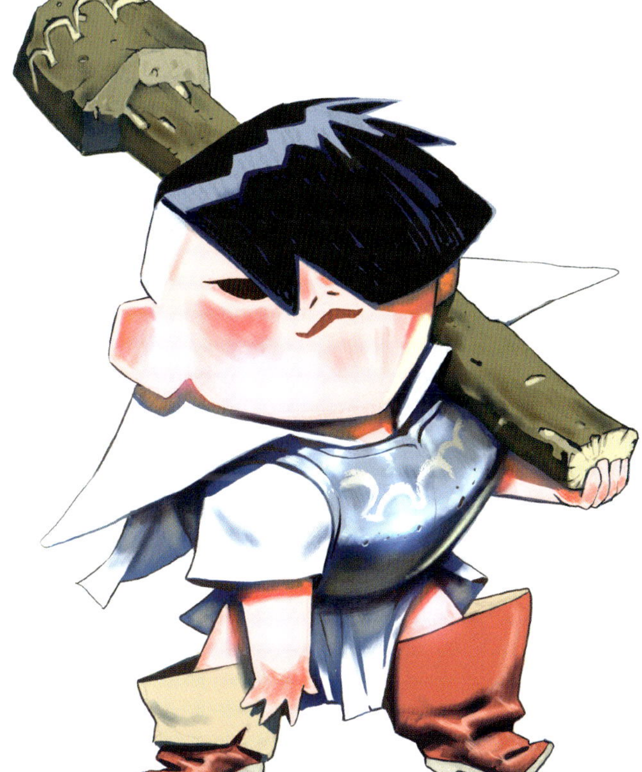

Artwork © Enrique Fernández

CHARACTER BOOKS

If you're looking for further resources to help you develop your character design expertise, take a look at some of the other titles available in the 3dtotal library. If you want to develop a particular style, try *Beginner's Guide to Creating Manga Art* or *Beginner's Guide to Comic Art: Characters*. If you are looking for general inspiration and advice, *Sketching from the Imagination: Characters* features a look inside the sketchbooks of fifty artists, while *The Artist's Guide to the Anatomy of the Human Head* examines the skeletal and muscular structures of the head and how to capture expressions and emotion in your artwork.

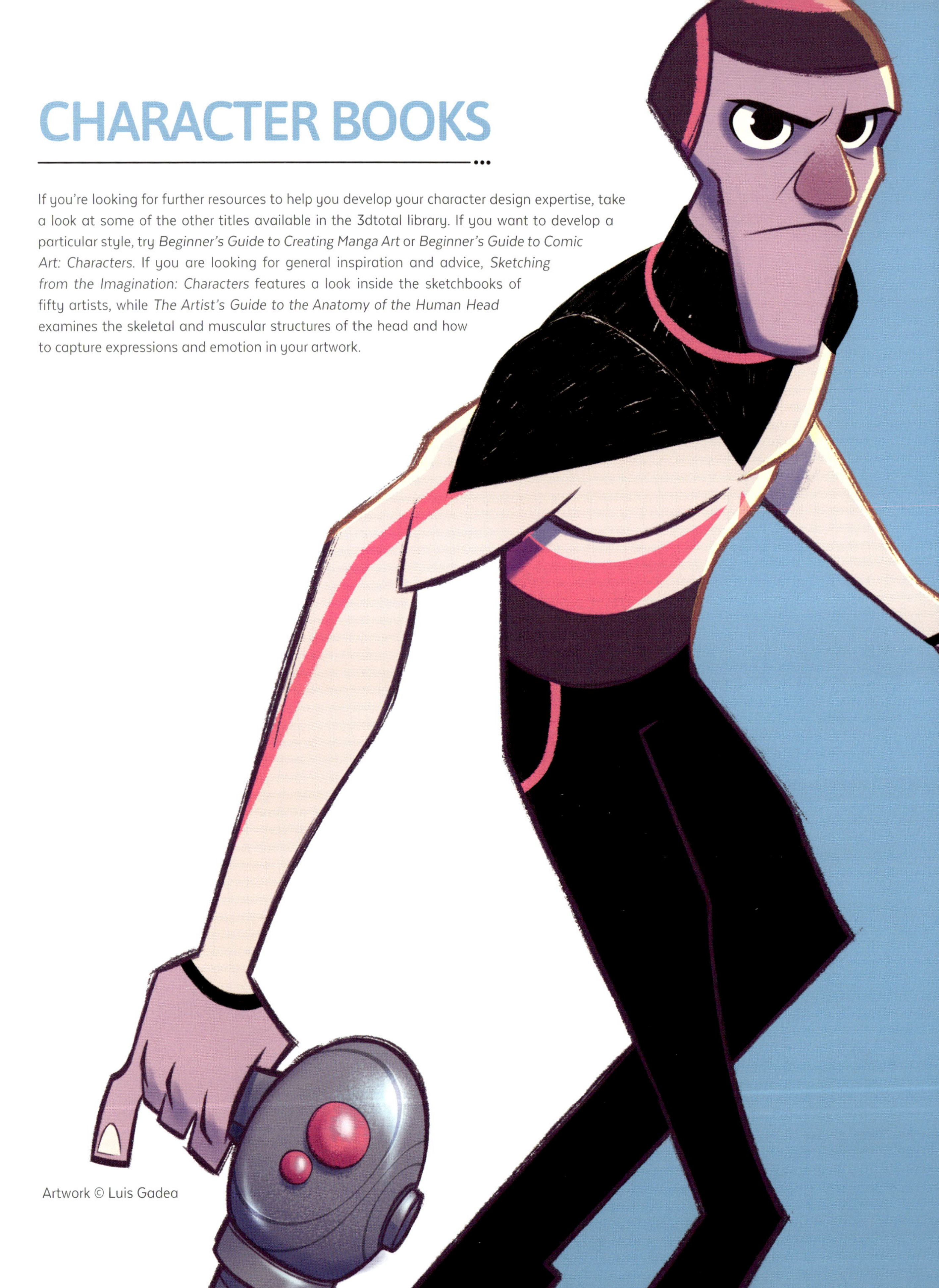

Artwork © Luis Gadea